Great Catholics

GREAT CATHOLICS

EDITED BY
CLAUDE WILLIAMSON, O.S.C.

Roman Catholic Books
A Division of Catholic Media Apostolate, Harrison, New York
Distribution: Post Office Box 2286, Fort Collins, CO 80522

NIHIL OBSTAT
ARTHUR J. SCANLAN, S.T.D.
Censor Librorum.

IMPRIMATUR
✠STEPHEN J. DONAHUE, D.D.
Adm., New York.

New York, January 9, 1939.

ISBN 0-912141-48-4

CONTENTS

CONTENTS

Rev. C. C. MARTINDALE, S.J., M.A.

PAUL ; APOSTLE, MARTYR

A.D. ?-62

SAUL OF TARSUS was destined to live a stormy life in any case, and after his death by beheading his history has been no less storm-tossed. At first, no one could believe that he had really been converted, his welcome amongst the older Christians was nervous if not chilly. He was responsible for the first real clash of opinion within the Church. The time came when the " reformers " made such ill-use of him that even Catholics were found to fear lest he might be somehow " rather Protestant " ; the Domes of Rome and of London came to seem almost symbolically to confront one another. Then arrived the period when it was customary to say that no one ever had written the books to which their name, as author, was affixed ; so a " Paul " was practically washed out : finally critics found a certain entertainment in saying that if Christ had founded Christianity, Paul had invented the Church, and that it was he who, drawing upon pagan " mysteries," had sacramentalized the innocent first-beginnings of the new Faith. Having thus been battered and mauled from every angle, St. Paul seems to be resuming the place that always should have been his, which Catholic tradition in fact had always assigned to him, namely, that of a Christian obedient to Christ, completely at one with the older Apostles as to doctrine, but endowed with a colossal personality, and held in thrall by a vision which he knew he was called to communicate to the world at large.

. . . .

Tarsus was a self-satisfied city, not without reason. We need not dwell on its enormous pagan history, simply because the Jewish community within it kept rigidly aloof from all that, and because the little Saul, " Hebrew, son of Hebrews ; Pharisee, born of Pharisees," grew up with a quite undiluted and unentangled psychology. The family must have been rich, because he was ". born " a citizen of the Empire, and citizenship, in Tarsus, was bestowed only on an inner circle of the wealthy. This did not prevent him, of course, from being taught a trade ; the Jews considered that a boy who had been taught no trade had been taught to be a thief. Hence later on he was always able to earn his keep by working at that black Cilician hair-cloth of

I

which they made waterproofs and the like. He went to school in Jerusalem, and " sat at the feet of Gamaliel "—literally, because boys squatted round their Rabbi who made them learn the Old Testament by heart and then, as we say, catechized them. To the intensely sensitive small boy, this visit to Jerusalem must have been everlastingly impressive. He returned to Tarsus and is not heard of in Jerusalem again till the martyrdom of St. Stephen, and passages in his letters afterwards make it clear that he never saw our Lord.

He breaks suddenly into the Scriptures as holding the cloaks of those who had thrown them off that they might the better stone St. Stephen into pulp. And immediately after that, a kind of blood-lust infected him ; he went straight to the High Priest (probably still Caiaphas) and offered himself to join in an absolute war of extermination. The memory haunted him till the end. He " forced his way even into private houses," and dragged Christians off to gaol ; " with zeal I persecuted the Church—even to excess I persecuted the Church of God and was ravaging her—I was a blasphemer, a persecutor, an insolent—I persecuted this doctrine even unto blood, putting both men and women into chains and casting them into prison—In my excess of madness against them, I would pursue them even into distant cities." Such were the sentences that this memory was to place upon his lips.

There is no trace at all that this view of himself had been falsified by a morbid brooding on the past. All the more exorbitant does this positive persecution-mania appear. One can understand the young man duly obedient to Authority, taking the views of the princes of his people, and rebuking or even boycotting the Christians. But this violent taking of the initiative ; this hunting of the believers out of their very homes, this pursuit of them, this ferocity even towards women—here are reactions that require explanation, unless indeed we yield to the temptation to suppose that diabolic agency was at least to some degree directly responsible for them. And we agree that the frenzy which beset the Reformers, causing them to destroy everything even remotely connected with the Mass, and again much of what has recently been happening in Spain, does strongly suggest a hellish invasion of the soul. And we certainly do not think that St. Stephen's speech, provocative to infuriation-point as it must have seemed, would have sufficed to create so enduring and unbridled a passion. Had Saul's rage been suddenly lashed into mania, it would probably have expired fairly soon. We are accustomed by now to seeing in these fierce psychological reactions a symptom of an interior urge that is being repressed with a violence that seeks its compensation as well as its disguise in behaviour such as Saul's was. In persecuting the Christians, he may well have been savaging his own soul.

Later expressions used by St. Paul show how intolerable the venerated yoke of Pharisaism had in reality been, and indeed that of the Law itself as by then interpreted. The Law showed him what was good, what evil, but provided him with no help to pursue the one and eschew the other. " The evil that I would not, that I do." I do not see this adolescent to have been a sinner : he would have been infinitely more at peace—peace of a de-spiritualized sort—if he had been. But I do see in him a tumultuous temperament rigidly reduced into austerity ; whether or no, left to himself, he would have found fairly soon that he was at breaking point, we cannot tell, though we may think it probable. But a Christian student would at once recognize that he was *not* left to himself. There was a goad already stabbing at his soul within him, and—to use a humble simile—as a man may actually hurt himself *more* to get rid of this pain or that pain, so Saul began " kicking " against that goad, and hurt himself worse still. There are pains which are compensatory for one another.

Possibly it was the " face as of an angel " that he, " looking stead-fastly " upon Stephen, had seen, which gave him the first of that long series of stabbing torments. To see peace and joy in the eyes of one who is denying what you hold most dear and yet feel you are being false to, can be maddening. You can see that he would have joined in the stoning of Stephen, had he been allowed to. Why was he not ? No matter. Possibly because the judges of such a case were also normally the executioners, and Saul was still too young to be permitted to sit as judge. Possibly because he was beset by a scruple that might almost have driven him, by the conflict that it engineered, to delirium— he may have considered that the whole procedure was (as indeed it was) illegitimate, the application of a sort of mob's lynch-law ; so that he had to forbid to himself what he so desperately wanted to do. Anyhow, he did the minimum that he could. He " held their clothes," and stared at the ghastly spectacle—which *we* describe so lightly, " they stoned Stephen " . . . but dare we let ourselves imagine it ?

The Road to Damascus followed. " Breathing out threats and murder," he prepared his caravan, and after a week's riding saw Damascus lying beautiful below him. Then came the shattering experience. A light out-blazed the noon : he saw a figure—he knew not whom (" Lord, who art Thou ? ")—and he heard the words, spoken in Aramaic, " Saul, Saul, why persecutest thou Me ? " And, on his enquiry, he was told, " I am Jesus, whom thou art persecuting." He asked what he was to do, and was sent to a Damascene Jew, Ananias, who should tell him the answer to that.[1]

We have, then, I think, the right to see that Saul had had no

[1] I think the futile attempt to detect discrepancies between the three narrations of this episode has been abandoned.

consciousness at all of being wrong ; indeed, that he thought he was
right in persecuting the Christians as cruelly as he possibly could, but,
that his interior conflict (if indeed it existed at all, even unconsciously)
regarded precisely *them*, and not Christ.   He had not known Christ
in the flesh ; he had no memories, even bitterly beaten down, of His
sweet attractiveness ; he knew of Him only as a rebellious heretic
who had been squalidly executed : possibly it made his hatred for the
sect of Christians[1] the more hot, because they alleged allegiance to so
mean a man.   But his " goad," so far, had been concerned with
Judaism versus Christianity, not a personal struggle—Saul versus
Christ.   But it was, precisely, *Christ* who appeared to him, and
Christ, moreover, identified with His Christians, " Why persecutest
thou *Me ?* "

Saul was " received into the Church " by Ananias and ate, and
recovered his strength, and asked what he ought to do next (that is a
psychological change, if you like !).   Ananias told him, vaguely, that
he was a " casket," specially selected for the carrying forth of Christ's
name to all the peoples of the world.   Saul went away at once—not to
do *that*, but into Arabia, though no one knows just where within it,
and there he " went into retreat."

What mysteries then took place within him ?   Certainly a double
crisis was involved.   He had nothing to change in his beliefs about
God.   The Pharisaic belief in God was pure.   Nor yet in what concerned the nature of man : nor was Saul the man to doubt the existence
and immortality and responsibility of the soul, nor the fact of Sin that
had streamed like a " black flood," death in its train, into the world as
from Adam.   But, as St. Paul himself says (Gal. i, 16), " Christ *was
revealed in me*."   Jesus, whom he had persecuted, now became the
centre of his personal life ; but, inasmuch as by persecuting Christians,
he had been persecuting Christ, it followed that Christ was also the
centre of all Christian lives, so that Paul and they had one life common
to all of them—Christ's life.   This was to become an essential element
in his existence alike and his preaching.   This was to be the " angle "
from which he contemplated both the world at large, and the Church.
Hence I hardly think that just now the thought of his destiny in regard
to the pagans came *first* in his mind.   I think that having seen the rôle
that Christ was to play in the world, he simply could not have excluded
the pagans.   Consequential details as to religious observances were
hardly likely just then to have troubled him.   All such casuistry was
subordinate.   What he had never guessed, what now he brooded upon
till the thought of it became literally a " second nature," was this
Incorporation into Christ, to which the world was summoned, and to

[1] This name did not yet exist, but it is convenient so to describe the followers of
Jesus.

which he was to summon the world ; and the immediate consequence, his own co-corporation with every Christian—and all men were potential Christians. Every veil that had shrouded the earth was now torn away for him : the Church—Christ—were to become co-extensive with the world, and with every man for ever. It was his special vocation to preach that.

But the second crisis must surely have been a moral one. However heroic a man may be, if but he is sensitive (and Paul certainly was that) he cannot feel anything but appalled by the thought that he, who has lived in a blaze of publicity, whose name has been created in one way, must now come forth into no less a publicity, renouncing everything that so far he has proclaimed. Paul had not yet learnt humility—at least, he had not had time to practise more than a very little of it ; undoubtedly the vision of Christ had hurled him once and for all off the pinnacle of his pride, but the " old self " was many a time to make itself felt, and to return to his own people, preaching Christ, and foreseeing what indeed happened, that the Christians themselves would be incredulous of such a conversion, and that he might find himself if not excluded from their community, at least anxiously received and chillily into it and being a man belonging nowhere and to nothing—that was appalling ! Save that he knew himself to be as truly now " in Christ," as Christ was " in him." " *Christ was revealed in me.*"

Saul returned to Damascus and, as one might have expected, roused the orthodox Jews to an absolute frenzy of passion and they vowed to murder him. He escaped to Jerusalem, but there it was the Hellenized Jews whose fury blazed up against him (why it should have been they, it is hard to see ; just possibly he approached them first, feeling that the others would be hopelessly obdurate), and again, at the urgent request of the Faithful, who were, I take it, afraid for their entire community, for they did not yet thoroughly know and appreciate the disconcerting convert, he fled.

He went home to Tarsus, and there, proving that it was not any fanaticism of his that had stirred up these savageries, he remained working quietly for a minimum (so I should calculate) of three years and possibly more. Nor did he return southwards till he was fetched by Barnabas who had befriended him in the nervous days at Jerusalem. Barnabas had been sent to see what was happening at Antioch, whence tales of pagans being received into the Church were arriving. Barnabas was so impressed by what he saw that he went off in person to Tarsus and fetched Saul back with him.

In A.D. 43 a prophet Agabus announced that a great famine was impending, and the Antiochene Christians anticipated it by making a collection which they sent by Barnabas and Saul to Jerusalem. Herod

Agrippa's persecution must just then have been raging there, but that king died suddenly and horribly while celebrating games in honour of the Emperor and after having himself been acclaimed as a god. This altered the whole situation. Rome resumed the government of the territories that had been given to Agrippa and the pagan power ensured peace for the Church, just then, such as Jewish rule never could. And coincidently with this not only was Saul transported in ecstasy to the " third heaven " and heard " words that never can be spoken " (for it was too at this point, we hold, that the spiritual marvels related in 2 Cor. xii, 2–4, may best be referred), but, it was revealed that Saul and Barnabas were to be " set aside " in view of a special work, which was, in fact, the first deliberately organized missionary journey equipped by the Church. The Apostles and their associates had travelled into Samaria, up to Antioch, proselytes and pagans had already become Christians, the Antiochene Christians had in fact become so numerous as to receive that very name as a *nickname ;* but casual events had dictated this. A world-mission, spontaneously undertaken because according to the Will of God, was something new.

This new *sort* of enterprize is what is here important, rather than the details of its implementing. We do not propose to relate the missionary journeys that now continuously succeeded one another. It is the whole colour of the Christian Church, henceforward unmistakable, that concerns us. She definitely is determined to *Christianize the world*, and it can be shown that when she was not missionary in act, this was because for various reasons (such as persecution or war) she could not be. Herein the Catholic and Catholicizing idea clashes with the modern spirit save in so far as that spirit is Communist. Communism too is a missionary creed and proposes to change not only a class or a country but the world. In very many ways the Christian and the Communist movements and indeed the imperial Roman idea and system could be compared. Shall we say that the Communist works by means of violence and hate ; the Roman Cæsar-god, by means of violence and scorn ; the Christian, by peaceful methods and with love ? There is enough, in those words, to go on with. They do not exhaust the facts, but they are more true than false, and all of them are antagonistic at any rate to the average English sentiment, which is individualist, dislikes propaganda of any sort, and objects strongly to interference either with opinion or with " conscience." Yet after all, Paul was to come up against something of that sort later on.[1]

The expedition began quietly enough. They went to Cyprus, which not only was close at hand, but was Barnabas's home-island. The chief event of their stay there was the abrupt transformation of

[1]As a matter of fact, we are just beginning, politically to use " propaganda," in sheer self-defence against the flood of anti-British propaganda too often broadcast.

Saul into Paul, and his unquestioned emergence into first place. And whatever Barnabas may have thought of Paul's decision forthwith to cross the water into the malaria-haunted, brigand-infested ravines and mountains of Pamphylia, the young John Mark, a cousin of Barnabas, who also was with them, decided to go home and in fact went. Later on, when Barnabas proposed to Paul that they should again take him with them, Paul flatly refused, so that an embitterment occurred between him and Barnabas, who was replaced by Silas. However, later still, Mark became not only the assistant and " secretary " of St. Peter, but was of the highest assistance to St. Paul.

Religious art has perhaps accustomed us to all-too placid a picture of the Apostles and of St. Paul in particular. The ferocious youth did not suddenly curb the tumults that at a moment could rage up within him. But never was there anything mean or petty, idle or merely resentful about Paul's wrath. He was the most generous-hearted of men, as a score of passages in his letters show ; the most sensitive, most " temperamental," as we should say, the most mercurial of men. He was capable of black depressions and also, we recall, often felt ill ; he could blaze up into exultation ; he was infinitely tender ; he was liable to be almost overwhelmed with gratitude both to God and to man ; he held, together with his vast visions, an intimate memory and appreciation of individuals ; he felt loneliness acutely, yet was ready to deprive himself even of his last companion, if but he could thus be of service to others who were in need.

We spoke of his " vast vision." Yet we do not think, as Sir W. M. Ramsay loved to argue with much skill, that Paul deliberately formed a mental map of the Roman Empire, saw in it an organization geographically " Christianizable " ; that he valued the Greek city-state as contrasted with oriental despotisms and the Jewish legalist theocracy ; and that though he practically never, or never, mentions art, philosophy, politics, history and the like, he was well-educated in all of them. I believe that Paul acted direct from his "revelation"; that he proceeded or refrained according as he felt himself urged or checked by the Spirit, and that his education had not been of the sort that Ramsay pictures. I fear that that admirable student, who has done more than most men to display to us the material world through which Paul moved, is none the less too anxious to make us Englishmen think well of him as of a man who had had a " liberal education " and was also an organizing genius. Paul managed his journeys sensibly : he proceeded according to a very simple plan from place to place, and he was apt to come back over the same ground " confirming the churches." He was " methodical " in due measure, but not a sort of missionary Napoleon ; and it is perhaps because Ramsay does not really grasp Paul's supernaturalism that he does not realize how far out of perspective all those other elements would have sunk for him, if not have vanished altogether.

Of course I do not mean that Paul never adapted himself to circumstances, but he was far more prepared to expect circumstances to adapt themselves to him, or rather, to God. He preached a really charming little sermon of " natural religion " to the rough Lystrians ; and at Athens he really does seem to have tried to talk " philosophically," and even quoted an abstract line about God from a Greek poet ; but the experiment did not succeed, and he went on to the far less promising mercantile and most licentious town, Corinth, very depressed, sick, frankly frightened, and all the more determined to " know nothing " amongst the Corinthians save " Christ and Him crucified." " Wiser than men is God's folly ; stronger than men, His weakness . . ." (1 Cor. i, 25). Who but Paul would have had the courage to say just that ?

What he had already realized and now saw with extreme clarity was, that Christianity was continuous with, and yet in essence different from Judaism, and that this involved the complete liberation of the Christian—not indeed from the moral Law proclaimed by Moses, but from all the ritual regulations of the Older Testament, not to dwell on the thousand-and-one customs that tradition had piled up during the centuries. We need not discuss in any detail this negative aspect of his message. He had to fight for his view, but at Jerusalem Peter settled the matter dogmatically in Paul's favour, indeed he had himself already proclaimed the same truth—against, to be sure, his instinct. Remember that the Jew *loved* his hereditary possessions even when they irked him. Of course a number of " casuistical " questions cropped up. Pagan converts were not obliged to submit to Jewish regulations—even circumcision—granted ! But what of the Jewish convert ? Might *he* discard them ? Would it be, not obligatory, but laudable, in the pagan convert, to adopt those immemorial practices ? And so forth. The first half of Paul's Christian missionary career was occupied with questions of this sort.

But also, and far more positively, and constructively, with the Free Gift of God, which we now call technically " Grace." And therefore, with no abstraction, but with Him who *was* that Gift—" If but you knew the Gift of God ! " " I, who am speaking with you, am He." *He* saves. Not the Greek philospher, not the Hebrew legalist, could save the world. " We, we preach Christ, Christ crucified—to the Jews, a shocking thing ; to the Greeks, a silly thing ; but to *us*, to us who are called, whether Jew or Greek, Christ the Power of God, and the Wisdom of God ! " Then follow the words we quoted above.

This led up to something still more positive and more " vital." Christ did not save us *instead* of us. What He did, living, dying, and

rising, was done *for* us, not *instead* of. Herein is cleft the chasm that
separates the Catholic from the " Reformer," who emphasized just
that " instead." God does not accept Christ " instead of " us : He
accepts Him, because in Him we are incorporate : He accepts us,
because in us is now Christ and the life of Christ. " If a man be in
Christ—lo ! a new creature ! . . . We, in Him, are to become the
Righteousness of God ! " (2 Cor. vi, 1). " With Christ am I co-
crucified ; I live, no longer *I*, but Christ is living in me." (Gal. ii).
" All you who have been baptised into Christ have *put on* Christ.
There exists no more Jew versus Greek, there exists no more slave
versus free man, nay, no more so much as female versus male—all you
are *one person* in Jesus Christ." (*ib.* iii, 27). " To be circumcised—to be
uncircumcised—that is nothing ! But a *new creation !* " (*ib.* vi, 15).
Such was the theme that Paul expounded to the untutored uplander
Galatians no less than to the hearty sensualists the Corinthians, and
again, in much greater development, to the Romans. And at what
cost—

Bruised, but not broken ; dismayed, yet not despairing ; hunted,
yet not fainting ; stoned, but never slain—ever bearing about in our
very body the killing of the Lord Jesus, so that the Life too of Jesus
may be revealed in this our dying flesh ! . . . *Therefore* play we not
the coward ! but even though this our outward man be being
worn away, yet from day to day our inner self is being renewed ;
for the trivial anguish of the moment works out for us overwhelmingly,
overwhelmingly, an eternal weight of glory—for we look, not on
things visible, but on things unseen ! (2 Cor. iii, 7-18).

Oh, I reckon the sufferings of the moment as not worthy to be
counted in view of the glory to be revealed in our regard ! Creation
itself is eager, expectant, of the revelation of God's Sons ! Creation
was once enthralled and made perverse . . . but she preserved hope,
seeing that she herself shall be freed, one day, from her destructive
slavery into the freedom of the glory of the Children of God. Yes—
we know that the whole of creation until this very time joins in our
groaning, travails along with us, yearning for your adoption, for the
ransom of our humanity . . . Ah ! we know that for those who love
God, He maketh all things to work together for good ! . . . What
then are we to say to that ? If God is for us, who is against us ? *God*—
who spared not His own Son, but gave Him over for us all—how then
shall He not give us *all* things together with Him ? Who can lay
charge against the elect of God, ' God ' ? But God *justifies* us !
Who can condemn us ? ' Christ Jesus ' ? But *He* died—no, rather,
He rose—He is at the right hand of God, and is interceding for us !
Who then shall separate us from the love of Christ ? Affliction, or
stress, or persecution, or hunger, or nakedness, or danger, or the
sword ? . . . But in these very things we *more* than conquer, through
Him who loved us ! Ah—I know well that neither death nor life,

nor angels, nor spirits, nor the present, nor the future, nor powers, nor height, nor depth, nor any thing created shall be able to separate us from the love of God that is in Christ Jesus, our Lord ! (Romans viii).

You see here that the ecstatic acclaim of the divine Charity, which raises the 13th Chapter of the First Letter to the Corinthians to a level reached by no uninspired document in world, was *realized* in Paul. He had passed into a world where not the Jewish nationalism, and certainly not the confused and tormented aspirations of any part of the pagan world could any more preoccupy him, but Christ only, and God in Christ, and Christ in him.

You can read in the Acts the vigorously told story of Paul's arrests, culminating in that which brought about his appeal to Cæsar, and his transportation to Rome, and his first sojourn there. Did St. Luke mean to write a second volume about Paul ? Possibly, and I think that in fact he did ; if he did, it is lost to us, as many of Paul's own letters are lost. But enough survive to enable us to see into whatever sublimer realms this supreme doctrine of our incorporation into Christ lifted Paul, especially in regard to its consequences in the Christian.

The great Epistles which matter to us here are those to the Philippians, the Colossians and the Ephesians, of which the last bears somewhat the same relation to the second as Romans does to Galatians, save that it was meant to be an Encyclical and sent from one church to another. Disliking to insist on what Paul was *combating*—seeing that what has mattered in him was his positive, embracing, and constructive vision and work—we can say very briefly that what was to be called " Gnosticism " dawned already from beneath his horizon. There are those who hold that when St. John, in his Apocalypse, brings upon his scene a *delegated* Wild Beast who " spoke like a lamb . . . " but none the less was doing exactly what Satan's supreme representative the Wild Beast " from over-seas," Imperial Rome was doing, he meant by this Second Beast, so mealy-mouthed, that flattering philosophy which says that everyone is right—after their fashion ; religions are but variant symbolical forms of the One ineffable Truth. Thus no form of religion need be reprobated save one which might say that it was the *only* authenticated Faith, the only quite true-Truth. St. Paul undoubtedly alludes quite often to this rising Theosophism, of which we have so much nowadays, over against the crude atheism of the thorough-paced Communist. But, I repeat, I wish to conclude with what was Paul, not by insisting on what was anti-Paul or that against which he wrote.

There now comes into his letters, again and again, the word *Pleroma*. He means by that, first, that the Plenitude of the Divinity resides totally in Christ, and is not gradually diluted through a whole series

of intermediate beings like " spirits " until man be reached.   He means
too that in Christ is the full storehouse of all those graces in which we
are meant, through Him alone, to participate.   And finally, by
" Plenitude," he means that Perfect Christ, that Christ who is still
growing to His " maturity " ;   that Christ who is " the Head of the
Church that is His Body, the Fulfilling of Him who is thus fully
fulfilling Himself in all."   (Eph. i, 23).

Christ is—

The reflection of God the Invisible,
Born first, before all creation.
Yes, *in* Him were created all things,
Things in heaven, or on earth,
Things visible or invisible—
Be they thrones or dominations, principalities or powers—
By means of Him, and unto Him, they all of them were created.
And Himself is prior to all,
And in Himself do all things hold together ;
Yes, and Himself is the Head of the Body, that is, of the Church,
He who is Origin, and again, Firstborn from the dead,
So that He might in all things stand forth First—
For in Him it has pleased the Father to make the whole Plenitude to
dwell.

God has willed to make known the richness of the glory of this Mystery
among the very pagans—namely, *Christ in you*, our hope of glory !
Him we proclaim, urging it on every man . . . that we may present
every man mysteriously perfected in Christ.   Yes—for *this* do I
strain and struggle, in the measure of that energy of His that
energises so mightily in me ! (Eph. i, 12-29).

   All this God set forth in Christ's person, to be dispensed to us as
the ages grew to their fulfilment. He willed to bring all things as
to a head in Christ—things heavenly and things earthly alike—in
Christ, seeing that in *Him* we have our lot assigned to us. . . .
(and I pray) that you indeed may know what is the hope to which
He calls you—what is the wealth of His inheritance among the
saints ;   what is the overwhelming greatness of His power towards
you who believe . . . for it is on the scale of the energy of the might
of His strength that He made to act in the person of Christ, raising
Him from the dead. . . . Yes, all things hath He set under His feet,
and Him hath He set as Head Supreme for the Church—that is,
His Body—the fulfilling of Him who is fulfilling Himself, fully,
in all things. (*Ibid.*)

   I would have wished to quote much more from St. Paul, including
that Epistle to the Hebrews that has been too rashly dissociated from
him. I should have liked to dwell on his martyrdom which must have

been almost quite solitary.   The " Healthful Fountains " still whisper beneath the whispering trees where they beheaded him, and you may find it easier to pray to him there than in his vast basilica under which still his body lies.

But I have no space for that.   I have wished to indicate certain turning-points in his career ; certain ways in which he was made to be a fit instrument in the hands of Christ, for the Christianization of the world, and, I might say, for its salvation even temporal.   For until man, and men, are understood and treated as Paul knew them, and was fain to treat them, no method is likely to be devised even for their earthly welfare individual or social ; and no method at all can be invented for the gathering of them together into the everlasting divine-human Society.   Negatively, Paul had to labour at the tedious task of convincing many among the first Christians that salvation was in *no* way bound up with the Mosaic ritual ; positively, he had to proclaim with all the force of his Christ-indwelt personality that it *was* bound up with Christ and with Him alone.   This, and again his own experience, led him to insist on the *freedom* of this redemption ; on Grace.   And this, in its turn, to insist on the consequences of Grace—Incorporation into Christ ; co-corporation with all who were thus incorporate in Him.   Hence the construction of the only true Society, both on this earth, and in heaven ; for, in God's plan, human nature is destined for and called to Super-Nature, and, save, in Christ, man does not reach its true self at all.   From this, flowing downwards, come all those consequences of charity, unity and peace, which not one of our modern political, economic, diplomatic or other schemes have even begun to produce.   We need not enter further into those consequences ; anyone can see that our world at present— schismatic, unstable, mendacious, is unlike, antagonistic to, GOD, the One, the Eternal, and the True ; and that our hatreds, wars, and bitter divisions between men, are hostile to the Eucharistic virtues of Charity, Peace and Unity.   Others, writing in this series upon great Catholics will (even unconsciously) show how these were the very things for and by which they lived.

ENID DINNIS

ST. PAULA

A.D. 347–404

THE HISTORY OF St. Paula (A.D. 347–404) is in one sense the story
of a Movement—the great monastic movement amongst women
in the Christian Church. Paula's name is not to be separated from
that of her daughter, Eustochium, of Melania, Marcella, and other
great Catholic women of the period that succeeded the persecutions,
a period when Christianity was kneeling at the tombs of the martyrs
without emulating their spirit.

It was the hand that greedily collected and conserved the writings
of St. Jerome that fortuitously preserved for posterity the story of
Paula. It remains enshrined in the letters of that mighty scribe, and
St. Paula is ours to-day with all the rich detail of her wonderful life
and achievement, no cold, classical figure carved in marble, but a
flesh-and-blood woman, inasmuch as Jerome, her friend and biographer,
was a flesh-and-blood saint, a drop of whose heart's blood was mingled
with the ink in which he wrote her story. It comes to us as warm
and living as the story handed down by tradition, although the
succeeding ages have not clothed it in the warm garments of
legendary lore.

St. Paula lived in an age in many ways akin to our own. She is
far more modern than the saints of mediæval times. Christianity at
the time that she enters into our story was out of the catacombs.
Christians were making mixed marriages. Paula's husband was a
pagan, although her own family was devoutly Christian. She came of
one of the noblest families in the Empire. St. Jerome lays careful
stress on her high birth, inasmuch as it became the instrument of a
great renunciation. Paula's marriage was a perfectly happy one.
She had five children, of whom Eustochium was the fourth. The
youngest was the only boy, and he remained unbaptized. The four
girls were brought up to be devout Christians like their mother.

We see Paula leading the life of a Roman patrician lady ; mixing
with the pagan world, scornful of its follies but falling in with its
conventions. She painted her face as the other Roman ladies did ;

wore gilt shoes ; was carried about in a litter by slaves, and took her daily bath in luxury which our own day might comprehend but which would have amazed the Victorians.

Paganism was dying ; Christianity was in the ascendant. The Pope occupied the Imperial Palace, vacated for political reasons by the Emperor. The danger to Christianity came from friendship rather than enmity with the unbeliever. Softness and luxury, not to say vice, were creeping in. Against this state of things there came a strong reaction. Certain groups of Christians adopted an austere form of life. Many fled to the desert and lived in cells remote from the perils of the pagan cities. These were the famous Fathers of the Desert.

In Rome itself there were seen Christian virgins and widows who exchanged their finery for a rough brown gown and veiled their heads in place of an elaborate head-dress. These consecrated their lives to God. Paula made her friends amongst them. Foremost was Marcella, whose name figures in the Martyrology.

Marcella was an immensely wealthy woman who at her husband's death had consecrated herself to a single life and her goods to the poor. St. Athanasius, as a monk from the desert, had stirred her heart, as Rufinus had stirred the heart of the valiant woman Melania, who was now established in a convent of virgins near Mount Olivet, in Palestine. Marcella turned her palace on the Aventine into a convent for the young maidens who had vowed themselves to virginity. The sister of St. Ambrose, Marcellina, was one of those whom she mothered, and it was for her community that the saint wrote his famous treatise on virginity.

Paula looked upon Marcella as a sister, and the little Eustochium regarded her as a second mother. It was to Marcella that Paula took the child when the stunning blow of her husband's death fell upon her.

Paula was left a widow at the age of thirty-one. Her grief was tempestuous. She became ill enough for her life to be despaired of. Strong human feelings found a free vent, but in her soul there was no spirit of defeat. She accepted her husband's death as a sign that God had called her to a higher life. When she turned her back on the world to embrace the consecrated life it was no sullen hugging of a life-sorrow, but a ready response to a call to a new and higher enterprise.

Complete retirement from the world was impossible, for she had her children to bring up, but the radical change which took place in Paula's life was that which is called conversion. Not, indeed, the abandonment of an evil life for a good one, but the ceasing to measure out the ointment—Paula broke her alabaster vase over the feet of her Lord. She was as extravagant as Mary Magdalen, and incurred as much censure.

She fasted and prayed ; visited the sick and the poor in their hovels, and practised severe mortifications, keeping pace with Marcella and her virgins with whom she loved to spend her time, chanting the psalms and studying the Scriptures.

The Christian spirituality of that era was derived from a deep study of, and delight in, the Holy Scriptures. Piety expressed itself in visits paid to the tombs of the martyrs which the reigning Pope had restored and beautified. Paula and little Eustochium frequently made these visits together. The latter was destined to become her mother's companion through all the high adventures to which she was being led. Paula's other daughters remained attached to the world until the sudden widowhood of Blesilla, the eldest, after seven months of married life led to her conversion to a life that rivalled her mother's in austerity.

Paula's pagan relatives—there were many on her husband's side—made a great outcry against her new mode of life ; nor were certain of her Christian friends over-pleased. Her excesses rebuked their mediocrity. Even some who wore the brown gown and demure veil were not above getting the best of two worlds. Marcella and her following had all the stern qualities of the Fathers of the Desert—their counterblast to the softness which was sapping the strength of the Christian life was no timid one. Yet a gentle child like Eustochium could hear in it the voice of the Good Shepherd of the catacombs.

In the year 382 came events which were to develop Paula's life on the lines she had chosen. The bishops of the Church were assembled in Rome and Paula was chosen to act as hostess to St. Epiphanius. From the latter she heard stories of the desert monasteries and the wonderful lives led by the monks there. Far from the glitter and turmoil of pagan Rome, Paula pictured that peace in which God speaks to the heart which He has called forth into the solitude. That symbolic desert place of the Scripture was still to her a geographical one.

But there were her children. She was still tied to the world.

It is at this juncture that St. Jerome appears on the scene—one had almost said " screen ", for Paula's life makes a series of pictures that form themselves in the mind as one reads it. St. Jerome ; the fierce monk from the desert, the genius with the artist's temperament—the man of letters who had cast off the spell of Greek and Roman profane literature and made the Holy Scriptures his sole library. Jerome the saint.

It was Jerome who was to bring Paula to her full spiritual stature.

As for St. Jerome ; in Rome, the benighted city given over to softness and vice, he made a discovery. There existed a body of noble Christian women who had the courage to lead a life of prayer and amazing austerity. Pope Damasus appointed Jerome to give a series of conferences on the Holy Scriptures to these same women. The monk was somewhat afraid of the other sex, but he had no choice. Paula was one of those who attended the conferences. St. Jerome gives us an idea of the red-hot enthusiasm of the members of this Study Circle. He was kept busy by the urgent demands of Paula and Marcella to elucidate the difficult passages which they encountered when he led them into " the meadow of the Holy Scriptures." They would send their own solutions along to him by a messenger who was instructed not to return without an answer. Jerome wrote these answers at night after his other work was done and the messenger must have exercised much patience. They formed valuable little treatises on the subject under discussion, extracted from him by the wiles of his feminine pupils. It was a preliminary to the part which Paula was to play in regard to the literary output of the Master-theologian. In years to come the bright shadow of Paula would fall across many a priceless script produced under duress when Jerome's temperament was at war with the magnitude of his task.

From Jerome Paula learnt the hidden wisdom of the Sacred Text. She made contacts with the Mind of God concealed from the reader who does not pierce the rind and reach the pith. She and Marcella set themselves to learn Hebrew so that they might enter more perfectly into the study of the Scriptures. They chanted the Psalms in Hebrew in the convent where Marcella gathered her religious family.

St. Jerome called these studies " the food of prayer ", and such they certainly were, for prayer was the main occupation of Paula's life. Nevertheless, her duty to her children was performed faithfully and with passionate devotion. Her outburst of grief at the untimely death of her eldest daughter, Blesilla, was as stupendous as her widow's grief had been. We find Paula making a very human lapse into her natural self on this occasion. There was pomp and splendour at Blesilla's funeral. As time went on Paula collected a community to live in her own house. St. Jerome called it " the domestic church." Rome became agog with the scandal of these patrician women who were enticing young girls to give up the idea of marriage and lead lives of austerity. St. Jerome turned the scourge of his pen on these critics. He knew how to do it. His invectives have come down to us together with his other writings. It was doubtless this warmth of expression that made him many enemies.

Paula was charged with squandering her children's patrimony—
she was indeed fast spending her substance on the poor and on good
works. She arranged to make over a great part of her fortune to her
children. She had come to loathe Rome, with its glittering paganism,
its shallow and inadequate expression of Christianity. One can
picture the comfortably-off Christian ladies being carried by their
slaves to the tombs of the martyrs as a sort of fashionable devotion.
Even the sermons of the stern men from the desert may have had
a value as a society diversion ? Paula's day was very much like ours.
At any rate Rome had become intolerable. In the solitudes alone
could peace and union with God be found.

Her great longing was to visit the Holy Land and if possible take
her virgins with her, and her daughter Eustochium. The latter was
now wearing the brown garment and veil of the consecrated women.
From her other children she would have to separate herself. It was
a terrible thought. The two youngest were still children. Paula
faced it out. Her life was formed on heroic lines ; but she had a
heart of flesh. " Have I a heart of iron ? " St. Jerome had cried, when
faced with a sacrifice of human affections, " Am I made of stone, and
was I suckled by a tigress ? " Paula could have said the same. But
she held by her purpose. Reproaches were showered upon her by
her pagan relatives. St. Jerome came in for his share—from his
fellow Christians. Amongst other things they brought charges against
him of mutilating the Scriptures in his translations. They also
attacked his moral character—and Paula's. Jerome retaliated,
scathing the vices of the age. Paula did her best to restrain the wrath
of the fiery man of God—that was to be her rôle for many a year to
come. The death of Pope Damasus occurred about this time. Rome
had become hateful indeed. In the desert alone would be found peace
and opportunity for service.

Jerome left Rome for the East in the August of 385. Paula completed
her preparations and followed him soon after with Eustochium and
some of her virgins and widows. A description of her departure has
come down to us from St. Jerome's vivid pen. As the vessel that
was to bear her away broke loose from its moorings Toxotius, her
young son, stood on the shore with outstretched arms as though he
would follow her. Her youngest daughter, Rufina, was there weeping
silently. Paula's heart was torn in two. Paulina was happily
married, but these two were still children. St. Jerome would have
it that Paula's love for her children was greater than that of any
other mother. Christianity strengthened rather than lessened the
natural love. There were her friendships, too. Marcella had been
pressed to accompany Paula on her journey, but the former's aged
mother was still alive, and that constituted a tie in the eyes of the

Christian woman who would so readily have sacrificed everything. There were other friends whom she would never see again in all probability. Eustochium alone was at her mother's side. The two are never separated in Paula's story.

Paula journeyed first to the Isle of Cyprus where she visited St. Epiphanius, her former guest. At Antioch she found St. Jerome awaiting her to be her guide on the pilgrimage to the Holy Land which she had undertaken to make before visiting the monasteries in the desert.

The story of Paula's travels, her wanderings in the desert, her journeying midst many perils, her various visits to the Holy Places, would be too long to describe even in outline. One may make a picture of the caravan. Jerome and his companions riding on horses, Paula and hers on asses. Paula saw now with her bodily eyes the land into which she had made so many spiritual excursions, the land of the Old Testament and the New. She refused to lodge in the Pro-Consul's palace at Jerusalem, choosing a humble lodging near Calvary. The Central event of History was then removed by a space of less than four hundred years. It was as near to Paula as the Elizabethan times are to us. The new church erected by St. Helena had but recently arisen on the site of Calvary. The rediscovered holy Cross of our redemption was there to receive adoration. But it was the cave at Bethlehem that made its supreme appeal to the imagination of Paula. It was the Bethlehem of the Nativity. She saw there the manger in which Our Lord was laid, before which she was to spend so many hours in prayer and ecstasy. " Here," she cried, " I have found my rest ! "

Paula decided that when her journey to the desert of Egypt was accomplished she would settle down with her community at Bethlehem.

Near Mount Olivet there stood the monasteries governed by the pioneers, Rufinus and Melania. Paula and her companions visited these. The meeting between the two women must have been a memorable occasion, worthy of an artist's brush. It has been passed over by the biographer's pen for sad reasons to be explained later in Paula's story.

Before settling at Bethlehem the travellers crossed the Nile and visited Alexandria, a city of immense intellectual activity. They were entertained by the Bishop and attended conferences on the Holy Scriptures at the great Christian School. After this they adventured into the desert in search of the monks and anchorites, the men of the solitude who lived for the things of Eternity alone. They journeyed, going at times without food or drink, encountering crocodiles with open jaws, foundering in quagmires. In wild and terrible deserts they guided themselves by the stars. Such was St.

Paula's pilgrimage. She was rewarded by being at length introduced to men of whom she cried in rapture, " these are not mortal men but angels ! "

Alack ! Human nature was to betray itself later on, even in the Solitudes.

The journey took the best part of a year. Paula then found herself once more in Bethlehem, free to develop her great scheme for founding a monastery for women near to the Church of the Nativity. She also set about providing a house for St. Jerome and his companions. During the building of the monasteries they found temporary quarters, and the new life shaped itself. On her return to Bethlehem Paula was greeted by the news of the death of her young daughter Rufina. The lesson of the anchorites had not dehumanized her. Paula wept for Rufina as she had wept for Blesilla. It broke another link with the world she had left.

Peace permeated the life led by Paula and her companions. They cultivated their garden, and walked out on the hillside singing psalms and drinking in the beauties of nature. Paula alluded to Rome as a dungeon. Not even the superintending of the building of her new convent came between her soul and God. As for St. Jerome, he was plunging more deeply than ever into the Holy Scriptures in the cave which he had made his cell. Paula and Eustochium persuaded him to read the entire Bible through with them, and incited him to embark on the commentaries and translations which might almost be called their united gift to the Church. St. Jerome was an indefatigable worker when once started, but he had the temperament, apparently, which is given to magnify difficulties at the outset. The strong spirit of Paula was at grips with his despondency all through.

It would seem that the solitude had given Paula and Jerome the peace which they sought. When Albina, Marcella's aged mother, died, the three, Jerome, Paula and Eustochium made a drive to get Marcella to come and join them. The letter written to her by Paula and Eustochium has come down to us. " Friendship does not know how to contain itself : impatience admits of no delay," they wrote. It was quite an impenitent impatience : " We conjure you to come to us, to give us back our dear Marcella, sweeter to us than any name on earth." Every argument is brought forward to induce Marcella to exchange Rome for the land where her friends had found their rest. Marcella is wooed by descriptions of the life in Bethlehem, challenged by trenchant comparisons. " Here all is simple and peaceful, and save for hymns and psalms nothing interrupts the silence. You hear the peasant, driving his plough, chanting the Alleluia : you see the reaper, binding up his sheaves, humming a psalm : the vinedresser, tending his vines, repeating to himself the songs of David."

Paula's letter ends delightfully : " Oh, when will the day come when a breathless courier will bring us the good news, ' Marcella, our Marcella, has landed in Palestine.' Already we see ourselves rushing to you to throw ourselves in your arms."

St. Jerome also wrote a long letter in the same strain. But in spite of the united eloquence of the three, Marcella withstood the invitation. She remained in Rome ; and time was to prove that the escape offered to her from the persistent humanness of Human Nature was not as complete as had been represented.

But for the time being all went well. Pilgrims flocked in immense numbers to Bethlehem. Paula's hospice became famous. By the end of three years, both monasteries, with their churches, had been completed. The description of them is interesting. Each building was surrounded by a high wall and guarded by a watch tower. The rule followed was that of the cenobites. Paula's community met at stated times in the chapel to sing the psalms and recite prayers. They were wakened by the Alleluia, and it summoned them to choir at the third, sixth and ninth hours, and in the watches of the night. The entire Psalter was sung daily, and each one had to learn it by heart. On Sundays the community went for the celebration of the Holy Mysteries to the church of the Nativity. They wore a habit of white wool and used no linen except for wiping their hands. Paula and Eustochium always undertook the meanest offices ; a stranger would have taken them for the humblest members of the community.

St. Jerome wrote exultingly to Pammachius, Paula's son-in-law, " These daughters of the Scipios and the Gracchi, delicate women who at one time found silken dresses too weighty, who could not step on the muddy roads and only went out borne by slaves in a gilded litter, now wear a coarse habit, and having become hardened to toil, they may be seen lighting fires, cleaning lamps, sweeping, preparing vegetables, cooking and serving dinner and running hither and thither like slaves."

During these peacefully ordered days we do not learn anything of Paula's intercourse with Melania and her community. They were not far away, and intercourse there must have been. But, alas ! there was destined to come about an estrangement between Jerome and Rufinus in which the two noble women were fated to be involved.

From this point Paula's story becomes one of long-continued trial and the bitterest sorrow. The serpent had entered Eden. The holy men who had placed a desert between themselves and " the gaudy porticos of Rome " whilst renouncing everything else had carried their human nature with them. Spiritual pride, with its attendant vices, reared its head where the sins of the flesh had been crushed out of existence. A bitter controversy broke out concerning the teachings of Origen, the great Christian apologist. Origen's teaching was found by the Church to contain unsound philosophy leading to dangerous errors. St. Jerome, who was a great admirer of Origen's genius, accepted what was good and rejected the errors. Certain others however, and notably Rufinus, embraced the erroneous doctrine as a new and highly spiritual development of truth. They accused their opponents of grossly material views of the Godhead. Controversy raged in the very solitudes where men had fled to find unity with God and their fellow-men. Rufinus became St. Jerome's bitterest enemy and traducer. The Bishop of Jerusalem sided with the heretics, and bringing some trumped-up charge of insubordination against Jerome, forbade both his community and Paula's to enter the church of the Nativity. Thus Paula was deprived of that which made Bethlehem her " House of Bread." A condition of things that lasted for three years.

For three years Paula's gentle strength was pitted against the impetuosity of Jerome " the wounded lion." She restrained him from entering into an open breach with the persecuting bishop who had deprived him of his sacerdotal rights. During that time she was subject to incredible insults, instigated, it was said, by Rufinus. The story is a long and intricate one. Fabiola, Paula's friend and fellow-worker, visited Bethlehem during these sad years. She also visited Melania's convent. The latter was in a cruel position. St. Jerome could not forgive her for her partizanship with Rufinus ; she herself could have had no wish to be in opposition to the friends who had followed in her footsteps. Fabiola's position was also full of difficulty.

In the end it was Melania and Paula who contrived to patch up a peace between Jerome and Rufinus. It was not, alas, a lasting one. Before that was achieved there was the interpolation of a menace from the invading Huns who were said to be on their way to attack Jerusalem. Paula and her community seem actually to have had to flee for a time to Joppa to be ready to embark and make their escape if necessary. The danger was averted however. Fabiola returned to Rome, and later on Melania returned thither with Rufinus. It was Paula who was destined to remain in the place where she had found her rest—a peace which was not that which the world calls by that name.

St. Jerome, who had journeyed to Rome to face and refute his traducers, returned to Bethlehem. Once more " spreading his sails to the wind of the Holy Spirit " he took up his pen. He continued to write commentaries. " You will it and I must obey," were his words to Paula. His correspondence was colossal. All the world seemed to be coming to learn theology from him. In the well-known picture he is represented in his cave with a tame lion lying by his side as he writes. Paula, who had tamed the lion in Jerome, does not appear in this picture, but she hovers, an invisible presence near his side, with Eustochium, who was to carry on her office after her death and coax from the semi-blind, tired old man, fresh works to add to the heritage of the Catholic Church.

Eustochium was the only one of Paula's children to survive her. News came of Paulina's death. The mother wept, as she had wept for the others. Her son, Toxotius, was cut off in his prime. He left a little daughter, who was sent out to Paula and Eustochium and who became Paula the Younger, the delight of her grandmother's ever-human heart. Anxieties crowded in on her. She had come to the end of her wealth and had to borrow for the completion of her extension to the hospice—she was indeed the mother of the harassed heads of religious houses ! The austerities that she practised hastened the end of her life. In the year 404, at the age of fifty-six, Paula breathed her last in the arms of Eustochium. Alleluias and psalms of joy greeted the passing of her great soul. The Church was too near the age of the martyrs to accustom itself to the Dirge. But the poor and the afflicted—and Eustochium—wept, and Jerome in his cell refused to be comforted. They laid Paula to rest in a cave near to the Manger. Four hundred years later her body was sent to Sens, in France. St. Paula in heaven would not have protested. She had learnt, even in this life, that a resting-place is not to be geographically defined.

Paula's story does not end with her death. She lived on in her daughter Eustochium. It was Eustochium who gently urged St. Jerome to the completion of his gigantic work, the translation of the Bible from Hebrew into Latin, when his enemies were " still barking round him " ; she who prayed and urged him on whilst he struggled with his commentaries on Isaiah and Ezekiel with the news of the sack of Rome ringing in his ears. Eustochium, who received the exiles from Rome, fleeing from the barbarians, into her hospice. Marcella was not one of these, for she had gained the crown of martyrdom in the act of protecting her foster-child, Principia, from the savagery of the invaders. Rome had justified its claim on Marcella.

Eustochium witnessed the destruction of the monasteries which her mother had built, by the Pelagian heretics. She saw them rebuilt. She had the happiness of seeing the monasteries on Mount Olivet once more flourishing under the rule of Melania the Younger, and happily united in friendship with her own. The wind calms down and the waters become smooth, and Eustochium goes forth to join her mother in the Land of the Living, after fifteen years of patient waiting.

There was one year more left for St. Jerome.   He fell asleep in the year 420. Paula's grandchild, Eustochium's foster-child, Paula the Younger, was there to minister to his last needs.   We know no more. The story has ended, for Jerome has laid down his pen.

The writer of this article would acknowledge her indebtedness to the nuns of Talacre Abbey for their translation and adaptation of *The Life of St. Paula* by the Abbé F. Lagrange.

Rev. HUGH POPE, O.P., S.T.M.

ST. AUGUSTINE

Bishop of Hippo

A.D. 354–430

I

THE LIFE OF ST. AUGUSTINE

THE BROAD OUTLINES of the life of St. Augustine of Hippo are familiar. Born A.D. 354 at Tagaste, at school at Madaura whence his delicate health compelled his removal for a time, passing to Carthage where his excesses distressed his saintly mother, St. Monica, he was yet the child of divine predilection and his conversion to the Faith and to a saintly life when thirty-three years of age is one of the greatest of Christian romances.

Northern Africa had not forgotten him when he returned to begin his real life's work ; and while some recalled his youthful aberrations and made unfair capital out of them, others—his life-long friend St. Paulinus of Nola for example—hailed his elevation to the Episcopate as marking the dawn of a new era for the harassed Church of Africa. Valerius, then the aged Bishop of Hippo, realised the opportunity God had offered him and promptly consecrated him, though in so doing he unconsciously infringed the Canons of Nicæa decreeing that there should never be two Bishops in the same See at the same time.

To appreciate the forty years that followed we have to form some idea of the state of Africa in general and of the African Church in particular. The Roman domination seems on the whole to have sat lightly on the subject peoples, and it is not easy to discover in African literature traces of discontent or rebellion during Augustine's lifetime. But the African races formed a motley crowd : they seem to have resembled the Athenians " ever employed in hearing or telling some new thing." Among the Christians heresy was rife, while the Manichæan philosophical speculations which had for nine years ensnared Augustine himself, were widespread. Schism was perhaps an even greater evil. For since Julian the Apostate, 361-363, the Donatists held most of the Catholic Sees, churches and property, and cruelly persecuted the Catholic remnant. Later on another heresy, Pelagianism, the worst and most long-lived of all, was to exercise its baneful influence on the much-enduring African Church.

If we would form any just estimate of Augustine as the Bishop of his flock, as the controversialist and the letter-writer we must bear in mind that from the moment of his Ordination, and still more from the time of his Consecration, he lived for his people, for the flock entrusted to him that he might teach them the way to heaven. If he teaches them the profoundest theology it is only because in St. Jerome's words " rustic ignorance must not be mistaken for sanctity," for the Bishop was convinced that the more he could make his hearers think the more solid the foundation of their piety would be. It was the same with his immense controversial work. He was never set on refuting his adversary by bludgeoning him, but by winning him. There were times, it is true, when the tactics of his opponents compelled him, as P. Monceaux expresses it, to " hit, hit hard, keep on hitting " ; but as a rule his controversial methods were confined to preaching the truth, to propaganda and publicity ; with this end in view, he read everything his adversaries wrote, he set forth Catholic truth on every possible occasion, and he never shirked a conflict.

But no one reading the *Confessions* or the earlier Letters can fail to realize that the life of a Bishop was the last that Augustine would have chosen for himself. For he was by nature the speculative thinker, the contemplative philosopher and theologian. Those early years after his conversion, when at Cassiciacum or later in his monastery at Tagaste, were his ideal. Here he was in his element. Reading, discussion, dictating, these filled his life. Had he been left to that life of leisure he would have taken rank as one of the world's profoundest thinkers. But it was not to be. To his intense dismay he was torn from his nest and made a Bishop ! How pathetic his laments that now he can no longer hope to know anything about his Bible—laments repeated to the end, even when consecrating his successor, Heraclius. He had revelled in the classics, had been wont, as he himself tells us, to read half a book of Virgil a day, was steeped in his Horace and Cicero, and of course as a loyal African knew his Terence well. Yet all this was laid aside for the needs of his flock. Instead of those " profane " authors, Holy Scripture and the Christian writers occupied his time. His familiarity with these latter is amazing. He seems to have read almost everything St. Jerome had written, though they were contemporaries. When arguing with Julian on Original Sin he quotes freely from SS. Cyprian, Hilary, Ambrose, Chrysostom, Gregory of Nazianzen, Jerome, Irenæus, Basil, Reticius, Olympius and Innocent ; these he styles " præclarissimos episcopos eloquiorum divinorum tractatores," " præclara Ecclesiæ lumina."

Nor was Augustine's Episcopal work confined to the pulpit or to his desk. From the outset he was a public personage who ranked high in the councils of the Roman officials. Some of these where Christians, even saintly Christians. But the majority were pagans who, however, treated the Bishop with immense deference when he had occasion to appeal to them. For this he often had to do ; so much so that his enemies, and even some of his own flock, accused him of being a " tuft-hunter," and the Bishop felt bound to point out that he only frequented the civic authorities in the interests of his flock.

II

THE KEY TO HIS LIFE

Every well-ordered life—and what is a Saint's life but a well-ordered one ?—has its key, its master-thoughts. What were these in the life of Augustine, the restless spirit, once the slave of his passions, trying in vain to feed his soul on the husks of a false philosophical system, throwing himself at length on the bosom of Holy Mother Church, becoming a priest against his will, then a Bishop—still more against his will—and dying at last with the Penitential Psalms pinned to the wall by his bedside ? The key to this wonderful life will be found, we fancy, in what we may term the " passions " of his soul : Truth ; the Church which led him to that truth ; Holy Scripture which led him to that Church ; the Apostolic See of St. Peter and his successors— the heads of that Church militant on earth ; and finally the possession of God hereafter, the goal of all his desires.

(a) *Truth—through the Catholic Church*

Augustine's *Confessions*, or *The Praises of God*, penned about A.D. 400 when he had been a Catholic some thirteen years and a Bishop for five years, tell only of his early struggles in his search after the Truth—the ruling passion of his life. Those undying pages depict the harassed voyager who has at length come into harbour. For it was in the Catholic Church that Augustine had found "the pearl of great price ", that Truth for which he had, all unknowing, sought all his life, even during those passionate years which he has described with such poignancy in his *Confessions*. For him that Church is simply the " Catholica "—the adjective for the concrete.[1] " We must," he says,

---

[1] The term " Catholica " occurs 240 times in Augustine's writings : in *De Baptismo contra Donatistas*, 59 times, *Contra Litteras Petiliani*, 20, in his *Epistles*, 35, in *Sermons*, 40 times, *cf.* Leclercq, *Dict. d'archeologie*, 2631, note, *s.v. Carthage*. This use of the adjective alone died out in the seventh century but reappears in St. Bernard, *Sermones in Canticum canticorum*, Sermon lxiv. 8, see Tertullian, *De Præscriptionibus*, 26.

" be in communion with that Christian Church which is ' Catholic,' which too, is called the ' Catholica ' not only by its own members but its enemies too. For whether they like it or not, heretics and schismatics—when talking with strangers, though not when talking among themselves—mean by the ' Catholica ' nothing but the Catholic Church ; for they would be misunderstood if they failed to use a term which the whole world applies to her alone."[1]   A good instance of this occurred when the Donatists had occasion to appeal to the Roman courts. For when the presiding magistrate asked if there were not some other Donatist Bishop present the Roman officials replied : " We acknowledge no Bishop save Aurelius the ' Catholicus '."[2] Aurelius being of course the Archbishop of Carthage.

(b) " Securitas "

In that Church, then, Augustine had found the " security " he had so long been seeking.   Hence his love of the very words " securus " and " securitas " ; they appear again and again in his Sermons and letters, also in his controversial writings. All know the classic phrase : " Securus judicat Orbis terrarum " since Wiseman drew Newman's attention to it, with world-shaking results.[3]   But few know its context or that it is but the crystallization of a long-drawn-out argument for the Catholic Church and the " security " she alone can provide.[4] Augustine's audience must often have smiled as the familiar word fell from his lips as he preached : " In security I rise superior to all else when He upholds me who is superior to all things,"[5]   " His promises make us ' secure,' for He predestined us before we came into existence,"[6] " with what ' security ' we sing in Christ ; for on that path there are no robbers,"[7] " with what ' security ' does not Christ's Passion provide us, what consolation, how it restores the weak and tempest-tossed soul ! "[8]   Once more : " The Lord is thy staff ; on it a man leans ' securely,' for He will never give way (securus homo incumbit quia Ille non succumbit—one of the many rhyming phrases which are impossible to translate). Say, then, I am ' secure ' ; love to be ' secure ' ; hope to be ' secure ' ; for it is Holy Scripture that says it."[9]

(c) Eulogies on the Church

The debt he owes to the Church is one Augustine feels that he can never express. Were we to give even a small selection of the in-

[1] De Vera Religione, 12, cf. De Utilitate credendi, 9, Contra Epistolam Fundamenti, 5.
[2] Enarr. ii, 31 on Ps. xxi.
[3] Dublin Review, Aug. 1839, also in Collected Essays, 1853, II, p. 224.
[4] Contra Epistolam Parmeniani, iii, 24.   [5] Enarr. i, 2 on Ps. lxi.
[6] Enarr. ii, 4 on Ps. lxxxviii.   [7] Enarr. i, 6 on Ps. lxvi.   [8] Enarr. i, 18 on Ps. liv.
[9] Enarr. iii, 17 on Ps. xxxii ; cf. Mgr. P. Batiffol, Le Catholicisme de S. Augustin, 2 Vols., 1920.

numerable passages in which he eulogises the Church we should weary the reader. Some, however, we must give : on his lips the Church is always " pia Mater Ecclesia "[1] ; " let us love the Lord our God, let us love His Church ; God as Father, the Church as Mother "[2] ; " We are brethren because one Mother Church bore us ; you are my children, for in the Gospel I begot you. . . . Love, then, the Lord who loves you ; throng the Church your Mother who bore you . . . you will prove yourselves not ungrateful for all the blessings He has showered upon you if you offer Him the due service of your presence here in His Church. For no one can expect to find God a merciful Father if he has shown contempt for the Church his mother."[3] All are familiar with the famous declaration, " I myself would not believe the Gospels did not the authority of the Catholic Church lead me to do so "[4] ; but perhaps we are not so familiar with such even more compelling pronouncements as : " Do but recognize the Catholic Church, and therein you will find an end to all controversies "[5] ; " if the wife is her husband's glory, so is His Church Christ's glory "[6] ; " I profess the Catholic faith and I am confident that thereby I shall attain to certain knowledge "[7] ; " I belong to that Church the members of which are all those churches of whose foundation and establishment by the labours of the Apostles we read in Canonical Scripture."[8] For Augustine " Veritas " and " Ecclesia Catholica "[9] were synonyms. When falsely accused of being a persecutor he solemnly takes an oath " by the Person of ' the Body of Christ,' that is by the Church of the Living God which is the pillar and firm foundation of the Truth and which is spread throughout the entire world," that he has never in his life persecuted.[10] Hence his repeated exclamation " O Catholica ! Pulchra inter hæreses ! "[11] " beautiful " because " here is a most solidly established truth : the Church has lasted and still lasts,"[12] " that Church of God none shall ever blot out from the earth."[13] There is almost a ring of triumph in the words : " We are members of that Church which, though spread throughout the world, is, by God's mercy, one mighty body under One mighty Head."[14] And how profound the remark that : " The marvels which take place in the

---

[1] *De Baptismo contra Donatistas*, vi, 4.

[2] *Enarr.* ii, 14 on Ps. xxxviii ; *cf. Sermo* ccxiii, 7 ; &c.

[3] *Sermo* xcii *ex Sermonibus ab Angelo Mai editis, cf. Miscellanea Agostiniana,* 1930, i, p. 332.

[4] *Contra Epistolam Fundamenti,* 5 ; the whole section should be read.

[5] *Ad Donatistas, post Collationem,* 24.   [6] *Sermo,* cclxvi, 5.

[7] *Contra Epistolam Fundamenti,* 17.   [8] *Contra Cresconium,* iii, 39.

[9] *Contra Litteras Petiliani,* iii, 59.   [10] *Ibid.* ii, 237.

[11] *Sermon* xii, 5 ; cclxxxv, 6 ; *Sermon* xvii, 3 ex *codice Guelferbitano* ; *Contra Epistolam Parmeniani,* ii, 28.

[12] *De Baptismo contra Donatistas,* vii, 9 ; *cf.* " Ecclesia mansit manet, manebit," *Contra Epistolam Parmeniani,* iii, 11.

[13] *Ep.* xliii, 27.   [14] *Ep.* cxlii, 1.

Catholic Church are accepted precisely because they take place in the Catholic Church ; but the converse is not true, namely that the Catholic Church is to be accepted on the ground that such marvels do take place in her."[1]

III

HOLY SCRIPTURE

Through the Bible Augustine had been led to the Church. But it was only comparatively late in life that St. Augustine had taken up the study of Holy Scripture for which he had always felt a distaste till St. Ambrose set him on the right path.[2]   Then those Scriptures became " castæ deliciæ meæ,"[3] so much that we find him literally steeped in them by A.D. 394 when he wrote his *De Sermone Domini in Monte*. Yet we find him writing to Januarius *c.* A.D. 400 : " In ipsis sanctis Scripturis multa nesciam plura quam scian."[4]   When preaching he always had the Bible in his hands : " What I am holding in my hands, namely the Bible which you see. . . ."[5]   From those Scriptures we learn our faith, " for one who dwells in the City of God, that is the Church, believes the Holy Scriptures, the Old as well as the New Testament, what we call the Canonical Books ; from them is conceived that faith by which the just man liveth, whereby, too, we journey on our way unhesitatingly so long as ' we are absent from the Lord ' " (2 Cor. v, 6.)[6]

But Holy Scripture does not stand alone : " the authority of our Scriptures," he says, " is confirmed by the agreement of the whole world, by succession from the Apostles and Bishops, and by Councils "[7] ; and while conceding that we are unable to adduce any arguments from Scripture on such a question as re-Baptism he adds, " yet we are holding to the true Scripture-teaching on the subject when we adhere to the teaching of the Universal Church whose authority is affirmed by Holy Scripture. Since, then, Holy Scripture cannot mislead us, anyone who is afraid of being misled on this obscure point should consult that same Church, for to her the Scriptures point without any ambiguity."[8]

The spirit in which Augustine studied his Bible may be gauged from the following among many similar passages : " Can anyone really understand Holy Scripture if he does not read it or listen to it with a devout mind ? If he does not acknowledge its supreme authority, nor dislike certain passages because they show up his own sinfulness,

---

[1] *De Unitate*, 50.   [2] *Confess.* v, 24 ; vi, 5–8.   [3] *Ibid.* xi, 3.   [4] *Ep.* lv, 38.
[5] *Sermo* xxxvii, 1 ; *Tract.* xxxv, 9 ; xl, 1 *in Joann.*
[6] *De Civitate Dei*, xix, 18.   [7] *Contra Faustum*, xiii, 5.   [8] *Contra Cresconium*, i, 39.

but is pleased to find his sins corrected ; rejoicing, too, to find that they are not spared because being set right ?   When certain statements in Scripture seem obscure or even ridiculous such a man does not straightway set out to prove them wrong, but prays for understanding of them, ever bearing in mind that it is his duty to revere and respect what is so authoritative."[1]   He writes in the same strain to Maximinus :

" If you really do pray, as you say you do, that you may become a disciple of Holy Scripture, then do not allow yourself to be distracted by questions which are merely profitless ; prefer a prudent silence to a torrent of idle words when you fail to discover an answer to some patent truth."[2]

IV

THE APOSTOLIC SEE

The Bible depends on the Church which alone can interpret it authoritatively, and alone can declare what are its contents.   And the Church itself is built on the Apostolic See.

Augustine constantly refers to the " Apostolic Sees " or those actually founded by the Apostles, and he insists on the authority attaching to them :   " The kindly Ruler of our Faith has, both by largely-attended assemblages of the peoples of all nations and tribes, and by the Apostolic Sees, provided His Church with an authoritative citadel ; and through the labours of a few, but truly learned and spiritual-minded men, He has plentifully furnished her with an armoury of invincible arguments from reason.   Schismatics, however, well aware that if their authority was to be weighed in the balance against Catholic authority, their own would be hopelessly discredited, strive to undermine by specious arguments and by insinuations—which, so they claim, are based on reason—that solidly established authority of the Church."[3]   " Try and realize," he says elsewhere, " what this authority of the Catholic Church means ; for she is solidly established by, first of all, the Sees founded by the Apostles themselves, secondly by the series of Bishops who have followed one another in those same Sees and thirdly by the consent of so many nations."[4]

Yet in the eyes of this African Bishop the " Apostolic See " *par excellence* is always that of Rome and the replies of Pope Innocent to the African Synods are those of the " Apostolica sedes et Romana "[5] ;

---

[1] Cf. *Ep.* cxliii, 7, *De Genesi ad Lith.* i, 37–41.
[2] *Contra Maxminum*, ii, 14.   [3] *Ep.* cxviii, 32.   [4] *Contra Faustum*, xi. 2.
[5] *Contra Julianum*, i, 13.   Hence Eugenius, Archbishop of Carthage, A.D. 481–505, said to the Vandals : " I will write and ask my fellow-Bishops to come ; they, and especially the Roman Church which is the Head of all the Churches, will be able to demonstrate to you the faith which we hold in common," Victor of Vita, *De Persecutione Vandalica*, ii, 15.

for " in the Roman Church has always flourished the Primacy of the Apostolic See "[1], and " the teachings of even bad pastors (in it) are not really theirs so much as God's, for God established the teaching of Truth in the Chair of Unity "[2]. St. Augustine's conclusion is characteristic : " How, then, can we hesitate to cast ourselves into the bosom of that Church of Christ which, as the whole human race concedes, has, by the succession of Bishops in the Apostolic See, attained to such a pitch of authority ? And this, remember, despite the yappings of heretics who have, however, been condemned partly by the judgement of the people themselves, partly by weighty Conciliar gatherings, partly owing to the awe inspired by miracles."[3]

In A.D. 416 the Bishops assembled at Carthage to discuss the case of Pelagius wrote to Pope Innocent saying : " We feel that the line of action we have taken for the salvation of many souls and to correct the obstinacy of certain people should be brought to your notice in order to secure the support of the Apostolic See for our modest decisions."[4] The Bishops assembled at Milevis at the same time and for the same purpose wrote to the same effect, adding, however, that " the authority of his Holiness is based on the authority of Holy Scripture."[5] These letters were followed by one from Aurelius, Augustine, Alypius, Evodius and Possidius urging Pope Innocent to add his authority to their condemnation of Pelagius ; for they are confident that once Pelagius realizes that his writings have been condemned " by the authority of the Catholic Bishops—and more especially of Your Holiness whose authority will, we feel sure, weigh far more with him—he will himself condemn those writings."[6]

In his reply Pope Innocent speaks of " the various anxieties and preoccupations of the Roman Church and Apostolic See " ; the African Bishops have, he says, " quite fittingly consulted the Apostolic dignity, and in so doing have but adhered to the long-established practice which, as you and I know, has always been observed by the world . . . well aware that replies come from the Apostolic fountain-head to all such as, throughout the provinces, ask for them ; this more especially when it is question of the Faith, for I deem that all our Brethren in the Episcopate should on such a point have recourse to Peter alone."[7]

---

[1] *Ep.* xliii,. 7.   [2] *Ep.* cv. 16.   [3] *De Utilitate credendi*, 35.
[4] *Ep.* clxxv, 2 ; " modest " " mediocritatis nostræ ; " in *Ep.* clxxvii, 19 the African Archbishop terms his authority a " rivulus " compared to the " largus fons " of the Pope's authority.   [5] *Ep.* clxxvi, 5.   [6] *Ep.* clxxvii, 15.
[7] *Ep.* clxxxii, 2. Innocent's words echo St. Irenæus' famous *dictum* : " Ad hanc enim Ecclesiam propter potiorem principalitatem necesse est omnem convenire Ecclesiam, hoc est qui sunt undique fideles, in qua semper ab his qui sunt undique, conservata est a quae est ab Apostolis tradita," *Adv. Haer*, iii, 3. On the whole episode see Mgr. Batiffol in *Rev. Biblique*, Jan. 1918.

On this, St. Augustine remarks :

" What other answer could Pope Innocent have made to the African Councils except that teaching which the Apostolic and Roman See with all the other Churches had held ? "[1]   A little later came the famous declaration : " The findings of two Councils were sent to the Apostolic See ; thence came the rescripts ; Causa finita est, utinam aliquando finiatur error ! "[2]

v

ST. PETER AND HIS SUCCESSORS

The Church, then, was an organized body and its centre of authority was at Rome, and that authority was St. Peter's. That Apostle suffered in Rome and his body lies buried there.[3]   The first of the Apostles,[4] he held the primacy among them.[5]   His name was originally Simon : " Had he been from the beginning called Peter no one would have thought of the mystery of the ' Petra ' ; Christ, then, would have him first called by another name so that from the change of his name the inner meaning of the mystery might be brought home to us "[6] ;   " in his very name ' Peter ' the Church is symbolized "[7] To him were entrusted the keys ; for just as he had professed his faith in Christ as the spokesman of the rest, so too did he as an individual receive those keys, and thus personify Unity[8] of which Unity indeed Peter becomes the symbol,[9] nay more :   Christ " would even make him one with Himself."[10]

There are, it is true, many passages in which St. Augustine seems to insist that Christ did not build His Church on Peter personally so much as on the faith he had just professed, even on Christ Himself " non supra Petrum quod tu es, sed supra petram quam confessus es."[11] But in every one of those passages Augustine is dwelling on Peter's subsequent denial of Christ ;   the lesson he is inculcating is that because Peter was to be so great he had to learn humility,[12] that " columna firmissima " had to fall,[13] therefore " Laudo Petrum, sed prius erubesco pro Petro "[14] ; it was only because of his threefold denial that he came to receive the threefold commission.[15]   The final word

---

[1] *Contra Julianum*, i, 13.   [2] *Sermon* cxxxi, 10.   [3] *Ep.* xxxvi, 21, *Sermo* ccxcvi, 6.
[4] *Sermo* ccxcv, 1, &c.   [5] *Enarr.* i, 1 *on* Ps. vciii, *Contra Julianum* i, 6.
[6] *Tract.* vii, 14, *in Joann.*   [7] *Sermo* iv, 19 ; lxxv, 11, &c.
[8] *Sermo* cxlix. 3 ; *De Agone*, 32, &c.
[9] *Sermo* xlvi, 30 ; lxxi, 1 ; cclxx, 2 ;   *Tract.* cxviii, 4 *in Joann.*
[10] *Sermo* xlvi, 30.   [11] *Sermo* ccxliv, 1 ; cclxx, 2, &c.
[12] *Sermo* cclxxxvi, 2 ; ccxcv. 3.
[13] *Tract.* cxiii, 2 *in Joann* ; *cf.* " Ille amator, subito negator," *Sermo* ccxcv. 3.
[14] *Sermo* cclxxxvi, 2.   [15] *Ep.* cxlvii, 30, &c.

on the subject has been given us by Augustine himself who in his
Retractations says, apropos of the lost *Contra Epistolam Donati hæretici* :

" Somewhere (in that work) I said of the Apostle Peter that on him,
as on a rock, the Church was founded, an interpretation which is
familiar to many owing to St. Ambrose's line ' Hoc ipsa petra Ecclesiæ
canente, culpam diluit.' But I am aware that on many subsequent
occasions I expounded the Lord's words ' Thou art Peter and upon
this rock I will build my Church ' as meaning that (it should be built)
on Him whom Peter confessed when he said ' Thou art the Christ, the
Son of the living God ' ; and thus Peter, being so called from the
' Petra,' would personify the Church (personam Ecclesiæ figuraret)
which is built upon this rock and received the keys of the kingdom of
heaven. For it was not said to him ' Thou art " petra ",' but ' Thou
art " Petrus ".' Whereas the Rock was Christ whom Simon confessed
as indeed the whole Church confesses Him—and he was therefore
called Peter. But the reader can choose which of these two opinions
he thinks the more probable."[1]

Clearly all that Augustine means here is that the essential conditions
for Simon's becoming the " rock " are (*a*) his faith in Christ's Godhead and (*b*) that Christ—the " Rock "—should endow him with a
share in that " rock-like " character. But this does not preclude—
nay it rather demands—that the Church should be built on the person
of Peter. For faith is a quality, and—as Pelagius himself said in
another context—" a quality must be resident in some substance "
" neque abseque re esse qualitas potest."[2]
So the Church was built on Peter owing to his faith ; and to Peter
were entrusted the keys. " But Peter is dead and has left us ! Who,
then, now looses or binds ? I dare to say that we too have those same
keys."[3] Peter, then, lives on in his successors. Hence Augustine's
reverence for the occupant of Peter's See. Hence he can say to Pope
Innocent when urging his support against Pelagius : " Altius
presides "[4] ; hence he can urge Pope Coelestine to the same course
" by the memory of the Apostle Peter."[5]
" He who holds to Holy Mother Church is ' secure ' ; no one will
snatch from the Catholic Church." " In the ' security ' afforded by
the peace of that Church let a man do good work, and let him
preserve in it to the end." " Unto the end," in that thought lay
another secret of Augustine's life : his mind was ever fixed on that
supreme goal. Without any exaggeration, his thoughts were ever

---

[1] *Retract.* I, xxi, 1.   [2] Quoted by St. Augustine, *De Natura et Gratoa*, 11.
[3] *Contra duas Epistolas Pelafii*, i, 1–2.
[4] *Sermo* xvi, 2 *ex Codice Guelferbitano, Miscellanea Augustiniana*, i.
[5] *Ep.* ccix, 8–9, *cf. Ep.* clxxxvi, 28–29.

on heaven, on that next world which, as he dwells on it in his Sermons, seems to have been as real to him as the African world in which he was living—but for a space, that eternal goal which now is his " ubi jam quod sitivit internum gustat aeternum . . . securusque de reliqua " as the Office for his Feast expresses it.

Few preachers can have more consistently spoken to their hearers about heaven and the need of preparing for it. " Brethren, I implore you, love God with me ! Hasten on the road with me by your faith ! Let us all yearn for that glorious Fatherland, yes, yearn for that, ever realizing that we are but pilgrims here."[1] That is the ending of but one sermon, and there were many like it. The Bishop's flock found his enthusiam so infectious that more than once they burst into applause when he had been speaking on the joys of the next world.[2]

---

[1] *Tract.* xxxv, 9 *in Joann.*
[2] *Enarr.* ii, 8 on Ps. xxvi, i, 31 on Ps. lxxii.

G. ELLIOT ANSTRUTHER, K.S.G.

HILDEBRAND, POPE AND REFORMER

A.D. 1020–1085

AGAINST THE CHEQUERED political background of the eleventh century, the figure of Hildebrand, Pope St. Gregory the Seventh, stands out as that of one of the greatest reformative influences of the Middle Ages. While directed in the first place to churchmen and things ecclesiastical, since the abuses which he fought had entered into and affected the Church's life and government, Gregory's reforms, of their very nature, led to a cleaning up also of much in the secular field. Imperial encroachments on religious liberty were curbed. " So far and no farther " was a lesson which an emperor was made to learn, almost literally, upon his knees. Most important of all, election to the Papal office was placed upon a basis which thenceforth secured freedom from the will and dominance of lay powers.

The following sketch is limited in length and character. There can obviously be little more in it than a relation of the chief events in Hildebrand's life ; and here it is well to bear in mind that in considering the man the emphasis must rest upon " Hildebrand " rather than upon " Gregory the Seventh." It will be seen that the reforming spirit actuated by that heart and mind affected church history throughout the reigns of five pontiffs before Gregory himself was acclaimed. We may even question whether the reformer's lifework might not have been still more fruitful if he could have remained the friend and counsellor of Popes, instead of having to face difficulties, enmities, from powerful factions both within and without the Church as himself a successor of St. Peter.

Soana, in Tuscany, was the birthplace of the future champion of the Church's liberty. There Hildebrand saw the light in the year 1020. Some historians have striven to claim high lineage for him ; it is more probable that he was the son of a Tuscan carpenter. Of his childhood and early life much is known, but much also is conjectural. As a boy he was attached to the Benedictine monastery on the Aventine in Rome, where St. Odilon of Cluny was among those from whom he imbibed religious knowledge.

It was as a young monk in Rome that Hildebrand had his first taste of the state of things against which all his principle, all his strength, was before long to be arrayed. Pope Gregory the Sixth, John Gratian, had appointed him his chaplain, and between master and servant in this respect there was a real affection. A prelate of upright life, the pontiff had none the less to confess before a synod held at Sutri that his acquisition of the papacy had been by methods laying him open to the charge of simony. Humbly and submissively he stripped himself of his pontifical robes and went into exile in Germany. Hildebrand faithfully followed him. The unfortunate Pope did not long survive his deposition : within two years he died.

Whether Hildebrand spent some further time in Germany after Gregory's death, or whether he went to Cluny as a member of the community of that house, is a question in debate so far as historians are concerned. What is of more importance, for our present purpose, is the circumstance beyond dispute that in 1049 he met, at Besançon, the saintly Bruno, formerly Bishop of Toul, himself a monk, who in the previous year had been elected Pope, taking the title of Leo IX. From that meeting great results were to spring, since now Hildebrand began that personal and courageous assertion of principle by which he is famous in the annals of the Church.

Leo's election had been by the personal authority of his cousin, the Emperor Henry III. On that ground Hildebrand ventured to reprove it, with such result that Leo, it has been said, threw off, for the time being, the symbols of his pontificate. Commanding the young reformer to go with him to Rome, he there received canonical election to the Chair of Peter at the hands of the Roman clergy. Thus Hildebrand struck successfully his first blow against usurpation of church authority on the part of lay princes.

Almost immediately afterwards the Pope bestowed upon his outspoken critic signal marks of favour. He withdrew him from outside Benedictine jurisdiction (? at Cluny : the point is obscure), made him a Cardinal, and gave him the post of administrator of St. Paul's Outside the Walls. Also he leant graciously towards the younger man's opinions and advice concerning reformation of church discipline, a matter in which his own spirit was in the fullest accord. During the five years of his pontificate he never ceased to labour in the cause of reform.

Leo IX's reforms were directed, in the main, against the sale of benefices to unworthy clerics, and the violation of the law of celibacy. In concert with Hildebrand and others like-minded, he took steps for the formal condemnation of these abuses. Publication of the decrees was made from various councils, in particular that held in 1049 at Reims.

It was not all plain sailing, and at Reims the assembly was

vigorously opposed. The French Sovereign, Henry I, together with many of his licentious nobility, feared exposure at the hands of the Church. There were French bishops, too, who failed to do their duty. It may be that some of these prelates had obtained their sees unworthily and were only too ready to excuse their absence from the council by laying stress upon the action of the King. Leo was able to gather to his side only twenty bishops, but he had the presence and support of fifty Benedictine abbots. The desired end was secured. Canons were issued condemning evils, and several guilty prelates were deposed. In addition the Reims council vindicated officially the principle that elections to ecclesiastical offices were valid only with the consent of the clergy and people. The Church's authority was proclaimed inviolate. Well might the powers of intrigue and corruption view the outlook with consternation !

Leo IX died in 1054. Worthily he is honoured as a saint in the Roman martyrology. The death of this high-minded pontiff brought Hildebrand to the fore in a new and startlingly important rôle. Gladly would the Roman clergy have made him Pope, but that honour the young man declined ; whereupon he was commissioned to go to Germany and there to choose, from among the prelates of the Empire, a worthy head on which to set the tiara. The choice, when made, was to be approved by the Emperor—a much more limited exercise of the secular power, be it noted, than that which not so much farther back had made or deposed pontiffs by the imperial will.

The choice fell upon Gebhardt, Bishop of Eichstadt, who was crowned in Rome in 1055 as Pope Victor II. The Emperor had not been friendly to this elevation, but his objections, as well as those of the Pope-elect, who was Henry's friend, were overcome by Hildebrand.

Victor II was swayed by the counsels of reform, and continued the campaign to this end begun under his predecessor. One of his first acts was to appoint Hildebrand to France as his legate ; in that capacity the latter assembled reformatory councils and did not hesitate to bring about the deposition of simoniacal or otherwise unworthy prelates.

It was in 1056, while the effects of Hildebrand's reforms were still causing excitement and consternation throughout a large portion of Western Christendom, that the Emperor, Henry III, died. His son and successor, Henry IV, was then a small boy, hardly six years old ; he was smaller still when, some two years previously, he had been recognized as king of the Germans. If only the spirit of illumination could have foretold what his character and attitude would be when he would assume, as a young man, the imperial office and responsibility ! History can surely hold few cases in which the saying " like father, like son " was more set at naught.

During Henry's childhood and youth, his mother, the Empress Agnes, acted as Regent ; but in 1070 when barely twenty years of age, he took the reins into his hands.   He was a prince of combative and independent disposition, strongly imbued with the sense of imperial power, and unwilling to meet the new spirit within the Church by keeping his secular fingers out of the ecclesiastical pie.   Hence arose the memorable and protracted duel, between the Empire and the Church, which was to bring out on rival sides the strong qualities of both Henry and Hildebrand.

Pope Victor lived but a short time after the third Henry's death. To the last term of his activity he helped Hildebrand in the efforts for reform, and when he died matters were so well advanced in the right path that the clergy determined there should be no intervention by the imperial authority in the matter of his successor.   In the case of Victor's own election, as we have seen, the Emperor was supposed to approve the choice, though the fact that on the contrary he objected strongly in no way prevented Hildebrand from securing the election of the nominee.   Now, however, the Church's freedom of action was to be tested altogether apart from what might be the wishes of the Imperial Court.   Henry IV being but a child of tender years, the fact of the regency strengthened the attitude taken up by the Roman clergy.   Accordingly these hastened to elect the new Pope. Their choice fell upon Frederick of Lorraine, Abbot of Monte Cassino, who assumed on his election the title of Stephen X.

Less than a year was the brief span of Stephen's pontifical life ; yet during that period he managed to extend still further the reform movement among the clergy.   Hildebrand, naturally enough, he regarded with high favour, sending him on missions to France and Germany and showing him other signs of confidence.   The Pope lived to see new and purer monastic houses rising to carry on, in Italy and elsewhere, the rule which previous corruptions had in some places disfigured.

Nor was Hildebrand himself neglectful of his duties as administrator of St. Paul's.   Into that abbey he introduced swift and rigorous and much-needed reforms.   The initiative was his, also, which sent into the arena, armed with the title and authority of a cardinal-bishop, one of the greatest champions of the Church's liberty, St. Peter Damian.

Stephen died in March, 1058, begging that there might be no appointment of a successor until Hildebrand's return from the Court, whither he had gone as legate to the Empress-regent.

It was hardly to be supposed that the forces of evil would submit calmly to a pontiff who by free choice had ascended the papal throne. If Stephen X encountered no active resistance on the part of the

Court and the Roman nobility, that fact may probably be attributed to the shortness of his reign. No sooner, however, was the Pope's death made known than the tyrannical house of Tusculum, nursing-mother of more than one indifferent Pope, roused itself for a further effort at usurpation. Troubling nothing as to the probable action of the Roman clergy, and in spite of the decree of the Reims Council, this faction elected, in the person of Benedict X, an antipope favourable to their ambitions.

Much as he disliked imperial interference in Church matters, Hildebrand liked even less a state of things by which the pontiff would reign by the will of a corrupt aristocracy. It was a case of two evils, with imperialism as the lesser. Consequently his next step was one of diplomacy. He gathered to his aid the German nobility, with Agnes the regent at their head, and still further strengthened his position by the support of that section of the Roman party which was still pledged to orthodox election.

The combined forces proved more than the rebellious barons could withstand. The antipope yielded his usurped throne and retired into obscurity. The power of Tusculum was broken for ever. With Hildebrand's approval, joined to the imperial consent, the Bishop of Florence, Gerard of Burgundy, became Pope Nicholas II. His election was thus the result of a compromise, but its validity was assured by the concurrence of the clergy.

From the pontificate of Nicholas II dates one of the most important reforms ever introduced into the discipline of the Church. Through long previous ages, right up till the time of the council at Reims, the Popes depended for their election upon forces and circumstances which might work for good but often worked for ill. Elections were sometimes the result of political conspiracy, family corruption, the mandates of immoral emperors, or the fortune of war. Looseness of discipline resulted in the election of not a few unworthy pontiffs. This situation violated the original practice of papal election, a practice vested in the Roman clergy and people, to whom Hildebrand restored it by the action of the Reims council.

It was determined now to utilize the reforming spirit born of the three previous pontificates in order still further to safeguard the liberty of the Church in electing her Popes. In April, 1059, a council assembled, in Rome, at which upwards of a hundred bishops attended. This assembly confirmed the condemnation previously directed against simony and the marriages of clergy. The council ordained also that the election of the Roman pontiff should in future rest with the cardinals, who, however, would respect the wishes of the emperor and would ask ratification of their choice from the Roman clergy and people.

Among the signatures to this decree is that of " Hildebrandus, monachus et subdiaconus", and the French historian Montalembert suggests that " it is not risking too much to impute to him the responsibility " for the decree itself. At a later period in history the power of election was made to rest absolutely and finally with the cardinals. Thus for upwards of eight centuries the pontifical throne has been protected by a method of election which although not in every case productive of an exalting Pope has at any rate contributed to a state of things much purer than that which preceded it.

Between the imperial party, on whose side the simoniacal bishops and clergy were ranged, and the Church as represented by Pope Nicholas, Hildebrand, and the Roman conclave, there was now an open rupture, one so threatening that it became needful to secure military support in order to maintain the reformed system of Church government. For this, Hildebrand looked to the Normans. It was at his suggestion that the Pope conferred the title of Duke of Apulia on the Norman chief, Robert Guiscard—to give him his nickname, Robert " Wiseacre." Guiscard promised by oath to defend the free election of future pontiffs. Another lay-champion invoked was the pious William de Montreuil, whose forces waged successful war in Southern Italy against simony and other evils. The energetic pontiff himself lived only long enough to see the beginning of these good results. He died in 1061, after a reign of little more than two years.

Within a few months a successor had been chosen and consecrated, and this by free election on the part of the cardinals. Before the election took place, and agreeably to the decree of the Roman council, a report had been sent to the Court. Its bearer had not been received, so the cardinals proceeded to act, with the advice of Hildebrand and the Abbot of Monte Cassino. Their choice fell upon Anselm, Bishop of Lucca, member of an illustrious Milanese family and one whose election offered a guarantee for the liberty of the Church. When legate in Lombardy this prelate had zealously combated simony in that country. He was regarded as a man of resolute will and perfect courage, qualities which he was not slow to demonstrate. He adopted on his election the title of Alexander II.

It was not long before the opposition united in efforts for the new Pope's overthrow. Lombard bishops were among the disaffected, indisposed to acknowledge any save one of their own countrymen ; the elevation of the Milanese was therefore urged as excuse for an effort to depose him. The Lombards conspired to bring about the election of an antipope in Cadalous, Bishop of Parma, whom they proclaimed at Bâle as Pope Honorius II, the Empress-regent approving.

Although the antipope had the imperial favour, and gained also the support both of Germany and of Constantinople, he was not able to withstand the lawful power of Alexander. The latter gathered to his side not only the influence of Hildebrand, who was now created Chancellor of the Church, but also the great houses of Cluny and Monte Cassino, and the strong arms of the Norman knights and soldiers.

Right and might were in this manner combined in the Pope's forces, and although there was for a time a ding-dong struggle for supremacy on the part of Honorius and his supporting faction, with a vacillating standpoint on the side of the Romans, Alexander was finally recognized. Agnes the regent was deprived of the administration of the Empire. A few years later she made her peace finally with the pontiff and she spent her last years in tranquil piety. At a council held at Augsburg in 1062, at which the young Henry IV was present, Hanno, the Archbishop of Cologne, declared that Alexander's claims were to be recognized as indisputable.

Now indeed it became every day easier to estimate the altered state of religious life due to the efforts of Hildebrand and his friends. On all sides a holy enthusiasm was aroused against corrupt practices and lax discipline. Among those who set themselves to propagate this zeal the Benedictines were prominent. These men hastened to make new foundations and to bring the masses of the people nearer to God. Monasteries were gradually freed from harmful associations or were dissolved and replaced by others more firmly ordered. Into this work both the Pope and Hildebrand threw themselves with crusading ardour, helped by the labours of such men as St. Peter Damian, St. John Gualbertus, and St. Peter Igneus. In Tuscany a sustained campaign was carried on by the monks of the new order of Vallombrosa. Worldly prelates and congregations found themselves faced by a reforming spirit so determined, so active, that resistance was useless.

Meanwhile, the councillors of the boy Emperor were trying by all possible means to sow disaffection and rebellion against the Holy See. Encroachments on the temporal power centred for the time being in Germany. Henry, acting as bidden, persecuted with rigour the people of Thuringia, attempting to extort church moneys unjustly, while forbidding any appeal to Rome. The Saxons were pillaged without ruth. On every side the cry of the people went up against the tyranny of Henry and his favourites.

Pope Alexander heard with indignation of this abuse of kingly power. He excommunicated some of the councillors and summoned the Emperor to appear before him in answer to many charges. But the pontiff himself was not permitted to see the further unfolding of the ranged antagonism of Church and Empire. He died in 1073, after an eventful and meritorious reign of twelve years, during which time the independence of the Church had been steadily maintained and strengthened.

Hardly were the funeral ceremonies of the dead Pope ended when the popular Roman voice clamoured for the election of Hildebrand to fill the papal throne. Cries of this desire had been raised at the funeral service itself. At that solemn function the Chancellor was presiding. Hastily mounting a pulpit, he sought to quell the unseasonable tumult ; but one of the cardinals present forestalled him and made an appeal for Hildebrand's election. The response was immediate. Cheers rang through the great church of the Lateran, and in the excess of their enthusiasm the people cried that St. Peter had elected Hildebrand as Pope.

In spite of his protestations, his tears even, the pontiff-elect was crowned and enthroned. Thenceforth a new situation faced the opposing ranks and influences. They who had previously reckoned only with the monk, the sub-deacon, the Chancellor, now found themselves confronted, in Pope Gregory VII, with the strong arm of papal power. Hildebrand was Pope—"Hildebrand", a name to be interpreted whether in admiration, by his friends, as "a pure flame", or in hatred, by his enemies, as "the brand of Hell"!

An historic reign now began. Seeing that the new pope was himself a monk, it is not surprising that he sought auxiliaries of reform in the monasteries. From their abbots he drew his most trusted counsellors. He was determined, too, to protect the religious orders not only from the interference of lay-princes, but also from high-handed doings by the secular episcopate. The spirit of the cloister was strongly implanted in his character : the word "monk" itself was hurled against him as a reproach.

The influence of the papacy was cast strongly in favour of the monks as against seculars and laymen. When a quarrel arose between the monks of St. Remy at Reims and the Archbishop, Gregory defended the monks. On another occasion there was some difference between the monks of St. Vannes and Bishop Thierry of Verdun, leading to the religious being shown the street by that wrathful prelate. Here again Gregory's protecting hand was extended, and the banished monks found a new home at Dijon. Other instances might be cited in proof of the pope's strong and, as some think, excessive partiality towards the monastic houses, to which he certainly gave privileges and dignities far beyond anything accorded by his predecessors.

It was not the case, however, that the pope depended only upon the monks for support in his policy. In Gregory's party were not a few zealous bishops who owed their Sees to the favour of laymen, while many of the laity themselves rallied to Gregory's side. But these together made only a small minority. Speaking broadly, it

can be said that the regular clergy were with Gregory, while the
seculars, for the most part, clung to the imperial party under Henry IV.

In 1075 the pontiff issued his edict, under pain of excommunication,
against the practice of investiture to sacred offices. To explain adequately the nature, origin, and growth of investitures would be to
enter upon a subject fraught with many technicalities ; moreover, it
would take us rather far afield from the biographical course. It may
be said briefly that the practice meant that kings and emperors who
wished to give bishoprics or other offices of dignity to favourites, worthy
or otherwise, did so by sending a ring and a crozier in sign that the
temporalities of a particular benefice had been bestowed upon the
recipient. These symbols were then carried to the Metropolitan, who
returned them as intimation that sacred office had been conferred
upon their holder.

As might be expected, such a system gave rise, in many cases,
to grave abuse, and Gregory determined to put a stop to it. He was
especially indignant that the two symbols, the crozier and the ring,
had been deemed to typify temporal gifts ; the one he regarded as
the sign of pastoral authority, the other as an emblem of the celestial
mysteries. His prohibition struck a heavy blow at simony, and
while it roused his foes to still more violent resistance to his authority,
it stimulated in faithful clerics a stronger hope of victory for the
Church as against the world.

The pope's own words will best explain and justify his action with
regard to investitures. Writing to the clergy and people of Aquilæa,
Gregory declares : " There is an ancient and well-known law,
sanctioned not by men, but by Christ our Lord and Saviour in the
fulness of His wisdom, which says : ' He that entereth in by the door
is the shepherd of the sheep ' ; but if he ' climbeth up another way,
the same is a thief and a robber ' (St. John x). For this reason, that
which has long been neglected on account of sin—that which had been,
and still is, corrupted by a detestable custom—we wish now to restore
and to renew, for the honour of God and the salvation of Christendom,
so that in every church the bishop charged to govern the people of
God, ordained according to the Word of truth, may be neither thief
nor robber, but worthy of the name and office of a shepherd. Such
is our will, such our strong desire, and such shall be, by the mercy of
God, as long as we live, the object of our unwearied efforts."

This action towards investitures supplied the imperial party with
further fuel for hostility, and matters swiftly approached a crisis
between the pope and the emperor. Henry IV faced opposition
from two quarters : the purer clergy and the oppressed peasantry of
Thuringia and other places. The Saxon spirit was in rebellion
against the tyranny of the Court, and it was easy to foresee on which

side the common people were likely to be ranged. More than once Gregory's legates had been sent from Rome to make stern representations to Henry about both his morals and his government. As long as it seemed likely that the wars upon which he was engaged might prove disastrous, the emperor was ready with promises of reform ; but when, after a sharp campaign, Henry conquered the Saxons, he set the Holy See at defiance, refused to relinquish the practice of investiture, and openly declared his enmity to the papal cause. It was the old story :

> " When the devil was ill, the devil a saint would be ;
> But when the devil got well again, the devil a saint was he ! "

The results were that the pope excommunicated several councillors and bishops of the empire, while Henry, for his part, multiplied scandalous promotions and recalled and restored to their benefices churchmen who had previously been deposed.

The pope now cited Henry to appear before him to answer for his offences. Far from complying, the emperor called a council at Worms, early in 1076, at which he had sentence of deposition pronounced against Gregory, who retaliated by excommunicating Henry and in turn proclaiming him deposed.

The events thus sketchily related followed upon an act of personal violence against the pontiff. While saying midnight Mass in St. Mary Major's at Christmas, 1075, Gregory was attacked by an armed band and was carried off to a fortified tower beyond the city walls. He was captive but a few hours. Learning of the outrage, the Roman populace stormed the place and conducted their pastor back in triumph to the church, where the Mass so rudely interrupted was resumed. Whether the emperor personally had any guilty knowledge of the previous night's attack has never been established : he is entitled to the benefit of the doubt.

We pass to October, 1076. In that month the German princes met at Tribur. As a result of their meeting Henry was told that unless he made his peace with the pope, and received absolution, another king would be elected ; meanwhile the royal authority was in abeyance. In this uncertain state matters remained until the early part of 1077, when a new assembly, over which Gregory was to preside, was called at Augsburg to pronounce upon the charges against the king.

Now, truly, the peccant emperor was in a coil. He had to act, and to act quickly. He had worldly wisdom enough to see that for the time being, at any rate, he was not a match for the powers against him. Humble pie is no pleasant meal ; but humble pie he must eat, or lose his throne. So there looms before us what was in one respect the central incident in the history of Pope Gregory's pontificate—the episode of Canossa.

The castle of Canossa, now in ruins, stands some fourteen miles from Reggio. It was a seat of Matilda, Countess of Tuscany, a woman devoted to the pope and the papal cause. There Gregory was making a stay, and to Canossa, in a seemingly penitent frame of mind, the fallen emperor followed him. From what ensued the expression " to go to Canossa " has come to bear the implications of a humiliation so deep that by comparison the ostracism of being " sent to Coventry " is but a pale ghost of suffering.

Exactly what happened is not clear. For the sake of Gregory himself we may hope that there is no literal truth in the picture of the emperor standing at the gate hour after hour, day after day, in cold and misery, turning imploring eyes towards the lighted windows whence came no ray of assurance that the pope would see him. It seems unbelievable, apart from the implied cruelty, that the *porta di penitenza*, as the gateway was afterwards called, witnessed for three days the spectacle of a shivering suppliant.

But though we may rule out the harrowing and incredible picture which some writers have painted, there remains the fact that for Henry the journey to Canossa, and the interview which at length was granted to him, was his life's bitterest pill. The meeting with the Pope took place on January 28th. All that was asked was promised in the way of obedience and reform. Too trustful, perhaps, of a disingenuous character, Gregory pardoned the suppliant, and for a time there was peace—but that time was short.

As to the wisdom of the papal attitude at Canossa, by which the emperor was re-admitted to favour only after he had drained the cup of self-abasement to the dregs, judgment on that score can be left to others. But it may be said here that, with such a chafing character as Henry's, less humiliation might have brought a better sequel.

The peace, as has been said, was short. Yielding to persuasion by the Lombards, Henry quickly thrust aside any thought of implementing the promises made at Canossa. He had hardly returned to Germany when intrigue and simony once more raised their ugly heads. The royal authority was resumed in Italy also. Episcopal favours were given with a lavish hand. Two papal legates, Anselm of Lucca and Gerard of Ostia, were imprisoned. In all this Canossa was soon forgotten—or ranklingly remembered.

Despairing now of all reform from Henry, the German princes, at the Diet of Forchheim, elected a new king. Their choice fell on Rodolph, Duke of Suabia. Between that monarch and Henry there ensued a bitter war which disturbed for three years the peace of the empire and tended also—on one side, unwittingly—to cramp the energies of the Church. In this struggle Gregory held aloof, during that period, from political support to either side ; he was content to counsel efforts for peace.

At length, however, in 1080, the Pope yielded to Saxon solicitations and intervened. Unable to get any reparation from Henry, he excommunicated and deposed that offender for the second time and declared himself on Rodolph's side. Again this action was met by a counter-deposition. An antipope was put forward in Guibert of Ravenna, who called himself Clement III—a cleric not to be confused with the legitimate Pope of that title who reigned towards the close of the following century. Rodolph died in battle, Hermann of Luxemburg succeeding him as king, elected by the Catholic party. The pope's position was strengthened by the sworn allegiance of the Norman leader, Robert Guiscard.

Adversity, we know, limits nicely as to bedfellows. In his extremity Henry turned to the schismatic emperor of Constantinople. Their combined forces entered Italy and laid siege to Rome. For three years (1081-84) the struggle continued, until temporary victory fell to the allies. Henry entered the city in triumph and caused himself to be crowned there by the antipope. What of Gregory ? By Tiber's banks, in the Castle of St. Angelo, the pontiff was virtually a prisoner, while Rome was given up to his unscrupulous opponent.

But help was at hand. Faithful to his oath of vassalage to the Holy See, Guiscard hastened to the Pope's defence. With thirty thousand Normans he came to Rome. Gregory was freed and Henry was forced to depart whence he had come. The Norman invasion had its sinister side, however, for Guiscard's troops pillaged and laid waste some of the fairest spots in the city and carried numbers of the inhabitants into captivity.

Little remains to tell of Hildebrand's life-story. Worn by the strain of continuous exertions, the Pope sought rest and peace at Monte Cassino. His spirit had always been that of the monk, his sympathies all for the religious life ; and now, for a while, he returned to the bosom of his Order. From Monte Cassino he went to Salerno, where on May 25th, 1085, he died, in his sixty-fifth year. Plaintively, in his dying hours, he murmured the reflection : " I have loved justice and hated iniquity ; therefore I die in exile."

" Therefore I die in exile." In these words there seems the confession from the great reformer that ultimately his work has been brought to naught. Hildebrand has in fact been regarded by many as one of the world's splendid failures, as a man who strove against forces and circumstances over-great for his strength and died with his mission unaccomplished. It is a superficial view. If St. Gregory VII did not succeed entirely in destroying the cancer of corruption, at least he played mightily one man's part. He feared neither the imperial frown nor hostile armies. He secured the freedom of papal elections, a reform which by itself is worthy to be his monument. Hildebrand delivered the Church from the imperial yoke, waged war against simony, purified the religious houses, enforced the principle of clerical celibacy, and in all ways sought to restore to Christendom the primitive piety and purity which in apostolic times had signalized the Church's divine mission.

Various have been the estimates of Hildebrand from those who have written about him. Among chroniclers adverse to his memory are the French authors Condorcet and Voltaire. The former roundly wrote him down a knave ; the latter remarked : " the Church counts him a saint and the sages count him a fool." If such a career is thus foolish in the eyes of Voltaire, who among us would wish to be wise ? To Sir James Stephen, on the other hand, Hildebrand's was the hand which " kindled the torch of reform and bore it aloft with clear and steady brilliancy to the gaze of the Christian world." From Paul Bernried comes a tribute touched with hyperbole but with that in it which the Catholic reader, from what has been here set down, is likely to endorse :

" He endured perfidy and temptation, perils, insults, captivity and exile, for the love of God. By the grace of that same God, and by the aid of the apostles—kings, tyrants, dukes, princes, all the jailors of human souls, all the ravenous wolves, all the ministers of Antichrist . . . were vanquished by this invincible athlete."

Hildebrand lies buried in the church of St. Matthew at Salerno. He was beatified by Pope Gregory XIII in 1584, and in 1728 Benedict XIII proclaimed his canonization.

ERNEST OLDMEADOW

ST. ANTONY OF PADUA

A.D. 1195–1232

I

READERS OF FICTION often come across a short story which, despite wide variations of authorship, of material and of handling, is essentially the same story. Rudyard Kipling was only one of its many artificers. In its commonest form, it has for prelude a few lines which picture a group of worldly men absorbing whisky-and-soda in some such place as a golf-pavilion. They believe themselves to be hard-boiled, no-nonsense materialists. By-and-by, one of them narrates a more or less grisly tale of " the supernatural." When he has finished, an awed hush arrests the sizzling of siphons, the striking of matches ; and one of the party is sure to bring out the lines :

"There are more things in heaven and earth, Horatio
Than are dreamt of in your philosophy."

It is a piquant fact that the writers and the most admiring readers of these Horatio-tales have been, like Kipling himself, persons with a contempt for Catholicism. What they despise as gross and silly superstition in Catholic men and women no less intelligent than themselves, they accept and respect when it comes from the pens of " rationalists " with whose general intellectual position it is not compatible.

But at one point—or rather in one person, the person of Paduan Antony—Catholics and countless non-Catholics find common ground. " I don't hold with Catholics, but I do believe in St. Antony " is a common saying among Protestants. Catholics are always being asked by Protestants to say where is the nearest statue of St. Antony " with his money-box for the poor," so that their gratitude for some undoubted favour may be expressed. Indeed the writer of these lines has met not only non-Catholics but even anti-Catholics who, when they are at their wits' end over a lost key, " ask St. Antony for it "—and get it. " I must admit that he isn't small-minded," was the unconsciously droll remark of one anti-Papist on finding that this good-natured Saint does not restrict his beneficence to those who fully share his theology.

Not in a polemical, point-scoring spirit but for their good, we ought to reason frankly with these paradoxical persons who in one breath denounce Catholic superstition and in the next beg St. Antony's aid. It is they, not we, who are toying with superstition. As the evidence for certain sequels, when St. Antony has been invoked, is too plentiful to be pooh-poohed as nonsensical self-delusion, two alternatives present themselves for choice. Either there is a Wonder-worker (whom his clients identify with the Saint of Padua) or there is the Magic from which clean souls recoil. The Superior Person will smile at this dilemma and will refuse either horn ; but we must insist on it. If the name of a long-defunct Portuguese, intentively pronounced, often—very, very often every day—induces certain results, although that Portuguese, instead of being puissantly alive in the presence of Almighty God, is as dead as a nail, then the magicians are right and the fashionable crystal-gazers of London and Paris are useful members of society. As De Maistre said, " Close the churches and you re-open the wizard's caves." Catholic Antonianism, with its whole context of doctrine on the Communion of Saints and the Church Triumphant, is intellectually and morally respectable ; but the Antonianism which mumbles the Paduan name like an African negro's incantation is not.

II

Although the *Restitutor Perditorum* has a clientèle which overflows the One True Fold—by the way, many " Orthodox " Easterns, whose forefathers separated from the Roman unity two hundred years before Antony was born, revere and invoke him—he must not be treated as if he does little more than find the keys of suit-cases and trunks. The Paduan was a man whose life-work was many-sided ; and on every side splendid.

Born in 1195, Antony sojourned in this world only six and thirty years. Thus his earthly life was not much longer than his Divine Master's. But it is not true that, like his Lord, he was born in a stable. Although few of the many cruising travellers who disembark at Lisbon on their voyage to Madeira are taken to see it, the Antonian pilgrim may still visit the very room where St. Antony was born. It is one of the few structures which survived Lisbon's great earth-quake. To-day it seems a strait and humble place ; but spacious building had not begun in Lisbon in the twelfth century. Even the cathedral had a stinted ground-plan. Moreover, we have con-temporary evidence that Antony did not spring from humble stock. A biographer who set to work within a year of the Saint's death had it from the Bishop of Lisbon and other first-hand witnesses that the young Fernando, who afterwards changed his name to Antonio, came of a noble and powerful family. (The claim that he was a descendant of Godefroi de Bouillon was not heard until the eve of the Protestant Reformation and is absurd. Antonio was pure Portuguese.)

Antony of Padua is a Saint who, unlike the poets, was made, not born. One of the wrong notions which hold back many of us from essaying the path of sanctity is the notion that a Saint can't help being one and that his sainthood is congenital, like his tallness or shortness, his black hair or brown. It is true that some natures have a stronger bent than others towards religious reverence ; but, as it is a bent which brings its peculiar and strong temptations, it spells no advantage. A Sinner becomes a Saint not through being Heaven's pampered darling but through bearing his cross daily and through wholly merging his own will in the will of God.

At the age of fifteen, young Fernando decided that he could not preserve his purity of mind and body amidst the hard-pressing temptations of everyday life. He became an Augustinian—a Canon of Saint Cross. St. Augustine did not found an Order of St. Augustine as St. Benedict, St. Francis and St. Dominic founded the Benedictines, the Franciscans, the Dominicans. None the less, the Augustinian Rule of Saint Cross was based on the great Bishop of Hippo's teachings and the Doctor of Doctors himself was held in reverence by the Canons of Holy Cross. St. Augustine's *Confessions* must have confirmed the belief of Fernando that his retreat into a pious house had been wise. But St. Vincent's Priory, just outside (*fora*) Lisbon, was not sufficiently remote from the disturbing world. Friends and relatives came thither too often for the earnest student who was one day to be an honoured theologian and teacher. Therefore he obtained a transfer to an older and more renowned priory of his Order—Santa Cruz at Coimbra.

To-day, a young Portuguese who leaves Lisbon for Coimbra is like a young Englishman leaving London for Oxford ; but, seven hundred years ago, Coimbra was certainly not " in the provinces." It was the capital of Portugal, in every way greater than Lisbon ; and its splendour was largely ecclesiastical. When Antony first beheld the city on the Mondego, the building now known as the Old Cathedral was of new-cut limestone, fresh from the chisels of French-trained masons. But the great Catholic glories of Coimbra were spiritual. Already Santa Cruz had its Saint, Prior Theotonio. This holy man had walked and talked with some of the older Canons who were still alive when young Fernando arrived from Lisbon ; and the English Pope Adrian IV (Breakspeare) had forged one of the many links which bind our country to Portugal by according to Santa Cruz signal privileges.

Fernando remained ten years with the Canons—two years in Lisbon, eight in Coimbra. When he left Portugal for ever, he had spent under its gentle skies more than two-thirds of his allotted years on earth. In eleven more years—some say only ten—his life's work was to be done. It is important to grasp these time-factors in order to understand that although we speak of Antony of Padua (his death-place) our Saint was Antony of Lisbon, who spent thrice as much time in Portugal as in Italy, and only a year or two, all told, in Padua.

III

Many persons now living remember the time when even educated Britons reckoned St. Antony's century as part of " the Dark Ages." When the spread of the Gothic Revival drew attention strongly to the unsurpassed cathedrals and other churches of that century, they somewhat modified their harsh verdict. The thirteenth century, they said, was a Bright Age for architecture but a Dark Age for Science and Religion. Fuller popular knowledge concerning the Universities and concerning the intellectual life of which St. Thomas Aquinas was the chief ornament, have made anti-Catholics less sweeping in their condemnation of the Medieval Church's attitude to Education ; yet the notion still remains that She was no Kindly Mother to Her children but a harsh schoolmistress, rapping their knuckles or giving their backs the rod in a spirit of tyranny.

The truth is that nowhere and never in history has a great institution shown more amenability than did the Catholic Church in the thirteenth century. If this were a study of St. Francis instead of St. Francis's disciple and coadjutor St. Antony, striking facts could be adduced, showing how not only Bishops but Cardinals and even Popes gave kindly hearing to the Little Poor Man of Assisi and helped him to realise his ideals. But our business is with Antony ; and to him also the greatest personages in the Church gave sympathy and understanding.

The Canons of Santa Cruz, in their rochets of fine linen, lived piously but not meanly in rich and busy Coimbra. Theirs was a solid monastery with a worthy church and a library.[1] They were not subject to the Bishop. In short, they were an autonomous community of such high prestige that their rule forbade any Canon to exchange his status for that of a mere monk. Yet their spirituality was so sensitive that they set the rule aside when Fernando was divinely moved to become a Franciscan.

" To become a Franciscan " would have been regarded by less

[1] The Manueline buildings which have made Santa Cruz architecturally famous were not raised until 300 years after Antony's death.

holy men as a humiliation. At that time (1220) the Franciscans had not truly become an Order. Only ten years had passed since the first little band of Franciscans (literally only twelve disciples) had obtained the blessing of Pope Innocent III. It is true that, during these ten years, thousands of earnest men had joined the movement; but it was an unorganized throng of clerics and laics, celibates and married men, young and old, high and low. Moreover, it was already at sixes and sevens, because its founder had been for two years in the Near East, trying to convert the infidels, and his lieutenants had got things into a sad mess. As there were no vows and no school of novices, many enthusiasts had come in only to go out again. Indeed many saintly men looked upon the whole thing as a mere flash in the pan.

What made the humiliation of giving up one of their best subjects more bitter to the Canons of Santa Cruz was the fact that this inchoate Franciscanism, in all its crudity, was at their very door. That " distance lends enchantment to the view " and that " familiarity breeds contempt " are true proverbs. If Coimbra had known nothing of the Friars Minor except as far-off, picturesque mendicant evangelists, it would have been easier to let Fernando join them. But Coimbra already had its own poor little Franciscan house. It was a place without dignity, and its inmates were illiterate. So wretched was the state of these ragged starvelings that they came often as beggars to Santa Cruz, craving the crumbs which fell from the Canons' table. Indeed, it was through his duties as almoner that Fernando came to know them. Of Franciscan glory as well as Franciscan poverty and humility he was already aware ; because the Heir-apparent to the Portuguese throne, Dom Pedro, had lately given to Santa Cruz a golden reliquary containing the bones of the first Franciscan martyrs of Morocco.

Not Franciscanism but missionary zeal—a zeal fully willing to accept a savage death for the Gospel—drew Fernando to the Friars in the first instance. If some of them had already gone to preach and die in Africa, why could not he, Canon Fernando, do the same ? Indeed, it is on record that he made a bargain along these lines. He would turn Friar, he said, on condition that he was sent to Morocco. The humble Franciscans of Coimbra took him at his word ; and the very next day they came to stately Santa Cruz carrying the sack-cloth and the rope-girdle which were henceforth to be his garb. Meanwhile Fernando had persuaded the reluctant Prior and Canons not to oppose his missionary effort ; and thus took place the drab little investiture of which Portugal has been proud ever since.

A truly Dark Age would have forced up poisonous fungi of pride ; but from the Age of St. Antony—an age warmed and quickened by the light of Faith—sprang sweet flowers of simplicity and humility. One of the thirteenth century's bequests to posterity was those *fioretti*—" little flowers "—of St. Francis in which St. Antony is not the meanest or the least fragrant bloom.

IV

Their poor friary near Coimbra had been named by the few Franciscans there after St. Antony of Egypt, and Antony was the new name which they gave to their neophyte from the goodly courts of Santa Cruz.

In the prime of his manhood, Brother Antony took shipping for Morocco. To ordinary voyagers the pains and perils of the sea are made tolerable by thoughts of happy days in the desired haven. For the young friar there was a different and, to him, a still more comforting hope. Could he but land safely, proclaim the Gospel faithfully, and seal the testimony with his life's blood, he would be content. But martyrdom at Moslem hands was not his destiny. He disembarked in Africa only to find himself a strengthless invalid. Fever seized him and held him until he was forced to decide upon a return to Portugal for recuperation. Not that his project was renounced. He was more set upon it than ever. Health and strength were to be retrieved for Christ's and the infidels' sake.

When the master of the ship which was to carry the sufferer home found himself being steadily blown eastward instead of northward, no doubt he cried out against the contrary winds ; but they were contrary only to human convenience. They were fulfilling God's Will towards one of the greatest of His Saints. The vessel was driven to Sicily ; and never again did Fernando of Lisbon behold Portugal.

At Messina, a consolation was given to him. In that port, he fell in with some Friars who broke to him the great news that Brother Francis was home again from the East and was about to hold a Chapter at Assisi. They themselves were bound thither. Antony joined them, or some similar band.

It was spring-time. From Messina to Assisi was a hundred leagues. There would be much discourse between the brethren on the way. But the one-time Augustinian Canon does not appear to have told the humbler wayfarers that he was a scholar and a priest. They arrived at the meeting-place of the Chapter, where some thousands of the Friars Minor were gathered together. There Antony, humblest of the humble, first beheld Brother Francis. Little did he foresee that he was to become one of the Poverello's most beloved and trusted colleagues—so trusted that Francis would one day call Antony " my Bishop "—and that he would preach in the Eternal City itself with the Supreme Pontiff and a bevy of Cardinals among his hearers.

Antony's first sermons, delivered in the Romagna (in north-eastern Italy) were against the so-called Cathari, whose heresies were so grievous that the teachings of the sixteenth-century Protestants are mild in comparison. They had no baptism, no Mass and, except in a weird sense of their own, no priesthood. Many of them held a dualism which made Satan almost a god in the temporal sphere. It was when the Cathars ridiculed his preaching on the river bank at Rimini that Antony turned away from them and called out " Oh, ye little fishes, I have a message for you from Christ."

Catholic painters have loved to depict this miracle. From the pure Tuscan of the *Fioretti* they learned how the fish " all held their heads out of the water and all attentively faced St. Antony, in great peace and tameness and order ; so that in front were the smallest fishes and after them the middle-sized and behind, in the deepest water, the largest fishes." As for the sermon, the disciple Antony certainly based it upon the discourse of his master Francis to the birds ; but Arthur Christopher Benson did the disciple an injustice when he described the sermon to the fishes as " a pompous and heavy-handed parody, suggesting a full grown man trying to gambol like a child."[1]

That the sermon to the fishes was not necessarily an arbitrary attempt to graft the bird-sermon of St. Francis upon the Antonian legend is proved by what we know of Antony's character.[2] He had a great love of Nature. While he preached, he looked upward ; and his very last weeks on earth were mostly spent in a little tabernacle which had been built for him at his earnest request in the leafy heart of a giant chestnut-tree. There, amidst the rustling of foliage and the songs of birds, he toiled at sacred studies—as his earliest biographer says—" like a bee in a hive."

Antony's sainthood, however, came out in other things besides apostolic preaching in crowded cities and solitary searching of Holy Scripture in lonely forests. For example, it was he who persuaded Padua to pass a humane bankruptcy-law, under which a debtor who had assigned his property to his creditors could not be immured and kept (as had been the harsh practice) in gaol. The museum of Padua still preserves the original document.

This brief paper cannot tell Antony's full life-story. But it must be related that St. Francis, who was not himself a priest, made use of the

[1] Long before the Catholic Revival in the nineteenth century Antony's Sermon to the Fishes was known to English Protestants. A delightful translation was published by Addison, after his travels in Italy. It is printed as an Appendix to this chapter.

[2] The Portuguese are proverbially kind to animals. When some well-meaning Britons wanted to lecture the public of Oporto against cruelty, the Portuguese simply could not understand it. At Portuguese bull-fights the bull is not killed and there is none of the slaughter of old horses which so long disgraced Spain.

ex-Canon's learning and allowed him to teach theology. Unhappily not even the smallest fragment of his lectures has survived. Nor do we indubitably possess any of those sermons which had so much drawing-power that the ladies of Padua would leave their beds before daybreak on cold mornings and would go by torchlight to church to hear them, while the congregation was swollen by thieves, usurers and notorious libertines.

Of the ten years or so which Antony lived outside Portugal, two at least seem to have been spent in France. To the French years belong some of the most picturesque Antonian miracle-stories, such as the stopping of the rain over the heads of an open-air audience and the replenishment of the wine-barrel after a poor woman had forgotten to turn off the tap. Some say that France was also the scene of that apparition of the Infant Jesus which is represented in popular statues of the Saint. And this brings us to the question of miracles said to have been wrought by Antony during his lifetime. Recent writers reject these *ante-mortem* miracles, on the ground that they are hardly mentioned in the earliest Lives of the Saint.

Although, as his concluding paragraphs will show, it would suit the present writer's argument to rest the fame of Antony the Wonder-worker almost solely upon his *post-mortem* miracles (as indeed Pope Gregory IX did when he canonized Antony) we must not indecently hurry to join the sceptics or minimizers. The Saint's first panegyrists did not profess to write as exhaustive biographers. Some of them, indeed, essayed no more than brief memoirs for liturgical use ; and they followed the Church in not dwelling on the earlier wonders.[1]

v

There is presumptive evidence for some Antonian *ante-mortem* miracles at least. The phenomenal fame of Antony, still a young foreigner at the time of his death, can hardly be explained by his eloquence and benevolence alone. When the boys and girls of Padua on June 13, 1231, rushed through the streets crying, " The Saint is dead, St. Antony is dead," the whole city was moved. Indeed, for

[1] An instance of excessive scepticism towards these wonders in Mr. Ernest Gilliat-Smith's *St. Anthony of Padua* (London, 1926), in many respects a good and useful book. After stating that the earliest account of the Sermon to the Fishes is in the Florentine Legend (c. 1275, or 44 years after the Saint's decease) he adds : " Note this, the miraculous element enters into it hardly at all." Yet, as Mr. Gilliat-Smith's own excerpt shows, the Florentine Legend explicitly says that the fishes " came at Antony's call, and remained with their heads out of the water until he had finished speaking to them and had given them his blessing and then they went away." Surely there is enough of " the miraculous element " here for anybody. Can it be that Mr. Gilliat-Smith has kept company with those whose fish-stories are so tall as to dwarf even St. Antony's ?

several days, the Paduans could talk of nothing else ; and a dispute as to his place of burial even led to a short and sharp little civil war.

Less than a year (May 30, 1232) after his decease St. Antony was added to the Calendar of Saints by the Pope (Ugolino) who had known and revered him in the flesh. But let it be carefully noted that Gregory IX did not act on mere impulse. His commissioners visited Padua and held an investigation of the most rigorous kind. They rejected every wonder-story which did not come unscathed out of their critical crucibles. In the end, they accepted as indisputable forty-six miracles, of which no less than forty-five were wrought *post-mortem.*

Since that year of 1232, Antonian miracles have become as numerous as leaves in Vallombrosa. There is no speech nor language in which their fame is not heard. It would be no exaggeration to say that the forty-six have grown to forty-six thousand and more. If all these had been written down and scrutinized, it would be found that the deponents are not visionaries or persons obsessed with the supernatural. Nor are they mainly those full-time church-folk who are known by the clumsy name " religious." They include hard-headed men of science and of business by the scores of thousands, as well as equally sane and practical working women. Literate and illiterate, old and young, earnest and careless, can alike testify to the efficacy of St. Antony's intercession.

Although " lost things " are prominently mentioned in the Friar Julian of Speyer's famous Responsory *Si quaeris miracula* and are the best known *materia* of the Saint's wonder-working, St. Antony of Padua has, throughout seven centuries and more, proved himself a Thaumaturge in countless other ways. Not only as a mission-preacher in his own day but as the celestial ally of evangelists and Christian apologists ever since he has deserved his name " Hammer of Heretics." Not only for the bankrupts of Padua and the forgetful Provençale was he a Father of the Poor but also for thousands past numbering who have invoked him in their misery. And the same is true of his other glorious titles—Consoler of the Afflicted, Medicine of the Sick, Hope of the Despairing, Tranquillizer of Factions, Deliverer of Captives, Trumpeter of Truth.

So now we are brought round again to the thesis which was adumbrated at the outset of this paper ; namely, that St. Antony of Padua is not only precious to us as a friend-at-court in highest Heaven but has an incalculable evidential value for Catholic apologetics. Unless millions of witnesses—even within a few years of his death *Veneti, Lombardi, Sclavi, Aquilei, Theutonici, Hungari* were flocking to his tomb— have been fools or liars, the testimony to the continuous existence, in a higher state, of the mortal born near Lisbon Cathedral in the year

1195 and dead at Padua in 1231 is too multitudinous and massive to be brushed aside. And, if it cannot be brushed aside, reasonable men must face its implications. Far-fetched attempts to explain it on the lines of that ignoble and mis-called " Spiritualism " with which our noble as well as holy Mother the Church sternly forbids us to toy, are incompatible with the rich history of Antonian miracles. Those miracles have always been miracles of celestial compassion, having nothing whatever in common with morbid and irreverent attempts to pull aside a curtain which God Himself has lowered and to pry into mysteries which mock the Peeping Toms with nothing more useful and uplifting than alleged materialisations of the clown Grimaldi or " Raymond's " supra-mundane cigarettes.

The Catholic explanation of Antony the Catholic is as simple as it is lofty and inspiring. The Incarnate God in Whose love Antony lived and died promised that because He lives, we shall live also, and that those who do His Father's will shall be one with Him, " even as He and the Father are one." That " Christ is risen " is among the best authenticated facts of history. Not only risen but ascended, He sits at the right hand of God. With Him in beatitude eternal are those " Friends of God," His Saints ; and part (if we may use a most finite word) of their happiness is expressed in the promise of another Wonder-worker, " The Little Flower," of Lisieux, who said, " I will spend my Heaven doing good upon earth."

ADDISON'S VERSION OF ANTONY'S SERMON TO THE FISHES

Although the infinite power of God, my dearly beloved fish, discovers itself in all the works of His creation, as in the Heavens, the Sun, the Moon, the Stars, in man or in the other perfect creatures ; nevertheless the goodness of the divine majesty shines out in you more eminently. For, notwithstanding, you are imprisoned in the deep abyss of waters, tossed among billows, thrown up and down by tempests, deaf to hearing, dumb to speech, and terrible to behold, the divine greatness shews itself in you after a most wonderful manner. In you are seen the mighty mysteries of an infinite goodness. The holy Scripture has always made use of you as the types and shadows of some profound sacrament.

Do you think that without a mystery, the first present that God Almighty made to man was of you, O ye fishes ? Do you think that without a mystery, among all creatures which were appointed for sacrifices, you only were excepted, O ye fishes ? Do you think there was nothing meant by our Saviour Christ that, next to the pascal lamb, he took so much pleasure in the food of you, O ye fishes ? Do you think it was by mere chance that when the Redeemer of the world was to pay tribute to Cæsar, he thought fit to find it in the mouth of a fish ? These are all of them so many mysteries and sacraments that oblige you, in a more particular manner, to the praises of your Creator.

It is from God, my beloved fish that you have received being, life, motion and sense. It is He that has given you, in compliance with your natural indications, the whole world of waters for your habitation. It is He that has furnished it with lodgings, chambers, caverns, grottoes, and such magnificent retirements as are not to be met with in the seats of kings or in the palaces of princes. You have the water for your dwelling, a clear transparent element, brighter than crystal : you can see from its deepest bottom everything that passes on its surface : you have the eyes of a Lynx or of an Argus : you are guided by a secret and unerring principle, delighting in everything that may be beneficial to you and avoiding everything that may be hurtful : you are carried on by a hidden instinct to preserve yourselves and to propagate your species ; you obey, in all your actions, works and motions, the dictates and suggestions of nature without the least repugnancy or contradiction.

The colds of winter and the heats of summer are equally incapable of molesting you. A serene or a clouded sky are indifferent to you. Let the earth abound in fruits or be cursed with scarcity it has no influence on your welfare. You live secure in rains or thunders, lightnings and earthquakes : you have no concern in the blossoms of spring or the glowings of summer, in the fruits of autumn or in the frosts of winter. You are not solicitous about hours or days, months or years.

In that dreadful majesty, in that wonderful power, in that amazing providence did God Almighty distinguish you among all the species of creatures that perished in the universal deluge ! You only were insensible of the mischief that had laid waste the whole world.

All this ought to inspire you with gratitude and praise toward the divine majesty that has done you so great things for you. And since you cannot employ your tongues in the praises of your benefactor and are not provided with words to express your gratitude : make at least some sign of reverence ; bow yourselves at His name ; give some show of gratitude according to the best of your capacities ; express your thanks in the most becoming manner that you are able.

ST. CATHERINE OF SIENA

A.D. 1347–1380

IT IS SOMEWHAT strange that St. Catherine of Siena has not had a wider appeal in our age, considering what an attraction St. Francis has recently exercised, and that in circles far removed from anything that could be called Catholic. Although the interest in St. Francis has been fostered by emphasizing what was romantic and humanitarian in his temperament and concern, nevertheless there is much in this attachment to him, however one-sided it may be, which is to be welcomed ; for it may prove an introduction to that which is far deeper in him, his profound personal religion and its Catholic setting, since these are the sources both of his simplicity and of his strength.

It is therefore highly desirable that St. Catherine also should become better known, for there is perhaps even more in her activities and her teaching which might make a special appeal to our generation and prove a means for drawing it, at least nearer to understanding the Catholic Church, and why it is what it is and ever must be. It is remarkable and promising therefore that our saint appealed to Swinburne, of all unlikely souls ; and not only because of her striving for peace ; for his appreciation of her hidden life of prayer reveals an unexpected sympathy and even insight. This is so strikingly displayed in his poem on " Siena " that some lines from it can be quoted, quite suitably, it is hoped, in order to illustrate the following essay to do something to popularise her memory and extend her still vital influence.

While there is much in St. Catherine's career and character which should naturally interest our age, there is also much that must challenge it ; but which might then lead it deeper. St. Catherine should make a special appeal to our age, first of all because she was a woman. For ours is the age which has had to bow to women's demands for a public career and political equality with men ; though it should then appear all the more remarkable that she took the commanding place that she did, acting almost as the unofficial ambassadress of peace to Europe, and being the most powerful figure of her generation, yet without having to claim or strive for anything. And all this was before the Renascence had come, which gave to a few women great influence, not always for good, and if to a few also in literature, never so powerful a place as St. Catherine attained, yet without having any learning at all. In the second place, she took an active and effective part in the politics of her times, and she was an intense lover and advocate of peace. This activity was however inspired by her attaining heights of contemplation, from which she could see so clearly and descend to act so swiftly and successfully. She had prepared herself for all this by a novitiate of silent seclusion and ascetic discipline ; and it was to a hidden life of mystical adoration that she turned at the end, when everything external seemed to have failed and further activity was blocked by the collapse of her overstrained physical frame.

The comparative neglect of this, one of the most remarkable women that ever lived, considering what she was and wrought, and how closely she touched the most vital and pressing concerns of our own age, may be partly due to the complexity of the times in which she lived. For although she cut like a sword through its tangled web—or rather, since she had so little faith in the sword, more like a flash of summer lightning, piercing the heavy clouds and illuminating the dark landscape—the disturbed and confused state of her world wants to be studied somewhat closely if the significance of her actions is to be understood, as well as the clarity of her wisdom and the courage of her character rightly appraised. For this better understanding of her, we do not as yet possess anything like the number of popular biographies and varied studies which so many have attempted in order to make St. Francis live again for our inspiration and example. We have Edmund Gardner's magnificent study of the Saint ; but while its literary flavour is of the finest and his spiritual insight altogether worthy of the subject, the telling outlines of her life are almost lost for the ordinary reader in the richness of the material dealt with, as well as by the high scholarship that is brought to its discovery and treatment. Miss Alice Curtayne's life is much shorter and simpler, while no less attractive in the force and beauty of its treatment, and should do much to bring the Saint's example and encouragement to the notice of a wider public. But there is nothing between these and the excellent, though somewhat brief and therefore necessarily bare, outline of her life in the Catholic Truth Society's twopenny tract. What is still needed is something specially designed to bring out the application of St. Catherine's life and teaching to our modern problems and perplexities. Moreover such a treatment, written specially in view of the needs of our age, would make a very powerful advocacy for the power as well as the truth of the Catholic Faith. This, not only because her saints are always the Church's best apologists ; but this saint's particular contribution would perhaps help to dispel the disappointment so many feel when confronted with the all too human elements of the Church's vast organisation, and the often terribly complicated issues its officials have to face in this modern world of ours. And while it would point to the necessity of digging down deep to the substratum of faith, to the wells of devotion, and to the rich resources of prayer, if anything is to be effected, especially at this stage of the world's history, it would also show how reverence for an essential office and centre of unity such as the Papacy was divinely instituted and commissioned to serve, can be combined with a frank criticism as well as a commanding appeal to the person who may be its actual representative ; a combination it would be a great gain to recover.

There are, however, it must be admitted, certain obstacles to be overcome before a wide and popular understanding of the Saint, as well as a devout attachment to her memory, can be looked for. There are elements in her type of temperament, as well as in her mode of action, which must remain only as a rebuke to our own age and its mentality. There are, first, her almost incredible austerities and sheerly miraculous abstinences. There are her visions and their often trance-like effects upon mind and body, both far removed from modern experiences, and beyond even what psychological research into similar though quite different states may seem to have illuminated. On the other hand it has to be realised that these were an absolutely necessary preparation for her divine vocation, as well as for her ability to cut through conventions without at the same time endangering her influence on her own generation, or clouding the purity of her character for posterity, by suspicion and calumny. For although these actually arose at the time, they were soon found false, and fell off her unstainable purity, or rather were consumed like smuts and smoke, pitch or charcoal, in the flaming fire of her love.

Such was the strength of this woman's personality—that thing about which we talk so much, without either defining or exemplifying what we mean. In her it was obviously derived from her absolute dedication, summoned as it was by divine revelation, and enforced by supernatural grace ; so that she did not, as we seem doomed to do, simply organize opposition parties, in order to accomplish reforms or resist wrong, or, more often, only gather meetings together in order to pass ineffectual resolutions of protest. She rather went straight to the fount of the evil, whether by her personal presence, or by her letters, which were almost as arresting ; and even then, not so much to condemn the evil, however unmistakeable and reprehensible, but to appeal to the good buried in souls that might have seemed to others beyond hope of understanding or response. She did not advocate reforms therefore : she started them ; she did not agitate until her womanhood had been granted political power or had been acknowledged to possess public sagacity ; she seized the one and displayed the other. Where others might have been strangled by conventions, dismayed by the dangers, or merely irritated by resistance, she launched herself, with the Gospel on her lips and sanctity flashing from her soul, full at the heart of the trouble, whether enshrined in false values or embedded in weakened wills. But before she could have carried anything through, or produced any effect, there had to be those years of silence, and her long vigils of prayer ; all softness of body had to be conquered, and all cloudiness of mind cleared away. The one had to be attained by the discipline and hardening of every sense, and the other by long dwelling in that " secret cell of self-knowledge " which she built for herself in her mind : a sphere where all things are crystal-clear, beyond any possibility of self-deception, the innermost secret of other hearts is reflected, and self-consciousness is lost in the consciousness of God, at once transcendent and near, Dread Sovereign Majesty, and yet the Loving Bridegroom of the soul.

Even to those who have cherished some dream of attaining that holiness without which, after all, not only can no man see the Lord, but there is no hope of inward peace or real outward power, St. Catherine presents a double challenge, whether of hope or warning. Her sanctity was won, not only through asceticism and prayer, in which the more immediate hindrances in the self were brought into subjection, but also against constant hindrances without ; whether found in disappointing characters, and misunderstanding minds, and these, not only among worldly souls, but among those who ought to have been in verity, as they were by vocation, religious. Turbulence and temper, vanity and violence, characterized the ordinary social life of the time ; while in the Church there was corruption even among the hierarchy, unworthy examples in the priesthood, secular or religious, timidity and mediocrity everywhere. Her earliest foes were those of her own household ; her tormentors and traducers often those of the " household of faith." With our Saint there was, therefore, no gliding into sanctity in an atmosphere of uninterrupted quiet, whether in the home or in the sanctuary ; everywhere there was chatter and clatter, confusion and disturbance. Everything had to be not only heroically attempted but heroically endured. The lesson she has left to aspirants after sanctity, who should not be any fewer in our days, for they are as much needed, but are perhaps too easily discouraged is that sanctity is most called for when everything is adverse, and is generally only achieved when everything seems contrary.

Even then St. Catherine's life and achievements contain a lesson hard enough to our coarse valuations and measurement by outward success. For the things she actually sought to bring about either altogether failed, or, when they succeeded, only seemed to bring worse evils in their train. The secret of a success which lies hidden in failure has to be learned both in appraising and in following her.   For out of all her magnificent efforts, and even most startling achievements, there was found nothing of solid and permanent gain but this : the sanctification of her own glorious soul and its saving influence on others. Even her wonderful letters, for all the practical effect they had would seem like writing on sand, which the cruel storms of evil or the lazy waves of compromise would have wiped out, were it not for their spiritual power and beauty which remain.   In addition we have her greatest literary bequest, which still lives to fertilize souls with high thoughts and holy contemplations, the mystical treatise known as " the Dialogue," dictated by her swiftly in a state of ecstasy as fast as the astonished scribes could take it down.

St. Catherine ought to attract our age, but she is bound to rebuke the modern mind ; nevertheless she might show us how to save both— at present so perplexed and cast down.   It is with some such hope that this brief outline of her life is here set forth.   It may move some to read the larger works and original sources, and encourage some writer better qualified to bring out the significance of her life and set it forth in such force and beauty as shall attract the wider attention it deserves.

It was in a steep side street of proud and turbulent Siena, a still medieval and crowded city, that, about the middle of the fourteenth century, there was born to the Benincasa family a child who, in her swift short life, was to make such a mark upon her country's history and an even more indelible mark upon the Church's memory by its well-merited canonization of her sanctity.   One can still stand and look

" Up the sheer street :

And the house midway hanging see
That saw Saint Catherine bodily,
Felt on its floors her sweet feet move,
And the live light of fiery love
Burn from her beautiful strange face.

It was a busy and bustling household into which our Saint was born ; the father a well-to-do craftsman and merchant, the mother of somewhat better social inheritance, giving birth thus to her twenty-fifth child, and this time twins ; though the sister twin soon died, as had twelve others of this numerous family beforehand.   These are facts which might well awaken varied reflections in the minds of those who are concerned about infant mortality, obsessed about the limitation of births, or wondering about God's ways in sending souls into this world.   Nevertheless, there can be little doubt that here was a soul marked out with special graces from earliest days.   For beside her christened name of Catherine, the family called her Euphrosyne, the name also given by botanists to that little meadow flower known to our countryside as Eyebright. We might well remember her by it, for though it is so humbly small, yet when looked at carefully, it is seen to be as unusual in form as it is beautiful in colour. Such was she as a child ; gifted not only with light brown hair which the Sienese girls so much admired that they bleached their more common black locks to obtain it, but with a beauty (however soon marred by smallpox) that must have caused the attention which was soon fastened on her, and have contributed to the extraordinary effect which merely to look upon her had all her life—and that upon everyone, however reluctant they may have been to desire her presence or believe in her power. But far more certain than beauty of face must have been the grace that diffused itself around her, and the light that shone from her soul ; for that was obvious and arresting from an early age.

The growing child had soon begun to make prayer the chief among her concerns ; going up the stairs of her lofty house, she was accustomed to make each step part of a rosary. As early as at six years of age there occurred the first of that series of visions that was to lift her eyes to heaven and draw her so near to Christ, though making it all the clearer to her what was crying out to be put right in the world and in the Church. Coming home from a visit one day, above the Dominican Church near her home, with which her religious life was so much connected, and where at last her head was to be enshrined as its most precious relic, she saw a vision of Christ, accompanied by saints and angels, smiling upon her and giving her the priestly blessing. It may be difficult in any given case to decide what objective reality such visions rest upon, but it is impossible in St. Catherine's case, at any rate, to explain them away. It is allowable to hold that such visions owe something to the recipient's own mind, stored, as hers may well have been, with images remembered from the pictures on the walls or in the windows of the Churches ; but all that may only provide furnishing or translation of what was an immediate touch of God upon the soul, calling it to high commission and sealing it with sanctity. Anyhow nothing for Catherine could be quite the same again, and she now set herself to seek for its meaning and to prepare herself for what it entailed.

The preoccupation that now began to hold her mind, and almost blinded her eyes to ordinary things, was soon noticed by her somewhat fussy and managing mother, and various distractions were invented to disentangle her mind's attention, or improve her health, for one or the other was naturally suspected to be not quite normal. She began to dream of being a nun, a missionary, or a martyr ; and in order to stamp as final her resolution to renounce all ideas of marriage, which was thought of for her, as was usual in those days, very early, at her confessor's advice she cut off all her lovely-coloured hair. Now ensued a tussle of wills ; and not only with her mother's, for the whole family strove to break hers to follow theirs. All privacy was denied her ; the family servant was sent away, and she was made to take her place and wait upon them all ; and her days were made weary with drudgery. With her swift power of extracting the best from the worst, Catherine set herself to look upon her father as Christ, her mother as the Virgin, and her brothers and sisters as the twelve Apostles ; and thus she served them with interior devotion. For the loss of any place in which to pray alone, she reverted to that " secret cell of self-knowledge ", as she called it. It was soon obvious that whatever hindrances and humiliations were heaped upon her, she was winning the victory ; and after her father had seen a vision of a snow-white dove hovering over her, when he caught her at prayer in her brother's room, he demanded that the persecution should cease, and a room of her own be given her. With this privilege, always so precious to a young girl, but welcomed by her for deeper reasons, she set herself to live like an anchoress, reducing food and sleep to an inhuman minimum, and going out only to her Communions at St. Dominic's close by.

> " For years through, sweetest of the saints,
>   In quiet without cease she wrought,
>   Till cries of men and fierce complaints
>   From outward moved her maiden thought."

Very soon there now began that other marked phenomenon of her mystical life, the trance-like condition which the reception of the Sacrament so often induced. It is not surprising that these happenings attracted attention and wakened suspicion. The cruel test of piercing her foot with a knife showed however that she was really beyond sensible feeling. Yet these were no mere stupors, as was afterwards apparent ; for in these frequent attacks of insensibility there was no blank unconsciousness, but rather such a consciousness of God's presence and the pressure of spiritual power, that everything of sense was cut off, and the body left almost as if the soul had departed from it. Unlike the common effects of false mysticism, these happenings only increased her desire to know what God had already revealed by His spoken word, and she also used her years of retirement to learn to read the Scriptures. How she did this is so unknown, that it is believed it was miraculously acquired ; for she seemed to be able to gather the sense when she did not even know the letters or how to spell the words. She must also have learned to write, though most of her voluminous correspondence was dictated, and sometimes at the rate of three letters at once to different secretaries.

One of these raptures took an unusual form, and has been represented in famous pictures, one by Luini, familiar to many from reproductions, as well as one by David which is in our National Gallery ; though no doubt she would think they did little justice to what her inner eye saw of glory and beauty. This was however a vision of her espousals as " the bride of the Kingdom of heaven." The ring of gold, with its pearls and diamonds, that sealed the ceremony, she declared that she could always afterward see shining on her finger. Lest anyone should dismiss this as an extravagant conception of her relationship to Christ, it might be remembered that all nuns wear a wedding ring in token of their dedication to Christ alone ; and since, in these days, a sensual basis is suspected for even the highest religious experiences, it might be recalled that Christ Himself, when speaking to His Apostles, called Himself the " Bridegroom." Indeed every human soul is unpartnered, and must at last become desolate, unless it is attached to Christ by supernatural love ; while the joy of heaven that all must attain, or remain in the outer darkness, is symbolized in the Apocalypse as the Marriage Supper of the Lamb. There is a secret here not easily attained ; yet if any soul does not know it, what else it does is of little value. In mystical theory the spiritual marriage is generally placed as the highest experience of the soul's converse with its Redeemer ; but it is then expected to be fruitful in works, and in the begetting of spiritual children ; that is, in the conversion of souls. So it soon was in the case of St. Catherine. For this vision marked the end of her life of seclusion and sent her forth to minister what she had gained and impart what she had learned.

> " Then in her sacred saving hands
> She took the sorrows of the lands,
> With maiden palms she lifted up
> The sick time's blood-embittered cup,
> And in her virgin garment furled
> The faint limbs of a wounded world.
> Clothed with calm love and clear desire,
> She went forth in her souls attire,
> A missive fire."

At first she set herself to minister to those who had not only the greatest physical but also the greatest spiritual need, working in the hospitals and taking her place in tending the sick, even penetrating into the very lazar-houses, then so plentiful, and often places of moral as well as of physical corruption. One disagreeable character there she tenderly nursed, only to be repaid with curses and abuse ; and before she could win her love and bring her to a pious frame of mind, Catherine had herself contracted from her some symptom of the

dreaded plague. On the old woman's death, however, she was consoled
not only by bringing her to penitence at last, but because the dreaded
marks disappeared, leaving behind only a luminosity where the leprous
spot had been before. It was her discernment of the soul's need, and
her power of speaking to its condition, that began soon to earn for her
a new fame ; and all kinds of persons now came to see her and sought
her guidance. Among these came priests and theologians, hermits
and religious, as well as lay folk of every walk and station ; and
sometimes with suspicion, or malicious intent. But with all of them
it was soon enough to see her face, and to hear her heavenly conversation, perfectly orthodox and humble, but decorated with strange
beauty and alive with spiritual fire. Those who had been helped
then brought others, and especially those who needed to be converted
from blasphemous talk and evil living and generally, despite reluctance
or bravado, they left changed, not only in their opinion about her,
but about everything else ; for to all she commended love and
forgiveness, holiness and humility.

It is not surprising that some persons began to get envious and
some to suspect pride and even worse disorders to be at work. Sermons
were preached publicly against her and her cult—for it was fast
becoming nothing else. She was delated to the heads of her Order,
for she had earlier become a Dominican tertiary, and at length
summoned to its General Chapter. Whatever accusations were made
against her, they were easily answered by the willing witness of those
who had known her intimately from her earliest days, and this, together
with the testimony of her own simple and radiant spirit secured her
complete acquittal. A special confessor was appointed for her,
everything ending, therefore, in the recognition of her sincerity and
soundness, and with the practical approbation of her character and
work.

It is a mark of her extending and deepening influence that there
now gathered round her a band of those who were dependent upon
her inspiration, and devoted to her service : a Fellowship, consisting
of old and young, men and women, priests and laymen, poets and
politicians, some of them rescued from lives of laziness and vice, many
from merely worldly concerns, and others from the feuds and fighting,
which were equally trivial, to purposeful living and the pursuit of
holiness. Some of these, doubtless the once gay and frivolous, who had
now become her known friends and slaves, were called after in the
streets, *Caterinati* ; but that was a name fast becoming a mark of honour
and dignity. Both priests, and laymen who could do so, took down
her conversation, and offered their services to write the numerous
letters which began the next stage of her ever-widening apostolate.

Catherine's way and success in dealing with individual souls, whatever their need and distress, was so remarkable and beautiful, that it must be illustrated by one example, which can fortunately be told in her own vivid and moving words. A certain Niccoló di Toldi, a Perugian, had been condemned to death simply for speaking slightingly of the Sienese government. All attempts at reprieve were sternly rejected, mainly because Siena and Perugia were then at war, and the young man's death was looked upon as a kind of reprisal ; or rather as an outlet for the hate and vengeance which always spring up at such times all too easily everywhere, but hardly anywhere more fiercely than in Italy at that time. The poor fellow was naturally raving at the injustice that was going to deprive him of life, when so young and for so small a crime, and he had therefore repulsed all attempts on the part of the local priests to prepare him for death. So Catherine undertook the difficult task. Writing to her director after all was over she says : " I went to visit him of whom you know, whereby he received such great comfort and consolation that he confessed, and prepared himself right well ; and he made me promise by the love of God that, when the time of execution came, I would be with him ; and so I promised and did. Then in the morning, before the bell tolled, I went to him, and he was very glad. I took him to hear Mass, and he received Holy Communion, which he had never received since the first. His will was attuned and subject to the will of God, and there only remained a fear of not being brave at the last moment. He said, ' Stay with me and do not leave me, and I die content.' He laid his head upon my breast, and I said, ' Be comforted, my sweet brother ; for we shall soon come to the nuptials. You shall go there bathed in the Blood of the Son of God, with the sweet name of Jesus ; and I will wait for you at the place of execution.' His heart then lost all fear, and his face was transformed from sadness to joy. I waited for him therefore at the place of execution with continual prayer, and in the presence of Mary, and of Catherine, Virgin and Martyr. I besought and implored Mary for this grace : that he might have light and peace of heart at the last moment, and that I might see him return to God. Then he came like a meek lamb, and, seeing me, he laughed, and asked me to make the sign of the Cross over him. I did so, and said, ' Up to the nuptials, my sweet brother ! for soon you shall be in everlasting life.' He knelt down with great meekness ; and I stretched out his neck, and bent over him, reminding him of the Blood of the Lamb. His lips said nought save Jesus and Catherine. And so saying, I received his head into my hands." She goes on to declare that she then had a vision of God receiving his soul, and that he turned back and looked at her " like a spouse who has reached the threshold of her new home, who looks round and bows to those who accompanied her, showing her gratitude by that sign. Then did my

soul repose in peace and quietness, in such fragrance of blood, that I
could not bear to have removed from my garments the blood that had
fallen on them.   Wretched and miserable that I am, I will say no
more ; I remained on earth with the greatest envy."

Comment is needless on this tragic story, thus transformed into
such heavenly beauty ; but there are points in it which are illuminated
by events that went before.   It should be noted, however, that those
nuptials which had been granted to herself in vision, are here shown to
be the destiny of every cleansed soul ; and her insight into the meaning
of the Precious Blood and its efficacy, which enabled her to overcome
any natural repugnance to this most unnatural blood-shedding, had
been strengthened and sealed by another mystical experience just
previously granted.

One morning after Mass, her director, who was making his thanksgiving, noticed her gaze fixed on a crucifix painted on the wall.   She
knelt upright, flung out her arms, and, remaining thus for a while,
then sank back on the floor as one dead.   She whispered to her
confessor, who hurried to her aid, that she had received the stigmata,
and believed that she was dying.   The suffering from this experience
continued several days ; but she eventually recovered and, fearing
publication of this dreadful favour, she had prayed at the time that
the marks should be hidden.   They never were actually visible, though
the pain was felt by her, and sometimes acutely, to the end of her life.
All this is in the realm of high mystical experience, and yet, surely
not beyond comprehension or even sharing ; for those who would
come at the last to the Marriage Supper of the Lamb will have to
have had some life-and-death contact with the Cross, or will only be
cast out for not having on a wedding garment.

Catherine now began to be called upon to intervene and arbitrate
in the feuds, whether between families or cities, which were a constant
plague of that violent age.

> Across the might of men that strove
>   It shone, and over heads of kings ;
> And molten in red flames of love
> Were swords and many monstrous things :
> And shields were lowered and snapt were spears,
> And sweeter-tuned the clamorous years :
> And faith came back and peace, that were
> Fled . . ."

Her one message to all was that of refusing to judge and being willing
to forgive ; and such was her grace and power that she was generally
wonderfully successful.   This both invited and impelled her to try her
skill as an ambassadress of peace upon the greater conflicts that were

distressing the world. To understand the need and scale of what she now attempted, it must be realized how deep was the confusion and violence of social life at that time. Not only were the Republics of the time governed by a series of factions, but within the same country, city was set against city, the nations were at war with one another, and Christendom was still harassed and threatened by conquests and onsets of Islam.

One of the most obvious needs therefore—and it seemed to her it might also be the clearest and simplest way out of the many local feuds and international strifes—was to get the irrepressible fighting spirit of the age enlisted upon an adventure that would rid Europe of a dire peril and bring unity at home. The Pope had proclaimed one more crusade against the Saracens, and Catherine lent all her powers to make it a success by trying to secure the adherence of active support of factions now at war with one another, as well as of persons who might thus redeem their lives from futility and vice. So she began to dictate a series of letters to notable and notorious people, in which the simplicity of her own mind and her power over others are reflected. She tried to appeal to such filibusters as Sir John Hawkwood, an Englishman, willing to sell his services to any one who would buy them ; not only calling him " dearest brother" but, recognizing the nature of the man she had to deal with, beseeching him, since he delighted so much in war and fighting, at least to fight for something just and noble, which he now had the chance of doing if he would take the sword under the sign of the crusader's cross. She even tried her powers of persuasion on the ill-famed Queen of Naples. In both cases she received the promise of support. Catherine may have shared the romantic conception of war, on which the Crusades themselves were going to inflict such a fatal blow ; and she seems to have hoped it would somehow make salvation accessible to the Saracens. Anyhow the crusade never even got started ; and from what we know of other attempts, it is perhaps as well. She soon learned to lean more on the cross as the weapon that can prove effective without the sword and to trust for the deep healing of the world's wounds to those wounds of love that can be suffered in union with Christ Crucified.

But a fundamental weakness in the whole situation, she discerned, as did many others, to lie in the residence, or rather the exile of the Papacy at Avignon. This Babylonian Captivity of the Church, as it came to be called, had been brought about partly because of the intolerable strife in Rome, and the indignities and hindrances which surrounded any Pope who tried to govern either city or Church from the Vatican. So under Clement V the Papal Court had removed to Avignon, and the Papal States were left to be ruled by Legates, who soon also became Frenchmen. This exile of the Papacy from Rome had gradually come to be looked upon as almost part of the natural order of things ; but in Catherine's time the need for the Pope's return to his own city had been made evident by the rebellion of the Papal States against the mismanagement and tyranny of the French Legates ; while some hope of its fulfilment had been aroused by the fact that Urban V had actually returned for a while to Rome. But he could stand neither its climate nor its quarrels, and although another great saint and seer, St. Bridget, had endeavoured to dissuade him, he returned to Avignon, where he soon died. It was the new Pope, Gregory XI, that St. Catherine now urged to attempt more bravely, and therefore with the promise of more permanence, to return to the holy city. This she advocated first by letters, and then in person. It must be remembered that when Catherine undertook this amazing task she was a woman of under thirty. She had already written to the Abbot of Mamoutier on the subject. He was an altogether unworthy person, but he was the Pope's nephew and it is evident that she hoped her advice would penetrate to the Pope's ears ; for in her letter to him she says : " To reform the whole you must destroy right down to the foundations. I beg of you, even if you have to die for it, to tell the Holy Father to remedy all this iniquity, and when the time comes to make ministers and cardinals, not to make them for flattery, nor for money, nor for simony. But with all your power implore him to look for virtue and good repute in the man, not considering whether he is noble or plebeian ; for it is virtue that makes a man noble and pleasing to God." Afterward she wrote direct to the Pope himself. The tone of this letter has been described as staggering. But what is most worthy of notice about it is the combination of respect for the Papal office with her bold words of reproof and advice to its then holder ; and yet, even these uttered, not with contempt or scolding, but with love and hope. For she urges upon the Pope that he should gather only good men around him, and that he should also deal gently with those that had revolted against his rule. Only her form of address can be quoted here : " O babbo mio," she writes, " sweet Christ on earth " ; but these will serve to bring out the combination of strong belief in his august office with her loving concern for him, whom she dares to counsel to find a remedy for all things in crushing self-love and loving God alone.

Soon however there came an opportunity for appealing to the Pope in person ; and she could hardly have been ignorant by this time what her powers were, if she could only be brought face to face with anyone. The cities of the Papal States had revolted against the rule of the Legates, had formed themselves into a league of resistance, and the important and powerful city of Florence had now joined the rebels.   Although Catherine realised the abuses that gave every excuse for their revolt, she believed that rebellion was no remedy, especially when it was against the head of the Church.   So she writes first to the authorities at Florence counselling submission, even to the interdict that had been imposed, and then to the Pope, advocating reconciliation : " O my sweet, most holy *babbo*, I can see no other means for you to have back your little sheep, who like rebels have strayed from the fold of holy Church.   Wherefore I pray you in the name of Christ Crucified, and I would have you do this mercy for me, conquer their malice with your benignity."

The consequence of this correspondence was that Catherine was first invited to Florence, and sent thence as its official ambassador to Avignon.   It must have been a strange meeting, when the Pope and the Saint faced one another ; and not perhaps without a sense of strain on either side.   For Gregory had already had experience of how this woman could write ; and he had reason almost to fear her personal presence.   She also must have trembled, if not for herself, yet for the success of her mission ; for she was concerned for three things : peace with Florence, the Pope's return to Rome, and the organization of the crusade.   Anyhow her spirit must have been deeply disturbed at Avignon ; the Cardinals all against her, the women, of whom there were many, and by no means all of un-blemished character, curious and contemptuous ; and in addition to these sinister influences she had to fight with all her strength to put resolution into the Pope himself.   It was a further distress for her that while she was there the Florentines arrived, but only to repudiate her position as their ambassador, and her advice in the negotiations. Nevertheless she so far won that, despite every device to dissuade him, including warnings from a reputed holy man that he would only be killed if he went, the Pope set out at last for Rome.   Their respective return paths crossed at Genoa, and there is a story that he there visited her, no doubt seeking fresh courage, but not courageous enough to come, save secretly and disguised.   But she knew him at once, and knelt for his blessing.   Anyhow the outcome of that visit was that he went on his way, though slowly and apprehensively, to Rome.

Her victory seemed remarkable and complete.   It proved to be short-lived, indeed entirely deceptive.   An outbreak of plague put an end to all further thoughts of the crusade ; and she had to bend herself once again to nursing the sick, by her prayers saving many of her friends who fell before it.   But no sooner had this trial passed than a far worse was upon her.   The Pope died in Rome, and another had to be elected.   This election took place amidst the greatest confusion.   Now that the Romans had got back their Pope, they were determined to have a Roman as Pope.   A Neapolitan was elected, but in fear of the rioting populace, the cardinals actually dressed up a Roman, Tebaldeschi, and despite his maddened protests, showed him to the people as Pope. The real elected, who took the name of Urban VI, was however enthroned and crowned. It was expected from all that was known of him that the new Pope would be a reformer, and so he proved ; but he began to carry out his reforms, not with firmness so much as with intolerable and domineering rudeness. The French cardinals were in the majority, and the Pope fatally delayed in redressing the balance. Fierce quarrels between them and the Pope led to their departure from Rome in a body ; to their open repudiation of the Pope's authority; and finally to their declaration that the election of Urban had been invalidated by fear. Even the Italian cardinals, outraged by the Pope's brusque ways, deserted him, and went over to the opposition. The terrible upshot of all this was that a French cardinal, Robert of Geneva, who was chosen by the rest partly because he had promised to take them all back to Avignon, was elected as Pope, taking the name of Clement VII. Catherine was desolate with distress and shame. She immediately sided with Urban as the rightful Pope, and promised him not only her support, but that she would come to his side, if he asked for her. But immediately things grew worse. The rival Pope established his position by creating fresh cardinals ; and sides began to be taken, not only between nation and nation, but between city and city, Order and Order, and even between members of the same family. The actual circumstances of Urban's election began to get confused in report and record, and despite Catherine's confidence and exhortations, good and holy men began to take the opposite side. Moreover, Urban soon showed himself anything but capable, buttressing his disputed position by outrageous brutality, instead of using the force and dignity which were needed if Christendom was to be won to his side. Bulls of excommunication began to flow from both sides ; and the only crusade the Pope was now concerned about was a crusade against his rival. Even Catherine's own followers began to falter, and if not to prove faithless, prove unequal to the burden of endurance or wise action. Her own director and friend, being sent on a mission to France to win it over to the right cause, failed even to get as far, and had to endure Catherine's reproaches, however much allowance she made for the difficulties that had daunted him.

Meantime, at the Pope's request, Catherine had gone to Rome ; but she had gone only to die. Some premonition of this may have moved her, before she left home, to dictate her great mystical treatise, the Dialogue, so rich with profound theological thought and spiritual insight. We can here take from it nothing but a few extracts showing her wonderful way of reconciling the two great commandments, the love of God and of our neighbour, which she showed can be fulfilled only by loving our neighbour as God loves us. She records Christ as speaking to her thus : " I require of you that you love Me with that love wherewith I love you. This you cannot do to Me, because I have loved you without being loved. All love that you bear Me you owe Me as a debt, and not as a free gift, because you are bound to give it Me ; and I love you freely, not in duty bound. You cannot then, render to Me the love that I require of you ; and therefore I have set you in the midst of others, in order that you may do to them what you cannot do to Me; that is, love them freely and without reserve, and without expecting any return from it ; and then I consider done to Me whatever you do to them. So this love must be flawless, and you must love them with the love wherewith you love Me. For there is no love of Me without love of man, and no love of man without love of Me ; for the one love cannot be separated from the other."

Arrived at Rome Catherine found the cause of Urban going from bad to worse, his methods and manners only contributing to the defections from him. The confusion and her perplexities deepened hour by hour, and she wrote again to the Pope a letter in which there still mingles with her customary courtesy, both boldness and humility : " Pardon my presumption, most Holy Father, that I have ventured to write confidently to you, constrained by the Divine Goodness. I should have come instead of writing, but did not want to weary you by coming so often. Have patience with me ; for I shall never cease from urging you by prayer, and by word of mouth or letter, as long as I live, until I see in you and in Holy Church what I desire, for which I know you desire, much more than I, to give your life." And again, and now for the last time : " Pardon me, for love makes me say what perhaps need not be said. For I know that you must know the nature of your Roman children, that they are led and bound more by gentleness than by force or by harsh words ; and you know also how necessary it is for you and Holy Church to preserve this people obedient and reverent towards your Holiness, because here is the head and beginning of our Faith. I beseech you humbly to strive prudently, always to promise only what you can completely perform, so that there follow no shame or confusion. Pardon me, sweetest and holiest Father for saying this to you." As she finished this letter she fell unconscious. It would seem to have been a stroke ; but it was just as probably something due rather to the overwhelming effect of her mystical intercourse ; for she herself, when able to write to her confessor about these seizures says : " I could not move my tongue or any other member, no more than a dead body. I therefore left the body as it was ; and my intellect remained fixed in the abyss of the Trinity. My memory was full of the needs of Holy Church and of all Christian people. I cried out in God's sight and confidently demanded divine aid, offering Him my desires and constraining Him by the Blood of the Lamb and all sufferings borne."

She was now left to face the failure of her plans and hopes ; and she could only turn to prayer. The prolonged vigil on which she now entered was to be her last great spiritual conflict and adventure ; its victory as hidden as the fight was fierce.

> ". . . she turned
> Back to her daily way divine,
> And fed her faith with silent things,
> And lived her life with curbed white wings,
> And mixed herself with heaven and died.

For every day was now alike, spent in an agony of intercession. Her own words again are the best way of letting us know what was going on in her soul. She writes to her confessor : " God imposed this obedience on me, that during this holy season of Lent I should offer up the desires of all my family, and have Mass celebrated solely with this intention, for Holy Church ; and that I should myself hear Mass every morning at dawn. By this and other means, which I cannot relate, my life is consumed, I doing in this way what the glorious martyrs did with their blood. I pray the Divine Goodness soon to let me behold the redemption of His people. When it is the hour of Terce, I rise from Mass, and you would see a dead woman going to St. Peter's. I enter anew to labour in the little bark of Holy Church. I remain there praying until nearly the hour of Vespers ; and I would fain not leave the place, neither day nor night, until I see this people pacified and reconciled with the Father. My body remains without food, even without a drop of water ; and with such sweet physical torments as I have never before endured ; so that my life is hanging by a thread." So it was. Lent ended for her with another seizure, which now paralysed her from the waist downwards. She was carried to her lodging, never to leave it again ; but a month spent in agony both of body and soul went by before release came. Her friends and followers were gathered round her, distressed at her wasted frame and still more by her spiritual sufferings. It was no easy passing for her ; and her last words, were " Blood, Blood, Blood ! "

If we may take upon ourselves to interpret this pain-racked, but profoundly penetrating apostrophe, it meant that she saw in vision, what she had long held by faith, that the blood of this world's sins, its murders and its feuds, its wars and wounds, can be cleansed only by the Blood of Christ, and only then as Christians, entering into the fellowship of His sufferings, and being crucified with Him, are willing to shed their blood for love of Him, rather than shed the blood of their neighbours or even of their enemies, whom they should love, even as He loved us ; as he did when we were sinners, indeed, His enemies.

They buried her body in Santa Maria sopra Minerva, and there the visitor gazing at the beauty of that Gothic Church, the only one in Rome, and looking perhaps first on Michelangelo's " Naked Christ," and then on the tomb of Fra Angelico, may be astonished to discover that the body, which can be seen lying exposed under the High Altar, is hers. This is even that Church's greatest treasure ; and he will be a strangely unmoved soul who does not kneel to ask her prayers for our world, once more again so much like that of her own time, needing just such an intercessor of peace as she was and realizing afresh how nothing but the Blood of Christ can cleanse and turn back the tide of this world's bloodshed, until it cries no more like that of Abel for vengeance from the ground, the nations as well as individuals shall have learned the strength there is in love, and the peace that comes from forgiveness.

W. J. O'DONOVAN, M.D., O.B.E.

THOMAS LINACRE

A.D. *circa* 1460–1524

THE MATERIAL FOR a Life of Linacre, whose name is a household word in medicine, is hard to find.

There is a good account of him in the *Encyclopædia Britannica*.

In the Roll of the Royal College of Physicians an abbreviated account of his life appears. It covers ten pages in a volume of 520 pages by William Monk, published in 1878.

His life had a great attraction for Sir William Osler who, among modern medical men, had in the writer's student days a reputation that extended wherever English was spoken, and whose textbook of medicine was the foundation on which tens of thousands of doctors built their life's work. William Osler wrote a Life of Thomas Linacre and read it as the Linacre Lecture at St. John's College, Cambridge in 1908. This is a small illustrated volume of 64 pages.

Sir George Newman, Chief Medical Officer to the Ministry of Health, gave a Linacre Lecture in Cambridge in 1928. His lecture was privately printed and it dealt with the " Influence of Linacre on English Medicine," giving a few biographical details.

Linacre's Life was also published by the Catholic Truth Society of London in 1912. Under the heading of Catholic Men of Science, *The Life of Thomas Linacre, Scholar, Physician and Priest* was written by J. P. Pye, M.D., D.Sc., Professor of Anatomy and Physiology at University College, Galway. This sixteen-page pamphlet was sold for a penny.

Dr. Payne was entrusted with the Life that appears in the Dictionary of National Biography, but the standard work to which all refer is " *The Life of Thomas Linacre, Doctor in Medicine,* Physician to King Henry VII, the Tutor and Friend of Sir Thomas More, and the Founder of the College of Physicians in London, with Memoirs of his Contemporaries, and of the rise and progress of learning, more particularly of the Schools from the ninth to the sixteenth century inclusive," by John Noble Johnson, M.D. This work was first published, in 1835, by Edward Lumley.

Dr. Johnson complains that the results of searching for materials for his text of biography do not correspond with the difficulties which attend the search.

In a copy of this book in the Radcliffe Library, Oxford, is a manuscript note on the fly-leaf, " As this book did not sell I destroyed all but a few for presents only.—Ed Lumley." In a bookseller's catalogue of the time it is described as " Octavo, boards, uncut, scarce, 6s."

The registers of the Archbishop of Canterbury, preserved in the library at Lambeth, contain only two trivial notices with regard to Linacre. There are a few biographical documents in the Bodleian Library.

In the index of the Roll of the Royal College of Physicians for the year 1937, a list of the Harveian orators since 1894 is set out on pages 230-231. William Harvey, the discoverer of the circulation of the blood, was a lecturer on anatomy and surgery at this College. He gave it during his life-time his patrimonial estate at Burwash in Kent, then valued at £56 a year. The purpose of his gift, indented on the 26th June, 1656, was to provide a small collation at the monthly meetings of the Censors of the Royal College of Physicians, and also that there might once a year be a general Feast kept within the said College " for all the Fellows that shall please to come."

In this index the name of Linacre, the founder of the College, does not appear. In the Calendar of October 1937, it is noted that Thomas Linacre died in 1524, and the list of the Presidents of the College from its incorporation is headed by " Thomas Linacre, M.D., Padua et Oxon.," elected 1518. This is in marked contrast with the references to Harvey who is commemorated by a special yearly lectureship.

The shortest books of reference will tell us that Thomas Linacre lived from about 1460 till 1524 ; that he was physician to Henry VIII and that a Charter of Incorporation was granted to the College of Physicians in London through his influence on September 23rd, 1518.

Perhaps the most critical honour has been done to the memory of Thomas Linacre by Sir George Newman, in his Linacre Lecture. He tells us that he was first the pre-eminent restorer of Greek scholarship in England ; that he was the friend and teacher of Sir Thomas More, and that it was due to Linacre's inspiration that his book is almost a textbook of preventive medicine ; and that to him we owe our conception of the splendour and amplitude and the high purpose of the science and art of medicine. " His personality comes down to us across four hundred years with an aroma and a virility alike creative, winsome and enduring."

Linacre was born in Canterbury, probably in 1460. He was educated first at the Priory School under William of Selling. He then went to Oxford ; no one has discovered which was his college ; where he lived or how he lived there is not known. In 1484 he became a Fellow of All Souls.

In 1488 Henry VII sent Prior Selling on a mission to the Pope in Rome and he chose his late pupil to accompany him. There are records of his stay at Bologna and at Florence, where he studied under Poliziano at the Court of Lorenzo the Magnificent. The future Pope Leo X was a fellow-student with him under this tutor, and another of his teachers was the world-famous Greek scholar Demetrius Chalcondyles.

In Florence at that time were Michael Angelo and Pico della Mirandola. Later in Rome, where he studied in the Vatican libraries, Linacre became a firm friend of Hermolaus Barbarus. It would almost seem that Linacre modelled his life on this extraordinary man, who appears to have made him a life-time student, turned his interests towards medicine and made him a confirmed admirer of Aristotle.

It was under this genius that Linacre began to undertake the collation of manuscripts. Here in the Vatican he studied the scripts of Galen's medical works which he later published, and he became known to the local Vatican population as one of the *calligraphi*, or transcribers of the early Greek manuscripts.

Linacre then went to Venice, where he occupied himself at the printing establishment of Aldus and he edited and corrected proofs of the *editio princeps* of the Aldine *Aristotle*. There is a superb edition of this work, printed on vellum, Linacre's own private copy with his autograph, in the library of New College, Oxford.

Next he went to Padua, where he obtained the degree of doctor of medicine with more than the usual " applause."

It seems pretty certain that Linacre spent six or seven years in Italy before returning to Oxford to teach Greek and practise medicine. St. Thomas More was his pupil and here he became a life-long friend of Erasmus, who wrote, " What can be more acute, more perfect or more refined than the judgment of Linacre ? "

Sir William Osler, the greatest of modern physicians, used to say that a Physician may have the science of Harvey and the art of Sydenham and yet there may be lacking in him those finer qualities of heart and hand which count for so much in life. " Many of the greatest physicians," said Osler, " have influenced the profession less by their special work than by exemplifying those graces of life and refinements of heart which make up character. These have been the leaven that raised our profession above the level of business. Of such as these Linacre was one." In Harvey Cushing's *Life of Sir William Osler*, 1925, Volume II, page 232, is a pretty conceit in which the great Professor is photographed leaning against the mantelpiece above which are pictures of Linacre, Harvey and Sydenham.

There have been physicians, especially in England, well known for their attainments as classical scholars, but, since Linacre, there has not come to a member of the medical profession a distinction in the field of classical studies comparable to Osler's election to the Presidency of the British Classical Association in 1919.

Osler claimed and publicly said that he could never pick up a textbook on the subject of Greek " without a regret that the quickening spirit of Greece and Rome should have been for generations killed by the letter with which alone these works are concerned. It has been a great comfort to know that neither ' Pindar nor Æschylus had the faintest conception of these matters and that neither knew what was meant by an adverb or preposition or the rules of moods and tenses ' (Gomperz). And to find out who invented parts of speech and to be able to curse Protagoras by his Gods has been a source of inexpressible relief. But even with these feelings of hostility I find it impossible to pick up this larger work of Linacre without the thrill that stirs one at the recognition of successful effort—of years of persistent application. No teacher had had such distinguished pupils— Prince Arthur, the Princess Mary, Sir Thomas More, and Erasmus, the greatest scholar of the age."

Linacre's Paduan degree of Doctor was confirmed to him at home by an act of incorporation soon after his arrival at Oxford, and it is probable that this was followed by a similar act at Cambridge, since he subsequently founded there a lectureship corresponding to a foundation he had given to Oxford, one at Merton and one at St. John's.

Early in the century he became teacher and physician to Prince Arthur. Soon afterwards he began to occupy the important post of domestic physician to King Henry VII, and in due course he became physician to King Henry VIII. Among his patients were the Lord High Treasurer, Sir Reginald Bray, Thomas Wolsey, Archbishop of York, Cardinal Priest of St. Cecilia, and William Warham, Archbishop of Canterbury. Truly the Lord Dawson of his age.

About the year 1509 he began to receive preferments in the Church. He was Rector of Mersham in Kent and in the same year he had a prebendary stall in Wells Cathedral ; in 1510 he was Vicar of Hawkhurst in Kent, and in 1517 Canon and Prebendary of St. Stephen's Westminster. He had a prebend of South Newbold, York, in 1518, was Rector of Holworthy in Devon in the same year and Precentor of York in 1519. He was indebted for this last appointment to Cardinal Wolsey, to whom at this time he dedicated his translation of Galen *On the Use of the Pulse*. In 1520 he was Rector of Wigan in Lancashire and was made Rector of Freshwater in the Isle of Wight on August 8th, 1520. In this year he was ordained a priest.

During his ecclesiastical career his medical practice continued. Why all these preferments were accepted and why they were so quickly resigned has not been elucidated, but it is probable that the expense of institution exceeded the profits which were derived from them during the period of possession.

He continued his professional work as Court Physician and at the same time assiduously continued his translations. The most noteworthy of his medical translations was Galen's *De Sanitate Tuenda*, which he dedicated to Henry VIII. There is a beautiful copy of this in the British Museum with an illuminated title-page. A manuscript almost as famous, dedicated to Cardinal Wolsey, was the *Methodus Medendi* published in Paris by Mathew in 1519. There is in the Bodleian Library a very fine copy of his third translation of Galen's *De Temperamentis*, which was one of the first books in England with Greek type. A. J. Leland's list of his translations is as follows :

Proclus	..	De Sphaera, 1499.
Galen	..	De Sanitate Tuenda, 1517
,,	..	Methodus Medendi, 1519
,,	..	De Temperamentis, 1521
,,	..	De Naturalibus Functionibus, 1523
,,	..	De pulsuum usu, 1523
,,	..	De Symptomatibus, lib. iv ; De Symptomatum Differentis, lib. i ; et De Causis, lib. iii, 1528.

Linacre took his share with Grocyn and Latimer in Hermolao Barbaro's plan to translate the entire works of Aristotle into Latin. This design executed in part was never completed owing to the separation of the parties and a difficulty of intercourse and of a comparison of the allotted portions with each other. Linacre was in London, Grocyn in Maidstone and Latimer at Saintbury in Gloucester. Erasmus and Sir Thomas More testify that Linacre completed his share but it seems lost for ever.

More famous still on the Continent was Linacre's reputation as a grammarian. True Colet did not accept the Grammar he prepared for the boys of St. Paul's School, but his second attempt, called *Rudimenta Grammatices*, dedicated to Princess Mary, became for two generations the mental nurture of French boys. Browning described in verse his studies and his painful death from stone of the bladder.

" Back to his book then ; deeper drooped his head ;
  Calculus racked him."

His most famous grammatical work, *De Emendata Structura Latini*

Sermonis, was published in 1524, two months after his death. Concerning this Philip Melanchthon said " Here is offered a book of a most learned man, Linacre . . . and so to me indeed no more perfect writing of this character seems to be extant."

At Padua in 1467 there were thirty-five teachers in the Medical Faculty. It is therefore inescapable to conclude that it was there that Linacre conceived the idea of founding lectureships in England. Only eight days before he died a Diploma Regium was issued and provision was made for the two lecturers at Oxford and one at Cambridge previously referred to. The fame of many a Linacre lecturer is still to seek, but this founder's name is still indissolubly associated with that most important foundation, the Royal College of Physicians of London. Linacre left his library to this College, which was destroyed in the Great Fire of London.

The Medical Act of 1511 provided that no one should practise as a physician or surgeon in London or within seven miles of it except with a licence from the Bishop of London or the Dean of St. Paul's, with the aid of competent doctors of physic as assessors ; and it was Linacre's zeal for the advancement of medicine that led him to obtain by Royal Letters Patent a Charter from King Henry VIII made out to himself and five other physicians for the foundation of a College of Physicians of London, for the regulation of the practice of physic in London and for seven miles around, and for the punishment of offenders. Four years afterwards these privileges and responsibilities were confirmed by statute and extended to the whole country.

The establishment of this College was due to Linacre's munificence, and its first meetings were held in his own house situated in Night Rider Street, which from the time of Linacre until 1860 remained in the possession of his College, when it was taken over by Act of Parliament in order to provide a site for His Majesty's Court of Probate.

Within a century this College had built for itself a comprehensive institution for scientific advancement comprising anatomical and special lectureships, a physic garden, a museum, a library and the publication of the London Pharmacopœia for the standardization of drugs. In this most potent germ, conceived in the mind of Linacre, lay all the developments of modern medicine, the British Pharmacopœia and the world-famous British Medical Schools.

Linacre's portrait may be found at Windsor Castle and there is a sketch in the British Museum copied in 1600 from some picture which cannot now be traced. A bust of Linacre in bronze, by Sir Henry Cheere is in the library of All Souls' College, Oxford.

He was buried in Old St. Paul's Cathedral in a spot which he himself selected and expressly specified in his Will. For many years no tombstone marked his resting place, but in 1557 Dr. Caius, then

President of his College, erected in gratitude a monument to the founder at his private cost, with the following inscription :—

" Thomas Lynacrus, Regis Henrici VIII Medicus. Vir et Graece at Latine, atque in re medica longe eruditissimus : Multos aetate sua languentes, et qui jam animam desponderat, vitae restituit ; Multa Galena opera in Latinam linguam, mira et singulari facundia vertit : Egregium opus de emendata structura Latini sermonis, amicorum rogatu, paulo ante mortem edidit. Medicinae studios Oxoniae publicas lectiones duas, Cantabrigiae unam, in perpetuum stabilivit. In hac urbe Collegium Medicorum fieri sua industria curavit, cujus et Praesidens proximus electus est. Fraudes dolosque mire perosus ; fidus amicus ; omnibus ordinibus juxta clarus ; aliquot annos antequam obierat Presbyter factus. Plenus annis, ex hac vita migravit, multum desideratus, Anno Domini 1524, die 20 Octobris.
Vivit post funera virtus.
THOMAS LYNACRO clarissimo Medico
JOHANNES CAIUS posuit, anno 1557

I do not think we can close this memoir of Linacre, who was among the earliest of his countrymen to be influenced by the " New Learning " and to whose labours England stands strongly indebted for the know-ledge of the finest language of antiquity, and to whom medicine owes its right to rank among the liberal arts, without reprinting his Will, to be found in the Registry of the Prerogative Court of Canterbury. Bodfield 21, fol. xxxvi :—

" Testament of Thomas Lynacre, Doctor in Medicine.
" In the name of God, Amen. The xixth day of Juyñ, in the yere of our Lord god a thousand fyve hundred and xxiiij, and the xvj yere of the reigne of Kyng Henry, Henry the Eight, I, Thomas Lynacre, doctour of phesike, being hoel of mynde and in good memory, lawde and praysing be vnto almighty god, make, ordeyn, and dispoase this my present testament and last will, Westmynster. Item, I bequëth to Thomas Lynacre, my brother, xlˢ. Item, I bequëth to my two neses, Agnes and Margaret, eche of them a bedde, with all things to it complete, after the discrecions of myn executours, so that Margaret shalhave the better. Item, I bequëth Mr. William Dancaster a fether bed and two Irishe blanketts, with a bolster. Item, I bequëth to John Plumtre these boks, Palax, Thuchiddes, wᵗ that that foloweth, Theodor and Apolones, Libanius Declamacions, Theocrita with the Coment, Pynderus with the Coment, the Coment vpon Omer. Item, I woll that my funeralls and burying shall be doon in moderat maner, after the discrecions of myn executours. Item, I bequëth to Richard, my seřunt, a blak gowne of iijˢ a yarde and xlˢ in money, for the good service that he hath doon to me. Item, I bequëth to eche of John Appulby and

Edward Tagge, my seŕunts, a blak gowne a pece of iij^s a yarde and
vj^{s}viij^d a pece ; and I woll that all my seŕunts and housholde have
mete and drynke for a moneth next after my decesse.   Item, I
bequĕth to my cosyn Robert Wright of Chester, a doblet cloth of
blak satyn, beyng in the keping of my sister Alice.   Item, I bequĕth
to Richard Wright a black gowne and xx^s in money.   Item, I
bequĕth to Elizabeth, my mayde seŕunt, a blak gowne and hir wages
after the rate of xxvj^s viij^d by yere.   The residue of all my goodes,
whatsoever they be after that my detts be paide, in manner and
fourme following ; that is to witt, ffirst I bequĕth and recomende
my soule vnto Almighty, &c., and my body to be buried within the
Cathedrall Churche of Saint Poule, of London, before the rode of
North dore there, bitwene the longe forme and the wall directly
over agaynst the said rode.   And I bequĕth for my buriall there
to be had suche convenient sūme of money as shalbe thought by the
discrecions of myn executours.   Item, I bequĕth to the high awter
of Saint Benet, where I am a pisñen, for my tithes forgotten in
discharge of my soule and conscience, xiij^{s}iiij^d.   Item, I bequĕth
to the high awter of Saint Stephyns, in Walbroke, for my tithes
there forgotten in discharge of my soule and conscience, vi^{s}viij^d.
Item, I woll that such due detts as I owe of right or of conscience
to any maner psone or persones shall be well and truely contented
and paid.   Item, I woll that Alice, my suster, shall yerely during
hir lyfe have the londes to be bought for my lectour at Cambridge,
syse pounds sterlinge to be paid to hir halfe yerely.   And I woll that
Joane, my suster, shalhave during hir lyfe fyve pounds sterlinge
of the landes to be bought for the said lector, in like maner and
fourme to be paide, or ells the said sūmes to be yerely xceyved of
the profits of my lands in Kent or in London, after the discrecions of
my Lorde of London, Sir Thomas More, Knyghte, and Maister
John Stokesley, Prebendary of Saint Stevyns at my funerall charges
doon, and these legacies and bequĕts expressed in this my present
testament and last Wille fulfilled and perfourmed, I woll shalbe
solde by myn executours ; and the money comyng of the sale of the
same to be applyed for and towards the pformauns and fulfilling of
this my present testament and last Wille.   And of this my present
testament and last Will I make and ordeyn my Lord Cuthbert,
Bisshop of London, Sir Thomas More, Knyght, and Maister John
Stokesley, Prebendary of St. Stevyne at Westminster, myn
executours, desiring and requiring them to substitute and make
som honest proctour vnder them, to take the labours aboute the
pforming of this my testament ; and the same proctour to be
rewarded for his diligence in that behalfe w parte of my goodes,
after the discreciõns of my said executours.   These witness Maister
William Dancaster, Clerk, William Latymer, Clerk, John Wylford,
Notary, Richard Hardyng, John Appulby.

There are points of great interest in this last testament.   Sir John

Cheke, Regius Professor of Greek in the University of Cambridge gave currency to the suggestion that Linacre was unorthodox, the story was intrinsically improbable and received no credence, the wording and dispositions of the will are wholly Catholic. We may note, sadly, that Colet receives no parting gift. This is a curious incident in so quiet tempered a life. Linacre was hurt that Colet could not use his Latin Grammar for the young beginners in St. Paul's School ; there was no quarrel and no reconciliation, both were men with forceful characters : both men have left memories treasured from England's Catholic past.

FELIX HOPE

LE CHEVALIER DE BAYARD

A.D. 1474–1523

IF EVER A man was a hero to his valet, that man was the famous
Chevalier, *sans peur et sans reproche*, whose death marked the passing
of the age of chivalry, and whose " right joyous, merry and entertaining history " was written by his " Lord Serviteur." Tradition—
confirmed by the researches of M. J. Roman in his well-known edition
of Le Loyal Serviteur's history, and more recently by M. G. Letonnelier,
Archiviste de l'Istère at Grenoble, in his *Étude Critique* (1926)—has
always pointed to Jacques de Mailles as the author of this work, which
was published in 1527, about three years after Bayard's death. Mailles
had been a secretary of the great Chevalier and an archer in his company on some of his campaigns. He was a native, like Bayard, of that
picturesque province of Dauphiné.

To be fearless and without reproach in the eyes of his contemporaries was far from implying ascetic abstinence from the pleasures
of the senses. But if Bayard was no saint, his knightly deeds and
character had become a legend already during his lifetime. The
" Loyal Serviteur," whoever he was, did not create it. But he
enshrined it in a work of art which, thanks to his genius for narrative
and his obvious sincerity, coupled with great felicity in selecting
incidents and phrases, reached a very high pitch of excellence. It
lives on its own merits, and has immortalized the name and character
of the *gentil Seigneur* it portrays. The author, indeed, was a creative
as well as a selective artist. When he was short of facts he invented
them. But his fictions are nearly always probable, and always in
harmony with the character he describes. Modern criticism has
done much to correct the blind acceptance of all the incidents
recorded on what had long been regarded as the unimpeachable
testimony of so intimate an acquaintance of the very gentle and
perfect knight. But it has not invalidated the legend of Bayard.
There are other sources by which that can be checked, such as
contemporary correspondence and writers, like the pedantic
Symphorien Champier and the chronicler Aymar du Rivail, both
relatives of the Chevalier, as well as Claude Expilly and Brantome,

and the greater historians of the age, from Commines to Guicciardini. From them all, when collated and corrected by the latest historical criticism, as has been done by Dr. Samuel Shellabarger (1928), emerge unaltered in all essentials the character and actions of the Bayard whom the Loyal Serviteur so lovingly depicted. A story may have to be discarded here, a picturesque incident there, a scene or a date altered, and a qualification added, but the portrait is authentic.

It is good in these days, when so many of our childhood heroes have been taken off their pedestals and roughly handled by modern historians, to find one of the dearest emerging from the searching test of present-day criticism on an even higher pedestal than he formerly occupied.

The Chevalier Bayard is still a name to conjure with. When all is said and done, he was truly a knight *sans peur et sans reproche*, a perfect flower of chivalry in that twilight period before the rising tide of the Renaissance had made a mockery of the faith, the self-sacrifice, the courage and loyalty of knighthood. And if there is in his life some faint suggestion of Don Quixote, fighting bravely in a world that has passed him by, one is not inclined to smile, for this man won his battle and made the world he lived in seem a poor thing by comparison.

Dr. Shellabarger's book is one of those rare histories which gather together all the threads of a subject and leave no loose ends for future historians to pick up. Except, perhaps, from an interpretative point of view, and barring future discoveries, he has said the last word on Bayard. These are points of controversy, but they are perennial, where one man's guess is as good as another's.

It happens to be a subject in which the sources are not too unwieldly or conflicting. Bayard had his Boswell—Jacques de Mailles, the loyal servant who, if he sometimes was more like our own Parson Weems than the biographer of Johnson, was still accurate enough for all practical purposes. Without him, as Dr. Shellabarger points out, Bayard would have been as shadowy a figure as many another illustrious *homme d'armes* of his period—brave men all, great soldiers and perfect gentlemen ; but their figures are shrouded in the mists of four centuries. Only one stands out clearly, a man of flesh and blood, and, at the same time, a legendary hero.

Many men have achieved a place in history by living before their time, but Pierre Terrail, Seigneur de Bayard, has gained his fame by living after his. It would be difficult to find a character in history whose tangible accomplishments bear so little relation to his celebrity. Born in 1474, in a valley in Dauphiné, and isolated from the significant movements of his time, he inherited the ideals and traditions of chivalry and of medievalism. It is as the last great champion of medieval chivalry that the renown of Bayard has come down to posterity.

The best modern and scholarly account of Bayard was published in 1828 by Terrebasse, but since that time new manuscripts have been discovered and many monographs have been published. The book of Dr. Shellabarger is an excellent example of graceful and valuable scholarship. It is well documented, yet it possesses very considerable literary merit. In its pages we find a deep under-standing and appreciation of the Middle Ages. The author presents a spirited and convincing defence of certain phases of medieval life. His book is not only a life of Bayard, but a history of the momentous period in which Bayard lived, and the author has caught its colour and spirit and drama, with much of the grace and gusto with which the Loyal Servant first wrote.

In an age of artful and frequently cultivated condottieri, when battles often resembled an elaborate game of chess between treacherous mercenaries where nobody much was hurt, it was quite natural that the defenders of declining chivalry should make the best of a really fighting soldier like Bayard. The Italian mercenaries practised war as a profession, and were chiefly terrible to rich and defenceless citizens ; so long as they obtained good pay and booty they were not on the look-out for hard knocks. Bayard on the other hand, was one of those singular persons who love fighting for fighting's sake. What is admirable about him is that he really was chivalrous ; he possessed all the rare virtues of his profession and none of its vices. If we may believe the stories of him, he was just, liberal to a fault, a kindly man to the weak and helpless, sincerely pious, and at the same time a most dashing soldier. It is a little difficult to estimate Bayard's military attainments, especially since warfare was then so different ; but he appears to have excelled as a tactical rather than a strategical commander. Even in tactical warfare he seems to have preferred the skirmish and the brilliant cavalry raid tactics to action on a large scale. His admirers tell us that the jealousy of great men at Court prevented the King from granting Bayard the higher commands which should have been his. But it is significant that the " Loyal Serviteur " himself tells an anecdote to the effect that Louis XII offered Bayard the command of a thousand foot, but that the captain preferred to take half that number.

Pierre Terrail, Seigneur de Bayard Chevalier, as he proudly designated himself, was born at a time when the vocation of a soldier was generally regarded as the most honourable of professions. War was then the one great opportunity of profit and honour for a youth whose earliest manhood, as Gargantua explained to Pantagruel, was the moment when he must begin to learn *la chevalerie et les armes*. From the Castle of Bayard in the Dauphine young Pierre was sent for his schooling to the household of the Duke of Savoy. As a page at that court, and in the train of the Duke on his constant journeyings and petty wars, he acquired that restless love of action and danger which was to make him for the rest of his life, as Brantome puts it, " ever seek out peril." There, too, in the sports of the pages and the tilting-yard he developed his horsemanship and his natural gifts as an athlete. On the death of the Duke of Savoy he entered the household of the King's favourite, the Count of Ligny, and ere long, as a man of arms in his company, set forth with the army of Charles VIII to the conquest of the kingdom of Naples. For the most part the ensuing campaigns in Italy were ideally suited to one of Bayard's temperament. Under Gonsalvo, the great Spanish captain, and Nemours, the French general, war was conducted largely according to the tradition of the fourteenth and fifteenth centuries. A series of petty sieges and isolated skirmishes gave openings to the individual eager to display his personal skill and courage. Bayard seized his opportunity. He was foremost on the bridge at Garigliano, last in the retreat to Gæto. It was characteristic of a century when the use of artillery in the field was only in its infancy, when the introduction of the musket and the arquebus was deplored as giving an advantage to the cowardly, and when Pescara's successful use of them was denounced as destructive of all good order of battle and the science of war, that the prowess of the individual knight still commanded the admiration of the armies. The reputations of the most gallant gentlemen of France were known to all. Before long his name, Pierre Bayard, was added to the list of such heroes as Le Sieur d'Urfe, Louis d'Ars, Yves d'Alegre, La Riviere, La Chesnaye, Montdragon, and Bonnivet, names which ring throughout the pages of chroniclers like so many battle-cries. Homeric combats were still the order of the day, and when ten thousand onlookers assembled on the walls of Trani to behold eleven champions of France engage eleven knights of Spain, Bayard distinguished himself above all by his feats of coolness, courage and skill.

The age was one of violent contrasts and strangest contradictions. Professor Cartellieri writes :—

> Wild orgies of immorality and gluttony were followed by spontaneous acts of penitence ; exultant hymns in praise of the rose-

garlanded Goddess of Love by stammering prayers to the gracious image of the Virgin ; untamed and boundless arrogance and aggression by acts of the deepest humility and contrition. Unbridled passions were concealed beneath a rigid ceremonial . . . noble chivalry based on honour was stained with cowardly violence against the weak. While a rigid code of rules controlled the jousts and tourneys, we find an utter failure of knightly ideals in battle . . . It was an age of fiery enthusiasm and weary nonchalance ; of senseless waste on the one hand, and grinding poverty on the other ; of childish naïvete and sophistical cunning ; of noisy and flamboyant achievement contrasted with a simple and genuine striving after beauty which trembled in the presence of the wonders of creation.

Knights were cast in heroic mould, and personal bravery knew no limits. At Agincourt King Charles was counselled not to accept the aid of the Paris craftsmen, for then the French army would be three times as strong as the English ; and that would contravene the principles of knightly honour. Hand in hand with " the glowing impulse for renown " went love. " An esquire or knight without his lady love was unthinkable," and Professor Cartellieri cites the case of " the foolish young Jehaim de Saintre " who blushingly and tearfully confessed that his mother and sister were his love. But this passion for women was too often only a means and motive to degrade her. One of the most interesting women of this epoch was Christine de Pisan, the first Frenchwoman to defend her sex's rights. In the story of woman's long fight for her rightful place honoured remembrance is her due. In jubilant verse she greeted La Pucelle, and, perhaps happily for her, did not live to see the shameful end of the maid.

Nor, indeed, was it at all probable that the legend of Bayard, which had sprung up during his own lifetime, not only among his own comrades-in-arms, but also among his Spanish, Italian, Swiss and English foemen, could be without substantial foundations. When Francois I had won his spurs at Marignano it was the Chevalier whom he chose to knight him on the field of battle. For his grim, momentous defence of Mezieres against the imperial troops he was hailed as a national hero, the saviour of his country. It is usually stated that he was inadequately rewarded ; but the promotion and distinction conferred upon him by Francois I were sufficiently munificent. Pope Julius II sought to entice him into the Papal service, but unsuccessfully. He was the perfect type of the happy warrior, the dashing individualistic French soldier, to whom blows were dearer than ducats, and to whom honour was more than life. To serve God and the King, to have at the enemy, and to relieve those in distress—this was for him the end and glory of existence.

From Fornuovo to Marignano and from Ravenna to Pavia his military career embraced all those campaigns in which French soldiers under three successive kings crossed the Alps and descended upon Italy, seeking fortune, fame, and adventure, and finding, so many of them, death in the lovely and fatal land they ruined. For thirty years the name of Bayard occurs in practically all the principal battles of the period. Everywhere he appears as the typical representative of a dying ideal, of medieval chivalry in the land of the Renaissance, as a knight of the tourney and the charge in an era which witnessed the birth of modern warfare. It is upon depicting him in this aspect of a great heroic figure, typical of a passing age, that " Le Loyal Serviteur " has lavished all his art, and rightly insists upon this as his true significance.

Why should this man, who played no important part in the history of his time, who performed no commanding achievement, who was not one of the great nobility, be a household name for succeeding generations ? How did he become, in Dr. Shellabarger's apt phrase, " one of history's most distinguished gentlemen ? " The author poses the question himself on the first page of his biography, and when he is through one realizes the answer, though it seems as hard to define as ever. Dr. Shellabarger's explanation, in his final chapter, is as follows :

Not only a personality of his times, not only a Frenchman, not only a soldier even, indeed, but secondarily these ; he becomes representative of universal issues—of that faith, to be sure, of which chivalry was a manifestation, and which, though neglected, can never die ; of medievalism, with its verile emphasis on loyalty and sub-mission ; but primarily, and to us more immediately, of reverent manhood ; faithful to its heritage of few but clear ideals, whose dignity is duty and whose honour, steadfastness. He represents the generations of obscure men, who are gentlemen by virtue of holding fast what the race has bequeathed for guidance in conduct and character, by virtue of discipline and self-control, of constancy and helpfulness. These are the important men, these conservatives. They insure progress by upholding continuity. They form the vertebra of any national life. And of such, we repeat, Bayard becomes an almost legendary example.

Pierre Terrail lived the life of a gentleman of his day (" gentleman " in the true sense of the word, meaning nobleman, aristocrat). His creed was the simple one of duty to sovereign, the service of honour (*honneur acquerre*), and the responsibility of nobleness (*noblesse oblige*).

He was born in 1474 at Bayard, thirty miles north of Grenoble. Though he could neither read nor write, he was thoroughly educated in the more important accomplishments of riding, hunting, hawking, jousting, swordsmanship, and proper social behaviour.

At the age of twelve he entered the household of Duke Charles I of Savoy as page, and six years later took service with the Count of Ligny, the King's favourite, as man-at-arms. Under de Ligny's lieutenant, Louis d'Ars, he went on that amazing expedition of Charles VIII to Italy which was to revolutionize Europe. It was the first of many such campaigns which were to cost France so dearly in life and treasure, but which were to give Bayard so many opportunities for glory.

The high-lights are few. He first gained international fame by his duel to the death in January, 1503, with Don Alonzo de Soto-Mayor, a Spanish knight. In 1512 he fought brilliantly under Gaston de Foix, one of the most vivid figures in the military annals of chivalry, if not of all time. After the bloody victory of Marignano, it was Bayard who had the honour of knighting King Francis I, his sovereign. In a critical emergency, when the fate of France hung in the balance, Bayard held Mézières, the key to France, against the Spanish forces.

From an obscure man-at-arms he had risen to Captain-in-Chief with a hundred lances of his own, a position usually accorded only to princes of royal blood. He was over in the front rank when an attack was launched ; and it was he who was always entrusted with the rearguard in retreat. Though often sick and weak from wounds, he was always where fighting was thickest, and he died a soldier's death, mourned by all the soldiery of Europe : " Tell the King " he said, " that I die happy in his service, and sword in hand, as I have always wished. And I have no regret in dying, except that I lose the means of serving him any more."

Adrien de Croy, one of the enemy knights, wrote to the Emperor : " A beautiful death, and, sire, although Lord Bayard was the servant of your enemy, still it is a pity of his death ; for he was a gentle knight, beloved by all, and who lived as nobly as did ever man of his estate."

To anyone whose childhood memory has left nothing but the dim figure of a knight who was "without fear and without reproach," his biography is recommended as a means of getting better acquainted with the age idealised by Scott and Kenelm Digby. " What Bayard was," to quote Dr. Shellabarger's last sentence, " he is now more completely than during life—a rare expression of that valour, chivalry and devotion which marks the gentleman of every age."

One might vainly ransack the pages of authentic history to find another character so completely of a piece as that of Pierre du Terrail, Chevalier de Bayard, who has descended to posterity embalmed in the immortal phrase of his loyal servant, a biographer worthy of his subject. From the moment when he first emerges from obscurity at the battle of Fornovo to the moment when, twenty-nine years later, a chance shot ended his heroic life at an all-too-early age, there is no word or act recorded of him which is not consonant with that splendid eulogy.

Yet the upholder of the old tradition was himself to be a leader of the new army. When Louis XII, preparing, as a member of the League of Cambrai, to march against Venice, began to organize the French infantry, he chose Bayard, among other famous captains of horse, to command it, and to lend to the new force the prestige of their names. In this second Italian campaign Bayard served under a soldier of real military genius, Gaston de Foix. It was a campaign in which the value of the new arms, artillery and infantry, was triumphantly demonstrated. Ravenna, the first great modern battle, sealed the fate of that chivalry at which the first blow had been struck at Crecy, when the English yeomen shot down the knights of France. Gaston de Foix himself died at Ravenna in the hour of victory, charging a troop of Spaniards, as in the rays of the setting sun of chivalry. Bayard lived on in its afterglow, to be taken prisoner at the Battle of the Spurs, and to be killed by a bullet before Pavia.

Naturally, the " Lord Serviteur " tells us less of Bayard's more important attainments than of his spectacular feats, while he abounds on the theme of his hero's private virtues. Thus we learn " *Comment le bon chevalier sans paour et sans reprouche, durant le siege de Padoue, fist une course aveque ses compaignons, ou ils acquist gros honneur,*" and numerous feats of the same kind. The Loyal Serviteur also relates several anecdotes of Bayard's chivalrous kindness to poor girls and women, and indeed claims that he provided marriage dowries in nearly a hundred cases. The manner in which Bayard received his death wound is well told :—

En ces entrefaictes, le bon chevalier, asseure comme s'il eust este en sa maison, faisoit marcher les gens d'armes, et se retiroit le beau pas, tousjours le visage droit aux ennemys, et l'espee au poing, leur donnoit plus de craincte que ung cent d'autres ; mais comme Dieu le voulut permettre, fut tire ung coup de hacquebouze dont la pierre le vint frapper au travers des rains, et luy rompit tout le gros os de l'eschine. Quand il sentit le coup, se print a crier : "Jesus" et pius dist : " Helas ! mon Dieu, je suis mort." Si print son espee par la poignee et baisa la croisee en signe do coiis, et en disant tout hault : " Miserere mei, Deus, secundum magnam misericordiam tuam," devint incontient tout blesme, comme failly d'esperits, et cuyda tumber ; mais il eut encores le cueur de prendre l'arson de la selle, et demoura en estant jusques a ce que ung jeune gentilhomme, son maistre d'hostel, luy ayda a descendre et mist soubz ung arbre.

Thus died in the year 1523—and buried at Grenoble—Pierre de Bayard, leaving behind him universal regret and the fame of a most valiant and most perfect knight. And if legend has embellished his figure somewhat more than critical scepticism will accept, who will complain?

LAURENCE W. MEYNELL

ST. THOMAS MORE

A.D. 1478–1535

No ONE WHO delights in quick, brilliant conversation of the sort that Beaumont described at the Mermaid Tavern where it seemed as if men would " put their whole wit in a jest," can do otherwise than lament that he was not one of the guests, in 1499, at Sir William Say's house in London, when the chief honours were carried off by a young lawyer from one of the Inns of Chancery and a distinguished foreign visitor.

It is clear that introductions in those days were no better carried out than they are to-day, for halfway through the meal the foreigner, delighted at finding such ready inventive wit in a country which he had visited with some apprehension, fearing it would prove as depressing as its notorious climate, leaned across to the young man who was giving as good as he got in the verbal duel, and said in the tongue which was then the universal speech of cultured men : " *Aut tu es Morus aut nullus* " (" If you are not Thomas More, you're nobody "). To which the young Englishman, pardonable pride mingling with a certain amount of reverence in his singularly attractive voice, made answer " And if you aren't Erasmus, you're the Devil himself " (" *Aut tu es Erasmus, aut Diabolus* ").

They were both right. Sir William Say had got lions at his table that day. What the rest of the company was doesn't matter much now ; any host would be well content to have under his roof the foremost scholar in Europe, the leading light of the Renaissance ; and the young man who was rapidly establishing a reputation as the wittiest talker in London.

Thomas More at that time was twenty-two years old. He had been born in a house in Milk Street, one of the crooked, narrow, noisy, insanitary streets of old London, in 1478. It was a significant date, for in that same year in the neighbouring city of Westminster, which you reached by taking a muddy road along the strand of the river (the same road which is now called The Strand), a man called Caxton had set up a new-fangled device for printing books. Thomas More and books went well together.

More's father was a lawyer and a successful one ; he subsequently became a Judge of Common Pleas and a Justice of the King's Bench. He was good stock to breed from ; shrewd, careful in money matters, conservative and industrious ; he didn't come from Yorkshire, but he might very well have done so.

Young Thomas More was born into a troubled England (perhaps that is true of every child in every age) ; but things were mending, and when the battle of Bosworth Field ended the reign of terror of Richard III in 1485, John More, the father, began to look round for a school for his eight-year-old son.

There was not such a vast, nor such a readily accessible store of knowledge in those days ; and such boys as went to school did so earlier and were expected to work harder.

Of the present famous schools only Winchester and Eton were in existence, and they were considered comparatively small beer. Thomas was sent to St. Anthony's School in Threadneedle Street, under Nicholas Holt, which was probably the best place in London.

Here practically the only subject of instruction, and certainly the only medium for imparting information, was Latin. This is a significant fact, and what lies behind it does a good deal to explain More's life. What it signified was that there was then in existence a thing called Christendom with common ideals, a common basis and a common language ; a real, tangible, entity that men believed in, considered permanent, and thought worth fighting for. That thing has since disappeared ; and the League of Nations has hitherto proved an ineffectual substitute.

At the age of thirteen More entered the household of Archbishop (later Cardinal) Morton, the Lord Chancellor of England and one of the most powerful men in the Kingdom.

Morton had a pretty shrewd admixture of worldly wisdom with his Christianity, and he was notoriously a good judge of men. Young More must have seen a good deal of " great life " in that manor house at Lambeth, and caught whispers from the conversation there of many men who mattered. The old Archbishop liked the boy, and said of him : " This child here waiting at table, whosoever will live to see it, shall prove a marvellous man." It was young More's facility for extempore wit that was most noticeable ; William Roper says that " though he was young of years, yet would he at Christmastide suddenly sometimes step in among the players and, never studying for the matter, make a part of his own there presently among them, which made the onlookers more sport than all the players beside."

His rather dour old father probably thought the Archbishop's house, with its full meed of praise and fine words, rather a dangerous forcing-house for his boy, and in 1492 Thomas was sent to Oxford, to that

Canterbury College which was afterwards absorbed into Wolsey's Christ Church.

It was a tremendous time in Europe, was the end of the fifteenth century ; and tremendous for a reason which probably could only be appreciated to its full at a university.

The monasteries, which had more than nobly served their turn as the great preservers and distributors of traditional knowledge when all Europe was barbarian and dark, were waning. Their reputation was impugned ; their power imperilled. The long and bitter civil wars of England had cost the country dear in the loss of men which it could ill afford to lose, younger sons of the great houses which had always been the traditional patrons of learning. On the Universities themselves the paralysing hand of the over-subtle schoolmen still lay heavy.

But all England : universities, aristocracy and Church, showed signs of imminent change ; and the change was coming from what has caused nearly every change in the structure of the body politic, a shifting of power from one part to another.

And this shifting of power, if it did not entirely spring from it, was at any rate largely influenced by yet another thing—the Renaissance, the New Learning, which like many " new " things in the world was an old thing rediscovered.

It is always difficult to recapture the temper of a past time ; and now, when the wheel has gone full circle, and the only word of Greek which most people know is Kinema, it is hard to believe that men literally shook with delight, and cheerfully endured every sort of hardship merely to be allowed the privilege of being taught to speak the same language as Homer, Sophocles, Aristotle and Plato.

There were giants in these days : Grocyn, Linacre, Latimer and Colet, these are names even now to conjure with. Then they must have seemed like gods, as they came drunk with the new thing which was like wine in all men's throats ; white-hot from having tasted it at its source.

More knew them all ; quicksilver will go to its kind, and his mind leaped with theirs. But of them all John Colet, who afterwards founded St. Paul's School, influenced him most. Colet was æsthetic and burningly sincere ; and when More made the older man director of his spiritual life he put himself in good hands.

All this newfangled and fanatical nonsense must have seemed strange to Thomas's father, who had probably never even heard of Picco della Mirandola ; and he must have thought that in moving his son from Morton's household to Oxford he had only shifted him from the frying-pan into the fire. At any rate in 1494 he took Thomas away from Oxford, and told him to settle down to something of some practical use ; so the young man entered New Inn, and later Lincoln's Inn, for the study of law.

Probably it was the best thing that could have happened to him ; the closeness and logical severity of a legal training gave rigidity to an intellect which in all conscience was fluid enough by nature. And, no doubt greatly to his father's surprise, Thomas showed that whatever else he might have picked up at Oxford he had certainly absorbed a passionate fidelity for the old religion.

This co-existence in one intellect of an eagerness for the New Humanism, and a rigid devotion to the traditional and ritualistic religion has puzzled many people. For the matter of that the 49th. proposition of the first Book of Euclid has, at one time or another, puzzled many people ; but it is not insoluble for all that. A great deal depends on the point of view. I remember looking with a non-Catholic friend at the criss-cross iron grille from behind which members of the Carmelite order are occasionally permitted to see visitors. My friend was horrified. "But it's terrible," he said, "being shut in by bars, like that." Whereat the nun behind the grille got as near angry as a Carmelite may do. "You stupid man," she admonished him, " these bars don't shut us in ; *they shut the world out*." A lot depends on the point of view. More thought that inside the Church was safety, not only for the souls of men, but for the social structure by which they lived ; and outside the Church, anarchy and danger to these things. He wanted reformation as much as any man ; but his idea of it could not conceivably embrace any question of doctrinal change.

It was whilst he was studying for the bar that he met Erasmus at Sir William Say's house. Erasmus was a thing common then (though getting rarer) ; to-day, almost non-existent ; a European. There was much in the two men that was similar, they were both quick-witted ; both were lively, often to the point of verbal absurdity ; both liked to laugh at silly things and were eager for new. Erasmus had a positive genius for making friends ; he made them everywhere he went, amongst every sort of person ; but it is to be doubted whether he liked anybody better than he did More. " I love the man so much " he once wrote, "that I would jump about in a dance if he told me to."

Contact with the mercurial Erasmus naturally increased More's already strong bent towards the rising tide of classicism, which exasperated his father still further ; so that some sort of difference arose between them, which was settled, amicably enough, by More leaving his father's house and taking lodgings, with Lily,[1] near the Charterhouse. It was whilst he was lodging here that he gave his

---

[1] That Lily who had been to Greece ; made a Pilgrimage to Jerusalem ; had Grocyn for a godfather ; and was later made by Colet the first headmaster of St. Paul's School.

remarkable series of addresses on St. Augustine's *de Civitate Dei* at the
Church of Saint Lawrence in the Old Jewry.

It was touch and go, at this time, whether he should enter the
service of that City of God more fully or not. He was strongly inclined
to become a Franciscan friar ; and for the four years that he lodged
by the Charterhouse he observed as far as he could the discipline of
the Carthusians ; but by 1504 he had definitely decided to remain
in the world ; and he promptly set about the most important individual
act a man of the world does—he got himself a wife.

He married, early in 1505, Jane, the elder daughter of a Mr. John
Colt who lived in Essex. The story, as told by Roper, is that More
really liked the second daughter best ; but, not liking to cast any slur
on the elder girl, '' he, of a certain pity, framed his fancy toward her,
and soon after married her.''

Be this as it may, Jane made him a very good wife and they had
six happy years together in Bucklersbury, near Wallbrook, where she
bore him the four children, Margaret, Elizabeth, Cecily and John, who
grew up to be the things that he loved best in all the wide world.

More had been called to the Bar in 1501 and he was rapidly making
a reputation, and no doubt a rising income, as a barrister of exceptional
promise. Some time after being married he entered Parliament, and
in 1508 he made his first journey to the continent, when he visited
the Universities of Paris and Louvain, and, like the good Englishman
he was, found nothing there superior in any way to what could be
found at Oxford, or even Cambridge.

In 1509 the crafty, mean, suspicious and unpopular Henry VII died,
and all England rejoiced at the accession of his son. In these days,
when Monarchs are the devoted and untiring servants of their people,
it is not easy to realize how much then even the common man was
dependent upon the individual temper and characteristics of his king.
The new Henry had all the many virtues of the Tudors, and he added
to them a tremendous zest for every form of living, and such an
enthusiasm for music, literature and the New Humanism generally
that it was confidently thought a golden age for learning had dawned
in England. Erasmus came back to England post-haste and went to
stay with More at Bucklersbury. It was on this visit that he wrote
the *Praise of Folly* (*Encomium Moriae*) which put him in the front rank
of popular writers.

More had time to laugh with his friend, he always had time for that,
but he was a busy man ; in 1510 he was made Under-Sheriff of
London ; and at this period of his life he was making and that without
corruption—a rare circumstance in those days—an annual income
equivalent to something like £6,000 to-day.

In the following year his wife died and More wrote her epitaph :

" Dear Jane lies here, the little wife of Thomas More," only a gentle spirit, I think, would have put in that word " little ". His eldest child was then only five, and he had three younger ; an awkward problem for a busy man. He solved it in a very few months by marrying again, another little woman by name Alice Middleton. Alice had many excellent qualities, but she was short-tempered and sharp-tongued, and didn't see much sense in all the joking and leg-pulling and verbal acrobatics that More loved to indulge in with his friends. When someone asked him why he chose little women for wives he answered " if wives are necessary evils, is it not wise to choose the smallest evil ? " A disarming reply. Whatever his friends may have thought about Alice, and she was not popular with them, no man ever loved his home life more, or got more pleasure out of it than did More.

In the year 1515 the current of More's life began to set in a definite direction when he was asked to go with four other men on his first diplomatic mission abroad. No great matter was at stake, only the arrangement of a Trading Agreement between this country and the Netherlands, and More does not seem to have enjoyed it much ; in any case he hated being away from home, being encumbered with the old-fashioned superstition that, after his duty to God, a man's most immediate business should be with his own wife and family. The trip is important in his life, however, because on it he began the composition of his book *Utopia*.

Utopia was originally written in Latin, More's natural medium of expression, but it was translated before long and became, and has since remained, one of the books most widely read by young spirits. There is a great deal in it which is sheer nonsense, being based on the assumption that in this imaginary, far-off state there existed a human nature devoid of selfishness, innocent of greed, incapable of envy, and unmoved by anger. Given the universal existence of such qualities it would not be difficult to build the Ideal State anywhere, even in Russia. Unfortunately human nature is not cast in that saintly mould, and all systems of reform based on the supposition that it is, will be short lived. But More's *Utopia* is valuable because it pointed out many of the crying evils of his day and laughed at them, and the greatest purgative of all is laughter. If all armies were compelled to dress in striped pantaloons and to wear fools' caps and carry rattles recruiting and war would slump badly.

In any case *Utopia* is, and always has been, good reading ; and if we take it more seriously than its light-hearted author meant us to, that is our fault and not his.

Henry VIII, in many ways the greatest of the Tudors, had one Tudor virtue *in excelsis*, that of being able to recognize talent when he saw it. More's ability, of which he must already have been aware by hearsay, was brought sharply to his notice when in the Star Chamber a case of *Pope v. the King* was brilliantly argued, with complete success for the Papal side, by young Thomas More. It was a foretaste (though neither man knew it) of things to come. Thomas More believed in a lot of things in his life, but in none more implicitly than in the importance to Western Culture of the Catholic Church ; and the vital necessity, to that Church, of preserving its fabric and teaching intact.

Henry was not going to have so able a man against him ; and in an astonishingly short space of time More was made a King's Counsellor and a Judge in the Court of Poor Men's Causes (as it was then called). This extension of his sphere of life brought him into contact with a very remarkable man with whom he was to be associated for some years to come ; a man sharper, cleverer, more cunning than he was ; his undoubted superior in diplomatic strategy, and just as undoubtedly his inferior in moral worth—the great Wolsey, already Archbishop of York and Cardinal, and soon to be made a Papal Legate *a latere*.

To know Wolsey, the great Minister, was but a preliminary step to getting to know his great Master, the King.

It is always difficult to capture the prevailing temper of days gone by ; we are apt to apply our own backgrounds and beliefs, forgetting that a man at forty may have the same eyes which served him as a youth of fourteen, but that they see different things. If we are to read More's life aright we must remember that though many men in his day grumbled at the principle of an absolute monarchy, none disbelieved in it. The King was a person apart ; individually he might have almost every fault imaginable (which Henry did *not*) ; but he had been touched by the finger of the hand of God and Divine Right was in him. About such a theory it will suffice now to say that if it is foolish to believe in the Divine Right of one man, it is many million times more foolish to believe in the divine right of the whole mass of men, the Proletariat, lumped together.

More respected the King ; found his company entertaining ; liked him ; but he never failed to stand up to him where a moral issue was involved, owing allegiance, as he did, to a King from whom earthly Princes drew their limited power. Nor, even when the King's favour was at its height and when the great royal mountain of a man walked with More by hours together in that little country garden at Chelsea, his arm about his favourite's neck, was More deceived.

" If my head should win him a castle in France," he reminded Roper, " *it should not fail to go.*"

Being pressed into the King's service (Erasmus said that his friend was " dragged " to Court, emphasizing the word ; and More himself said that he was as uncomfortable there " as a bad rider in the saddle ") left little time for literature ; but in 1518, when the Court moved to Abingdon to escape the epidemics of London, More found occasion and time to compose his celebrated *Letter to the Fathers of the University of Oxford*, his finest piece of Latin prose and a most telling stroke for the New Learning against the diehards.

Wolsey at this time was one of the most powerful men in Europe. His capacity for political intrigue was enormous and his flair for it unrivalled ; and by working in close contact with him More must have become acquainted with a great deal that went on behind the scenes. Like the wise man that he was he kept his own counsel, and what he delighted in most was not the impressive state that my Lord Cardinal kept, nor the mad magnificence of such gestures as the Field of the Cloth of Gold, but the times that he could snatch to be away from such things surrounded by his own family at his own fireside, or in his own garden.

His children were his chief delight, and the fact that the three eldest of them were girls was a lucky circumstance for women generally. In an age when it was as rare to find a housewife who could write, as it is now to find one who can cook, men of letters must have been astonished by the family conversations under More's roof. Of all the splendid things that Holbein did none is more pleasing than his sketch (the finished picture, if it was ever made, is lost) of the More family. Here they all are : father and mother ; grandfather ; children ; various in-laws ; and even the household fool, charmingly grouped in the harmony which must in fact have prevailed there. William Roper who lived for upwards of sixteen years in the house said that he never knew his father-in-law " as much as once in a fume."

It was probably the fact that they took him away from the home that he loved so much, which was the chief thing that More objected to in the various diplomatic and political missions on which he was sent abroad.

Clouds were already beginning to show on the horizon ; no bigger than a man's hand, at first ; no bigger, indeed, than the fanatical hand which in 1517 nailed the famous Protest to the church door at Wittenberg. More wanted reform, but he did not want it in the shape of heresy. There was a certain English stupidity in the man which made him protest that if the windows were dirty, it was not necessary to pull the house down to remedy the defect. In 1521 when the King's book against Luther was produced (we still see the effect of it on any coin of the realm), More had a hand in editing it, and it may well be that he did not then fear much what Luther could do. But Luther was not the only cloud. In 1527 there were rumblings in the Royal sky. Henry, who had gone to a great deal of trouble in 1509, to get Papal permission to marry his brother's widow, had got tired of her, and seen Anne Boleyn " the little lively brunette with fascinating eyes." He now wanted an annulment of his first marriage so that he might contract another one ; and Wolsey was sent to France in the summer of 1527 with instructions to leave not a stone unturned (nor, presumably, any avenue unexplored) to secure what the King had set his heart on. More went with the Cardinal, and, just before he left, he said gloomily to Roper, " I would to God, son Roper, upon condition three things were well established in Christendom I were put in a sack and here presently cast into the Thames."

The three things were that whereas all Christendom was at war, it might be at peace ; that whereas the Church of Christ was torn with dissension and heresy, it might be unified and perfected ; and that the matter of the King's marriage might be brought to a good conclusion. Thus do time and events, changing, remain ever the same !

Wolsey did not have his usual success abroad, and although he returned home in ostensible triumph, with his customary pomp and pageantry, his star was already setting ; and his astute mind must have known it. He had failed in the matter of the divorce, thereby alienating Anne Boleyn. Even Cardinals cannot afford to get on the wrong side of fascinating brunettes with sparkling eyes !

Pope Clement now came in for a *mauvais quart d'heure*. He was in the hands (by reason of the fall of Rome in 1527) of Charles V, nephew to the English Queen, who took a very strong line indeed about his Aunt being slighted. On the other hand Clement had not the slightest desire to offend Henry, and was fully alive to the dreadful danger of losing England out of Christendom. No doubt heartily cursing the weakness of his predecessor for being ingenious enough to find excuses for granting the original dispensation for a marriage, he did what ninety-nine men out of a hundred would have done, and appointed a Commission. It availed him nothing. Catherine would not budge an inch, nor would the fascinating brunette ; the Commission was recalled to Rome and the King began to turn to his friends and to separate the sheep from the goats.

Wolsey was the first to feel the blast. He had failed in the matter of the divorce, so in 1529 a bill of indictment for *praemunire* was brought against him and he was brought to ruin.

So much for a long parenthesis, which is necessary to explain how in 1529, on the 25th of October, the King personally handed the Great Seal of England to Sir Thomas More in the Privy Chamber at Greenwich.

Henry had already sounded More on the question of the divorce, and had promised him that there would be no pressing for a decision one way or the other ; that promise was repeated after More took the oath as Chancellor. Both promises were subsequently broken.

In many ways More was an ideal Chancellor ; he was a lawyer and he was a hard worker ; and it was under his regime that the unheard-of circumstance occurred that he was able to leave his Court and go home because there were no more suits pending.

> " When More some time had Chancellor been
> No more suits did remain
> The like will never more be seen
> Till More there be again."

In an age which delighted in puns it was something to have a name like More !

Events were happening on the stage of history which were going to cut short so promising a Chancellorship. In 1531 the King was acknowledged to be " the supreme Head " of the Church " in so far as the law of Christ allows ". For Thomas More who, when it came to moral issues, believed in plain speaking, it was a fairly obvious progress from that moment to the later one on May 15th, 1532 when he handed back to his Sovereign the Great Seal in its white leather bag enclosed in crimson velvet.

He was Chancellor no more ; as he jokingly announced at the door of his wife's pew (taking the place of the servant who ordinarily gave notice of the fact that he had left the church), " My Lord has gone, my lady."

No doubt the step eased his conscience ; but it infuriated his good wife. She enjoyed being the Chancellor's Lady, and the ornate barge with its eight liveried watermen meant a good deal more to her than tender scruples.

Nor did tender scruples mean much to the man who was rapidly worming himself into Royal favour ; the erstwhile servant of Wolsey, a man without a tenth of the ability of the great Cardinal, without a ten-thousandth part of More's moral worth—the cunning Cromwell.

It is a bad day for states when kings and princes gather round them the worst counsel they can get, rather than the best, being flattered by the one and fearing the other.

Indeed Cromwell and the King between them badly bungled the business of trying to get rid of More, which they were now determined to do. There were charges about writing a pamphlet against a King's Proclamation—which was nonsense and proven so. There were accusations of receiving bribes, which he easily refuted. There was the ridiculous business of the Holy Maid of Kent, in which he had acted with most commendable circumspection. There was the absurd endeavour to find fault with his part in the King's book. All these broke down to the intense annoyance of the King who, like all Tudors, was a good friend, but a very bad enemy. But on Sunday, April 12th, when one of the King's officers ordered him to appear before the

Commissioners next morning to take the new oath Thomas More
knew that they had got him at last.

Next morning he did what had always been the prelude to any
important matter in his life ; heard Mass and went to the Sacraments.
Thus fully equipped to face the worst that the world could do, he left
his happy home and household in Chelsea for the last time, and with
what must have been a heavy heart came to the Archbishop's Palace
at Lambeth—that same Palace where as a boy he had served in Morton's
household and made them all laugh by extemporizing in the Christmas
plays.

Of course he would not take the Oath ; nor would the saintly Fisher.
Such men have a scale of values other than the mere earthly one.
He was willing to accept Anne Boleyn's accession as Queen as an
accomplished fact ; but nothing would persuade him to say that it
was a fact justified by Christ's law.

It is possible that Henry, by himself, might have been satisfied with
some sort of compromise ; but not so Anne and Cromwell ; between
them they had their way, and after four days of delay More was sent
to the Tower.

Of his year's imprisonment why say much ? His jests with his
jailers ; nay, indeed, his jests with his executioner, are common
knowledge.

He was comforted throughout his stay in the Tower by the untiring
devotion of his daughter Margaret who was (as she wrote at the end
of one of her many lovely letters) his " most loving obedient daughter
and bedeswoman, always, which daily and hourly is bound to pray
for you."

The drawn-out story of the attempts to entrap him, and the
lamentable farce of his trial make poor reading for English justice.
Indeed More had more than once to put the Chancellor who presided
over the Court right in matters of procedure ; and finally when the
ill-advised Chancellor interrupted him with the unfortunate question
" What, you wish to be considered wiser and of better conscience than
all the bishops and nobles of the realm ? " More had ready the crushing
answer which will serve its turn yet in many cases : " *My lord, for one
bishop of your opinion, I have a hundred saints of mine ; and for one Parliament
of yours, I have all the General Councils for a thousand years ; and for one
kingdom, I have France and all the kingdoms of Christendom.*"

Answers like that were not popular ; and on the unsupported evidence
of one man, and that a suborned one (the despicable Rich), Thomas
More, Knight and-one time Lord Chancellor of England was condemned to death.

The day before he died he sent his hairshirt to his beloved Margaret
and a letter written with a coal ; a letter such as only a good man

could have written and which it does all men good to read ; and on July 6th he was taken out to the place of execution and killed.

Morally the act was, of course, plain murder ; politically it was stupid in the extreme, and it raised such a storm of scorn in Western Europe as startled even the blind Henry. The Emperor Charles V declared that he would sooner have lost the best city of his realm than such a man, and Christian men told one another everywhere that " this day a prince is fallen in Israel."

Many historians nowadays find that they can write More's life in two sentences. *He enjoyed Royal favour ; he flourished. He was foolish enough to incur Royal displeasure ; so he died.* And there they write their *Hic jacet.* One won't quarrel with the summary, provided it be remembered that, dying, More left something of value behind.

What he left behind of value was not the *Utopia ;* not the fact that he was a good judge ; not his learned writings, nor his witty conversation ; but the fact that he saw the necessity of a yard-stick for measuring the things of this world. Even in worldly matters More had this essential sense of balance. The Field of the Cloth of Gold was very magnificent ; but it lacked the solid importance of his own hearth rug. It was pleasant to walk and talk with kings ; but more urgent to keep in touch with his children. Affairs of State had to be seen to ; but only when family matters had been settled first.

And when it came to a comparison of the matters of this world and the next More still had his yard-stick. He believed in what all Christendom had believed in for over a thousand years, what had held all Christendom together, and given it unity and purpose—the Divinely guided teaching of a Divinely instituted church. When matters of this world, however pressing and important, ran counter to *that*, Thomas More knew how to judge.

The importance of home life ; and the supremacy of the Church— who shall say that these two things will never be in peril again ? Nay, who shall say that, here, in England, Englishmen may not be called upon to defend them within the next decade ? If such a call comes, it will be well for us to remember that a greater Englishman than any living to-day has thought such things worth dying for.

ST. IGNATIUS LOYOLA

A.D. 1491–1556

[We accept, with Astrain and other historians, the date of Loyola's birth as 1491. Dudon, his latest historical biographer, prefers, but with much hesitation, 1493. Apart from the external evidence, we would suggest that the actual events in the Saint's life favour the earlier date.]

THE FAMILY FROM which Inigo Lopez de Loyola came was Basque. It was a noble house ; its sons had distinguished themselves for centuries, consistently on the side of the ruling monarchs. Of this family, in his generation, Inigo was the youngest of thirteen children ; therefore, according to a common custom, he was destined for the Church. But the boy had little inclination that way, and left the rectorship of his village to his brother, Pero. His father and mother had died before he was fourteen ; his brothers had scattered, one to seek his fortune in America ; Inigo himself had grown up at home, with such smattering of education as his surroundings provided. At the age of sixteen (1507), he accepted a post under a relative, Juan Velasquez, the king's treasurer, which would give him every chance of seeing and enjoying life in the gay cities of Spain, and round about the court of Ferdinand the Catholic. There he remained for eight years, that is, till he was twenty-four ; no better, it would seem, but perhaps no worse, than other gay young courtiers about him. Of those years he tells us himself that he just enjoyed himself ; he was fond of the life as he found it, he delighted especially in its tournaments and feats of arms ; there was a lady at court high above him to whom he became devoted, like Dante to Beatrice, but it does not appear that this was more than an ardent youth's romantic dream. At length a scrape, in which his name was involved (1514) made it advisable that he should seek occupation elsewhere, and Inigo's life at court came suddenly to an end.

Perhaps he was not altogether disappointed with the change, for the next phase in his career promised to be still more in accordance with his ambitions. From the counting house and the court he entered the service of another relative, Antonio Manrique de Lara, Duke of Najera, who in the following year (1516), the year of the marriage of Ferdinand and Isabella, was appointed Viceroy of Navarre. It promised to be a good time ; civil war changed it all. At the siege of Najera (1520) Inigo had his first baptism of blood, and during and after the battle proved himself for what he was. When the town was taken, contrary to the custom of the time, he insisted that there should be no looting. " Pillage," he said, " became neither a Christian nor a gentleman " ; and it is worthy of note that the young captain was obeyed. The civil war, thanks in no small part to Inigo's shrewd counsel, came partially to an end, but developed into a French invasion of Navarre. André de Foix, with his French army, supported by many Navarrese, arrived before Pampeluna, where Inigo was stationed, the last and surest stronghold of the king. The town capitulated forthwith, for defence was hopeless ; still, though defence was hopeless, and against the judgment of the commandant, Inigo persuaded his comrades to defend the citadel to the last. In the struggle that followed a cannon ball broke his leg, and with his fall resistance ended. Inigo was then (May 19, 1521) just thirty years of age.

His captors treated him with honour. Their physicians were placed at his service ; he was given back his sword ; after twelve days the French themselves carried him to his brother's castle at Loyola, in the neighbouring Basque Province. In the enemy's camp as well as in his own Inigo commanded the esteem of men. At Loyola he went through an ordeal. The leg had been badly set and would henceforth be crooked ; he had it broken again that it might be made straight. There was an unseemly bone protrusion ; Inigo ordered that it should be sawn away. The leg when set was too short ; he insisted that it should be stretched. With all this the convalescence was very long. To fill up the time the invalid called for books, tales of romance that had been his delight in the old days at Madrid. But no such books were forthcoming in the castle ; all that could be found were a life of Christ, and a volume of lives of the saints. For want of something better he read them. They set him thinking, and his present plight drove the thoughts home. Inigo, the romantic troubadour, the chivalrous soldier, the man easily loved by follower and victor, suddenly found a new vent for his romance, and chivalry, and love. These men of whom he read were heroes, every bit as much as a leader of men on a battlefield ; they fought and died for their King and His cause, quite as truly as any soldier. Nay, they were more heroic ; for their service cost them more, it was given without thought of reward, it was given to a King whose cause was far more worth serving than any other. What a reign His had been, and what a

conquest ! There had been no battles, no killing ; there had been no
guns, nor any thraldom ; there had been only a great love which had
engendered love, and it had won the world. These were the men
whose lives had altered Christendom, and had not merely won a
petty battle. Why could not he be what these had been ? Why could
he not take service under One whom to serve was so worth while ?
He would alter his life ; he would be like the master of men, Dominic,
the winner of men, Francis ; he would be a Carthusian, he would be
anything at all, so long as he could serve the King of kings whose
kingdom brought peace and goodwill to men. He would love this
King and serve Him ; he would put away all other service for His sake ;
he would fight as they had fought, with no other weapon but love ;
he would be the knight-errant of love, with love he would go and
conquer the world.

As soon as he was fit to travel Inigo kept his word and set out,
whither he did not know. His first goal was the Benedictine monastery
of Montserrat. There he made a general confession of his life ; he
kept the knight's vigil before Our Lady's altar ; he hung up his sword
at her shrine ; he went out into the world absolutely penniless and in
a beggar's garb, for he changed his clothes with a beggar on the road.
He came to a village called Manresa, intending to hide there for a few
days ; he stayed ten months. He begged his bread every day ; he
slept wherever good people were willing to receive him ; and again
there soon appeared the same phenomenon as before, of men and
women being drawn to the stranger who only asked for alms, so that
there were many doors open to admit him if he wished to enter. But
he preferred to live alone ; he spent almost all his time in prayer ;
years after, when asked about matters in the spiritual life, he would
say : " I learnt that at Manresa." Still he must fulfil his purpose of
going to the Holy Land. He left Manresa with nothing but the clothes
he was wearing and one or two books on his back, begged his way to
Barcelona, thence to Rome, thence to Venice, thence even to Jerusalem.
There he found his heart's desire ; he was happier in Jerusalem than
he had been anywhere in all his life before. He told himself he would
stay there all the rest of his days. He would live the life of Jesus on
the spot ; he would be as like Him as he could be, he would do His
work, he would preach to the people as He preached, perhaps like Him
he would one day be put to death. Such was Inigo, and such was
his state of mind, in the Autumn of 1523, when he was now thirty-two
years of age. But his hopes were frustrated. Single-minded
enthusiasts like Inigo, lovers like him who knew no barrier to their
love, were dangerous guests in a land of Mohamedan fanatics ; besides,
in the short time he was there, he ignored the ordinary rules laid down
for the security of pilgrims. The Franciscan Provincial of Jerusalem

interfered ; Inigo was ordered back to Europe, was forbidden to stay in the country under threat of excommunication ; here, as at Pampeluna, it required much to move him from his purpose. He had no choice but to do as he was told ; he arrived again in Venice, a beggar in rags, in January 1524.

What was he now to do ? His first plan had utterly failed, yet he knew he had a mission. He would wait and see ; in the meantime he would study for the priesthood. He came back to Barcelona ; there this palmer of thirty-three settled down in a free school for small boys to study Latin grammar. He found a lodging in a garret over a little shop ; he begged his bread from day to day ; he let the soles of his shoes wear through, telling himself that it was cheaper to go barefoot. After two years of this he made his way to the University of Alcala. There he tried to learn everything at once, with the result that he learnt nothing, though he stayed a year and a half. Meanwhile, as he had done at Barcelona, he could not keep himself from doing good, trying to make people care for Jesus as he cared. The Inquisition got on his track ; he was put in prison for forty-two days ; once more he found it advisable to move on. He tried the University of Salamanca (1527) ; but there he suffered an even worse fate. Within a fortnight of his arrival he fell under suspicion. He professed to teach others, having himself learnt nothing, and from a book written entirely by himself. He was again thrown into prison ; he was released on condition that he kept his teaching to himself. Inigo's decision shows where his heart was ; since he could not help people any more in Salamanca he would go elsewhere. He would leave Spain altogether ; he would go to the University of Paris, the centre of all learning, and there he would begin life all over again.

Inigo arrived in Paris in February, 1528. He was thirty-seven, and his life so far, had come to nothing. He began once more from the beginning ; a year of grammar, four years of philosophy, two of theology. He shared rooms with a Savoyard peasant, Pierre le Fèvre, and an impecunious Navarrese nobleman, Francis Xavier. While they helped him with his studies, he helped them in other ways. Soon, like other men, these two fell victims to Inigo's fascinating love. Other students followed ; Inigo did not pick his men ; he took those who came to him. On August 15, 1537, seven of them came together and took a solemn vow to give their lives, in some way, for this King of whom Inigo had spoken. What they would do they did not know ; only this, that, like him, they would begin their new life in Jerusalem. It was all very foolish and romantic, but there it was ; they had caught the love of Inigo, and, like him, love made them want to do foolish things. Still it was not all foolishness ; if Inigo would be a fool for Christ's sake, he did not forget at least some human prudence. He took his own degree in 1534; he insisted that these first disciples should finish their own studies, though it would take them three years more. Meanwhile he would go back to Spain, and settle his own and their affairs. They would meet again in Venice, in 1537, for their pilgrimage to the Holy Land ; after that their King would tell them what he would have them to do. We may leap the intervening years, for so it came about ; on January 8, 1537, they assembled in Venice, their numbers increased. It was fifteen years since Inigo had set out for Palestine, at the age of thirty-one ; now he was forty-six, and had come back to the same point. There was just this difference ; that whereas before he was alone, now he had a group of men about him, fired with his own desire. There was no other bond to bind them together ; no superior, no obedience, nothing but the realisation of the truth of Jesus Christ and love of Him, nothing but the common longing to be of service to Him, to be what He was and to do what He would do were He in their place there and then. Beyond that they had no further ambition ; that they should found a religious order had not so much as entered their minds. After all only one of them, Le Fèvre, was as yet a priest ; Inigo himself had not yet received ordination.

But now circumstances began to alter their perspective. At the time it was not easy to go to Palestine ; the Mohamedan ships were scouring the Mediterranean, and merchants refused to sail. Inigo and his disciples could not waste their time while they waited ; they began at once with such service as the thought of Christ suggested, the tending of the sick in hospitals, and the records tell us of the extremes of self-conquest to which they went. Next was devotion to the Blessed Sacrament, what may be called the special devotion of Inigo Loyola. In the city, as in many places elsewhere, it had become almost extinct ; these laymen set to work to revive it. Careful now, after his lessons elsewhere, to secure approval for his work, Inigo sent two to Rome to ask for papal approbation ; they were examined and approved, which gave them a still greater sense of brotherhood. In consequence, all now received the priesthood, and renewed together the vows they had taken three years before at Montmartre. But the voyage to Palestine still remained impossible ; until there was more hope they would divide into groups, and scatter themselves over North Italy, looking for what good they could do. They waited and waited, but in vain ; in the end, after a year of waiting, the Palestine dream had to be abandoned. Very well, they would go out to win the world for Christ, starting from where they were. They would go to His Vicar on earth, and offer themselves to do whatever he might wish them to do. But who were they ? If anyone asked them, what were they to say ? Already they were beginning to be called

Iniguists, but Inigo would have none of that. It was about this time that Inigo became Ignatius ; one suspects the change had something to do with the name. In the end they hit upon a title that satisfied them all ; it summed up in a word their whole ideal, it contained the only bond and rule they needed. If enquirers asked them who they were, they would say, quite simply and unequivocally, they were " the Companions of Jesus." Just that and no more.

Still, though at first they did not recognize it, they had made two far-reaching decisions ; the decision to remain in Europe, and the decision to keep together as a corporate body. They next decided that their headquarters should be in Rome, and Ignatius went there with two others to establish themselves there. In Rome they behaved as elsewhere, giving retreats and preaching ; their work came to the notice of the Pope, and he told them that Rome must be their Jerusalem. And it was only then after four years of companionship, that the followers of Ignatius began to feel the need of a closer bond of union. They came together in Rome, all that could come. They decided on some form of Constitution ; they would vow themselves to poverty and chastity ; but what more ? They would bind themselves to obedience to the Pope, would go wherever he might choose to send them, would undertake whatever he might ask of them. But, among themselves they must also have a head ; they must become an order of religious. The vote for a head was taken ; all but one chose Ignatius. He protested ; he gave them back their votes, bade them pray and vote again. But the result was the same. Their vows were renewed in his hands ; their foundation was formally approved (1540) ; the seed sown in Paris six years before had come to fruit. Ignatius Loyola, the first General of the Companions of Jesus, was in his fiftieth year.

And now at last, when he was appointed General and must speak, the soul of this conqueror of men began to show itself. All through his life to this point one cannot but be struck by the way men were drawn towards him, no matter in what guise he came among them. The soldiers at Pampeluna, the French that held him prisoner, the family retainers at Loyola, all testify their enthusiastic admiration for this leader of men. When he turned beggar, and refused from anyone more than his daily bread, or his means of transit from place to place, at Manresa, at Venice, at Barcelona, in a short time men and women gathered round him, eager for the privilege of maintaining him, even eager to submit themselves to his guidance. He became a poor student, at Alcala, at Salamanca, at Paris, and within a few days, at each university, fellow-students and many more sought his company and leadership ; so many that his influence brought him into suspicion and trouble. When the time had seemed ripe, and he had found the men he wanted, he laid open his soul to one or two, told them of his love for, and longing to be like, Jesus Christ ; and at once this poor scholar, of over forty years of age, won the hearts of ambitious youths of twenty, and found them longing to love and live like himself. He set out before them what must have seemed a wild-goose chase ; wise men who heard of it shook their heads, did all they could to prevent these promising cadets from throwing away their lives, even threatened Inigo himself with punishment, for so diverting youth. But he was not moved, nor were they. They would beg their way penniless to Jerusalem, there to do they scarcely knew what ; and these young men who had come to know him, with no other· influence upon them but the man himself, had surrendered brilliant careers, and had vowed themselves to follow him wherever he led. He had tested their devotion by leaving them for two whole years to themselves, away from him, in their own surroundings, with their natural ambitions telling on them as before ; and it had stood the test. There had been no question of a superior, or of obedience, or even of organisation of any kind. The only bond had been the personal admiration and love of these men for Ignatius, and the personal love of Ignatius for each one of them ; a love, in both cases, buried in one still more absorbing, the personal love of them all for Jesus Christ their Lord.

This was what now became the more manifest in everything he said and wrote. His men must not be called Iniguists ; they were not the Companions of Inigo, they were the Companions of Jesus. They were not obedient to him, they were obedient to the voice of Jesus Christ. Obedience to a mere man would never make them do what he wanted them to do ; no, not even obedience to Christ, if it were just obedience and no more. But with love, and such love, what might he not hope for ? And he would quote the saying of Augustine, as a sort of motto for them all : " *Ubi amatur, non laboratur, aut si laboratur, labor amatur* " ; " Where there is love there is no labour, or if there is labour the labour is loved." No, not even obedience, if obedience there must be, should be their bond or their inspiration. They wished him to write rules, to draw up a Constitution for their guidance ; whatever else he wrote, this should appear in the very first sentence : " More important than any written Constitution is the interior law of charity and love." So would he be guided throughout. Poverty ? He would not bid his subjects to remain poor men ; he would bid them to " love poverty like a mother." Humility ? He would not tell them to be humble ; he would tell them to " love and ardently desire " humiliations. He would not demand obedience ; enforced obedience he would expressly repudiate. Instead, he would insist that subjects love their superiors, and that superiors love their subjects no less. He would not say much to them of the apostolic life ; instead he would fill them with love for their fellow-men, love for all men, " *quidam universalis amor*," which would take them all over the world, doing good of whatever kind, to everyone, everywhere, at whatever cost, out of this same pure love of mankind. He would not have them look for any reward, not even any fruit of their labour as such ; love should be its own reward, and the emblem of love was the cross rather than the crown. So would they " imitate and follow " their Lord, so would they reproduce His life in their own, " desiring with all their souls whatever Christ our Lord loved and embraced." This was the man who now revealed himself, in the Constitutions he took more than ten years to write, and in the letters of guidance and affection which now began to come from his pen.

And where had this love already led them ? It was only six years since the little group had gathered together at Montmartre ; only three years since they had reassembled at Venice. In those three years they had scattered themselves over North Italy, teaching the people, serving the sick, caring for the poor and depraved, and already the Church, from the Pope and his Curia downward, had begun to take notice of them. Not all were friends ; a saint never has all friends, the best loved of men is usually the most hated. There were suspicious cardinals, resentful ecclesiastics who would have nothing to do with these intruders, jealous fellow-preachers who would point to their heresies, deserters who would tell lying tales about their lives at home, debauchees who were indignant that these begging priests should interfere with their pleasures ; even in these first three years all these had set themselves to malign the Iniguists as upstarts, heretics, schemers, intruders, immoral. And then Ignatius had come upon the scene. He had encountered the profligate, and made of him a bosom friend. He had talked with a resentful rival, and the two had become zealous supporters of each other. He had gone to Rome, and all opposition had ceased. Ignatius was too genuine, too lovable, too true to Christ and the work of Christ for men to have any doubt. *Digitus Dei est hic* ; " The Finger of God is here," a Pope could at last say ; and from that time, whenever there was anything of serious consequence to be done, he knew that, if other resources failed, he could apply to his faithful, and loving, and unflinching Ignatius.

Hence in this very year, 1540, when for the first time these Companions of Jesus asked for a Constitution, Ignatius's beloved Le Fèvre was already in the heart of Germany, still a young man in the thirties, the first apostle of the Counter-reformation. A few weeks more, and his other beloved, Francis Xavier, was off at a day's notice for the mysterious Indies ; Xavier, who later would hear from Ignatius : " I will never forget you. Always your own, Ignatius," and would read those letters on his knees. To the end of his life Xavier knew no other rules of his Order ; instead, when he would describe his Institute to his fellow-apostles, we find such as this in his letters : " The Company of Jesus is nothing more than a Company of love." But it was not only these two ; now that the floodgates were opened and the General, who rules as yet by love only and without any regulation, could direct his men where he would, the waters began to flow. The Pope needed theologians for Germany ; they were sent. Kings asked for chaplains for their soldiers ; they were provided, the first army chaplains in history. Rome wished to know the actual state in England, Ireland, and Scotland ; two were appointed for the perilous mission, the first Jesuits to visit these islands. Things were not happy in the University of Paris ; the great Maldonatus and others were soon in the city. Missionaries were needed in Barbary ; others in Abyssinia ; others again in Austria, Hungary, Poland ; and they were found. It seemed as if young men of spirit had only to come in contact with the person of Ignatius, and all the world became too small for the exercise of their " universal love."

Such was the growth of the tree whose seed was sown on the sick-bed in the castle of Loyola, twenty years before. How different, perhaps, from anything the sick man himself had then imagined ! For then his first thought had been the surrender of everything and prayer. He had discovered Jesus Christ ; Christ had become necessary to him ; not for all the world, not for all the work and conquest in the world, would he let Him go. And yet, with all the difference between the ideal and its realisation, how much was there that still remained the same ! The General of the Companions of Jesus, whose men were writing to him from all over the world, who in return was responding to them with letters full of love and interest, of prudence and guidance, who was being appealed to by rulers in Church and State, was to be found every morning on his knees before the altar, with tears running down his cheeks, clinging to the Christ whose love these twenty years had only rendered deeper ; in the evening might be found on the verandah outside his window, lost in ecstasy as he contemplated God, manifested in the beauty of the stars. Once he had thought to become a Carthusian ; in spite of all his labours and distracted life he had never ceased to be a contemplative. He would teach sinners and all men to pray as best they could ; but his own prayer, to which he would invite all who could reach it, was the intimacy of perfect union with his Beloved Lord. So did he, in an astonishing way, seem to forget his own existence ; to suspect Ignatius of worldly ambition or falsehood is merely ignorance. Three times he asked to be relieved of the management of the Company ; his health was too precarious, he could be more useful elsewhere, it would succeed much better under an abler General. When the news came of great things done by his disciples, the colour would rise to his face, to think that he sat there at home doing nothing. When men spoke the praises of his Order in his hearing, he would wonder how it had all come about. Though, as is manifest in his Constitutions and letters, nothing was of greater interest to him than the spiritual lives of his disciples, of his own spiritual life he could be induced to say little or nothing. It is only through some chance notes, written for himself alone to see and discovered after his death, that we know of his daily prayer, his intimate knowledge of the Blessed Trinity, his familiarity with the saints, his spiritual canticles of the purest ecstasies of love.

To complete the portrait of Ignatius it would be necessary to speak of his other works, besides the Company of Jesus ; the " Company of Orphans," which he also founded, drawing laymen into it to help him, the House of St. Martha for fallen women, the work on behalf of the Jews of Rome, and more. But we are not writing a book. From the days at Manresa, where he had broken his constitution by the rigour of his life, he had always been a sick man ; he had endured stomach trouble ever since, once at least he had been near to death. When he settled in Rome, in 1540, at the age of fifty, he became worse ; the climate of Rome never suited him. In his last few years he was a permanent invalid, and was compelled to do much of his work through the hands of others ; on this account he asked again to be relieved of his office, but his disciples would not consent. On July 30th, 1556, when he was sixty-five, he had been visited by his doctors, but they had feared nothing unusual ; Ignatius, it would seem, knew better. That evening he carried on his ordinary business ; he showed the same interest, but some noticed that his mind was more aloof than was his custom. During the night the infirmarian, who slept within call, heard him pouring out his soul from time to time in simple words of pure love. In the early morning of the 31st he went in to him as usual. He found him at the point of death. He ran for help, but it was too late ; quietly and unconcerned, without a parting word to anyone, without the last sacraments of his Church, without any sign that it mattered one way or another, this universal lover of men passed to the love of One whom he loved yet more. He died, and immediately all Rome was moved ; not so much, it would seem, as with other saints, because men had been struck by his sanctity ; but because of his meekness and clemency, of the affection and love they had borne him, of the ideal and example his quiet life had been to them all, prelates and layfolk alike.

ERNEST C. MESSENGER, Ph.D.

CARDINAL POLE

A.D. 1500–1558

A PLACE SHOULD certainly be found, in a volume devoted to Great Catholics, for Reginald Cardinal Pole. It is a matter of ordinary historical knowledge that he was chiefly responsible, together with Queen Mary, for the brief restoration of England to unity with the Holy See in the middle of the sixteenth century, and that he was the last Archbishop of Canterbury to acknowledge the supremacy of the Pope. But his personal greatness, and his accomplishments in other spheres, are not so well known, and I purpose in this essay to sketch them very briefly.

Reginald Pole was of royal descent. His mother, the Lady Margaret Pole, was a niece of King Edward IV, and therefore connected with the Yorkist family. His father enjoyed great favour at the court of the Lancastrian King Henry VII, and was attached to the household of the King's eldest son, Prince Arthur. As all the world knows, Arthur married Catherine of Aragon, but died shortly afterwards. Catherine then married Prince Arthur's younger brother, Henry, by papal dispensation.

Reginald was born in the year 1500. We gather from one of his letters that his pious mother dedicated him to God from his earliest youth[1] and it would seem that she hoped from the first that he would embrace an ecclesiastical career. Reginald's father died in 1505, but the Lady Margaret was at once assisted by Prince Henry, who even before his accession to the throne made himself responsible for Reginald's education. The boy was first sent to school at the age of seven, to the Carthusians at Sheen. It is interesting to note that Reginald thus came under the same salutary influence as did his great friend Sir Thomas More.

At the age of twelve, Reginald entered as a student at Magdalen College, Oxford. Here he had for tutors the famous Thomas Linacre, who was devoted to medical science, and physician to the King, and also William Latimer, a well known humanist. Reginald was evidently a very promising student, and he was admitted Bachelor

[1] Letter to the Countess of Salisbury, Cotton, App. L, 79, British Museum.

of Arts at the age of fifteen. Two years later, i.e. in 1517, he was presented by King Henry to the prebend of Boscombe in Salisbury Cathedral. In 1518 he received the collegiate church of Wimbourne, and in 1519 the prebend of Yatminster, also in Salisbury Cathedral.

It is often said that Pole held these benefices as a layman. The only basis for this statement is the fact that when later on he was raised to the Cardinalate in Rome, he had his head shaved. But it seems quite probable that Reginald received the tonsure in England shortly after he took his degree. Certain it is that he is described as a " clerk " in the announcement of his presentation to Wimbourne. Again, sons of nobility and gentry in those days often received the tonsure at an early age, even though they had no intention of proceeding to the priesthood, in order that, having thus entered the clerical state, they might possess the revenues of ecclesiastical benefices. These had to be forfeited on marriage. It would seem, indeed, that occasionally dispensations from these requirements of Canon Law were granted. At any rate, after he had revolted from the Holy See, Henry VIII, as Pope of his new Church, gave one dispensation to a layman to hold a benefice, even though married.[1] Even so, we gather from this that a dispensation was necessary if a layman was to hold a benefice, and therefore we are surely justified in saying that when Pole held these benefices, he was either tonsured, or else expressly dispensed by ecclesiastical authority. The early age at which these benefices were conferred upon him, and the plurality involved, were not contrary to Canon Law as it then stood, and therefore no blame attaches either to Reginald or to those who conferred them upon him. The Council of Trent later on put an end to these abuses.[2]

As has already been said, Reginald's mother probably hoped from the first that he would eventually become a priest. But others had different plans for his future, and in particular, Catherine of Aragon cherished the idea that the best way to prevent a revival of the feud between the houses of York and Lancaster would be to marry her daughter Mary (afterwards Queen of England), to one of the sons of the Lady Margaret. It was doubtless with this end in view that she arranged for the Countess of Salisbury, as the Lady Margaret had now become, to be appointed governess to her daughter. This was calculated to ensure that the Princess Mary would be much in the company of the sons of the Countess. Her eldest son was already married by this time, and there can be little doubt that Reginald was the one on whom Catherine's hopes were fixed as the future spouse of her daughter. King Henry himself did not sympathize with this

---

[1] See Frere, *Marian Reaction*, p.58.
[2] See my work *The Reformation, the Mass and the Priesthood*, Vol. II, p.13, and the *Catholic Encyclopædia*, Vol. II, pp. 475–6.

scheme, but at any rate the possibility of such a marriage between the parties was mooted again and again during Pole's lifetime, as we shall see.

In those days, a gentleman's education was thought to be incomplete if it did not comprise a stay abroad, and accordingly, at the age of 19, Reginald went to Padua in Italy, for the purposes of continuing his studies. The high favour he enjoyed at this time in the eyes of King Henry is shown by the fact that His Majesty made him an allowance of 500 crowns, in order to defray all his expenses abroad. The University of Padua was then one of the best in Italy, and during his stay there, Pole met many of the most famous scholars and prominent ecclesiastics of the time. He was a constant guest at the house of Pietro Bembo, afterwards Cardinal, " the prince of humanists," and during his six years' residence at the University, he gathered round himself a very brilliant circle of scholars and students.

From time to time Pole visited other Italian cities. Thus in 1525 he paid his first visit to Rome. Meantime he had not been forgotten in England, and in 1524 he was appointed a Fellow of the recently established College of Corpus Christi at Oxford. But the Pole family were by now somewhat under a cloud. Reginald's elder brother had been sent to the Tower by the irascible Henry because of his connection with the ill-fated Duke of Buckingham, the father-in-law of Ursula Pole. But the Countess of Salisbury herself was still in favour, and so was her son Reginald. When he returned to England in 1527, he received a warm welcome from both the King and Queen.

The Princess Mary had by now been designated as the spouse of either the King of France, or his heir, and thus Reginald was free to proceed in his ecclesiastical career. He was almost immediately appointed Dean of Exeter (August 12th, 1527). But instead of taking a prominent place in affairs, he withdrew once more to Sheen. This rather noticeable retirement from Court most probably had its explanation in the domestic complications in King Henry's household. Henry had for some time ceased to be faithful to Catherine of Aragon. A natural son by one of the Queen's ladies had been created Duke of Richmond. He had also had immoral relations with Mary Boleyn, and now he lost his heart to Mary's younger sister, Anne. Already steps had been taken to try to establish that his marriage with Catherine had been invalid from the beginning. Reginald Pole may well have desired to keep clear of these questionable proceedings.

Nevertheless, he was soon approached by Thomas Cromwell, at that time in the service of Cardinal Wolsey. Cromwell asked Pole his views on these matters of the King's business. Reginald replied that the King's servants ought above all to recommend that which was most in accordance with the prince's honour and interest.

Cromwell thereupon proceeded to explain the Machiavellian views which he himself held. The King's inclinations, he said, were to be studied carefully, and then furthered, without, however, sacrificing the appearance of religion or virtue. He recommended Pole to study Machiavelli's book, *Il Principe*, rather than Plato. Pole promised to read the work, but did not commit himself further.

The affair of the King's Divorce dragged on. Browbeaten by Henry's envoys, the Pope, in May, 1529, at last appointed a commission to examine into the validity of the marriage with Catherine. The Commission sat in England in June, 1529, but Catherine appealed from the Commission to the Pope. That meant that the cause would have to be finally settled at Rome. Henry had good reason to fear that in that case the decision would go against him. In view of his headstrong character, the future outlook was indeed uncertain and dark, and Pole thought it prudent to ask to be allowed to go abroad once more for the purposes of study. It seems quite clear that his object was really to avoid being entangled in the difficult and delicate situation in England.

But though he went abroad, he was not left in peace. In August, 1529, about two months after Pole had left for Paris, a certain Thomas Cranmer was introduced to the King by Cromwell, as one who had a good plan for solving Henry's matrimonial problem without having recourse to the See of Rome. The first point in this plan was that canonists and universities should be persuaded to declare that the marriage with Catherine was invalid. The King welcomed this idea, and as Pole was now at Paris, Henry commissioned him to sound the Doctors of the University there, and to do his best to persuade them to pronounce in his favour. Pole begged to be excused from this unwelcome task, and pleaded his inexperience. But the King merely sent others to assist him. After much pressure had been brought to bear on the Doctors of the Sorbonne, a majority declared in Henry's favour, and this result was duly sent to the King by Pole.

But Henry was not yet satisfied. He wanted to gain Pole absolutely to his cause, and so he recalled him to England in 1530, and offered to him the Sees of Winchester and York. As Canterbury was still occupied by Archbishop Warham, the King was thus offering to Pole the highest ecclesiastical positions then vacant. It must have been a great temptation to Reginald. His whole life had seemed to indicate some such destiny and position. He had been marked out for the Church from the first, and benefices and dignities had been showered upon him. Undoubtedly he was faced with the first grave crisis in his life. Should he accept, and throw in his lot with his King, humouring his whims as counselled by Thomas Cromwell ? Or should he refuse, and thereby place his future, if not his very life, in jeopardy ?

His family were asked to do their utmost to ensure a favourable decision, and they did so. Every possible consideration was urged upon him, and he tells us[1] that at length he thought he had found a way to satisfy both the King and his own conscience. He went to the King to explain his plan, but strange to say, when about to do so, his lips refused to move, and when at last he found himself able to speak, he uttered every argument against the idea he had come to defend.

The King was furious, but nevertheless consented to read a document which Pole drew up explaining and defending his attitude. Cranmer bears witness to the persuasiveness of this document.[2] In it, Pole urged Henry to leave the matter to the Pope's judgment, and warned him that one step further would drown all his honour. But Henry had already practically committed himself, and, urged on by Cromwell, he finally decided to break with Rome.

Pole decided once more to leave England, for his continued presence could do no good, but rather harm. Accordingly he betook himself to Avignon early in 1532, but the climate there proving unsuitable, he went on in September of the same year to Venice, where he was within reach of his beloved Padua. Here he renewed his acquaintance with his old friends, and in addition, made many new ones. Thus he came into contact with Contarini and Caraffa, both afterwards Cardinals, and the latter destined to occupy the See of Peter, and to be one of Pole's greatest enemies. He also met Cortese, Sadoleto, and others, and had long conversations with them on the ecclesiastical position, the need of a reform within the Church, and other matters which interested him and them.

Meanwhile, affairs in England were going rapidly from bad to worse. In November, 1532, Pope Clement VII drew up a bull threatening Henry with excommunication if he did not separate from Anne and take back Catherine, pending the Papal decision as to the validity of the former marriage. But so far from obeying the Pope, Henry actually married Anne Boleyn secretly in January, 1533, and four months later Cranmer, now Archbishop of Canterbury, by a solemn farce pronounced the marriage with Catherine to have been invalid. On May 29th, Anne was crowned at Westminster as Queen of England.

The Pope, of course, could not ignore this flagrant act of disobedience. On July 11th, 1533, Clement again threatened Henry with excommunication for contracting a second marriage while the consideration of the first was still pending in the Roman Court. Henry's only

[1] Letter to Edward VI, Epistles, i, 251–62.
[2] Letter from Cranmer to Lord Wiltshire, Lansdowne MS. 115 ; Strype, Cranmer, App. No. 1.

answer was to appeal to a General Council, though he had already refused to have anything to do with the Council which the Pope had summoned.

On September 7th, 1533, Anne brought forth, not the son and heir for which Henry had married her, but a daughter. Thus the question of the succession to the throne of England was still uncertain, and the Emperor's ambassador wrote to that monarch suggesting that Pole might well succeed eventually to the Kingdom, and once more mentioning the project of a marriage between him and the Princess Mary.[1] But the Emperor did not favour the idea.

Meanwhile, Henry continued in his headlong course. In 1534, Parliament was persuaded to pass the Act of Supremacy, declaring the King to be the Head of the Church. A similar declaration had already been extorted from Convocation. In January, 1535, the bishops were ordered to surrender all bulls of appointment obtained from Rome, and to take out fresh commissions for the government of their dioceses, acknowledging that their authority emanated from the King. The schism was thus complete.

Henry had not forgotten Pole's existence. In February, 1535, he charged Thomas Starkey, one of his chaplains, to obtain from Pole his opinion on the validity of the marriage with Catherine, and on the authority of the Pope. Whatever may have been Henry's motive in this, Pole decided to comply, and to set forth his opinions at length in a book. While he was preparing this work, news reached him of the martyrdom of John Fisher, Bishop of Rochester, and of his old friend Sir Thomas More. He also found other matter to deal with in anti-papal books written in England by Sampson, Bishop of Chichester, and Gardiner, Bishop of Winchester. It seems that these books had been sent to Pole by Henry's orders, in the hope that he would see his way to adopt their sentiments. But Henry had mistaken his man. Pole's mind was made up, and the book, *Pro Ecclesiasticæ Unitatis Defensione*, vindicated the Papal authority and directly attacked the Royal Supremacy and the new religion thereby set up in England.

Henry was furious, but he dissembled his rage, and tried once more to persuade Pole to return to England and discuss the matter. Pole remarked that, like the fox, he had seen many animals going into the lion's cave, but none coming out again, and wrote to the King declining the invitation, inasmuch as by the Act of Supremacy, everyone refusing to acknowledge the King's headship of the Church had been dubbed a traitor.

Meanwhile, Pole was actually reproached for his loyalty to the Holy See by Tunstall, Bishop of Durham, who added in a letter that Pole's own mother and brothers were likely to suffer in consequence of

[1] Gairdner, *Letters and Papers of Henry VIII*, Vol. VI, No. 1164.

his opposition to the King. And to emphasise this, Pole actually received letter of protest from his mother, the Countess of Salisbury, and his elder brother, Lord Montague. Further letters were sent, as we shall see. It seems strange that Blessed Margaret Pole, who was so soon to lay down her life as a martyr for the Faith, should write to expostulate with her distinguished son for refusing to accept the unlawful spiritual claims of King Henry. But the true explanation is without doubt that given by Dean Hook, in the account of Pole contained in his *Lives of the Archbishops of Canterbury*. Hook points out that the original draft of these letters is amongst the Government papers in the Record Office, and remarks :

> " There can but be one inference deduced from this fact— namely, that the letters received by Pole were a mere transcript on the part of his relatives of letters composed by order of the government, and when we consult the documents themselves, this natural suspicion is fully confirmed by internal evidence."[1]

This candid avowal from an Anglican writer rather unsympathetic towards Pole is also quoted with evident agreement by Canon Dixon in his *History of the Church of England*, Vol. I, p. 483, note.

Pole wrote his mother a very touching letter, asking her to remember " that ever you had given me utterly unto God. . . . This promise now, madam, in my Master's name I require of you to maintain." Thus did Pole resist the apparent attempt on the part of his mother and brother to make him untrue to his conscience.

A day or two after this letter was written, Pole was summoned to Rome by Pope Paul III, who had succeeded Clement VII. At last definite steps were being taken to bring about the long-desired reformation of the Church from within. The Pope had decided to call a General Council, and desired Pole's advice and help. Pole, as in duty bound, promised to go to Rome, but at the same time he wrote to King Henry informing him of the position, evidently in order to avoid any widening of the breach already made. But it soon became obvious that Pole was now regarded as the King's enemy. Even so, he was faithful to his conscience. Others in England, when faced with the cruel dilemma of choosing between the Pope and the unlawful claims of their lawful King, had, for various reasons, chosen the latter alternative, and temporised with their consciences. Pole was made of sterner stuff. He fully realised the price he might have to pay. He knew the fate which Henry had meted out to his best friends in England, and we gather from his letters and from other sources, that henceforth he was more than once in danger of his life from Henry's hired assassins.

[1] *Lives of the Archbishops of Canterbury.* Vol. VIII, p. 102.

Pole set out for Rome in September, 1536. When he had reached Verona, a messenger arrived from England with further letters, including two from Pole's sorrowing mother and brother. Writing at this time to his friend Cardinal Contarini, Pole says that these letters touched him so deeply that he almost changed his plans. But he was confirmed in his original purpose by Bishops Caraffa and Ghiberti, who were accompanying him, and he contented himself with " doing what he could to satisfy his relatives."

Pole duly arrived in the Eternal City, and was at once appointed by the Pope to the Commission which was preparing for the forthcoming Council. At the end of this year 1536, Pole was suddenly, and almost against his will, raised to the Cardinalate. His present friend but future enemy Caraffa was made a Cardinal at the same time. Pole received many congratulations from his friends, but from England there only came reproaches.

The Commission of which Pole was a member in due course drew up an important report, the *Consilium delectorum Cardinalium de emendanda Ecclesia*. It is a noteworthy document, remarkable for its outspoken condemnation of abuses in Papal administration, and the fact that Pole had a hand in drawing it up shows how anxious he was for the reform of the Church.

In February, 1537, Pole was appointed Nuncio to England. The Pilgrimage of Grace had just taken place, and raised hopes in Rome of a restoration of the authority of the Holy See. It was thought that Pole might perhaps be able to encourage another similar movement, and that perhaps even Henry himself would find it prudent to seek reconciliation with the Church. Henry was apparently willing to send certain persons to confer unofficially with Pole in Flanders. But it soon became evident, not only that there was no hope of Henry's submission, but also that Pole would receive no help or support either from the King of France or from the Emperor. The deceitful Henry had even requested the French King to capture Pole and hand him over to the English. The King of France could not consent to that, but instead he requested Pole to leave his dominions. Similar opposition to Pole was offered by the Emperor, for political reasons. Henry's agents constantly endeavoured to murder the Cardinal, and eventually, as it was impossible to fulfil his mission, Pole returned to Rome.

Two years previously, i.e. in August, 1535, the Pope had drawn up a bull definitely excommunicating Henry, deposing him, and pronouncing various spiritual pains and penalties against his adherents. But its publication had been suspended, doubtless in the hope that more peaceable means might produce the desired effect. But Henry had gone from bad to worse. He had dissolved the remaining monasteries, and sacked the shrine of St. Thomas at Canterbury. Thereupon the Pope decided, in December, 1538, to publish the suspended bull, and Pole was sent to the Emperor, then at Toledo, and to the French King at Paris, to urge them to carry out the undertaking they had already given to do all in their power to restore England to the faith.   In particular, they were to be requested to publish the bull of excommunication in their dominions.

Pole set out on this second mission.   At Bologna he received the sad news that all his relatives had been committed to the Tower, and shortly afterwards came the news of the execution of his elder brother, Lord Montague.   Pole's mission failed, as before.   The Emperor and the French King were too engrossed in considerations of political expedience to further the cause of the Church of God, and Pole had to return once more to Rome.   On his way, he heard that his mother had been sentenced to death, and later on came the news of her martyrdom.   The Cardinal's comment on this crowning loss was a noble one :

" Until now, I had thought God had given me the grace of being the son of one of the best and most honoured ladies in England . . . Now He has vouchsafed to honour me still more, by making me the son of a martyr . . . Let us rejoice, for we have another advocate in heaven."

Yet Pole cherished no feelings of enmity or hatred towards his mother's murderer, and he declared that if his own slaughter could bring about Henry's conversion, he would desire it at once.

In August, 1541, Pole was appointed Governor of Viterbo and the Patrimony of St. Peter.   He ruled the province for some five years, with great discretion and humanity—so much so that, as we shall see later on, his enemies complained of his leniency towards heretics there. But the Cardinal was destined for more important work, and in 1545 he went to Trent as one of the three Papal legates appointed for the opening of the great Council of the Church.   In preparation for this, Pole had written an excellent treatise on General Councils, and in January, 1546, there was read, at the second session of the Council, an address written by him, emphasising the threefold purpose of the assembly, namely, the uprooting of heresies, the reformation of ecclesiastical discipline and morals, and the external peace of the whole Church.   It is a wonderful address, candidly acknowledging the partial responsibility of ecclesiastics for the evils of the day.[1]

Pole's ill-health compelled him to leave Trent in March, 1536, but he continued to take an active part in the discussions of the Council.

---

[1] An English translation has recently been made by Father Vincent McNabb, O.P., and published by Burns and Oates under the title *Cardinal Pole's Eirenicon.*

In particular, he was very much interested in the discussion and definition of the true doctrine on Justification. Some years previously, his friend Cardinal Contarini had endeavoured to bring about the reconciliation of the Lutherans with the Church, by setting forth what was undoubtedly an insufficient and inadequate account of the Catholic doctrine on Justification as eventually defined at Trent. Pole at that time undoubtedly sympathized with Contarini's view, though he realised that it was contrary to the Augustinian and Scholastic tradition. But it must be borne in mind that at that time there had been no Church decision on the matter. The subject was long debated at Trent, and the Council's proposed decree on the subject was sent to Pole for his observations, and there can be no doubt that he loyally accepted the doctrine as eventually defined.

Pole did not return to Trent, but was summoned back to Rome in October, 1546, where the Pope made great use of his services in matters of official correspondence.

At the end of January, 1547, Henry VIII died, and Pole wrote to the Pope suggesting that it might now be possible to restore England to communion with the Holy See. The Pope appointed him as legate, and Pole forthwith wrote to the Privy Council, begging them to receive him in the Pope's name. But the Council refused even to read his letter, and it became only too plain that under the new king, Edward VI, England was to recede still further from the true Faith. But Pole continued to keep in touch with home affairs. The Protector Somerset actually wrote urging him to abandon the " errors and abuses of Rome," and sent for his approval a copy of the First Prayer Book of Edward VI. He also invited him to return to England, but Pole of course declined the invitation.

Pope Paul III died in November, 1549. Cardinal Pole stood high in favour in the Conclave. At the third scrutiny he received 26 votes. Two more would have sufficed to make him Pope, and a move was made that evening by a group of Cardinals to have him proclaimed Pope at once by " adoration." But Pole declined, and said that, if elected at all, he must be elected after Mass the next morning, in accordance with the usual practice. Eventually Cardinal Del Monte, one of Pole's fellow legates at the Council of Trent, was chosen. He took the name of Julius III. Pole's humble comment on. his own failure to be elected was that " the Lord did not require this particular ass."

Actually, Pole had enemies as well as friends amongst the Cardinals, and it was urged against him that he had consorted with heretics at Viterbo and elsewhere. This was a specious accusation. Pole had throughout been anxious for the reform of the Church, and had encouraged all who seemed to desire to promote the reform of discipline, from within. But some of those whom he supported did not confine themselves to matters of discipline, but later went on to attack the Church's doctrines, and eventually apostatized. Amongst these was Peter Martyr and Ochino, who both went to England to support the new Anglican Church. Naturally, this sad ending to promising careers was made the most of by Pole's enemies. Doubtless also his support of Contarini's ideas on Justification was also brought up against him. It was also urged that he had been lax in his government of Viterbo, and had not inflicted capital punishment as often as he should have done. It was even said that he had a natural daughter, a certain English girl whom he had befriended and succoured in Rome.

Pole was preparing to defend himself in a public work against these charges, but the new Pope dissuaded him from doing so. Cardinal Caraffa also dissuaded him, and expressed his sorrow that such accusations should have been made against him. Yet Caraffa himself revived some of these accusations against Pole later on, when he became Pope. Meanwhile, Pole betook himself to the Benedictine Monastery of Maguzzano, on Lake Garda.

Early in July, 1553, the short reign of Edward VI came to an end, and after a brief and unsuccessful attempt to put Lady Jane Grey on the throne, the crown of England came to its rightful owner, the Princess Mary, daughter of Catherine of Aragon. The Pope's delight was unbounded, and at once Pole was appointed Legate to England, to bring about that reconciliation with the Holy See which had been so long delayed, but now seemed certain.

The immediate sequel is fairly well known. The dominant power of the Emperor was once more exercised for political reasons, to the detriment of the spiritual welfare of England. The Emperor had conceived the idea of marrying his son Philip to the new Queen of England, and as Pole would probably not favour this match, the Emperor determined to keep him out of England as long as possible. He succeeded in doing so until November, 1554, when, Mary being safely married to Philip, Pole was allowed to land in England to fulfil the mission entrusted to him by the Pope. But it must not be thought that he had done nothing in the meantime. From various places on the Continent, he had taken an active part in purging the Church in England from its Protestant elements, and preparing the way for its reunion with Rome.[1] At long last, the difficulties were all overcome, and Pole had the inexpressible joy of receiving the submission of the kingdom, and of absolving both Parliament and Convocation, and of publicly reconciling the realm to the Holy See, on November 30th, the Feast of St. Andrew.

[1] An account of Pole's activities throughout Mary's reign will be found in the second volume of my work, *The Reformation, the Mass, and the Priesthood.*

Space will not admit of a detailed account of the important work Pole now had to do in England. One matter that occupied his attention was the repression of heresy. The laws against heresy were revived by Parliament, at the request of Convocation, in 1554-5. Some measures against heretics were undoubtedly necessary.[1] But there is no need to suppose that Cardinal Pole thirsted for their blood. His own sentiments on the matter are set forth in a letter he wrote to the Bishop of Augsburg :

" I do not deny, in the case of a man's opinions being extremely pernicious, and he no less industrious to corrupt others than depraved himself, I might say such a one should be capitally punished, and as a rotten member, cut off from the body. But it was my constant declaration that this remedy was not to be applied till every gentler method had been made use of . . . The fact is so notorious that on account of my lenity in punishing erroneous doctrines, I have hardly escaped a suspicion of favouring their cause whose persons I screened."[2]

Pole expressly requested the bishops and clergy " to entreat the people and their flock with all gentleness, and to endeavour to win the people rather by gentleness than by extremity and rigour."[3] But undoubtedly, if all other measures failed, Pole held that the extreme penalty could and should be applied. Even so, he himself took little part in the actual persecution. He pardoned at least three heretics who had been condemned by Bonner. Archbishop Cranmer was one of those who suffered the extreme penalty. At the request of Philip and Mary, Pole was appointed to the See of Canterbury in his place, and somewhat reluctantly, he accepted this arduous post in addition to his office as Legate.

There is one task of Pole's which deserves especial mention, and that is his great plan for a reformation of the newly reconciled English Church. This was evolved in a Convocation in October, 1555, which was almost immediately transformed into a National Synod. Plans were drawn up for a new Catholic translation of the Bible, an authoritative exposition of the Creed, a set of homilies for reading in Churches, etc. But above all, a great Constitution was passed regulating the ecclesiastical life and discipline of the country. Pluralities and other abuses were to cease. The duty of preaching was to be performed regularly by those with the cure of souls, at least on Sundays and holidays. Special care was to be taken by the

---

[1] See my book, *The Reformation, the Mass and the Priesthood*, Vol. II, pp. 156-160.
[2] Pole's *Epistles*, iv, 156.
[3] Foxe, *Book of Martyrs*, VI, pp. 587-8. Collier defends Pole's attitude in *Ecclesiastical Records*, VI, p. 101.

bishops to ensure the suitability of those admitted to holy orders, and steps were taken to root out all simony. The bishops were ordered to set up diocesan seminaries, under the care of the Chancellors of the Cathedrals, and the diocesan benefices were to be taxed for their upkeep. The Constitution also promulgated the Decrees of the General Council of Florence concerning the Primacy of the Roman See, and the doctrines of the Seven Sacraments. If only time had allowed this new Constitution to be put into practical effect, the Catholic Church in England might have proved too powerful for even Elizabeth to shatter and destroy.

But the time was too short. Mary's reign, and Pole's own life, were both drawing rapidly to a close. And Providence had reserved for Pole's latter days the hardest cross of all. Pope Paul IV had quarrelled with Philip of Spain, and very drastically decided to withdraw all Papal legates from his dominions, including Pole from England. Pope Paul—the Cardinal Caraffa who had previously repudiated unworthy suspicions of Pole's integrity, was an old man, and in his old age was displaying much obstinacy, and little wisdom. The rumours of Pole's unorthodoxy were revived, and this time they seem to have been given credence by the Pope.

While we condemn the Pope's unreasonable attitude, and lack of prudence in this matter, we may allow that there were some superficial grounds for this mistrust of Pole, in addition to the earlier accusations which had, though unjustly, been made against him. To begin with, Cardinal Pole while in England had been assisted and advised by Bartholomew Carranza, Archbishop of Toledo, and he had proposed to adopt his Catechism for English use. But Carranza himself had fallen under the suspicion of the Inquisition for unsound views on the subject of Justification. This naturally recalled Pole's own earlier views on the subject, and enemies might suggest that he still retained these views, though they had been condemned at Trent. Again, as Carranza himself pointed out in a letter to Pole, the latter laid himself open to severe criticism by not residing in his See of Canterbury. (Pole rightly urged that business of state kept him much in London.)

In any case, Pope Paul had evidently made up his mind to remove Pole from his Legation. He even summoned him to Rome. Protests from the Queen, Parliament, and the Hierarchy of the whole country were sent to the Pope, but were disregarded. Mary even took the drastic step of forbidding the Pope's messenger to land in this country. But the utmost Pope Paul could be prevailed upon to do was to appoint another Legate in Pole's place, and for this purpose he selected a feeble old Franciscan, utterly unsuitable for the post, who died almost immediately, after vain efforts to decline the honour forced upon him.

Pole at first drew up a strong protest, defending his impugned orthodoxy, but when he had finished it he destroyed it, saying " *Non revelabis pudenda patris tui.*" He did, however, when appealing to the Pope on behalf of his friend Priuli, protest against the way he was being treated, and pointed out the harm that was being done to the cause of Catholicism in England :

> " I am already informed by what steps the enemy begins to triumph in this realm, especially with respect to those proceedings which have been carried on against myself. For whereas I had gathered together my scattered flock chiefly by my own invariable adherence to the faith which I exhorted them to embrace, as soon as it was rumoured that my rectitude in that belief was questioned, the enemies of that cause thought they had an opportunity of calling off the sheep to a greater distance from the voice of the shepherd."[1]

But as his protest was of no effect, Pole retired to his See of Canterbury, and ceased to exercise any Legatine functions. Pope Paul IV's strange and unwise conduct did tremendous harm to the Catholic cause in England, and it is not altogether surprising that when Archbishop Heath, of York, spoke against the Supremacy Bill introduced into Elizabeth's first Parliament, he remarked :

> " If by this our relinquishing of the See of Rome there were none other matter therein than a withdrawing of our obedience from the Pope's person, Paul the fourth of that name, who hath declared himself to be a very austere stern father unto us ever since his first entrance into Peter's Chair, then the cause were not of such great importance as it is in very deed."[2]

The end was at hand. Mary died on November 17th, 1558, at 7 o'clock in the morning, and Cardinal Pole, her faithful cousin, died later on the same day, at the age of 58. His great friend Priuli said that—

> " As in health that sainted soul was ever turned towards God, so likewise in this long and troublesome infirmity did it continue thus until his end, which he made so placidly that he seemed to sleep rather than to die."

One of Pole's last acts was to send a messenger to the Princess

---

[1] Pole's *Epistles*, V, 31.
[2] See my book, *The Reformation, the Mass and the Priesthood*, Vol. II, p.193. Heath goes on to explain that the Supremacy Bill meant that they " must forsake and fly from the Unity of Christ's Church, and by leaping out of Peter's Ship, hazard ourselves to be overwhelmed and drowned in the waters of schism, sects, and divisions." *Ibid. :* Heath, like all Catholics, made a clear distinction between Papal authority in itself, and an unwise use of Papal power.

Elizabeth, with a note. The letter is extant, but we do not know the nature of the verbal message. We can however easily guess that it was an exhortation to Elizabeth to keep the Catholic Faith which she had professed during her sister's reign. But Elizabeth decided otherwise.

Pole was duly buried in his Cathedral of Canterbury, not far from the Shrine of St. Thomas. But his brick tomb has been woefully neglected. Cardinal Vaughan presented a panel, which now hangs over the tomb, with Pole's armorial bearings.

Dr. Parker, the new Archbishop of Canterbury, described Cardinal Pole as " *carnifex et flagellum ecclesiæ anglicanæ*." That verdict would be repudiated as manifestly unjust by all right-minded people, and there can be little doubt that Reginald Cardinal Pole was one of the noblest of men, and one of the greatest Archbishops that sat in the Chair of St. Augustine.

Bibliographical Note.—The standard English biography of Cardinal Pole is that by " Martin Haile " (Mary Hallè). The article on Pole by James Gairdner in the *Dictionary of National Biography* is also invaluable. Both have been consulted in the present study.

VERA BARCLAY

ST. TERESA

(*Born at Avila, Castille*)

A.D. 1515–1582

AFTER FOUR YEARS of enclosure in the first little convent of the
Reform, St. Teresa writes : " As time went on, my desires to be
of some good to some soul somewhere went on increasing ; and I
often felt like someone who is in charge of a great treasure and desires
that all should benefit by it, but his hands are tied so that he cannot
give it out . . . And so it is that when we read in the lives of the
saints how they converted souls, it raises in me more ardour, more
emotion, and more emulation than all the martyrdoms which they
suffered ; for this is the disposition which the Lord has given me."

Is it not true to say that this is the disposition which the Lord gave
to all " great Catholics " ? Without it they would probably still have
been great—but not great Catholics. That is why St. Teresa will be
shown in this study, not as a great mystic or a great writer (the aspects
under which she is best known) but as one greatly active " for the
good of souls," to use her own expression.

I shall not try to give an outline of St. Teresa's life as a whole. My
aim will be to help the reader form a freshened and more vivid picture
of St. Teresa herself—not by the methods of the portrait painter, but
rather in the way one might collect a number of intimate and
characteristic snapshots of a great personality and arrange them with
care in an album. Those who turned its pages would feel their memory
refreshed and their affection stimulated.

The snapshots in this case are the lively accounts St. Teresa has left
us of the small as well as the great events of her very active life. We
are fortunate in possessing them. How many of the saints lose not
only their charm but their own identity as the hagiographer presents
them to us, more concerned with our edification than with the writing
of history or the true portrayal of character.[1]

---

[1] In the case of St. Teresa, it is rather the portrait painters who fail to do her
justice. That she was beautiful we know. But none of the portraits given in lives
of her suggest this. We have her own comment on one of these. She sat for it by

140

The point of the present study, then, is to let her speak for herself as far as possible. The quotations will not be taken from the " Life," which she wrote in obedience to her directors for their use in guiding her, but from her later book, *The Foundations*. This was also written in obedience, but was intended, not for the scrutiny of puzzled spiritual directors, but as a book to be read by her own nuns—which makes the style more lively and more personal. And as in writing this book she drew largely on the log of her journeys, and wrote the final chapters while she was actually engaged in the work, the accounts are more vivid than those for which she had only her memory to draw on. She wrote quickly, in moments snatched from busy days, without reading over what she had written. This gives her style freshness and spontaneity.[1]

The quotations are not meant to give a complete account of any of the foundations, but simply to show St. Teresa in action, journeying, buying houses, dealing with scores of individuals of very varying types, and talking to our Lord about it all as to the constant companion of her journeys and, indeed, the instigator of her incredible doings.

St. Teresa's great longing to work for the good of souls was answered by our Lord with the words, " Wait a little, my daughter, and you shall see great things." The words puzzled her. But six months later she understood their meaning, when the General of the Carmelites visited St. Joseph's at Avila, and delighted with this return to the primitive ideals óf the order, gave Teresa licences to found more convents. Here is St. Teresa's description of her arrival with six nuns and her faithful chaplain, Father Julian of Avila, at midnight, to found the first of her new convents in a town—Medina de Campo—where the project was looked upon as "great folly." It was important, she felt, to take possession of the house secretly, and be fully established before break of day.

" We arrived at midnight, and alighted at St. Anne's, so as not to make any noise, and went on foot to the house. It was just the time when the bulls which were to fight next day were being driven to the enclosure, and it was a great mercy that some of them did not toss us." They entered the *patio*. The local Carmelite Prior who had found the house for them had said the entrance could be adapted as a chapel. " The walls looked to me very ruinous, but not so bad as by daylight I afterwards saw them to be. The Lord seems to have been

---

obedience, and when at last she saw the result of the clumsy lay-brother's work, she laughed and said, " God forgive you, Brother John ; after making me go through no one knows what, you have turned me out ugly and blear-eyed." It is a pity her death-mask is not better known.

[1] For English readers a good deal of the charm depends upon which translation is used. I shall give extracts from the *History of the Foundations*, published by the Cambridge University Press.

pleased to blind that good father so that he should not see how unfit
it was to place the Blessed Sacrament there " (the Lord evidently
being on the side of the reckless—a favourite thought of St. Teresa's).
" I went to see the entrance. There was a good deal of earth to be
shovelled out ; it had an open roof, and the walls were unplastered.
The night was short, and we had only brought with us a few hangings—
I think three—which were not nearly enough to cover the length of
the entrance, and I did not know what to do, for I saw it was not fit
to set an altar there. It pleased the Lord—for He desired that it should
be done at once—that the lady's steward had in his house a great
deal of tapestry of hers, and some blue damask bed-hangings ;
and she had told him to give us anything we wanted ; for she was
very good. When I saw such good furnishing, I gave praise to
the Lord, and so did the others. We did not know what to do for
nails, nor could we buy any at that hour ; but we hunted in the walls,
and at last with a good deal of trouble we found plenty. Some put
up the hangings ; we nuns cleaned the floor ; and we worked with such
a will that when morning dawned the altar was set up, and the little
bell in a passage ; and Mass was said at once. . . .

" Up to this time I was very happy, for it is my greatest pleasure to
see one more church where the Blessed Sacrament is reserved. But
my joy was short-lived ; for when Mass was over, I went to look at the
patio through a little window, and I saw that all the walls were fallen
to the ground in places, so that it would take many days to repair
them."

The Blessed Sacrament had been reserved. " *Oh valamé Dios !*
What anguish filled my heart," writes St. Teresa at that memory,
for the tabernacle was practically in the street. " And together with
this arose in my mind all the difficulties which those who disapproved
of our venture had spoken of, and I saw clearly that they were right.
It seemed impossible to go forward with what I had begun." She
was even tempted to doubt that it was God's will at all, and to think she
had been deluded by the devil. " Of all the burden of distress which
weighed me down I said nothing to my companions, because I did not
want to give them any more distress than they already had. I went
on in this unhappiness until the evening, when the Jesuits sent a
Father to see me, who greatly comforted and encouraged me."

All St. Teresa's foundations for nuns were dedicated to St. Joseph,
to whom she had a great devotion. And he seems in almost every
case to have lived up to the traditional idea that if you seek St.
Joseph's help he will play a practical joke on you by apparently letting
you down and then making things come right after all. While we are
on this question of St. Teresa's bad moments before each new success,
some other passages may be given even though they belong to later

foundations. Her way of writing about them shows her real humility—
to her, one of the two essential virtues (the other being charity).

For instance, there is the time heavy rain threatened to swamp a
great occasion. " I kept on lamenting, and I said to our Lord,
as it were complaining, that I would He would either not command
me to engage in these works, or would set this trouble right. That
good man Nicholas Gutierrez . . . told me very gently, not to distress
myself, for God would set it right. And so it was : for on Michaelmas
Day, at the time when the people were to come, the sun began to
shine. This moved me to devotion, and I saw how much better that
dear good man had done with his trust than I with my worry."

On another occasion St. Teresa admits to " creeps." It was on
All Hallow-e'en, at Salamanca. A friend provided a house for the
foundation, but this was occupied by students, and they were only
cleared out the day St. Teresa and her companion took possession,
leaving the place in a filthy condition.

" The night of All Saints I and my companion remained in the
house alone. I can tell you, sisters, that it makes me inclined to
laugh when I think of the terror of my companion, Maria of the Sacrament, who was a nun older than I, a great servant of God. The house
was very large and rambling, and had many garrets, and my companion
could not get the students out of her head, thinking that, as they were
so angry at having to go out of the house, one of them might have
hidden in it. They could very well have done so as regards hiding
places. We locked ourselves into a room where there was straw,
which was the first thing I had provided for founding the house,
because with its aid we could do without a bed. We slept in it that
night with a blanket apiece which had been lent us.

" When my companion found herself locked into that room, she
seemed a little reassured as to the students ; yet notwithstanding,
she did nothing but look from one side to the other ; and the evil spirit
must have helped to put thoughts of dangers into her mind in order
to upset me ; for with my weak heart, a little suffices. I asked her
why she was looking about when nobody could get in. She said,
' Mother, I am thinking, if I died here° now, what would you do all
alone ? ' This, if it should come to pass, seemed to me a dreadful
thing. It made me reflect a little, and be frightened too ; for even
when I am not nervous, dead bodies always give me a curious feeling,
even when I am not alone. And with the tolling of the bells into
the bargain—for, as I said, it was the night of All Saints—the devil
got a good start for making us lose our wits with childish trifles. When
he sees that people are not afraid of him himself, he seeks other devices.
I answered her : ' Sister, when this comes to pass, I will think what
to do ; now let me go to sleep.' As we had had two bad nights, sleep

soon drove away our fears. Next day they were ended by the arrival of more nuns."

We have seen that Campo de Medina was the first new convent founded. Before St. Teresa began this foundation, however, her mind had been full of a more ambitious project. No sooner had the General departed than she sent an express letter after him, urging the importance of starting monasteries of the primitive rule for friars (a project of which the Bishop of Avila had spoken to him). Her very eloquent letter moved him to send her licence to found two, as long as the present and late provincials agreed.

Busy and distracted as she had been at Medina, "while I was there," she writes, " I was always thinking over the monasteries of friars ; and since, as I said, I had not one friar, I did not know what to do. So I determined to talk to the Prior[1] about it in strict confidence, to see what he would advise ; and so I did."

What follows gives us a glimpse of St. Teresa in conversation, and her genius for understanding individual people and dealing with them appropriately (even if sometimes a little astonishingly). There are several conversations with this delightful and quixotic prior, and comments on his actions. We can hear them both laughing ; or see Teresa smiling at her thoughts of him.

When he had heard of Teresa's wish to found a monastery for friars " he was very glad and promised to be the first himself. I took this for a jest, and so I told him : for although he was a very good brother . . . recollected and very studious and a lover of his cell, and was learned, I thought he would not have the energy, nor be able to endure the necessary hardships for he was delicate and not used to them." He assured her he would, and was indeed thinking of becoming a Carthusian. " For all this I was not quite satisfied ; and I asked him to let us put it off for some time, during which he should practise the things which he would have to promise ; and so he did." A year passed so, in which the Prior had many troubles, and also " made great progress." Then turned up a young friar, later to be known as St. John of the Cross, who delighted St. Teresa, and promised to join the Reform. " When I saw I already had two friars to begin with, I thought the thing already done ! However, as I was not altogether satisfied with the Prior, and also we had nowhere to commence, I waited some time." (She used to call them her " friar and a half," because St. John of the Cross was so very small).

A good man offered a very small house in the country for the purpose of making a start with the friars. St. Teresa with one sister and Father Julian set out, and after tramping all day looking for it, found it at nightfall, " in such a condition of extreme dirtiness that we

[1] Fray Antonio de Heredia, Prior of the Carmelites at Medina.

dared not spend the night there." It consisted of an entrance, one room, a kitchen and a garret. She at once saw the entrance as a chapel, the attic as a choir for saying office (it had " squints " into the entrance, which went up to the roof) and the room to sleep in. Her companion was horrified, and said, " Assuredly, mother, there is no one, however good, whose spirit could stand this ; do not think of it." And Father Julian thought the same.

When, however, the Prior (now Fray Antonio) heard about it " he answered . . . that he was ready to live not only there, but in a pigsty. Fray Juan of the Cross was of the same mind."

It was not the poverty of the place that made Teresa think it so propitious for the great venture (she never chose the uncomfortable for preference, and she abhorred dirt and unhealthy conditions) but she knew human nature and she felt sure the Provincials would not give leave " if they saw us in a well-appointed house ; but in that little place and house they would think it did not matter."

While Fray Antonio started to get together what he could for the new house, Fray Juan of the Cross accompanied St. Teresa to Valladolid, where she visited the Provincial—" an old man, of very good stuff and straightforward. . . . I said so much to him of the account he would have to give to God if he hindered so good a work, and His Majesty so disposed him to agree, that he softened greatly towards our projects."

Fray Juan went back to prepare the house and Fray Antonio came to speak to St. Teresa at Valladolid, " very happy, and told me what he had got. It was very little. Only with hour-glasses was he well provided—for he was taking five—to my great amusement. He said he did not like to go without the means of keeping the appointed hours. I do not believe he had got anything to sleep on." He resigned his priorship, and " went off to his little house with the greatest content in the world." During Advent the first Mass was said there, and the first monastery of Barefoot Friars was an accomplished fact. " In the following Lent," writes St. Teresa, " when I was going to the foundation of Toledo, I went that way. I arrived one morning. Father Antonio was cleaning out the doorway of the chapel, with the happy face which he always has. I said to him, ' How is this, Father ? What has become of your dignity ? ' He answered, telling me of his great happiness in these words : ' I execrate the time when I possessed it ! '

" As I entered the chapel, I stood amazed to see the spirit which the Lord had inspired there ; and not only I, but two merchants, friends of mine, who had come with me from Medina, who did nothing but shed tears. There were so many crosses, so many skulls ! I shall never forget a small wooden cross there was for holy water, which had fastened to it a paper image of Christ which seemed to excite more devotion than if it had been of the finest workmanship. The Office Choir was the garret, half of which was lofty enough for standing to say the hours ; but they had to stoop a great deal to enter it and to hear Mass. They had made at two extreme corners next the chapel two hermitages, where they could only be prostrate or sitting : these were filled with hay, because the place was very cold, and the roof was close over their heads ; they had two openings facing the altar, and two stones to rest their heads on ; and there were their crosses and skulls. I found that when Matins was finished they did not go away again before Prime, but remained there in prayer, so absorbed in it that sometimes when they returned to their places for Prime their habits were covered with snow, and they had not noticed it."

They were joined by two other friars. "They used to go to preach at many neighbouring places which were destitute of any teaching ; and that was another reason why I was pleased that the house should have been founded in that place. . . . In so short a time they had gained such esteem that it gave me the greatest joy when I heard of it." They used to go barefoot two leagues, to preach and hear confessions, " in much snow and frost. . . . They were so happy that they minded all this very little."

At Toledo great objections were raised to a foundation. St. Teresa and several nuns lived in lodgings while negotiations were going on. A house was found for them by a very poor young man, called Andrada, a student, whom a Franciscan friar who had heard his confession, sent to help them—though when he first presented himself, " it amused me much," says St. Teresa, " and my companions more, to see what sort of assistance the holy man had sent us." Andrada " thought it an easy thing " to find a house, and the very next day spoke to Teresa at Mass, saying he had got a house, and here were the keys. Soon after, he reported that the nuns could take their furniture in. " I told him there was but little to be done, since we possessed nothing but two mattresses and a blanket. He must have been astonished. My companions were vexed at my telling him."

" We went on some days with the mattresses and the blanket, without more to cover us, and one day we had not even a bit of wood enough to broil a sardine, when the Lord moved someone—I know not whom—to put in chapel for us a little faggot, with which we did better. At night we suffered a little from cold, for it was cold ; however, we covered ourselves with the blanket and with the serge cloaks which we wore over our habit, which have often been useful to us."

St. Teresa adds that this extreme destitution taught them the sweetness of poverty ; and that when rich friends supplied all their needs, they felt very sad, and the sisters said : " What is the matter, Mother, that we seem to be no longer poor ? "

"From that time forward there grew within me the desire to be very poor."

Cheerfulness in bearing hardships always appealed strongly to St. Teresa. On the journey to Seville it was the heat that tested their spirit. "I can tell you, sisters, that when the whole force of the sun was beating down on the carts [covered wagons] going into them was like going into a purgatory. What with sometimes thinking of hell, at other times feeling that they were doing and suffering something for God, the sisters travelled very contentedly and cheerfully." Of a good priest who accompanied her on a journey that was not only dangerous on account of precipices but most annoying because of the faithless and inefficient guides, she writes, "his goodness was so deeply rooted that I do not think I ever saw him out of temper : which made me marvel much and thank God that temptations have so little power when anyone is radically good."

On another journey her ever faithful Father Julian comes in for a little bit of sarcasm, however. At Seville they found themselves mixed up in a great popular festival when they had hoped to hear Mass quietly, one Sunday morning.

"When I saw this I was greatly concerned ; and to my thinking it would have been better to go away without hearing Mass than go down into such a hurly-burly. Father Julian thought not ; and as he is a theologian, we sisters all had to bow to his judgment ; for the rest of our escort perhaps would have followed mine, which would have been very improper." It would have been wiser, though, for the sight of their habits promptly raised a great commotion among the people. "I can tell you, daughters . . . it was for me one of the worst moments that I have ever passed, for the uproar among the people was as if bulls had come into the church." They had to be locked into a chapel.

It was always when her nuns were involved in dangers that she was troubled. They were truly like so many beloved children to her. In one place she writes, "I can tell you that, loving my daughters so deeply, it has not been my smallest cross to have to quit them when I went away from one place to another, especially when I thought that I should not return to see them, and I saw their great emotion and weeping : for though they are detached from other things, this detachment God has not given them—perhaps in order to give me the keener pain. For no more am I detached from them. . . ."

The dangers and discomforts of St. Teresa's journeys are beyond our imagining—broiling heat, precipices, floods, and, almost worst of all, the inns. She would proceed with these journeys even though suffering from severe fever ; and some of the most trying of them took place when she was over sixty. After describing the journey to Burgos, one of the most dangerous she ever undertook, she writes,

" I myself was suffering from a very bad sore throat : the pain was so severe that it prevented me from entering as I otherwise should into the amusement of the adventures of the journey."

It is worth quoting some rather long passages on this question of suffering, for in them St. Teresa lets us into her confidence even more intimately than usual.

The Bishop of Palencia had asked her to make two foundations, one at Palencia and one at Burgos. While at Valladolid she caught an epidemic that sounds very much like our influenza, especially in its after effects. The illness left her " with so little energy and feeling it so impossible to do anything," that she began to oppose the idea of these foundations. Looking back on it she says,

" It frightens and grieves me—and I often complain of it to our Lord—to see what a great share the poor soul has in the weakness of the body ; so that it appears to have nothing to do but observe its rules, laid down according to its needs and sufferings. This seems to me one of the greatest troubles and miseries of this life, when the spirit is not so high as to master it. For I reckoned nothing to be ill and suffer great pain—though it is a trial—if the soul is vigorous ; for the soul knows that this comes from the hand of God and continues to praise Him. But to be on the one hand suffering and on the other inactive is a fearful state, especially for a soul which has experienced strong desires never to rest inwardly or outwardly, but wholly to employ itself in the service of its great God. There is no help for it in this state but in patience and the confession of its own wretchedness, and in resigning itself to God's will, to be made use of as He pleases and for what ends He pleases. This was my condition at that time : for although I was already convalescent, yet I was so weak that I had lost even the confidence which God is wont to give me when I have to begin any of these foundations. Everything seemed impossible to me. . . ."

A few pages on she writes something that draws a useful distinction between the determination always to do God's will (which never falters in the saints) and the kind of zeal which may well wax and wane even in such dynamic saints as Teresa.

" One day, while in doubt and not resolved to make either foundation, I besought our Lord, just after my Communion, to give me light, that I might do His will in everything : for my lukewarmness was not such as to make me falter one hair's breadth in this desire." The words she heard in answer tell us the secret of her truly supernatural endurance.

" Our Lord said to me, as it were reproaching me, ' What dost thou fear ? When have I ever failed thee ? What I have always been, the same am I now. Thou must not fail to make these two foundations.' O Great God, how different are Thy words from human words ! These words left me with such resolution and spirit that the whole world would not have been strong enough to oppose me ; and I began at once to set to work, and the Lord to give me the means."

The foundation at Palencia was duly made ; and then came the journey to Burgos, the Provincial accompanying the party. There were bad floods. " It was really foolhardy to set out from Palencia when we did. It is true that our Lord had said to me that we could very well go, that I need not fear, for He would be with us. I did not tell this to the Father Provincial at the time ; but to me it gave assurances in the great difficulties and dangers which we met with." At a certain crossing called the Pontoons " the water was so high that the passage could not be seen or guessed at. . . . To see ourselves go into a world of water without a way or a boat, even though our Lord had given me an assurance, I was not without fear. What then must my companions have felt." It is interesting to see from these two passages that St. Teresa did not confide even to those intimate companions in their great danger the words of Christ which she had heard in prayer. From the frequency with which she quotes these in her writings one might have imagined her speaking of them.

The terrible journey was rewarded by opposition being unexpectedly raised to the foundation. This makes St. Teresa write, " O my Lord, when anyone has done Thee some service, how certain it is to be at once repaid with a heavy cross ! And what a precious reward it is to those who truly love Thee, if once it is given us to realise its value ! But " (she adds with her usual candour) " that time we did not welcome our gain, because it seemed to make everything impossible."

The difficulties were raised by the Archbishop himself. " The Archbishop always said that he desired the foundation more than anyone ; and I believe it : for he is such a good Christian that he would not say it if it were not true. His conduct did not show it ; for he imposed conditions which, to all appearance, we could not possibly fulfil : this was the devil's device to prevent the foundation. But, O Lord, how well it is shown that Thou art mighty ! For the very means which he devised to stop it, Thou didst adopt for making it better. Blessed be Thou for ever ! "

St. Teresa was, as usual, more concerned for others than for her own disappointment. " I was grieved for the distress of the Father Provincial, and very sorry that he had come with us. . . . While I was in this trouble . . . our Lord, without my being in prayer, said to me these words, ' Now, Teresa, stand firm '."

Several very trying months followed, during which various friends bestirred themselves on St. Teresa's behalf. A wealthy lady, Catalina de Tolosa, provided the endowment and constantly visited the nuns in the draughty attic where they were lodged. " And because of this people kept continually saying disagreeable things to her. . . . She answered with a prudence which she possesses abundantly, and bore it so well that it showed God was teaching her the art of pleasing some and putting up with others, and was giving her courage to bear it all. How much more courage for great things have the servants of God than the high-born people who are not His servants !—not but that Catalina herself was of the purest descent ; for she is very much of a hidalgo."

At last a house was found, with the help of a man who became a great friend of Teresa's—the licentiate, Aguiar. " We may truly say that, under God, it was he who gave us the house. A good head for business is worth much. His is first rate ; and God gave him the good will." Of the house he helped to find she writes, " Well did our Lord repay us for what we had been through, by bringing us into a paradise—for with its garden, its views, and its water it seems no less. . . . The Archbishop heard of it immediately, and was delighted that all had turned out so well, and put it down to his own obstinacy—and quite rightly." ·

The convent was duly founded, and a High Mass sung by a Dominican Prior, " with great magnificence of musicians, who came of their own accord. All our friends were rejoicing, and so was almost the whole city. . . . The joy of the good Catalina de Toloso and of the sisters was so great as to move my devotion."

And then follow some words on enclosure that are well worth quoting.

" No one who has not experienced it could believe the fullness of satisfaction we feel in these foundations when at length we find ourselves enclosed where no secular person may enter ; for however dearly we may love them, it does not prevent us from being delighted to find ourselves alone. It seems to me like as when a number of fishes are taken out of the river in a net, which cannot live unless they are put back into the water. So it is with souls which are used to living within the flowing waters of their Spouse : when they are drawn out thence and find themselves in the net of worldly affairs, they really do cease to live until they find themselves back again. This I see always in all these sisters."

The quotations given will have helped the reader to form some idea of St. Teresa's personality—her courage and childlike simplicity, her sympathy for others, her humour, her great practical good sense, and her almost audacious optimism. But perhaps the most striking effect of reading her story in her own words instead of in those of the reverential biographer, is that they make us feel, as no comment could do, the essential humility of great saints.

Burgos was the last foundation St. Teresa made and she finished writing the *Fundaciones* while she was there. Her last painful journey was soon to begin, and she had not many months more to live. Praying about her new family she heard the words : " '. . . Thou mayest safely depart.' I at once arranged to be going, for I felt I was no longer doing anything here, except enjoying myself in this house which I so much like ; while elsewhere, although with more difficulty, I might be doing more good." Words which are a fitting conclusion to this study, for they are almost the same as those with which we began, and they show us St. Teresa in the same mind as when she set out on her great adventure, twenty years before.

ST. CHARLES BORROMEO

A.D. 1538–1584

THE DIOCESE OF Milan numbers among its bishops thirty-five canonized saints. It claims as its principal patron the great St. Ambrose, Father and Doctor of the Universal Church. The blood of illustrious martyrs has sanctified its soil—SS. Gervasius and Protasius, St. Victor, SS. Nabor and Felix, SS. Nazarius and Celsus, but St. Charles Borromeo is its special pride. In him it honours a pastor who not only restored its ancient glories but who, in the short space of twenty years, accomplished a work that has made him for all time the perfect pattern of the Christian episcopate. To his own flock at Milan and indeed to the whole Catholic world he is the living realization of the priestly ideal, a great bishop who in his days pleased God and was found just.

He was born in an age when some people used to say " If you want to go to Hell become a priest." It is hard for us to realise the dreadful state of religion in the early part of the sixteenth century. For instance, until St. Charles took possession of his See in 1565 no Archbishop had resided at Milan for eighty years. The non-residence of bishops was one of the crying abuses removed by the Council of Trent, as was also the plurality of benefices. No one seemed to mind if one prelate held the revenues of a dozen abbeys or if a mere child were head of a religious house. Charles himself was twelve years old when his uncle Giulio Cesare Borromeo handed over to him the Abbey of Arona with its revenue of thirteen thousand pounds a year and the boy startled his father by insisting that the money should be spent on the poor. As for the clergy, secular and regular, the lives of many of them were openly scandalous. They walked the streets in lay dress complete with sword and pistol. Churches were in a half-ruinous condition, the sacred vessels corroded with rust, the vestments moth-eaten. The Cathedral of Milan was a public thoroughfare for traders and their cattle. In country districts the priests lived in open concubinage and regarded Confession as necessary only for the laity. Many of them did not even know the formula of absolution. It is not surprising that many of the laity went to the

Sacraments once in ten or fifteen years, perhaps never at all, and that the poor did not know the Pater or Ave or even how to make the Sign of the Cross. Religious houses, monasteries and convents were equally lax, if not more so. When afterwards as Archbishop Charles tried to reform the Fratres Umiliati, three members of the Order who were actually rectors of churches, hired a deacon to assassinate him. The attempt failed, but not through any fault on the part of the brethren !

In sharp contrast to all this spiritual squalor the Borromean household was a model of solid piety. Count Gilbert, the father of Charles, used to recite the Divine Office daily, went to the Sacraments every week—an extraordinary thing in those days—and carried the virtue of almsgiving almost to excess. Countess Margaret, sister of John Angelo Cardinal de Medici, afterwards Pope Pius IV, was a devout Christian woman. She died, however, when Charles was nine years old. The territory by Lake Maggiore, the Castle of Arona and the palace in Milan formed the family estate, to which Frederick, being the elder son, was heir. To Charles there were only two possible careers, the Army or the Church. He had been tonsured at the age of seven and so was technically a cleric. At twelve as we have seen, he was Abbot of the Benedictine Abbey of Arona. Two years later he entered the University of Pavia. Intellectually he was not brilliant, but he had a tremendous capacity for hard work, not at all a bad asset in a young man with ambition, especially when coupled with noble birth and powerful family influence. His career was assured. At twenty-one he was a Doctor of Civil and Canon Law. But there was more to come. At the end of December, 1559, his mother's brother ascended the Papal Throne. Charles came to Rome for the Coronation and the very day after his arrival was appointed Protonotary-Apostolic and Administrator of the Archdiocese of Milan. Dignities and offices began to fall like rain. In quick succession he became Legate of Bologna, Ancona and the Marches, which brought a handsome revenue. He received also an annual grant of a thousand crowns from the diocese of Ferrara. On January 31st, 1560, the Pope created him Cardinal Deacon of the title of SS. Vito and Modesto ; then Papal Secretary of State, Grand Penitentiary, Protector of Portugal, Lower Germany, the Catholic Swiss Cantons, the Orders of Franciscans, Carmelites, Umiliati and others. Charles Borromeo was at this time just over twenty-two years of age.

It would be difficult to imagine a more unpromising preparation for sainthood. Yet the signs had not been wanting. Pius IV, with his Lombard commonsense, his shrewd judgment of men born of a wide experience of many countries, had not acted without knowledge of his nephew's character. The stocky, round figure of the Pope was a

familiar sight in Rome striding beside that of the tall young Cardinal
with the blue eyes and big nose and the rather pale smooth face, for,
as the servants complained, he scarcely gave himself time to eat or
sleep.   The talk was on one topic, reform and the necessity of re-
opening the Council of Trent.   The Council had lingered with many
interruptions since its first session fifteen years ago (December 13th,
1545).   Four or five times the sittings had been suspended, once with
an interval of four years.   It had last met at Trent in 1551, ten years
ago, and the obstacles in the way of a resumption were almost
insuperable.   To Charles as Secretary of State the Pope entrusted the
work of reassembling the Council and of superintending its actions.
Though devoid of any diplomatic experience he succeeded in overcoming the objections of Germany, France, Spain and Switzerland
and at last in January, 1562, the Council, consisting of two Cardinals,
one hundred and six bishops, four mitred abbots and four generals of
religious orders met at Trent.   The deliberations lasted almost two
years and during this time the whole guidance of the Holy See over the
Council passed through Borromeo's hands.   Thirty-five thousand
letters written in his long sloping hand bear witness to days and nights
of restless labour, to infinite patience and tact and an intense
application not only to large issues, but to minutest details.   The
confirmation of the Council by the Constitution *Benedictus Deus* in
January, 1564, and the publication of the Catechism of the Council
of Trent brought Charles's career in Rome to an end.   On the death
of his elder brother he had had himself ordained priest, much against
the advice of his uncle who was anxious for the Borromean line.
He was consecrated Archbishop of Milan on the feast of St. Ambrose,
1563, and after the death of Pius IV three years later, persuaded the
new Pope, St. Pius V, to allow him to reside in Milan among the flock
he so ardently longed to serve.   He had visited his diocese a few
months previously and during a stay of some nine weeks had managed
to hold his first Provincial Council.   The Conclave had necessitated
his return to Rome, but in April, 1566, he re-entered Milan.   Thus at
the age of twenty-seven he began to exercise the fulness of the Pastoral
Office.

The diocese was one of the largest in Italy, extending over a hundred
miles on its northern side towards Germany and comprising the Duchy
of Monteferrato, parts of Venice and Switzerland.   Southwards it
stretched to the shores of the Mediterranean.   It contained two
thousand two hundred churches, three thousand clergy, one hundred
communities of men and ninety convents of women.   Twenty of the
latter Charles subsequently suppressed.   All told there were some
six hundred thousand souls under his care.

For the remaining eighteen years of his life the driving force behind all his activities was his high ideal of the priestly state. He clearly saw that our great High Priest in laying upon the Apostles His own priesthood imposed also the obligation of walking in His footsteps and imitating Him ; that His Priests were to be living images of Himself, other Christs manifesting His own Divine perfection, communicating it to others, perpetuating it to the end of the world, and that consequently the priesthood is not a state instrumental to the acquisition of perfection, but of its very nature imposes the obligation of exercising a Christlike perfection already presupposed. All this Charles perceived with a wisdom and a discernment that was the fruit of a growing union with God in prayer. His life, in public and private had always been blameless. Even the sharp-witted Romans, keen critics of clerical conduct had had no fault to find. But for some time, especially since the death of his brother, he had begun to devote himself more and more to the service of God. He had made over to the Sovereign Pontiff the revenues of twelve benefices, resigned the Principality of Oria with its yearly income of ten thousand ducats, bestowed the Marquisate of Romagnano on one of his relatives and sold his three armed galleys and even the valuable furniture he had brought from Rome. The proceeds of the sales went to the poor. His object was to free himself from everything that would in any way interfere with the exercise of the pastoral office. In contrast with this vision of the exalted dignity and dreadful responsibilities of the priesthood he saw how many bishops and priests had abandoned the high standard of their state. The light that was to shine before men was rapidly becoming dim, the salt was losing its savour, and the world in consequence was threatened with ruin. With all the energies of his mind and heart Charles determined to restore to the priesthood its light and savour that men might live enlightened by its brightness, seasoned by its purity. This determination found its concrete expression in the six Provincial Councils and the eleven Diocesan Synods which he held in the course of his episcopate, the record of which is contained in the Acts of the Church of Milan, a monumental collection of ecclesiastical and spiritual legislation unique in the history of episcopal government. These Acts include also his minute regulations for numerous Confraternities and especially for the Congregation of Oblates of St. Ambrose, rules for his own household, edicts on the discipline of clergy and laity in general, on the manner of observing Feasts, Vigils, Synods and so forth, instructions as to preaching, administration of the Sacraments, fabric of Churches, etc. In fact Charles effected nothing less than a precise and perfect application of the decrees of the Council of Trent to the whole complex system of provincial and diocesan administration. The spirit which animated his reforms is manifest in the address which the young archbishop made to his suffragans and clergy at the second Provincial Council : " Fathers, this is our duty and our office, placed as we are in the exalted seat of episcopal dignity, to look out for dangers as from a watch-tower, and to repel them when they threaten those who are resting under our charge and care. As parents we ought to have a fatherly oversight of our sons ; as pastors never to take our eyes off the sheep which Jesus Christ has delivered by his holy death from the mouth of hell ; and if any are being corrupted by the impurity of vice, to heal them with the sharpness of salt ; if any be wandering in moral darkness, we ought to hold the light before them ; for as the Supreme Creator of all things, when in the beginning He made the Heavens which we behold, adorned them with a multitude of stars illuminated by the splendour of the sun to shine by night upon the earth, so in the spiritual renewal of this world He has placed in the Church, as in the firmament of Heaven, prophets and apostles, pastors and doctors who, like stars illuminated by the light of Christ Our Lord, the everlasting Sun, preside over the darkness of this clouded world, to drive away darkness from the minds of men by the splendour of a noble and holy discipline."

It is impossible in such a brief sketch to give an adequate idea of the difficulties with which Charles had to contend in carrying out his work of reform. There were three principal sources of opposition, the clergy, the civil authorities of Milan and the people. The first two were by far the most troublesome. The majority of his colleagues in the episcopate had long been accustomed to reside at a distance from their Sees and to live in princely fashion on the revenues of their numerous benefices. One bishop in answer to Charles's demand that he should return to his See declared that he would not have enough to do. The lesser clergy, secular and regular, were in a worse condition since to the scandal of non-residence many added that of flagrant immorality. On one occasion the Archbishop met with physical violence, the Canons of La Scala barricading the doors against him and firing on the Archiepiscopal cross. Again, but for Divine intervention he would have been murdered at the altar by the Fratres Umiliati. The great plague broke out in 1576 and hundreds of the clergy fled in panic, leaving the stricken populace without Mass or Sacraments. Charles gathered around him the few priests who were willing to stay and face the danger. It was the example of his own life and character that gave them courage and where he led they followed, ready if necessary to lay down their lives. He supplemented the little band with priests from religious Orders, principally Capuchins from the Swiss Cantons, and bishop and priests together, in perfect unity of self-oblation, gave themselves as living sacrifice to the service of their Divine Master. In this voluntary and complete offering of self, inspired by the love of souls for God's sake, Charles saw the return of the old ideal of sacerdotal perfection, the ideal portrayed by the Good Shepherd Who did not hesitate to offer His life for the sheep and Who requires a like offering of those on whom He stamps the sacred character of His priesthood. It was a renewal of the law of the priestly life, a new stirring of the vital impulse inherent in the divinely instituted organism which was to work on the souls of men, assimilating them to itself, transforming them into the likeness of its own Divine Exemplar.

In the year after the plague, 1578, Charles founded his Congregation of Oblates, a body of secular priests who, as the name implies, offered themselves by a voluntary promise to obey him and his successors in the service of the diocese. The Congregation was the logical outcome of his deep, penetrating vision of the relationship between the Pastoral Office and the Priesthood in the universal cure of souls. The universal cure of souls demands an intimate mutual relationship between the priesthood and the episcopate ; on the part of the priesthood, of willing obedience and close personal co-operation ; on the part of the episcopate, of prudent guidance and fatherly solicitude. It is therefore a relationship of pastoral authority and priestly obedience based on a common duty and responsibility towards the flock of Jesus Christ. Charles, in forming his new Congregation, impressed on it this distinctive character, that the priestly perfection of its members, fostered and preserved by community life and rule, should be exercised in the diocesan cure of souls under the government and direction of the bishop of the diocese. The Oblates by virtue of their act of oblation, which if necessary could be confirmed by a simple vow, were thus united with the Bishop as members of the body are united to the head, sharing in his spirit, his zeal and his desire for the glory of God, ready at any time to undertake any mission he might entrust to them. Charles instituted societies or *consortia* of Oblates throughout the arch-diocese. These *consortia* consisted of groups of diocesan priests directed by a president who in turn was responsible to the Provost of St. Sepulchro, and he to the Archbishop. Thus the salt regained its savour, the light of the priesthood was rekindled and to-day, after almost four hundred years the spirit of Charles Borromeo still animates with undiminished vigour the Church and clergy of Milan.

Before mentioning the difficulties Charles had to encounter with the Spanish Authorities—difficulties which lasted almost to the end of his life—it would be well to group together his other pastoral achievements which have left their mark on not only Milan, but on the Universal Church. His first care on entering the diocese was to re-organise the education and training of young men for the priesthood in accordance with the new decrees of the Council of Trent. Three things he had to provide—educated and cultured professors experienced in parochial administration and well equipped with the necessary theological learning ; a sufficient number of priests to fill the numerous vacancies caused by the abolition of pluralities ; and lastly, adequate means for the support of the system. In the diocese of Milan alone he succeeded in establishing six seminaries fully staffed and endowed, accommodating over seven hundred students. He also founded the Jesuit College at Brera (1573) and the Swiss College in Milan (1579) which provided a native clergy for the Grisons and proved as important an outpost of the Faith for Switzerland as was the College of Douai for England. This seminary system, planned strictly according to the mind of the Council of Trent, was the pioneer of the great movement which renewed the life of the Church throughout the seventeenth and eighteenth centuries and still remains the standard pattern for the formative education of the clergy.

Charles was responsible for another institution which has had a world-wide influence on the Church. Within the first year of his episcopate he began the Confraternity of Christian Doctrine (April, 1566), an organisation of lay catechists or *pescatori* as they were called, who undertook the work of instructing children and preparing them for the Sacraments. The confraternity developed under his personal direction and at the time of his death there were seven hundred and forty schools, over three thousand catechists and forty thousand children under instruction. The modern Sunday school and the Confraternity of Christian Doctrine recommended to all parishes by the present Holy Father are direct descendants of this first confraternity of St. Charles.

The reform was not confined to the secular clergy and the laity but embraced also the religious orders. With tremendous difficulty he succeeded in uniting two branches of the Franciscans, the Amadei and Chiareni, and joined them to the general body of the Order. He also compelled two other branches, the Conventuals and the Observantines to give up their private property and return to the spirit of poverty in accordance with the rule. The Umiliati, after several attempts at reform, were finally suppressed by St. Pius V. Charles obtained permission from the Pope to use six of their houses for his own foundations and to apply the revenues of several others to the maintenance of the Cathedral. He had a profound admiration for the Society of Jesus, which was as yet in its infancy, and introduced the fathers into his diocese. They became the first directors of his seminaries. He also developed the Congregation of Barnabite fathers and employed them in various offices of the diocese, chiefly as missioners and preachers.

Switzerland, of which Charles was Apostolic Visitor, claimed a large share of his attention. Though technically the northern parts of

Switzerland lay within the jurisdiction of the Archbishops of Milan, in actual practice they had been for years without any form of ecclesiastical government, and were consequently in an appalling state of spiritual disorder. Clerics bought and sold their benefices with impunity, engaged in secular trade and business and were ignorant of the most elementary functions of their sacred office. The Blessed Sacrament was treated with shocking irreverence and the churches were scarcely recognisable as places of worship. Charles tactfully invited the cantonal authorities to co-operate with him in restoring order and to his surprise, the invitation was well received. Envoys were sent to accompany him in his visitation of the three valleys and backed by their authority he succeeded in removing the greater abuses and laid the foundation of lasting reform based on the Tridentine decrees. He made a second visitation in 1570 and so great was his reputation for sanctity that even the Swiss Protestants, overcoming their natural antipathy to a Catholic bishop, paid him the tribute of an official welcome.

The Milanese authorities, however, were not inclined to be friendly. The city at this period was under Spanish domination, with a Governor appointed by the King. Trouble broke out soon after Charles held his first Provincial Council. The Senate objected to the punishment of lay offenders by the ecclesiastical courts and accused the Archbishop of trespassing on the royal prerogative. Both sides appealed to the Pope and in the interim the difficulty of the situation was aggravated by a savage attack on the Archbishop's sheriff. Charles excommunicated the instigators, including the chief of police, and the Senate in revenge, organised a campaign of malicious slander, accusing him of personal ambition and hypocrisy. A general edict was passed instituting severe penalties against all who should infringe in any way on the jurisdiction of the King, the effect of which was to bring the machinery of all the ecclesiastical courts to a standstill, and the Governor even threatened to expel the Cardinal from Milan. Charles laid the facts before the King of Spain, who, much to the Senate's annoyance, decided in his favour. The Governor also received a sharp reprimand from St. Pius V. The Pope died in May, 1572, and Charles spent six months in Rome for the Conclave. On his return there was a fresh outburst of hostility. The new Governor, Requesens, had at one time been a personal friend of the Cardinal, but now, anxious for popular favour, he published some letters from the Court of Spain containing prohibitions extremely damaging to the authority of the Church. The letters had been written during the previous controversy, but the late Governor had prudently kept them secret. With their publication the ancient hatred flared up again and Charles vainly tried to persuade Requesens to withdraw them. Eventually he was compelled to excommunicate the Governor, who in retaliation forbade the meetings of religious confraternities without the presence of a magistrate, seized the Castle of Arona, Charles's family stronghold, and placed a guard around the archiepiscopal palace. The King of Spain eventually put an end to the affair by removing the Governor to Flanders. His successor made some rather feeble and stupid attempts to renew it. He sent an embassy to Rome to complain of the Archibishop's harshness in forbidding carnivals and jousts in Lent and ordered a carnival to be held in front of the Cathedral one Sunday morning while Charles was celebrating Mass. But the people had by this time learnt to appreciate the true worth of their pastor. They boycotted the carnival and packed the cathedral to the doors. Shortly afterwards the Governor fell ill and Charles, who was absent in Brescia, hastened to his bedside and administered the Last Sacraments. He died reconciled to God, and with his death the long-standing quarrel came to an end. It had lasted over twelve years and never once had Charles failed in patience or charity even when compelled to enforce his authority by extreme measures. It is interesting to note that he had a great regard for St. John Fisher, the martyred bishop of Rochester, and found in his heroic sacrifice in defence of the Holy See the inspiration of his own undaunted courage throughout this long and bitter trial.

One must read the life of Charles Borromeo in order to appreciate his character. It is a life full of varied incident, of intense restless activity among men and affairs of momentous import in the world of his time. Princes and statesmen and great ecclesiastics, he knew them all and they knew him. Had he wished to do so he could have lived according to the prevailing standards, no better and certainly no worse than many of this contemporaries. There would have been few indeed to blame him. Instead he became a saint, his sanctity grew and flourished not in the calm shelter of the cloister but in the turbulent atmosphere of an evil and corrupt society. It was of that highest type which unites the inner life of contemplation with tremendous external activity, the pure unselfish love of God expressing itself in a complete and absolute oblation of himself to the apostolate of souls. When but a young man of twenty-five he seriously thought of resigning the cardinalate and of retiring to a monastery there to live, as he put it, " as if only God and myself were in the world." God's will seemed otherwise, so he determined that if he must live in the world he would never be of it. He was a firm believer in the principle that the spiritual life admits of no stagnation, that the soul must ever make fresh advances in the way of perfection. So as the years went by and the cares and anxieties of his office continually multiplied he gradually increased his austerities. During the last decade of his life

he took but one meal a day, if meal it could be called, for it consisted
almost entirely of bread and water and sometimes a few dried figs.
He rarely slept longer than four hours and on the occasion of the
consecration of an altar or a church, the translation of relics or any
important liturgical function would spend the whole of the previous
night before the Blessed Sacrament. Every minute of the day was
devoted to some part of the administration of his vast diocese—planning
and organising Provincial Councils and Diocesan Synods, founding
convents, religious houses, seminaries and colleges, supervising the
discipline of his metropolitan cathedral, visiting the parochial and
collegiate churches of the archdiocese which numbered over two
thousand, and also conducting canonical visitations of the sixteen
dioceses subject to the metropolitan See of Milan. From his earliest
years he had trained himself in the hard school of penance and prayer,
merciless to his own lower nature, but gentle and sympathetic to the
weakness of others. This complete mastering of himself was the
secret of his power of ruling and guiding men, of his magnetic influence
over the hearts of his people. Himself immovable, resting on the
sure foundation of unshakable faith, he moved others, used them for
God's service, attracted them to himself that he might bind them more
closely to God, fought and defeated them when they opposed the work
of God. Intellectually he had the large vision and breadth of concept
one associates with the mind of a great architect, or a great legislator,
a mind clear, concise, direct, spacious and essentially simple in creation
and construction, intensely practical in application. The force and
determination of his personality were softened by an extraordinary
tenderness, often manifested in a hundred little ways. Sometimes
when on a visitation he would sleep on the floor or a table, rather than
a servant should go without a bed. His money he kept in three
purses, one for household expenses and two for the poor. During
the great plague he would vest in full pontificals and walk from door
to door, baptising, confirming and administering the Last Sacraments,
handling pitiful wrecks of humanity with tenderest care while his
servants looked on in horror from the street. Or he would often be
seen sitting by the wayside teaching little children to pray. One of
the last acts of his life was to catechise the boatmen who rowed him
across Lake Maggiore when he returned, a dying man, to Milan.
In appearance he was above the average height, his frame proportioned
and well knit though somewhat stooped in later years through weariness
and lack of nourishment. His forehead was broad and calm, the face
long and rather narrow with blue eyes, large aquiline nose and
sensitive mouth. The whole impression was that of interior peace,
of quiet strength tempered by a winning kindliness.

The end came on November 3rd, 1584. He was forty-six years old and had been a bishop for over twenty years. He died worn out with labour at an age when most men are coming to their prime. His words at the hour of his death were symbolic of a life of perfect oblation in the spirit of the Incarnate Word at His coming—" *Ecce venio,* behold I come."

The Rev. LEWIS WATT, S.J., B.Sc.

FRANCISCO SUAREZ

A.D. 1548–1617

O N A CERTAIN Sunday in November, 1613, a Protestant minister
preached at Paul's Cross a sermon against those who had incurred
the displeasure of King James I by refusing to admit royal absolutism,
and threw into the fire which had been kindled there a number of
their books, including one which had particularly annoyed the King,
the *Defensio Fidei Catholicae* by a professor of theology at the University
of Coimbra, Father Francisco Suarez of the Society of Jesus. Not
content with this symbolical attack on the author, James set himself
the task of having him repudiated and condemned by other governments. In January of the following year Sir John Digby reported from
Madrid to his royal master that, in accordance with instructions
received, he had requested the King of Spain, Philip III, to testify
publicly his disapprobation of the book. In consequence of this request,
a committee was set up in Spain to examine the doctrine defended by
Suarez, and after some little time reported that it was true and accepted
by the doctors of the Church ; moreover, that the book contained
nothing which was injurious or out of place with regard to the King of
England. The Spanish Ambassador in England was accordingly
directed to make this known to James I, and to declare to him how
greatly Phillip III desired his security and happiness adding that the
best means of obtaining them was to show much confidence in his
Catholic subjects. James met with greater success in France, where
Huguenots and Gallicans were united in their hatred of the Society of
Jesus. In 1613 the French ambassador in London and the English
ambassador in Paris were urged by him to press for the condemnation
of the book which had so excited him. It was some months before it
found its way into France, imported from the Frankfurt Fair by
Huguenot booksellers, but when it did arrive the attack upon it began
immediately in the *Parlement*, with the ulterior object of discrediting the
Society in France, and culminated in another public cremation of the
Defensio. The French hastened to announce this to James I, who was,
naturally, overjoyed. The Archbishop of Canterbury asked the Anglican
clergy to make the fact of the French condemnation known as widely

as possible, and the Puritans suggested public rejoicings. The Spanish ambassador, on the other hand, was very uneasy, seeing a threat to Spain in the Anglo-French *entente* against Suarez and his doctrine, and Pope Paul V strongly protested to the French government against the decree of the *Parlement*. Suarez himself published a criticism of that decree.

To understand all this European turmoil caused by the publication of a book which did no more than reassert, in a systematic and logical way, traditional Catholic theology and political philosophy, it is necessary to bear in mind not only the religious situation of the times (Protestant against Catholic, the Kirk against the Church of England, Gallican against Jesuit) but also the political views and ambitions of James I. Perhaps in reaction against the very democratic teaching of George Buchanan, who had been his tutor, the King constituted himself the official spokesman of royal absolutism and the champion of kings against ecclesiastical claims, whether presbyterian or papist. Both in *Basilikon Doron* and in *The Trew Law of Free Monarchies*, which the royal author published in 1599, he maintained the divine right of kings, in the sense that all rulers receive their political authority from God directly to Whom alone they are responsible for their actions, and that the duty of all subjects is entire obedience to the will of their ruler, their constitutional rights (if any) being mere concessions granted by him. This thesis involved James in a controversy with St. Robert Bellarmine, a controversy which was intensified and embittered by the anti-Catholic Oath imposed by Parliament in 1606, after the Gunpowder Plot. This Oath, which was condemned by Pope Paul V, was defended by James I in his *Triplici Nodo* (1608), revised and republished in the following year to meet Bellarmine's criticisms, only to meet with more destructive criticism by the famous Cardinal. The central point of the controversy was the power claimed by the Popes to intervene in civil matters when the spiritual welfare of souls was at stake, but a discussion of this point leads inevitably to an examination of the foundations of political authority. Suarez was drawn into the controversy, reluctantly, at the desire of the Pope, but his health and his other occupations made his preparation of the reply to the King a slow affair, so that its composition, revision at Rome and printing took three years. The news that Suarez was at work upon it came to the ears of James I, who instructed his agent at Madrid, Sir John Digby, to send it to him as soon as possible. Digby's letters to his Sovereign during the years 1612-13 frequently refer to the book, the first part of which he forwarded in January, 1612, and the second part in February. In June, 1613, he mentions that he is sending the fifth part, and that there only remains to be sent the sixth part. In the autumn James received the entire work, which was entitled *Defensio Fidei Catholicae adversus Anglicanae*

Sectae Errores.[1] The impression it made on him is sufficiently shown by the public burnings of the book already described. He also had it " refuted " in a public disputation at the University of Oxford.

The *Defensio Fidei* is a large book, far too long to summarise here. In the Paris edition of 1859 it covers more than seven hundred pages printed in double columns. Its first two parts are devoted to a defence of the Catholic Church against the Anglicans ; the third, which contains the traditional Catholic theory of political power, discusses the authority of the Roman Pontiff and of secular rulers ; the fourth treats of clerical immunities ; the fifth (since James had called the Pope anti-Christ) deals with that title ; and the sixth is an examination of the Oath of 1606.

It will not be out of place to give a short account of the political theory which Suarez opposed to James's defence of the divine right of kings. This theory was stated so clearly and expounded so systematically by Suarez that it is sometimes known as the Suarezian theory. Such a title, however complimentary to Suarez, does less than justice to the theory, for it seems to suggest that he was the first to put it forward ; indeed, some writers, even Catholics, have made this suggestion a statement. But, whether suggestion or statement, it is completely erroneous as Professor O'Rahilly has demonstrated by quoting sixty Catholic authors who expounded and maintained the theory before Suarez wrote.[2] Bellarmine defended it, and there is no reason to doubt that Suarez is correct in saying that it was the traditionally accepted theory in the Catholic Church. It was set forth by Suarez not merely in the *Defensio*, where he uses it to refute the exaggerated claims made by the King for civil rulers, but (and even more completely) in his great treatise on Law, *De Legibus*, which, though not published till 1612, contained the matter of the course of lectures which he delivered at Coimbra University from 1601 to 1603.

Historically, Suarez explains, civil society (or " the State " in one of the meanings of this term) developed from the family. The multiplication of families and their need for mutual assistance and cooperation disclosed the necessity for some greater society with a wider purpose than the family naturally possesses. Juridically, this society, civil society, comes into existence as and when families agree, explicitly or implicitly, to form it. It is, like the family, a " natural " society, one which the nature of man postulates as a condition of a satisfactory human life. It is willed by God, the author of nature. Now it is impossible for any society to achieve its purpose if there be no person

---

[1] The history of the events narrated above is told more fully by Fr. J. Brodrick in his *Life and Works of Blessed Robert Cardinal Bellarmine, S.J.* (Burns Oates and Washbourne) and by Père R. de Scorailles in his *Francois Suarez* (Lethielleux).

[2] *Studies*, March, 1921.

(physical or moral) vested with the authority necessary to regulate and co-ordinate the activities of its members with a view to the attainment of the good of the society. In the case of a natural society (family or State) that authority is willed by God, since, willing the society, He must will all that it requires for its existence and progress ; and the extent of that authority will be measured by the natural purpose of the society. It is perfectly true, then, to say that political authority comes from God, and, indeed, Scripture confirms this. But there is the further question to be considered, on whom does God confer political authority ? He has, of course, a perfect right to select some individual and confer it upon him, manifesting His will that this individual shall be ruler, as with Saul or David. But what if there is no such explicit manifestation of the divine will ? In such a case, replies Suarez, political authority is vested in the community as a whole, as a *corpus mysticum*, for there is no particular person (physical or moral) within the community unmistakably provided by nature with political sovereignty. It should be noted that, according to Suarez, political authority is not the gift of the members of the community to the community as a whole. It includes powers which, as individuals, they never possessed. Its direct source is God Himself.[1] This contention, apart from other points, is enough to differentiate Suarez's theory from other theories which bear a superficial resemblance to it, such as that of Rousseau.

A further important difference between Suarez and Rousseau lies in their attitudes towards the transfer of sovereignty by the community to some particular person (physical or moral). For Rousseau, the sovereignity of the people is inalienable ; for Suarez, it is not. He maintains that the community may, for the furtherance of the general welfare, set up any form of government apt for this purpose. It may (explicitly or tacitly) transfer its sovereignty to a monarch, or vest it in a group ; if it does so, a contractual relationship arises between sovereign and community, the former being bound to govern in the interests of the subjects, the latter being bound to obey the ruler within the limits of his authority. These limits are set by the natural purpose of the State, viz. to secure and foster the temporal welfare of its members, and by any conditions limiting the transfer of authority to him. Consequently the ruler is not empowered to make such laws as he pleases, without regard to the general welfare of the community, nor are subjects bound to submit to his arbitrary will. Particularly in the matter of religion he may not regard himself as the spiritual head of the commonwealth, a position which rightfully belongs to the Roman

---

[1] Gierke's accusation that " in defending such a paradox even the ability of a Suarez could only produce an ingenious *jeu d'esprit* " has been rebutted by Professor Ernest Barker. See *Natural Law and the Theory of Society*, by Otto Gierke ; translated by Ernest Barker (Cambridge University Press) ; Vol I, p. 46 and Vol. II, pp. 241, 243.

Pontiff. Suarez thus rejects the doctrine of the divine right of kings in the sense in which James maintained it. But on the other hand he denies that civil authority is derived from the Pope. In purely civil and political matters (outside the States of the Church) the Pope has no jurisdiction, though he is entitled to intervene in them when the good of souls is at stake. In other words, Suarez agrees with Bellarmine that the Pope's jurisdiction in the temporal affairs of the non-papal States is indirect only.[1] Put in the language of to-day, this amounts to saying that, while sovereign States are politically independent in all purely temporal matters, they must look to the Christian Church for guidance when religion or morality are concerned, and that they exceed their proper function and authority when they enact legislation which conflicts with the teaching of the Christian Church. The world is coming to see, in this thesis, a safeguard of liberty against totalitarianism, but it is not surprising that to James I, holding the views he did, it was entirely repugnant. It is rather piquant to find a Spanish theologian defending a reasonable liberty of citizens against an English king who stood for absolutism.

The importance of Suarez as a jurist must be pleaded in excuse for this long account of his controversy with James I. Much could still be said under this heading, and would have to be said did this chapter profess to be an adequate exposition of Suarez's philosophy of law.[2] But Suarez was much more than a jurist. He was an eminent philosopher and theologian, and had a very distinguished career as professor at Rome and in the Iberian Peninsula. He is one of the leading figures of the great age of Spanish theology. As a preacher he did not prove a success, both because he carried into the pulpit the expository technique of the professor and because his voice was early weakened by an illness following on his efforts to evangelize the country districts round Segovia, where he taught philosophy from 1571 to 1574. His vocation was to be that of a lecturer and writer ; much more of the former and much less of the latter than he would have chosen, had he been his own master. We have twenty-three large volumes from his pen (ten being published after his death) ; yet he was forty-two years old before he published anything, having then been engaged in study and teaching for twenty-five years. For long he held the principal chair of theology at the University of Coimbra ; and previous to that

---

[1] An interesting discussion of this question will be found in Brodrick, *op. cit.* Vol. I, ch. 12.

[2] On Suarez's doctrines in the field of international law, see *The Catholic Conception of International Law*, by Dr. J. B. Scott, Trustee and Secretary of the Carnegie Endowment and President of the American Society of International Law ; and *The Catholic Tradition of the Law of Nations*, by John Eppstein (Burns Oates & Washbourne). The Carnegie Endowment for International Peace is soon to publish a selection from Suarez's juristic writings with introduction and notes.

appointment (forced on him by Philip III) he was professor of theology in the Colleges of the Society of Jesus at Valladolid, Segovia, Avila, Alcala and Rome.

It is a remarkable fact that in his oral teaching he dispensed with notes, speaking in his rather weak voice with great clarity of enunciation and lucidity of thought.   In those days text-books were unknown, and in the opinion of Suarez there was a real danger lest those who attended lectures should find, at the end of their course, that they retained very little of what they had heard unless the professor spoke sufficiently slowly for them to copy down what he said.   Undoubtedly the method of dictation has its disadvantages, but the ability to take intelligent longhand notes of a lecture delivered with conversational rapidity is possessed by few, nor can the professor be sure that his audience is able to write some form of shorthand.   The pedagogical difficulty is, then, a very real one.   At Alcala and at Coimbra Suarez found the method of dictation in general use, and he followed it himself.   It seems also to have been the method he employed in preparing his theological works, for his biographers make reference to his dictating to secretaries (chosen from among his students).   Some indeed, speak of his dictating to several secretaries together and on different topics. In a letter to the General of the Society of Jesus, in which he defends himself against certain attacks that had been made against his doctrine, he says that his method of teaching differs from that of most other professors of his day.   They were accustomed, he says, to proceed on traditional lines and along well-beaten tracks, handing on the teaching they had themselves received, whereas for his part he tried to go down to the roots of each question in order to discover the truth.   This gave a misleading appearance of novelty to his doctrine, a novelty which is necessarily suspect in a professor of Catholic dogmatic theology.   The most common accusation brought against him, then as now, was that he departed from the doctrine of the great master St. Thomas Aquinas.   How far this charge can be justified is a matter which cannot be examined here, though it is necessary to remark that he himself considered his views on all major points to be identical with those of the great Dominican, whom the Society of Jesus had officially chosen as its theological Doctor.[1]

It is regrettable that we have very few details about the personal appearance and temperament of Suarez.   One who had been a student at Coimbra and attended his lectures describes him as of medium height, very thin, with hollow cheeks and blue eyes.   The events already mentioned which left his voice impaired also weakened his chest and lungs, and this caused him much trouble throughout his life.

[1] A vindication of the Thomism of Suarez will be found in de Scorailles, *op. cit.*, Vol. II, ch. 2.

As he grew old, he suffered from rheumatism, which interfered a good deal with his work, particularly since it crippled his hands. His biographers speak of his neuralgia and digestive troubles. His health was never really sound, and when he applied in 1564 for admission into the Society of Jesus one of the reasons for which he was refused was his poor health. The other reason was his lack of talent, a point to which we shall return in a moment. In order to smooth out as far as possible the obstacles put in his way by his physical condition, his Superiors, on the advice of the doctors, made special provision for his food and accommodation, not without causing dissatisfaction to certain critics who objected to the privileges accorded to him. It may well have been this lack of health which explains the impression made on some of his contemporaries, who describe him as rather sombre, and his reputation for being retiring and withdrawn from contact with others, though this may also be explained by the enormous labour he imposed upon himself. His self-control was well shown in an incident which took place while he was professor at Coimbra. He was challenged by another professor of the University, one who seems to have been definitely jealous of him and his reputation, to a sort of academic joust, much in favour in those days. A large audience assembled, and party feeling ran high. At the proper moment Suarez proposed to his opponent a syllogism with a major premiss which was to form the basis of his whole argument. This premiss was promptly denied. To the astonishment of the audience, and no doubt to the annoyance of his friends, Suarez offered no proof of it, but remained completely silent. When the unpleasant affair was over and he was back at home again, he was asked why he had not covered his disconcertment by opening some other line of argument. In reply, he took down from the shelves a volume containing the canons of the Church's General Councils, and showed the inquirers that one of these was identical with the major premiss which had been denied. Reproached now with not having vindicated himself earlier, he answered that he had preferred not to injure the reputation of his opponent by revealing the error he had made. Living in different times and in a different atmosphere, we may think this but a small matter ; but under the conditions in which the affair took place it reveals something like heroism.

Few, if any, nowadays, or even in his own day, would deny Suarez the title of genius. But it is an undoubted fact that this genius was late in developing. Its first signs were so unusual as to constitute a psychological mystery, if not evidence of supernatural intervention. The occurrence can be best described in the course of a brief biographical sketch. He was born on January 5th, 1548, at Granada, in Andalusia, of a family which had for centuries played an important part in the history of Castille, ecclesiastical, civic and military, particularly distinguishing itself in the wars against the Moors. After the capture of Granada in the closing years of the fifteenth century, Suarez's grandfather received an estate there from Ferdinand and Isabella, in recognition of his services. His eldest son, Suarez's father, had eight children ; four sons, three of whom entered religion, and four daughters, three of whom became nuns. Francisco was the second son. The family was wealthy, but later fell on evil times, so that Suarez had to obtain permission from his superiors to assist his eldest brother and other relatives financially, out of the money received for his books.

Suarez received the usual education of a boy of his time and class, probably at the young University of Granada ; but when he was thirteen years old he was sent, along with his brother John, to the great University of Salamanca, where he entered as a student of law (ecclesiastical and civil). There was a College of the Society of Jesus at Salamanca, and three years later Suarez applied there for admission into the Society. He was one of fifty who applied in that year (1564), and of all the fifty he alone was refused, on the ground of lack of sufficient talent and health. He appealed to the Provincial of Castille, who ultimately agreed to admit him, but only after overriding the unanimously unfavourable verdict of those appointed to examine him. In June, 1564, he entered the Jesuit novitiate, but before the year was over he was back at Salamanca, trying to understand the course of philosophy at the Jesuit College. His efforts were all in vain, he could make nothing of it. His fellow-students christened him " the dumb ox," as St. Thomas Aquinas had been christened in earlier times. His professor put him under the care of another student, who was to try to make him understand the lectures. The failure of this experiment was so signal that Suarez, determined not to leave the Society of Jesus but seeing no hope of passing the examinations necessary for the priesthood, applied to his superior for permission to pass into the ranks of the lay-brothers. This permission was not granted, and he was told to pray for success in his studies. A little time elapsed, and then came, suddenly and unexpectedly, the extraordinary change to which allusion has been made. One day, after his youthful mentor had laboriously explained to him a lecture in the simplest terms he could find, Suarez asked to be allowed to give his version of it. He gave it with such extraordinary ability that the professor was informed without delay. Suarez was submitted to a public test, from which he emerged with great distinction. Thereafter he outdistanced all his contemporaries in the College. Explain it as we will, naturally or supernaturally, the fact of this sudden intellectual awakening is attested by all his biographers, even the earliest.

From 1566 to 1570 he studied theology and exegesis at the University of Salamanca, one of his professors being a Dominican, another an Augustinian. Loyal to the official decrees of the Society, Suarez took as his master St. Thomas Aquinas, but he also studied the Franciscan Doctor Scotus. In private he revised his philosophy, particularly metaphysics. In 1572 he received Holy Orders, and said his first Mass on the Feast of the Annunciation. The whole of his life thereafter was spent in fulfilling the duties of a professor of theology and in that amazing literary activity which gave him a European reputation even in his own lifetime. When one looks at the long row of large tomes which comprise the published works of Suarez, one is irresistibly impelled to ask how he ever found time to compose them, in addition to fulfilling the duties of the professorate and of a priest of the Society. Fortunately the time-table he followed during the last twenty years of his life (that is, while professor at Coimbra) has been preserved. To read it is to be filled with the half-incredulous awe that is produced in the ordinary man by reading about the mortifications of the saints. The time of his lecture, which lasted an hour and a half, was half-past six *in the morning* during the summer months, an hour later in the winter. He rose never later than half-past three in the summer, half-past four in the winter. After an hour and a half of mental prayer, followed by the recital of the Little Hours of the breviary, he went to his books. By the time most people in England are breakfasting, Suarez was settling down to a couple of hours' work with his secretaries. He did not break his fast till mid-day, for it was his custom to say Mass daily at eleven o'clock in the morning. After a very light breakfast, he said Vespers and Compline, recited his Rosary and read some spiritual book. At two o'clock he anticipated Matins and Lauds of the following day. Then he settled down to five hours of mental toil before his second meal of the day. After that a short conversation with some of the members of his community, lengthy night prayers, and bed. All this for twenty years at least, and Suarez a man of feeble health ! A contemporary who lived beside him describes him as being as regular as a clock in following his time-table, a point of similarity with Kant. Another point of similarity is that just as Kant had Lampe to look after him, so Suarez had the help of a lay-brother (Pedro de Aguilar), who assisted him for twenty years, but who never had to be dismissed as Lampe was.

A man is not entitled to be called a Great Catholic merely because he was an intellectual giant. To justify that title there must be something more than merely human greatness ; there must be at least something of sanctity. Reflecting on Suarez's utter self-renunciation, complete dedication to the service of God, as manifested in his outward life, one is forced to ask whether his mere tenacity of purpose is not evidence of a sanctity which transcends that of even fervent religious. But there is other evidence. " Never in my life," said the Bishop of Coimbra, " have I known anyone who united so profound a humility with such wide learning, who was so esteemed by everybody and who thought so little of himself." As to his union with God, we have seen what a large part of the day he gave to prayer. He once said, " If I had to choose between our morning meditation and the knowledge I have spent so many years in acquiring, I would willingly give up all that knowledge rather than one hour of prayer." There is evidence, written by an eye-witness and made public after Suarez's death, that he had ecstasies in prayer. His devotion to Our Blessed Lady showed itself in his books. He was the first theologian to treat in a strict scholastic way of her position in the Christian economy. His charity to his fellow-men was shown over and over again in his lifetime by many acts of kindness, and by the invariable courtesy with which he treated, both in his writings and in spoken word, the many critics and adversaries he encountered.

He died, after a short illness, at Lisbon on September 25th, 1617, having been a Jesuit for fifty-three years and a professor of theology for forty-three, twenty of which he spent at Coimbra. On his death-bed he uttered a phrase which has often been quoted : " I would never have believed that dying is so sweet."

In his lifetime, Pope Paul V referred to him as " *eximius et pius*," and the title " *doctor eximius* " has been given him by posterity, following Pope Benedict XIV. He has an assured place in the line of great Catholic philosophers and theologians. As a jurist, he is attracting more and more the attention of modern thinkers concerned to find a sound basis for society, national and international.

E. I. WATKIN, M.A.

DOM AUGUSTINE BAKER

A.D. 1575–1641

SOME MAY BE surprised at the inclusion in this gallery of great Catholics of a man who may seem a minor figure. Fr. Baker's life was not outwardly eventful. It was, what he would have wished it to be, a life of retirement and seclusion. Not for him the martyr's crown or a prominent place in the apostolate of England. And though a prolific writer—*Sancta Sophia* was compiled from more than forty treatises— he cannot be regarded as a writer of high literary rank. He is too diffuse, too rambling, too formless. Indeed it would be impossible to publish his works as they stand. Happily, the outstanding editorial ability of Dom Serenus de Cressy, his disciple and biographer, has compiled from his writings an orderly and well proportioned treatise, a comprehensive guide to contemplative prayer, *Sancta Sophia*. Nor did he possess the imagination and original invention indispensable to great literature. Even his style, though lucid and pleasing, is of no outstanding beauty.

Even in his special field, contemplative prayer and mystical theology, he is not among the supreme masters. When he wrote, he had experienced of the higher mystical prayer which he terms passive contemplation, only a single ecstasy. When towards the end of his life he entered permanently into this state of prayer he wrote no more. He is not an exponent of this supreme mysticism.

Nevertheless, no Catholic teacher of the spiritual life has a more valuable message for us than Fr. Baker. Others have been far greater, holier than he. But not one among them is a better guide to the life of prayer. By all but a tiny majority, the highest states of mystical prayer can be studied only for their witness to God's glory and the power of His work in souls, as matter for adoration and a testimony to the truths of faith, not as having any practical bearing on our spiritual life. Moreover, to read the works of the great mystics, a Rueysbrook or St. John of the Cross for practical instruction, is not without grave dangers. Guides to the highest mystical union, they demand the utter renunciation indispensable to its attainment and describe the spiritual purgatory through which those alone can and must pass who are invited to enter the earthly paradise, which, like Dante's, is situated above purgatory.

As Fr. Baker shows, these sufferings are not given to souls of lower call who have not received the strength to endure them. Their description therefore, if regarded with personal application, is apt to frighten souls from the life of inner prayer.

Fr. Baker, while faithful to the principles worked out in their utmost rigour by a St. John of the Cross whose works he had read, tempers their application to the weakness of the vast majority even of prayerful souls. Hence his writings can be put with safety and profit into the hands of any who are invited to the life of prayer.

The snow-clad peak climbed by St. John of the Cross is likely to deter those who are not Alpine climbers of the spirit, so that they remain comfortably seated in their hotel garden. The more accessible uplands to which Fr. Baker summons us, the downs, or at most the high moors of his native land, encourage even those of moderate vigour to climb after him.

And if there be any called to even higher ascents they will find Fr. Baker's doctrine in conformity with the sublimer teaching they will need, a stage on their way to the summit.

In this moderation, this consideration for human weakness, which nevertheless is never false to the immutable, because intrinsic, principles which determine man's union with God, Fr. Baker is true both to the spirit of his order, the discretion which renders St. Benedict's rule the masterpiece of wisdom that it is, and the tradition of English mysticism.

His doctrine of contemplation follows closely the anonymous fourteenth-century *Cloud of Unknowing* on which he commented chapter by chapter. He also made considerable use of Walter Hilton's *Scale of Perfection*. He is thus in the direct line of pre-Reformation English mystics, as the Congregation to which he belonged is in the direct line of mediæval English monasticism.

Fr. Baker's life is so essentially the record of his doctrine as lived by himself and taught to others that it is not easy to decide of which to speak first. But perhaps it will be as well to begin with his life. Its best source as regards his life of prayer is the confessions contained under a thin veil of anonymity in his commentary on the Cloud, the Secretum. Making use of these, Serenus de Cressy wrote his life, published for the first time a few years ago together with a shorter life by another Benedictine contemporary Dom Peter Salvin. A third life by Dom Pritchard still awaits publication. There is also for his earlier life an unpublished autobiographical fragment.

Fr. Baker was born at Abergavenny in 1575, the thirteenth child of Lord Abergavenny's steward. His parents had conformed with no particular enthusiasm to the Established Church. Christened David, he was educated at Christ's Hospital, London and at Broadgates Hall, Oxford. He was then called to the bar, working with an elder brother.

Though his fastidious temperament kept him from gross vices he lost hold of religion and even doubted the existence of God. His father recalled him home and obtained for him the post of Recorder of Abergavenny. A project of marriage, however, fell through. In the year 1600, as he rode home absent-mindedly, he suddenly found that his horse had taken him onto the middle of a high and narrow footbridge over a mountain stream, the Monnow, " where he could neither go forward nor turn " . . . In this extremity he framed . . . such an internal resolution as this : " if ever I escape this danger I will believe there is a God who hath more care of my life and safety than I have had of His love and worship." Immediately he found his horse's head turned by no means that he could discover and the danger escaped. This led him to return to a serious practice of religion and to enquire into the controversy between the Protestant and Catholic religions. It resulted in his conversion. At his first confession " there sprang up a desire of spiritual perfection to be purchased with the loss of all sensual pleasures and abandoning all secular designs." It was not long before he had converted his mother and sister.

Desirous of embracing the religious life, he met in London some English monks affiliated to the Italian Cassinese congregation. He went out to Italy and was clothed, taking the name Augustine, at the monastery of St. Justina in Padua on May 27th in 1605. Here he began the practice of mental prayer, his " first conversion ". Knowing of no other method than meditation, little adapted to his temper, he soon found himself a prey to aridity and gave up mental prayer entirely. As his health was bad, his superiors sent him home when still a novice to his native air. Though he had intended to travel slowly and visit places of interest, a powerful impulse made him travel post-haste, so that he arrived in time to procure his father's deathbed reconciliation with the Church. He made his profession in London. At this time the English Congregation was restored, or rather continued, by the affiliation to it and Westminster Abbey, of two Cassinese monks by the last surviving monk of Westminster, Dom Sigebert Buckley. Though there is no doubt of this affiliation, its time and circumstances are reported very differently by those in a position to know the facts and with no motive for misrepresenting them—an instructive warning against overconfidence in historical details.

Dom Baker joined this revived congregation, and when later in 1619 it was fully organized, he became a monk of Dieulouard Abbey in Lorraine, the parent of Ampleforth. Rather strangely, however, he never lived there, though he spent later many years at Douay, the parent of Downside. This great light of English Benedictinism may therefore be claimed by both houses. For the time he was in England.

He returned to the practice of mental prayer, his " second conversion," and after a few months was raised to " passive contemplation," an ecstasy produced by " a speaking of God to the soul." It lasted at most a quarter of an hour. Fr. Baker believed that this rapid spiritual advance was assisted by the mortification of his inability to satisfy his hunger without very serious effects to his digestion. With a man's appetite he could digest no more than a small child. Later in life his digestion became normal, though his health was never robust. This ecstasy made his prayer " far purer, far easier, less painful to nature and more abstract from sense" than before, "yea, it wrought a stability or perfect settledness of prayer." It produced an interior illumination whereby he understood the meaning of spiritual books. It replaced fear of death by an eagerness to die. Further, it gave him a conviction of the truth of Catholic doctrine. " I would tell you of the wonderful proof and satisfaction that a soul hath of the verities of Christian religion by one of the said passive contemplations. . . . The soul most clearly seeth that all is most assuredly true that in such work is manifested or told unto her, as are the verities and mysteries of Christianity. O happy evidence of our belief. No thanks to them that believe after such a sight. A man may say that God is not beholden to them for believing that which they have so clearly, evidently and manifestly, as it were, seen with their eyes and handled with their hands. Such sights of the soul are far more clear than are the sights or feelings of our outward senses."

This apprehension of Catholic truth by which we must probably understand a perception of what may be termed the inner substance of dogma ; to spiritual significance is not an essential part of mystical contemplation. It is, however, a frequent accompaniment. Malaval, the blind mystic of Marseilles, speaks of it in the same terms as Fr. Baker.

This contemplation was, however, followed by the desolation inevitable in the higher mystical way. Fr. Baker, having no experienced director, and not having yet studied the mystical theologians who treat of it, did not understand its nature or the attitude he should adopt. Perplexed and discouraged, he again abandoned interior prayer at the threshold of the Night of Spirit, as he had abandoned it before when faced with the Night of Sense. Years of life followed with no practice of mental prayer, the spiritual void being covered by legal activities, in themselves valuable and largely charitable, but not in conformity with Fr. Baker's profound call. About the year 1613 he was ordained priest.

After twelve years he returned to mental prayer, never again to abandon it. This was his third, in the *Secretum* he calls it his " second, conversion ". Though he attained a high degree of what he terms active contemplation, he had not been raised again to " passive " when he composed his works.[1] A simple prayer of aspirations, acts of love, elicited by God in His higher will, became his usual prayer, increasingly simplified and abstracted from all sensible images or even mental concepts. At the beginning of this renewed spiritual life he was in Devonshire, chaplain to Mr. Philip Fursden. Here, by avoiding controversy and recommending a prayer of humble resignation, he converted Mr. Fursden's mother-in-law, a staunch Protestant, whom the arguments of other priests had merely irritated.

From 1621 to 1624 he was in London engaged, by his superiors' command, in antiquarian research into the history of English Bene-dictinism. It is interesting and pleasant to notice that in these researches he had the assistance and sympathy of Protestant antiquaries. To mobilize scientific research in the service of a state ideology has been reserved for the modern totalitarians, Communist, Nazi or Fascist.

In 1624 he went to Douay but was at once sent to Cambray as a spiritual director to the English Benedictine nuns who had just founded a convent there, the present Stanbrook. A most influential nun was the great-great-grand-daughter of St. Thomas More, Dame Gertrude More. In fact, the convent could not have been founded without the financial support of her father, Crisacre More. She had inherited a good measure of her ancestor's humour, love of learning, critical intelligence, and mental curiosity. To this she added a strong will. All these qualities, reinforcing her position as the daughter of the practical founder, had made her a dominant influence in the convent. Moreover, they turned her away from the interior life to external interests, in Baker's terminology to extroversion rather than intro-version. Even her religious vocation was not perfectly clear to her. It was, in part at least, a distaste for marriage, the only practical alternative, and she had made her profession half-heartedly. However, she had also what Fr. Baker calls "a wonderfully strong propensity in her rational will to seek after God and eternal felicity and a disesteem or contempt for all the transitory things of this life." This propensity, in which also she resembled her martyred ancestor, drew her inwards to seek God in the soul, towards introversion. Indeed, it was no doubt the true motive of her religious vocation, as it had drawn St. Thomas to make trial of the Carthusian life. Torn between these two conflicting tendencies and moreover harassed by the disease of scruples, Dame Gertrude was unhappy, restless, and in consequence rather bitter and very critical. At first, therefore, she

[1] See, however, below, page 227.

would have nothing to do with this new director to whom she was not bound to go, since he was not the nuns' official confessor. Indeed, we may suppose that it was to give the nuns the choice between two types of direction that he was not appointed confessor. At last, however, she came to him, for the first time, eleven months after her unconsoled profession. A few months later she returned to him and became his most enthusiastic disciple, as also was the Abbess Dame Catherine Gascoigne. He put her into a course of affective prayer, acts of love in which her propensity to God could find expression and exercise unhampered and unretarded by the multiplicity of images and concepts involved in meditation. This course proved most beneficial, and its fruits are embodied in the outbursts of affective prayer known as *Confessiones Amantis*, a lover's confessions. Fr. Baker left her at liberty to follow the inner guidance of the Holy Spirit both in regard to her prayer and those external matters not regulated by her rule. Though her weak health made her unable to undertake extraordinary mortifications, she could not indeed fulfil the rule completely, and she found it necessary to continue a measure of secular reading and conversations and to engage in a large number of external activities, since these things were regulated by the guidance of the Holy Ghost obtained by prayer and subordinated to a unifying, because simple contemplation, Dame Gertrude advanced rapidly. Her prayer was directed to the incomprehensible Godhead apprehended by faith. And although affective it was not sensible devotion, but an exercise of the spiritual will aspiring and adhering to God. Any sensible affections were secondary, the concomitant, and so to speak, by-product of the exercise of will. Indeed, Dame Gertrude was tried and purified by much sensible aridity, the Night of Sense.

Fr. Baker remained at Cambray nine years, 1624 to 1633. It was during this period that he began to compose the host of treatises with translations and adaptations in which his doctrine is contained. In the *Secretum* he tells us of some peculiar psychophysical results of his prayer, motions of arms or legs and an apparent drawing of his prayer activity upwards to the head. Finally on Mid-Lent Sunday, 1627, " there happened upon his head and body such an alteration that he greatly wondered at it nor could he tell what to make of it." Of the phenomenon itself we hear no more. But whereas before he had suffered from a mental dullness due to the drawing of his spiritual activities into the centre of his soul, though it left him capable of all his duties, he now " had free use of his wits and senses in greater clearness and perfection than ever before." He " found himself enabled to write or discourse of spiritual matters." In the strength of this new light he produced all his writings. As we have seen, *Sancta Sophia* was compiled out of more than forty treatises. And the bibliography appended to Dom Justin McCann's edition of the Salvin and Cressy lives enumerates no less than 68 items. Of these, however, some are translations or adaptations, others fragments. Nevertheless, it was a most prolific output. Indeed, it would seem as though many mystics, knowing that they cannot adequately convey their sublime spiritual apprehensions, yet under a strong urge to impart their knowledge for God's glory and the benefit of others, cannot refrain from expatiating on the same topics, repeating themselves in the vain effort to express themselves to their satisfaction. Moreover, the instruction of the Cambray nuns was a powerful inducement to composition.

As always, a novelty or apparent novelty, however good, provoked opposition. The opposition at Cambray was headed by the nuns' regular chaplain, Dom Francis Hull. Though personal jealousy may have played a subconscious part, the liberty left to the individual by Fr. Baker, the seeming illuminism of his insistence upon Divine calls and inspirations, the very subordinate place assigned to meditation, then widely regarded as the ideal form of mental prayer, and above all his denial that Superiors had a right to prescribe their subjects' method of prayer were grounds for genuine though mistaken alarm. Moreover, Dame Gertrude's enthusiasm and her naturally assertive temper which, though subdued by prayer, could not have been wholly eradicated, may well have made her tactless and a trifle overbearing in defence of the doctrine which had liberated her soul. Fr. Hull, on his deathbed, declared to Dom Salvin that he had not opposed Fr. Baker's doctrine in itself but merely the abuse made of it by indiscreet disciples. In any case, the controversy produced two good results. It effected a final purification of Dame Gertrude's soul in view of her holy death from small-pox in August, 1633, at the early age of twenty-seven. Not only did she bear the pain and the loneliness of her disease with exemplary courage, as also the lack of viaticum, since she could not swallow the Host; but she proved how thoroughly she had assimilated Fr. Baker's teaching by refusing to see him, since it was unnecessary, and she would be left alone with God.

The other good result was the formal examination of Fr. Baker's writings by order of the General Chapter of the congregation. For it resulted in their unreserved and wholehearted approbation. In fact, *if* the English Benedictines can be said to possess any official body of spiritual doctrine, as the Jesuits the *Exercises of St. Ignatius*, surely it must be the doctrine of Fr. Baker. I hasten to add that although in his writings Fr. Baker had primarily in view the monks and nuns of his order, he expressly points out that *mutatis mutandis*, his doctrine is applicable to all, whatever their state of life, who are called to seek

God by the practice of contemplative prayer. In fact, when we remember that of the sixty-five years he lived, Fr. Baker spent less than six in a monastery, and during his five years at Douay took no part in the choir, it is clear that he was a monk rather in the spirit than in the letter. But the spirit alone has any intrinsic value. For souls surrendered to God, Fr. Baker tells us, all employments undertaken by a Divine call are equally valuable, " even labouring for the conversion of souls is of no greater price with God than is the keeping of sheep."[1]

To return from this digression. Though the General Chapter approved Fr. Baker's doctrine it was thought wiser to remove both protagonists in the controversy from Cambray. Fr. Baker therefore now spent five years at Douay. Except for his daily Mass and his meals he confined himself almost entirely to his room. This soon became a centre of spiritual guidance, not only for members of the house but for outsiders, for example, the English Franciscans and the students and teachers at the seminary for secular priests. It may, therefore, be said that during these years Fr. Baker was spiritually forming the confessors and martyrs of the English mission where the Civil War would shortly rekindle the persecution relaxed under King Charles.

This unofficial influence, with the body of enthusiastic disciples it brought into being, alienated from Fr. Baker a powerful theologian who had hitherto supported him, but who was of too active and dominating a temper to practise his doctrine himself, Dom Rudisind Barlow. Even so the trouble would not have come to a head had Fr. Baker not felt himself obliged to compose a treatise on the conventual life, aimed under the thinnest of disguises at Dom Rudisind. This error of judgment exasperated Dom Rudisind, to whom Fr. Baker had actually presented in person the attack upon himself, and though infirm, Fr. Baker was sent to England in 1638.

We are not, however, entitled in Dom Rudisind's case, any more than in Fr. Hull's, to charge Fr. Baker's adversary with deliberate and conscious jealousy. As Fr. Baker himself points out, the good are often permitted by God to oppose the good for their spiritual profit without wilful fault, but from lack of light withheld by God. In this instance Dom Rudisind may well have regarded Fr. Baker as a centre of dissension in the house and as encouraging by his personal criticism of himself an undesirable spirit of criticism and insubordination. Any personal jealousy or pique at work as a motive

---

[1] I cannot altogether agree with this. No doubt all employments performed in obedience to God are equally sanctifying. It does not follow that they are equally valuable in themselves, therefore in God's estimate, Who must judge values as they objectively are.

may well have been completely hidden from his conscious knowledge for want of the light to discover it, obtainable only by prayer.

In England, Fr. Baker spent the last years of his life partly in Bedfordshire, partly in London. Towards the end he had often to change his lodgings to escape arrest. For the Long Parliament was bent on extirpating Popery. But this banishment from Douay, which he could have avoided by accepting an offer to reside at the seminary, and its consequent sufferings were the final detachment enabling Fr. Baker to receive the higher " passive " contemplation which he had lost so long. Since he had ceased writing we know nothing of his final prayer. We may perhaps console ourselves by reflecting that the practical utility of his work is, as we have seen, partly conditioned by its confinement to the lower slopes of the mystic Carmel. There are others to speak of the summits, notably the doctor of mystical theology, St. John of the Cross. Fr. Baker's silence is thus profitable for us as well as his speech, and like the latter the result of his Divine call. All we know is a revealing phrase in a letter that he was *totus in passionibus*, wholly in a passive state. When his correspondent misinterpreted these sufferings as privations and was arranging for a supply of money, Fr. Baker explained that the sufferings he meant " were the greatest tastes of heaven that this life is capable of, his prayer being now become wholly passive." He died of a pestilential fever in the house of a Mrs. Watson, who described his peaceful and resigned death in a letter to her daughter. " His body was weak but his sickness violent and the pangs of death extreme strong ; but perfect resignation and a total subjection to the will and good pleasure of Almighty God was plainly seen to be performed by him to his last breath. The day before he died he took a leaden pen and wrote thus : ' Abstinence and Resignation I see must be my condition to my very expiration.' His happy departure out of this world was on the ninth of August, 1641, upon St. Laurence's Eve." He was buried in St. Andrew's, Holborn. But no doubt his grave is as unknown to-day as that of his disciple Dame Gertrude More, buried somewhere in what was the Convent cemetery and is now a private garden.

Sixteen years later his enduring monument was to be erected by Dom Cressy, *Sancta Sophia*.

Fr. Baker's method of prayer was essentially one of the will. Acts of will at first deliberately elicited, " forced acts " become gradually more affective and under the operation of grace ultimately become " aspirations ", acts elicited by the Holy Spirit and produced, therefore, with greater facility and more spontaneously, also fewer, since each continues longer. And there is a corresponding progress in their spirituality and simplicity. Moreover, these acts and aspirations are predominantly addressed to the incomprehensible Godhead apprehended by faith.

The substance of this method can be found already in the *Cloud of Unknowing*, on which, as we have seen, Fr. Baker commented. But it is worked out in greater detail and divided into stages. Although it was no novelty, it ran counter to the method of mental prayer then most popular, though not so universal as it became after the Quietist controversy had brought mysticism into discredit and suspicion. This method was that of discursive meditation, of which *St. Ignatius's Exercises* were the most important example. Fr. Baker himself agreed that for many souls of active and extroverted temper meditation is the best form of mental prayer, indeed probably the only form of which such souls are capable. And all souls, he thought, should begin with meditation, even if they continued it no more than a few months, before they were called to replace it by acts of will.

There can be no doubt that meditation or some equivalent exercise, such as deeply pondered reading, is indispensable. For its object is to transform an exclusively or predominantly notional assent to the truths of faith into the real assent by which alone they are assimilated into our mental and spiritual life and move the will. Indeed, if our spirituality lacks the foundation of such realised doctrine, the exercise of the will elevated to the incomprehensible God which Fr. Baker recommends, may prove too empty of content, the vague undenominational and undogmatic worship of a God not only above knowledge but wholly unknown, in fact agnostic. When Fr. Baker wrote, however, there was a tendency to treat meditation not, as what it is, the foundation of mental prayer but as being itself mental prayer, though as he shows, prayer is an act of will, not of understanding. Indeed it was widely regarded as the sole mental prayer.[1] This was due, I believe, to the fact that the Reformation had disclosed a widespread ignorance and at best lack of effective realisation of Catholic truth. Because Catholic doctrine had too often not been assimilated by Catholics, vast numbers had yielded to the assault of a heresy whose doctrine was the vital conviction of its adherents. The most urgent need, therefore, was to replace a formal and customary Catholicism by an intelligent and living understanding of the Catholic faith. For this there could be no better instrument than the methodical meditation practised and preached by the Jesuits, who set the tone of counter-Reformation spirituality.

But however valuable and indispensable this method might be, if it is regarded as the sole or even the best method of prayer, it must prove a fatal hindrance to the soul's Godward ascent. In fact, the mystics had never ceased to protest against meditation when pursued

---

[1] Where meditation is and must be a soul's prayer to the end the strict prayer is not the meditation itself but the resolutions and other acts of will which the meditation produces.

beyond the point up to which it is necessary. Fr. Baker had many predecessors and contemporary writers to support him. It was an uphill fight all the same and destined to a lengthy, though not complete or final defeat.

Fr. Baker's doctrine, never more than a rough sketch, of passive contemplation, is less satisfactory. It seems to me clear that the prayer he describes as active contemplation, aspirations as opposed to forced acts, and in particular the prayer of interior silence, corresponds with St. Theresa's Prayer of Quiet and its highest stage probably with her prayer of Full Union. These, however, are states of infused or passive contemplation. Fr. Baker tells us that aspirations as opposed to the immediate acts produced by our own effort are elicited by the Holy Spirit. Is not this a passive rather than an active prayer? Since the entire development of prayer in the state of grace is the supernatural operation of God, we should not expect any very clear line of demarcation between the lower states, in which the Divine action is more or less concealed behind the action of the subject, and the higher, in which the conscious relation between these factors is reversed. Active contemplation passes gradually into passive, as spring into summer. Moreover the only passive prayer which Fr. Baker has described was, as he says himself, " rapt ", ecstasy. This, however, follows in St. Theresa's scheme, two states of passive prayer, Quiet, and Full Union.

The persuasion that passive contemplation differs essentially from active and is clearly distinguishable from it even in its lowest form arises, I believe, from a confusion between the substance and common, but not universal, concomitants of mystical prayer. These concomitants are vivid apprehensions of Divine Truth, e.g. the evident conviction of Catholic truth of which Fr. Baker speaks, or illuminations of the Divine Glory. These communications are so vivid that they are sometimes described as a sight, a vision, or as by Fr. Baker in his *Secretum*, a speech of God. We may well believe that the medium of these communications, since open vision is impossible on earth, are in fact the " infused species " of which Fr. Baker speaks. Abbot Butler, who disagreed with Fr. Baker on this point and rejected his theory of infused species, had in view the substantial mystical prayer : Fr. Baker, I think, the concomitant. In fact, they were speaking of different things.

Moreover, since these concomitant apprehensions are transitory acts, Fr. Baker having in mind such a concomitant experience, denied that passive prayer could be a state. Later on, however, he was himself to enter a permanent state of high passive prayer. But as he had ceased to write he could not modify his former statement.

We may also observe that the text on which Fr. Baker comments, the Cloud, speaks of the highest prayer in such terms as suggest an apprehension of God's glory of this type and which is in fact the concomitant, not the substance, of mystical prayer. "Then will He sometimes peradventure send out a beam of ghostly light, piercing this Cloud of Unknowing that is betwixt thee and Him and show thee some of His secrets." (Ch. 26.) Such an experience, while corresponding to that described by Fr. Baker as God's speech in his soul, and justifying his belief that the medium is infused species and that the experience cannot be an abiding state, is, as certainly, not the substance or essence of mystical "passive" prayer.

The substance of mystical prayer, even in its highest degree, the transforming union, is not any kind of illumination. It is the soul's conscious union with and occupation by the incomprehensible Godhead. As the union is a high degree of charity, the reception of God's will, the intuition of it is a high degree of faith, the reception of God's self-knowledge. And the seat of the union-intuition is the centre or ground of the spirit, the root of will and understanding alike. The union-intuition in which this prayer consists is thus the direct continuation of the union with the Godhead apprehended by faith, which is Fr. Baker's active contemplation. Fr. Baker was obliged by his authorities to make room for this dark adherence to the Godhead in passive prayer, side by side with the illuminations often concomitant upon it. But whereas he could clearly distinguish and demarcate the latter from his lower active contemplation, it is hard indeed to distinguish his account of the former (*Sancta Sophia*, Sec. IV, Chap. IV, paragraphs 5, 6) from his account of active contemplation (*ibid.*, Sec. IV, Chap. I, paragraphs 14-17). That he places the former prayer in the will, the latter in the centre beyond will and understanding is not a significant distinction. For the centre is pre-eminently the root of the will which is the actuality of the soul ; *nihil aliud sumus quam voluntates*.[1] And as the union advances and deepens, the union becomes increasingly central, in this ground rather than in any more superficial actuition of the will.

Moreover, active contemplation is described in terms applicable only to a high degree of infused prayer. " In which union (above all particular images) there is neither time nor place, but all is vacuity and emptiness, as if nothing were existent but God and the soul ; yea, so far is the soul from reflecting on her own existence, *that it seems to her that God and she are not distinct but one only thing ;* this is called by some mystic authors the state of nothingness, by others the state of totality ; because therein God is all in all, the container of all things." This absorption of self-consciousness by God-consciousness is evidently a sublime effect of the Divine operation and a very high degree of union,

[1] " We are nothing but wills "—St. Augustine.

far above any active contemplation in which the soul is the conscious agent and the conscious source of her acts. It is unfortunate that we cannot tell whether this passage was written from personal experience or taken from mystical writers. If written from experience, Fr. Baker must have been raised to a completely infused contemplation already but failed to recognize the fact because there was no ecstasy and no concomitant illumination, such as he had received on his second conversion.

In so far as we can distinguish between acquired and infused, active and passive contemplation, and it is a distinction of degree, not of kind, I believe that the forced acts of will, even when, as in Dame Gertrude's case affective, since they are enforced, that is consciously elicited by the will are acquired contemplation, aspirations on the other hand being consciously elicited by the work of the Spirit are infused or passive contemplation, corresponding to the prayer of Quiet. If Fr. Baker, though distinguishing aspirations from enforced acts, precisely by the conscious Divine production of the former, nevertheless terms them an active contemplation, it is because he was misled by his ecstatic illumination into the belief that such illumination always accompanies passive prayer, as in fact, we may suppose it did during those final years when Fr. Baker recognized his prayer as passive. And these illuminations may well have accounted for his abstinence from writing, as an illumination of Divine Truth made St. Thomas unable to continue his unfinished *Summa*. Like St. Thomas, Fr. Baker may have been impressed with the impotence of human language and thought to convey the Infinite Reality of Divine Truth.

That it was in fact for the profit of souls, the vast majority of contemplatives, called only to a lower degree of mystical union, probably the Prayer of Quiet or Full Union which illuminations do not normally accompany, that Fr. Baker kept silence about the higher degrees of prayer and their concomitant illuminations and, therefore, also of the desolation, the Night of Spirit bound up with them, we have already seen. His motive, however, was more probably the sense of impotence to express them.

It is interesting to observe that Fr. Baker had already recognized that these illuminations of Catholic truth apprehended from within in mystical prayer, are identical in nature, though not in authority, with the illuminations, in which God conveyed truth to the original organs of His public revelation, prophets and apostles.

In his teaching on mental prayer and the degrees of its progress Fr. Baker does but expound with a peculiar felicity, clarity, discretion and practical usefulness what had been said by others. The most distinctive and most valuable element in his spiritual teaching is his doctrine of Divine calls and inspirations.   Here also he can and does appeal to authority.   Holy Scripture, the liturgy, the Fathers of the Desert, Cassian and his own Patriarch St. Benedict have much to say of Divine guidance obtained by prayer.   Nevertheless, during the reaction against Protestant individualism, to insist upon the necessity for spiritual progress of seeking and obeying the inspirations of the Holy Spirit must have seemed dangerous.   Was it not the doctrine of the Spanish illuminists and in contemporary England of the Quakers, who, moreover, had not yet acquired their reputation for impeccable respectability and harboured a number of enthusiasts who alleged Divine inspiration for such vagaries as walking nude through the streets ?   Did it not refuse obedience to superiors and directors in favour of selfwill masked as Divine inspiration ?   In his preface to *Sancta Sophia*, Dom Serenus Cressy is obliged to refute such objections and in particular the assimilation of Fr. Baker's doctrine to heretical illuminism.   This doctrine is in fact, as Fr. Baker pointed out, con-tained in the Collect which asks God to prevent our actions by His inspiration and does but explain St. Paul's text " as many as are led by the Spirit, they are the sons of God."   It is a doctrine of spiritual liberty without the least taint of licence.   Every heresy, it is said, is the revenge of a neglected truth.   And the unguarded and exclusive emphasis laid by the Quakers on immediate inspiration was the revenge of the long neglect into which the genuine Catholic doctrine of inspirations, as Fr. Baker expounds it, had been suffered to fall.   Indeed, precisely by meeting and satisfying what was true in the Quaker doctrine, it was the best antidote and remedy for what was false in it, though it must be admitted, that, as far as contemporary Quakers were concerned, the language used about them by implication both by Fr. Baker and still more by Fr. Cressy was not calculated to make this remedy applicable in practice.

    In our time the doctrine of Divine inspirations has become the distinctive and most essential tenet of an important contemporary religious movement, the Oxford Groups.   According to them every action of the day, however trivial or secular, even the choice of a tailor or a train must be decided by Divine guidance, to be sought by and expected from daily silent prayer.   And it is no doubt the truth and value contained in both practices, regular mental prayer, and seeking Divine guidance, which has attracted so many to the movement and given it so much strength and vigour, in spite of the exaggeration and onesidedness with which they are presented.   For the former practice has been neglected by the majority of Protestants, the latter by almost all modern Christians, whether Protestant or Catholic.   Fr. Baker's doctrine, which safeguards and duly incorporates in the entire body of Catholic truth the practice of seeking and following individual guidance is thus our best answer to Group excesses, because it recognizes the truth they contain.

As against all illuminism Fr. Baker denies that we are to expect Divine illumination on matters already made known by public religious authority, such as the doctrines of faith and moral laws. The illuminations of passive prayer are extraordinary, not to be sought, and always confirmations of truth already declared by the public revelation in the Church's custody. Nor do the Divine inspirations concern actions already prescribed or forbidden by the duties of our vocation or the command of lawful superiors. They are confined to actions in themselves indifferent which can without sin be performed or omitted. For although such actions or omissions are in their matter indifferent, they are not so in the concrete. A good intention makes them positively good, and a bad intention correspondingly evil. Moreover, it requires that we should do or omit, as is, not necessarily in itself, but for us here and now, the most perfect course. How are we to secure this pure intention, and the choice of the more perfect course for us to adopt? Only the inspiration of the Holy Spirit will cleanse our motive from the impurity of self-seeking and enlighten us to choose rightly, where from the nature of the case no external rule is applicable. Indeed, we shall need the inspiration of the Holy Ghost to perform even obligatory actions and omissions with a pure intention and in the best way. Unlike the Groups, Fr. Baker does not extend inspirations to secular matters in so far as they have no spiritual relevance. For example, though we might ask and expect Divine guidance in choosing a morally unobjectionable investment, we could not expect it, to find the most profitable investment. Perhaps, however, Fr. Baker, writing as he does, primarily for religious, does not sufficiently allow for cases in which success in a secular undertaking is necessary for subsistence. For example, though I could not expect Divine inspiration to enable me to make a fortune on the stock exchange, I might surely ask for it to prevent my losing my savings by a bad investment.

This, however, is a side issue. The object of the Divine calls and inspirations is our spiritual progress, our gradual emancipation from selfwill and attachment to creatures, to detachment from self and creatures and abandonment to the will of God. It is in this spiritual progress that every soul must observe her individual calls, follow the inspirations obtained by mental prayer for her spiritual guidance. In contrast with the Groups Fr. Baker tells us we must not expect the inspiration and guidance to be given in our prayer itself. To expect it then would tend to distract our prayer from God to our needs and problems. Having laid our problem before God in prayer, we must banish it from our thoughts till our prayer is finished. Then the guidance will be given either by an enlightenment of our reason or, if, after careful consideration of the arguments in favour of both courses, the mind remains doubtful, by a blind impulse of the will. If neither form of guidance is received, we may choose at random, even by lots, tossing up as we should say, and take the result as God's will. But no doubt Fr. Baker would have regarded this solution as applicable only where the pros and cons are balanced so evenly that there really is very little to choose between the alternatives and the sole spiritual value of the choice made consists in the desire to obey God, to discover and perform His will. Indeed, as we have seen, Fr. Baker thought that all lawful actions are spiritually indifferent and receive their value solely from our obedience to God's will in performing them.

This indifference as to the matter of these acts and omissions is probably bound up with the most important difference between Fr. Baker's teaching and illuminism. Illuminism claims that if we follow Divine inspirations we shall always choose the course in itself the best and the wisest, i.e. it promises infallible guidance. Fr. Baker admits that, even when we have sought Divine Guidance in the way he prescribes, we may still make a mistake in the matter of our choice. God may nevertheless allow us to choose what will prove the wrong or the less wise course. But the mistake thus permitted, if not indeed apparently inspired by God, will be the best for our spiritual advancement. A choice itself an error and more or less a failure, for our soul will be more advantageous and more successful than would have been the choice in itself better and more successful. We may, therefore, say that whereas illuminism promises infallible guidance, Fr. Baker promises only infallibly profitable guidance, profitable, that is to say, for our soul's progress to God. And it is obvious that (objectively) infallible guidance would not be infallibly profitable guidance. For constant objective success would be inconsistent with the mortification and humiliation necessary for spiritual progress, and would in fact tend to foster the attachment, self-satisfaction and pride from which it is the object of prayer to deliver us. It would also make religion a means to worldly success. On the other hand such measure even of objective success as is good for the individual under his particular circumstances—itself, of course, a most varying and unpredictable measure—is guaranteed by the infallibly profitable guidance taught by Fr. Baker.

Fr. Baker's life affords, I believe, an instructive example of infallibly profitable, as opposed to infallible guidance. His well intentioned but tactless criticism of Dom Rudisind which led to his leaving Douay was no doubt written only after prayer for light and in accordance with what he believed to be the Divine Will. In itself his action was, so far as we can judge, mistaken. Nevertheless, it procured him that final purification of his journey to England which was, it would seem, indispensable for his advance to a higher degree of prayer. It was, therefore, by God's infallibly profitable guidance, that he was permitted to make what appears to have been the objective mistake of attacking Dom Rudisind. We may, however, wonder whether in the end the latter, however indignant at the time, did not profit by Fr. Baker's rebuke.

It should be observed that according to Fr. Baker, the Divine inspiration inclines in case of doubt to omission rather than positive action. For a multiplicity of activities not demanded by the duty of our state hinders contemplation and the simplicity it induces. It turns us outward, makes us extroverted, instead of inwards to the soul where God dwells and works. This passivity contrasts strikingly with our modern worship of activity, the hustle and bustle of constant business and exciting amusement. But it is precisely what the modern world needs, if the spiritual life is to revive and the voice of God to be heard. Modern psychology tends to regard the introvert as a pathological case. He is in fact the man who alone lives a worthy human life, possessing his own soul and finding there his God. It must, however, be admitted that introversion without prayer is indeed pathological. For the irreligious introvert finds only his empty self with its illusions and daydreams. It is the road to madness and a state even more unhealthy than that of the extrovert. The introversion preached by Fr. Baker is Godward, not selfward. Moreover, all works of obligation must be punctually performed, however many and however distracting and, if performed with the right intention, cannot hinder union with God, though they will, I think, hinder the conscious awareness of that union. And in the higher degrees of contemplation external activities no longer interfere with contemplation in the apex of the spirit above their tumult of images and thoughts. For there is no longer any attachment to them.

As regards the Sacraments, Fr. Baker keeps the happy mean between the excess which believes that their use automatically produces a high degree of holiness and their depreciation, if not disuse, by many Protestants. For, while duly valuing the Sacraments, he warns us that without interior prayer they will not enable us to overcome our faults and advance far on the road towards God. Only the assiduous practice of mental prayer enables the grace they confer to operate effectively.

His doctrine of Divine guidance diminishes the rôle assigned by Fr. Baker to the human director. It is not for him to prescribe the details of prayer and conduct. For he cannot have sufficient knowledge of the soul's state and call. He can but supply general instructions whereby his penitent or directee can enable himself to receive the guidance of the inner Director. Hence for contemplatives following

the way of prayer through the will, he is opposed to the constant
self-examinations and repeated confessions of the same faults then so
popular in many quarters, though he does not deny that they may
be useful in awakening and maintaining a tender conscience in those
active souls whose consciences are not enlightened and cleansed by
God in contemplative prayer.

It must, I think, be admitted that Fr. Baker undervalued the Divine
Office as a means of sanctification. He was, indeed, well aware that in
primitive monasticism the vocal recitation of the Psalter was the
prayer of the monks. He also recognized that it is possible to say the
Office, as a prayer of aspirations, if the Holy Spirit so enables and moves
an advanced soul. He had in fact prayed it himself thus. He
even says that such vocal-mental prayer is the safest, being least liable
to harm the head and spirits, in modern language strain the nerves.
But he thought that under contemporary conditions the Office could
not ordinarily be used as mental prayer.

If, however, the Office can be prayed aspiratively why can it not at
a lower stage be prayed as a prayer of forced acts? It would seem
eminently adapted for this. Some modern representatives of the
Bakerite tradition maintain that the function of the Office is not
to be a mental prayer, but solely to fulfil man's obligation to worship
God. But in the last resort what is worship, if it is more than external,
but the raising up of the soul to God, and its surrender to His Majesty?
Does not the *Gloria Patri* involve in principle the complete abandonment to God which the spiritual ascent with its degrees of prayer
progressively realises? And what is the 118th Psalm, recited on so many
days of the year, but a series of acts of submission to, and aspiration
after, the law, that is the will, of God, the essence therefore and object
of the immediate acts recommended by Fr. Baker? Certainly where
the Office is recited in choir at a pace allowing no return upon distractions or slowing down and the regular life admits them, there
will and should be set times for mental prayer apart from the Office,
though, even so, a portion of the latter might well provide the material
of acts. Where, however, circumstances do not allow more time for
prayer, the Office recited in whole or part is surely the best form of
prayer. For its acts are made in unison with the Church and guided
by her appointment, in accordance with the scheme of redemption
celebrated in her liturgical year. Even Fr. Baker was not unaffected
by the liturgical decay which had already begun.

These differences on points of detail do not affect my conviction that
Fr. Baker's spiritual doctrine is the most practically valuable that
I am acquainted with for all who desire a life inspired and guided by
prayer. Many writers hold up a very high and difficult ascetical ideal,
without showing how it may be attained, others are too emotional

if not sentimental, others are rather theoretical than practical, others take our devotion no further than the Saints and the Sacred Humanity,[1] and others describe summits to which only a minute number are called.   Fr. Baker, especially if read together with the *Cloud* on which he commented and illustrated by the inner life and devotion of his great-hearted disciple, Gertrude More, leads us with gentle yet firm guidance towards God.   He asks us to correspond with, not to outstep grace, to observe our individual call instead of burdening our souls with the practices and prayers of others, even if in themselves more perfect than ours.   Though he does not hide from us that the ascent is rough and steep, he assures us that we shall be guided and supported by a Guide who will not ask for any exertion beyond the strength which He alone can accurately gauge, since He gives it Himself. The principles of what was known in Fr. Baker's lifetime as Bakerism can be taught to all of ordinary intelligence, while inexhaustible by the most intelligent.   They can and should be the foundation of the spiritual education of Catholic children.   If this were the case there would not be such a lamentable tale of lapsed Catholics.   Those trained in the school of the Spirit will have received the best security against the materialism of the modern world and its human idolatries. The conversion of Mr. Fursden's mother-in-law would be repeated time and again by the employment of the same Bakerite method. No one to whom Catholicism had been presented, as Fr. Baker presents it, could possibly imagine that priest, director or saint, not even Our Lady or the *humanity* of Our Lord came *between* The Catholic and God, or interfered with his direct access to the Triune Godhead, incomprehensible in His transcendence yet apprehended by faith and intimately present in the soul, as nothing created can be, however holy.

Fr. Baker's doctrine is so simple, so discreet, so replete with sanctified commonsense, that it is difficult to convey its distinctive quality, traditional originality—if the oxymoron may be excused—and homely sublimity.   The Abbe Brémond might have done justice to Fr. Baker and Bakerism, though he would perhaps have over-refined and subtilised them.   I can but implore any readers who do not already know their Baker to make his acquaintance.   If *Sancta Sophia* seems too large a mouthful to begin with, though selections could easily be made, there is his own abridgment of Bakerism in his *Inner Life of Dame Gertrude More*.   Or if we would begin with his biography, there are the autobiographical portions of the *Secretum* excerpted and arranged by Dom Justin McCann under the title *The Confessions of Father Baker* and the two longer lives by Salvin and Cressy, edited together by Dom

---

[1] Like the author of *The Cloud*, Fr. Baker observes the Augustinian rule *per Christum Hominem ad Christum Deum*.

McCann. Finally, there is the book to which Fr. Baker owed so much and which we cannot separate from him, a book which has lately attracted, though not without serious misconception, Aldous Huxley. I mean the *Cloud of Unknowing*, now published with Fr. Baker's commentary. Those who desire to practise Fr. Baker's prayer of acts, assuming of course they have the requisite call, will find his own collection at the end of *Sancta Sophia*. And there are the acts from which he partly derived them, those compiled by Blosius. Or there are the longer affective prayers by Dame Gertrude More, published in a special volume. Her *Idiot's Devotions*, however, are not hers but Fr. Baker's, consisting in the main of the acts appended to *Sancta Sophia*. In one way or another come to Fr. Baker. The result will not fail to be a large addition to the Bakerites. And I know no better, wiser or safer school of prayer. So I end by echoing Fr. Baker's petition :

"The blessed spirit of prayer rest upon us all."

Rev. J. LEONARD, C.M.

ST. VINCENT DE PAUL

A.D. 1581–1660

A FEW YEARS AGO, at the annual meeting of *The Mental After-Care Association*, the Chairman, in the course of his report, after pointing out that this work " for poor persons convalescent or removed from institutions for the insane " calls for the highest qualities and energies of a staff as it demands patience, knowledge, tact, ability and personality, went on to say : " in its work the Association is carrying out the injunction of the almost forgotten but great and farseeing Vincent de Paul who was certainly the first to proclaim that mental disease was not different from bodily disease and that Christianity demanded of the humane and the powerful to protect and the skilful to relieve the one as well as the other." And Lord Wakefield of Hythe, in his opening address at this meeting (1933) declared that " there can be no finer task than that which seeks to lighten the darkness of night in mortal minds."

It is true, no doubt, that the name of Vincent de Paul is almost forgotten, if indeed it was ever remembered, outside Catholic circles in the English-speaking world, but in those circles the name of " this great and far-seeing man " has been for over three centuries a household word, and his long life was devoted in a wider and nobler sense than perhaps Lord Wakefield intended " to lighten the darkness of night in mortal minds."

Vincent de Paul was born on April 24th, 1581, in the hamlet of Pouy, a few miles from the town of Dax in the old French province of Gascony. Both his father and mother, Jean de Paul and Bertrande de Moras, were of yeoman stock and he was the third of their six children, three boys and three girls. Like all country lads he helped in the work of his father's farm and was never tired of telling his noble friends in later life that he had herded swine in his youth. As he was both industrious and intelligent, his father sent him, whilst still quite a child, to a College directed by the Friars Minor in Dax where he made such a good impression that he was to all intents and purposes adopted by the resident magistrate of the district, a certain M. de Comet. When he had finished his classical studies, he proceeded to Toulouse, then second in the estimation of the learned to the great University of Paris, to pursue his studies in philosophy and theology which lasted for seven years.   He was ordained sub-deacon and deacon in 1598 and, two years later, on September 23rd, 1600, was raised to the priesthood.   He opened an " Academy for the sons of the nobility and gentry " and in 1605 was summoned to Bordeaux to the Duke of Epernon, a relative of one of his pupils, who wished to nominate him to a bishopric.   Nothing, however, came of this for, on his journey homewards, whilst travelling from Marseilles to Narbonne by sea, he was captured by Barbary pirates and then began a series of adventures which the late Abbé Bremond described as " the last of the Arabian nights."   He was first sold to a fisherman and then to an old alchemist who employed him as an assistant in the pursuit of " the philosopher's stone."   He was subsequently purchased by a renegade Savoyard on one of whose three wives, a Greek schismatic, he made such an impression by his conversation that she reproached her husband for having abandoned the religion professed by his slave. The renegade resolved to attempt an escape from Barbary, and accompanied by Vincent they succeeded in reaching Aigues-Mortes in the summer of 1607.   They went on to Avignon where they were welcomed by the Papal Vice-Legate who shortly afterwards took them along with him to Rome.   Two letters written by the Saint to M. de Comet have been preserved in which he gives a vivid, racy and amusing account of his adventures.   The reader can see from them that at this time Vincent de Paul was a young man, anxious to acquire information of every description, especially scientific, easily able to make friends, kind-hearted, generous, anxious to please, adventurous, ambitious for preferment and withal devout and possessed of an unlimited trust in Providence.   After a year and a half in Rome, he was entrusted with a diplomatic mission to Henri IV and arrived in Paris towards the end of 1608.   After some time, he obtained the post of chaplain to Queen Marguerite of Navarre.   In 1610 he passed through a severe spiritual crisis which determined the course of the remaining half century of his life and set his feet definitely on the road to sanctity from which they never subsequently wandered.

One of his fellow-chaplains, a learned and distinguished theologian, suffered from such violent temptations against the faith that he contemplated suicide.   He poured out his troubles to Vincent who gave him good advice which, however, proved unavailing and, in the end, moved by the wretched theologian's mental agony, Vincent prayed to God to be allowed to bear the other's burden.   His prayer was answered and for four or five years he was the victim of appalling doubts not only concerning the Christian religion but even the existence of God.   Those doubts were subsequently overcome but not until after he had resolved " to honour Jesus Christ more fully and to imitate Him more perfectly " than he had hitherto done by " devoting his whole life, for the sake of Jesus Christ, to the service of the poor." Up to this time he does not seem to have lived a life any way different from that of the average, contemporary, devout ecclesiastic, but from then onwards he set out determinedly to imitate as closely as he could the life of Our Lord Jesus Christ.

He was then thirty years of age, " of medium height, well-built and well-proportioned." His hair was black, his complexion olive and he wore the slight moustache and closely-cropped beard then usual with the French clergy. He had a remarkably fine head ; the brow was high, broad and " majestic," the nose large and fleshy, the jaws clean-cut and determined, the chin square and strong, the mouth wide and close-lipped. But the most striking feature of his counten-ance were the eyes " which were dark, deep-set, and twinkling with humour, mischief and irony." All his life long he bore the marks of his race and early environment and though his natural gifts and qualities were purified and ennobled as he advanced in holiness, he never utterly ceased to be a Gascon son of the soil. Even as a young man, he was possessed of a remarkable fund of good sense and he could not easily be imposed on by even the greatest and most learned. He had indeed a profound respect for the powers that be in Church and State, great prudence and powers of discrimination, a marked reserve of manner with a tendency to secrecy and self-communing. He spoke easily and well and his conversation was enlivened by a spice of mischief which revealed at times that not only was he a man of undoubted originality but that he had never fully lost his Gascon sense of humour and love of adventure.

When he had set out on the road to Christian perfection he was enlightened and guided by two remarkable men, Cardinal de Bérulle and St. Francis de Sales. Bérulle, according to St. Vincent, " was endowed with such solid learning and holiness that his like could not be found." His powerful and original mind, after long meditation on the Scriptures, set forth a body of doctrine that was to prove of lasting importance to the Church of France. " He saw God in everything and everything in God and taught a lesson of utter self-renunciation, absolute detachment from creatures and an entire immolation of self, combined with a continual absorption in God and an unceasing reference, not only to the example but to the ' states ' of the Incarnate Word." The essentials of his mystical teaching were subsequently translated into simple language by St. Vincent for the benefit of his disciples, both men and women, but much more effectively and strikingly in his own daily life. In 1619 he became acquainted with St. Francis de Sales and was soon on terms of intimate

friendship with " the blessed bishop of Geneva." There can be little
doubt that the example and writings of St. Francis exercised a
stronger and more lasting impression on St. Vincent than did those
of any of his contemporaries. According to Pope Pius XI, the great
truth for which St. Francis de Sales stands is that holiness of life is
not a privilege of the few to the exclusion of the many but that all
Christians are called to it and the obligation of arriving at it is
incumbent on all. He combated " the prejudice that true holiness
appears to be surrounded by so many difficulties that it cannot be
attained by those living in the world," and, " set out to show how
holiness is perfectly reconcilable with every kind of duty and every
condition of civil life." It may be said that in these words Abbot
Butler summarises the history of St. Vincent's propagation and
extension of the fundamental doctrines of St. Francis de Sales.

In 1613, Vincent, guided by Bérulle, accepted the cure of souls in
the parish of Clichy, than a suburb of Paris, and this, according to
himself, was the happiest time of his life. However, he did not enjoy
it long for, again acting on Bérulle's advice, he took up the post of tutor
to the children of Philip Emmanuel de Gondi, General of the Galleys,
and chaplain to his household. St. Vincent was destined to spend
twelve years with this family, save for a brief interval when he acted
as parish priest of Châtillon-les-Dombes, and it was through the
influence of the General and his wife that the Saint was enabled to
begin a number of those great works of charity for which he became
famous. The first of these was begun in a very small and simple way
and the same holds true of all St. Vincent's enterprises. At Châtillon,
he established an association of ladies to look after the material and
spiritual needs of the poor in their own homes. The venture, thanks
to the wise regulations he drew up for its guidance, proved successful
and, on his return to Paris, he founded a " Confraternity of Ladies of
Charity " in several parishes in the city and also in towns and villages
on the de Gondi estates. He also established similar Confraternities
for men with this difference, that while the women's associations were
primarily concerned to serve the sick poor in their own homes, the men's
were concerned with poor persons who were able to work. It was
on this model that Frederick Ozanam, two centuries later, established
" The Society of St. Vincent de Paul " which now has branches
throughout the whole world.

One winter's night in 1625 whilst Vincent was staying with the
de Gondi's in their château at Folleville in Picardy he was summoned
to hear the confession of a dying man. On the following day, the
man declared in the presence of Madame de Gondi that he had been
making sacrilegious confessions for years and that, if he had not had the
opportunity of confessing to St. Vincent, he would have died in his sins.

This incident made a profound impression on the lady, who conceived the idea of inviting members of religious Orders in Paris to go round her estates, instructing the peasants on the principal mysteries of religion and on the benefits of making general confessions. She laid aside for this purpose the sum of £20,000, the interest on which was calculated to defray all the expenses of these missions, but as none of the Orders approached were able to undertake the work she turned to her chaplain and prevailed on him to make a beginning. With a few friends he took up his residence in an old College of the University of Paris called *Les Bons Enfants*, of which he had been made Principal, and in this way the Congregation of the Mission came into existence.

De Gondi, as General of the Galleys, was responsible for the lot of the convicts condemned to man the galleys and the state of physical, moral and religious degradation in which the wretched men were compelled to live was appalling. St. Vincent reminded the General of his obligations and a serious attempt was made to better their condition. Hospitals for sick convicts were provided in Paris and Marseilles, and the Saint's untiring efforts for the material and spiritual welfare of those wretched men resulted in his being appointed Chaplain General of all the King's Galleys by Louis XIII in 1639. In his old age he once remarked : " If God has been pleased to make use of the most miserable of men for the conversion of some heretics, they themselves declared that this was due to the patience and kindness that were shown them. Even the convicts with whom I lived were won over by no other means and if I chanced to speak coldly to them I spoiled everything ; on the other hand, when I praised their resignation, sympathised with them in their sufferings and kissed their chains, then it was that they listened to me."

After the death of Madame de Gondi, Vincent went to reside permanently in the Collège des Bons Enfants. In 1632, he moved to the ancient and extensive Priory of St. Lazare which became his headquarters and the centre of all his activities until his death on September 27th, 1660.

The preaching of missions in country districts made him realise that if this work were to prove permanently fruitful it was essential to provide the people with a zealous and devout pastoral clergy. He knew from experience that the clergy and especially the country clergy were, in general, ill-fitted for their duties. The first step he took for their reformation was to bring together candidates for ordination before they received Holy Orders and, whilst arousing their fervour by means of a spiritual retreat, to supply them with a brief course of pastoral theology. This experiment was begun at Beauvais and proved to be a success. Subsequently, thanks to the generosity of his friends, he was able to supply free board and lodging for all ecclesiastics who made a retreat at St. Lazare and this work was developed and extended during his life-time to other European countries. In the course of time, gratuitous retreats for laymen were also given at St. Lazare and, within the period that elapsed from their institution until his death, more than twenty thousand laymen had made a spiritual retreat within the walls of the old Priory.

The spiritual welfare of ecclesiastics, however, was Vincent's work of predilection and in 1633 he established an association of priests who met every Tuesday at St. Lazare to confer on moral, religious and spiritual topics and from this body some of the most eminent bishops of the Church of France in the XVIIth century were drawn. Bossuet, who had been a member, wrote : " When raised to the priesthood, we were associated with this group of ecclesiastics who met weekly to treat together on divine matters. Vincent was its author and its soul. Whilst we listened hungrily to his instructions, there was not one of us who did not feel that the words of the Apostle were being fulfilled : ' If any man speak, let his speech be that of God '."

A further extension of the training of the clergy and one destined to be more fruitful and permanent than any yet attempted by St. Vincent was the establishment of seminaries. The Council of Trent had called for the erection of clerical seminaries but up to this time the few and scattered attempts to carry out its recommendations had proved of little avail, especially in France. In 1635, after Vincent had moved to St. Lazare, he started what would now be called a " petty " seminary in the Bons Enfants where the boys received a semi-literary, semi-religious education with a view to the priesthood. He was dissatisfied with the results, transferred the seminary to a building in the grounds of St. Lazare and, in 1642, established a " major " or " great " seminary in the Collège des Bons Enfants.

As his Congregation increased in numbers its activities were multiplied. He was asked by Rome to send his missionaries to various European countries, including Scotland and Ireland, and willingly did so. Mr. Compton Mackenzie says that the preservation of the Faith in the Hebrides and portions of the Highlands was mainly due to the efforts of those priests and that St. Vincent de Paul deserves to be known as " The Apostle of the Hebrides." As time went on the missionaries were sent to preach the Gospel in pagan and infidel lands and the history of their apostolic labours in Barbary and Madagascar is one of the brightest pages in the annals of the propagation of the Faith in the XVIIth century.

Whilst all this work was going on for the reform of the clergy and the preaching of the Gospel, St. Vincent never ceased for a moment to look after the spiritual and temporal welfare of the poor and afflicted. The Confraternities of Charity were intended to provide opportunities for women of wealth and position to manifest their love of God by the exercise of the corporal and spiritual works of mercy. It soon became evident that, partly owing to inexperience and the legitimate demands of their family and social obligations, their efforts needed to be supplemented by some regular, trained, permanent body. It was this that led to the foundation of the Company of Daughters of Charity who were intended to co-operate with and complete the work of the Ladies. The beginnings of this new Society, at the present day the most numerous and widespread Order in the Church, were very simple. In 1634, one of the most active and experienced of the Ladies of Charity received four or five devout country girls into her home and undertook to provide for their maintenance and their spiritual and professional training. This lady was Louise de Marillac, a niece of Marshal de Marillac and his brother the Keeper of the Seals, who was by now the widow of Antoine Le Gras, the private secretary of Marie de Medici. Louise was of an ardent and generous disposition but of a rather restless, unhappy and scrupulous temperament. Under the guidance of St. Vincent she learned to be calm, serene and even gay and ultimately attained to such heights of heroic virtue as to be canonised by Pope Pius XI.

The Daughters, or Sisters, of Charity began with visiting and nursing the sick poor in their homes but as their number increased, they gradually extended their ministrations until these embraced nearly every form of Christian charitable endeavour. In 1638 they opened a Foundling Hospital. For many years those unfortunate babies had been allowed to die of hunger and neglect ; they were even sold to beggars who mutilated their limbs to arouse the sympathy of the public and extort alms. It is estimated that, during the first quarter of a century after the foundation of the Hospital, more than forty thousand children had been rescued from starvation or death. In 1653 they undertook the management of a Hospice of the Name of Jesus which afforded a home for forty poor men and an equal number of women who were saved from a life of mendicancy, and this institution proved to be the forerunner of many similar establishments. Three years later, St. Vincent was asked to undertake a much more difficult task. The streets of Paris swarmed with able-bodied beggars whose numbers were estimated at not less than forty thousand and whose ranks were filled with thieves, prostitutes and criminals of every kind. The Government determined to open a General Hospice for all beggars who would be compelled to clear off the streets and go there. The idea of compulsion was utterly distasteful to St. Vincent. He wished to begin with a couple of hundred volunteers who, by showing that they were content with the way they were being treated, might induce others to enter the Hospice freely. Though his proposal was rejected, he did his best to make the lot of the inmates more tolerable by sending the Sisters of Charity to manage the institution. The manifold labours of these devoted women were not confined to Paris. Before their founder's death they were at work in many cities of France and had even gone as far afield as Poland.

The establishment of the Company of the Daughters of Charity was a daring experiment. Hitherto, devout women who wished to devote their lives to the service of God had had to retire within the walls of a monastery and Vincent de Paul was now sending them out not only into the streets and slums of great cities but also to the battlefields of Europe. The success of this experiment was due to the fact that, in conformity with his principles and ideals of government, he was prepared to allow vital concepts to develop without undue interference, that he was always ready to learn from experience and never in a hurry to promulgate fixed sets of rules and regulations. He was fond of quoting St. Luke's statement : " Jesus began to do and to teach " and based his methods on that text. When he did set down rules in writing it was only after they had been tested by years of experience and even then he allowed them to be modified by local conditions and needs. He was prepared to face any contingency and had learned the secret of turning obstacles, in which he recognised the guidance of divine Providence, into means of action.

On the death of Louis XIII in 1643, the Queen Regent, Anne of Austria, established a council to deal with the ecclesiastical affairs of the kingdom and summoned Vincent to take his place at the " Council of Conscience," as it came to be known. Despite his reluctance, for he had made it a principle never to discuss, still less to intervene in, affairs of State, he was forced to accept the honour and remained a member of the Council for ten years when he was dismissed by Mazarin whose policy and statecraft were antipathetic to all that St. Vincent held most dear.

The bulk of the work of the Council fell on the Saint's shoulders and he laboured courageously and untiringly for the welfare of the Church of France. He co-operated with the men and women who were bent on restoring the primitive fervour of their respective Orders by securing the nomination of Abbots and Abbesses who were worthy of their position. He endeavoured to have devout and learned ecclesiastics appointed to vacant benefices and especially to bishoprics. In this he was not always successful for he had constantly to withstand the open or concealed opposition of Mazarin who looked on a valuable benefice or great bishopric as a means of securing supporters of his political schemes. Vincent de Paul had also to see that the provisions of the Edict of Nantes were observed and although he did not love heresy he certainly did not hate heretics. " He acted firmly but never bitterly ; it was always evident that it was never his intention to wound Christian charity and that he well knew how to discriminate between men and their religious opinions. He was fully convinced that persuasion and not force is not only the better but the more successful way of leading men's minds back to the truths of religion and never failed to render justice to his Huguenot fellow-countrymen." As a member of the Council he had to oppose Jansenism and no episode of his career does him greater honour. He had known the leaders of the party intimately and had for years been on terms of close friendship with the " patriarch of Port-Royal "—the enigmatic Abbé de Saint-Cyran, whose life he saved when threatened by Richelieu's suspicions. As a man of action he had a natural antipathy to subtle theological controversies and was convinced that the energies and abilities of " the gentlemen of Port-Royal " might have been more profitably expended in labouring for the salvation of souls. Pascal, indeed, in the last months of his brief life, would seem to have reached the same conclusion.

Finally, he was called to play a part in the civil wars of the Fronde and here he adopted the ungrateful rôle of " honest broker." In January, 1649, he made an attempt to secure peace that nearly cost him his life when he left Paris to persuade Mazarin to retire at least for a time from public life. He failed and characteristically laid the blame on himself. The civil wars were carried on for three years and during this dreadful time, one of the darkest in the history of France, he worked unceasingly to provide the unfortunate people, harried by the troops of both parties, with the consolations of religion and with supplies of money, food, clothing, seeds, agricultural implements and tools. The Lieutenant-General of St. Quentin, in a letter thanking him for having saved the lives of hundreds of thousands of poor men and women, saluted him with the title of *Pater Patriae*, and surely no man ever better deserved the noble title of Father of his country.

It surely can be no matter of surprise that the character and career of Vincent de Paul has aroused feelings of sympathetic admiration even in the most unexpected quarters. Voltaire, for instance, in a letter to the Marquis de Villette, writes : " Vincent de Paul is my saint ; he is the patron of founders. He has left more useful monuments behind him than did his sovereign Louis XIII. Amidst the wars of the Fronde he was equally respected by both sides. He alone could have prevented the massacre of St. Bartholomew. He desired to have the infernal bell that gave the signal for the massacre demolished. He was so humble of heart that he declined to wear, on the feasts of the Church, the vestments that had been presented to him by the Medicis."

St. Vincent de Paul's love for his fellow-men was, however, based on more noble and enduring principles than those dreamed of by the philosopher of Ferney and his associates. He had realised, like every Catholic saint, that the great fundamental truth of the Christian religion is the Fatherhood of God Who, because He is Father, loves His divine Son and, in Him, all men. St. Vincent showed by words and example that men are bound to love one another with the same love with which God loves them and that if men will not love their brethren in Jesus Christ neither do they love God nor does God love them. This was the truth that guided and inspired his life and that earned for him the glorious title of Patron Saint of all works of charity in the Catholic Church, which was conferred on him by Pope Pius X.

MONTAGUE SUMMERS, M.A., F.R.S.L.

JOHN DRYDEN

A.D. 1631–1700

THERE ARE FEW, if any, among the greatest names in the annals of our native literature who during past centuries have suffered more reverses from the ebb and flow of time than John Dryden. His genius was amply recognized by his contemporaries. He was honoured and rewarded by two kings ; indisputably he dominated, and justly dominated—living and dead—the whole field of English letters, criticism, poetry, the drama, for full a hundred years. Yet even during his own life his creed and politics were detested : he was insulted and deprived by a usurper ; amid the ribald laughter of a turncoat town he was held up to scorn and reprobation in libels of almost unexampled foulness and brutality. Among the professed critics, the phlegmatic Addison, as we might have expected, at once proved niggling, spleenful and unfair. Jacob Tonson used to attribute this ugly caprice to sheer jealousy. He was " so eager to be the first named " himself, said the shrewd old publisher, but at the same time it is also clear that his rigidity and narrowness could not endure the splendid glow of Dryden's faith. In conversation too Addison's tongue was that of a common backbiter, so " that he and his friend, Sir Richard Steele, used to run down even Dryden's character as far as they could," to the loudly expressed indignation of Pope and Congreve who warmly championed the friend they had so dearly loved. Alexander Pope, indeed, and Pope's mighty school hailed Dryden as the Master ; to the Augustans his " energy divine " was a ceaseless inspiration. Dr. Johnson eloquently argued his supremacy, but did not set himself to solve the secret of that supremacy. Barely two generations later T. B. Macaulay shows himself (as his wont) insolent and currish and dull in his attacks which are plainly begotten of bigotry or prejudice. Not a few Romantics (and Gray who should have known better is but lukewarm) even from Joseph Warton's day had been eyeing Dryden with a certain grudging, a certain ungenerous suspicion. The personality and influence of " our immortal bard " to use the phrase of Scott, a passionate admirer, they were perforce bound to recognize, but curiously such men as Wordsworth, Southey,

Coleridge could not see that Dryden is essentially a romantic poet and yet one would have thought this must be self-evident to a reader, however casual, of those glorious tragedies " Tyrannick Love," " The Conquest of Granada," " Aureng-Zebe," " Don Sebastian," or the St. Cecilia Odes, the songs, " The Hind and the Panther," the " Fables " —to cite no more. That Dryden is a romantic poet was plain enough to Dr. Johnson when he wrote : " Dryden's page is a natural field, rising into inequalities, and diversified by the varied exuberance of abundant vegetation ; Pope's is a velvet lawn, shaven by the scythe, and levelled by the roller." " Do you wish for invention, imagination, sublimity, character? Seek them," bids Lord Byron, "in the Fables of Dryden, the ' Ode of Saint Cecilia's Day,' and ' Absalom and Achitophel.' "

If the Surrealists of to-day were gifted with real penetration instead of lamenting over Dryden as an artist who was hampered and repressed by the conventions of education and social environment they would appreciate that in Dryden we have a striking figure of the man who so far from conforming to any stale academic tradition or accepting the current norms of taste had a power of intellectual strength to rise above his age, towering like a Titan, that he was the man who moulded his age, not only deciding questions of literature and art but guiding it along subtlest lines of philosophical inquiry and above all directing it in religious debate. Those of that following who are blind to this confess themselves self-betrayed.

By common consent the position of Dryden is at last stabilized. It is conceded by all (a few eccentrics except) that he has his place in the very front of English literature. He is to be named with the greatest, with Chaucer and with Shakespeare. To my mind it is neither fanciful nor impertinent to emphasize that all three were Catholics, for Dryden achieved his noblest and most thoughtful work after his conversion. Inevitably their Catholicism gave these three poets a broader outlook, a deeper understanding, a more determined and steadier standpoint.

John Dryden was born on the 9th August, 1631, at the residence of his maternal grandfather, the rectory of Aldwincle All Saints, a Northamptonshire village of small size or note. It lies rather more than a league from the market-town of Thrapston, which is to say, that it is distant five-and-twenty miles from Peterborough. In 1931 the population of the two parishes, Aldwincle All Saints and Aldwincle St. Peter's, only numbered 316. Concerning Erasmus Dryden, the poet's father, whose seat was at Titchmarsh, nearby, little is known save that he was regarded as a person of considerable importance during the Commonwealth, being spoken of as " a zealous committee-man " on one of the abominable Sequestration Boards, and that he

was long a busy Justice of the Peace for the county, activities which
in those dark days are only too sadly indicative of his views.   Mary
Dryden, his wife, was the daughter of the Rev. Henry Pickering, a
divine of the starch Genevan opinion, who served the ministry of
Aldwincle All Saints for forty years, dying in 1637.   The poet in
fine came of dour Puritan stock, as indeed his rabble of opponents
never missed to remind him and generally in very scurrilous language,
although it was a circumstance for which he quite clearly was not
responsible, and which he could neither alter nor avoid.   It is worth
remarking, however, that there are absolutely no grounds, save for
the accident of the Parish Registers of 1631 being lost, for the canard
that Dryden as an infant was never baptized, since the baptisms of
nine of his brothers and sisters, including his sister Agnes who was
carried to the font only fifteen months after his own birth, are duly
recorded at Titchmarsh.

The boy Dryden received part of his earlier education at Oundle
Grammar School whence about the time of the Civil War's breaking
out he was admitted a King's Scholar at Westminster under the
regimen of our English Orbilius, the celebrated and *plagosus* Dr.
Richard Busby.   On the 11th May, 1650, he proceeded, a Westminster
Scholar, to Trinity College, Cambridge, and here he matriculated
on the following 6th July.   His Cambridge career was interrupted
for a month or two at least by the death of his father from whom he
inherited a small estate.   He took his B.A. in 1654, after which we
lose sight of him for a short while, and it is uncertain, perhaps un-
important, whether he continued to keep terms at Cambridge or resided
in the country on his own holdings.

Of one thing we are very sure, he occupied those formative years
in study, not only of books, but of systems, living ideals and men.
" For my own part who must confess it to my shame . . ." he cries
in his *Life of Plutarch* (1683), " I never read anything but for pleasure."
Now pleasure for Dryden did not imply a mere passing and easy
entertainment, it meant the permanent and abiding satisfaction of an
intellect of the first order, which was always vivid, always eager and
inquiring, always consciously or unconsciously on the quest for beauty
and the ultimate truth.   *Immortalitatem sapientiæ concupiscebam æstu
cordis incredibili* says the great Doctor of Hippo, and in his degree,
surprising as the parallel may appear, Dryden nearly resembled the
student St. Augustine.

" A man should be learned in several sciences, and should have a
reasonable, philosophical, and in some measure a mathematical head,
to be a complete and excellent poet ; and besides this, should have
experience in all sorts of humours and manners of men."   Such was
Dryden's considered judgment.   A Cambridge contemporary bears

witness how whilst yet an undergraduate he had " read over and very well understood all the Greek and Latin poets." Let modern educationalists—so called—assert what they will, there is no surer foundation of a complete and universal culture than a knowledge of the Greek and Latin classical authors. It is a significant detail that Dryden preferred Rome to Hellas ; he was more at home with Vergil and Lucretius than with Homer and Theocrite.

He did not aspire to the immense erudition of a Burton, nor was he prepossessed by the precise pedantry of Thomas Farnabie. On the other hand he was perfectly familiar with the great critics, Longinus and Aristotle, together with the Italian Commentators on Aristotle, Vettori, Robortello, Castelvetro, Minturni, Vida, Father Tarquinio Galluzzi, S.J., Beni, Archbishop Piccolomini, and the rest. Congreve, himself no mean scholar, used to express his wonder at Dryden's unfailing memory. He is indeed never at a loss for the happiest illustration from Persius, or Seneca or Claudian or Plutarch to under-score the point he makes. Very beautifully and elegantly he can turn a passage from a Latin poet for one of his heroic dramas, such for example as the admired soliloquy of Cortez in Act III of " The Indian Emperour " :

> All things are hush'd, as Nature's self lay dead,
> The Mountains seem to nod their drowsie head ;
> The little Birds in dreams their Songs repeat,
> And sleeping Flowers, beneath the night-dew sweat ;
> Ev'n Lust and Envy sleep, yet Love denies
> Rest to my Soul, and slumber to my Eyes.

The ideas are suggested by Statius, in the ode " To Sleep " in the " Sylvæ." True, Dryden is often careless enough in the letter of his quotations. But what matter if recalling a line from the " Georgics " he writes *quamvis sit rustica* instead of *quamvis est rustica*, or has *nec tingeret* for *neque tingeret* in the seventh " Æneid " or varies Martial's *Qua possis melius* to *Ut melius* ? His was the true spirit of the finest classical scholars, not the grammarians, not the academies, old and new, so nicely correct, so dull and dead, but the spirit of those whose hearts burn with the loveliness and who are ennobled by the dignity of Latin literature, which the modern hectic world is so fast learning to forget. In one place Dryden says that when reading some poet or historian, or to use his own vivid phrase when he hears his author speaking, he is ready to think himself engaged in actual conversation " with the greatest heroes and most prudent men of the greatest age," and, he adds, " This sets me . . . on fire " . . . *æstu cordis incredibili.*

He was for ever turning over and over the Latin poets, ever finding some new beauty, ever lighting upon some vein of thought he would work deep to enrich our native English tongue, and from the poets, from Virgil chiefest of all, he absorbed in his own character something of the true Roman virtue, *virtus* in its highest and completest sense, that quality which was to stand him in good stead when against overwhelming odds conscience called upon him to make and to maintain the most momentous decision that it is given for men to cast. That he often stumbled on his road, early and late ; that he often fell far below his own ideals ; that he even seemed to contradict himself and was indeed inconsistent, is not to be denied. Dryden's admirers have often deplored these vagaries. I would emphasize the fact that so soon as he became a Catholic they ceased to exist. Even ten years previously in the Dedication of his tragedy " Aureng-Zebe," published in 1676, he gives a pretty good account of himself : " I will not be too positive. . . . As I am a Man, I must be changeable : and sometimes the gravest of us all are so, even upon ridiculous accidents. Our minds are perpetually wrought on by the temperament of our bodies, which makes me suspect : they are nearer alli'd, than either our Philosophers or School-Divines will allow them to be. . . . An ill Dream, or a Cloudy day, has power to change this wretched Creature, who is so proud of a reasonable Soul, and make him think what he thought not yesterday."

When the crucial moment was reached Dryden was not found wanting, he embraced what he knew to be Eternal Truth, he made his submission to the Holy See, and his duty once plain to him, his word once given, suffer as he might he never for a moment wavered, he never looked back from that allegiance. There was much of the spirit of heroic virtue—I use the term in its strict theological signification—in John Dryden. A little later we shall see something of what his conversion entailed from a purely temporal point of view.

The most striking feature in the development of John Dryden's ideas is the man's sheer intellectual honesty. His was an argued conviction, arrived at logically step by step, that a certain course was the right and hence the only course, and that course he adopted, regardless of consequences. There were, in a sense, no half-measures. Before he was convinced, whilst his religious views were still indeterminate he had no scruple about writing " The Assignation," a comedy which in spite of many brilliant passages and scenes of some considerable beauty it is hard to excuse from the charge of profanity, and he had dedicated " The Spanish Fryar " " a Protestant Play to a Protestant Patron." Once convinced, he was capable of rising to heroic heights of sacrifice. Nor was he supported by that passionate enthusiasm, which seems to sweep some happy souls with irresistible force. His conversion was—so to speak—absolutely cold-blooded, absolutely sincere.

There were no easy transitions for a convert in the days of Charles II. When a man became a Catholic he must indeed have felt himself a stranger in a strange land. Furiously hated and attacked by those whom he had left, he was too often a suspect in the eyes of those whom he had joined, since the older folk for the most part showed themselves anything but cordial to new-comers, and they are hardly to be blamed inasmuch as they were surrounded on all sides by feed falsehood and the most murderous treachery. The convert had to learn new ways, a new language, to acquaint himself with a multitude of observances which must for a while at any rate have perplexed him as alien and unknown. Pepys records how one Christmas midnight curious sightseers, and he among them, crowded the Queen's chapel at Somerset House for the High Mass, agog to gape at the fantastic cradle and live infant that (rumour went) would be solemnly exhibited with all kinds of pageantry and theatrical show, rivalling Bartlemy Fair in full swing. Sadly mistaken and disappointed the good gossips proved to be. To-day there are High Anglicans who (as Father Woodlock said in Farm Street pulpit), bating one great essential, preach and practice nine-tenths of the Faith. In her recent intimate biography, *Three Ways Home*, Miss Sheila Kaye-Smith observes that although her allegiance has been transferred from Canterbury to Rome, from shifting sand to the Rock of Peter, her beliefs and religion have never changed. Such a statement would have been impossible in Stuart England. We may instance as a typical High Anglican of the most advanced school the pious Nicholas Ferrar of Little Gidding, the " Protestant Nunnery " as it was generally dubbed. Ferrar was a learned and devout recluse, an ascetic much given to good works, something of a mystic, the author of *Contemplations on Death* and other serious treatises, commonly reputed to be a hot papist, and one who for his way of life and his opinions suffered much from puritan persecution and annoy. Yet Ferrar solemnly averred that if he knew Mass had been said at any time in a room of his house he would level that room to the ground and utterly demolish it.

In the Preface to *Religio Laici* Dryden declared that he was " naturally inclined to scepticism in philosophy," which is hardly to be surprised at since he lived during a critical period in the history of thought, that juncture when the new and supple experimental science was attacking the established scholasticism, a conflict of systems in which the latter, although on English soil seemingly worsted for a while, has signally triumphed in the end, as we are happy enough to bear witness to-day. Fortunately Dryden was well trained and exercised in the scholastic habit, and from first to last he shows himself a practised disciple of the schools in his method of distinguishing and ranging his thoughts and arguments. " He delighted to talk of liberty and

necessity, destiny and contingence," says Dr. Johnson, whilst Swift
sarcastically summed up " The Hind and the Panther " as " a complete
abstract of sixteen thousand schoolmen from Scotus to Bellarmine."
It is interesting to note that in " The State of Innocence, or The Fall
of Man " when Adam " as newly created " rises from " a Bed of Moss
and Flowers," he cries :

> What am I ? or from whence ? For that I am
> I know, because I think.

Which is, of course, the " *Cogito, ergo sum* " of Descartes.   What is
yet more significant is Eve's line : " The sin which Heav'n makes
Happy in th' event."   The theology is correct.   In the Paschal
Præconium the Deacon sings : " *O felix culpa, quae talem ac tantum
meruit habere Redemptorem !* "

It must not be forgotten that Dryden was a keen student of and
indeed an adept in astrology.   His own nativity and that of his son
Charles, very exactly cast, are preserved at Oxford among the papers
of Elias Ashmole.   Towards the close of his life we find him writing to
his two sons, who were then at Rome and members of the Papal household, to tell them that he has himself cast Charles's nativity, and so can
assure the boy he will soon recover his perfect health, " and all things
hitherto have happened accordingly to the very time that I predicted
them."

The one sad blot—an early but a grave error—that stains Dryden's
character is the poem " Heroick Stanzas," which he wrote on the death
of Oliver Cromwell, 1658, and which appeared in print with two similar
copies of verse by Waller and Thomas Sprat respectively in the
following year.   It is, of course, possible to exaggerate the significance
of these unfortunate quatrains, and throughout after years his enemies
were never tired of twisting and colouring his panegyric (for a panegyric
it must be confessed to be) to their worst ends, but it is revolting to think
that their malice should have professed to discover in these " Stanzas "
such enormities as an approval of the murder of King Charles I,
although nothing of the sort is hinted at or intended.

In 1657, Dryden who was then aged twenty-six, had been appointed
secretary to his relation Sir Gilbert Pickering, than whom few stood
in higher favour with the usurper.   Sir Gilbert indeed had occupied
many political posts of the first importance.   Thus he served on
each of the five councils of state of the Commonwealth, acted as
" Lord Chamberlain " of the " Protector's " court, and cut a fine
figure in the Cromwellian mock " House of Lords."   To what more
useful patron could a young cousin from the country on the threshold
of his career apply in the hope of advancement ?   It was in these
circumstances that Dryden wrote the " Heroick Stanzas."

After this unhappy passage it is with relief that we pass swiftly to the ringing sincerity of the *Astræa Redux*, "A Poem On the Happy Restoration and Return of His Sacred Majesty Charles the Second," 1660, and the right loyal rapture of "To His Sacred Majesty, A Panegyrick On His Coronation." Both were published by Henry Herringman the leading bookseller of the day, for whom at this time Dryden was doing a good deal of work. It was through Herringman that he met a son of the Earl of Berkshire, Sir Robert Howard, who had till the eve of the King's return been lying a prisoner, and for a while under sentence of death, at Windsor Castle, since the Puritans hated and feared him as the most dangerous of malignants and a notorious " favourer of Roman Catholicks." Sir Robert, himself a poet, essayist, and with some capital plays to his credit, soon became intimate with Dryden, and the friendship of this " ingenious Person " who enjoyed considerable influence with the King proved of inestimable service to the younger author. On the 1st December, 1663, Dryden married Sir Robert's sister, the Lady Elizabeth Howard.

Sir Robert not only wrote comedy and tragedy with equal facility and success but he had financially interested himself in the Theatre Royal, the King's own playhouse. Charles II was a keen and discerning patron of the stage, and when after the theatre had been silenced for eighteen years by the rebels, two houses were opened under royal patent in London at the Restoration, the actors naturally called for new and up-to-date fare to entertain their audiences. In a very few years Dryden had won his position as the leading dramatist of the day, upon which Dr. Johnson aptly remarks that " the composition and fate of eight-and-twenty dramas " includes no small part of a poetical life.

His ninth play, produced at the Theatre Royal in June, 1669, is particularly interesting, and (as I think) this exquisite tragedy gives us clear insight into his opinions at that time. " Tyrannick Love ; or, The Royal Martyr " was written in compliment to Queen Catherine of Braganza, and the plot which tells the history of St. Catherine is directly derived from the hagiography of Symeon Metaphrastes. The figure of the Saint is beautifully drawn and designed with the utmost reverence, her famous contention with the Pagan philosophers being treated with no ordinary skill. In her " apologia " for Christianity, the heroine, with the keenest dialectic, fearlessly employs argument and illustrations which the most solid apologist might study with profit and conviction. It is pleasing to know that " Tyrannick Love " proved a tremendous success, and during its run, which was something extraordinary for those days, this " *godly out of fashion Play* " drew crowded houses. Moreover, it remained in the repertory for more than thirty years.

For the splendid wedding festivities which celebrated the arrival
in England of Mary Beatrice of Modena, the bride of the Duke of
York, the laureate Dryden composed an Opera, " The State of
Innocence : and Fall of Man," which when printed, three years later,
in 1677, he dedicated to that amiable Princess with courtly compliment.
Here he treats of the profoundest religious and philosophical problems
such as that which conciliates moral liberty in man, the *liberum
arbitrium* of the Schoolmen, with divine foreknowledge.   St. Raphael
and St. Gabriel discourse with Adam who inquires :

> Freedome of will, of all good things is best ;
> But can it be by finite man possest ? . . .
> Grant Heav'n could once have giv'n us liberty ;
> Are we not bounded, now, by firm decree,
> Since what so e'er is pre-ordain'd, must be ?

The resolution briefly is that human responsibility cannot be explained
to a limited intelligence.   Actually Dryden in this " Poem of Paradise "
presents a defective and incomplete view of the problem since out of
respect he omits from consideration the dogma of man's Redemption
and grace.   " The State of Innocence " was primarily designed for
representation, and it would have been indecent and unbecoming to
discuss the most sacred and profoundest truths of Christianity in a
stage play.   Yet the very nature of the subject which Dryden chose is
sufficient witness how deeply his mind was preoccupied with and how
keenly he debated the dogmas and mysteries of religion.

From the time of his first comedy in February, 1663, Dryden had
been intimately connected with the King's company, to whom he was
bound by contract, so that the theatre, year in year out, provided him
with a fairly steady income of three or four hundred pounds, in those
days no inconsiderable sum.   He was naturally on friendly and familiar
terms with the leading actors and actresses, and he is spoken of as a
particular admirer of Anne Reeve, a lady who although unfortunately
lacking in any remarkable talent was one of the most beautiful women
on the boards.   Little is known of her as she only appeared in very
minor rôles, waiting-women and the like.   In the spring of 1675,
Anne Reeve left the London stage to enter a foreign convent, probably
Bruges, although this is uncertain.   " She died a religious," says *The
Gentleman's Magazine*, February, 1745.   At the time her retirement
and taking the veil caused an immense sensation, and the coarse-
grained satirists of the town were not sparing of their gibes and sneers.
Rochester, rough and ribald, mischievous and mean, in a biting pasquil
bade Dryden, " turn Priest since *Reeve* is turn'd Nun."   Obviously
Anne Reeve would have discussed her vocation and her future with
Dryden upon whom this event made more impression than he was

immediately aware. I do not question that her prayers in her distant cloister were by no means the least powerful factor in his conversion.

During the fevered frenzied years of Oates's plot, from 1678 to 1682, a time of revolutionary madness, of half-crazed hysteria, of murder and martyrdoms not a few, Dryden carried himself with singular dignity and restraint. A loyal supporter of the throne he was soon made a target by the savage foul-mouthed crew whom the villain Shaftesbury had hired to debauch and defile the country with their rancorous attacks upon King, law and order. The land was flooded with seditious fire-brand filth, and in consequence the world has been enriched with three masterpieces, the two parts of " Absalom and Achitophel " and " The Medal." The portraits—some damned to eternity in a line, some drawn full-length—of Buckingham, of Lord Howard of Esrick, of Titus Oates, of lean Sheriff Bethel, and in the second part of " Absalom and Achitophel " (which was mainly entrusted to Nahum Tate) of Jack Hall, of Pordage "the Wizard's son," of Shadwell and Elkanah Settle are of the first order of things. Shadwell received a second castigation in " MacFlecknoe," but the character of Titus Oates sketched again in " Albion and Albanius " is not so generally known as it deserves. This ruffian " for Mighty Mischief born " is described as :

> The basest, blackest of the Stygian band :
> One that will Swear to all they can invent,
> So thoroughly Damn'd that he can n'er repent :
> One often sent to Earth,
> And still at every Birth
> He took a deeper stain . . .
> One who has gain'd a Body fit for Sin ;
> When all his Crimes
> Of former Times
> Lie Crowded in a Skin.

The short sharp lines like strokes of a hammer drive home the point with irresistible force. The theology may not be correct—after all we are quoting from an allegorical Opera, but the *tout ensemble* is exact.

When in November, 1682, very soon after " The Medal " and the second part of " Absalom and Achitophel," the " Religio Laici "—a Layman's Faith—was published, even the most obtuse must have seen the logical outcome of Dryden's reasoning. He halts for the moment, it is true, but the event is sure.

> Dim as the borrowed beams of moon and stars
> To lonely, weary, wandering travellers,
> Is Reason to the soul. . . .

Where does truth lie ? It cannot be in a blind following of a printed page, the Bible, for since it was translated into our tongue ignorant and fanatic Protestants have used it so, as if their business was not to be saved, but to be damned by its contents. Better had it remained in the honest Latin of St. Jerome. If there were only some infallible authority to direct and decide !

> Such an omniscient Church we wish indeed :
> 'Twere worth both Testaments, cast in the Creed.

What is the argument against the Catholic Church ? Merely a political notion. The Church will not teach the Divine Right of Kings as absolute dogma. Heretical and excommunicated monarchs are to be withstood on points of conscience. When Elizabeth banned Holy Mass and made the exercise of any priestly function a penal offence theologians taught she must be resisted and disobeyed. Mariana, Bellarmine, Emmanuel Sa, Campion, Parsons, and a score beside are agreed on that. So Dryden stays where he is—for the moment.

Less than three years later, shortly after, if indeed not before, the accession of King James II, Dryden, as the logical outcome of his philosophical and intellectual development was received into the Catholic Church. His wife and at least one of his sons had preceded him. It must be clear to any reader of his works that this was the inevitable and ultimate solution of the many debates he had loved to argue with himself his whole life long. To question his sincerity is not merely to show oneself ungenerous but completely lacking in perception. T. B. Macaulay wrote : " Finding that, if he continued to call himself a Protestant, his services would be overlooked, he declared himself a Papist. The King's parsimony immediately relaxed. Dryden was gratified with a pension of a hundred pounds a year, and was employed to defend his new religion both in prose and verse." To quote Dryden's own words on another occasion : " Now there are three damn'd lyes crowded together in a very little room." A Treasury warrant of 6th May, 1684, directs the payment to the laureate Dryden of certain arrears since 1680 on a pension of £200 a year, and of further arrears since the same date on " an additional annuity." The latter was approved by James II, and it is this which is declared to have been a new bribe, " the price of apostasy." Macaulay, to-day generally discredited in his rôle of literary critic and ignored in his rôle of historian, was probably quite deliberate in his misrepresentations. To apply his own phrases to himself : " he was perpetually acting against his better knowledge. His sins were sins against light." Dr. Johnson, Malone, Scott, and every honest critic recognize the absolute sincerity of Dryden's conversion.

On 19th January, 1686, the sententious Evelyn—who for all his good qualities was more than a bit of a prig—gravely shakes his head : " Dryden, the famous playwriter, and his two sons and Mrs. Nelly (miss to the late——) were said to go to Mass." So far as Nell Gwyn was concerned this bit of gossip proved utterly false. And Evelyn adds what seems to me an absolutely abominable comment : " such proselytes were no great loss to the Church." The unction and smugness of Mr. Pharisee !

That Dryden upon his conversion was to be pelted with the most blasphemous and most libertine libels need not, I suppose, occasion any great surprise. There was not a paid Protestant pamphleteer in town who failed to throw mud and dirt helter-skelter, penning dialogue and tract and epigram, prose, and verse hardly to be distinguished from prose. We need not dwell on these things. They are forgotten utterly, and even in their day all decent folk regarded them as beneath contempt.

King James shortly called upon his historiographer to reply to Dr. Stillingfleet, the Dean of St. Paul's, who had plunged headlong into controversy. The occasion was this : Anne Hyde, the King's first wife, left a paper which stated her reasons for becoming a Catholic. This was now published, and Stillingfleet, who no doubt according to his own lights was a very good man but who quite certainly according to any light was a very stupid man, essayed to answer it. It was necessary that there should be some rejoinder, a task authority very effectively entrusted to Dryden.

As yet the great poet had given the world no reasons for his change, but feeling that some account was justly required of him he composed " The Hind and the Panther," 1687, that magnificent allegory in which the " milk-white Hind, immortal and unchanged," the Catholic Church, so nobly and so convincingly argues against the Anglican Panther " the fairest Creature of the spotted Kind," and the hundred impure vagrom sects, the Independents, the Anabaptists, the Arians, the Freethinkers, the Latitudinarians, the Huguenots, the Brownists, typified as " the bloody Bear," " the bristled Baptist Boar," " false Reynard," " the buffoon Ape," and the rest. There are portraits too in the poem—" The Buzzard, Bishop Burnet " " Invulnerable in his impudence."

" The Life of St. Francis Xavier," which Dryden translated from the French of Fr. Dominic Bonhours, S.J., 1688, is a fine piece of work, and a notable contribution to our hagiography in English, a field of religious letters which is only too apt to be barren or hard. To this period also belong many of his versions of Latin hymns, lyrics of the first quality. It is probable that of the one hundred and twenty hymns which make up the Primer of 1706, all or nearly all were Englished by Dryden between the years 1685 and 1700.

At the Revolution of 1688 when " a company of men perhaps as destitute of honour and as God-forsaken as any which history has record " succeeded in driving from his throne their King who was to die a Saint in French exile—miracles were worked at his tomb and by his intercession—Dryden fell with his royal master. He refused with scorn to take the oaths to the Dutch usurper, and forthwith he was ejected from his posts of laureate and historiographer royal. He lost all for truth and conscience sake, and this surely is heroic fortitude.

Having ceased his dramatic activities for the space of four years he was now obliged to turn once again to the stage for support. The first piece he produced after the Revolution, " Don Sebastian," has for a hero a truly romantic figure, that great and gallant Catholic knight Dom Sebastian of Portugal, and by many it is esteemed his finest play. Indeed much of his best work was done during the twelve years when he was hated and persecuted for religion's sake. It was now that he wrote " Alexander's Feast " and the " Fables " ; that he translated Vergil. Old and weary, at a time when he had earned and had a right to expect independence and repose, he was bound to take pen in hand as busily as during the vigour of his youth and prime. He was tied to his desk until the last. " A Secular Masque " was finished and sent to Drury Lane early in April, 1700, and on the 30th of that month " The Postboy " announced that " John Dryden, Esq., the famous poet, lies a-dying." On Wednesday, 1st May, at three o'clock in the morning he died, fortified by the last rites of the Church, and " taking of his friends so tender and obliging a farewell as none but he himself could have expressed."

John Dryden was not a Saint. He had too many human weaknesses and failings for that. But he also had some of the rarest and most difficult qualities which are essential to the character of the greatest Saints. He obeyed the dictates of conscience simply and sincerely, heedless of loss, heedless of the enmity of the world, and of whom else save such as he was it once said : *Beati, qui persecutionem patiuntur propter justitiam : quoniam ipsorum est regnum coelorum ?*

7

ST. MARGARET MARY

A.D. 1647–1690

Je me consumais en Sa présence comme un cierge ardent, pour Lui rendre armour pour amour.

THE FIFTH CHILD of Claude Alacoque, royal notary of Vevrosvres in Burgundy, and of Philibert, his wife, was born on July 22, 1647, and baptised three days later. Margaret's godparents were her father's cousin, Antoine Alacoque, parish priest of the village, and Madame de Fautrières, of Corcheval Château close by. Claude's business, as lawyer officially appointed to transact legal affairs in the district, brought him into contact with the landed gentry ; and in any case there was less distinction in the country in France between his class, *noblesse de la robe*, the legal upper middle-class, and *noblesse de l'épée*, the old feudal nobility. So it was not surprising that Madame de Fautrières, without children of her own, should practically adopt her little goddaughter (1651), probably feeling it a pity that such an attractive child should be left to run more or less wild. Margaret spent most, if not all, of the next four years at Corcheval. She was full of life, loving gaiety, noise and movement, but sensitive, affectionate and responsive. In the middle of a wild, riotous game she would at once become quiet if told that such behaviour was not pleasing to God.

Many children have a very vivid realisation of the presence of God but in Margaret's case this was phenomenal. Whenever she could not be found in the château or garden she was always to be discovered in the chapel on the terrace, kneeling still and silent before the Blessed Sacrament. Her godmother put her in charge of two women, who were to teach reading, writing and the catechism. One of these petted and cossetted the child, the other was bad-tempered and sharp-tongued. It was thought odd that Margaret avoided the first and was fond of the other. Only later was it known that an instinct of supernatural purity had perceived behind the pleasant façade a corrupt nature and bad life.

These four happy years (1651-1655) slipped by in lovely surroundings. The old castle, destroyed by Coligny during the wars of religion, had been rebuilt during the reign of Louis XIII and was surrounded by a spacious park shaded by noble hornbeams.   The quiet solitude of these shady, grassy glades had an irresistible fascination for Margaret, in whom a desire for silence and remoteness alternated with outburst of noisy high spirits.

Monsieur de Fautrières died.   Madame was about to marry again and Margaret, now eight, returned to her own home in the little hamlet of Lautecour.   The house consisted of two great square blocks, separated by a courtyard, in the middle of which the old well was roofed by one heavy slab of granite.   The block known as the *maison de cabinet*, because the notary had his office there, was rebuilt after a fire at the time of Margaret's brother's marriage (1666), which is commemorated by the allegorical paintings on the old rafters and ceilings, bearing the Alacoque arms, a cock and lion *gules* on a field *or*. A square tower at the far end, now a chapel, is traditionally the spot of the saint's birth and, probably, the room she occupied as a child.

Margaret came home to a typically patriarchal household, her father and mother, five brothers, the two elder at School at Cluny, a sister younger than herself, who died as a child, her father's spinster sister, Catherine, his married sister, Benoîte, her husband Toussaint Delaroche and their three children.

The garden sloped down, beyond the house to a narrow valley whose steep sides were thickly covered with oak trees.   The whole countryside has a fascination all its own.   Huge granite boulders thrust up through oaks and pines, like the ramparts of legendary castles, or crop up in wide open spaces, their greyness half hidden by the yellow and purple of broom and heather.   Man can only wring his livelihood from this poor soil by hard work and sweat, for the famous wine country of Beaune and Burgundy lies beyond the horizon of serrated hills.   One sheer rock, twenty feet or more high, rises in the little valley near the Lautecour house, completely screened by the thicket of oaks, and this was Margaret's favourite haunt.   It is such a secret hiding-place as any child would love, but Margaret went there, like the Maid at the Fairy Tree of Domrémi, not to play and invent stories but to listen to God and His mother.   " Oh my only Love," she wrote over thirty years later, " how much do I owe You for having marked me out from my earliest youth by making Yourself master of my heart."

The child who escaped alone to be with God was soon drawn into even closer relations with Him.   Claude Alacoque died (1655), leaving his affairs in some disorder and his widow, strong neither in character nor in health, felt unable to cope with all her children, so Margaret was sent to school at the Urbanists (a branch of the Poor Clares) at Charolles, a few miles from home.   There the nuns were so struck

by the little girl's supernatural gift of prayer that they allowed her to
make her First Communion at the then amazingly early age of nine.
Still gay and eager, full of life and enjoyment, she tells us that " This
First Communion filled all my childish pleasures and games with such
bitterness that I no longer cared for them."

An illness, which kept her bedridden for four years (c. 1657-1661)
completed her detachment and as she lay, helpless, immobile, sleepless
and racked with pain, all her thoughts and desires were wholly turned
to God, with a mystic comprehension of the spiritual value of suffering
amazing in one so young. " My heart was burnt up by desire to love
Him Who gave me such an insatiable longing for Holy Communion
and for suffering."

Suffering, bodily, mental and spiritual, was indeed to be all her
life the seal with which her Divine Lover marked her for His own.
No one more than she has shown so clearly the impossibility in this world
of separating love from suffering. He who does not know sacrifice
and pain does not know the true meaning of love. Like St. Teresa
of Lisieux—that other French saint whose fame, two centuries later,
was to blaze from her cloister through the world—Margaret's longing
for pain and humiliation knew no limits. Her prayer was granted
and in full measure.

Brought home by her mother, cured apparently miraculously after
a promise to become " a daughter of Mary," Margaret had to endure
years of misery and mortifications made the harder to bear because
her dearly loved mother was as ill as she. If Toussaint Delaroche
treated his unfortunate sister-in-law and niece no better than paupers
and beggars, his wife and Catherine Alacoque were worse and, cruellest
of all was that worst of tyrants an old family servant, whose brutality
was only equalled by her ignorance. When her mother was ill,
her recovery proclaimed impossible by a village quack called in to
bleed her, Margaret had to beg food from the neighbours and perform
surgical work and dressings of which she was entirely ignorant and
from which her sensitive, highly strung nature shuddered in revolt.

Madame Alacoque's hopes that her sons would take command when
they came of age were dashed by the death at twenty-three first of one,
then of another, but with the majority of Chrysostom, the third, better
days dawned. Toussaint Delaroche, with all his faults, had nursed
the estate so well for his brother-in-law's children that they were now
comfortably off. Jacques, the third surviving child, was twenty and
studying for the priesthood at Cluny. Chrysostom married well in
1666 and Madame Alacoque was anxious that her daughter also should
marry and so provide her with a peaceful home for her old age.

Lautecour became quite gay. The young couple entertained and
suitors for Margaret's hand were not wanting. There is no contem-

porary portrait of her but those painted from descriptions of her
fellow nuns must show her distinctive features. She was slight and
graceful, good-looking, with straight nose and curved mouth. The
heavy, low-arched eyebrows show character and the hazel eyes have
the " inner " look of the mystic. She had charm, gaiety, sympathy,
was sensitive, quick and affectionate. Quite as important as all this
in French eyes, she was promised a substantial *dot*.

She tells us in her autobiography that, during these years (1666-1671)
she became frivolous and worldly. The fact that, during one
carnival, she went to a masked ball, assumed to her the aspect of a
deadly sin, so the rest of her self-accusation can be judged by this
instance. Yet to her it represented a falling short of her high vocation
which needed to be expiated by merciless mortifications. Her
visions and divine revelations were continuous but she was left
without human help in her spiritual life. Her godfather, the curé
of the village, seems to have been a good, ordinary soul, with all the
material commonsense of the French peasant but incapable of understanding what he regarded as eccentric nonsense.

The poor girl was torn in two between her inner conviction of her
vocation to the religious life and the insistence of her relations,
including her godfather, on her duty to marry and provide a home
for her mother, whom she loved more than any human being. If
she were to go away to a convent, it was urged, she would be her
mother's murderess. She tried to persuade herself that she could
answer the divine call by local good works, was told that she was
giving away food and money which was not hers to give. Even the
good-natured Chrysostom remonstrated when he found the house
filled by a crowd of wild, noisy and dirty children to whom his sister
was trying to teach the catechism.

At last came help. A Franciscan friar came to Vevrosvres to preach
the Jubilee which Pope Clement had proclaimed on his accession
(1670). " He came to the house and slept there to give us time to
make our confessions," and in him Margaret found a wise director.
The friar told her to give herself wholly to God, showed her how best
to pray and do penance. He spoke to Chrysostom, now the head of
the household, and told him it was dangerous to oppose a genuine
vocation. Chrysostom spoke to his sister. Was she really determined
to be a nun ? " Yes, rather death than to change my mind."

She went on a visit to an uncle at Mâcon, where he and his daughter,
a nun in the Ursuline convent there, tried to persuade her to enter the
convent, so as to be near home and with relations. " Never, but some
distant convent, where I shall know no one . . . where I can forget the
world and be for ever forgotten by it." Margaret, who had taken the
second name of Mary at her Confirmation (1670), went with her brother

to the Visitation Convent at Paray-le-Monial and, hardly was she inside the parlour than she heard an interior voice : " It is here that I wish you to be." She only returned home when her reception had been arranged. Such was her joy during her last few weeks at home that neighbours murmured that such riotous high spirits scarcely showed a religious vocation ! But, at the last moment, as she was ready to start for Paray, June 20, (1671) came the final struggle. " I endured such terrible agony that I think I shall suffer no worse at the hour of death. It felt as if my very bones were torn one from another."

From that day till her death (October 17, 1690) Margaret Mary never left the enclosure, in which two months later she was clothed and (November 6, 1671) made her solemn vows at her profession. Her life, like that of St. Teresa of Lisieux, was entirely uneventful in the eyes of the world, because it " was hid with Christ in God." It seemed indeed that her desire to live " the world forgetting, by the world forgot " was to be fulfilled.

France was then at the apex of her fame, the reign of Louis XIV, which even the mocking spirit of Voltaire acknowledged to be one of the three most glorious periods of human history. Round the splendour of the *Roi Soleil* shone such a galaxy of stars as Descartes, Pascal, Bossuet, Fénélon, Racine, Corneille, Molière, Condé, Turenne, but no breath from the outer world troubled the calm of the Visitation Cloister at Paray.

Paray-le-Monial has changed little, if at all, from the day when Margaret Mary came there. The typical small French provincial town, with its tall, gabled houses, its cobbled streets shaded by great plane trees, clusters round the towering bulk of the eleventh-century basilica, built by St. Hugh, Abbot of Cluny, as a model for that at Cluny. A little east of the basilica rises the sharp gable of the Visitation Convent, built in 1642. A cloister runs round the square court, with a fountain in the middle. Community rooms, sacristy, chapel, refectory and novitiate open off the cloister and two staircases in the corners lead up to the nuns' cells on the first floor. That of Margaret Mary is now a chapel of the Sacred Heart, but Bougaud describes it as he saw it, just over sixty years ago, unaltered from the time of her life and death, small and narrow, the only furniture a bed, table and chair, the whitewashed walls bare but for a wooden Crucifix and a crude drawing of the Sacred Heart.

When Margaret Mary was professed, Mother de Saumaise was superior (1672-1678), and the affectionate relations between them continued after she left, to be succeeded as superior by Mother Greyfié (1678-1684). The latter, more practical and austere, was thanked by the saint for the way she tried the revelations by mortifications and humiliations. The novice-mistress, Mother Thouvant, gave to the new postulant, in answer to a question about the best way to pray, the historic words : " Place yourself before Him like a blank canvas before a painter." Margaret Mary obeyed, though, as she tells us, not understanding and not daring to ask an explanation. The " blank canvas " soon became a living likeness of God.

Her desire to be " consumed like a burning candle to give back love for love " was soon fulfilled. Every spare moment was spent in chapel. When the Blessed Sacrament was exposed she would kneel before It the whole night for twelve hours or more, eyes fixed, hands folded, motionless, testified her companions, " as a marble image." When one of them asked how she did it, she answered simply that, at such times, she no longer knew she had a body. The word " obedience " alone could recall her from her ecstasy, for her Lord had told her that only by obedience and strict observance of the Rule could she please Him.

St. Jane Frances Chantal, when she had founded the order, under the direction of St. Francis of Sales, had discouraged any great corporal austerities and mortifications. Indeed, the rule of enclosure was not adopted till eight years after the foundation in 1610. It was only natural that many of the older nuns, some of whom remembered the foundress, should look with an unfriendly eye upon the extraordinary behaviour of the new novice. Her profession was delayed for several months and she was heart-broken at the possibility of being sent away as unsuitable to " the daughters of Mary," as they were called locally.

Mother de Saumaise tested her by mental and physical asceticisms which tried the delicate body and sensitive, affectionate nature almost to breaking-point. The infirmarian, an energetic, bustling, practical woman, continually found fault with a help who, in spite of superhuman devotion to the sick, so often fell downstairs or forgot some part of the régime. It was the same in the kitchen. Plates slipped from Margaret Mary's hands on her way to the refectory as if the devil himself were in them and all the humility with which she picked up the dusty portions and put them on her own plate, did not excuse her clumsiness. On another occasion she was called away in the middle of sweeping the chapel and was confronted by the pile of dust as she came in with the other nuns to Office. She was set to watch an ass and foal to see that they did not break into the vegetable garden. Drawn as by a magnet, she was found pressed against the chapel wall while ass and foal rioted among the vegetables. Paray tradition, however, has it that not a hoofprint nor a sign of theft marked the invasion. A still worse trial was in store. It was revealed to her that she must announce to the nuns the Divine choice of her as victim to expiate the sins of half-a-dozen tepid souls. A more terrible task could scarcely be imagined for one so sensitive, loving and humble, whose one desire was to efface herself.   It was done, without the support of Mother de Saumaise, who was ill in bed.   The resulting taunts and rebuffs added to the strain of an inimical atmosphere which was torture to her.

The day she made her profession she had written in her own blood, " Everything for God, nothing for self."   Her longing to suffer was only less than her love for God, Whose continual presence she was granted.   Again and again in her autobiography and letters she expresses this love of sacrifice and suffering.   " You will find neither peace nor quiet till you have sacrificed everything to God," she wrote to her brother Jacques, curé of Bois Sainte Marie (1686).   " I have only one desire, to love (God), to forget and annihilate myself." " Three desires so ardent that I regard them as three tyrants, which make me suffer a continual martyrdom, without leaving me a moment's peace . . . to love my God perfectly, to suffer much for His love and to die in that burning love " (1690).

" I cared no longer for time nor place, since my Sovereign accompanied me everywhere."   This continual communion with God, these almost continual revelations of the divine love and will, were supra-sensual and, like all the experiences of the great mystics could not be adequately expressed in words.   " I could not explain what happened then," " it seemed to me,"—she knows that so many of her experiences can only be set out in symbols and forms which, like the Platonic Ideas, when materialized, are only feeble mirrors which distort even as they reflect.

Mother de Saumaise, feeling that all this was beyond her power, called in some th·ologians, who, says Languet, the saint's earliest biographer, " condemned without examination everything which appeared to them miraculous, unusual or supernatural."   " I no longer doubted that I was abandoned, since I was told that it was not the spirit of God guiding me, and yet it was impossible for me to resist this spirit."

Early in 1675 a new superior was appointed to the Jesuit house at Paray, young Father Claude de la Colombière, formerly tutor to the children of the great statesman and financier, Colbert, and remarkable for his intellectual and spiritual gifts and his personal charm.   As was customary the new superior came to give a conference to the Visitation nuns and, no sooner had Margaret Mary seen and heard him than her divine Master told her " This is he whom I send to you." Encouraged by Mother de Saumaise she opened her heart to the Jesuit and told him of the three special revelations she had already received of the devotion to the Sacred Heart.

The first had taken place on December 27, St. John's feast, 1573, when Margaret Mary, having a little leisure, was kneeling before the Blessed Sacrament exposed. Pressed close against the grille, she suddenly felt herself " Entirely clothed " (*toute investie*) with the divine presence, so that, no longer conscious of outward things, she was rapt in ecstasy. " He let me rest a long time upon His divine breast, where He revealed to me the marvels of His love and the incomprehensible mysterious secrets of His Sacred Heart, which He had always kept hidden from me till then and which He now opened to me for the first time." Then, taking her heart, He drew it into His own, " a tiny atom which was consumed in that burning furnace," and returned it, like a live flame, to her side, while she was named " the beloved disciple of My Sacred Heart."

The second great revelation took place on a Friday in the early part of 1674, the third during the octave of Corpus Christi, 1674. " The divine Heart was shown to me on a throne of flames, more radiant than a sun and transparent as crystal, with this adorable wound, surrounded by a crown of thorns to symbolise how our sins pierce it, and crowned by a Cross."

Devotion to the Heart of Jesus had existed since the earliest days. St. Augustine, St. Bernard, St. Catherine of Siena, Benedictines, Franciscans, Dominicans, had all expressed it. The thirteenth-century St. Gertrude, Abbess of the Benedictine convent of Rodelsdorf, prophesied in her *Revelations* that the secrets of the Sacred Heart were only to be proclaimed in a later age, when love of God should have grown weak and cold.

A special devotion is needed at every period of history to counteract the evil of the age. That to the Sacred Heart came when France most needed it. When Louis XIV ascended the throne as a child of five (1643) France was devastated by nearly a century of civil and religious wars. Huguenots had destroyed and desecrated churches. Religion was practically dead in some districts and to reclaim the people from savagery and paganism it had needed missionaries as heroic as St. John Francis Regis in Auvergne and Fathers Nobletz, Maunoir and Huby in Brittany. Jansenism, made formidable by the genius of St. Cyran and Pascal and the influence of the nuns of Port-Royal, taught, like the Calvinists, that Christ had not died for all, so that few, and they only rarely, might approach the Sacraments. Gallicanism, which had sprung to full strength when Catherine de Medici had summoned a national assembly in opposition to the Council of Trent, shared with Jansenism a denial of Papal authority even in some things spiritual. The court, during the first forty years of Louis' reign, was a centre of moral corruption. Religion, even when practised, tended too often to a cold formalism. A new devotion was required to set cold and tepid hearts on fire. God chose to proclaim it to the little country girl, who had never been twenty miles from home till she entered the convent which she was never to leave.

Claude de la Colombière was destined to be partner with Margaret Mary in the promulgation of devotion to the Sacred Heart of Jesus. He alone realized that her visions and revelations were of God and she in her turn recognized in him the soul chosen by God to share in her work.

There is perhaps no human relationship so perfect as friendship between saints, such as those of St. Francis of Assisi and St. Clare, St. Francis of Sales and St. Jane Chantal. There was such a spiritual affinity between de la Colombière and Margaret Mary and their names are for ever intertwined in the history of devotion to the Sacred Heart—a closeness symbolized by her vision, as she advanced to receive Holy Communion at his hands, of their two hearts being taken into the Heart of Christ and there fused into one.

The last great revelation took place while the Jesuit was still at Paray, the octave of Corpus Christi, 1675. It laid down the commands which have distinguished this devotion ever since—the Holy Hour before the Blessed Sacrament exposed on Thursday night, in memory of the Agony in the Garden, " which will reduce you to an agony harder to bear than death," and Communion on the first Friday of every month, customs now universal throughout the Catholic Church. There was another command, that a new feast was to be instituted, the Friday after the octave of Corpus Christi, a feast of special love and reparation to the Sacred Heart. " I promise thee that my Heart shall abundantly shed the gifts of its divine love upon those who render it this homage and induce others to render it."

Accordingly, on the Friday after the octave of Corpus Christi, June 21st, 1675, Margaret Mary and Blessed Claude de la Colombière both dedicated themselves to the Sacred Heart and three months later he left Paray for London, where he had been appointed chaplain to Mary of Modena, wife of James, Duke of York.

It is good to know that London was the first place after Paray in which devotion to the Sacred Heart was taught and preached by de la Colombière during the two years of his work there. Then, in 1678, broke out the madness of the Titus Oates " Plot," the most degraded page of English history. Thanks to his French nationality, the young Jesuit was saved from the martyrdom of his English brethren, but weeks of imprisonment in Newgate aggravated the delicacy of his health so that he returned to France in January, 1679, a dying man. During the ten days he spent at Paray on his way to Lyons he was able to have several long interviews with Margaret Mary and the new superior, Mother Greyfié. He was again there, sent by his superiors in hope of arresting the galloping consumption, before his death (February 15th, 1682), but this time, almost too weak to speak or move, a mutual friend was the bearer of messages between him and Margaret Mary. Only two meetings were possible. He wrote of one : " It was the greatest difficulty for me to speak. Perhaps God willed it thus so as to let me have the greater pleasure and opportunity of speaking to her heart."

Once again Margaret Mary was deprived of human help. Attempts to further the new devotion were indeed successful among the novices, of whom she was appointed mistress (1684-1685) and who were devoted to her. One in particular, Nicole de Farges, whom she called her " little St. Aloysius," was a great help and consolation. The novices resolved to celebrate the feast day of their mistress by a surprise. When she entered the chapel of the novitiate on July 20th, 1685, she was transported with joy to find a little altar erected to the Sacred Heart, before which she and the novices knelt and dedicated themselves to this manifestation of Christ's divine love. " What joy for me that the adorable Heart of my divine Master should be known, loved and glorified," she exclaimed to her novices. " It is the greatest comfort I can have in my life."

But trials were not over. A novice who ran to beg the nuns to come and join them was sent back with the words, " Go and tell your mistress that sound devotion is to be found in the practise of our Rule and Constitution and that this is what she should teach and you should practise."

Even the allusions in Father de la Colombière's *Spiritual Retreat*, read aloud in community early in 1685, to the new devotion, the revelations made by God " to the person whom one is justified in thinking after His own heart," did not bring victory. Margaret Mary wrote in Lent of the following year to Mother Greyfié, " I feel myself tortured and persecuted in many ways, one of the most violent being to regard me as a toy of Satan." Indeed some of the older nuns went so far as to asperse her with holy water whenever she passed, to drive out the devil of whom they believed her possessed. Bodily illness and pain were added to her mental and spiritual woe. Her longing for suffering was indeed fulfilled.

Father Rolin, S.J., superior of the Jesuit house at Paray, 1685-1687, succeeded to Claude de la Colombière's work. It was he who induced Margaret Mary, under obedience, to write her autobiography. He encouraged her and helped the spread of devotion to the Sacred Heart to other Visitation Convents and Jesuit houses and corresponded with her till her death.

At last came peace and triumph. On June 21st, 1686, the Feast of the Sacred Heart was solemnly inaugurated in the Paray convent.

" I shall die happy now that the Sacred Heart of my Saviour is beginning to be known," Margaret Mary wrote to Mother Greyfié. In all her activities as infirmarian and assistant during the next four years, she lived continually in communion with God. " I shall not live much longer, since I no longer suffer," she was heard to say in 1690 and on the 17th October she died, in the arms of her dear " little St. Aloysius " and Françoise Verchères, another of her favourite novices. " I no longer need anything but only God, and to lose myself in the Heart of Jesus Christ," were some of her last words.

It has been said that dogma is imposed from above but devotion springs up from below. We have seen an example of this in our own day, in the way in which love of St. Teresa of Lisieux swept the world and might also be said to have " forced " her canonisation. The spread of devotion to the Sacred Heart was slower, for the world was wider two and a half centuries ago. There was opposition even within the Church from Jansenism, but in 1765 Pope Clement XIII authorized some churches to celebrate the Feast of the Sacred Heart, which was extended to the whole world in 1856 and is now one of the most popular and widely spread of devotions. Margaret Mary was not beatified till 1864—eight years after the Feast was made universal, and canonized in 1920.

Blessed Claude de la Colombière, who first preached devotion to the Sacred Heart, and was Margaret Mary's best spiritual help and adviser, has not yet been canonized in spite of his sanctity and heroic virtues.

J. LEWIS MAY

FRANÇOIS DE SALIGNAC DE LA MOTHE-FÉNELON

Archbishop and Duke of Cambrai

A.D. 1651–1715

AN ELDERLY GENTLEMAN of courtly manners who used to visit my father's house when I was a child—he would be at least a hundred and twenty if he were alive to-day—used occasionally to grow reminiscent and discourse of his school-days, and at such times he rarely failed to recite in an accent of great purity the following sentences from Fénelon's *Télémaque : Calypso ne pouvait se consoler du départ d'Ulysse. Dans sa douleur, elle se trouvait malheureuse d'être immortelle.* I heard those words so often that in the end I came to know them by heart. I loved them and love them still, not only because they are associated in my mind with the memory of an old friend, and with a leisurely grace of manner that somehow seems to recall spinets and jars of *pot-pourri*, but for themselves, because they have a singular charm and fragrance of their own.

For a long time my acquaintance with Fénelon did not progress beyond those two sentences. Fénelon remained a shadow to me and might have continued to do so to this day, had I not, many years afterwards, come across, in Pater's *Imaginary Portraits*, the passage that runs as follows :

On the last day of Antony Watteau's visit, we made a party to Cambrai. We entered the cathedral church : it was the hour of Vespers, and it happened that Monseigneur le Prince de Cambrai, the author of *Télémaque*, was in his place in the choir. He appears to be of great age, assists but rarely at the offices of religion, and is never to be seen in Paris ; and Antony had much desired to behold him. Certainly it was worth while to have come so far only to see him, and hear him give his pontifical blessing, in a voice feeble but of infinite sweetness, and with an inexpressibly graceful movement of the hands. A veritable *grand seigneur !* His refined old age, the impress of genius and honours, even his disappointments, concur with natural graces to make him seem too distinguished (a fitter word fails me) for this world. *Omnia vanitas!* he seems to say, yet with a profound resignation, which makes the things we are most of us so fondly occupied with look petty enough. *Omnia vanitas!* Is that indeed the proper comment on our lives, coming, as it does in this case, from one who might have made his own all that life has to bestow? Yet he was never to be seen at court and has lived here almost an exile. Was our " Great King Lewis " jealous of a true *grand seigneur* or *grand monarque* by natural gift and favour of heaven, that he could not endure his presence?

The author of *Télémaque*! At once, those words of my old friend came back to me, like music borne upon a perfumed breeze—back out of the haunted past—*Calypso ne pouvait se consoler du départ d'Ulysse. Dans ِa douleur elle se trouvait malheureuse d'être immortelle.* And Cambrai! In that name, too, there was music. And who was he, this great ecclesiastic, who was also a genius and a *grand seigneur*? And what were his disappointments, and what was the reason of that profound resignation which led him to sigh, or seem to sigh, *Omnia vanitas?* I determined to discover.

And so it was thus, in this seemingly chance fashion, that I came to call back from the shadows into which he had vanished more than two hundred years since, one of the most gifted, one of the most fascinating, and one of the most unfortunate figures in history.

In the heart of *le Périgord Noir*, a land of dark ravines and rushing torrents, of shadowy woods and jagged heights, haunt of the wolf and the wild-boar, a land whose memorials of the past go back beyond the dawn of history—here in the ancestral château of his race, in the year of grace 1651, was born François de Salignac de la Mothe-Fénelon. His father, Pons de Salignac, Comte de la Mothe-Fénelon, having been left a widower with twelve children, married again when he was well on in life, and the future Archbishop of Cambrai was one of the four children of this second union.

The family, though very noble and very ancient—its records go back to 997—was by no means rich, and the task of supporting so large a family and of educating them in a manner appropriate to their station must have been anything but an easy one. Fénelon was delicate, and was at first brought up at home under the care of a tutor. Who that tutor was and whence he came, no one can tell ; but, whoever he was, he instilled into his pupil a love of high literature, and especially of the great writers of Greece and Rome, which abode with him through all his days, and in which, when the shadows of sorrow and disillusionment fell across his path, he was to find, next to his religion, his deepest and most unfailing consolation—*decus et solamen.*

To a younger son, and a delicate one, of an aristocratic but impoverished family the Church seemed naturally to offer a career, particularly in this case, as Fénelon's uncle, his father's brother, was Bishop of the neighbouring town of Sarlat, a see which for generations had been a sort of fief or appanage of the Fénelon family. But apart from such worldly and practical considerations, apart, too, from his quick and lively intelligence, his studious temperament, his taste for literature, especially classical literature, there was a mysterious grace, as though an aureole, about the child, an indefinable suggestion even in those early days of the *noli me tangere*, which seemed to hint that he was destined to be one of those of whom people come to say that they are " in the world but not of it " ; that he was destined for the sanctuary.

At the age of twelve, probably on the advice of the Bishop of Sarlat, who had early conceived high hopes of his promising nephew, the boy was sent to the university of Cahors to follow a more definitely ecclesiastical line of study. There he remained until he was sixteen, when he was sent to the Collège du Plessis in Paris. In the metropolis he came under the tutelage of another of his father's brothers, the Marquis de Fénelon. This uncle, whose name was Antoine, had had a tumultuous past and had been a famous duellist in his day. Later on, suddenly abandoning his wild courses, he became the friend and coadjutor of the saintly Olier, the founder of St. Sulpice. The Marquis Antoine was a member of the Company of the Blessed Sacrament, whose aim was nothing less than the moral and spiritual regeneration of France. He was in the good graces of the King, who had granted him quarters in the Abbey of St. Germain des Prés. It was his uncle who facilitated his introduction to the de Chevreuses and the de Beauvilliers, who formed a sort of coterie, at once aristocratic and devout, an inner ring within the Court, of which Mme de Maintenon herself was one of the most important adherents. Though he may have been indebted to his uncle for his initiation into this exclusive and highly cultivated group, his rapid advancement in the regard and affections of its members he owed entirely to himself, to that union of grace and charm, intellectual attainments and austere unworldliness which constituted at once his mystery and his fascination. St. Simon in a celebrated passage of his memoirs notes the diverse and seemingly contradictory elements which in Fénelon resolved themselves, as by a miracle, into the most enchanting harmony.

" Everything," he says, " was there in combination, and the greatest contradictions produced no lack of harmony. In him were united seriousness and gaiety, gravity and delightful manners, the scholar, the prelate and the *grand seigneur* ; the prevailing characteristics, in his face, as in his whole bearing, were refinement, intellect, graciousness, decorum and above all *noblesse*. It was difficult to take one's eyes off him. . . . His perfect ease was infectious, and his conversation was marked by the grace and good-taste which are only acquired by habitual intercourse with the best society and familiarity with the habits of the great."

On taking orders, about the age of twenty-three, he devoted himself to humble parish work, toiling with unwearying zeal among the poor, the downtrodden and the outcast. He taught the catechism to little children. Even then his fame was beginning to get abroad and many were the distinguished men and women who came to see and hear this very exceptional catechist at his expository labours.

One of Fénelon's half-brothers had gone as a missionary to Canada (where he was fated to leave his bones) and Fénelon himself, also fired with missionary zeal, ardently desired to follow in his steps. The project was vetoed by his two uncles, the Bishop and the Marquis, on the grounds that for one so delicate as he to face the rigours and the hardships of missionary life in so inhospitable a climate would be to court swift and certain death. His thoughts then turned to the East and he wrote half-seriously, half-playfully (the mixture is characteristic) telling of the project he so ardently cherished. For whom the letter was intended is uncertain ; it was probably Bossuet. " At last, Monseigneur," the letter ran, " I am about to set forth ; I almost feel as if I could fly. Greece lies spread out before me. The Sultan is recoiling in terror. Already the Peloponnesus breathes the air of freedom, and the Church of Corinth shall put forth new bloom, and the voice of the Apostle again be heard in the land. I shall not forget thee, O Isle made sacred by the celestial visions of the beloved disciple, O happy Patmos ! I will go and kiss the footprints of the Apostle and dream that I see the heavens opening above me." Playful rhetoric ! A young man giving rein to his ebullient fancy. Some have found fault with the tone and called it flippant. The flippancy is superficial. No man was ever more sincere than Fénelon, but the last thing he would do would be to make a parade of his piety.

In 1681 his uncle of Sarlat resigned the Priory of Carennac in his nephew's favour. Carennac is a delicious little town in Quercy, on the banks of the Dordogne. Fénelon wrote to his cousin, the Marquise de Laval, giving her an account of his reception. All the *gros bonnets* of the place were there to do him honour ; the local nobility and gentry, the clergy, the military, the big farmers and the common people. Everybody came out to acclaim his arrival. The *élite* of the soldiery were there in force and there was a prodigious letting-off of muskets. " The air," he writes, " was thick with smoke, and the noise of the firing was deafening. My prancing steed, fired with

noble ardour was for plunging incontinently into the river. I was
more prudent and came down to *terra firma*. The guns fired, the
drums rolled. I crossed the beautiful Dordogne, which was hardly
visible for the boats that were escorting me. At the water's edge,
the venerable monks, drawn up in a body, gravely awaited my landing.
Their address of welcome was full of the loftiest encomiums ; my
response was gentle and friendly, but not without a touch of the
sublime. From countless throats the shout went up, ' He'll be the
apple of our eye ! ' Next, no less a person than the Orator-Royal
delivered his harangue. He likened me to the Sun ; then to the Moon.
Anon, all the brightest planets had the honour of being compared to
me. Then we came to the elements and the meteors and finished up
appropriately with the Creation of the World. By this time the Sun
had gone to bed, and to confirm the likeness between us, I retired to
my room and prepared to follow his example."

That is the letter of a young man written when the world was opening
out before him, and the future bright with promise ; but it exemplifies
a trait in his character which never deserted him, and that was his
complete naturalness in all things. There was never in him a trace of
the bigot or the pedant. He had an amused contempt for all that was
pompous, or self-important, or pretentious whether in manner or discourse. He was an ascetic, but he never showed it. He was learned,
but no one ever wore his mantle with an easier grace. It was said he
was ambitious in those days. If to be ambitious is to know one's power,
to realize one's gifts and to wish to use them, to make them shine,
then Fénelon was ambitious. One of the gifts he possessed in perfection
was *l'art de plaire*, the power to charm, and if by its means he sought
to win a gentle dominion over the hearts and minds of the men—and
women—with whom he came into contact, of the youthful converts
at the *Nouvelles Catholiques*, of the dour and stubborn Huguenots of
Saintonge and Aunis, of the aristocratic men and women of the court,
can this be imputed to him as a fault ? A touch of the feminine in his
composition—of the feminine, not the effeminate—which is the almost
invariable concomitant of genius, gave him a wonderful insight into
the female heart. Yet it was this sympathy, this subtle understanding,
combined with his generosity, his charity, his sense of *noblesse oblige*
that was fated to bring upon him the supreme trial of his life.

Fénelon's success at the *Nouvelles Catholiques*, where he went to
instruct and confirm in the faith girls newly converted from Protes-
tantism, led to his transference to a very different portion of the
mission field. In 1685, he was sent to Saintonge to collaborate with
the soldiers in bringing back the Protestants to the Church. There
his patience, his persuasiveness and his sympathy worked miracles.
He had little faith in the secular arm as an instrument of conversion.

He thought it more important to count hearts than heads, and deemed that one soul really won to the Church was worth any number of " converts " dragooned into outward compliance by *force majeure*.

" It seems, M. l'Abbé," said de Harlay, the worldly Archbishop of Paris, whose offers of preferment Fénelon had coldly rejected, " it seems that you wish to be forgotten. Well, you shall be." But de Harlay was wrong ; Fénelon was not forgotten, nor will be. One of the things by which he will be remembered is his *Traité de l'Education des Filles*, a little book dealing with the education of girls, which he wrote at the request of Mme de Beauvilliers.

Mme de Beauvilliers had a numerous family. The girls alone numbered eight, and there were several boys. She asked Fénelon to advise her regarding their education, particularly that of the girls. And so he produced this delightful little *Manual for Mothers*, a jewel of pedagogic wisdom, from which mothers and teachers even in these " advanced " days might derive many a useful lesson. Fénelon begins by saying that female education in those days was practically non-existent. And yet a woman's occupations are scarcely less important to the common weal than a man's. She had a house to manage, a husband to bless and children to educate. And how can she educate them if her stock of knowledge is limited to curtseying, dancing and knowing how to enter a room ? Here are a few specimens of the advice he gave to Mme de Beauvilliers : " Never let lessons become associated in the learner's mind with boredom and restraint. Don't scare children into obedience by frightening them with bogies of black-robed priests, or ghosts that walk by night. Make your lessons entertaining, attractive ; reduce rules and discipline to a minimum. Don't bore and discourage children by perpetually talking to them in schoolmaster's jargon about things they cannot understand. Don't let the words ' school ' or ' class ' spell only gloom, constraint, everlasting lessons, silence, uncomfortable postures, fault-finding and perpetual threats. However, if you *do* threaten, do what you say you will do, or it will be good-bye to discipline." He looks on it as a serious disqualification in a teacher to exhibit any physical abnormalities likely to repel or disgust the pupil. " People," he says, " may be models of all the virtues, and yet be anything but agreeable to look upon. It is a mistake to try and force children to take to them."

In contrast to Sir Austin Feverel, Fénelon had little faith in " systems." He believed rather in suiting the education to the character and temperament of the child who was destined to receive it, with due regard to the position which he or she was afterwards to fulfil. The curriculum for girls is not a little interesting : " There is not much use in letting a girl spend a lot of time over Italian and Spanish ; a little Latin would be far more to the purpose. She should of course be thoroughly conversant with the three ' R's,' and, if it is a country-house she is going to run, then some acquaintance with estate-management would not be amiss. She must know some history, and be familiar with the works of the best standard writers in prose and poetry. Painting? Music? Yes, perhaps; but sparingly. The main thing for a woman—next, of course, to her religious duties—is to know how to manage her house; no easy matter if it is to be done well. Let her be thrifty, but not fussy. And she must have practical, first-hand knowledge of her servants' duties. It is no good blaming the cook for an unsatisfactory omelette, if you don't know how to make one yourself."

There is no doubt about whom he was thinking of in all this, or of the house he had in mind. His model was his mother who, without being stingy, was yet so " careful of the gear," not only for the sake of her own family, but that she might have the wherewithal to befriend the poor about her gates. As for the house, that was surely the beloved old home—*la pauvre Ithaque* as he called it—by the Dordogne, with its great rooms and tarnished splendours, where his happy childhood had been spent.

On the 17th August, 1689, Fénelon was appointed by the King tutor to the Duc de Bourgogne, and at once became one of the great notabilities of the Kingdom. Congratulations poured in upon him from every side; a chorus of compliments and adulation. Only one letter struck a different note. It came from his old friend and former tutor, M. Tronson of St. Sulpice. " It cannot be denied," so ran his words, " that, in the ordinary course of things, promotion makes the way of salvation harder. It opens the door to the prizes of this world; take heed lest it close it against the everlasting blessings of the world to come. No doubt," he went on, and his words show how accurately he read the heart of his cherished pupil, " your friends will comfort you by telling you that you did not seek the post. And that is certainly a thing to thank God for. But beware of laying that unction too freely to your soul. A man often has a great deal more to do with his own advancement than he himself imagines. We may not actively solicit promotion, but we are sometimes very adroit in removing the obstacles that hinder it." And he concludes, " After all the fulsome compliments you have doubtless received, a little plain-speaking from me will not come amiss."

The Duc de Bourgogne, wayward, wilful, capricious, subject to ungovernable fits of temper, but clever, and sound at heart, was a terribly difficult pupil. But Fénelon was gifted with unerring tact, inexhaustible patience and an unbreakable will. None knew better than he how to combine the *suaviter in modo* with the *fortiter in re*. When, later on, he came to look back on his handiwork, it is said that he sometimes wished he had not done it quite so thoroughly, for the once wilful, high-spirited, violent-tempered child had been transformed into a meek, retiring, and entirely unenterprising young man. It seemed to him then that he ought to set about the opposite and more difficult, task of restoring the spirit he had so effectively subdued. Fénelon composed his own text-books, *Fables* in the style of Perrault, charmingly written, and each with a suitable moral ; *Dialogues des Morts*, imaginary conversations between historic personages ; and lastly *Télémaque*, which its author describes as " an heroic poem (it is written in prose) like those of Homer and Virgil, introducing matters suitable to be taught to a prince destined to the throne—all the virtues necessary for the good governance of a state, and the faults to which sovereign power is liable." There was no reference intended to the King. So said the author. Many thought, or pretended to think, otherwise ; among them the King himself—and Bossuet ! But all this was later. At present Fénelon is in high favour. The barometer is set fair. So much so indeed that in 1694 the King bestowed on him the wealthy abbey of St. Valéry. A year later he appointed him to the Archbishopric of Cambrai which carried with it the title of Duke and revenues amounting to two hundred thousand livres *per annum*, permitting him at the same time to retain the office and emoluments of tutor to the royal princes.

But now, when he seemed to be on the crest of the wave that should raise him sooner or later to the highest position in the realm, when present greatness seemed but the harbinger of greater things to come, the tragedy of his life was at hand.

It is impossible—indeed it would be beside the mark—to attempt here to discuss in detail the character of Mme Guyon and the long and bitter Quietist controversy which brought about the irremediable estrangement of two great Churchmen, turning their love into bitterness and gall, and sending one of them, the most gifted, the most fascinating, the most ethereal spirit of the age, into an exile that endured until his death.

Who then, and what, was this Mme Guyon ? A saint fired with the mystical ardours of a St. Teresa, or a St. Jeanne de Chantal ? Or was she a victim of delusional insanity and, in plain language, mad ? Mad or not mad, she was a woman of extraordinary personal charm. The fact that she had brought Mme de Maintenon for a time beneath her spell is sufficient proof of that.

It was in the autumn of 1688, or the spring of 1689, that Fénelon met Mme Guyon for the first time. He had heard of her wanderings up and down the country with her strange, gaunt Barnabite monk, Père La Combe ; of her visions, her " preachings," her numerous and voluminous writings. He had made enquiries about her at Montargis, her native town, on his way back from Saintonge, and the result of his investigations did not tend to allay his prejudice against her. On the contrary. But then he met her face to face at the Duchesse de Charost's (the Château de Beynes) and they returned to Paris in the same coach. Mme Guyon took advantage of this *tête-à-tête* to expound her doctrine, and Fénelon eagerly imbibed it. " From that day," says d'Aguesseau in his *Memoirs*, " they became close friends and Fénelon shared all her illusions. He was perverted, even as the first man, by the voice of a woman, and his genius, his fortunes, even his good name were sacrificed, not to the illusion of the senses, but of the mind."

Now, her doctrine of *l'amour pur*, or the mystical love of God, a state in which the soul loves God so absolutely as to be regardless even of its own salvation, loving Him without any expectation, indeed without any thought of recompense, might, a generation or so earlier, have passed more or less unheeded, but the Molinos scandals had intervened and led the ecclesiastical authorities to scrutinize with great care any new manifestations of mystical enthusiasm. Molinos had taught that the soul and the body were perfectly distinct, and that the soul was neither soiled by, nor responsible for, the sins committed by the body Mme Guyon entirely rejected that pernicious doctrine, but her own teaching was, her opponents held, calculated to weaken the ritual and sacramental system of the Church. It would take too long here to go into the details of the controversy that raged about her voluminous writings, especially the famous *Moyen Court de faire oraison*. In the end, a council consisting of Bossuet, Tronson and de Noailles was held at Issy for the purpose of sifting the true mysticism from the false. As a result of these deliberations thirty-two articles were drawn up, and to these Fénelon, who added two more, attached his signature. The whole matter seemed satisfactorily settled when Bossuet, in order to explain and amplify the decisions arrived at, brought out a book which he invited Fénelon to approve. Fénelon refused, on the grounds that the book, under cover of exposing false doctrine, was in reality a personal attack on Mme Guyon as cruel as it was unwarranted. Mme Guyon, if she had erred had erred in the letter, not in the spirit. That was the position taken up by Fénelon. He was her friend, and he claimed to know what was in her heart more truly than her other judges, who knew her only by her writings. Fénelon then brought out a book which he called *Explication des Maximes des Saints*, setting forth his view of true mysticism, basing it on the writings and teaching of the great mystics, St. John of the Cross, St. Francis de Sales and others of equal weight. Thus the controversy began again with greater bitterness than ever.

If an inhabitant of some neighbouring planet had been able to look down upon France just at that time, he would have noted some strange phenomena. He would have seen two erstwhile friends, both men of genius, both loyal sons of the Church, confronting and denouncing one another in terms of unparalleled ferocity. He would have noted unprecedented activity in the episcopal palaces of Meaux and Cambrai and an amazing output of polemical compositions—attack and reply, rejoinder and counter-rejoinder, and so on without end. And if he had been able to investigate the cause of this extraordinary, this unexampled commotion, he would have learnt to his amazement that it concerned the mystical and disinterested love of God.

Fénelon sent his book to Rome—a bold step seeing how jealous at that time the church in France was of its " liberties "—and begged that the Pope would pass judgment upon it. This act of " ultramontanism " added fuel to the fire that was already raging furiously enough. The King ordered Fénelon to retire forthwith to his diocese and to remain there. That meant exile—and he knew it—and the downfall of all his hopes. Once, and only once, they revived like the dying flicker of a candle. In 1711, when the Dauphin died, the Duc de Bourgogne, Fénelon's one-time pupil, who had never ceased to love his former tutor, became the direct heir to the throne. The great King Louis was old and in failing health. In the natural course of events, the Dauphin's accession could not be long delayed, and when it came to pass, Fénelon would be the power behind the throne and in a position to instigate those measures of humane and enlightened government which he had had so long at heart. After nearly two years of deliberation *les Maximes des Saints* was condemned. The blow must have been a heavy one, but Fénelon bore it without a murmur, and with complete submission. The voice of the Church was the voice of God. And the Church had spoken.

* * * * * * * * *

Years have gone by. The Archbishop is still an exile in his diocese at Cambrai. The *art de plaire*, the old magnetic charm, has not abandoned him and he has endeared himself to all his people. But day by day he seems to grow more detached from the world. The young Dauphin, on whom rested his last hopes of playing that distinguished part in his country's affairs to which his splendid gifts and his enlightened patriotism entitled him to aspire—the Dauphin is dead ; cut off in the flower of his youth. Death too has been busy among his dearest friends, those staunch companions of good and evil days, who had remained steadfast when all the world had turned against him. First, de Langeron was taken, the friend of his youth, who had served him so long and loyally and whom he loved with a

love passing the love of women. " I have lost the greatest comfort
of my life," he wrote to de Chevreuse, " and the best helper God has
given me in the service of His Church." And in another letter, " I
have lost a friend who has been the delight of my life for thirty-four
years." *Quid moror altera?* we seem to hear him cry from the depths
of his solitary anguish. Soon another friend, hardly less intimate,
the Duc de Chevreuse had followed de Langeron to the grave. " He
is not gone from us because we see him not," he wrote to the Duchesse ;
" he sees us, loves us, feels all our needs. He himself has reached his
haven and prays for us who are still exposed to the perils of the deep."
Singula de nobis anni predantur euntes! Two years later, the Duc de
Beauvilliers followed, the last to go of that little group of friends who
had clung to him more closely than brothers. " If only," he sighs,
" all great friends could wait for each other and die on the same day ! "

Of Fénelon's life at Cambrai we get a vivid glimpse from an
unexpected source. Bossuet is dead and his secretary, Le Dieu, whose
principal motive seems to have been curiosity, paid a visit to Cambrai
soon after his master's death. He presented himself to the Archbishop, a little doubtful as to the reception in store for him. His
misgivings proved groundless. " His manner," Le Dieu sets down in
his diary, " was gentle and exquisitely polite. Courteously, but
without effusion, he invited me to his room . . . The Archbishop was
attired in long violet robes, cassock and chimere, with rose-coloured
button and button-holes. There were no gold tassels or gold fringes
on his girdle, and round his hat was a plain cord of green silk . . .
When dinner was announced, he invited me to a seat at his table . . .
The Archbishop said grace and took his place at the head of the table
with the Abbé de Chanterac (his Grand Vicaire) on his left. I had
chosen an inconspicuous place among the general company, but the
seat on the Archbishop's right being vacant, his grace signed to me
to come and take it. I thanked him and observed that I was already
seated and served. With great courtesy he insisted, saying, ' Come,
your place is here.' So I obeyed without further demur." The
visitor then goes on to describe the " tasteful magnificence " of the
repast, the many varieties of meats and game, the excellent red wine,
the choice dessert " peaches and grapes first-rate, albeit we were in
Flanders "—the spotless napery, the massive plate, the liveried
servants. Then he goes on, " The Archbishop did me the honour
to help me with his own hand to everything that was choicest on the
table. Each time he did so, I raised my hat, and each time he did
the same to me. He also paid me the compliment of raising his glass
to me, which he did with grave and gentle courtesy." But amid all
this state and dignity the Archbishop himself lived in all respects a life
of the strictest self-denial.

Fénelon's life at Cambrai varied little from day to day. As a rule the only thing that interrupted its regular routine—and there was no lack of routine-work, for the diocese was a vast one—would be a visit from one of his kinsmen, nephews or great nephews—he adored children—or a pastoral journey to preach, or to hold a confirmation, in some outlying town or village. His flock worshipped him ; his gentleness, his meek-hearted dignity, his burning sincerity, his unselfishness, his charity, the indefinable impress of genius that seemed to surround him like an aureole, his voice so infinitely sweet and clear, his kindness to the poor and suffering, his love of children—all these things, united with his own sorrows and tribulations so nobly borne, had won him an abiding home in the hearts of his people. *Nom omnis moriar*, he might have said, had he guessed how his memory would live on undimmed, and his story be handed down from generation to generation. " The days are long," he wrote pathetically to one of his kinsmen, " but oh, how short the years ! " And again, " Old age is stealing insensibly upon me . . . I feel like one in 'a dream, or a figure in a shadow-show." And, sometimes, in a moment of despondency, " Life seems to me like a poor play on which the curtain will soon be rung down." But such moods are rare and swiftly pass. For the most part his temperament was sunny and serene. This letter reflects the calm cheerfulness that marked his usual mood : " Your letter delighted me, my dear nephew. Its little poetic flights amused me and its affection warmed my heart. I live on friendship, and of friendship I shall die. I only realise that it is springtime now by the trees in our poor little garden here,

iam lento turgent in palmite gemmae."

Then follow three more quotations—from the *Georgics* these—to illustrate his love of trees. " Oh, how I wish you were here beneath their shade ! "

Fénelon is a prince of humanists and nowhere is his love of the humanities more attractively displayed than in his famous " Letter to the Academy." That exquisite literary *causerie* proclaims Fénelon one of the most penetrating and delicate of critics. It was his last work, written in fact but a few months before his death. Yet it shows no trace of weariness of mind or body.

The Abbé de St. Pierre, a member of the French Academy, had submitted for the approval of his colleagues a syllabus of works to which in his opinion it was meet that they should address themselves. The Academy thereupon decided that all its members should be individually consulted in the matter, and invited each to send his comments on the syllabus presented to him, or, if he preferred, to submit an alternative scheme of his own. Fénelon chose the latter course, and his reply reached the Academy towards the end of May, 1714. It was regarded by his fellow Immortals as a delightful piece of work, but not conspicuously practical. " Full of lofty, delicate and carefully meditated ideas," said the Abbé de St. Pierre, " expressed in terms of gracious elegance, it is well calculated both to charm and to instruct." " But," he added, " it leaves us as much in the dark as ever as to the nature of the work to which we should devote our energies. At the moment, we have to decide *what* to do ; the question *how* to do it will follow later." And this, perhaps, is what was to be expected from one whom the King had described as the most gifted, but the most chimerical mind in his kingdom ("*C'est l'esprit le plus bel mais le plus chimerique de mon royaume*"). There is, at any rate, no doubt about the *bel esprit* of this little essay. One might say of it what Sir Arthur Quiller-Couch says of Newman's *Idea of a University*, namely, that " it is so wise—so eminently wise—as to deserve being bound by the young student of literature for a frontlet on his brow and a talisman on his writing wrist." If, however, we compare it with Newman's *Idea*, we shall see that it is much less closely knit ; that it is an informal *causerie*, rather than the orderly and logical development of a thesis. If it be asked what the book is about, I suppose one might have recourse to its sub-title and say that it is composed of " Reflections on Grammar, Rhetoric, Poetry, and History." But that would not tell you much. It might even lead you to avoid it, for Grammar, Rhetoric, History, Poetry itself, are, alas, subjects whose expositors do not always escape dullness. But this essay, from beginning to end, is pure crystal. Fénelon is learned, but no pedant. His heart is with the Ancients—however much he may strive in this *opusculum* to do justice to the Moderns. He is steeped, as they say, in the classics, and if he wants to illuminate a truth, or to drive home an argument, it is to Virgil, or to Horace, or to Homer, rather than to any modern writer, that he will go for his illustration. Those who, like George Eliot's Parson Irwine, or Mgr. Dupanloup, have a taste for classical quotation, who care for these things, not only for their own sake but, like the hero of Stevenson's *Ebb Tide*, for the associations which they call to mind, will love the " Letter to the Academy."

Towards the end of 1714, when the autumn was flaming away and the trees in his palace garden had changed from green to gold, Fénelon went to spend a few days with his friends at Chaulnes, where he was ever welcome. It was his last taste of earthly joy. A little before Christmas, as he was returning to Cambrai after a pastoral visit, the carriage in which he was driving collided with the parapet of a bridge. One of the horses was killed, but Fénelon himself escaped with a severe shaking. He never recovered from the shock. On January 1st,

1715, the Feast of the Circumcision, Fénelon was seized with illness. From the first onset of the malady, he knew that he would not recover. He had himself carried from the little " grey room " in which he habitually slept, into the great State Bedchamber with its crimson hangings, in order that he might take leave of all who might wish to bid him farewell. As the news of his illness got abroad and it became known that he was dying, a great number of the townsfolk whom he had befriended, counselled and consoled came to look their last on him and to ask his blessing. On the morning of the Feast of the Epiphany he received Extreme Unction. At times he was delirious, but in his intervals of consciousness his kinsmen and some others, his friends, came and knelt at his bedside, one after another, to receive his blessing. Afterwards, all his servants came and, weeping, begged that he would bless them also. This he did, very gently. Abbé Le Vayer, a member of the Congregation of St. Sulpice and the Superior of the Sulpician Seminary at Cambrai, then recited the prayers for the dying ; after which, lying for a space in perfect stillness, he breathed his last, quite peacefully, at a quarter past five in the morning of the 7th January, 1715.

And now, as we bid him farewell, what words more apt could we apply to him than those with which a great English poet saluted the shade of Virgil, with whose noble and tender spirit Fénelon, " majestic in his sadness," has so much in common :

> Light among the vanished ages,
>   Star that gildest yet this phantom shore,
> Golden branch amid the shadows,
>   Kings and realms that pass to rise no more !

CHARLES CARROLL OF CARROLLTON

A.D. 1737–1832

IT IS DIFFICULT within a restricted space to present the life and times of a man who lived during one of the most stirring periods of American history—from the early years of the last English colony of Georgia to the end of the " Era of Good Feeling "—almost a century. It was a century that witnessed the culmination of the inter-colonial wars, the final defeat of France in the western world in 1763, the growing spirit of independence in the English colonies, the War of Independence from 1774 to 1783, the launching of a new nation founded upon the democratic principles of liberty, justice and equality, the stabilization of that independence through the War of 1812, and the successful organization of the federal government up to Jackson's triumph in 1828-1829.

However, there is this advantage : no other Revolutionary character offers a better focus for these years (1737-1832) than Charles Carroll of Carrollton. He was born about the same time as the outstanding men among the Founding Fathers, and he outlived them all. There is the added advantage in reviewing this great epoch through Carroll's participation in it : we are dealing with the largest plantation owner of the day, probably the wealthiest man in the English colonies, and without any doubt, one of the most cultured spirits of all those who had a share in founding the American Republic. That he was born a Catholic, that he remained a Catholic in spite of all the legal proscriptions both before and after Independence against his Faith, and that he gloried in preserving his Catholic Faith until death—this last factor in his life must endear him to all Catholic readers.

First of all a word about the Carrolls. The two principal branches are Irish in origin, but their genealogy in Maryland is somewhat uncertain, since the same Christian names occur in each branch— Charles, Daniel, John, Mary and Elizabeth. The older branch begins with Charles Carroll, the attorney-general (1660-1720), whose son Charles Carroll of Annapolis lived from 1702-1781, and whose son is the subject of this sketch. The younger branch begins with Daniel Carroll of Upper Marlboro, two of whose sons attained fame—Daniel

Carroll, a signer of the Federal Constitution and one of the three Commissioners appointed by President Washington to lay out the capital city, and John Carroll, who was the first American bishop and archbishop, his See being Baltimore. Both branches married into the Darnall family, and so were of the blood of the Calverts—the Lords Baltimore who founded Maryland.

Much might be written on the unfortunate social, political and religious condition of the English and Irish Catholics in the Maryland Province at this time, but it may be summed up in a word : the ostracism was complete, all-embracing, deadly. It must be remembered also that the fourth Lord Baltimore had apostatized in 1713 in order to obtain proprietary rights over Maryland. In no phase of social life was the penal legislation against the Maryland Catholics more vicious than in the matter of education. In my *Life and Times of John Carroll* (Vol. I, pp. 15-16). I have attempted to describe the situation in a paragraph :

Nothing more noble in American life can be found than the determination of the Catholic parents of Maryland to preserve amongst their children the Faith for which their ancestors had fought, suffered, and died. The transmission of the doctrines and the discipline of the Church was a sacred obligation imposed upon them by their conscience ; and at a time when to apostatize from the Catholic Faith was the open road to social and political advancement in the English dominions, there was a strength of purpose in the hearts of these Maryland mothers comparable in every respect to the mothers of the martyrs. To see their children go from their side for a sojourn of ten or fifteen years, and to be bereft of the happy, innocent faces of their boys and girls during that period when they are a parent's consolation, knowing that even on their return as educated gentlemen and gentlewomen they would be politically outcasts, demanded a nobility of soul which is one of the brightest factors in the drab colourless colonial history of America. Apart from the fact that Catholic parents could not compromise in the matter of education, there was added reason why they refused to enter their children in the colonial schools of Maryland. The appalling description of the immoral conditions of these schools, as painted by the historians of the Anglican Church of Maryland and Virginia, needs but to be read to understand the abhorrence in which such educational masters must have been held by Catholic Maryland women. Children of cultured families like the Carrolls could not be trusted to schoolmasters unworthy of their calling, and with the laws ever on the alert against the establishment of Catholic educational institutions, one avenue of escape alone was opened to the colonial families, that which the Catholics of England, Ireland and Scotland had taken for two centuries, namely, the English colleges and convents in continental Europe.

Charles Carroll was the victim of the illiberal attitude of his day, but he was to benefit by these years of training abroad and was to return as a leader in the struggle which eventually won freedom for his fellow-Catholics in the new republic.   To a boy of his age, the perils of the long journey across the Atlantic were forgotten in the joyousness of the great adventure, but there had been implanted in his young heart memories of the political and religious intolerance against his people, and the vision of the tear-stained faces of his parents as he said good-bye had its place in determining his judgment when the call came to break for ever with the motherland.

Charles Carroll of Carrollton was twenty-eight years old when he returned to his father's house in Annapolis in 1765.   The years spent abroad at the English Jesuit College of St. Omer, where he had as his companion the future bishop, John Carroll, then the years at the College of Louis le Grand in Paris, and later at the Middle Temple in London—these formed the great character he was to become. Eleven of those seventeen years had been spent under the instruction of the Jesuits, who almost alone among the educators of the day, in the face of the dominant non-Catholic doctrine on the divine right of kings, had kept alive in their classrooms the fundamental democratic principles of equality, justice and freedom ; it was their training in history, politics and jurisprudence which served him and his country admirably once Americans decided to place these old and well-tried Catholic principles at the basis of their national life.

At this point, a word should be said about his father, Charles Carroll of Annapolis or Doughoregan.   With his great wealth and high social standing he might easily have sent his son to any one of the better known classical colleges of the day—Harvard, Yale, or even the nearby William and Mary College of Virginia, where Jefferson, Monroe and John Marshall were once students.   But there was no stronger determination in the hearts of Maryland's Catholic fathers and mothers than that of giving their boys and girls a sound moral Catholic education.   Rather than have their sons subjected to the danger, remote as it may have been in those days, of losing their faith and their moral Catholic code in these institutions, the parents of boys like Charles and John Carroll willingly saw their sons set out on the long and perilous journey across the Atlantic to find safe harbourage in the schools of Catholic France.

His return in 1765 coincided with the violent opposition of the Americans to the Stamp Act, and it has recently been shown from his letters, that "he was one of the first, if not the very first, to see the probability of successful revolution and eventual independence " as a result of the storm of indignation aroused by the Act.

It must be realized that, in spite of his wealth, education and culture, in spite of the social standing of which the anti-Catholic laws of Maryland could not rob him, Charles Carroll of Carrollton, as he was henceforth known, returned a disfranchised citizen, with no voice in the political affairs of the province. As a Catholic, he was only a little better politically than the slaves on his plantations. He was denied the public exercise of his religion, and was forced by these same laws to pay a double tax for the support of a clergy that could never be his own.

Events, however, of far-reaching importance were soon to brush aside this civic disability, and before he quite realized it, he was in the thick of the political controversies of the day.

The Carroll-Dulany controversy gave him a victory over the acknowledged head of the American bar, and he came out of the newspaper strife as the " First Citizen " of Maryland. Carroll's famous reply toward the end of the battle of letters—" *Meminimus et ignoscimus* "—" We remember and we forgive "—has been the watchword of American Catholics in every nativistic attack since his day. American historians now recognize that the real significance of this controversy (1773) lies in the fact that the struggle against bigotry and intolerance had been at last won. Although the laws of Maryland disfranchised Carroll, his fellow-citizens ignored them and appointed him to important colonial committees. From 1775 on he was Maryland's principal political leader, and in 1776, he was one of the three Commissioners appointed by the Continental Congress to go to Canada for the purpose of securing the co-operation of that province in the fight against England. He signed the Declaration of Independence on August 2, 1776, the only Catholic to have that privilege.

There is one chapter in his life which has only recently been given an adequate appraisal. No educated American to-day would deny the fact that without the help of Catholic France, the American Revolution was doomed to defeat. It may be true, as Carroll wrote to an English friend in 1774, that once hostilities began, the Americans would never surrender. " If we are beaten on the plains," he said, " we will retreat to our mountains and defy them . . . we have no doubt of our ultimate success." These are the words of a loyal patriot, but the statesman in him realized that a victorious American Revolution could only be achieved through an alliance with England's century-old enemy, Catholic France.

The American cause was in a desperate state in 1777, even after the victory over Burgoyne at Saratoga in October of that year, and Carroll's knowledge of France and of French political leaders was to be of infinite value during the negotiations. Efforts were made to have him go to Paris as the envoy of the new Republic, but he wisely declined ; for, on all sides the rank and file of the Americans would rather have gone back to the rule of England than form a compact with a Catholic king and a Catholic people. To offset bigotry, negotiations had to be made in secret. When the Franco-American Alliance became known in 1778, the outcry from American pulpits was even more violent than that against the Quebec Act in 1774, by which the English Parliament gave freedom of worship to the Catholics of Canada.

Every school-boy knows the result of that famous Alliance. When Admiral de Grasse arrived in the waters of Chesapeake Bay in the summer of 1781, at the head of a fleet of twenty-five war vessels, with a military force of almost 22,000 officers and men, and with nearly ninety Catholic chaplains, the war was virtually at an end. In October that year, Cornwallis surrendered at Yorktown.

Carroll's services during the Revolution were many and varied. He was the chief assistant to Robert Morris in financing the war. He was a member of the first War Department of the United States. He followed the American army everywhere and spent part of the terrible winter at Valley Forge with George Washington. He was instrumental in exposing the famous Conway Cabal. He refused the presidency of the Second Continental Congress, and was almost alone in condemning the confiscation of loyalist property. Later on, in 1793, he was to be spoken of as Washington's logical successor in the presidency of the United States. While he was not present at the Constitutional Convention in Philadelphia in 1787, having declined the nomination, it is fairly well ascertained that his influence was felt in the proposal of his cousin, Daniel Carroll, which broke the worst deadlock of its deliberations, namely, the method of electing the president of the new nation. This method—the electoral college— is said to have had its origin in Carroll's explanation of the way in which the College of Cardinals elect the Pope. A recent writer has said : " It is safe to state . . . that Charles Carroll of Carrollton was the father of the electoral college." As Maryland's first Senator in the Federal Congress of 1789, he, with Daniel Carroll, Maryland's first Representative in the same body, was responsible for the celebrated clause in the First Amendment—" Congress shall make no laws respecting the establishment of religion or prohibiting the free exercise thereof."

With the turn of the century, Carroll ceased to take an active part in national affairs, but his letters up to his death display his keen patriotic interest in all that concerned the principles of American democracy.

In a letter written shortly before his death to George Washington Custis Parke, Charles Carroll said :

When I signed the Declaration of Independence I had in view not only our independence from England but the toleration of all sects professing the Christian religion and communicating to them all equal rights . . . Reflecting, as you must, on the disabilities, I may truly say, of the proscription of the Roman Catholics in Maryland, you will not be surprised that I had much at heart this grand design, founded on mutual charity, the basis of our holy religion.

In 1827, in a letter to a Protestant minister he wrote :

Your sentiments on religious liberty coincide with mine. To obtain religious as well as civil liberty, I entered zealously into the Revolution, and observing the Christian religion divided into many sects, I founded the hope that no one would be so predominant as to become the religion of the state. That hope was thus early entertained because all of them joined in the same cause with few exceptions of individuals. God grant that this religious liberty may be preserved in these states to the end of time and that all believing in the religion of Christ may practise the leading principle of charity, the basis of every virtue.

The opening years of the nineteenth century in the United States were among the most remarkable through which the nation has passed. There was the Louisiana Purchase of 1803 which must have recalled to Carroll one of his father's letters during his student days in Paris, when a movement was started by the Catholics of Maryland to leave that province in a body for Louisiana where they could worship God in peace. The aftermath of the French Revolution with the rise of Napoleon he understood better than most Americans of the day, and he took part in the defence of Baltimore during the War of 1812. He lost his only son, Charles Carroll of Homewood, in 1825, and he had seen his three grand-daughters marry into the British nobility. One became the wife of the Marquis of Wellesley, the Lord Lieutenant of Ireland and the brother of the Duke of Wellington. The second became the Duchess of Leeds, and the third, Baroness Strafford. In 1827, he was named chairman of the Committee for the incorporation of the Baltimore and Ohio railroad, and on July 4, 1828, he laid its foundation or corner stone which may still be seen in the old Camden Station in Baltimore. To this period belongs the meeting again after so many years between Carroll and Lafayette in 1824, when that national hero was the guest of the United States. To these years belongs also that more striking episode—the visit of the prelates of the First Provincial Council of Baltimore in 1829 to Doughoregan Manor to pay Carroll honour. Few scenes in American Catholic history are comparable to this.

All his life long, he was a faithful son of Mother Church. Neither the luxuries of Paris nor the temptations of London dampened his religious zeal and devotion ; and certainly no young Catholic man of the day received more stirring letters from his father to keep true to Catholic principles of life and action. It was on his death-bed that he gave utterance to one of the noblest thoughts that ever came from his lips : " I have lived to my ninety-sixth year ; I have enjoyed continued health ; I have been blessed with great wealth, prosperity, and most of the good things which the world can bestow—public approbation, esteem, applause ; but what I now look back upon with the greatest satisfaction to myself is, that I have practised the duties of my religion."

Perhaps, the most dramatic moment of his life occurred on the occasion of the golden jubilee of American independence—July 4, 1826, for on that day two of the three remaining Signers of the Declaration, Thomas Jefferson and John Adams, entered into their eternal reward, leaving Carroll to bear for the last six years of his life the title " Last of the Signers."

On August 2, 1826, at Faneuil Hall, Boston, Daniel Webster, the greatest of American orators, paid Charles Carroll of Carrollton this tribute :

Of the illustrious Signers of the Declaration of Independence there now remains only Charles Carroll. He seems an aged oak, standing alone on the plain, which time spared a little longer after all its contemporaries have been levelled with the dust. Venerable object ! We delight to gather around its trunk while it yet stands, and to dwell beneath its shadow. Sole survivor of an assembly of as great men as the world has witnessed, in a transaction one of the most important that history records, what thoughts, what interesting reflections, must fill his elevated and devout soul ! If he dwell on the past, how happy, how joyous, how full of the fruition of that hope which his ardent patriotism indulged ; if he glance at the future, how does the prospect of his country's advancement almost bewilder his weakened conception ! Fortunate, distinguished patriot ! Interesting relic of the past ! Let him know that while we honour the dead we do not forget the living, and that there is not a heart here which does not fervently pray that Heaven may keep him yet back from the society of his companions.

When they laid him to rest in the chapel of his beloved Doughoregan, in mid-November, 1832, the entire nation went into mourning. Panegyrics were delivered by leading orators in the chief centres, and the American press was unanimous in its praise of a long life of perfect devotion to God and country. The nation had lost a common father. He was the last link with the past, with the founders of the American Republic.   When he died, a new generation was in the seats of the mighty, never to forget that their legacy of American idealism came from the Catholic Carroll as truly as it had come from Washington, Jefferson and Hamilton.

REFERENCES :

The biographies of Charles Carroll of Carrollton upon which this text is based are: Rowland, *Life and Correspondence of Charles Carroll of Carrollton* (New York, 1898, 2 Vols.) ; Leonard, *Life of Charles Carroll of Carrollton* (New York, 1918), and Joseph Gurn, *Life of Charles Carroll of Carrollton* (New York, 1935).   Other important sources are : Russell, *Maryland, The Land of Sanctuary* (Baltimore, Md. 1907), and J. Moss Ives, *The Ark and the Dove* (New York, 1934).

RIGHT REV. DR. JOHN G. VANCE

JULIE BILLIART

A.D. 1751–1816

O F THE LIFE and character of Julie Billiart we can but give a
brief and inadequate sketch. She was born in 1751 and died
in the year 1816. Her life, therefore, spans what, until our own
day, was the most unstable and tumultuous period in modern history.
It is an age full of declarations of rights and of independence ; of
revolutions and counter-revolutions ; of plots and revolts ; of
constitutions and mighty wars ; of systems, of treaties and of
congresses. Rarely has there been a period comparable for
unsteadiness, unless it be the last eventful years.

Julie Billiart was born of humble peasant farmer stock, of people
who for generations had owned their own poor fields. She thus
had the soil of France, and of Picardy in her blood. She enjoyed a
radiant childhood. Her mother was a dear and saintly woman, and
her father was both good and devout. The tone of the household
was entirely Catholic, and the family enjoyed the ministrations of
a remarkably devoted parish priest.

It was clear at an early date that Julie was especially wrapped in
the things of God. She took a vast interest in her Catechism, and
especially in repeating it to others. Nothing seemed to affect her
so definitely as the thought, presence and companionship of God.
Her childhood, the little we know of it, was singularly beautiful.
She naturally engaged in the ordinary household work and in the
farm work until, through disaster, her people lost their fields. Then
she perforce worked as a hireling in the harvest fields of another.
Whether she was selling goods in the market, working with the
reapers in the fields, or resting for the mid-day meal, there clung
about her the beauty of holiness and a wonderful enthusiasm—the
enthusiasm of a lover—for God. A long period of sickness ensued,
during which she was half crippled. From the age of thirty-one
to the age of fifty-three, for twenty-two long years—the long years
that are chronicled in one short sentence—she was completely
crippled and bed-ridden. She passed that time, as indeed she had
passed all her active life, in intimate communion with Almighty God.

In these days of sickness and illness she knew what it was to be forced to flee from the violence and brutality of the revolutionary forces. She knew and heard of the civil constitution of the clergy and of the utter desolation of the Church. She heard Mass and received Holy Communion sometimes from priests who had been proscribed, or sometimes from those who were at the moment being ruthlessly hunted. But all the brutality, clamour and violence of her day seemed to her in her preoccupation like the sound of distant voices. Her soul was wrapped in God. Not that she was insensitive to the pain of others or the disasters affecting the Church. She was touched and wounded deeply on hearing that sixteen of the Carmelite Nuns who had been so gentle and encouraging to her as a child had been taken to Paris and there guillotined, one after the other, as they stood murmuring the *Salve Regina*. This always seemed to her the way to die, unbending and unbroken for the love of Christ. Though it would be well to linger over the period of pain and suffering in Julie's life, or better still to try and estimate what it meant in the unfolding of her heroic spirit, we must pursue our breathless chronicle.

At the age of fifty-three, at a time of special devotion and religious revival, she was commanded by a priest to take one step for the love of the Sacred Heart of Jesus Christ. Julie took the one step, then a second, then a third, and her paralysis was cured.

Thereafter she had but twelve years to live, and in that short interval she founded the Institute of Nôtre Dame, informed its spirit, fixed its labours, drew up its regulations and rule of life, founded some ten or more convents, and animated her daughters in Christ with something of her own magnificent enthusiasm and restless zeal for God. To effect this mighty work she had to travel much, and many dozens of long journeys are recorded, particularly through the north-east of France and in Belgium. She would travel the long journeys sometimes on foot—it is recorded that one day she walked twenty-eight miles—or by the rocking stage coach, or partly on foot and partly in the farm carts that lurched along the uneven roads. She knew every manner of trouble and anxiety that can overwhelm a human soul. Real poverty and want she indeed experienced, but these she scarcely seemed to notice. She met, too, with profound dislike in some quarters. She was persecuted by some of the clergy— bitterly and persistently persecuted by one priest who did much to turn the hearts of people in high places away from her. She was persecuted, moreover, by the bishop of the diocese in which the congregation had been cradled. She faced schism in her own community of nuns, and before her death she knew what it was to suffer profound and terrible misunderstanding even from those of her own Order whom she had most loved and trusted. At the age of sixty-five, having wrought a mighty work in the foundation of a great teaching order which has rescued hundreds of thousands of children for Christ both in Europe, and in the far-away mission fields of India, Japan, Africa and China, she gave up her radiant soul to God, murmuring the words of the Magnificat :

"My soul doth magnify the Lord, and my spirit hath rejoiced in God my Saviour."

We turn to a brief appreciation of this truly wonderful life. In Mère Julie, we discern the simplicity and literalness of a child, which, in passing, we may expect to find in all great lives. It is indeed one of the indisputable signs of greatness. One sometimes finds it in the lives of great philosophers : one finds it always among the great saints like Teresa, John of the Cross and Ignatius Loyola. Smaller minds and weaker personalities try to interpret and explain, and are thus led to compromise, until, their deeds half done, death comes silently to capture them. Not so Mère Julie. Christ, for instance, has said "If anyone will come after Me, let him deny himself and take up his Cross daily and follow Me." Julie, hearing these words wished to follow Christ. She therefore denied herself, took up her Cross daily and sought His Footsteps. Again Christ had said "Happy are the poor in spirit : happy are the meek : happy are they that mourn : happy are they that suffer persecution for justice sake," and Julie took the words, in literalness and simplicity to heart. She was genuinely happy when she was reviled and persecuted : she gave praise to God in moments of sorrow and desolation, believing quite simply that the Eight Beatitudes were Christ's code of happiness. Christ further had said "Unless ye become as little Children, ye shall not enter into the Kingdom of Heaven." Julie thus became, as all the great saints have become, as a little child to fit herself the more fully to understand the words of Christ.

But Christ did not only say that His followers should become as little children to enter into the Kingdom of Heaven. On one occasion He said "The Kingdom of God is for the violent, and only the violent carry it away." This quality of violence in Mère Julie is to be sought in her inexhaustible and undaunted courage. She did indeed view life and its events as a " battered caravanserai " jolting now slowly, now more swiftly, towards eternity. Everything that transpired, whether for joy or suffering, assumed in consequence its true proportion. Thus no word of men, no power of men, no threat, no anxiety, no inner dereliction of spirit could break her wonderful courage that was founded upon God. This is much to say of one who was tried in almost every way in which we human beings can suffer. At least she underwent all the graver and more terrible anxiety of evil report, misunderstanding, calumny and abuse. Only once in the biographies do we hear of an occasion when, broken in health and overcharged with anxiety, she burst into tears. Nor in so doing did she detract in any way from her high courage.

Herself undaunted, she inspired her whole Congregation of Nuns with her own splendid courage. They led hard lives without seeming to reflect for a moment on their hardship, as everything was transformed into joy by their love of God. Boys who go camping or picnicking will undergo want and grave discomfort because the picnic or camp is a new experience. They see in it something novel and inspiring, and they relish, whatever be the discomfort, the delightful absence of restraint. This spirit of children picnicking or camping with their supreme disregard for trifles was the spirit that Mère Julie infused into her Congregation. When the sisters had food, they ate it gladly. When they had none, they uncomplainingly went hungry. When they found beds they slept in them with comfort. When they found none, they were content with a mattress on the floor, or some straw, and as the " caravanserai " moved along they found in all these and similar privations nothing but trifles.

Mère Julie's courage was shown too in the way she handled money, and that courage again was shared by her sisters. She thought and believed that, if the sisters worked for God, He would provide at least for their elementary needs. So, on one occasion she left one franc with the Sister Superior of a newly founded Convent. On another occasion she left five francs, but for Mère Julie this was almost capital. Her own courageous belief must indeed have been shared by the poor Sisters Superior. In Julie's undaunted spirit and high womanly courage, therefore, we find that character of violence which Christ demanded of those who would enter His Kingdom.

But how can one convey anything worthy of this strikingly beautiful figure with the gentle voice, the tender wistful care for all her children, and the radiant smile of holiness ? Yet where we must perforce fail to delineate the personality, we may attempt to assess the work.

In the Political and Social History of the time we read of great names, of revolutions, consulates, and empires, and of all the personalities and forces in the different hemispheres that shaped and coloured these stirring events. Praise is given to the soldier, the statesman, to that far-seeing constitutionalist, or to this Prime Minister who could withstand the violence of a Continental System. Throughout the whole recital you will hear no reference to the person and work of Mère Julie. In omitting her name and that of others who have wrought foundation-work of Christian education, the historians greatly err, for they omit one of the most significant forces of the period.

Let us, in order to have some standard of comparison, consider for a moment the case of Napoleon. By the magic of his name and person he could, even at the end, gather about him the remnants of a great army. That army was defeated and dispersed. Mère Julie, by the magic of her person, and the saintliness of her life gathered about her an army which has steadily grown into a mighty force spread throughout the whole world. That army has never known defeat, has never lacked recruits, and has never lost sight of its objectives. Again Napoleon, long before his death, saw the dreams of his life, his work, his great political structures mostly shattered and in ruins. In the event scarcely anything of his constructive work was to remain. Mère Julie saw her work founded, extended and consolidated during the twelve magnificent years of her active life, and in the intervening century that work has grown in extent, in spirit, and in power. Lastly, Napoleon's name is known to the many. The name alone can still evoke grand enthusiasms and sometimes extravagant praise : it can still, almost as it were a living thing, call forth words of utter disparagement. All who know Mère Julie, on the other hand, and her beautiful life—her children's children now number a mighty family of many millions—speak of her with joy and love, and they invoke her aid in struggles and difficulties.

Why then do the Political and Social Historians continue to err by omitting references to so mighty and indomitable a force as Julie Billiart ? But perhaps Julie herself would have preferred to share with other saints the silence of history. She loved her God ; she bore her Cross ; she followed Christ ; she wrought the work Christ gave her to do ; she now reigns with Him in glory.

BIOGRAPHICAL DATES.

1st Period	EARLY YEARS.
(to age of 16).	

July 12th,	1751	Birth at Cuvilly, Picardy, France. Daughter of Jean François Billiart, a small farmer, and Marie Louise Antionette Debraine. Education at village school of Cuvilly.
	1760	First Communion.
	1764	Confirmation by Cardinal Bishop of Beauvais.
	1765	Vow of perpetual chastity.
	1767	Ruin of the Billiart farm.

2nd Period
(to age of 23).

YEARS OF POVERTY.

1767-1774   Work in fields. Apostolic zeal among labourers.

About 1770   Admission to daily Communion.

1774   Paralysis caused by shock resulting from attempt on her father's life.

3rd Period
(to age of 53).

YEARS OF PHYSICAL SUFFERING.

1774-1790   " The Saint of Cuvilly." Work for God from her sick-room.

1790-1794   Attempts on her life by Republicans. Flight to Compiègne. Frequent changes of lodging. Her vision of the future Institute of Nôtre Dame.

1794   Removal to Hôtel Blin at Amiens. Meeting with Marie Louise Françoise Blin de Bourdon (co-foundress).
First beginnings of Religious Life.

1797   *Petite Terreur*. Removal to Bettencourt. Instructions continued in sick-room.

August 5th, 1803   Return to Amiens. First foundation of Institute of Nôtre Dame.

February 2nd, 1804   First Religious vows.

June 1st, 1804   Sudden cure of her paralysis.

4th Period
(to death at age of 64).

FOUNDATIONS OF NÔTRE DAME.

October 15th, 1805   Final vows.

February 2nd, 1806   Revelation of expansion of Institute.

1806-1808   Foundations in dioceses of Amiens, Ghent, Namur, Tournai, Bordeaux.

1808   Persecution by ecclesiastical authority at Amiens.

1808   Gift of healing : 23 sisters cured of typhoid.

January, 1809   Expulsion from Amiens, departure for Namur.

1807-1814   Foundations at Saint Hubert, Zele, Gembloux, Andenne, Fleurus.

1813   Visit to Pope Pius VII at Fontainebleau.

1814-1815   War in Belgium. Courageous visitations of convents within war-zone.
Persecution by the Sisters. Final martyrdom of the spirit.

April 8th, 1816   Death at Namur.

May 13th, 1906   Beatification by Pope Pius X.

CHRISTOPHER HOLLIS, M.A.

JOHN LINGARD

A.D. 1771–1851

IT TOOK TWO hundred years after the Reformation in England before the Catholic body was stamped out. Throughout those two hundred years the Catholics were an ever-decreasing, but still important, minority. After the rebellion of 1745 the Catholic body, as a body, almost ceased to exist. Catholicism became the creed of a very few, scattered individuals. For almost exactly a hundred years from the death of Pope in 1744 and the rebellion of 1745 Catholicism dropped out of English life. In the 1840's came the revival, the " second spring."

The new Catholicism was the product of a wide variety of causes. The sharp addition to the numbers of practising Catholics in England was mainly due to the Irish immigration, consequent on the famine. There was also a lesser trickle of immigration from other Catholic lands. Converts were chiefly the result of the Oxford Movement and the influence of Newman.

Yet, while so much has been written, and justly written, of the influence of Newman and the Oxford converts, it is strange and ungenerous to underrate, as is now commonly done, another influence, in its way as remarkable as that of Newman—the influence of John Lingard, surely the most remarkable man that has been born of English Catholic parents since the seventeenth century. The present writer found himself seated at dinner a year or two ago near two of the best-read of living English priests, and was astonished and shocked to find that neither of them ever read Lingard, that they did not believe that anyone else ever read him and that they thought praise of him was an exercise of the foolishly pious rather than of the sincere and scholarly. Such an opinion is surely a disaster.

The great achievement of Lingard was this. The bias against tradition of the encyclopædist mind of the eighteenth century had raised a demand for the revision of history. " Why should we accept traditional stories ? " they said. " Let us go back to the original documents and find out what really did happen." The pretence, at least, of an acquaintance with original documents is to-day so common that we can no longer appreciate the originality of that demand. Yet it was an original demand a hundred and fifty years ago, and it was made by men who had not the least doubt that the consequence of satisfying it would be the explosion of the Christian religion. The Catholics in England, such as they were, were few and timid, few of them qualified to meet an intellectual challenge and the majority apprehensive that nothing but harm could come out of a Catholic engaging in controversy, whatever the controversy's result, grateful not to be physically persecuted, apprehensive that any provocative conduct might be a barrier to further emancipation. Lingard, as we shall see, had a full understanding of the importance of avoiding provocation. Yet he saw, too, that victories could not be won by timidity and that, when there was a bluff to be called, it was well to call it.

For it was his conviction—a conviction the justice of which he amply demonstrated—that the encyclopædist challenge was a bluff. Just as de Maistre had shown that there was no reason to fear that challenge in philosophy, so Lingard showed that there was no reason to fear it in history. Faith had no cause to fear a challenge. It could appeal to reason, and it could appeal to evidence, and could win the verdict. It was un-faith that was un-reason.

Yet Lingard, who was so great a historian only because he was a great statesman as well as a great scholar, very well understood how carefully a Catholic priest must tread, if he wanted to gain the attention of an English audience in the early nineteenth century. It was not enough for him to win most of his controversies ; he must win all his controversies. If he would correct mis-statements about the Church, he must confine himself to correcting those that could be exposed with absolute certainty. Accusations, where refutation was not yet quite demonstrable, must for the moment be allowed to go by default.

Thus in his private papers we find the record of his making a list of the errors in Macaulay and Carlyle and then docketing them away in a desk with the reflection that it would be best to leave a non-Catholic to expose the errors of the anti-Catholic writers. " Through the work," he wrote of his *History*. " I made it a rule to tell the truth, whether it made for us or against us : to avoid all appearance of controversy that I might not repel Protestant readers ; and yet to furnish every necessary proof in our favour in the notes ; so that, if you compare my narrative to Hume's, for example, you will find that with the aid of the notes, it is a complete refutation of him without appearing to be so. This I thought preferable. In my account of the Reformation I must say much to shock Protestant prejudices and my only chance of being read by them depends upon my having the reputation of a temperate writer. The good to be done is by writing a book which Protestants will read."

In particular he determined early on the necessity for making a great renunciation. No man was ever better qualified than he to expose the Glorious Revolution of 1688 for the cads' ramp that it was. Yet he saw that there was a limit to the amount of exposure that the British public would tolerate from one priest. His prime task was to expose the Reformation. Even such an exposure was to the English mind so great a paradox that, careful though he was to write in studied moderation and understatement, yet, even as it was, Macaulay was able to dismiss him with a " Dr. Lingard, a very able,and well-informed writer but whose great fundamental rule of judging seems to be that the popular opinion on historical questions cannot possibly be correct." Lingard felt that, should he go forward and attack 1688 as he had attacked the Reformation, however irrefutable both attacks might be, the force of both would be diminished.

That a Catholic priest should have been the first of scientific English historians is a happy accident, whose importance is sometimes overlooked. " It is a Providence truly," said Cardinal Wiseman, " that in history we have given to the nation a writer like Lingard. . . . This is a mercy indeed and rightful honour to him who, at such a period of time, worked his way not into a high rank but to the very loftiest point of literary position." Whatever may be the degree of anti-Catholic prejudice that is still to be found among English scholars, certainly the language in which the achievement of mediæval civilization is discussed to-day differs greatly from that in which it was commonly discussed in Lingard's day, and the most confident of rejoicers at the destruction of Christian unity in the sixteenth century would not to-day try to justify it with the careless and cocksure inaccuracy of a Froude. For that there are many reasons. One of them is most certainly the influence of Lingard—the conviction which he imposed on English historical scholarship that the deepest learning and the highest integrity might cause not a weakening but a strengthening of Catholic faith. It may have been strange that they needed such a lesson, but need it they certainly did. Mr. Belloc, with characteristic generosity and characteristic aggressiveness, has continually borne witness to Lingard's influence. He has acknowledged him as his master and he has accused his fellow-historians of " using Lingard as a quarry, and without acknowledgment."

If we consider the date at which he wrote, it is extraordinary how high was the level of accuracy which he maintained. Page after page of Macaulay is disfigured by the grossest errors both in text and reference. Froude gives as quotations sentences which are but paraphrases, if that, of their original. And their modern defenders plead that the age was not an age of accurate history. Lingard, working under enormously greater difficulties than Macaulay or Froude, covering an enormously larger period than they, can hardly be convicted of any important inaccuracy. Even where new evidence has come to light since his time, very often, as in the case of Chapuys' reports of the state of England to Charles V, it has entirely confirmed conclusions to which Lingard had already come.

The estimate of the influence of Lingard has been disputed, and it has been argued that, so far as nineteenth-century England was convinced that a man could be both a scholarly historian and a Catholic, he who convinced them was not Lingard but Acton. It is hard to agree. Lord Acton's influence was in exactly the opposite direction. Acton changed no man's mind. He was a victim of the dominant ideas of his time to an excessive degree. His influence on the academic world was to persuade it that, when there did happen to crop up an intelligent man who had had the misfortune to be brought up Catholic, he agreed with the academic world so far as he dared to. It was Lingard's greatness that, while he won the esteem of the academic mind, he never himself faltered in his contempt for it.

There is loss and gain in exclusion from the main educational stream of one's country. The average standard of the Catholic school then was probably, as it probably is to-day, lower than that of the non-Catholic, and students may lose intellectually, though they gain spiritually, from exclusion from non-Catholic schools. But for the exceptional man, able to learn for himself, it is a gain that he be able to learn, freed from the stereotyping influence of a strong tradition. Nothing but the happy accident of penal laws could have produced the great liberating influence of Lingard.

It is probably true that Lingard was too contemptuous of Oxford. Never having himself experienced those complex loyalties to and affections for an institution, by which Englishmen are so largely moved, he under-rated their power for good. For he himself loved Ushaw, but loved it rather as his child than as his parent. He judged the intellectual solely on his intellect and thus formed for him a perhaps excessive contempt. While other Catholics were congratulating themselves on the intellectual reinforcement of the Oxford converts, Lingard, while congratulating, yet could not conceal a measure of contempt for men who even for a time had been captured by the values of Oxford. It was no difficulty to him to understand how an active, unreflecting man accepted the values taught in England by nineteenth-century Church and State. But he could not understand how a scholar could accept them, gaping as they were with their inconsistencies. " There appears to me," he wrote, " a superabundance of wordiness and dreaminess in all the writings of the Oxford tractarians." And in a private letter he wrote, in a phrase of typically humorous petulance, of a group of them at Oscott, that they talked " as if they were all old women or lunatics."

He had, it cannot be denied, a certain prejudice against the Oxford converts, though in serious moments ready to recognize the good that they did and to advocate the wise policy that, with their differing background, they should go their way and he should be allowed to go his. It was important that there should be different sorts of Catholics, pursuing their different policies, the one hitting the mark here, the other there. " Let the converts write in their own way. They must know better than we do what is most likely to influence the Protestant mind." Yet it was his conviction that it was a highly untypical sort of Englishman who was attracted by the Oxford Movement and his fear that large hopes of a national conversion in the wake of that of Newman were doomed to disappointment. He has proved right in his fear and it may be that he has proved right in his belief that his apologetics were more calculated to appeal to, at any rate, a large class of Protestant Englishmen than those of some of the Oxford thinkers. It was his contention that there was no deep difference between him and the Protestants as to what the Catholic Church was ; their difference was whether that Church, as she now existed, did or did not resemble the organization of the primitive Christians. It was a question that could be settled by the appeal to history. But in a way his difference from the Puseyite was more profound than his difference from the Protestant, because one who held the branch-theory of the Church must attach so wholly different a meaning to the word " Church " to that which Catholics attached to it that it was difficult even to talk with him. When after his many spiritual wrestlings Newman decided that a branch-theory of the Church was not tenable, it was a momentous catastrophe to his disciples, but Lingard was not wrong in his expectation that the answer of ninety-nine out of a hundred even of educated Englishmen would be a shrug of the shoulders and an " I never supposed that it was."

One of the strongest battles which he fought was the battle against those who would be stricter than the mind of the Church. " All things are lawful, but all things are not expedient," he used often to quote. The passage of the generations had built up in the English soul a massive wall of anti-Catholic prejudice. The Catholic habits had come to seem to it bizarre and puerile—worse still foreign. It was most important that Englishmen should not be compelled to accept more than the Church definitely commanded. Once that the authority of a teaching Church was accepted, then the converts would form their own pious habits in time. That could be left to the future. But for the moment he was most strongly opposed to *les petites dévotions*—to the introduction into England of harmless but unnecessary Continental customs. He scorned the uncouth halter of the Roman collar, seeing no reason why the priest should be compelled to dress like a dog in order to show the world that he was not a layman. And he rightly rejected as an offence alike against English susceptibilities and against Catholic tradition the barbaric notion that a secular priest should be addressed as "Father." He was more than doubtful at first of the wisdom of reintroducing the Jesuits into England and determined to fight to prevent them from regaining control of the English College at Rome. Yet after Father Plowden's death and in the second half of his life his relations with the Jesuits at Stonyhurst grew much more friendly.

The waters of Lingard's great learning flowed along two widely different channels. On the one hand, as we have said, he started a tradition in academic circles which has endured to this day. "Talbot adds," he was able to record at the end of his life, "that my history had no small share in creating in the universities the spirit of enquiry into Catholic matters. . . . This, if it be true, is very gratifying." But his history also fell into the hands of a creature more wildly unlike a don than any that was ever erect upon two legs. William Cobbett acknowledged Lingard as his master.

Cobbett, a politician, aflame with indignation at the sufferings of the poor of his own day, a man of humble origins who had had no expensive schooling, had, he tells us, up till then accepted uncritically the conventional Whig history and believed that, if things were bad, they had at least always been bad. It was Lingard who opened his eyes, through whom he first learnt that there had been an England very different from that of the early nineteenth century. No two men could have been more different than Cobbett and Lingard. They had nothing in common save only the common advantage of having escaped the cramping influence of the academies. Cobbett had but little interest either in history for its own sake or in religious truth. His interest was in the social problems of his own day, and history to him a useful weapon, if it enabled him to pillory the rich by telling of another age in which things were managed very much better than in his own. Lingard showed him that there had been such an age, and Cobbett eagerly seized his Lingard, translated it into his own tremendous prose, used what suited him, omitted what did not suit him, blurred out all qualifications and set it out as a trumpet-call to bid the people rise for liberty.

Lingard had never believed in art for art's sake or history for history's sake. Like Trollope, he had always written frankly with a purpose. But his purpose had been a very different one from Cobbett's. He wrote to dissipate prejudices against religion, Cobbett to rouse men to revolt. As a result, therefore, Cobbett's story of the Reformation, though based upon Lingard, yet reads very differently from Lingard. Cobbett, for instance, for the purposes of his contrast, is inclined to romanticize the conditions of the pre-Reformation monasteries and to speak of the Reformation as a crime perpetrated by a few wicked men against a contented England. Lingard, as a true historian must needs have done, knew well that the Reformation could not have happened if there had not already been much amiss with the pre-Reformation England, and, if anything, he perhaps somewhat exaggerated the corruption of the pre-Reformation monks. They were " a time-serving lot," he wrote. He did not need to create imaginary paragons of virtue in order to heighten the contrast with the vices of the reformers. Yet the gap between Cobbett's mind and Lingard's mind was perhaps not so great as that between their works. For Lingard was, from policy, always understanding, while Cobbett from his policy—that of creating immediate excitement—was always overstating.

In any event the consequence of the Lingard-Cobbett critique, even though details of it have not proved tenable, has been important and beneficent. The England of Lingard's day worshipped at the shrine of the depressing materialistic goddess of progressive capitalism. A reaction against the horrors of capitalism was sooner or later inevitable but, if the reaction should come to a generation whose eyes were covered with the blinkers of Whig history, it was only to be expected that they would react from the Tweedledum of capitalism to the Tweedledee of Marxian Communism, thence to collapse into despair when they found that they had but exchanged prison for prison. What has kept England alive is the persistence in every generation of a small band of men who have rejected the false liberties of liberalism and Whig history and maintained the right of appeal to tradition. A motley band they are—Disraeli and the Young Englanders, Feargus O'Connor and the " back-to-the-land " wing of the Chartists, Ruskin, William Morris and, to a lesser degree, the other pre-Raphaelites; Mr. Chesterton and the Distributists of our own day. They all, to a large extent derived, whether they were conscious of it or not, from Cobbett and, through Cobbett, from Lingard.

They derived from Lingard, but Lingard must not, therefore, be held responsible for all their doings. When we come to the world of art an important distinction must be drawn. There can be no doubt that the Gothic Revival owed a great deal to the impulse towards a better understanding of the Middle Ages which Lingard gave. But for all that Lingard strongly disapproved of it. He disapproved of Pugin's mediævalism—perhaps because he knew so much more about the Middle Ages than Pugin did. It was his argument, not dissimilar to that of Mr. Eric Gill to-day, that every age must have its own artistic expression and that nothing was less of a compliment to the Middle Ages that to imitate their forms of architecture in an alien environment.

The external story of Lingard's life can soon be told. The son of a carpenter of Lincolnshire family, resident at Winchester, he was born in that city in 1771 and brought up there. Owing to the offices of Mr. Nolan, the local priest, a burse was obtained for him at Douai, whither he went at the age of nine. After his nine years of schooling there, he decided to stay on and study for the priesthood, expecting to receive his ordination at Douai, The troubles of the French Revolution came, and Lingard, like other English seminarists, had to flee to England. Once in Douai he had already been in danger of his life, when he had stopped the mob to ask of them why they were dragging a French acquaintance of his to the guillotine; a cry had been raised of *le calotin à la lanterne*, and Lingard had only saved himself by taking to his heels. Eventually he and three companions escaped from Douai by letting themselves by sheets from the windows.

Thus it happened that he received his ordination in England—one of the first Englishmen to do so since the Reformation. The England to which he returned was an England in which Catholics were still to wait almost another forty years for their full political emancipation. Yet it was an England, in which, for the first time since the Reformation, the Catholic religion was again tolerated. By the Second Catholic Relief Act of June 24, 1791, it was declared no longer a penal offence to say Mass publicly. Lingard went to teach at Douai's new home of Crook Hall, near Durham, and moved with the College to Ushaw in 1808. In 1811 he became parish priest of the little Lancashire village of Hornby and there he remained for the last forty years of his life.

Many opportunities of advancement came to him. But for his own strenuous opposition he could certainly have had a bishop's mitre and probably a cardinal's hat. But a brief spell in the temporary rectorship of Ushaw had confirmed the conclusion of his temperament that he was unfitted for executive office. He thought indeed that gifts of statesmanship were required in order to shape the policy with which the Catholics should meet their new opportunity and their new status, and there was probably no man in England who had so large a hand in the shaping of that Catholic policy as Lingard. But he preferred to work through advice and consultation rather than be himself the acknowledged leader. And, as an adviser, he played a part in Catholic councils very different from that of the average village priest. Nor was his influence confined to Catholic circles. He was able to occupy a position in general English life such as no Catholic priest had occupied for centuries and which it is extraordinary that a man without family connections should have been able to acquire. He was the confidential friend, in a day when such a relationship was indeed rare, of Blomfield, the Anglican Bishop of Chester, and boasted with good-humoured amusement to his Anglican neighbours that the Bishop had sent him a copy of his episcopal charge before he distributed it to his own clergy. In an age when travelling was by no means the easy business which it is to-day, Brougham, soon to be Whig Lord Chancellor, and Pollock, to be Tory Attorney-General, had a habit of making the difficult journey to remote Hornby in order to take the advice of its parish-priest.

In learning he was the complete man to a degree which it is rare to find in our hurrying age. French, owing to his education in France, was as much his language as was English, and, when elected a Member of the French Academy, it was no difficulty to him to write his qualifying essay in the French language. Greek and Latin were his companions, as they were those of all educated men at that day, but he had a contempt for those who confined their reading in those tongues to the conventionally termed classical authors. He was a master of prose and a competent versifier in four languages.

He achieved his mastery because he was willing to pay for it the necessary price of a secluded life. The telephone and the motor car have in our day made it fatally easy to obtain company and, as a result, there are few who are ready to find their first companions in their books, which is the necessary condition of great scholarship, or to commune with themselves rather than chatter to others, which is the necessary condition of great literature. It would indeed be a foolish falsehood to pretend that the average Englishman, Catholic or Protestant, lay or clerical, a hundred years ago was such a man as Lingard. There were but few like him in the country, and it may well be that the average even among the professedly educated was more ignorant than are we to-day. But one cannot but wonder, when one reads the life of such a man as Lingard, whether too high a price cannot be paid for raising the average level of information, whether there is not some value in a more frank division between the learned and the lewd and whether it is altogether better to have a society in which all claim to be lieutenants and none is willing to be private or able to be general.

Like all very able men, Lingard would doubtless have become both base and boring had his life not been disciplined by faith. He had a power of irony that a later age was to find tedious in Anatole France. " The sagacity of Mosheim," he wrote of Egypt in his *Anglo-Saxon Church*, " has discovered that this practice "—that of celibacy of the clergy—" owed its origin not to the doctrine of the gospel but to the influence of the climate." There follow two lines of learned references, and then, " If this be true we must admire the heroism of its present inhabitants, who in their harems have subdued the influence of the climate and introduced the difficult practise of polygamy in lieu of the easy virtue of chastity." He was sometimes almost brutal in his rebuffs to the distinguished who had, he thought, presumed too far. " If Dr. Wiseman should be of a different opinion respecting St. Thomas, I can only account for it by supposing, as is not unlikely, that he never studied the question." Or, in reply to a suggestion of a visit from Dollinger, whom he did not esteem as highly as did others in England of that date. " I hope Dr. Dollinger will think the conservation of his money preferable to my company."

Young men in a panic, old men in a frenzy, alike aroused his almost contemptuous amusement. He took a positive, perhaps sometime an almost cruel, delight in ridiculing what he considered affectation. When an over-enthusiastic nun begged him to bring back for her a memento from the Vatican, he complied with the request but sent also a flea which he had caught in the Papal antechamber. The driver of the stage-coach used to stop his coach opposite Lingard's house and say to his passengers " This is the house of Dr. Lingard, the famous historian of England." The passengers then stared in. So Lingard trained his dog to sit at a desk in the window in cap and gown with spectacles on his nose. The passengers imagined that they had seen the famous historian, while Lingard himself continued his work in another room at the back of the house.

Yet contempt and brusqueness in him never became inordinate, because there reigned over all the discipline of charity. He had a most profound sense of vocation. There were two tasks to which he felt himself called, nor was it for him to estimate their relative importance. He was called to minister to the scattered faithful of a large north-country parish and he did so for forty years with a devotion and a patience so great that even to-day the memory of " the old doctor " has hardly perished in the Hornby district. He was called to play a great part, if not the greatest part, in shaping the policy by which Catholicism should seize a new opportunity for the recapture of the lost province of England. There he engaged a battle, the event of which is not yet known.

EDMUND C. BUCKLEY

DANIEL O'CONNELL

A.D. 1775–1847

IN HER INCOMPARABLE adventures, Alice, that Marco Polo of Wonder-
land, once encountered the Cheshire cat. Ensconced on the
branch of a tree, the animal gradually faded away until nothing of it
could be seen save the grin. So is it that, with the passage of time, a
man whose stature once impressed a continent, may survive only in
the faint transparency of a name.

In Ireland " the Liberator," in England " the Irish Agitator," such
was Daniel O'Connell in the eyes of the great majority of the two
races. The two titles illustrate in their way the tragic differences
between them, which have painfully contributed to the making of our
island's story.

O'Connell was not the first nor was he the only worker in the struggle
for the smashing of the great social and ecclesiastical machine, based
on intolerance and greed, which held the Irish race bound for the
best part of two centuries. There were many others, both in England
and in Ireland, towards the end of the eighteenth century, who
realized the degrading injustice of the system of ascendancy and
worked, not without success, for its amelioration. But these were
for the most part English or Anglo-Irish politicians who had little or
no spiritual contact with the mass of the population. O'Connell,
on the other hand, was Irish of the Irish, born and fostered among
the glens of remotest Kerry, in a district and among a people to whom
English law and the English tongue were still strange ; remote and
inaccessible from the capital, but free and open to the wild Atlantic,
which made the markets of France and Spain the natural, if illicit,
outlet for a race of adventurous cattle-breeders, traders and smugglers.

It was at the end of an era that, in 1775, O'Connell was born.
With the realization of the penal laws against Catholics there was
achieved a measure of economic emancipation. But there was
still the aftermath of a great wrong and O'Connell's Ireland was a
country where, as Charles Lever vivaciously intimates, the administration of law had been brought into discredit.

By this chaos the O'Connells themselves were affected. Debarred as he had been from the usual opportunities of commerce and the usual right to own property, the chieftain of the family, Daniel's uncle, had become the most accomplished and admired smuggler in County Kerry. So strong was his scruple against contributing to the revenue that, when a tax was imposed on beaver hats, he changed his headgear and, for the rest of his life, was known as " Hunting Cap." Happily for Hunting Cap, the grand jury, though Protestant, consisted of his customers ; and when, inadvertently, a new official, Captain Butler, searched the cave where O'Connell kept his contraband, even he allowed the lady of the house to retain a silk dress from France. " You shall have it free, madam," he said, " if it costs me my commission."

The vicissitudes of the seventeenth and eighteenth centuries had brought the O'Connells down from their old position of tribal chiefs and rulers over a wide domain, but they still maintained a certain rude dignity of their own. They furnished recruits for the French King's armies, imported French wines and silks, paid for them in Irish cattle and sheep, and grew rich by trading with their inland neighbours, Protestant or Catholics, who were less favourably situated for smuggling purposes but who had no compunctions about profiting by transactions grateful and comforting to themselves although frowned on by English law. An uncle of the Liberator was a colonel in the French service, and as regular communication was kept up between the members of the family, it was natural that when young Dan came to the proper age he was sent to school in France, where he received a fair grounding in the " humanities." Whether he was to become a priest or an officer was still an open question when the outbreak of the French Revolution brought about a new order of things in which all his plans came to grief. In the clerical-royalist atmosphere of St. Omer the Revolution was regarded with detestation and horror ; things went from bad to worse until the college was occupied by Revolutionary troops and the pupils turned out. Young O'Connell made his way, not without danger and difficulty, to Calais. He and his companions were hooted and hustled as " young priests " and " little aristocrats." They were forced to wear the hated tricolour, but O'Connell's last act on leaving for Dover was to tear the cockade from his hat and throw it into the sea.

It is as a wild Irishman, making things hot for England, that Daniel O'Connell has usually been depicted. Certainly his personality was masterful ; certainly his career was tempestuous. If, however, he stands among the universals, it is as a symbol, not of anarchy, not of rebellion, but of order. In a world, encumbered with anomaly, his gospel was logic and his practice was law. He saw, on the one hand, the dangers of the excesses being perpetrated in the sacred name of " liberty," and the calamitous reprisals that were certain to follow ;

on the other, he beheld his country dejected, degraded, downtrodden in every way ; his religion persecuted, proscribed, and outlawed. He felt that he was born in servitude, and living a slave, and his noble spirit determined to be free.

Even in boyhood, his essential conservatism was revealed. But the radicalism of Robespierre was to him a peril from which he must make his escape. He returned to Ireland the royalist that he never ceased to be. In another respect, he was normal. Meeting his cousin, Mary, he remarked one day, " Are you engaged, Miss O'Connell ? " She replied, " I am not." " Then," he went on, " will you engage yourself to me ? " and she answered, " I will." Secretly, but happily, they were married ; there was a large family, and amid his agitations, O'Connell maintained his home. For twenty-five years he rose at 4 in the morning, lit his own fire and worked till 10 in the evening.

In O'Connell then we see the paradox which sometimes puzzles the student of the British Labour Party. He was no Bolshevist, eager to smash society. On the contrary, his grievance was that, in this society, he was not permitted to play his part as a loyal subject of the Throne. What made him so dangerous was the fact that he asked nothing at any times except the obviously reasonable. Of his two main demands, it may be said that both were merely expressions of the usual Whiggery. What was the Catholic Emancipation that so greatly enraged Wellington ? Nothing except the principle that no citizen shall suffer disqualification on account of his religion. What was " repeal of the Union " for advocating which O'Connell was sent to prison ? Merely the policy of allowing an English-speaking democracy to manage its own strictly domestic affairs.

The very fact that Catholics arrived at a measure of prosperity, meant that they were the more conscious of political exclusion. Take O'Connell's own case. As a " junior " at the bar, he only received £200 for his first seventy-eight briefs. Yet when his income rose to twenty times that figure, he had still to practise as a junior and was unable either to " take silk " as a King's Counsel or to sit on the bench as a judge. It was what South Africa would call a colour bar, but without the colour.

Ireland had been a nation before England had an alphabet. Now she was a downtrodden province, dominated by avaricious and intolerant blood-suckers. The ablest lawyers, including the Government's own Attorney-General, had declared the Union binding only until it could be successfully defied. The Parliament that passed the Act had no power from God or man to do so. Votes for it were obtained by open bribery and fraud at £8,000 a-piece. Upwards of a million sterling was expended in the purchase of the votes that carried it. Peerages, Protestant bishoprics, judgeships, positions in the army, navy, and Civil Service were bestowed in payment of votes. Public opinion in Ireland was despised during the negotiations. Public meetings against it were dispersed by force. Martial law was in full force, and the Habeas Corpus Act suspended. Intimidation to an alarming extent prevailed. Nearly one hundred thousand soldiers, with all the savagery of '98 attaching to their characters, occupied the island ; and, notwithstanding, seven hundred thousand were found to petition against the Bill, while only three thousand, including officials, could be marshalled to petition in its favour. Carried by perjury, corruption, and intimidation the " Union " became the law of the land.

Froude describes Ireland at the same period as follows :

> The executive government was unequal to the elementary work of maintaining peace and order. The aristocracy and the legislature were corrupt beyond the reach of shame. The gentry had neglected their duties until they had forgotten that they had any duties to perform. The peasantry were hopelessly miserable ; and, finding in the law, not a protector and a friend, but a sword in the hands of their oppressors, they had been taught to look to crime and rebellion as their only means of self-defence.

The cruelties inflicted on the Irish people by reason of the rebellion of 1798, to which they had been driven, and into which they had been actually incited by the Government, the unchecked lawlessness of the Orange Society, and the enforcement of martial law under which Ireland groaned, produced almost universal hopelessness amongst Irish patriots. As long, however, as the Irish Parliament remained, anti-Catholic and bigotted though it was, there were certain hopes of its having to allow liberty of conscience to the vast majority of the people it legislated for, and otherwise to promote their happiness and prosperity.

O'Connell's powers of vituperation and abusive oratory were immense. The age was one in which coarse rhetoric flourished, when even *The Times* could print epithets that would be barred to-day from gutter sheets, but O'Connell exceeded in scurrility all the coarse orators of his day. It was unlikely that the victims of his abuse would feel pleased with him.

Catholic Emancipation had its advocates before O'Connell, and in the easy-going sceptical eighteenth century it did not much disturb the " Protestant conscience " of England. The practical difficulty at the earlier period was that it would completely upset the balance of power in Ireland, based as it was on the impregnable rock of the Protestant establishment. After the Union this danger did not exist in the same form ; but in the interval there had been a great " Evangelical " revival, which by reviving the " No Popery " feeling among the masses of the people created a much more serious obstacle, the overcoming of which was O'Connell's great achievement.

He got little help or sympathy from the English Catholics, whose motto was to " let sleeping dogs lie " ; and the Irish Hierarchy, with one or two exceptions, favoured the same attitude. A considerable amount of practical toleration had been secured by quiet means under Grattan's Parliament in 1793 ; and the fear was that by over-hasty agitation and clamour things might be made worse rather than better for the timid Catholics who in Dublin and in the other large towns had been thriving and prosperous under existing conditions. O'Connell's attempt to found a " Catholic Association " in 1823 met at first with little encouragement : the body rented two small rooms in a side street, and sometimes there was the utmost difficulty in assembling a quorum to carry on the necessary business. The carrying of the agitation over the heads of the " country gentry and the rich traders of the towns," and getting it into the hands and the minds of the farmers and country priests was O'Connell's idea ; and on these lines he won. " A penny a month, a shilling a year " was his cry, and the " Catholic Rent " was started. This in time provided the necessary funds, and the movement spread till the country was fairly covered.

At this date we need not defend O'Connell against the insinuation that he made money by politics. The truth is rather that he gave up a magnificent practice at the bar and impoverished his inherited estate, dying almost without means. But, of course, his " penny-a-month plan for liberating Ireland," as the critics called it, resulted in the collection of what seemed to be enormous sums of money. In 1825 this penny " rent " backed by the priests, was yielding £1,000 a week, and O'Connell thus established a precedent the importance of which possibily he did not realize. Hitherto, constituencies and their candidates had been dependent on the finances of the few. But in Ireland there arose a democracy that financed itself.

But still O'Connell was powerless. No Catholic could sit in Parliament, and although some English Radical members occasionally took up their cause things were at a deadlock. Then came a stimulus in the form of a Government prosecution, based on the newspaper report of a speech in which O'Connell had warmly praised the South American Republics for their successful assertion of independence and had hinted that " if driven mad by persecution " Ireland might follow their example. But as Dublin Castle had not taken the precaution of sending an independent reporter, and as all the newspaper reporters had lost their notes and could not strain their memories to the extent of recalling the words used, the prosecution ignominiously collapsed and the movement secured a huge advertisement. The

Government then brought in a Bill for the Suppression of Unlawful Associations, and many speeches were made but nothing in particular achieved. When the association was suppressed O'Connell promptly founded a " New " Catholic Association, and things went on as before.

O'Connell had none of the qualities of a statesman. Compared with Parnell the great Protestant leader of the Irish, O'Connell seems like a Tammany Boss in the presence of Abraham Lincoln. He was emotional and superstitious and ludicrously vain. Words were a sort of dope to him and he came to a point at which he could not live without oratory, just as a drug addict cannot live without cocaine. Yet he achieved a great act of deliverance for the people of his faith. It was he, more than any other man, who removed disabilities from Catholics, and it is an odd fact, and one likely to provoke cynical reflections, that among the most strenuous opponents of his efforts to emancipate his co-religionists was a young Oxford don, who wrote to his mother, after Peel's defeat in the University constituency. " We have achieved a glorious victory ; it is the first public event I have been concerned in, and I thank God from my heart, both for my cause and its success." His name was John Henry Newman.

Freedom for his fellow-Catholics to practise their religion, eligibility for every position and office in the State, and similar freedom for every man to follow his own convictions, were the cardinal points in his demands for " Emancipation " ; and the power for his fellow-country-men to legislate under the Crown, through a House of Lords and a House of Commons thoroughly representative of the people of Ireland, was what he claimed as " Repeal."

O'Connell was, first and last, a man of law and order with an ingrained hatred of revolution and violence. While Wolfe Tone and Lord Edward FitzGerald and the wilder elements in Dublin and Belfast cheered for the Revolution in France and plotted rebellion in Ireland, young O'Connell joined the Militia and turned out in arms in support of the Government. His uncle and the other officers of the Irish Brigade placed their swords at the disposal of the English King ; and the whole O'Connell clan in Kerry, with their co-religionists, were enthusiastic loyalists and supporters of the Union which O'Connell himself was to spend most of his later life in denouncing. But here again he knew where to draw the line, for when at the very end Young Ireland was once more caught in the revolutionary whirlpool and tended to follow Davis and Mitchel (both Protestants) into rebellion, O'Connell withstood them, even at the risk of sacrificing all he had worked for, and went out alone to die a broken-hearted man on an alien shore.

O'Connell's career divides itself naturally into two movements which, although essentially and inevitably related, must be separately considered. The Union with England and the abolition of the Dublin Parliament were warmly supported by the Catholic Bishops, to whom that Parliament meant nothing but a hated ascendancy. Cork and the southern counties had no love for Dublin, and they too supported the Union. None were more vociferous in their clamour than the members of the junior Bar, and O'Connell in the first glory of wig and gown joined in the outcry with his fellows of the Four Courts. But it was Emancipation that held the attention alike of the Catholic Church and of the Irish people. It had the sympathy of all that was progressive and tolerant in English public life and over the civilized world. It was a tremendous struggle, and O'Connell was the hero of it. And when it was granted, nothing in particular happened ! A few wealthy Catholics could enter Parliament, but the Catholic peasant was still left to groan under the burden of the payment of tithe to a Church that was not his. The " Forty Shilling Freeholder " found himself disfranchised. Everything in Ireland went on much as before.

What was O'Connell to do ? He was no longer a young man ; he had necessarily neglected his profession while engaged in endless public work. The Bishops were prepared to rest and be thankful, but there was no rest for the " Liberator." And thus he inevitably drifted into his second great movement which was to lead him to failure as complete as his first had been triumphantly successful. As an " Emancipator " he had the support of the English Whigs, but on the matter of Repeal they were opposed to him. In Ireland most of the younger priests rallied to his support, but the Bishops and the elder priests were lukewarm, if not hostile. He had huge popular successes, huge meetings at which endless speeches were delivered. But what was it leading to ? His health gave way. His financial position was seriously involved. " Young Ireland " rose in revolt, and clamoured for war and bloodshed. It was a hopeless position, and O'Connell broke under its weight.

The turning-point came when in 1828 it was finally determined, in spite of the legal disqualification, to challenge an election for Parliament. Mr. Vesey FitzGerald, member for Clare, had been appointed President of the Board of Trade, and it was arranged to contest his re-election, O'Connell himself being the opposing candidate. The result is well known. The majority of the electors were Catholic tenant farmers, but never before had the landlord's right to the votes of his tenants been seriously challenged. The association had, however, changed all that ; and the tenants, headed by their priests, marched in platoons to the poll and voted for O'Connell. Mr. Vesey Fitz-Gerald wrote to Peel: " Nothing can equal the violence here. The

proceedings of yesterday were those of madness : the country is mad."
But O'Connell and his men had kept within the law, and his election
was not disputed.

There remained the obstacle of the Oath at the Table, containing
as it did a declaration against " Popery " which O'Connell could
not make. But there was no more fight in the opponents of Emancipation, most of whom were already tired of the conflict. Lord Anglesea,
writing from Dublin discovered, somewhat later in the day, that it
did not matter much after all and that the best way of " depriving the
demagogues of their power " was " by taking Messrs. O'Connell,
Shiel and the rest of them from the Association and placing them in
the House of Commons." So the objectionable declaration was
withdrawn. O'Connell was re-elected and took his seat. The
struggle that threatened revolution was at an end, and Peel and
Wellington discovered that nothing very remarkable had happened.
The question of tithe still remained to act as a cause of turmoil and
bloodshed ; but the main point was won, and O'Connell became the
hero of the Catholic world.

In normal circumstances this would have been the end. Indeed,
O'Connell himself had indicated that with Emancipation there would
be no more cause for agitation. " I say now," he cried, " that all,
all, shall be pardoned, forgiven, forgotten upon giving us Emancipation,
unconditional, unqualified, free and unshackled." But from one
cause and another this measure of agreement was never reached.
The Government took back with one hand what they had granted with
the other, the " Forty Shilling Freeholder " was disfranchised ;
O'Connell remained embittered and dissatisfied and before long
agitation for Repeal of the Union succeeded that for emancipation.
But that need not concern us here. The great concession that could
have been made without agitation thirty years before was at last
grudgingly made, and the lesson of successful agitation was learnt,
with result of which perhaps the end is not yet.

About his advocacy, there was heroism. In West Cork, an attempt
was made on the life of a magistrate. Dublin Castle undertook what
would have been a veritable massacre of suspects. In five minutes
a packed jury consigned four men to death and a second batch had
been scheduled to share the same fate.

Desperately a messenger made his way over the mountains to
summon O'Connell. Surrendering his briefs, Daniel set out on a ride
of ninety miles in a dog-cart. Without wig or gown or brief he strode
into the court, where they brought him a sandwich and a glass of milk.
The prosecutor continued his speech. Suddenly, O'Connell munching
the while, ejaculated, " That's not law," and it was not law. So began
a crashing counter-attack, under which the entire case for the Crown

collapsed. There was no verdict possible except an acquittal and
that verdict had to be accepted also for the men already awaiting
execution.

With the Protestant as such, O'Connell never had a quarrel. His
colour was " green," but he would say, " I kiss the Orange to my lips
and I press it to my heart." For years he was comrade to Grattan,
and when Grattan's Parliament was obliterated, O'Connell devoted
his first great speech to denouncing the Union. With the Protestants
of Dublin he fought against what was bound to be a loss of patronage
and prestige. But " the garrison " declined to reciprocate. One
alderman, D'Esterre, refused to support a petition to emancipate the
Catholics and was the first of many disputants to challenge O'Connell
to a duel. He was a little man and a good shot, but despite his bulk,
O'Connell met him. To the general surprise it was D'Esterre who
was killed, and of O'Connell we read :

" His conscience was bitterly sore. He had not only killed a man,
but left his widow and two small children almost destitute. He was
determined to do all he could to assist her. He wrote at once, offering
to " share his income " with D'Esterre's widow. She declined, but
consented to accept an annuity for her small daughter, which was
paid regularly for more than thirty years until O'Connell's death.
The memory of the duel haunted him for the remainder of his life.
He never went to communion afterward without wearing a white
glove on his right hand as a sign of penance ; and whenever he passed
D'Esterre's house he would raise his hat and murmur a prayer for the
dead."

He was a weak man in a crisis, and had scarcely any judgment
in difficult situations. His tactics and his strategy were equally poor.
He always imagined he had won the fight when he had merely won
the first round. He would found a society, such as the Catholic
Association, to support a cause, and then, at the first rumour that
the cause was won, would propose the society's suppression as " a
gesture " of friendliness towards his opponents. He may have put
his ear to the ground, but he could never hear anything, and could
neither be persuaded to believe that any person had a chance of
defeating the Beresfords in the pocket-borough of Waterford or that
the nomination of himself for the constituency of Clare could have any
value whatsoever. " Peel," he said, " is the merest man of words
that the world has produced." He might have been describing himself. What finally destroyed him was his behaviour at the monster
demonstration at Clontarf to demand the repeal of the Union. Peel
proclaimed the meeting, and O'Connell instantly came to heel.
" ' This must be obeyed,' the old agitator ordered," and thereby
established himself as a model for Professor John MacNeill to follow

in 1916. Once again O'Connell "immediately urged complete submission and recommended the dissolution of the Association," and compelled the editors of his newspaper to resign, and "ordered the unofficial law courts to suspend their activities." When Lord Chief Justice Denman delivered his judgment on the appeal against the sentence which sent O'Connell, in circumstances almost of luxury, to Richmond Gaol, upsetting the sentence and inflicting a heavy blow on Peel and his Ministry, O'Connell "received the news with blank incredulity." He never foresaw or anticipated anything that happened to him.

Such an achievement constitutes a great claim for honour and renown, and having rescued liberty from licentiousness and error, having shown it compatible with loyalty, as he did in his own person, as well as in the persons of millions of his countrymen ; and having supernaturalized it by religion, he exhibited it as one of the dearest earthly gifts of God to man, the safety of governments, and the basis of human happiness.

For well-nigh half a century, as Herculean agitator he toiled, with zeal unequalled and with wisdom unsurpassed. A bright and easy career of happiness was before him in an honourable profession. He renounced it, and when one would suppose him weary of the political warfare, he rejected its highest reward. His minutes literally counted as gold honestly earned as a lawyer in his laborious profession. Yet, no one devoted more time to his country's welfare. The whole burden of the Irish cause rested upon him. He bore it up. General apathy for a long time pervaded the masses. Suspicion, opposition, calumny, and contempt were hurled against him. Attacks on himself he paid back with interest and scorn, and from insult he defended himself, once sinfully indeed, but according to the mistaken code of honour that then prevailed, with the weapons employed in duel encounters. Insults to his country he drove back with pulverizing blows. Peel and Disraeli fell beneath them morally as completely as the unfortunate d'Esterre did physically. Him it was O'Connell's misfortune, for which he publicly repented, to have fatally wounded. The " Orange " Peel and " the legitimate descendant of the impenitent thief," are epithets of lashing invective that made the greatest men writhe beneath its inflictions, as witness their contemplated duels with him. Disappointments, baffled hopes, perfidy to pledges, in turn accosted him.

It was, moreover, O'Connell, more than any other man, who created the idea of the public meeting as we know it to-day. At a time when it was contrary to etiquette for statesmen to mount the platform, he was second to none as a popular orator and actually was under a perpetual threat of prosecution. His Catholic Association was forcibly suppressed ; so was his Anti-Union Association, but O'Connell always had the best of it.

With King George IV, as Prince of Wales, a Catholic like O'Connell did not suppose that he could have a quarrel. It was known that the Prince had married Mrs. Fitzherbert and Mrs. Fitzherbert belonged to the Roman Church. Years after that affair had ended, we have a glimpse of O'Connell, kneeling at the feet of King George IV and presenting him with a wreath of laurel as he says, " When your Majesty came amongst us, discord ceased and even prejudice fled."

It was his obsequious loyalty on which the King trampled, and the result was an embittered alienation. In a famous resolution, O'Connell and his friends learned " with deep disappointment and anguish how cruelly the promised boon of Catholic freedom has been intercepted by the fatal witchery of unworthy secret influences "—otherwise Lady Hertford, the divinity at Windsor. On the other hand, the King, seeing O'Connell at his levee, muttered " There is O'Connell ! G—d damn the scoundrel." In bitterness, in humiliation, thus spoke King George IV of England in London in May, 1829, just after the passing of the Act of Catholic Emancipation. For it was a humiliation for this bigoted, dropsical Hanoverian and his Court to be forced to do justice to his Catholic subjects, and O'Connell was the man whose brilliant political skill forced him. But O'Connell was more than a man in those days : he was a nation. He was Ireland. And Ireland won this freedom for herself and for us. As the late Bishop Ward said : " A comprehensive history of Catholic Emancipation can only be written from an Irish standpoint. . . . The struggle for emancipation in England was only an episode in it, though, of course, one of essential importance." And again : " Emancipation was from the beginning an Irish, not an English question. . . . Emancipation was forced from an unwilling Government . . . as the lesser of two evils, and because the state of Ireland had become such that it had become in their opinion ungovernable by any other policy." In 1836, O'Connell became co-founder with Bishop Wiseman, of *The Dublin Review*.

He gave a series of weekly breakfasts at Holmes's Hotel. If the government thought fit to proclaim political breakfasts, he declared, then they would " resort to a political lunch. If the luncheon be equally dangerous to the peace of the great duke, we shall have political dinners. If political dinners be proclaimed down, we must, like certain sanctified dames, resort to ' tea and tracts,' leaving us still to fall back upon the right to meet at suppers, until suppers also are proclaimed down."

So was inaugurated the tradition of an Irish humour in politics which, at its best, has been devastating.

There is not much need to unfold O'Connell's public character. He was a man of whom any country might justly feel proud. A lawyer—he was the most renowned of the Irish Bar. A statesman—he was the admiration of liberty-loving people in its true sense in all the surrounding nations. A champion of civil and religious freedom—by his labours and victory, all the millions of British subjects are ever since in possession of that inestimable boon. A constitutional warrior for the emancipation from thraldom and for the national liberty of his countrymen, for which he fought in every action of his life, he stands unique in history in that position which can best enlist the admiration of humanity, and evoke for his memory its most grateful veneration. Pope Pius IX describes him in words that should be inscribed in brass on the tablets of the Irish people as " the great champion of the Church, the father of his country, and the glory of the Christian world." His life was an eventful one. The battle he fought was a tremendous one. The victory he obtained was a glorious one. The cause in which he may be said to have died was a noble and glorious one, though as yet unwon, and his memory is a priceless and sacred heirloom for the scattered Irish race. To this day his reputation remains a tradition in all the democracies of the world. But in Ireland and in England, where he played so dominating a part in the evolution of modern politics, his fame has never recovered from the eclipse of those closing years of his strenuous life.

It is true that repeal was not carried until seventy years and more after his death, but it is not to O'Connell's fame that the delay has been a disaster. Looking back on the drama, we cannot be other than amazed at the folly with which the statesmen of England rebuffed a man who, being never happier than in the House of Commons, was pathetically anxious to keep within the law. The very pliability of O'Connell, as the stalwarts regarded it, is the measure of the madness which denied a reasonable response to his approaches.

Ireland has never had a more devoted servant than O'Connell. In her cause he sank all ambition for personal advancement ; so long as he knew that his country needed him, he gave her his service first and last.

In the last years of his life he lost some of the ground he had gained, but he continued to sacrifice himself to his country's call with that magnificent generosity which brings him vividly home to a new generation to whom he is little more than a name.

He died at Genoa, a man bereaved and broken. " The heart of O'Connell at Rome, his body in Ireland and his soul in heaven "—so he murmured—" is not that what the justice of man and the mercy of God demand ? " Enough that his wishes were carried out. At the Irish College there is a silver urn that enshrines the heart. A tall tower at Glasnevin stands sentinel over the rest of that mighty physique. Within a year of his death Ireland entered upon that prolonged series of insurrectionary offensives which ended at last in the establishment of the Free State. For the Diehards, progressive Britain has had to pay a heavy price.

> The heart that has truly loved never forgets,
>   But as truly loves on to the close,
> As the sun-flower turns on her god, when he sets,
>   The same look which she turn'd when he rose.

He was a great Catholic lawyer who sacrificed all hopes, and repeated offers of professional advancement, in order to retain his freedom to continue his self-imposed life's work of serving his country.

The great Montalembert addressing him a short time before his (O'Connell's) death, said :

> Thy glory is not only Irish—it is Catholic. Wherever Catholics begin anew to practise civic virtues, and devote themselves to the conquest of civic rights—it is your work. Wherever religion tends to emancipate itself from the thraldom in which several generations of sophists and logicians have placed it, to you, after God, is religion indebted.

The prejudice and passion which were at their height at the Liberator's death unjustly obscured the fame of one whom Gladstone called " the greatest popular leader the world has ever seen " but it will contribute to a revival of interest in one who was a veritable Titan in his time, and beyond dispute a genius.

His life story should be an inspiration to every Catholic and democrat, and of surpassing interest to anyone, in fact, who has a spice of romance in his character.

Perhaps the most paradoxical feature about Emancipation is that it was the logical outcome of the Reformation. The very liberty of conscience to which O'Connell appealed was the fruit of the Reformation, which, in its turn, had its origin in the centuries of intolerance.

DOUGLAS WOODRUFF

THE ABBÉ MIGNE

A.D. 1800–1875

JACQUES PAUL MIGNE came from the Auvergne country. He was born there on October 25th, 1800, and so just missed the last of the conscriptions of the First Empire. He grew up, the son of poor parents, a boy of all-round proficiency but of no especial brilliance. He was fond of swimming, rather good at games, of a good average capacity with books. He was offered a place in the seminary at Orleans, accepted it, and emerged as an ordained priest in 1824. He was appointed, in the ordinary way, to a succession of local curacies in the Auvergne countryside.

So far, until his early thirties there is nothing in his story to set him apart from hundreds of other young priests. The years during which the Bourbon Restoration was slowly failing to strike root again in a France transformed by the Revolution, were slowly disclosing the character of the new French society. What that character was is preserved for us and our posterity in the stories of Balzac. After all the vicissitudes of Jacobinism and foreign war and the Empire, the France of the nineteenth century emerged as the men of 1789 had dreamt of it, with the world made safe for private enterprise. The restored Bourbons, the more limited monarchy of Louis Philippe, King of the French and not of France, the Second Empire and the Third Republic, all succeeded each other without challenging or disturbing the new supremacy of private business and the quiet reign of the middle class.

The Church lived under the Concordat with which Napoleon had brought it back into the national life, and during the first years of the Abbé Migne's pastorate, the characteristics of the new form and spirit of society began to be appreciated for the profoundly uncatholic things they were. The new Catholic life took many forms. In alliance with the romantic spirit, and the rediscovery, in Germany and England no less than in France, of the forgotten middle ages, there came the movement of which the greatest name is Montalembert. There appeared, at a deeper level of spirituality, the multiplication of new religious orders, mainly for women, orders severe in temper and in opposition to the easy worldliness of an age primarily concerned with private accumulation for private comfort. In Lacordaire and Lamennais the new spirituality was directly concerned with the social ills of the new liberal economic order. The Concordat gave the French Government a veto on the appointments of bishops, and the nineteenth-century French hierarchy were in consequence safe and cautious men, from whose minds the French Revolution was never very far. They were attached to the civil order because they could not take it for granted as their highborn, assured, predecessors of the old regime had done. They were good men, but they were in their positions to maintain an understanding, to keep the Church's side of the bargain. Catholicism was the religion of France, but it was expected to live discreetly, and to allow the tone to be set by the State, and to accept the supremacy of lay opinion. The ancient monarchy had prepared the way, controlling and formalizing religion through the higher ranks of the clergy, and the nineteenth-century Church lived under a double handicap. It was suspected because of its old close association with the effective bureaucratic monarchy, and it had itself lost the habit of independence. One kind of weakness before the Revolution involved another kind of weakness after it.

It was its strength, as it is always the perennial strength of Catholicism, that its clear hold on doctrine enables it to stand partially outside the atmosphere of every age. Its priests brought away from their severe seminaries principles with which to measure the fashions of the hour, and if the new liberalism was of its nature hostile to the idea of a revelation which claims so much and expects so intimate an obedience, at any rate it provided the conditions for free and vigorous controversy. It was the purpose and the achievement of the Abbé Migne to provide the weapons for the secular contest. He was the armourer of the clergy of Europe.

When he first enters the larger scene, he is a young priest who has realized that every age differs in the difficulties and opportunities it presents to the Catholic apostolate, and that the great weapon of the Church in the nineteenth century was the printing press. Charles X had been driven away on the very issue of the press. The liberal era disclosed the freely circulating newspaper, and that provided opportunity for the Catholic as much as for anybody else.

A small local incident in the Auvergne, arising directly out of the events of 1830, had first awakened Migne to the new significance of the newspaper. He had become involved in a controversy over a political demonstration at a Corpus Christi procession, and he had written a pamphlet, *De La Liberté, par un prêtre*. As often happens to priests who write pamphlets, there had immediately been trouble with the bishop. It was the immediate occasion for his leaving the

Auvergne for Paris, where he arrived in 1833, afire to start Catholic newspapers, to educate not only the laity but the clergy, and perhaps the episcopate as well. He was a man of boundless self-confidence, worthy of the province which bore him and which has borne so many of the most practically gifted Frenchmen, and he brought away unimpaired from a seminary education an instinctive talent for publicity. He had, of course, no funds, and he had no grounds for supposing that the religious authorities of Paris would be particularly pleased at a young priest arriving to found newspapers devoted to religion, including the airing of grievances.

But he began, as he was to go on for the rest of his life, printing appeals and circularising possible subscribers, and then committing himself to the work without waiting to see if the funds were in hand. No sooner had he arrived in Paris, in 1833, than he issued prospectuses for *l'Univers Religieuse* and *Le Spectateur*. He never believed in under-statement, and this his first prospectus is characteristic of his advertising methods for the next forty years. He declared : " We shall present the most Catholic notions on the most interesting questions of the moment, dances, balls, theatres, novels, loans on interest, divers taxes, divorce, the salaries of the clergy, everything with the utmost reserve." These papers were launched in the waters which had been so deeply troubled by Lamennais. There was a ferment of ideas, and the papers immediately found a public. He then took over *La Tribune Catholique*, which had been founded also in 1833, to defend the ideas of *l'Avenir*, and to save the paper from the ruin which had overtaken Lamennais himself. *La Tribune Catholique* was merged with *l'Univers*, and eighteen hundred subscribers were collected in three weeks. In those days in France the owners of newspapers could think in small and reasonable numbers and did not have to envisage their readers, as modern popular papers do, by the hundreds of thousands. *Le Spectateur* never in fact managed to appear. There was a foretaste of the Abbé's unconventional business methods in the way those who had subscribed to *Le Spectateur* received instead *l'Univers Religieuse*. This paper, destined to become the most famous Catholic paper of the century, appeared in November, 1833, with the title *l'Univers Religieuse, Politique, Scientifique et Littéraire*, but it was destined to its great career not under Migne but under Louis Veuillot, one of the writers whom Migne had collected for the paper. Migne had the experience, a common one for editors, of many people giving their name but not in fact any active collaboration. In 1836 Migne gave up this editorship, but he reappears in Catholic journalism ten years later with a new paper, in collaboration with two other priests, *La Voix de la Vérité*, whose purpose was to give legal advice to priests, but it did not limit itself to advising them in disputes in the civil courts, it also took an all too keen interest in their disputes with their bishops. There followed immediately conflict with the bishops and suspension. This happened when Migne was already in much disfavour on other grounds. A certain impetuousness, a determination not to be balked or stopped, made conflict with the somewhat timidly conservative French episcopate probable from the first. At the beginning and the end of his public career Migne was in disgrace, but it was a disgrace compatible with a general recognition that few men in a very active season have done more valuable work for the Church. Migne withdrew from the *Univers*, because he had had another and a vaster idea altogether. He would not publish newspapers and live preoccupied with the passing affairs of the hour, each day affording doubtless the occasion for recalling a thoughtless and ill-educated generation to the majestic structure of Catholic thought. He would present the age with that whole majestic structure itself. A task, he declared, equal to tunnelling Mount Cenis or building ten cathedrals, " the greatest work of the century."

Accordingly he set himself in the course of 1836 to become a publisher, of a new kind, and on a scale that no one had attempted before. He proposed to himself no smaller aim than to bring back into circulation the whole of the written possessions of the Church ; to collect them and print them and sell them very cheaply. He worked at his task till his death nearly forty years later, leaving a name that is held in admiration whenever learned works are written and footnotes and references are written and read. Every considerable work on the first fifteen centuries of our era makes the continual acknowledgment to Migne, P.L. or Migne, P.G., Op. cit., loc. cit. " There is not an article in this encyclopædia," writes Dom Henri Leclerq, the editor of the great *Dictionnaire d'Archéologie Chrétienne*, " that is not indebted to him."

The French Revolution had destroyed or dispersed or nationalized the libraries of the religious houses. Sometimes, the authorities had made a new museum, and had filled it with the treasures of a neighbouring monastery ; so at Avranches a municipal building holds the books of the Abbey of Mont St. Michel. But that was the best that could befall. When the Abbé Migne began, few bishops and religious houses and extremely few parish priests had any good libraries. The Fathers of the Church were only to be procured in large and expensive folios, produced sumptuously, but spasmodically, and by chance in the seventeenth and eighteenth centuries, the fruit, for the most part, of Benedictine scholarship in the Benedictine abbeys. The position was closely parallel to that in England where at the same time and from the same motive, the scholars of the Oxford movement were producing by subscription their libraries of the Fathers, in English, to give English clergymen something more accessible than the expensive and cumbersome folios in which alone, and only in the larger libraries, the chief authorities for Church doctrine and Church history could be read.

Migne could not and did not aspire to bring out critical editions. He was content to make a reasonably sound text widely available. His editions have always been exposed to two major objections, that they are not really scholarly, and that they are produced, in double columns of small print on cheap paper, in a way that makes their reading needlessly fatiguing and unappetizing work. From Vienna and Berlin later and better editions have since his day been taken in hand, but they have followed his chronological plan of division.

The beginnings of the publishing business repeated the difficulties of the newspapers. Money had to be collected by a prospectus, and véry eloquent though the prospectuses were the response was always inadequate. Episcopal authority was watchfully unsympathetic, holding that such a business was forbidden by Canon Law to a priest. Migne argued that it was a recognized thing for religious houses to have their own printing houses. He pointed to the Benedictines. He said he intended to limit himself, as religious houses did, to printing his own publications ; he would not be conducting a commercial printing works. He may seem to have gained his point when Monsignor de Quellen, Archbishop of Paris, suggested that the undertaking should be transformed into a diocesan one with the Archbishop at its head. But such control he refused, and he continued suspended, but allowed to say Mass at Versailles, by kindness of the Bishop there.

Without episcopal approbation, the great undertaking began. In 1840 the first volumes of a general encyclopædia of theology were produced. A brief enumeration of the major works issuing from the press will convey an impression of its activity. There followed, before 1845, twenty-eight volumes on the Scriptures, and twenty volumes of Gospel commentaries between 1842 and 1853. Ninety volumes of Sacred Orators run from 1844 to 1866. Three successive Encyclopædias of Theology, in 52, 53 and 66 volumes appeared in the same twenty years. The greatest undertaking of all, and the one which is meant now by the word Migne, was the collection of the writings of the Latin and Greek ecclesiastical authors from the earliest times. The *Patrologia Latina* was sold at five francs a volume to subscribers, at 7.50 frs. otherwise. The *Patrologia Græca* with its more difficult type cost 8 francs by subscription or 10 francs otherwise. The Latin Fathers were tackled first, at the rate of twenty volumes a year. The work began to appear in 1844, and eleven years later there were 217 volumes, some 300,000 pages. The Greek Fathers were then tackled, and from 1857 to 1866, there appeared 162 volumes, for which new Greek types were made.

The Benedictines had been the chief precursors of Migne, and it was fitting that at the outset of his work, it was a Benedictine who was at hand to undertake the editing. The future Cardinal Pitra was the man. Little over thirty, he had already made his name as an archæologist, as the decipherer of the Early Christian inscription found at Autun. He had just become a monk of Solesmes under Gueranger, and on the completion of his noviciate had been made Prior of the Benedictine house at St. Germain-des-Pres in Paris. The future Cardinal lived hard years through the eighteen-forties. The attempt to revive Benedictine life in nineteenth-century France without endowments meant unceasing financial cares. The Paris house was from the first in difficulties which finally overwhelmed it, and too much of Pitra's time was spent travelling to Belgium, Germany, England, in the attempt to obtain gifts. In these painful years, the work which Migne entrusted to him formed the happiest part of his life. He protested against the name Patrologia for collections which were so much wider than patrology, but Migne was adamant. But in general he had a free hand, and he selected the texts, brought back into use the writings of many quite forgotten writers, and above all, prepared the summaries and guides which under the title of Conspectus so greatly add to the usefulness of the volumes.

The Abbé Migne, whose work was to bring back an old world to challenge the preoccupations of the new, used the methods of the enemy which he sought to destroy. His work was the sanctification of a secularized society, but his methods involved the use of competitive business practices. If he had not been a holy and disinterested man, he would have been a typical highly successful French entrepreneur. He obtained his labour when it was cheap. He employed gladly and very cheaply, for the works of proof-reading and correcting, priests who for one reason or other had fallen into disgrace and were glad to earn a mere pittance. For the less intellectual work, he employed orphan children. We must imagine him in his ever-growing premises at Petit-Montrouge in the suburbs of Paris, ruling with a strong hand over a great number of unfortunate people. The public is fond in those cases of passing a rather severe judgment on the payers of low wages, but the whole question is whether there are any profits out of which more could be paid. Of most Catholic good works it is true to say that if they cannot be carried on cheaply they cannot be carried on at all. The real paymasters are the ultimate purchasers, and it was the public, chiefly the clergy, who would pay five francs a volume but not more, who determined the pay the Abbé Migne could offer.

A traveller who visited the workshop in 1854, has left a vivid picture of the Abbé at work.

"The establishment contains within itself almost everything required : a type-foundry as well as steam-presses ; book-binding and hot pressing ; and the preparing glazed and satin paper ; everything, in short, except making the paper ; which, by the way, is now of a greatly improved quality from that of the earlier imprints. Two thousand volumes could be at any time produced in twenty-four hours by the actual day's work. The different rooms are large and lofty ; everything scrupulously clean and perfect in order and method. The walls are lined with the stereotype plates, whole volumes of leaden books of some tons weight. The modest apartment of Mr. Migne is entered through a library containing a single copy of each work he has produced, handsomely bound ; this forms his luxury. The excellent Abbé is a bright, brisk-looking man of about fifty. We have fallen on very matter-of-fact days ; still, I could have wished he had had something of an ecclesiastical dress, instead of his brown working coat ; and the sound of a bell, and a pause for the Angelus at noon, would have been pleasant, and a prayer at assembling ; he himself hears and says Mass daily at the adjoining small Church ; many of his workmen also attend it. Every day, and all day long, except from eleven to twelve o'clock, when he and his people take their meal, Mr. Migne is seated in the centre of a sort of raised glass room commanding the whole of the workshops, with about forty secretaries and editors at desks around him. At twelve o'clock precisely he unlocked the door of this room ; we had been sitting there the last few minutes previously, having entered it from the Abbé's private apartment, and then his fellow-labourers, who were waiting on the stairs below, entered ; five minutes of settling down and arrangement, and each was engaged in correcting proofs, collating, and the like, and all in perfect silence. The Abbé himself, with scissors and paste began, *pour s'amuser*, concocting paragraphs for *La Voix de la Vérité*, a newspaper of two editions, one daily and the other three times a week, which he has newly added to his other labours, for ecclesiastical distribution. He also engaged himself on a clerical commonplace book, alphabetically arranged in 640 divisions, each of double-columns, with sub-divisions for morals, dogma, discipline, etc. I whispered my adieu and trod gently out, feeling as if I had witnessed some grand institution of the 'Ages of Faith' advanced into the nineteenth century, and thinking that the patient old monks, while toiling over their manuscripts in the scriptoriums of those great Benedictine monasteries which so long adorned and blessed France, would have joyfully recognized their meritorious successor in this laborious and virtuous ecclesiastic. They preserved theological learning to our day—he had secured it, and has achieved, single-handed, an enterprise at which all Paternoster Row would stand aghast."

This same visitor found the Abbé Migne in a happy mood of optimism. He had just finished his *Cours Complet* and was embarking on the *Traditions Catholiques*. His past, he said, assured him of his future, and looking round his shelves, he quoted St. Augustine's sentence on Prophecy, " *Impleta cerne, implenda collige.*"

He had collected together the letters of thanks and testimonies he had received from all over the world in the course of the twenty years he had devoted to his task. They amounted to more than 50,000 and filled twelve quarto volumes. The autographs his visitor observed included Cardinal Wiseman, Archibishop Cullen, Cardinal Bonald, Monseigneur Dupanloup, Bishop of Orleans, the Archbishops Affre and Sibour and Bishops from furthest Asia. He had received the Holy Father's special benediction for himself and his labours. He gave his visitor a frank account of how the financial side worked. With no other capital than " *La bonne volonté*, the devotion of all he could command, his own fortune, and trust in Providence," the Abbé had made himself into a sort of banker. He received loans, mostly from the clergy, for which he paid 5 per cent. in money or 7 per cent. in books. These loans were generally in very small sums, but at the time of this interview, he had decided in future to refuse all sums smaller than 500 francs, the expenses of correspondence, etc. being so great. His caller was rather horrified at this, and ventured to hint at the possible risk, thinking of the poor priests of France, whose professional income was 1,200 francs a year, or £48, lending out their slender provision for old age and sickness to help on this great work.

" *Jamais*," replied the Abbé, "*jamais aucun de mes billets n'a éprouvé le deshonneur d'un protêt, même dans les jours les plus mauvais.*" There was also the sideline of supplying the Stations of the Cross, painted in oil and framed, which he sold at 1,500 francs, to which he had recently added the famous Murillo, the Conception ; these pictures were sold at 700 francs. He had never been ashamed of adopting any efforts which would help him to advance his great work, condescending without demur to the usual tradesman's artifices, such as offering reduction for large numbers or for subscriptions taken out in advance ; 290 francs' worth of books added to every 1,800 francs paid ; so many volumes having the privilege of being sent carriage paid with correspondence also free ; the right of sending other books from different booksellers in the same paid parcels ; premiums to those who procure 600 subscribers, and so on. What else could he do ? The only patronage he received was in the form of the promise in advance of considerable episcopal subscriptions for the books themselves, for presentation by the Bishop to the various diocesan seminaries. The largest of these was from Monseigneur Dupanloup, who ordered thirty copies of all the works. The Abbé's visitor was much impressed by these numbers, considering " that the aggregate income of all the sixteen Archbishops and seventy-one Bishops of France falls short of the revenue of the present Protestant Bishop of London, and exceeds only by a trifle that of the Bishop of Durham, as returned by those gentlemen themselves, and the actual receipts are probably much in excess of what actually appears in figures."

Migne pursued his steady programmes undistracted by the troubles of the Church in France under the Second Empire, but it is interesting to note how these troubles in fact closely affected him. The turning-point in the history of Napoleon III, his relations with the Church, comes just half-way through his twenty years of rule. In 1859 with the change in his Italian policy, and a certain hardening of anti-clerical temper in France itself, the precursor of the temper of the Third Republic. The revolution of 1848 was, in its early stages, led by men who were well disposed to the Catholic religion. The great influence of Lamennais and Lacordaire was strikingly shown in the way the Second Republic sought to avoid the disastrous quarrel with religion which had ruined the movement of 1789. From their side the Catholics were active in support of the revolution. But the fatality which lies at the heart of these movements, by which the centre of gravity shifts all the time further to the Left, destroyed the first fair promise and played into the hands of Louis Napoleon, who became President with a great measure of Catholic support which was not withheld from him even when he carried through his *coup d'état*. For ten years the Second Empire maintained close and good relations with the Church. They were years during which the reputation of Migne was steadily increasing. A provincial synod of the clergy at Périgueux gave him official praise in 1856, but it was not until 1862, when in fact the moment was no longer propitious, that his praises were sung in the French Senate, where an eloquent speech called a reproach on France that he should have been left single-handed to undertake labours which should have been collective, the joint work of the government and the clergy. For many years his friends had pointed out that it was a reflection on French scholarship that so many of the subscribers were foreigners, Englishmen or Greeks.

The tribute in the Senate came at the apogee of his work, for in 1861 he had completed the first series of Greek Fathers. He then wrote : " Now can we gaily sing our *Nunc Dimittis*, because with neither great help nor great virtue, it has been granted to us to be of greater use to the Church than many of the wise men and the saints, and that, laying down this book, fundamental to every serious library, *à l'édition duquel nous n'avons pu déterminer ni libraire ni communauté, ni gouvernement, nous pouvons, en quelque sorte, dire comme* St. Paul : ' *Cursum meum consummavi,*' and then, present ourselves with confidence before God, our *Cours de Patrologie* in hand."

Then there came great and, as it proved, irretrievable disaster. On February 11th, 1868, the printing works were destroyed by fire. His faithful friend Bonnetty has left a moving account of the way the Abbé met the blow.

" ' They are no more '—we heard these sad words from the mouth of the tireless and irreplaceable editor of all the works of the Greek and Latin Fathers. In these immense workrooms, where, under the master's eye, there toiled that army of workers by brain and by hand, reproducing the masterpieces of the human intelligence, the traditions of the Catholic Church, and, one may truly say, of the whole world, the title deeds of the beliefs and faith of our ancestors, we have seen that abomination of desolation of which the prophet spoke : a heap of smoking ruins, a mess of dust and burnt wood, of paper and lead all mixed together, with more than fifty fire-engines pouring water on it all, and a hundred and fifty firemen, axe in hand, carrying away what could be salvaged under the eyes of their officers—and in an obscure corner, the Master, the indefatigable Migne, overcome with grief and saying to the friend who tried to console him—' They are no more.' "

When the loss could be estimated, it amounted to six million francs. Migne was insured with over twenty insurance companies, and after three years of argument and litigation he succeeded in getting paid about half this loss.   But much no insurance company could restore. The stereotype plates from which the Latin and Greek texts had been made were lost forever, and lost, too, was the manuscript material which had been assembled in order to carry on the Latin Patrology from Innocent III to the Council of Trent.   Another two days and the last volume of the *Greek Fathers*, volume 162, would have been out.   It was destroyed, and so was the 223rd volume of the *Latin Fathers.*

But the great fire really came when the work of Migne was done. He was sixty-eight and he had laboured prodigiously.   But it was not in him to retire.   He set to work to re-establish his press, and the effort involved him at the end as at the beginning of his career in trouble with his Bishop.   He had little by little added all sorts of sidelines to his printing.   He was Washbourne as well as Burns and Oates.   He developed an ingenious scheme by which he collected the stipends for masses and gave the priests who said the masses not cash but books and Church goods. He allowed them a discount, they fared better than they would have done had they received the offerings and then come to spend them over the counter, and yet he made a good profit, for the books and articles cost him considerably less than the prices at which they were reckoned when delivered to the priests. On 1 franc 65 centimes, the normal mass offering, he cleared the 65 centimes. It is not surprising that the Archbishop of Paris, when he heard of this, declared that it must stop. Unfortunately the Abbé was in no mood to let go one of the life lines by which he hoped to regain financial ground. He defied authority, and authority replied by a decree on July 25th, 1874, by which Migne was suspended. It was the last blow, for a little over a year later, on October, 24th, 1875, the eve of his seventy-fifth birthday, he died.

A lifetime has passed since his death, and his labours can be appraised in retrospect. Was he, perhaps, *par excellence*, the publisher of works which are bought but not read ? Did he make Bishops, priests and librarians say " Yes, we ought to have that " without ever envisaging who would have occasion to sit down to " that " ? In large measure, it was so. But there is more to books than being read. It is important that they shall be known to exist, and they are not without effect, even when they seldom leave their shelves. Migne was in a pre-eminent degree, the publisher of works which were never intended to be read through but in. Silas Wegg emphatically said of Gibbon that he had not read him slap through lately, and every priest of France, although he might have been paying his 5 francs, had the same story to tell of his relation to Migne. Like the don who in days now remote said the purpose of a classical education was nothing so ambitious as to impart a real knowledge of Latin and Greek, but rather to leave an ineffaceable impression that both languages existed, Migne left an enduring mark even on the unscholarly and the slightly literate. There has never been an age less theologically instructed than our own. The books which were the fruit of his long and courageous activity were not the fashion of his time, or of ours. But equally they were not antiquarian pieces, the materials of scholarship and nothing more. They held the words and the spirit of the first twelve hundred years of the Church, the living testimony of some forty generations of Catholics. It was Migne's greatness that he did more than any other man in the last century to enable Catholics to recover touch with the earlier members of their great society. He fortified and enriched his own and succeeding generations and he was a true educator who knew, as the Christian tradition has always maintained, that it is not knowledge in itself which is of importance but knowledge of what it concerns men to know, not truth but particular truths. In a century so filled with a sense that it knew more than its predecessors and had little to learn from those who had had the misfortune to live in earlier days, Migne came forward, preparing his five-franc volumes and saying plainly that in all the great urgent questions of human destiny the nineteenth century must not do all the talking, but must listen also to the fourth or fifth.

SHANE LESLIE, M.A.

CARDINAL NEWMAN

A.D. 1801–1890

OUR FATHERS HAVE told us how their fathers told them of the magnetic and unforgettable influence of Newman upon his generation at Oxford. Before he gave the Catholic Church in England her second spring he had given the same to Oxford. It is difficult to know what Oxford stood for in the national life a hundred years ago. The Colleges were refined preserves of an old-fashioned Anglicanism. There was no Cause worth writing for save a memory of the Stuarts. There was no Theology save a certain patristic knowledge amongst a few old seniors. There was no Movement save when the wind of controversy stirred the ashes of the Nonjurors.

The University Dons had every reason to be satisfied with the best of sinecures in the best of worlds. Privilege met Power without being over worried by thought.

The solemn complacency of the University was rippled by the brilliant young Fellows of Oriel. Newman, who had already been stirred and sharpened by Dr. Whately, passed under the daring domination of Hurrell Froude. It was a short but a decisive spell. It turned his imagination and his logic like twin steeds together in the direction of all that was Catholic. Henceforth, as Tutor at Oriel or Vicar of St. Mary's (the University Church), he drove his chariot in one direction.

Amongst minds as eager as his he played his part in the Tractarian Movement. The outburst of these famous Tracts could be compared in the intellectual and theological world to the Gold Rushes in California. Men who had long been starved for lack of a philosophy or an ecclesiastical sense suddenly discovered nuggets of doctrine lying under their dry Creeds. Hurriedly they disclosed these and from Oxford spread word that this new gold was available. But the chief artificer was Dr. Pusey and the exquisite refiner thereof was Newman. Around him were the choice spirits of Oxford : the Wilberforces, the Froudes, Ward, Oakeley and the scores of writers, pioneers, poets and priests who were to swell the historical Oxford Movement. Few of them knew themselves yet in any guise save that of disciples but it was

Newman's influence and voice, and above all, his advancing thought which shaped, and often entirely disposed their destinies.

The century of the Oxford Movement has passed. The year 1833 is taken as the beginning. In June, Newman wrote, " Lead Kindly Light " which has acted ever since as a kind of dark lantern to the English-speaking people. In July, Keble preached his famous Sermon on National Apostasy and before the year was over the Tracts had commenced. They carried the Church of England by storm. Newman's measureless intellect and acute pen might easily have been cast on the side of the rising Liberal School. But in the unknown germination of his spirit he faced towards Catholicism. Then it was seen that he could raise but never lead a people. He inspired all who were thoughtful and liable to inspiration in the old Oxford.

Pioneers, leaders and men of action are quickly and finally described, almost defined within their area of history. But men of thought endure for ever. While a Cæsar or a Charlemagne can be historically analysed and pigeon-holed, no man can yet set limits to the influence of a Plato, an Aquinas, a Pascal or a Newman upon human life.

The actual happenings, triumphs, disasters, friendships in Newman's life can be reckoned and two superb volumes of biography cover all that can be gleaned of Newman's terrestrial life. But his philosophical and intellectual life has not ceased. Every fifty or hundred years the historians of thought must make a new cast and endeavour to appreciate his influence afresh. That is where the eternal and undying Newman persists. That is why amid the majestic monuments of his dead contemporaries—Whately, Wilberforce, Wiseman, Manning his legacy remains a living fountain. What Plato's works were to the early fascinated Churchmen so are Newman's to English-speaking Catholics.

That Life has been told and re-told. It is only necessary to sketch an outline.

The conversion of Newman came in 1845 : that famous event which, Disraeli said, could so often be apologized for but never explained : a conversion which many disciples had reason to add to the Conversion of St. Paul in their Church Calendars.

With his best friend, Ambrose St. John, Newman entered the Propaganda College in Rome. He was received by Pius IX at the beginning of the Pope's career and he met Cardinal Acton near the end of his. He was forty-five and he absorbed as well as he could, the theology and philosophy of the Church. He could not fashion himself into an Ultramontane Theologian nor really step into the current of thought which was running strong in the Church, and which shortly broke into one great Dogma and found high tide in another. Intellectually, Newman was a scout, furnished with all

the delicate gifts and acquisitions that are paralleled in a hero of
Fenimore Cooper. He was certainly not a heavy artillerist in the
Church's batteries. Dogma he was unready to define and excommunication he was loath to see wielded. This metaphor of the scout,
familiar as it reads, will explain much of the tragedy of Newman's
Catholic life. At the Propaganda he was simply learning to line up
as one of the Pope's grenadiers, when his talents were those of a free-
lance. England was in need of religious Orders and the converts
threw themselves into communities rather than into the dioceses.
Newman entered the Noviciate of the Oratory. As a link with the
past it is interesting that he met an old father who had enjoyed two
conversations with St. Alfonso Lighori.

Then followed the episode of the English Oratory, the Birmingham
Foundation and the Oratory School ; the Lectures in Controversy
and suddenly the restoration of the Hierarchy and the exquisite hailing
by Newman of the second spring. Surrounded by imprudent and
over-zealous converts with wary and suspicious Catholics of the old
stock in the background, Newman found his way difficult. All his
life he was at the nominal head of enthusiastic but confused armies.

As a thinker, a historian, a poet and philosopher, he needed the peace
and walls of a sanctuary. His life would have been happier could he
have been enclosed and kept behind the friendly fence of the Oratory.
There he might have achieved one of two immense tasks, for both of
which he was competent : a re-translation of Holy Scripture into
beautiful but Catholic language or a restatement of the dogma and
philosophy of the Church into language which would be intelligible
and attractive to the modern English mind.

Both these ideas he approached and though both paths were rich
with pitfalls and difficulties, there can be no doubt that his wonderful
subtle mind, his enthusiastic piety and his faultless English style
would have combined to achieve either. Certainly no one on the
Catholic side has appeared before or since capable of achieving success.

It is needless to point out the place of a popular and yet literary
version of Scripture in a country which has built not only its faith
for three centuries but its opposition to Catholicism upon a supremely
literary version. Newman seemed the divinely chosen instrument to
meet the need. His failure was not due to his own talent or good
will. The Church did not rally to the idea and a version by an
American Archbishop was already in the field. Newman was bitterly
disappointed.

His life became a litany of disappointments. He lost the suit for
libel brought against him by Dr. Achilli. It was Wiseman who seemed
to have let him down. He withdrew from his Dublin campaign which
he hoped would inaugurate and leave a completely functioning

Catholic University in Dublin. Cardinal Cullen and the Irish Bishops had let him down in this case. The episode produced intellectual works more than Halls and Academies. His University Lectures were an addition to English prose rather than to Irish Culture. But it was on the whole a bitter memory and Newman fell back on new undertakings in Birmingham. Still he was hedged by friends, disciples, subscribers and champions. Every scheme he initiated received immediate support, but history will be dubious whether he was wise ever to undertake practical schemes. His destiny lay in the intellectual and dim unforeseen future. Amid all the new Catholic schools and communities, amid new Bishoprics and a vast practical advance of Catholicism he seemed endowed with supreme gifts of apologetic and mastery of theory. Whatever troubles he had with certain books, when his exquisite English was translated into Latin or Italian, he was safe in the world of the intellect. His works were obviously appealing to the English public. Manning might convert his fifties but Newman was converting his hundreds.

Newman's method of conversion was different from any others and from the beginning it was so. Newman set out to make conversions by the intellect. Manning made them by colder reasoning and Faber by perfervid emotion. Already in 1846, Newman was writing with his " illative sense " in mind : " you cannot buy reasons for a crown piece—you cannot take them in your hand at your will and toss them about. You must consent to think . . . Moral proofs are grown into, not learnt by heart."

Newman believed that the intellectualism of the Liberal movement in Europe could only be met intellectually. Diamond only could cut diamond and by a Catholic Liberalism only could secular Liberalism be met. This was the key to his teaching life. It was unfortunate that his "*floruit*" lay between the end of the forties when the triumph of Liberalism in the State (often following revolutionary means) and the beginning of the seventies when the Church answered Liberalism in religion by the dogma of the Infallibility. But Newman's teaching was not for a period but for all time.

His famous essay on Development was troubling the theologians from the day of his conversion. In time it was realized that the essay was turning the flank of controversy. The Unitarians used parts of it exactly as the Modernists used passages of Newman after his death. But taken as a whole he always kept a middle and indestructible course for intellects that sought and followed him. Rome was at that time clearing the decks and misunderstood Newman's preferences for the " probability " of circumstantial evidence to clear-cut demonstration. Newman found this line of approach in the great De Lugo who compared belief in the divine authority to the human belief in the existence of India, which must be proved morally but cannot admit downright demonstration. This side of Newman runs like the recurrent chorus through the tragedy of his life and is brought out with the most circumspect and amazing ability by his choir-leader or biographer, Wilfred Ward.

It is best to accept the fact that Newman came into the Church at a difficult time for himself. When he wished to believe a thing, he could persuade himself with a wealth of parallel and a beauty of imagination, as for instance, in the Holy House of Loretto which was never a matter of Faith. In 1848 Newman wrote " I feel no difficulty in believing it, though it may be often difficult to realize." And probably the sceptic and the pious believer would equally accept his beautiful outburst on the subject : " He who floated the Ark on the surges of a world-wide sea and enclosed in it all living things, who has hidden the terrestrial paradise, who said that faith might move mountains, who sustained thousands for forty years in a sterile wilderness, who transported Elias and keeps him hidden till the end, could do this wonder also."[1]

Perhaps this passage as well as any other will explain Lord Acton's remark that Newman was a Sophist. So he was in a supreme sense and so was Plato ! It explains why he soon complained that he found so much courtesy in the Church and so little sympathy. Rome had been drawing in her ropes and she certainly did not believe in giving her most brilliant defender rope enough (as the extreme Ultramontanes thought) to hang himself! Even new expressions of old truths were suspect.

The disciple, the lover, the reader, the biographer of Newman, must make up his mind that he will only meet pricks and tears, rebuffs and raw reconciliations in reading the Catholic life of Newman. Only so can it be understood. Apart from the fragrance of prose which every separate crushing seemed to produce and the divine sense of humility which is so great a virtue in itself, the life of Newman was the slowly forming basis upon which intellectual defences of the Church have since been built.

Fortunately Newman was never crushed. His grand old Bishop Ullathorne saw to that. But he was continually frustrated, disappointed and reduced even to barrenness of the spirit. These facts are no doubt the dead bones which protrude from any faithful biography. But the spirit of Newman is not a spirit of failure. It is a living emanation. The Church passes into no intellectual or philosophical controversy in herself without Newman being invoked by both sides. This was especially the case during the Modernist struggle under Pius X. The fact that both opponents appealed to

[1] W. Ward : *Life of Newman*, Vol. I, p. 198.

Newman showed that he had found a golden mean, which without being a compromise, is nearer the final line taken by a Church which is the Church of the Ages.

The great controversy of Newman's time was not Modernism, which of course was posthumous to his life and labours. It was the Infallibility. It is known that Newman without denying its truth was on the side of those who wished to defer or at least extenuate the dogma. It is well known how in a famous letter to his Bishop he smote the extreme high Ultramontane view but he never accepted the corresponding Gallican lowness of view. He was able to accept the words of the final definition like so many others because of their sublime moderation. The dogma as Manning and Veuillot and the Jesuits wished it proved very different from the wording which the theologians like Cardinal Cullen and Dr. Murray (to name two Irishmen who dipped their fingers in the defining ink) finally imposed on so great and all-embracing an idea.

The subtlety with which Newman entered controversy added fuel to his own side and flame to his opponents'. As Wilfred Ward wrote : " He could very rarely bring himself to employ the positive and confident tone, the strong expressions, the one-sided statements, the would-be demonstrative proofs of many popular Catholic contro-versialists. His fastidiousness and his accurate sense of fact forbade it."[1]

The Infallibility was defined in 1870 and meantime he had harvested a good crop of seeming failures. There is no need to belabour the university he attempted to achieve in Dublin. Wilfred Ward wrote that " Dr. Cullen seemed to dread freedom for science." He might have added freedom for Ireland. Newman was impartial and friendly both to the pious scientists or Liberal Catholics and to the Young Irelanders. He slowly realized that the Catholic University was only wanted as a political weapon against the mixed education which the government was bent on giving Ireland. And the result—failure ? Again Wilfred Ward gives the final answer : " If the Rector failed, the Christian thinker succeeded."

His troubles thickened when he dabbled in Catholic reviews. Lord Acton was connected with the *Rambler* and was inclined to take the same impartial line in history that Newman was taking in dogma. The *Rambler* had upset the bishops by declaring that St. Augustine was " the father of Jansenism " in exactly the same way that Newman was after his death credited with the paternity of Modernism. The well-meaning and the well-informed could read through such over-whelming epigrams but the faithful were liable to be scandalized. There was a truth in such statements, perhaps even a half-historical germ, but they were not transcendently true. Newman accepted the

[1] *Life of Newman*, Vol. I, p. 265.

Rambler not to propagate his views but as a duty to save a Catholic periodical from dying and from censure at the same time. He persuaded the brilliant editor, Mr. Simpson, to submit, which no bishop could have achieved. Before long he resigned himself in deference to his bishop. What had happened was " one more to the list of tasks he had undertaken in hope and which had been frustrated by those who failed to understand its importance."

The failure of the *Rambler* was followed by that of the *Home and Foreign Review*. They seemed the only channels for Newman to express himself in and bishops condemned both. The *Dublin Review* was Ultramontane. It is clear that Newman was no more Gallican than Ultramontane but it was a time when he that was not on one side was supposed to be against it. The Temporal Power of the Pope was the burning question of the hour and Newman who believed the pen was a better weapon than the sword fell into a backwater. Sad years passed in which he felt convinced of failure. He had claimed a great mission twice in his life and twice the wave, which he should have ridden, had passed over his head.

Newman had every reason to be irritated with the powers at Propaganda or at Westminster. It was fortunate that his irritation did not find vent against either but was drawn into his famous *Apologia* against Canon Kingsley. Newman answered an accusation of dishonesty by a swift turning of the argument. Kingsley, thoroughly nettled, loosed a fierce and blind rejoinder which he described as " a score of more than twenty years to pay." The nation's attention was drawn and Newman saw his chance to break through the clouds. He produced a white-hot classic which thrilled the entire intellectual public. To those who had shared in the Oxford Movement it was the drama of their own life. To those, who had been contemporaries in Church or State, here was an opening of the books so sincere and so revealing that the day of Judgment seemed forestalled. For the first time in his life Newman was lifted upon a pinnacle of fame. To his generation it was a brilliant charge and an echoing challenge. What echoes of the past it must have rung on the memories of every Oxford man and of every Anglican or Catholic who had passed through the religious troubles that made the Victorian age one of controversy.

To the present day the *Apologia* is largely incomprehensible. It is only as autobiography, as logical defence, as an example of piercing English style that it survives. But the whole background reads to-day a little sepulchral and even the voice of Newman is as Manning said of the book—" a voice from the dead."

Public men are doomed to appear in their contemporary life as caricatures : not merely the victims of cartoonists but as the fantastic pen-sketches of critics and journalists. As a rule they leave posterity to strip the false from the real. Newman decided to achieve this for himself " that the phantom may be extinguished which gibbers instead of me." But his philosophy, his piety, his wonderful subtlety of faith, his piercing sweep through history, the power he had to be a believing Gibbon—must all be sought in his other works. The very fact that he was not a theologian made him so great and original an interpreter of the supernatural. If the English-speaking world ever approaches Catholicism, it will be through the words and steps and illumination of Newman.

But the 'sixties were not so triumphant or easy-going for him. They brought Newman his difficulties at Oxford first of all. He had all a great thinker's wish to share in the practical. He was not content to sit and enounce Catholic theory suitable for British consciences. He hungered to return to the scene of his Oxford triumphs. Catholics were going to the university despite the prohibition of the Holy See. Newman felt an urge to open a house to care for them. He did not realize how many Catholic fathers, who had not dreamt of sending their sons to Oxford, would haste to place them under the shadow of Newman. To come under Newman seemed an education in itself. This was also only too well realized by the new Archbishop Manning and the Holy See. Newman had realized that " to write theology is like dancing on the tight-rope some hundreds of feet above the ground." He now preferred the *terra firma* of Oxford which he knew and which knew him still as her one-time apostle. To the lasting disappointment of English Catholics Newman was prevented by authority from opening house at Oxford even after purchase of the site. An Oratory at Oxford without Newman would have been the play of *Hamlet* without Hamlet and the idea was abandoned.

Newman was sufficiently distressed by the continual opposition he met to send an embassage of friends to Rome to clear his orthodoxy. If he suffered from the downright criticism of his enemies he suffered more through imprudent friends who insisted on placing him at the head of a Liberal School which he was willing to guide but never to endorse.

The period of tightening the reins drew to a climax with the mighty controversy of the Infallibility. The Ultramontanes under Manning and Ward had stirred such doubts at Rome concerning Newman's writings that the Pope asked Cardinal Cullen for his private opinion. Though he had shown himself a poor friend to Newman in Dublin days, Cullen performed now a most admirable service. He cleared Newman's name so thoroughly that Newman was invited to be one of the official Theologians at the Council.

The outcome of the Council was a dogmatic triumph for Manning who had urged a definition in season and out of season. But for

Newman who had written to his Bishop a letter, which might be described as " ca'canny," the result was a moral victory.

Newman evidently felt invigorated and not crushed by the controversy which he preceded with his matchless *Grammar of Assent* and followed with his *Letter to the Duke of Norfolk* giving the reasons whereby he accepted the findings of the Council.

The *Grammar of Assent* is Newman's contribution to philosophy and it stands. For the logical sceptic it offers a by-pass to the Garden of Faith. Perhaps it is his most permanent and inexhaustibl ⸝.. Recognizing how difficult belief can be, he analyzes it under such categories as apprehension, inference, assent and certitude. And what might sound a dull and dry-as-dust book is illuminated by a dazzling beauty of metaphors and parallels mixed with touches of humour and poetry. At his age it was an astonishing achievement.

His resilient mind met the definition of the Infallibility with private protest to his own Bishop, with submission (though almost the submission of one stunned) when it was passed, but as soon as he read the exact terms he was " pleased at its moderation ! "

The Council represented the high tide reached by the Ultramontane movement which had proved so inimicable to Newman's personal views. The rest of the 'seventies were to prove a reaction in his favour culminating in the Cardinalate itself from the hands of a new Pope.

The sunset of his career was as bright and roseate as the dawn. He was one of the half-dozen Victorians who entered permanently into the religious history of England.

Nearly half a century has passed since the death of Newman. His stature has grown visibly and it is realized that his frame was built for the centuries and not for the narrow-cabined 'sixties of the nineteenth.

He set out to strengthen and to amplify the whole Christian position. He foresaw the rise of the sceptical and agnostic positions and had prepared the defences before the coming of the flood.

He did not believe that reason was sufficient in its human workings to meet and defeat the attack on the Church. He knew too well the meaning of Pascal's famous saying that there are reasons which reason herself knows not. He drew additional pillars and breakwaters to faith from his philosophy of history and from his experiments in psychology. Thanks to his style he drew an imaginative aid from that poetic instinct which he could express in prose as well and as often as in verse. He endowed English-speaking Catholicism with a permanent library which contains models of writing in philosophy, history and controversy.

The sorrows, frustrations and disappointments of his life are forgotten. They make the material of biography and they point the moralizations of the judicious. But Newman's monument is in himself. The religious mind is not likely to have easier paths in the future than those which he followed. The memory of his intellectual wanderings and stabilities is always at hand to guide and enlighten the chosen thinkers who act as the scouts to the main body of Christian thought. But Newman was more than a scout although much of his life was spent in lonely pioneering. How far was it possible to allow the Catholic mind to explore ? Where exactly could the front lines be safest drawn between sympathetic orthodoxy and honest doubt ?

To those in need to-day of illuminating belief, or mystical refreshment his name stands for more than a guide or scout. To posterity he has become again what he was to Oxford a hundred years ago— an apostle—the one radiant, discerning, unfailing, unageing apostle to all who seek Catholic truths in English speech.

MICHAEL DE LA BEDOYERE, M.A.

LEO THE THIRTEENTH

A.D. 1810–1903

I

"I'LL NEVER GIVE my vote save either to a great nobleman, like Chigi, or a saint, like Martinelli," exclaimed Cardinal Randi after the death of Pius IX.

Jovial, emotional, plain-spoken and practical Cardinal Bartolini was in despair. This Conclave in February, 1878, was unique : the first to be held after the loss of the temporal power, the first since the great secular world had wholeheartedly and finally accepted a philosophy of life that seemed in plain contradiction with Catholic Christianity.

" The Pontiff to be elected must be dear to God, of that there is no doubt," exclaimed Bartolini's lieutenant, Fr. Calenzio, to whose diary we owe the inner story of the election, " but must also be useful to the Church. . . . If you want a saint at any price, there's Ledochowski, Manning. . . . Why not a diplomat, Ferrieri, Franchi, De Luca ? But, whatever you think, this is essential . . . : that a Pope should be elected, first of all, well, and secondly, soon."

Bartolini was right, and his candidate was duly elected in two days, the shortest Conclave on record. The elect Cardinal, Pecci, was neither a great nobleman, nor a saint. He was something between the two : he was, in the very best sense of the word, a gentleman.

Vincenzo Gioacchino Pecci, Cardinal Bishop of Perugia and Chamberlain of the Holy Roman Church, was close on sixty-eight, frail and of only moderate health. " I cannot accept so enormous a burden," he muttered after the election, " I shall fall under it in a few days. It is not the Papacy but death that is offered to me."

An early death ahead of him, and sixty-eight years of no more than a moderately successful life, as great ecclesiastics go, behind him ; only the virtue of the Holy Spirit guiding the deliberations of the unusually excited Cardinals could fully explain the choice.

Who was this slight, dignified figure with that immensely intelligent head, those piercing black eyes set deep in a drawn, thin, stern face with a great Roman nose, and broad, firm mouth? One painter's brush brought Voltaire back to life on his canvas when seeking to interpret those features. Another might have seen in them more than a trace of that scholarly and poetic spirit which seems shared by the features of Virgil, Dante and Newman. The wife of an Italian Prime Minister, passing a little earlier through Perugia, had studied that face and guessed that it was a *papabile* face : " I have seen few such expressive heads as his," she wrote, "on which firmness, resolution and strength are so clearly stamped. . . . One thing is certain—he is no ordinary person. His voice is sonorous and full . . . His demeanour is majestic and full of dignity ; the chief impression one gets is that of asceticism and sternness, but this is softened by a certain benevolence especially when he unbends to children."

It was a splendid choice, this choice of a grand gentleman who, seemingly, had done little to deserve it but be himself, fully the diplomat, fully the bishop and now to be fully the Pope for so long as the Spirit who had inspired the choice cared to preserve him on the throne of Peter. Not a soul could have guessed that it was to be for a quarter of a century, and few could have agreed that the Church would be more skilfully steered through the storms by an inexperienced cleric-gentleman than by a great nobleman, used to the ways of governments and courts ; more wisely steered by a simple bishop, unpromoted for thirty years, than by a great saint who could find guidance through the sole contemplation of celestial lights.

II

A gentleman, in the very best sense of the word ! Joachim Pecci was of a family of squires ; the lords of the little community that dwelt in the mountain town of Carpineto in the Papal States. There they had lived, cut off from the world, unchanged, seeking only to live decent Catholic lives of give and take (mostly give) among the people of whom they were the visible heads, and, maybe, hoping every so often that one of their sons should attain to outward fame by climbing the rungs of the ladder of ecclesiastical preferment, the only outlet in this ecclesiastically-ruled land.

Joachim, the sixth child, was intelligent and ambitious. "To enhance the glory of the family," as he himself wrote, he embraced a Church career. A little later he explained that he desired " to rise in the hierarchical branches of the prelacy, and thus to increase the just respect which our family enjoys in the land." So might a younger son of an English peer or squire enter the diplomatic service with the hope one day of seeing his portrait in the ancestral dining-room as an ambassador. As an English gentleman, this spirited and intelligent younger son would fully accept all the values, the patriotic, the social, even the vague religious values that are involved in a great traditional career. So did young Pecci. But he was not English ; he was Catholic and Papal. In his very being, as well as in his career, the religious value was supreme, and after it came the value of learning. To a Catholic Papal gentleman the idea of being a great prelate without also being a holy and learned priest involved a contradiction. And therefore there was nothing odd or incongruous in the fact that the young cleric-diplomat, after some years of an almost purely secular career, should become an exemplary bishop and, one day, a great Pope. From careerist he grew into devout pastor, and from devout pastor into Papal holiness, and this growth was possible because, from the first, all the elements of a fully Catholic character, the desire to be holy, the desire to be learned, the desire to fulfil successfully any station in life that he might attain, were present ; all the true elements in fact of what we in England call being a " gentleman," but all transferred from the best English values to the best Catholic and Papal values.

Between the ages of twenty-eight and thirty-seven, Mgr. Pecci graduated in the knowledge of men and of the modern world. As Apostolic Delegate in Benevento and Perugia he was virtually ruler of primitive Latin communities, where secret societies, bandits and insolent nobles fought for money and power. Human nature at bottom is much the same all the world over, and when the young diplomat was trying to maintain order, throwing people into prison and even ordering out the army, he was learning the elementary lesson that authority and discipline, combined with understanding and sympathy, can never be replaced fully by learning and autonomy. There is an appetite in fallen man that can be repressed by learning, culture and progress, but never extinguished.

From Italy he was transferred to the very different world of Brussels, capital of the new Belgian State and symbol of the modern democratic enlightenment. Here he was in the midst of the good and the bad that seemed so inextricably mingled in the new world. He was amazed and thrilled by the wonders of the new age : " What a miracle ! " he wrote. " Six iron tracks which pass through Belgium in all directions furnish the kingdom with the most comfortable means of travel imaginable. . . . Nothing is more agreeable than riding like this at more than twenty miles an hour. The most delightful views, villas, country houses, and villages, sped past on our right and left like a dream or an optical illusion." Likewise he appreciated the greater freedom given to religion in this young country than had often been the case under reactionary rule. But the freedom went deep and strayed far : " After the revolution of 1830 a section of the clergy," he wrote, " was led astray by the ideas of independence and liberty preached by Lamennais, which had found many supporters in Belgium." Likewise the feudal lord was puzzled by the beginnings of " that division of society into two widely different castes " which appeared to be necessitated by industrial progress but was so much less good than the centuries-old social life of Carpineto and so much more evil than the human faults of Benevento. Whither were these gifts of God, these " sparks of the Creator," this new knowledge, these admirable inventions, leading man ? Must man turn his back upon them and upon all the social and intellectual changes that went with them ? Or was he strong and wise enough to adapt himself and to use them in accordance with that great maxim written up all over his old Jesuit school in Viterbo " For the Greater Glory of God ? "

Such questions were the subject of his meditations and his studies during the long years when he ruled men's souls in Perugia. In some strange way, Mgr. Pecci seemed from the first to be waiting in a shadow for a day when his qualities of mind and character would get their chance. As Nuncio in Brussels he had endeared himself to many and shown his interest in a changing age, but Rome and Metternich were not too happy about him. After the promise of a brilliant diplomatic career, the young Nuncio was virtually retired at the age of thirty-six to Perugia and nominated Cardinal *in petto*. Thus he was set upon the summit of a low mountain in the expectation that he would be isolated yet not dishonoured. This in truth seemed likely to prove the case. Through the years of revolution and war during which the temporal power of the Papacy was broken and modern Italy created, Cardinal Pecci kept himself aloof from politics, handled with the greatest tact the awkward moment when Victor Emmanuel visited Perugia, and devoted all his energies to the spiritual rule of his flock; but he also remained in the closest touch with the world, reading and studying every paper or periodical that he could obtain, seeing innumerable prelates from abroad—so many of whom halted at Perugia on their way to Rome—and, as it were, testing his own quality in a series of remarkable pastorals on subjects that bore closely on acute contemporary controversies as between Church and modern civilization. The illusion that here, retired but active, was the man of the future was all the stronger in that the powerful but die-hard Cardinal Antonelli, Pius IX's Secretary-of-State, had no love for the exiled prelate. Pio Nono, though never a man of intellectual brilliance, was of generous disposition, and it had only been the buffetings he had received at the hands of young Liberal Italy which had forced him to set up a high barrier between Church and world. Antonelli, on the contrary, had never had doubts, either intellectual or natural, about the answer to the questions which Pecci had been asking himself since the days of Brussels. But Antonelli predeceased Pius IX, and the latter looking back over his stormy Pontificate said : " I know there must be a change, but it will have to be left to my successor. I cannot break with the traditions of my reign." Meanwhile Cardinal Pecci's exile was over, for the ageing Pontiff in the year before his death had recalled Pecci to Rome and given him the high office of Chamberlain.

III

Great Churchmen live long and maintain their strength, but when one recalls the disappointment of Disraeli in having already reached the age of seventy before obtaining that power for which his whole life had been a preparation, one may understand the feelings of the keen and intelligent Leo on being elevated to the greatest position which it is given to man to hold at approximately the same age as the British wonder-statesman, and after that long career of disappointed promise. Not power to do good, but only death. " The exaltation of a ghost," said one observer.

It was but a momentary sense of weakness, and Leo began at once on a programme of his own with a mind made clear through years of attention and one made strong through prayer and work. He was too much of a realist to give a clear-cut answer to the questions that had been shaping themselves in his mind ever since the Brussels days. Was this Brave New World better or worse than it had looked to the unchanging persecuted Vatican? Was it possible to draw a clear and accurate line between the good and the bad in the new secularism and the new science? But if Leo refused to commit himself, but rather made up his mind to deal with every concrete issue as it arose on its merits, he was most clear as to the positive constructive programme which was needed, whatever the practical answers might be. If there were evidences in the outside world of a vast scientific development, it was certain that the Church would be all the better able to deal with whatever it might bring if she too bent all her efforts to the study of the thought upon which her claims and her position rested. " We are living on the intellect of a former age," Newman exclaimed. It was due to Leo that to-day when a man makes his choice between theism and agnosticism, that choice is almost certainly one between the principles of Catholic Christianity at its intellectual best or nothing. It was due to him that the present Pope has been able to set into operation a programme of *action*, driven, as it were, by a highly efficient and smoothly running theological and philosophical engine. That this *action*, moreover, is rallying to the colours millions of indifferent and thousands of ignorant or hostile is due to the second part of Leo's constructive programme.

A prelate in Rome had stated about this time : " We condemn the separation of the Church from the State, but we are running the risk of separating the Church from Society." In dwelling upon the contrast between the ancient unchanging Church and the aggressive, changing revolutionary Modern State, Rome had been in danger of conceding to the world the latter's claim to a monopoly of what the progressive, enlightened, humanitarian called good. Leo had not meditated upon a great development like the electric light, and called it " a spark of the Creator," in vain ; he had not directed his own poetic talents to the expression of wonder at the art of photography for nothing ; nor, on the other hand, had he contrasted the birth of the two nations in industrial Belgium with the happy relations of the people in his out-of-date home town without profit ; he had not omitted during his long years at Perugia to watch how a new spirit of hatred and selfishness among the strong and a new spirit of unrest and dissatisfaction among the poor were showing themselves to be the necessary accompaniment of emancipation, progress and outward wealth. What was called progress might raise many different questions for the Church, but it was certainly her opportunity. If the new State was determined to rebel against the religious spirit, then it meant that the Church alone could provide that justice and charity without which no society can endure and that final meaning of social life without which the very greatest of human inventions cannot be safely used and controlled. Separation of State from Church simply called for the need for a closer union between Society and Church, a union the need for which the Church could prove. " Only that can represent real progress," Leo said, " which leads to man's spiritual and moral perfection."

For these reasons the long and busy reign of Leo was given its positive character by two historic Encyclicals, *Aeterni Patris*, the charter of the Church's intellectual renaissance, and *Rerum Novarum*, the Church's challenge to the State and to secularism on behalf of the millions who make up the society that the State rules and that secularism enslaves.

When Leo was planning to raise Christian thought and scholarship to the level claimed by the secular world, he made up his mind to open the Vatican archives to historians. The boldness of the step alarmed his entourage. What dangers there might be in revealing to the world the secrets of the Vatican past. " *Teste piccole !* " (petty minds), exclaimed the irritated Pontiff, and a little later he declared to an audience of students : " Go back as far as you can, to the sources. We are not afraid of the publication of documents." It was in exactly

the same spirit that he ordered the whole body of Catholic teaching
to seek again in the original text of Thomas Aquinas the intellectual
springs of Christian theology and philosophy.

Aeterni Patris, like the opening of the secret archives, was a command
to dig deep into the past in order to strengthen the foundations on
which the present and the future could be built. To the world,
exulting in its own untamed progress and invention, it was a bold
challenge, but one the wisdom of which has been made more and
more evident by subsequent events ; to the Church itself, which had
grown afraid of the future and ignorant of the riches of the past, it
restored a lost heritage. The last thing Leo had in mind was retreat
or a burying of the Church's brains in the sands of the past. A
life-long student of St. Thomas he knew his to be the philosophy with
the widest sweep and the soundest framework for incorporating the
new discoveries which science was making ; " Far from denying,"
he wrote, " the conquests of experimental science, it fully admitted
that the human spirit only rises to the knowledge of things spiritual
through those apparent to the senses."

But there was more to Leo's policy even than this. In telling
scholars to go back to the *original text*, he was virtually telling them to
go back to something *new*. There could be no better way of breaking
through the superstructure of formalism and convention which were
preventing Catholics from thinking for themselves. Just as at Oxford
the young undergraduate is given profoundly important original
texts to study for himself, rather than encyclopædias to memorise,
in the hope that his mind will be trained and his curiosity to seek for
himself will be aroused, so this intelligent Pontiff was trying to stimulate
the Christian intellect and rekindle its curiosity. The re-discovery
of the Middle Ages and of pre-Tridentine Christianity with its profoundly important effects on secular as well as religious thought and
the consequent almost aggressive nature of Christian criticism of
contemporary philosophy were due to Leo's inspiration. Indeed
many held that Leo moved too quickly and murmured that the Pope,
who could tolerate the false conclusions of scholars on the ground that
in the work of discovery mistakes must be made before the truth is
laid bare, got no less than he deserved in the Modernist movement.
Doubtless the story of Modernism would have been different had
Leo lived another ten years, but perhaps the greatest tribute to Leo's
inspiration is to be found in the fact that the summary execution of
Modernism by his successor acted in the end, not as a deadly wound
to Leo's programme, but only as a wholesome purge. The strength
of the intellectual and devotional life created by Leo's breath can be
judged from this episode. To-day that past which Leo called back
to life is successfully challenging the present, but the world has

completely lost its faith in all the progressive liberal ideas which so terrified the *piccole teste* of the Vatican and so attracted those who had misunderstood the Leonine emancipation.

But brilliant as was Leo's intellectual renaissance, it could not be as spectacular as his lead in the social question. It was here that he saw his chance of turning the tables, as it were, on the world. With it he struck at the Achilles-heel of the new age.

Social disorder inevitably follows intellectual and moral disorder, but whereas men will be content for a long time to lead intellectually and morally disordered lives they will soon complain of the suffering that accompanies social disorder. Marx had not been wrong in his analysis of the situation and in his prophecy that the progressive world was heading for social disaster through the challenge of the proletariat for possession of the new wealth which it had created. Leo had watched the first stages of this revolution, and as an exemplary bishop for thirty years he had observed that the individual, forgotten when included in the discontented revolutionary masses, had genuine grounds for his grievances. Among the upper classes at the end of the nineteenth century this in itself was almost a revolutionary notion, so revolutionary that when the thought did really strike anybody he himself usually became a revolutionary, attacking both Church and State for the unjust order they had created. But the great majority were content either to appeal to the laws of economics or the laws of God, reluctantly retreating step by step when the masses began to look ugly.

But for Leo, the same Leo who when faced by the world's progress had bade his subjects think for themselves and rediscover the intellectual riches contained in their own heritage, the observation of the world's social disorder was simply the opportunity for re-discovering the social order that once followed automatically on intellectual and moral order. Agreeing with Marx in his analysis of the situation, he profoundly disagreed with his account of its causes. Social disorder was the consequence of moral disorder, not its cause. When the world was intellectually and morally ordered, what were the consequent principles of social order? Re-assert those principles, work towards the restoration of religious, intellectual and moral order, and the problem of social disorder will be solved. Here then the Church, the sole inheritor of those principles and the sole possessor of the truth whence the principles themselves derive, could alone bring to the world the solution for which the masses, Society, craved. The separation of Church from State was the means of reconciling Society with Church.

It was simple enough in theory, but the results of the rigorous application of the theory were surprising, not to say, scandalizing.

Rerum Novarum, the Church's solution to the social question, remains in 1938 a veritable Workers' Charter ; in 1891, it was almost a monstrosity, coming as it did from what was considered the most die-hard and reactionary body in the world.

Here are some of the surprising things it said :

> The condition of the working people is the pressing question of the hour. . . . Misery and wretchedness press unjustly on the majority of the working class. . . . Society is divided into two widely different castes : those who manipulate for their own benefit all the sources of supply, and the needy and powerless multitude, sick and sore in spirit. . . . Working-men have been surrendered to the hard-heartedness of employers and the greed of unchecked competition. . . . A small number of the very rich have been able to lay upon the teeming masses a yoke little better than that of slavery itself. . . . It may be truly said that only by the labour of working men do States grow rich. . . . It is shameful and inhuman to treat men like chattels to make money by. . . . A workman's wages should be sufficient to enable him comfortably to support himself, his wife and his children. . . . It is just and right that the results of labour should belong to those who have bestowed their labour. . . . If the State forbids citizens to form associations, it contradicts the very principle of its own existence. . . . Wage-earners should be especially cared for and protected by Government. . . . God has granted the earth to mankind in general, not in the sense that all without distinction can deal with it as they like, but rather that no part of it has been assigned to anyone in particular, and that the limits of private possession have been left to be fixed by man's own industry, and by the laws of individual races. The law should therefore favour ownership, and its policy should be to induce as many as possible of the people to become owners. . . ."

Rerum Novarum, nearly fifty years after it was written, remains as fresh, and for the " haves " as novel and scandalous, as it did then.

The only difference perhaps lies in the fact that to-day no one can dismiss it—things have gone too far—whereas then it fell on deaf ears. Leo's fearless appeal to the truths that lay hidden in the past of Christianity, had it been faithfully acted upon, would have gone far to reconcile the Church and society. Unfortunately, the power over society held by wealth proved a much tougher proposition than the power of the intellectuals, and it has required, not the spiritual and economic programme of Leo, but the threat of socialist dynamite to weaken that grip. Unfortunately, too, members of the Church proved almost as reluctant as did the rest of the " haves " to apply their great leader's programme. It is only fifty years after the

Encyclical that the social teaching of Leo is taking its place as an integral part of that intellectual, spiritual and moral re-birth of which Leo was the inspirer and Pius XI the leader in the field of action. It is because of what has taken place since Leo's death that the Church as a whole has been moved to follow his inspiration and the world has taken some notice of the only alternative to despair or crude power-worship.

These two great constructive answers to the world's challenge were not the fruit of deep scholarship, on the one hand, nor of any special study of sociology on the other ; they represented rather the brilliant insight and fearless confidence of the born statesman, the gentleman of learning and experience, the rooted, traditional Catholic mind, faced with the need of a masterly handling of a complex and difficult situation. Looking back from to-day with the experience gained through half a century of worldly stress and disillusion we can observe the remarkable fact that, whereas the philosophies, whether materialist or idealist, and the political theories of Leo's time have been exploded, the revitalized Christian theology and philosophy whose inspiration was *Aeterni Patris* have become the centre round which all who believe in a supernatural meaning to life gather ; the social and economic problems, too, for which he found the true solution in *Rerum Novarum* have remained the real ground on which men fight one another under the banners of Socialism, Fascism, Communism and even Christianity itself. It is the simple truth that Leo XIII in understanding the true nature of the challenge of his day and in answering it by an order to dig deep into the past and, on the basis of what was there discovered, to think again for oneself, put himself fifty years ahead of his time.

Time only has shown that these two Encyclicals were truly flashes of inspiration; Leo could not have been aware of the fact. They were his simple contribution where he saw his way perfectly clear. They fitted into the events of his long reign along with other actions and decisions of a less striking character.

Those twenty-five years of Supreme Pontificate were a splendid fulfilment, the ripening fruit of a balanced life. " Holiness is sanctified politeness " is a saying attributed to St. Francis of Sales. Leo XIII in his great office found the opportunity to sanctify the life of a Catholic and Papal gentleman and thus to make it holy, strong and commanding. Though he feared that death would result from his election, he seemed actually to grow stronger, and even when advancing age emptied his skin of the flesh within, that skin seemed to grow tauter and stronger like the finest parchment and the bared bones revealed more and more the firm steady chiselling of his striking face. The disciple of Aquinas, he became himself an example of the consubstantiality of body and soul, the body itself expressing the changes and growth of the spirit.

That balance of character, which in his early youth had manifested itself almost paradoxically in his making a clerical career the avenue of ambition and success, yet never allowing these ends to diminish or weaken the priestly quality of his vocation, showed itself again in the temporal side of the Papacy. He was artist enough to love its pomp and splendour, and he delighted in the fervent cheers of the crowds as he was carried in state on the *sedia gestatoria* with the great fans waving at his side. For a great occasion or to receive a distinguished visitor he would dress with special care and choose with a loving taste from the many gorgeous rings in his possession those that would best suit the occasion. Yet with this appreciation of magnificence in all that was public in his rôle, he lived the simplest of personal lives, just as he immediately broke through formality with a visitor, always asking him to be seated and to chat in comfort.

With the like dignity and commonsense he approached every question, and if he ever was in danger of losing that balance, it was through too great informality and trust, as when he once granted a personal audience to a famous journalist who wished to interview him, and found himself saddled with statements he had never made. In redressing the balance he was apt perhaps to react a trifle too sharply, as a sensitive yet generous man will. This often accounted for certain manifestations of unexpected severity that were disconcerting and made people feel that in matters of detail he tended to withdraw with one hand what he had given with the other.

It was unavoidable that during those twenty-five critical years of new dawn for the Church Leo should have to give practical answers to concrete difficulties, particularly in the political and social field. Though here one may miss something of the imagination and sweep of his constructive leads, he felt his way firmly and courageously. For a lifetime he had puzzled over such questions : now he decided as wisely as circumstances permitted. In Encyclicals, *Diuturnum Immortale Dei* and *Libertas*, he expressed the principles which guided him when deciding so practical a question as " what should a French Catholic do under a liberal, republican regime, or an Italian under a government bitterly hostile to the Church ? " Let it be remembered that the vast majority of Catholics whose voices could be heard found nothing to puzzle them in such questions. The " old regime " and " no compromise " were the obvious answers. But Leo, on the one hand, stated that " the Church does not condemn any form of government, nor does she condemn those Governments which for some weighty reasons, either for the sake of a good to be obtained, or an evil to be averted, tolerate various religions," and, on the other, reminded mankind that civil society did not create human nature, but that only from the laws, originating in God's eternal law, could men find an ultimate protection against the inevitable oppression that must come from man-invented legislation. With these truths as his guide, he did not fear to scandalize many by making peace with laicized France, and he began a series of negotiations with the great powers which together have been described as " a signal monument of suppleness, of penetration and of unerring judgment in regard to that re-grouping of forces in Europe," thus, in a word, restoring the Vatican as the watch-tower of Europe and indeed, of the world.

How far ultimate success, in fact, attended these many and complex negotiations, how far Leo's generous faith in mankind, balanced of course by his supernatural faith in God's Revelation and His Church, teaching the forgotten dogma of Original Sin, was right in leading him to support even erring scholars or over-sanguine Christian democrats and then, towards the end, forcing him to draw back with some sharpness owing to abuse of his generosity—how far, in a word, he was as wise in detail as he was sublime in his leadership is an unfair question to ask. At the age of ninety he saw the beginnings of the new century, the century which with its swift and dramatic changes, its staggering reversal of values, its despair and its crude hopes, its meaning and destiny still unknown, has confounded all the prophets, and has left standing, out of all those giants of the nineteenth century, only perhaps Marx and Leo : Marx who saw the coming catastrophe and the rise of social State despotism seeking or pretending to seek for a paradise on earth ; Leo who saw that only within the rich and varied heritage of Christianity, restored by him to new life, were to be found the principles of action that in leading man to a paradise of fulfilment in heaven could assure him a tolerable comfort in this world. Marx's option may be winning, but mankind has yet to realise the devastating consequences of that victory, consequences fully foretold by Leo, consequences that could still be avoided if Leo's voice carried further even to-day.

Three years after the opening of the century that could appreciate his greatness as his contemporaries could not, Leo muttered : " I do not know how men will judge me, but I know I have always greatly loved the Church and have tried to procure her good. So I die tranquil." Even in that supreme moment, especially for one chosen by the Holy Spirit to be Christ's Vicar for twenty-five years, Leo with calm and balance summed up his long life's work. Undramatic, untheatrical, not rising to the heights of saintly exaltation, nor to the depths of a sinner's self-reproach, quietly repeating to himself the true Christian's safest prayer : " Lord, I am not worthy," he relapsed into unconsciousness and gave up his soul to God.

He died, as he had lived, displaying that essential simplicity through which can shine greatness of Faith, greatness of tradition, greatness of culture. A great Christian gentleman, that is, a man to whom came, with equal poise and serenity, the greatest as well as the lowlier of the stations in the career he had chosen, a man who fully co-operated with the high gifts and opportunities willed for him by God, a man who in being chosen to fill the highest office on this earth almost inevitably grew to the sanctity, wisdom and, indeed, genius that that office requires. " He had," in the words of Cardinal Ferrari, " the gifts and merits of the great Popes of old, and at the same time the deeds and characteristics of a great Pope of our time."

PETER F. ANSON

AUGUSTUS WELBY PUGIN

A.D. 1812–1852

"IN THE LONG gallery of those who, in the last hundred years, have saved and increased, and handed down whatever there is of artistic life in England, one picture has been badly hung. It deserves to be hung in a better light. It contains the figure of a tough little man, with dark hair, and flashing eyes, and a hearty laugh, dressed in semi-nautical clothes." [1]

With these words Mr. Trappes-Lomax concluded his life of the man I have chosen for insertion in this gallery of great Catholics—Augustus Welby Pugin—one of the most neglected figures of the Catholic Revival in England, and one of the greatest architects of the last century. Until Mr. Trappes-Lomax published his biographical study of Pugin in 1933 this remarkable man had been allowed to fall into the background. We Catholics were largely to blame. We had been content to let Ruskin's opinions about Pugin and his work pass unchallenged. Ruskin hated everything that savoured of " Romanism," at least modern Rome, and believed that nothing good could ever be produced by a contemporary who had been so foolish as to be ensnared by the wiles of the Scarlet Woman. It was strange that he was quite oblivious that all the medieval Italians about whose work he wrote so enthusiastically in the *Seven Lamps of Architecture*, and *The Stones of Venice* were practising Catholics in communion with the Holy See !

Augustus Welby Pugin was the son of a French architect who came to England at the time of the Revolution, at least so it is supposed. He belonged to a family which claimed a noble origin, even if remote. In 1802 the elder Pugin married Catherine Welby, who belonged to an old Lincolnshire family. Their son, Augustus Welby, was born in London on March 1st, 1812.

He was educated at Christ's Hospital, and afterwards went into his father's office, where he found himself in company with a number of other young students of architecture. His father often took him to France on sketching tours. He soon became a rapid and dexterous

[1] M. Trappes-Lomax. *Pugin: A Mediæval Victorian*, p. 328.

draughtsman. But he was more interested in the theatre. For a time he was employed as a scene painter at Covent Garden. Then his ambitions shifted in quite another direction ; he decided to become a sailor, and bought his first boat, in which for a year or two he made trips to and from the continent. To the great disgust of his fastidious parents, he adopted not only the dress, but also the habits of a common seaman. At the early age of nineteen he married Anne Grant who died the following year. In 1834 he married a second time, and his wife, Louisa Burton bore him five children. After her death in 1844, Pugin remained a widower for four years, and in 1848 married Jane Knill as his third wife, who became the mother of two more children.

Pugin's mother a rigid Protestant of a Calvinistic type, had been a follower of Edward Irving. But the study of medieval art led her son to consider the claims of the Catholic Church, with the result that in 1834 he took the then most unusual step of becoming a Catholic. " I became perfectly convinced," he afterwards wrote, " that the Roman Catholic Church is the only true one. I learned the truths of the Catholic Church in the crypts of the old cathedrals of Europe. I sought for the truths in the modern Church of England, and found that since her separation from the centre of Catholic unity, she had little truth, and no life ; so without being acquainted with a single priest, through God's mercy, I resolved to enter His Church."

It must have been a great sacrifice to Pugin to leave the Church of England, and the step cannot have been taken without grave reflection. A century ago Catholicism in England was " the religion of small shopkeepers in the towns and peasants in the country who congregated round the chapels of their scattered manorial lords."[1]

He knew quite well that such a step would mean the loss of work and social status, for English Catholics in 1834 were indeed a body despised and rejected by their fellow countrymen. It must have been a wrench to give up worshipping in Salisbury Cathedral, even if the rendering of the Prayer-Book services was not very inspiring. The bare room with an altar at one end which then served as the Catholic chapel in the city was a poor substitute. After his conversion Pugin started to build himself a curious medieval house near Salisbury, which he called St. Marie's Grange. It was about this time that Sir Charles Barry obtained the collaboration of the young architect in the designs he was preparing for the new Houses of Parliament at Westminster. This collaboration continued with brief intervals for the greater part of Pugin's life. Barry did his best to destroy any evidence to prove just how much he owed to Pugin, and it is only within recent years that it has been discovered that not only the

[1] *Op. cit.*, p. 59.

Gothic umbrella-stands, ink-pots, blotting-pads, and other trivial details, but also the river façade and the clock tower are actually Pugin's work. He was also kept busy on other domestic work at this period, including the vast Gothic mansion Scarisbrick Hall in Lancashire. He also found time for writing, and in 1836 published his first important book entitled *Contrasts, or a parallel between the noble edifices of the fourteenth and fifteenth centuries, and similar buildings of the present day; showing the present decay of taste.* In the writing of this vehement and critical volume Pugin found a congenial outlet for his artistic convictions and his newly-found Faith.

* * * * * * * * * *

The opening of the chapel of Oscott College on May 29th, 1838, not only ushered in, as it were, the Second Spring of Catholicism in England, but established Pugin's fame as the leading " Christian " architect of the time.

He had been called in a few months earlier to advise on its decoration. Not content with this Pugin pulled down the east wall and inserted an apsidal sanctuary. Full of enthusiasm he went over to Belgium. Here he managed to secure the reredos, brass lectern, communion rail, and many other treasures from old churches.

The great day came at last. Bishop Ullathorne tells us how Pugin, with his dark eyes flashing, and tears on his cheeks, superintended the procession of the clergy, and declared that it was the greatest day for the Church in England since the Reformation. Certainly nothing had ever been seen in England so gorgeously decorated as the new chapel at Oscott. Its walls were blazing with gold and colour," the light passing through the windows that were as yet unclouded by the blown grime of Birmingham."[1]

The twenty-five-year-old Pugin was appointed professor of Ecclesiastical History at Oscott. Not only did he lecture to the students, but found time to design chairs, tables, cupboards, the paschal candlestick, the statue of Our Lady in the chapel, the outdoor shrine on the terrace, and the lodge gateway. The stone pulpit in the chapel became famous in later years, for it was here that John Henry Newman preached his famous sermon on the Second Spring.

The ghost of Augustus Welby Pugin seems to haunt Oscott even to-day a hundred years since the opening of his chapel. He has left a permanent mark on the college, even if he did not actually design the buildings. It is a pity that the Milner Chantry was never carried out. From the drawings which still exist, one can see that it was a most original conception.

[1] Trappes-Lomax, *op. cit.*, p. 146.

Pugin was now hard at work all over the country. St. Mary's, Derby, is noteworthy as being the first large building which was entirely Pugin's own work. It is also one of the few churches in which he employed the Perpendicular style of Gothic, another being St. Alban's, Macclesfield (1839-41).

Bishop Wiseman preached at the opening function at Derby in October, 1839. He described the church as " without exception the most magnificent thing that Catholics have yet done in modern times in this country, and quite worthy of ancient days. It is all of stone with three aisles, a glorious tower, and a very rich sanctuary ornamented with beautiful stained glass windows, and rich broad hangings ; all given, as well as very splendid vestments, by Lord Shrewsbury."

But Wiseman did not mention that these " very splendid vestments " were not worn at the opening Mass. For the donor refused permission unless the full orchestra and choir, which included female singers, were dismissed. Unless plainchant was sung, Lord Shrewsbury would not allow his vestments to be worn. Bishop Baines, always an enemy of Pugin and hating everything Gothic, said that it was too late to make any changes. In fact he and the sacred ministers had already started to vest in the sacristy. However, Lord Shrewsbury was adamant. So the cloth of gold vestments had to be set aside, and a dingy old set of French shape put on instead.

Six weeks later the foundation stone of St. Chad's, Birmingham was laid. It was solemnly opened on June 23rd, 1841, when once again, to the horror and disgust of Pugin and his noble patron, a full orchestra and mixed choir " performed " the music of the Mass.

The architect was much hampered by lack of funds when building St. Chad's. Rigid economy had to be practised, especially on the exterior. The style is of the utmost simplicity. The material of the walls is red brick, now toned down to a mellow brown by nearly a century of Birmingham smoke. There are two twin spires, and the whole grouping of the masses is very effective, particularly when viewed from the canal, above which the apsidal sanctuary of the church projects with striking effect.

In spite of Pugin's pathetic remarks in a letter to March-Phillips ; " I have given up all hope now of the church coming to anything really good ; it will look very well, *but it will not be the thing* " ; the interior is wonderfully impressive. The nave columns rise almost to the level of the roof and give an impression of great height. But the chief feature is the great rood screen, which Bishop Wiseman did his best to abolish. No matter how often one may revisit St. Chad's, one always derives a fresh pleasure from the study of this building. It is difficult to realise that it is the work of a young man not more than twenty-seven years of age ; even more difficult to remember that what one actually sees is no more than a poor makeshift when compared with the original design.

During his brief career, which lasted little more than fourteen years, Pugin built a large number of parish churches and chapels all over England.   How he found time to supervise so much work, when one considers the difficulties of travel in those days, will always remain a mystery.

Among these churches should be mentioned the following : St. Wilfrid's, Manchester (1839) ; Keighley, Yorks (1840) ; St. James, Reading (1840) ; Warwick Bridge, Cumberland (1841) ; Ackworth Grange, Yorks (1842) ; Old Swan, Liverpool (1842) ; St. Mary's, Stockton-on-Tees (1842) ; Brewood, Staffs. (1844) ; Highfield Street, Liverpool (1845) ; King's Lynn, Norfolk (1845) ; Kirkham, Lancs. (1845) ; Marlow, Bucks. (1845) ; Salisbury (1847) ; St. Thomas's, Fulham, London (1847).

Several of the smaller churches have been pulled down, and replaced by modern structures of doubtful merit.   These include King's Lynn, Shepshed, Leics. (1841) ; Whitwick, Leics. (1837).

Ambrose de Lisle March-Phillips, who was one of Pugin's chief patrons, became a Catholic at the early age of seventeen.   He owned vast estates in Leicestershire, and in 1835 built himself a manor house at Grace-Dieu from the designs of William Railton.   It included a Perpendicular Gothic chapel, complete with rood screen.   When Pugin saw this for the first time, he threw his arms round the neck of his host, and exclaimed with delight, " Now at last I have found a Christian after my own heart."

He not only found a rood-screen and a Christian after his own heart, but also services such as he loved.   There was a surpliced choir of men and boys, cantors in copes, and plainchant.   For no " cock and hen " choirs were tolerated by the squire of Grace-Dieu.   Pugin made several alterations and improvements in the chapel which can still be seen.   He rebuilt the chancel arch ; gilded and coloured the figure on the rood, (said to have belonged to Syon Abbey before the Reformation), and put in the graceful stone baldachino above the altar in the Blessed Sacrament chapel.   He always regarded this as one of his most successful works.

Within a few miles of Grace-Dieu is the famous Cistercian monastery of Mount St. Bernard.   It was founded by a small group of Irish monks from Mount Melleray, just over a century ago, and was the first community of this order to be re-established in England since the Reformation.   Encouraged by March-Phillips, the ever-generous Lord Shrewsbury defrayed almost the total cost of the buildings.   The plans were entrusted to Pugin, who must have revelled in such a congenial work. The first part of the monastery was opened in 1844. As they are to-day the buildings give only a poor idea of what Pugin intended them to be. For many additions and alterations were made after his death, including an awkward-looking octagonal-shaped chapter-house. Pugin's design, as may be realised from his drawings, conveyed the whole spirit of Cistercian austerity and simplicity. After being incomplete for nearly a hundred years except for the nave, the church has at last been finished, more or less according to the master's designs. But it would be interesting to hear what he would have to say about putting the High Altar beneath the central tower, with the people's nave at the east end ; a startling departure from both traditional orientation and English Cistercian planning.

Pugin also prepared two designs for Downside Abbey, which were never carried out, although a start was actually made. The scheme was on a most ambitious scale, and would have been even more impressive than Mount St. Bernard's. Interesting examples of other monastic buildings he executed can be found in the Convents of the Sisters of Mercy at Bermondsey, Liverpool, and Birmingham.

It has already been stated that Pugin got into touch with Lord Shrewsbury, who afterwards became his most generous patron and employer. John, sixteenth Earl of Shrewsbury, (the " millionaire-saint " as he was often called), who spent over £500,000 on building Catholic churches in England, summoned Pugin to Alton Towers in Staffordshire about 1836 and engaged him as his architect ; wishing to make " the gorgeous halls of his glorious Palace still more gorgeous, and the Palace itself still more glorious " (Trappes-Lomax, *op. cit.*, p.98). Pugin was kept busy for several years altering and adding to the " princely towers and enchanted gardens " at Alton, as Cardinal Wiseman once described this fantastic place. But how are the mighty fallen ! To-day the Arabian Nights dream of Gothic has become a sort of popular " Road House." Its halls and gardens in summer time are thronged with crowds of trippers from the neighbouring Potteries, and the lovely chapel is closed and derelict.

More fortunate has been the fate of the restored Castle which crowns the opposite side of the narrow gorge on the summit of a hundred-foot cliff. This re-creation of the Middle Ages—as Pugin visualized them—is now used as a school for little boys, in charge of the Sisters of Mercy. The same Order occupy the Gothic buildings of St. John's Hospital, erected by Lord Shrewsbury in 1842 as a home for aged priests, with " twelve poor brethren, a school master, and an unlimited number of poor scholars."

Even in its incomplete state the group of buildings is full of charm. The dim little church, with its rood screen, and painted glass windows, is a real gem and one of the most satisfactory of all his creations.

The group of buildings on the rock at Alton shows us, writes Mr. Trappes-Lomax, " how fine and simple the Gothic Revival might have become, and how the support of Lord Shrewsbury must sometimes have made it appear to Pugin, in spite of the hostility of the " Romanisers," that it was given to him to restore in England, both the spirit and the practice of medieval men " (*op. cit.*, p. 108).

It is only a few miles from Alton to Cheadle, a small market-town dominated by the lofty spire of Pugin's Catholic church. Heret he architect was faced with quite unusual difficulties in having too much money to spend on a comparatively small building. Lord Shrewsbury suddenly decided to increase the original £5,000 when the church was nearly completed. The result is that St. Giles' is a small parish church containing enough decoration for a large cathedral. The dim, dark interior can hardly be taken in at a first glance. Every window is filled with stained glass, and every inch of the walls, columns, arches, and ceilings, are covered with painted decorations ; sadly faded and tarnished after nearly a century. There can be no other church in England compared with Cheadle for such a reckless lavishness of decoration.

Even to-day one almost gasps at such a display of " *le luxe pour Dieu* " (as Huysmans would have described it, and how he would have revelled in this church !). But it is difficult to imagine what must have been the effect on the large congregation who took part in the consecration ceremonies on that September morning in 1846. What did the Vicars Apostolic of England make of this church, for they were all present at the consecration. Those older folk, who could recall the Penal Days, maybe even the Gordon Riots, must have rubbed their eyes in amazement when confronted by this amazing building, so utterly unlike the typical Catholic church to which they were accustomed ; seldom more than a large room, more akin to a Methodist chapel. What did they make of the gilded lions on the blood-red doors ; the great screen and rood loft ; the shining brass grilles round the Blessed Sacrament chapel ; the stained glass in the windows which effectually excluded most of the day-light, and above all, the blaze of gold and colour, no matter where the eye wandered ? To them it must have seemed that the " Second Spring " was already over, and that it was the time of the Harvest.

*   *   *   *   *   *   *   *   *   *

Work was now pouring in all over England, even abroad, for Pugin was being employed on several big jobs in Ireland, as well as on the chapel of St. Edmund's College at Douai in France. From 1840 to 1848 he was directing the building of St. George's, Southwark.

His original design showed a magnificent cruciform church with a central tower, obviously inspired by Lincoln Cathedral. But it was rejected by the committee on the grounds of expense ; also because it would take too long to build. Pugin was furious, and only after endless negotiations, agreed to a compromise. At last he promised to provide a church to hold 3,000 people at the maximum cost the committee could run to. But he took good care to make it clear that he could not build a cathedral with the limited funds at his disposal.

The result is nothing more than a spacious parish church. It would have been a striking building if the lofty tower and spire had ever been completed. But the exterior still remains in the same state as when the church was opened in 1848, and the effect is mean and sprawling. The interior is spoilt by the lowness of the roof, so designed from motives of economy. The side chapels and the three chantries contain some lovely Gothic detail, but the whole effect and proportions of the interior were completely ruined by the removal of the rood screen in 1885. Until this is replaced it is impossible to obtain any idea of what the architect intended this church to look like, for it was the chief feature of the interior. Once again poor Pugin had to endure an orchestra at the opening Mass, and even more than this—the advertised attraction of the famous singers, Mario and Tamburini, from the Italian Opera ; to hear whose voices thousands were willing to pay for admission.

Pugin built four other cathedrals besides Birmingham and Southwark —St. Mary's, Newcastle-on-Tyne (1844) ; St. Barnabas', Nottingham (1844) : Enniscorthy (1843-48) ; and Killarney (1842-55). Newcastle-on-Tyne recalls Southwark in some respects, and has been much altered in later years. But fortunately the rood screen still remains in position. Nottingham is a dignified cruciform structure in the Early English style, definitely planned as a cathedral, and not merely a large parish church. Both the Irish cathedrals are fine buildings, but Pugin bitterly complained of what he had to endure in connection with their erection. Of Enniscorthy he wrote, " It has been completely ruined. It could hardly have been worse if it had fallen into the hands of the Hottentots. I see no progress of ecclesiastical ideas in Ireland. I think it is possible that they get worse. It is quite useless to attempt to build true churches for the clergy have not the least idea of using them properly."

" Architect—and Something More " was the title of a illuminating study of Augustus Welby Pugin contributed by Mr. Trappes-Lomax to the American magazine Liturgical Arts in October, 1933. The author reminds his readers that only a few months before his death Pugin himself had written : " I believe as regards architecture, few men have been so unfortunate as myself. I have passed my life, in thinking fine things, studying fine things, designing fine things, and realising very poor ones."

Although one cannot go so far as to agree that all Pugin's buildings are " very poor " stuff, yet it is true that owing to circumstances over which he had no control, the actual realization of his designs, which look so beautiful on paper, often falls short of the original conception. But Pugin was not chosen for insertion in this gallery of great Catholics because he left behind him any really outstanding buildings, secular and religious, but because he was *something more than an architect*—because of his life-long fidelity to those ideals and principles, for which it can be truly said he laid down his life.

Had he lived longer he might have realized that he had been largely mistaken in his estimate of himself and of his mission to his contemporaries. As Mr. Trappes-Lomax has aptly expressed it. " He was like a man walking steadily forward while gazing fixedly back over his shoulder. He was in the uncomfortable position of being the first of the moderns, while looking on himself as the leader in a revival. As indeed he was. But he was the first of the moderns too." He suffered throughout his life from two very definite delusions. He believed that art and religion are identical, and that Gothic is the only kind of Christian art.

He was perfectly sound on the principles of architecture, but failed to see that if these principles are carried out, they do not necessarily produce Gothic architecture. He was only twenty-nine when he laid down the following axioms : " The two great rules for design are these ; (1) that there should be no features about a building which are not necessary for convenience, construction, or propriety ; (2) that all ornament should consist of enrichment of the essential con-struction of the building." And further on he emphasises these points : " In pure architecture the smallest detail should have a meaning and serve a purpose, and even the construction itself should vary with the material employed, and the designs should be adapted to the material in which they are executed."

This all sounds so " modern " that it is almost impossible to realize that it was written in 1836. One might compare Pugin to a John the Baptist in a mid-nineteenth-century wilderness, preparing the way for the " functionalists," whereas all the time he himself thought he was merely helping to rebuild the walls of a medieval Jerusalem. Pugin's writings and drawings help one to understand his character far better than the buildings themselves, for few of them have not suffered badly from the unconscious vandalism of those who ought to have had more respect for the work of a great master. So it requires a good deal of imagination to picture what the architect himself intended them to be, especially the interiors, only very few of which now retain the original altars and other liturgical fittings.

But fortunately the vehemence of his prose writings has not been tampered with in the same manner as his churches have been hacked about. Not many writers of English have ever equalled Pugin in his mastery of vituperation. He wrote just what he felt, and paid not the slightest attention to the feelings of his readers nor cared how much he might offend them. He was utterly convinced that what he wrote was true ; perfectly sure that his opponents were wrong. There is something about Pugin's writing that reminds one of William Cobbett. The latter has the heavy bluntness of the country farmer ; the former the breezy vigour of the seaman. Pugin's French ancestry may have helped to give an extra keen edge to the razor-like logic of his prose. The most important of his published works are : (1) *Contrasts* (1836) ; (2) *The True Principles of Pointed or Christian Architecture* (1841) ; (3) *An Apology for the Revival of Christian Architecture in England* (1843) ; (4) *The Present State of Ecclesiastical Architecture in England* (1843) ; (5) *Glossary of Ecclesiastical Ornament and Costume* (1844) ; (6) *A Treatise on Chancel and Rood Screens*.

They are all illustrated by drawings of exquisite delicacy and precision. Few men have ever surpassed Pugin as an architectural draughtsman. He had a style all his own which it is difficult, if not impossible to imitate.

* * * * * * * * * *

It was a life-long hunger for the sea that urged Pugin to start building himself a house on the chalk cliffs of Ramsgate in 1841. He was never so happy as when he was in the company of fishermen and sailors, and as has already been stated, from the time he was a lad chose to dress in semi-nautical clothes, which gave him the appearance of a deck-hand on a fishing smack, so that few persons who met him would have guessed that this burly figure was none other than that of the famous Catholic architect. Those early years spent on the sea during which he was wrecked off the coast of Scotland, not far from Leith, helped to form Pugin's character and influenced his whole after-life. They were certainly the happiest years of his life, and no doubt he often looked back, and regretted that he had not remained a sailor.

So there was good reason for his deciding to make a permanent home for himself as near to the sea as possible. Having decided on the spot, the first thing was to build a church, for at that time the nearest Catholic place of worship was at Margate. A small chapel would have sufficed to accommodate both residents and summer visitors at Ramsgate. But Pugin remembered the French fishermen who often put in to this port ; they too must hear Mass. What is more, it would be a help to sailors if there was a church with a spire visible many miles out to sea. So he decided to build a church which, for once in his life-time, would be the complete expression of his deepest religious and artistic convictions ; not merely a half-hearted compromise, like most of his previous works, where he was hampered either by lack of funds or by tiresome and difficult clients.

The foundation stone of St. Augustine's was laid in 1845, and not until six years later was it ready to be opened. It is unique among Pugin's churches, and unlike any others he built. It is best described as four-square and solid ; tough and dark, like the man himself ; its windows flashing like those eyes which used to flash when he was roused. The flint exterior is as homely and simple as the rough seaman's coat and trousers which Pugin wore. The interior, despite the graceful and delicate workmanship of the stone walls and columns, hardly suggests that over £15,000 had already been spent on it before the opening. But everything reveals sincerity of purpose and good craftsmanship. The tower and spire have never been completed.

*   *   *   *   *   *   *   *   *   *

Pugin did not long survive the opening of this church. He died on September 14th, 1851, worn out by mental strain and worry, for as the doctors had told him, he had worked one hundred years in forty.

Was there ever an architect, either before or since, who managed to carry on at the same time, and in face of such intense opposition, such a prodigious amount of work as Pugin ? Certainly few men have erected the number of churches that he did in the comparatively brief space of little more than sixteen years before his final mental breakdown at the early age of forty. There was always something flame-like about his best work, both in his writings and in his buildings. And the flame burnt itself out all too quickly. The over-stimulated brain and overworked body collapsed under the strain.

His mortal remains were laid to rest in the south transept of St. Augustine's, Ramsgate, within sight and sound of the sea, which next to Christian architecture, was the only thing in life which he felt to be worth living for.

The Rev. SIR JOHN R. O'CONNELL, M.A., LL.D., M.R.I.A.

ANTOINE FRÉDÉRIC OZANAM

A.D. 1813–1853

Frédéric Ozanam was born on April 23rd, 1813 at Milan, then under the sway of France. He was the third son and fifth child of Antoine Ozanam and Marie Nantas, daughter of a prosperous silk merchant of Lyons, of which city both were natives. Antoine Ozanam had fought gallantly in the Napoleonic campaigns—indeed it is recorded that he took his share in no less than sixteen battles—before severe wounds compelled him to retire from active service at the early age of twenty-five.

Antoine on his retirement settled down with his young family probably as a silk merchant in Paris, but unfortunately he was too generous and too confiding ; he signed some bills for an impecunious but pertinacious relative who, as not unusually happens, defaulted, with the result that Antoine Ozanam, being required to make good the default, was reduced to beggary and had to give up his business. Feeling that he could not remain in Paris, Antoine Ozanam emigrated to Milan, where he made a livelihood as a tutor while he took out a course of medical studies with a view to qualifying to become a doctor. Despite all sorts of obstacles he passed his medical examinations brilliantly and soon attained a position of some distinction as a capable and much respected doctor. And here in Milan Frédéric, the future Founder of the Society of St. Vincent de Paul, was born.

The French domination of Italy was not destined to be of long duration. With the disaster of Waterloo in 1815 the Napoleonic Empire collapsed and shortly afterwards the triumphant Austrian armies entered Milan and the French occupation came to an end. Dr. Antoine Ozanam was too patriotic a Frenchman to continue to live under an alien flag and shortly after he returned with his wife and young family to his native Lyons where he settled down as a medical doctor.

The Ozanams were far from affluent but Antoine and his saintly wife had qualities which raised them above the need of, or the desire for, great riches. They were deeply and sincerely religious, most charitable to all their poorer neighbours, helpful in all their troubles and trials, and united in the strongest bonds of love to each other and to their children. At a much later period of his life Frédéric Ozanam recorded his gratitude that he had been brought up in his childhood and youth in a home of that middle class which was neither harassed by grinding poverty nor demoralized by too lavish wealth. Before everything else Antoine Ozanam and his wife, during all their days, manifested a noble sense of duty, an unwearied practice of charity to the poor ; and it was in this atmosphere and under this inspiration that the young Frédéric passed his boyhood and his youth.

Although there was in the first half of the eighteenth century a widespread feeling of unbelief and of antagonism to Christianity throughout France, it was fortunate that at Lyons there was an excellent school, the Royal College of Lyons, staffed by learned and sympathetic teachers of whom the Superior ; the Abbé Rousseau ; had a widespread reputation. Another professor, the Abbé Noirot, the teacher of philosophy, was declared by the famous Victor Cousin to be " the best professor in France," and he it was who taking a special and understanding interest in his young pupil Frédéric Ozanam, dispelled those ideas of unbelief which were beginning to cloud the intellect and depress the spirit of the young student, and restored him to the stability of his belief. Dr. Antoine Ozanam was no mean classical scholar. He delighted especially in Homer, Virgil and Horace, and he took great pleasure in training his three sons in classical knowledge. When Frédéric at the age of nine became a day-pupil at the Royal College of Lyons he was, for his years, exceptionally well-prepared to benefit by the excellent teaching at that school. To this he added an insatiable thirst for knowledge and an unwearied diligence.

These qualities were manifested in a very remarkable degree some few years afterwards when Frédéric Ozanam had—at his father's urgent desire—become a student of law in Lyons. In April, 1831, two followers of Saint-Simon, Pierre Leroux and Jean Reynaud, arrived in Lyons to preach Saint-Simonism and " to announce the fall of the Christian God." They declared that the Christian God was out of date, that whatever benefit Christianity had been in earlier and simpler days it was now no longer of any use, and that it was incapable of coping with the terrible problems presented by the growth of modern industrialism.

Frédéric Ozanam, then a youth of eighteen, alone entered the lists against these champions of Saint-Simon socialism, and first in two articles contributed to the Liberal journal the *Precursor* in May, 1831, and subsequently in a pamphlet which appeared in the following August, entitled " *Reflexions sur la doctrine de Saint-Simon*," he showed with an amazing extent of knowledge and of detailed information that the true solution of the problems presented by Saint-Simon, was not to be found in any form of socialism or communism, but in the widespread and organized practice of charity based on the brotherhood of Jesus Christ, taught and observed in the Catholic Church.   In this early pamphlet Ozanam already manifested those qualities of sympathy and courtesy which all through his life were to characterize his work, qualities which while maintaining to the full his opinions yet respected the views, however erroneous, of those with whom he was in conflict ; and he struck the keynote of his future life work when appealing to the young men of his day he declared of the mission of the church " *Cette œuvre est à vous jeunes gens* "—" You have experienced the emptiness of physical satisfaction and hungered after truth and justice, seeking them in the schools of philosophy or running for them to the modern apostles who have nothing to say which can fill the void in your hearts. Behold, now, the religion of your fathers offers herself to you freely. Do not turn away, for she too like yourselves is generous and young. She does not grow old with the world but always new, puts herself in the forefront of human progress to conduct it to perfection. Already in the distance the dawn of beautiful days is breaking and religion, resting no more on a feeble sceptre and crumbling thrones but supported by the strong arm of science and art, goes forward like a queen to the centuries of the future."

In the autumn of 1831 Frédéric Ozanam went to Paris to pursue his legal studies. Paris at that time was the most godless of cities, " a rubbish heap ", as he describes it in one of his letters, " no life, no faith, no love ;" religion was neglected, the churches were empty, the clergy timid and neglectful ; " the age of reason," a cynical critical attitude to Christianity, everywhere rampant ; and not least in the halls and lecture-rooms of the Sorbonne which Ozanam had to attend. Ozanam, always sensitive and lonely, felt intensely lonely in this friendless, godless material city far from the happy home in which he had grown up and the affectionate parents and brothers who had all been so closely bound together in what there can be no doubt was an ideal Christian family. Yet one happy circumstance tended to relieve his sadness. He had a friend in Lyons named Perisse who had a cousin living in Paris. Frédéric, in his yearning to see a friendly face, called on Perisse's cousin and found in him the great scientist André Marie Ampère. Ampère with his quick gift of sympathy soon realized how lonely was this young man, away from his home for the first time, a stranger in an unknown city, and he invited Ozanam to make his home with him. Great as was Ampère's intellect and subtle as was his mind ; yet they were united to something finer still, a heart which declared " I should possess everything in the world to make me happy did I possess nothing at all but the ' happiness of others.' " Who can say how deep was the influence on Frédéric Ozanam of this great hearted scientist, who served God with all his heart, who worked so unweariedly in the pursuit of knowledge, and who in all his ways ever manifested the noblest ideal of a Christian life.

The first battleground of his faith had been in Lyons, when after much travail of spirit his doubts had been dissolved and his faith had been confirmed by " the best professor in France," the Abbé Noirot. The second battle was staged in the lecture-halls at the Sorbonne. One of the professors, Letronne, announced to his pupils that " the Papacy was only a transitory institution born under Charlemagne, dying to-day," and from this text proceeded to demolish the Papacy and all that the Papacy stands for.   Another professor, Jouffroy—who lectured on philosophy—assured them that Christianity was quite *passé*, quite *démodé*, and that mental science could only be acquired from the teaching of the Scotch philosophers.   This perversion of truth in history and philosophy had gone on unchallenged until Frédéric Ozanam appeared in the lecture-halls.   He soon found that there were other Catholic students there as well as himself who resented the anti-Christian tone of the lectures and although they were then a minority they presented to the professors a considered protest against some of the teaching, with the result that the professors modified their anti-Christian attitude and Jouffroy, one of the ablest of the free-thinkers, a professor in the Sorbonne, apologized to the students and assured them that never again would he offend any form of religious belief.   " Gentlemen," he said, " for five years I have received nothing but objections dictated by materialism.   To-day, there is a great change : the opposition is all Catholic."

These protests of the Catholic students had a result more far-reaching than the influence on the professional lectures.   It brought the students together and revealed to them their sympathy and their strength. Although at first comparatively few in number they were united by a great ideal and an inspiring mission.   They began to meet for the discussion of all sorts of problems and as they made these meetings open to all students irrespective of class or creed or political bias it is needless to say that there were often violent and heated debates. Gradually, but more and more, the discussions, however they began, veered round to religion and it was usually on some aspect of religion that the discussion finally settled and ended.   In all these debates Ozanam was the recognized leader and he came to be accepted by his friends, the young Catholic students of the University, as their leader and their spokesman.   No choice could have been more happy or more beneficial to the cause of Catholic Truth.   Ozanam brought to the task many of the ideal qualities of a Catholic leader of thought or of action.   He was essentially a seeker after truth ; he was eminently fair-minded ; he was gifted with an insight and a sympathy which enabled him to see his opponent's point of view, and the best side of

that point of view, even when he was about to demolish it.   He had a
well-furnished mind to which he was constantly and voraciously
adding new stores of knowledge of all kinds.   Above all, he had that
Faith which moves mountains and a charity, all-embracing and never-
failing, coupled with a charming modesty which disarmed all criticism
and everywhere won hearts.

About this time Ozanam, casting about him for a centre where the
Catholic students could make their headquarters, was fortunate enough
to make the acquaintance of M. Baily, a devout Catholic layman
who had just founded a new religious journal *La Tribune Catholique*,
non-political and inspired with generous sympathy for the workers
and the poor.   M. Baily introduced Ozanam to the then languishing
remnant of the once flourishing *Société des bonnes études* and he in
his turn brought in a number of his student friends, including his
companions Lallier Lamarche, Le Taillandier and Devaux, who were
later on destined to play such a beneficent part in the foundation and
development of the St. Vincent de Paul Society.   M. Baily, though
now middle-aged was blessed with a sympathy for young men and he
gladly gave the use of the rooms of his paper for the meetings of
Ozanam and his friends ; and he himself presided at their discussions.

It was at one of these discussions, when those assembled were
warmly discussing the Catholic Church and its position in France at
the time, that a young waiter of Voltairean propensities hurled a
bombshell into the meeting by insistently demanding " Show us your
works."   " By their works shall ye know them."   He declared that it
was of no use to speak of the tradition of the Church, of the great
history of the Church in the past, of the claims of the Church in France
at that time.   He asked what the Church was doing for the poor, the
desolate, the suffering ?   How was she trying to make life happier and
better here and now ?   How, in a word, was she fulfilling her first and
most insistent duty to God's poor ?

Ozanam answered as best he could this frontal attack, but he could
not fail to be conscious that in the France of the 'thirties and especially
in the Paris of that day, there was much to justify all that the anti-
Catholic had alleged against the Church—if it did not lack Faith it
was woefully wanting in good works ; it was allied to the Monarchy
instead of serving the poor, it had fallen into a cold and apathetic
formalism which took no account of the fact that the poor were drifting
further and further away from a Church that had apparently ceased
to have any regard for their sufferings or their welfare.

As Frédéric Ozanam left the meeting sadly and thoughtfully with
Lamarche and Devaux, he uttered the phrase which became the
war-cry of the new movement : " Allons aux pauvres."   He became
at once acutely conscious that the battle for religion, the struggle for

the soul of France, was not to be fought in the lecture-halls of the University, but in the slums of the cities and in the poverty-stricken tenements of the poor. The cry " Allons aux pauvres " continued to make itself heard in Ozanam's heart. Two ideas were deeply impressed on his mind ; one, the conviction that the battle for the Faith must be fought by the young men of France, and especially by the young men of the student and professional or business classes ; that this was a struggle in which the clergy could take little part and which must be carried on by the laity. Secondly, that in this crisis it was not sufficient to have Faith, to have loyalty to the Church, to have pride in her glorious past but that if Christianity was to be saved it must prove its mission by good works. In a word, that if the social order was to be saved from ruin it could only be by the Church devoting itself to good works of all kinds, inspired and directed in the spirit of Christian charity. Ozanam continued to discuss the need of some such active lay charitable work with his friends, who on their part were only too ready to undertake any work of the kind under his leadership and he obtained the cordial support of M. Baily who placed his rooms at their service, and promised to preside at their first meeting.

An inspiring chapter in the history of Christian charity was opened on that memorable day in May, 1833, when in the offices of M. Baily's journal, *La Tribune Catholique*, there was held the first meeting of the Society of St. Vincent de Paul. M. Baily was in the Chair and including him there were seven persons present, the others being Ozanam, Lather, Lamarche, Deveaux, Le Taillandier and a recent convert from Saint-Simonism named Clare. The essential ideas which were in the minds of all those present have never varied and continue to-day to guide the Society of St. Vincent de Paul, with its hundreds of thousands of members throughout the world, as it did those six young men who assembled under the guidance of M. Baily in his rooms in May, 1833. The Society was to exist for the personal sanctification of its members, attained by prayer and pious reading, by mutual edification, by fraternal charity and by charity manifested to the poor and suffering, who were to be visited in their own homes, where they were to be helped with food, raiment, fuel, even money, and any other help, spiritual or material, which might be necessary.

When visiting the homes of the poor, their spiritual and moral reformation was to be the first concern of the brothers of St. Vincent de Paul and it was towards the accomplishment of this essential aim and object that all their efforts were to be directed but, subject to this, the material benefit of the poor and the suffering was to be ever borne in mind. From this two-fold aim, the spiritual and the material, a number of other duties arose. Thus, if in their visits to the poor, the brothers found that those whom they visited had not been married

they were to endeavour to have the union regularised by inducing
the parties to go through the ceremony of matrimony ; if they were
neglectful of the Sacraments they were to be persuaded to enter on the
habit of Confession and Holy Communion.   If their children had not
been baptized or confirmed they were to be persuaded to have these
Sacraments administered.   If the children were not going to Mass or
to school every effort was to be made to get the children to go to Mass
and to attend school regularly, and some of the brothers usually
volunteered to accompany the children to Sunday Mass or to supervise their attendance at that ceremony.

From the intimate sympathetic charitable association with the
poor incidentally arose all sorts of other subsidiary charitable works.
The deaths of the parents rendered necessary one of the earliest of
these subsidiary works in the erection of orphanages for boys and girls,
the latter usually undertaken by the French sisters of St. Vincent de
Paul, sometimes under the general supervision of the numbers of the
St. Vincent de Paul Society.   The proverbial improvidence of the poor
early indicated the need for the institution of penny-banks or savings-
banks, managed by the members of the Society, where the scanty and
hard-earned savings of the poor might be safeguarded.   The sadly-
neglected spiritual condition of Catholic sailors evoked the sympathy
of the members of the Society, with the result that at various ports
the Society maintains Sailors' Homes where the spiritual and material
needs of seamen are provided for while their ships are in port.   In
like manner boys' clubs fitted with gymnasia, facilities for games,
reading, music, etc., have been founded and are being maintained
in various centres of population.   Wherever there is a special need, a
special form of charitable work has been begun and maintained
there to meet it and no form of charitable work has been excluded
from the list of the Society's activities.

It is unnecessary to say that when those seven men met for that
first meeting they had little thought of the growth and development
of the Society or of the multifarious activities in which it would
engage in some branch or conference in response to some exceptional
need.   But it may quite truly be claimed for its original members that
they started with the principle which has ever guided the work of the
Society from that day to our own : that no work of Charity should ever
be regarded as outside the scope of the work of the Society of St.
Vincent de Paul.

After the first meeting Ozanam went home and having chopped
up firewood, brought it to an old couple whom he was in the habit
of visiting.   The other members knew no poor people whose needs
they could supply but this was speedily remedied by Sœur Rosalie,
a valiant and devoted nun, a Sister of St. Vincent de Paul, who knew

all the poor people in the district. Sœur Rosalie speedily put the members in touch with the deserving poor and soon they were as busy as they could be. Assuredly there was no dearth of poverty in the slums of Paris in 1833 any more than there is a hundred years later.

And then within a very short time the most amazing thing happened. Quickly and almost imperceptibly the Conference grew and grew. Many and desirable men offered themselves for membership of that Society which demanded frequently tiresome and fatiguing work and offered nothing in exchange except the reward of charity. The original seven were reluctant to admit any more until Ozanam persuaded them to do so. In a short time the original seven had grown to a hundred so that the Society had to be split into three divisions allotted to separate parishes. Still the numbers grew and again had to be subdivided ; until the system was adopted of attaching a Conference to each Parish or to each Church or Chapel of a Parish.

Hardly less rapidly did the Society spread to other countries. In Italy there were Conferences established in Florence, Milan and Turin at an early date and also in Belgium and Holland. Just ten years after the foundation of the Society, a branch was erected in London, the first meeting being held in a house in Leicester Square belonging to a Mr. Pagliano, whose interest in the work which was being done in Paris by Ozanam and his fellow-workers had been aroused by a series of articles which had appeared a few weeks earlier in the *Tablet*. At the preliminary meeting Mr. Frederick Lucas, the editor of the *Tablet*, was present and took a leading part. After a second meeting a Central Council was constituted of which Mr. Pagliano became President, and he was succeeded in 1852 by Mr. George Blunt who occupied this position for many years. Shortly after the election of the Central Council in 1844, Conferences were established in the Church of Our Lady of the Assumption, Warwick Street, at the Church of the Immaculate Conception, Farm Street, and at Lincoln's Inn Fields. They still continue their beneficent and useful work.

It was typical of the retiring and humble character of Frédéric Ozanam that although repeatedly pressed to become president of the Society of St. Vincent de Paul, he consistently refused this position although it is beyond question that his inspiration brought the Society into being and his ideals were impressed on all the work of the Society. It is well known that one of the cardinal principles of the Society is that its relief shall be given and all its help shall be provided entirely irrespective of religious distinction—the only claim recognized by the Society being the need of the poor. This principle Frédéric Ozanam laid down at the earliest moment and insisted on as a fundamental rule of the Society which has ever consistently and invariably been observed. The essential idea of the Society was the law of charity, charity which unites the brothers to each other, and to the poor whom they serve for the love of God and in the spirit of the common brotherhood with Jesus Christ in the Sonship of Almighty God.

During these years Frédéric Ozanam was diligently pursuing his studies in the University of Paris. His capacity for work was immense and his curiosity insatiable, but he was torn between two rival—and as he thought—hostile interests, law and literature. His father was anxious that he should become a lawyer and qualify for admission to the Bar as soon as possible, possibly influenced by the knowledge that he could not provide for him or even for Madame Ozanam should he predecease her, while Frédéric was attracted to literature, to history, to poetry, especially in so far as these subjects related to and threw light on the origins and development of the Catholic Faith. Notwithstanding the time which he devoted to the active practice of charity in the work of the Society of St. Vincent de Paul, Ozanam spent most of his time in the study of law to prepare himself for his professional future though he could not entirely overcome his strong attraction to literature and especially to poetry. Speaking Italian with ease and fluency, he early became attracted to Dante whom he revered not only as one of the greatest poets but also as a great Christian philosopher. While it was then—as it has been since—the fashion to think of Dante as the disillusioned critic of a disappointed and dissatisfied age, Ozanam saw in the great Florentine a Christian poet inspired by the noblest aspirations of Catholic Faith and ideals. It was therefore with peculiar pleasure that in the summer of 1833, some months after the founding of the Society of St. Vincent de Paul, that Ozanam made a journey with his father and mother and elder brother Alphonse to Italy where they visited Milan, his birth-place, and Bologna and Florence, which had a profound influence on his studies and his life-work. In later years Alphonse, recalling their sojourn in Florence, wrote " From this first visit to Italy he drew the inspiration for his studies on the philosophy and literature of the age of Dante. From this time dates that passionate love which grew on him for that great philosopher and wonderful poet whose elevating doctrines he continued to study for the rest of his life. One may say that after his first visit to Florence the shadow of Dante followed him everywhere. The *Divine Comedy* became for him an inexhaustible source of treasures, so much so that, when one considers the whole of his literary work, it is easy to realize that the philosophy of the thirteenth century is at the back of all his writings. Thus the philosophical ideas of Dante which he chose as the subject for his degree in Literature, became the foundation stone of a magnificent edifice which he set himself the task of building, not for his own glory, but for that of God and as a vindication of Catholicity."

At the end of this journey in Italy Frédéric Ozanam returned to Paris where he devoted himself to the preparation for his two intermediate examinations in law and in literature, both of which he passed brilliantly. In the meantime, during the summer vacation which he spent in Lyons, he wrote an essay on *Two Chancellors of England : St. Thomas à Becket and Bacon* in which he contrasted the conduct of these two great Englishmen, pointing out that à Becket was a noble product of Christian civilization, while Bacon failed because he was a victim of rationalism. It would have been of even greater interest if Ozanam had dealt with another Lord Chancellor of England, St. Thomas More, for it cannot be doubted but that the character, life and martyrdom of this great English Lord Chancellor would have appealed even more strongly to the spirit of Frédéric Ozanam than either of those of whom he wrote. In the eighteen thirties however the character of this, the greatest Englishman that ever lived, had not yet come to be realized in its true significance. In April, 1836, Ozanam took his degree with honours in Law and thereupon became entitled to enter on the active practice of the law. Ever obedient as he was to the wishes of his father, he returned to Lyons to begin his professional career while still in his spare moments—which were not few at that early period—preparing the two theses required for the degree of Doctor of Literature, one in Latin and one in French. While thus engaged a sad blow befell the family in the death of Dr. Ozanam who had sustained a severe fall on a steep staircase leading up to a garret to which he had climbed on an errand of mercy. He died as he had lived, serving and succouring the poor.

" The keen edge of our sorrow," wrote Frédéric Ozanam, " is blunted when we remember my father's piety, deeped as it was during the closing years of his life by frequent use of the Sacraments. His virtues, his work, his sufferings, the dangers through which he passed during his life, must all have helped him to reach more easily the heavenly homeland where we too, if we are good, shall soon find him once more, in that eternal resting-place where there shall be no more death." The necessity of providing for the support of his mother owing to Dr. Ozanam's death in something akin to poverty caused by his benevolence to the suffering poor, decided Frédéric Ozanam to settle down in Lyons, where as an addition to his practice as an advocate he obtained the professorship of Commercial Law in the University of Lyons. The Rector of the University of Lyons was not slow to realize that in the young professor of Commercial Law he had secured the services of a man of more than ordinary ability and character and in order to bind Ozanam more closely to the University he offered him the additional Chair of Foreign Literature. The offer which was gladly accepted involved consequences little foreseen at the moment. The appointment, like all appointments in that bureaucracy-ridden country, had to be ratified by the Minister of Education, then the celebrated French philosopher Victor Cousin. Cousin had known Ozanam in his student-days in Paris and had been favourably impressed by him but he found a difficulty in making the appointment as there were other candidates in the field and other, unfavourable, influences were at work. Ozanam realizing the obstacles which were working against his appointment, went to Paris and called on Victor Cousin who received him cordially and told him that his appointment would be ratified but only on the condition that he would qualify for the post by competing for the Chair of Foreign Literature at the Sorbonne in Paris in an examination which was to be held in the ensuing September.

This Chair of Foreign Literature was one of much importance and it attracted the best intellects in France amongst all those devoted to foreign literature, and as the course was long and difficult all the candidates had been preparing for at least a year. Ozanam realized that he had less than six months to prepare for the examination but as Cousin promised that whatever might be the result Ozanam should be appointed to the professorship at Lyons if he sat for the examination, he could not well refuse. With that capacity for intense application which was one of his qualities Ozanam set to work, studying eighteen hours a day, during which he worked at four foreign tongues—English, German, Spanish and Italian. Completely worn-out by intensive study, the candidate seemed to himself to fail in the long written tests of the first day but when it came to the oral examination he manifested such wide and general reading that the examiners were quite carried away and when he had finished his discourse on Dante the crown was won. The public who crowded the hall burst into loud applause and the Minister of Education, Victor Cousin, expressed only the general opinion when he declared: " M. Ozanam, it is impossible to be more eloquent than you have been." This triumph had an unexpected but far-reaching effect on Ozanam's career, because instead of finding himself appointed to the professorship in Lyons, he had gained amidst universal applause the coveted position of Professor of Foreign Literature at the Sorbonne, the intellectual centre of Paris and of France.

From this time, although at the commencement he was only assistant professor to Professor Fauriel, Ozanam's life and work was centred in Paris, in the lecture-halls of the Sorbonne, and in the offices of the Society of St. Vincent de Paul, until his death some thirteen years later in September, 1853.

The appointment to this professorship, carrying with it as it did, the probability, if not certainty, of ultimately attaining to the full professorship of Foreign Literature, brought great joy into the life of Frédéric Ozanam. It justified him in abandoning the practice of the law for which he had no taste ; it definitely allied him with those studies in literature, history and philosophy to which he had always been so closely drawn ; and it enabled him to devote himself more and more to the direction and organization of the great charitable work of the Society of St. Vincent de Paul which was then continuing to grow and spread with a truly wonderful activity. Yet there were times when Ozanam could not but feel conscious of a loneliness which yearned for sympathy and companionship. He was too serious-minded to find the ordinary amusements of Parisian life congenial and too studious to make friends readily with those less intellectual than himself. Happily for Ozanam, he found in Amelia Soulacroix an ideal wife, affectionate, intelligent, accomplished, attractive, unselfish. She was the daughter of the Rector of the University of Lyons. Her parents were somewhat shocked at the idea of their daughter marrying a man so slenderly endowed with this world's goods as the young assistant professor at the Sorbonne and they pressed him to devote himself to the pursuit of the law in Lyons, which with the two professorships then at his disposal there would provide a sufficient income.

Ozanam, however, was not prepared to sacrifice all the opportunities which his lectureship at the Sorbonne gave him of putting the Mission of the Catholic Church, her great achievements for the betterment of humanity, her immense services to the education and happiness of the race before an age which had been taught only that the Church was the enemy of progress and the determined foe of enlightened thought. Nor was he willing to weaken his connection with his beloved Society in which he had such hopes for the improvement, both spiritual and material, of the conditions of the poor. Whatever the ambitions of her parents may have been, Amelia Soulacroix, unlike most French young ladies of that secluded age, was willing to face the future with the man she loved and accordingly they were married in the Church of St. Nizier in Lyons on June 23rd, 1841, by Frédéric's elder brother Alphonse, who had become a priest ; Charles, the younger brother, acting as server at the Nuptial Mass.

The remaining years of Frédéric Ozanam's life were spent in the discharge of his duties as Professor of Foreign Literature in the Sorbonne and in guiding the ever-growing activities of his beloved Society of St. Vincent de Paul. But in both these absorbing duties there was a difference between the way in which Ozanam fulfilled them and the manner in which most men would have been satisfied to perform them. Frédéric Ozanam approached his duties as professor as the discharge of a sacred trust. He felt that a great serious mission had been committed to his charge to make known the Truth ; to explain the Mission of the Catholic Church, to manifest her civilizing influence, her elevating work, to mankind throughout the centuries. To do this adequately involved not only a statement of her spiritual labours and of her moral teaching but also an examination of all that the Church of God has contributed to the happiness and elevation of mankind in Poetry, Science, Painting, Sculpture, Architecture and Music. It was under this influence that he repeatedly lectured on Dante, and his influence on medieval thought, and that he devoted so much labour to the task—at that time so unpopular and yet so necessary—of demonstrating the learning and the sanctity of the Church in the Middle Ages. The influence of Ozanam's lectures on the thought of his time was much increased by his wide and accurate knowledge, which enabled him to marshal all kinds of facts in support of the opinions which he expressed. While other professors spoke in vague generalities unsupported by anything except their own theories Ozanam could call on his wide knowledge and ready memory for the facts of history necessary to support his teaching. But he brought other qualities not less valuable to enhance his position as a teacher of history. He brought an obvious sincerity, a manifest desire for the Truth however it might affect the question, a singularly lucid power of exposition, and a most moving gift of eloquence.

Drawn as he was to Italy—may it not have been that the birth of this Frenchman in Milan made him half an Italian—he went there on his honeymoon in 1841, when he visited Naples, Salerno, Palestine, Capri, Pompeii and Rome. Again in 1846, Ozanam with his wife and young daughter, his only child, spent several months of the winter and the following spring in Florence and its neighbourhood. The result of these visits to Italy was Frédéric Ozanam's delightful work *The Franciscan Poets in Italy of the Thirteenth Century*, a work which as an eminent Catholic writer has said, " remains to this day one of the indispensable authorities for the history of literature, of Catholicism, and of Italy." This work at once placed Ozanam in the front rank of Franciscan students. " No other book," writes a modern critic, " reproduces so sincerely and truly the spirit of the Franciscan movement with all the glow of its religious ecstasy and all the charm of its innocent simplicity ; no other book expounds so clearly the gradual evolution of that spirit, or testifies so convincingly to its influence on all aspects of human life and art." To Ozanam we are indebted for the discovery of that most wonderful of all the Franciscan poets, Jacopone da Todi—that wild saintly Jongleur, echo of the Poor Little Man of Assisi himself—who gave to the world that most tender and

melodious lyric *Stabat Mater Dolorosa* and that other touching poem—
so different in its sublime note of maternal joyousness—*Stabat Mater Speciosa*, in which we see the Virgin Mother exulting in the birth of her Divine Babe. Ozanam believed that he had been the fortunate one to recover this exquisite lyric and he has in this delightful book done much to remind us of the debt of gratitude which we all owe to that mystic Jacopone da Todi, the greatest of the Franciscan poets, a servant of God the greatness of whose sufferings was only equalled by the sublimity of his inspiration. All lovers of St. Francis and his age must ever be grateful to Frédéric Ozanam for a work at once so original, so scholarly and so human, which has thrown a new light on the poetic aspect of the Franciscan movement.

In the twelve years which passed between his marriage and his early death, Ozanam continued his lectures at the Sorbonne. In 1843-1844 he lectured on the history of Italy during the so-called Dark Ages from the fall of the Roman Empire until the time of Charlemagne. In the following year he lectured on English literature and in 1844 he succeeded Professor Fauriel as Professor, he having been up to that time assistant professor. Many of his students have left grateful testimonies of his capacity and popularity as a professor, not the least being Ernest Renan, who though unhappily refusing that Faith which so strengthened and consoled Ozanam, records " I never leave one of his lectures without feeling strengthened, more determined to do something great ; more full of courage and hope as regards the future. Ozanam's course of lectures are a continual defence of everything which is most worthy of our admiration. Ozanam, how fond of him we were ! What a fine soul ! "

We have already seen that the condition of affairs in France could not fail to call for deep anxiety on the part of anyone to whom the welfare of the Church or the stability of the constitution was a matter of concern. It is true that during most of Ozanam's working life, from 1831 when he went as a student to Paris until the revolution of 1848, there had been a comparative lull in the unrest which preceded and followed this short period of quiescence. No one, however, who took the wellbeing of France to heart could fail to be profoundly concerned for a condition of affairs which was so threatening and so unstable. It is needless to say that Ozanam was full of anxiety and his apprehensions caused him to redouble his efforts to allay or anticipate the storm which he felt was rapidly approaching. In all his lectures, so carefully thought out and laboriously prepared, in his frequent addresses to conferences and meetings, in his innumerable contributions to the Catholic press, and in his work for the Society of St. Vincent de Paul, he laboured to prevent the social *débâcle* which he feared was imminent. In these unceasing efforts he overtaxed his strength and made himself vulnerable to the attacks of tuberculosis which later on seized hold of him. He went through the trying experiences of the Revolution of 1848 without apparent injury, even when Monsignor Affre, the Archbishop of Paris, yielding to Ozanam's request to negotiate between the insurgents and the soldiery, was done to death.

But the pressure at which Ozanam lived could not continue and in the autumn of 1852 he had a severe breakdown. Learning that the students were complaining of his neglect of his duties, Ozanam insisted in getting up from a sick bed—in spite of the protests of his devoted wife—and delivered at the Sorbonne a most brilliant and touching lecture. It was the last occasion on which he ever spoke. Shortly afterwards with his wife and child he sought the milder climate of Italy and settled down at Pisa where he passed the winter and the spring of 1843. In the summer he took a villa at Antiguano outside Leghorn. Here he gradually got worse. Early in September he made up his mind that he would like to end his days on the soil of France and he was brought by boat from Leghorn to Marseilles and here, surrounded by his family and strengthened with the Sacraments of that Church which he loved so deeply and served so faithfully, he peacefully breathed his last on the 8th September, the feast of the Nativity of Our Blessed Lady, 1853.

There are few men of whom it can be said with such absolute truth as of Frédéric Ozanam that " their works do live after them." There can be no question but that to Frédéric Ozanam we owe the inspiration, the origin, and the foundation of the world-spread organization of Charity, the Society of St. Vincent de Paul. If his humility prevented him from allowing himself to be elected as President, he nevertheless was the moving spirit, the driving force, the capable director of the Society from its foundation until his death over twenty years later. During this period he superintended its workings not only in France, but, wherever in Italy he could establish or encourage it. In the years which have passed since his death, thanks to the blessing of God and the wise and prudent system of charity laid down by Ozanam, the Society has marvellously spread throughout the entire world. There is hardly a corner of the Old World or of the New in which the Society is not established. Its members are counted by hundreds of thousands and are ever increasing. Their activities are ever multiplying, and as the needs of the day vary and change so do the activities of the Society, so that in very truth it fulfils the earliest rule laid down by its founder : that there is no form of charity which shall be considered foreign to the objects of the Society. All this great work has been accomplished, this wonderful spread of its activities has been achieved, because the Society from its foundation has ever and always been guided by the Spirit of Charity for the love of God and of Humility in honour of His Name.   So long as those two principles abide in the Society its days shall not end.

In these days there is no less need for Catholic action than in the days of Frédéric Ozanam.   To-day, as a hundred years ago, the Catholic Church is being challenged " to show her works " and the need is no less great for the laity to take part in a widespread movement of Catholic action.   The Catholic manhood of England are asked to give themselves, their leisure, their experience, their energy, their devotion and their initiative, as did the Catholic young men of Paris under the inspiring leadership of Ozanam, to the service of God's poor, the betterment of their lives, the improvement of their conditions, the education of their children, the brightening of their coming years, inspired to undertake this splendid mission by the same spirit which guided Ozanam and his companions, the love of the poor in the Brotherhood of Jesus Christ.

W. R. THOMPSON, F.R.S.

GREGOR JOHANN MENDEL

A.D. 1822–1884

W E ARE SO accustomed to rely on the technical resources of the civilization in which we live, that few of us ever come to realize how feeble is our grip on them, as individuals—how imperfectly we possess them. But it is pretty certain that an average non-technical citizen, if shot back by the time machine to the twelfth century, would find himself quite surprisingly incapable of making important material improvements in his surroundings. He could not, for example, even if he were a radio fan, construct a wireless set of the very simplest type. He might find a piece of galena, and he could easily build a simple condenser, but the coils and head-phones would, I fancy, defeat him, if only because of the difficulty of producing insulated copper wire. In any case, he would certainly be incapable of building a transmitting station. Even the making of such a simple thing as a box of safety matches would probably be quite beyond the technical powers of the average householder. It involves the manufacture of a box out of very thin slices of wood, covered with coloured paper and bearing a printed label which, in the one I happen to have before me, is decorated with a figure of a sailing ship, made, I suppose, from a zinc cut. The matches bear at the tip a rounded blob of some hard brownish substance which, when rubbed on the layer of material covering the sides of the match box, ignites. Though I have had a fairly comprehensive scientific training and have a theory about the composition of the material on the sides of the match box, I should not care to bet that it is correct, and though I think I could make matches with phosphorus and potassium chlorate, I should not like to be set the task of hunting for them in the twelfth-century world.

The fact is, that since society is in a sense an organism, which goes as a whole through a developmental process involving all its parts or elements, the discoveries made by its members require for their apparition, certain settings or predispositions and cannot come into being until their hour has struck. Though Roger Bacon looked forward to a time when men should fly through the air and move under the sea, we may doubt that this was in any true sense a scientific prevision or prophesy such as we find in *The Sleeper Awakes* or *The Servile State*, where the acute minds of Wells and Belloc have followed existing potentialities or tendencies to their natural conclusions. Bacon seems indeed to have rendered real services to science ; but though he says in his *Opuscula de Secretis Operibus Artis et Naturale* that it is possible to make vehicles which " without the help of any animal, will run with measureless speed," yet he could not have had any definite idea as to how this was in fact to be accomplished.

It has often been remarked that when the time for a scientific discovery has arrived, it tends to break out simultaneously in several places like measles. Sometimes, as seems to have happened with wireless, we have the apparition in rapid succession of bits and pieces that are eventually assembled in the final product. Sometimes the new idea emerges full fledged, but independently from a number of minds. A classical case is that of the theory of Evolution by natural selection, formulated in almost exactly the same terms by Charles Darwin and Alfred Russel Wallace, the evidence of independent origin being so clear that communications from the two authors were presented at the same meeting of the Linnean Society. The history of the differential calculus is another. The origins of this tremendously powerful mathematical method can actually be traced back through the works of Pascal, Fermat and Descartes to Nicholas Oresmus who died as Bishop of Lisieux in the latter part of the fourteenth century. But it attained its full development only in the late seventeenth century, through the work of Newton and Leibnitz. Each of these two great men claimed for himself the credit of the discovery and a bitter controversy ensued, lasting many years ; but good modern authorities consider that Newton was led to the idea through the lessons of his master, Barrow, while Leibnitz reached it through the study of a figure in Pascal's *Traité des Sinus du quart de cercle.* [1] The truth is that the fullness of time had come and that a natural convergence of forces was tending, almost inevitably, toward the creation of the new thing.

But though at such moments (as we can see after the event) the elements of the discovery lie, as it were, in the open and fully exposed to view, it is not given to everyone to pick them up. " It behoves us always to remember," says Sir D'Arcy Thompson[2], " that in physics it has taken great men to discover simple things. They are very great names indeed that we couple with the explanation of the path of a stone, the drop of a chain, the tints of a bubble, the shadows in a cup." Once the discovery is made a very ordinary person can

[1] M. Andoyer et S. Humbert, in Gabriel Hanotaux's *Histoire de la nation Française*, T. xiv.
[2] *Growth and Form*, p.8.

expound it and the pedestrian exploration of its implications may occupy a whole generation of workers. But the plucking of the intelligible whole out of what appears on the surface as a meaningless agglomeration is a work of genius. There is no doubt that certain individuals have an innate aptitude for it. We see them move from one subject to another, illuminating everything they touch, transforming every problem. It does not seem that the faculty can be created, though it can doubtless be developed. It does not necessarily imply either extraordinary erudition or deep philosophical insight. Its essential element appears to be a kind of intuitive process, by which we must not understand either the mere apprehension of the concrete, characteristic of sensory life, or the direct vision of essences that belongs to the *intellectus angelicus* but that instantaneous process of reasoning whereby the mind leaps from principles to conclusions without any formal enunciation of the arguments that logically connect them. In this process, it seems, the whole man is involved. The bodily predispositions play a part so that though the power of discovery and invention develops with exercise and may be favoured by circumstances, the conscientious labour of the ungifted will not of itself engender it. The writer was once told, of a well-known biologist, distinguished rather for the mass than for the brilliance of his writings, that he laboured every day into the small hours, searching the literature for new ideas. But his power of original thinking did not notably develop and though his name is associated with certain striking advances, the exact nature of his connection with them remains obscure. No amount of taking pains will replace genius. On the other hand, the great scientific figures have very generally possessed along with their originality, the ability to do a great deal of hard and extremely accurate work, without which, indeed, the most fruitful hypotheses remain sterile. The great discoverers are not in any pathological sense abnormal. They are, in most respects, typical products of their time, preoccupied with its problems and driven by its energies. But their insight and power of achievement surpass those of common men, so that they not only can foresee the new thing but can also bring it into being. To this little company belongs Gregor Johann Mendel.

We suffer a good deal nowadays from a superabundance of Sorcerers' apprentices, drawn from the ranks of science and its popularisers, each advertising and urging on us his special formula for the dissipation of our ills. One of the most objectionable of these is certainly the Eugenist of the simple-minded but very vocal school that equates hereditary value with cash. There is something to be said for the worship of the county family, now, alas, almost vanished away ; and one might even perhaps find some strange excuse for the adoration of Germanic Blood. But it is difficult to sympathize with those who make mere money-getting ability the touchstone of progress, as the Eugenists do when they suggest that if we can only prevent the poor from having children, everything will soon be all right. The remedy for social ills favoured by these would-be geneticists might actually have prevented the appearance of the Founder of Genetics, since Johann Mendel was in fact, the product of one of those poor and hard-worked families of peasant farmers particularly disliked by many of our modern Eugenists. The facts of his life so far as they are known to us, might, indeed, be drawn from one of those tales dear to the Christian story-tellers because they reflect or epitomise the spirit of Christian civilization, ordered yet free, hierarchical yet hostile to caste. Mendel was the clever poor boy who rose to be an abbot. It is moreover, a singular and significant fact that the career of Mendel, which meant so much to science, was made possible only through the institution of the family, in its humblest expression. One of his sisters sacrificed a large part of her small dowry to the payment of Mendel's school fees. Everyone acquainted with continental life knows what such sacrifices may mean. But the important point is not that the sacrifice was made, but that it could be made ; that there was within the family circle, the resource with which an emergency could be met. The opening of careers to talent by the institution of state scholarships is a thing that everyone with any democratic feeling must applaud ; but schoolmasters are not infallible judges, nor the examination system the only test of intellectual worth. It is well that the intimate judgments of the family should have some weight in deciding the careers of its members as against the impersonal selective mechanism of the state. It may be said that parents are notoriously subject to delusions about the capacities of their children ; but in this case, at all events, there was no delusion ; never was an investment more fruitful than the investment of the Austrian girl's dowry in the career of Mendel.

One of the most common complaints made against the Roman Church is that its clergy are sometimes not gentlemen : not, as the saying goes, out of the top drawer. This accusation often comes from persons fond of posing in other circumstances, as friends of democracy and is a good index of their real feelings. We need not attempt to refute it. In so far as it indicates a lack of those superficial characteristics that derive from the long-continued possession of wealth, it is simply an expression of the fact that the Church offers to those who have a genuine vocation for her work possibilities of personal development that they could find nowhere else. Mendel came at an early stage in his studies under a monastic teacher ; and it can hardly be a coincidence that when his studies in the gymnasium of Ölmutz were concluded, he applied for entrance into the order which had given him a teacher at his former school in Troppau. He entered the Augustinian Abbey of St. Thomas in Brünn[1] in 1843, passed successfully through the hard tests of the monastic novitiate and was ordained priest in 1847. In 1851, he was sent, at the expense of the monastery to the University of Vienna, for three years' work in mathematics and the natural sciences. It was apparently after his return from Vienna that he began, in the gardens of the Abbey, his celebrated experiments in heredity.

The education of Mendel was thus in large part not only religious but ecclesiastical and monastic. Now it is certainly a mistake to suggest that there is a necessary connection between religious orthodoxy and scientific ability. When we consider, says Maritain[2], that the Creator of the human mind has allowed some of his great contemplatives, St. Hildegarde, for example, to retain such erroneous ideas on cosmology, we seem led to infer that He is rather indifferent to our knowledge of the conformation of the universe or the laws of the winds. On the other hand, it does seem that the progress of a mind specifically devoting itself to the search for natural truths, cannot be positively hampered and may indeed be facilitated by its view of ultimate philosophical questions. The violent energy that the adherents of Communism devote to the extermination of religious doctrines in general and the idea of God in particular clearly shows that they, at all events, have no doubts about the matter. That one of the great biological discoveries should be made by a Catholic monk is from their standpoint, a disagreeable paradox. When Christians refer to the religious beliefs of early scientific workers, they are often met with the reply that in those days the implications of science were not fully realized. Nothing of this kind can be said about Mendel. During the period covered by his experimental work, which he began in 1854 and embodied in papers presented to the Natural History Society of Brünn in 1865 and 1869 the Darwinian revolution had swept over Europe. The daily work of Mendel must necessarily have brought him in contact with it since he was, during this time, a teacher of science in the Realschule of Brünn. Furthermore it seems that Mendel's investigations were to some extent stimulated by his dissatisfaction with the Darwinian doctrines.

There is no doubt that a great deal of the enormous modern development of biology is due to the doctrine of evolution and to the simple and plausible theory of natural selection which enabled Darwin and the Darwinian propagandists to ensure its acceptance by the general public. But it is also true that a good deal of the research engendered by the theory has consisted in chasing will-o'-the-wisps and has enriched biology *per accidens*, not through the attainment of

---

[1] Now Brno.   [2] *Reflexions sur l' Intelligence*, p. 184.

the ends sought, but by the incidental results of the search. From 1870 to 1900, says Caullery,[1] biology moved with the impetus given to it by Darwin along lines established by Hæckel. " The whole effort during the latter part of the nineteenth century, was devoted to an attempt at an effective reconstitution of the evolutionary process, to retracing the decent of the various animal groups with the help of the data of comparative anatomy and especially of embryology." Hæckel who must, on the whole, be reckoned a charlatan in spite of his admirable work in some fields, had formulated after his usual manner, his " Fundamental Biogenetic Law," according to which the life history of the individual retraces the history of the race. The story of embryology for some decades afterwards, consists in the main in its disproof. The results of the effort to reconstruct phylogeny from the data of comparative anatomy, extracted from existing forms are now seen to be largely illusory and unverifiable ; and though the material results of these chimerical researches may be considered as a justification of them it seems that embryology and comparative anatomy could have been more profitably studied in and for themselves.

The problem of heredity is one of the fundamental biological problems. It is also quite obviously one of the vital problems of evolutionary theory. Nevertheless the tide of evolutionary speculation carried biological work away from it. Investigators working in the eighteenth and early nineteenth centuries succeeded in establishing some vague and unsatisfactory general principles such as that a cross between pure breeds gives offspring similar among themselves, while a cross between hybrids produces forms showing a wide range of variation ; and that hybrids are generally more vigorous than the parents but tend to be sterile. But as the literature on the subject increased in volume, the results became ever more confused and unintelligible. The work of Mendel, admirably planned and brilliantly executed, cut straight through the indigestible mass accumulated by his predecessors and in the short paper published in 1865 he transformed genetics from something little better than an anecdotical rubbish-heap into an exact science provided with a perfectly definite method.

The great scientific figures of the present time live in a blaze of publicity. Of one of them it was said by an irritated colleague, that his fame surpassed that of Carpentier or Battling Siki ; that he went on tours like an actress ; and that pretty ladies stood in queues to see him. Their mental processes are exhibited to us in detail. But Mendel is an obscure figure and we do not know exactly by what steps he proceeded to his discovery. He tells us in his 1865 paper

[1] *Les conceptions modernes de L'Heredité* : Paris, Flammarion, 1935.

that he was led to it through attempts he made by artificial fertilisation to obtain new colours in ornamental plants. " The remarkable regularity with which the same hybrid forms returned, whenever the same species were crossed," suggested to him, he says, " The idea of new experiments having as their object the determination of the descendants of the hybrids." But others had doubtless made the same observations, without any spectacular consequences. The originality of Mendel's treatment of the problem had perhaps something to do with the fact that he taught mathematics and physics, as well as biology. At all events, his application of exact, quantitative methods to biological problems clearly marks him as one of the first of the moderns. Instead of trying to deal with the organism as a whole, which in this case inevitably leads to almost inextricable confusion, he concentrated on certain clearly definable characters occurring in sharply differentiated forms in the different varieties he had at his disposal. Thus, he crossed tall plants with dwarfs ; plants having green seeds with plants having yellow seeds ; plants whose seeds are wrinkled with plants whose seeds are smooth, and so forth. The progeny of such crosses show variations likely to confuse a novice in experiment, in characters other than the one selected for study. But Mendel avoided these difficulties by attending rigorously to the character chosen and following it through a long series of generations. Twenty-two strains of peas were used in the experiments and they were grown and studied throughout the whole period of the work so as to make sure of their constancy and genetic purity. These laborious and difficult investigations occupied eight years, but when they had been concluded, Mendel was able to make an absolutely fundamental statement of the laws of heredity in regard to characters of the type studied ; and the basic principles he established remain valid to this day and constitute the permanent foundation of all the modern work in genetics. He showed that the differential characters between varieties occur, so to speak in *couples*, now called *allelomorphs* and that the various couples are inherited *independently* in crosses. Each pair dissociates in the sex cells so that each of these contains only *one* element of the pair and is *pure* in respect to the character considered. The recombination of these elements takes place according to chance, following the laws of statistical probability. If we have n differential characters there will be 2^n categories of gametes, 4^n different possible combinations of gametes giving 2^n distinct " phenotypical types," the frequency of which is given by the coefficient of the terms of the expansion of the binomial $(a+b)^n$. Mendel also established, for the characters he studied in his peas, the law of *dominance* according to which a character that appears in the descendants of a hybrid may be apparently non-existent in the parent, where it must, nevertheless

" exist " in some sense, though it is, so to speak, masked or dominated by its opposite. This law is not an absolutely general one, but the idea connected with it, of the independence and continued existence of characters or " character-factors " remains the key-stone of the Mendelian system.

Mendel was thus the founder of the analytical and bio-mathematical treatment of the problem of heredity. The difference between his conceptions and that of the orthodox Darwinians of the time is seen very clearly, says Emanuel Rádl[1], if we compare Galton's theory of heredity with that of Mendel. " According to Galton, who in this respect was only expressing the views of his time, the characteristics of the parents have a resultant effect on the descendant, like that of two forces working simultaneously on one body. The result is uniform and nobody could resolve it into its components unless he knew the nature of those components from some other source. Following out this idea further, Galton believed that every individual is influenced, in a greater or less degree, by all his ancestors, so that no ancestor can appear pure in any descendant. According to Mendel, however, the characters of the parents are combined in the descendants, but do not fuse, so that they exist there, side by side, and can separate again in future generations. No fusion of characters takes place, and hence the ancestor can reappear unadulterated in his descendants."

Mendel's fundamental paper on heredity appeared in 1865. He made the mistake of publishing in the journal of the local Natural History Society. Nevertheless, this journal was accessible in the libraries attached to a number of the great scientific centres and his work cannot altogether have escaped attention. Furthermore, Mendel carried on a long correspondence with the distinguished botanist C. Von Nägeli who published in 1884 a theory of heredity based on the idea of representative particles and containing even the idea of dominance ; but he could not persuade Nägeli to take any interest in his discoveries. It was not until 1900 when the intoxication induced by Darwinian theory was beginning to wear off, that work on hybridization was resumed, Mendelian principles discovered simultaneously by de Vries, von Tschermak and Correns and the genius of Mendel finally recognized, sixteen years after his death.

Rádl expressed in 1909 and reiterated in 1930, his belief that Mendelian studies were undermining the foundations of Darwinism. It is probable that feelings of this kind were responsible for the long-continued antipathy for genetics displayed by many Darwinians.[2]

The mathematical treatment of Mendelian data developed by neo-Darwinians like R. A. Fisher and J. B. S. Haldane seems to have satisfied many of the doubters. In so far as the Mendelian conception

[1] *The History of Biological Theories.*   [2] cf. J. S. Huxley, *Nature*, April, 12, 1924.

implies an " atomistic " view of the organism, regarded as a mosaic of " characters," it is certainly much closer to orthodox old-school Darwinism than it is to " holistic " doctrines such as neo-Lamarckism, as is clearly shown by the attitude of biologists like Professor MacBride to the *gene-concept*, which is a modern development of Mendelism.

But in spite of the mathematical neo-Darwinians, it is not by any means certain that a satisfactory theory of evolution can be constructed on a Mendelian basis. The distinguished French biologist M. Caullery in his admirable little book devoted to Mendelism[1] which he fully accepts, nevertheless considers that while Mendelian genetics throw light on the notion of the species, on intraspecific variation and, to some extent, on the origin of closely related species, yet the data provided by genetics cannot really be the basis of the evolutionary process. Genetics, he says, is the study of the living thing in a state of specific stability. This is also the opinion of the American biologist H. S. Jennings, who concludes, after an exhaustive examination of the facts of Mendelian genetics, that they really throw no light on in and that we are still looking for the unknown cause of Evolution[2]. But Professor J. B. S. Haldane has asserted that " the uniformity of the nuclear mechanisms can be extrapolated with great confidence into the past, and that we can be reasonably sure that an Acanthodian or Pteridosperm nucleus was organised on modern lines." From this, it follows, he thinks, that " the principles of genetics and the method of evolution were very much the same in remote geological epochs as they are to-day."[3] This suggests that the difficulties of the Mendelian evolutionist are not restricted to the present as authors like Caullery are inclined to think, but are radical difficulties.

This is also the view of Lamarckian evolutionists like E. Rabaud and E. W. MacBride, who consider that it is impossible to extract either a theory of evolution or an intelligible notion of vital activity from Mendelian principles if these are given an all-embracing and fundamental significance. If the Mendelian idea is pushed to the extreme limit, the organism appears as a mosaic of characters, assembled according to the laws of chance. But the organism is an assemblage in which the possibility of vital action depends on certain precise co-ordinations and relations between the various parts. Lamarckians and Darwinians agree on this point but while adaptive power is *causal* in the Lamarckian theory, it is an *effect* in the Darwinian system and in spite of long-continued efforts and many subterfuges the Darwinians have never been able to produce an intelligible and convincing explanation of this effect. Mendelism has not alleviated their

[1] loc. cit.   [2] *Genetic Variations in Relation to Evolution.*
[3] In Darlington's *Recent Advances in Cytology.*

difficulties and when one considers the position as a whole one feels inclined to sympathize with those who say with E. S. Russell[1] that the phenomena of Mendelian inheritance are simply incidental and accessory phenonema and that we have not yet found a way of dealing scientifically with heredity in its basic aspect.

But the difficulties created by the impact of Mendelism on the theories of adaptation and evolution were not difficulties created by Mendel. Mendel was a man who followed his nose. He liked facts, and the only theories that seem to have appealed to him were those that emerge immediately from the facts. Rádl says of him that he imagined " that the organism is made up of characters, somewhat as substances are made up of atoms " ; but I cannot find any such statement in the papers he published, so that while he must be given the credit of discovering the most workable and scientifically fruitful method we possess for tackling the problem of heredity, the puzzles arising out of the philosophical development and extension of his results, cannot fairly be laid to his charge. If he had continued his work he might eventually have encountered and dealt with these problems, to the advantage of posterity. But he was obliged to give it up when, in 1868, he became abbot of his monastery and he was never again able to return to it. At the time of his election he was engaged in an attempt to confirm, on plants of the genus *Hieracium*, the results he had obtained with peas. Technical difficulties which were not cleared up till thirty years later, made the material unsuitable for study. The biographers of Mendel, who are inclined to regard the latter part of his career as a defeat and decline, usually suggest that chagrin due to the neglect of his discoveries and the unsatisfactory results of his Hieracium work, had a good deal to do with his withdrawal from the scientific field.

One may, however, venture to suggest that the biographers have not considered the position from the standpoint of Mendel. Mendel was a priest and a religious, and though he was, no doubt, greatly attached to his scientific work and much disappointed by the lack of interest shown by the scientific world in his results, we cannot doubt that, having a vocation for the things of God and putting first things first, his work as a botanist would appear to him as a very light thing when weighed against the responsibilities and opportunities of the abbatial office in a great religious house, and that he abandoned his scientific investigations simply because of his devotion to duties that he sincerely and rightly felt to be of a far higher order.

These duties were onerous and the responsibilities of office, in normal circumstances, a heavy burden. But in Mendel's period of office they were greatly increased by the action of the Austrian govern-

[1] *The Interpretation of Development and Heredity.*

ment, which imposed a special tax on monasteries. Abbot Mendel refused to submit to this tax, maintaining that all citizens are equal under the law. Other monasteries at first sided with him but gradually they weakened and one after another consented to pay the tax. Mendel continued to resist and though great pressure was brought to bear on him, he refused to give way, even allowing the goods of the monastery to be distrained upon by the fiscal authorities. The later history of anti-clerical operations in Europe shows clearly that Mendel behaved with good judgment, for the principle on which he acted was again and again proved to be the only practicable basis for the defence of the elementary rights of religious communities. Mendel's resistance was ultimately effective. The objectionable law was repealed. But before the Austrian government decided to take this step, Abbot Mendel died of Bright's disease, at the age of 62, on the 6th of January, 1884.

It is said that toward the end of his life, under the influence of difficulties, disappointment and disease, the temperament of Mendel deteriorated. To him, his career may well have appeared in a temporal sense, a failure. His great scientific effort, brilliantly planned, admirably executed and fundamentally successful, attracted no attention from the learned world. Those who should have been his allies in his religious battle, deserted him and he did not live to see its successful issue. But looking back from our vantage point in the present we see that he was, in the scientific field, the initiator of one of the most fruitful of scientific movements, and in the religious field, the defender of a position of pivotal importance. Gregor Johann Mendel was a great Catholic.

Rev. MARTIN D'ARCY, S.J., M.A.

GERARD MANLEY HOPKINS

A.D. 1844–1889

IN THE TWENTY years since the first volume of Fr. Hopkins' poems
appeared the literary world has come more and more to believe
in the high quality of his genius. There is as yet, however, no such
agreement about his character. From the poems themselves and
certain anecdotes often retold a legend of a poet born out of due
time, very sensitive and very eccentric, has sprung up. That he was
a priest and Jesuit gave a fillip to the imagination, and on the strength
of the later sonnets some critics conceived a vast pity for him—this
tender plant in the rough plantation of the Society of Jesus and the
Catholic Church ; they even suggested that his poetic gifts were
stifled in the vocation he chose, and that at the end he had misgivings
about his vocation and his faith. It is perhaps natural that those who
know little of the ways of God with individual souls—especially those
of predilection—should so interpret at first the sonnets of affliction.
Now however that, thanks to the industry of Mr. Humphrey House
and Professor Abbott, we have editions of his diaries and notes and
letters to Robert Bridges and Canon Dixon, there is less excuse for such
a view, and there is abundant material for a just estimate of Hopkins'
character. Nevertheless, Professor Abbott in his introduction to one
volume of the letters can write that, "it is our good fortune that his
name belongs to literature and not to hagiography." By this I suppose
he means that Hopkins can stand the test of poetic genius but not of
holiness. That this is his meaning appears from a comparison which
he makes between Milton and Hopkins. "There is a kinship of
spirit between the two poets. But what was possible to the resolved
will of Milton the heretic was beyond the powers of Hopkins the
priest. He lacked, so it seems to me, just that serene certainty of how
to serve God." It is always dangerous to make guesses about a
person's spiritual life, and Hopkins was never one to " tell secrets,"
but we may well ask whether the spiritual suffering of the priest did not
rest on a much closer intimacy with Christ and Him crucified, than
the grim and cantankerous outlook of a Milton.

As the impression of Abbott is shared by others and the legend of his frailty is still current, it is important to test this preconception by the evidence of the diaries and letters. Now on reading them disinterestedly no one, I think, can help feeling himself in the presence of a man of the highest sincerity and simplicity, a most delicate conscience and sense of honour and of steadfast loyalty to his vocation. On the other hand his poems show the marks of great interior conflicts and their great individuality does, it must be confessed, pass over into the eccentric at times. In the diaries again the observation is never weakly impressionist and seldom emotional ; it is so direct as to be almost impersonal, and from the effort to be truthful comes a minuteness of detail and singularity of language. This singularity of look would betoken strength, were it not that often it is the unusual in nature which attracts his attention. To my mind it is here the problem of his character is clearly marked. What was his virtue could also be his weakness. He was interested in others and what they could tell him, and he loved the conversation of his Irish brothers, in the novitiate, for instance. But throughout his life, he is far more the keen observer than the victim of introspection, and it is to be seen in the diaries written before he became a Jesuit. Were it not so, I might be tempted to see in this habit, his usual conscientious attempt to carry out the rule and regulations of St. Ignatius which emphasized the need of scientific and businesslike accuracy even in self-examination.

The letters to Bridges and Dixon betray this same combination of robust discrimination and singularity. In the correspondence with Dixon it is delightful to come across the gentle understanding of his friend and the wisdom of many of his observations ; but he worries the older man at times by the scrupulosity which even to his fellow Jesuits appears exaggerated. The story is told of him that when he was professor in Dublin, some friends asked him to stop for tea and he excused himself on the ground that he had not leave to do so. The same over-conscientiousness is seen in the fuss he makes about the possible publication of any of his poems, and in his reluctance as a priest to spend any time writing poetry for fear it would interfere with his job of teaching or preaching. In all this he is literal minded and refuses to distinguish between the serious and the light or fantastic, duty and that happy love which enables the children of God to act in full liberty of spirit. Quite possibly the fact that he was a convert and that he had been brought up in the atmosphere of rectitude which belongs so especially to Victorian religion, may help to account for some of the puzzles of his character. He was in sentiment and by education a thorough Victorian, and it was through this habit of mind a genius quite un-Victorian had to work. Other converts have exhibited the same unresolved tension. They have startled, and still startle the traditional Catholic by their inability to unbend.

But this at best is only a partial explanation, and we can get closer to the truth by looking for clues in the material provided by the diaries, letters and evidence of friends. From his photographs, Hopkins might be thought almost effeminate, and from these and the tradition that he was a delicate and unpractical poet, many have paid too little attention to evidence which contradicts this. In a letter of Mr. C. N. Luxmoore giving reminiscences of Hopkins' schooldays, we learn that " once roused by a sense of undeserved injustice, he, usually so quiet and docile was furiously keen for the fray, and only bristled the more, when as was usually the case, the authorities tried force and browbeating to silence his arguments and beat him down." There are clear traces of this same strength and passion for justice in his letters. It is joined with a very masculine taste in literature. He liked Dryden because " he is the most masculine of our poets ; his style and his rhythms lay the strongest stress of all our literature on the naked thew and sinew of the English language." Again it is not the Hopkins of popular fancy who could write : " I was fond of my people, but they had not as a body the charming and cheering heartiness of these Lancashire Catholics, which is so deeply comforting ; they were far from having it. And I believe they criticised what went on in our church a great deal too freely, which is d—d impertinence of the sheep towards the shepherd, and if it had come markedly before me I should have given them my mind."

It is fair to argue from these and similar passages that he had substantially a robust soul. I use the word " substantial " deliberately because it comes near to the kind of distinctions he would himself have used. (It would be well worth while to make a study of Hopkins in terms of the psychology he himself loved and thought true). He looked out and away from himself straightforwardly at things and persons ; he is stirred by the " inscape " of things and roused by wrong done to others. He looked, too, for " a dexterous and starlight order " ; he gives glory to God for " dappled things," the " Kingdom of daylight's dauphin," " The skies between fire mountains," and like the Queen of Heaven,. " All things rising, all things sizing," he sees, " sympathizing with that world of good, Nature's motherhood."

When he had to decide on his vocation and chose, in Bridges' quaint description, to be " a housecarl in Loyola's meinie," Newman congratulated him, saying that the Jesuit discipline was not too hard and that it would bring him to heaven. Evidently Hopkins had said something to Newman about the hardness of this discipline, and it had occupied his thoughts. Mr. C. Devlin in a penetrating essay has pointed out how intimate is the connection of the thought in the poems with the Exercises of St. Ignatius. Now those exercises start with the idea of the service of God and pass on to the service of Christ the King, and they are a military handbook of sanctity, stating with stark clarity the rules and discipline of Christ's army. The robust mind of Hopkins delighted in this and he lived and thought by those rules. It is not without significance that in seeing a soldier he should always be inclined to bless him, and that one of the tenderest of his poems should be about a bugle boy from barrack. Moreover, the inspiration from early years and his true love was Christ. In the early diaries occur these lines.

> " And other science all gone out of date
> And minor sweetness scarce made mention of :
> I have found the dominant of my range and state—
> Love, O my God, to call Thee Love and Love."

At first this love was no doubt mixed with romantic feelings ; he had been swayed by Keats and Tennyson and was touched by Dolben. In a sonnet on Easter Communion the thought and language are romantic, and he is sure that God " for sackcloth and frieze and the ever-fretting shirt of punishment " will " give myrrhy-threaded golden folds of ease." But he was too honest even in his youth to have romance without the test of fact. At the time he was writing in this way he sets down in his diary : " For Lent. No pudding on Sundays. No tea except if to keep me awake and then without sugar. Meat only once a day. No verses in Passion Week or on Fridays. Not to sit in armchair except can work in no other way. Ash Wednesday and Good Friday bread and water."

When he became a Jesuit the Exercises of St. Ignatius gave a steely strength and purpose to this love of Christ. For some years I think he was still like his Bowman Arthur. " His three-heeled timber 'll hit The bald and bold blinking gold when all's done Right-rooting in the bare butt's wincing navel in the sight of the sun." He was to find that God disposed of him in no such simple fashion. But throughout trials and disappointments he is quite clear of his vocation in the service of Christ and regards with abhorrence as disloyalty and treachery any suggestion of falling out of the ranks. In 1881 he writes to Dixon : " As for myself, I have not only made my vows publicly some two and twenty times, but I make them to myself every day, so that I should be black with perjury if I drew back now. And beyond that I can say with St. Peter : To whom shall I go ? *Tu verba vitae aeternae habes.*" In a letter of the same year he says again that he leaves questions like the publication of his poems to his superiors and tries to live on the principle of resting in the providence of God. " If you value what I write, if I do myself, much more does the Lord." This trust despite all appearances was not in vain, though Hopkins was to go into a darkness which left him no romance and not even faint rays of consolation. We can see the change and watch his constancy. In 1879 he tells Bridges that he has not the inducements and inspirations that make others compose. And then follows the revealing sentence. " Feeling, love in particular, is the great moving power and spring of verse and the only person that I am in love with seldom, especially now, stirs my heart sensibly and when he does I cannot always ' make capital ' of it, it would be a sacrilege to do so." The writer of that sentence surely has a name "which belongs to hagiography " and he is wiser and more heroic than the youth who wrote of the " myrrhy-threaded golden folds of ease," which Christ was to give.

In the last years even this rare stirring of the heart was, so he thought, withheld. His body is against him in Ireland, his work is a tread-mill, his companions wound him by their political antipathies. He knows that he is misunderstood and feels that those who are friendly think of him as a harmless eccentric. He sees himself an exile, doing nothing for Christ, " breeding not one work that wakes," and fighting against melancholy he is ware of " a rack where, self-wrung, self-strung, sheathed and shelterless, thoughts against thoughts in groans grind." Yet, as Mr. House, with his customary understanding points out, " at a time when he was most despondent, when the drudgery of routine work, marking examination papers, was threatening his eyes ; and his body was weak ; and plans for his own work all interrupted and deferred, he wrote in a notebook :

" Man was created to praise, etc," (these are the first words of the Exercises of St. Ignatius), " Praise by the office expressly meant for this ; by the Mass, especially the Gloria."
And the other things on earth—take it that weakness, ill-health, every cross is a help. *Calix quem Pater meus dedit mihi non bibam illud ? Facere nos indifferentes*—with the elective will, not the effective especially ; but the affective will follow.
I must ask God to strengthen my faith or I shall never keep the particular examen. I must say the Stations for this intention. Resolve also to keep it particularly even in the present state of lethargy."

No wonder Mr. House writes that " no single sentence better explains the motives and direction of Hopkins' life than this ' Man was created to praise.' He believed it as wholly as a man can believe anything ; and when regret or sorrow over anything in his life comes to a critic's mind this must be remembered." It is perhaps because of critics' ignorance of the Exercises of St. Ignatius that they have not followed Mr. House's wise advice. From beginning to end Hopkins remained faithful to the teaching in that book, and the quotation just given shows what is really a heroic resolve to follow out even its most difficult details. In the light of this no one should again raise the question of Hopkins' sincerity in his vocation or take the evidence of the sonnets as reason for doubting the firmness of his faith. Mr. G. W. Stonier in a review of his poems in *The New Statesman* is much nearer to the truth when he says that " religion hardened him morally and intellectually, provided him with a background infinitely better suited to his genius than Greek myth, and brought into his poetry the polyphony of style, parti-colour of pattern, and expanding, realistic and passionate force of his great work. In the face of this it seems to me absurd to speak of damage done to him by conflicts of art and religion, sensuousness and asceticism." If this be true then Mr. Abbott's contrast of Hopkins with Milton and his remark that Hopkins " lacked just that serene certainty of how to serve God " fails of the mark. Hopkins never swerved from a very definite rule and ideal of how to serve God, that, namely given in the book which begins with the praise of God and goes on to the way of serving and following Christ as a King. There is a problem, but it is not where Mr. Abbott would find it . . . Mr. Stonier accepts the verdict of a friend of the poet who wrote : " His mind was too delicate a texture to grapple with the rough elements of life." This perhaps is the impression which many must carry away after reading the poems and hearing something of his life story. But the emphasis, I think, is wrong, and it is not true to say that he did not grapple with the rough. Substantially he is robust and he has his eyes always open. There is no trace of fear ; he does not turn inwards to escape reality and substitute an imaginative and emotional world for the real one. In order, therefore, to understand his melancholy and the impression of broken nerves we must begin not with an emphasis on these latter traits, but on the natural wholesomeness of the man. He begins life open-eyed and cheerful and as Luxmoore tells us with a passion for fairness and truth. The cheerfulness never quite dies, as the tone of many of the letters to Bridges and their breeziness and slang prove. He remains also open-eyed to the end, but what is noticeable is that he preserves the delicacy and innocence which goes with childhood and suffers for it. Age did not bring him a harder skin, so that what was too ugly and harsh for a child had the same effect on him in middle age. The very chastity of mind which was his strength, proved also his torment. Just because he kept that fresh and singular outlook and was perhaps incapable of becoming common, of adapting himself to the mentality around him, he was unable to build up defences and be worldly wise. For most men, life has an element of hide-and-seek. They economize and make use of conventions to keep off what is hostile and hurting in order that they may seek out what they want and feel that they can do or be. Public opinion and conventional manners and ways are a mixed blessing. Hopkins missed their blessing ; he was left unprotected and grew more and more singular despite his own hatred of eccentricity. He gained, however, in this, that what he thought and wrote was marked by intense originality. Inevitably, however, what interested him was not what the chorus sang of, and so he grew by habit as well as nature to love " all things counter, original, spare, strange " and to use a language which scandalized his contemporaries by its obscurity. His moral and spiritual conscience too began to suffer for its isolation by growing in delicacy to the point when it became over-conscientious and almost scrupulous. The process, indeed, can almost be described in a set of words ; a pure and innocent outlook grows more distinctive and original and at the same time more singular, rare and unconventional and odd. At a critical moment of his development he came across the subtlest of philosophers, Duns Scotus, and there can be no doubt that " the rarest-veined unraveller of realty," as he described Scotus, had an immense influence on his subsequent habit of thought. Few at the time knew anything of Scotus and the Scotist Hopkins convinced his friends all the more that he was eccentric and of no use for the hurly-burly. The Scotist doctrine of individualism fitted too well with his own habit of mind, and when his innocence had grown so delicate that he could no longer decide without weeks of agonizing concentration whether the fourth decimal point in an undergraduate's marks were correct or not, he had reached a degree of singularity which left him without protection against the rough elements of life.

Hopkins suffered, therefore, because of the very quality of his mind and soul, and one cannot easily separate his triumphs from his sufferings. But I doubt whether spiritually or practically he would have been so haunted by failure had it not been for the exhaustion and collapse of his body. If one takes the trouble to notice in his diaries and letters the number of times he has to confess to physical weakness and consequent depression, the weariness unto death of his spirit, so manifest in the later sonnets, will not come with a surprise. " I can no more." " All life death does end and each day dies with sleep." Of many passages let these suffice :

In 1877-8, " Life here is as dank as ditch-water and has some of the other qualities of ditch-water : at least I know that I am reduced to great weakness by diarrhœa, which lasts too, as if I were poisoned."

In 1880, " I take up a languid pen to write to you, being down with diarrhœa and vomiting, brought on by yesterday's heat and the long hours in the confessional."

In 1880, " But I never could write ; time and spirit were wanting ; one is so fagged, so harried and gallied up and down. And the drunkards go on drinking, the filthy, as the scripture says, are filthy still : human nature is so inveterate. Would that I had seen the last of it."

In 1883, " Since our holidays began I have been in a wretched state of weakness and weariness, I can't tell why, always drowsy and incapable of reading or thinking to any effect."

In 1884, " I am, I believe, recovering from a deep fit of nervous prostration (I suppose I ought to call it) : I did not know but I was dying."

In 1885, " The long delay was due to work, worry, and languishment of body and mind . . . to judge of my case, I think that my fits of sadness, though they do not affect my judgment, resemble madness."

Here is a sad record and it is clear that his body and nerves failed him, and at that time there was no cure, if indeed there is now, for nervous prostration. The melancholy caused by weakness and nervous depression was bound to invade his mind and spiritual life, and in the last years he had this as a more or less constant persecution. It tempted him to think of his whole life as a failure and himself as " time's eunuch " and in the name of the justice he had always loved to plead pitifully with Providence. " Thou art indeed just, Lord, if I contend with thee ; . . . why must disappointment all I endeavour end ? " But what should strike the reader is the evidence of his unswerving loyalty and fidelity to the ideal of the Exercises of St. Ignatius throughout this trial, and the robust quality of the letters even at this time. He may have thought himself a failure, and some readers and critics seem to have been deceived by the tone of the sad sonnets and the superficial appearance of excessive fragility in his life. Because of his open-eyed innocence he could not but be hurt dreadfully by the sight of evil, whether physical or moral. " The filthy are filthy still." His senses and his conscience had become so thin that what would not have hurt his friends caused him untold suffering. But for this depression and pain he is surely hardly accountable. They came through his chastity, the perfection of his sensibilities and the burden of a body which drooped. Where he was truly himself, in the intimacy which as he believed and as Scotus taught, existed between Christ and himself, where Christ plays, " lovely in limbs, and lovely in eyes not his to the Father through the features of men's faces," he was, as the evidence shows, utterly faithful. Providence did not allow his heroic abstention from publication and readiness to sacrifice fame to be without their reward. It is surely remarkable that poetry so hidden from the world, so fated apparently to die, should now be praised wherever the English language is understood. It is time, I think, that his character should also be vindicated. He thought his spiritual life a failure and had many moments of dereliction. But amongst his last poems there is one in which he had a glimpse of his worth in the sight of God, which he was too humble to apply to himself. In the sonnet on the saintly, obscure lay brother, Alphonsus Rodriguez, who was afterwards canonized, he compares the glory which is flashed off exploits all the world can acclaim with a hidden martyrdom. "But be the war within, the brand we wield unseen, the heroic breast not outward-steeled, earth hears no hurtle then from fiercest fray."

It was his lot not only to think himself a " eunuch " and produce immortal poetry, but to feel himself a spiritual failure and be exalted on his cross. The poems express his anguish ; his letters and life show his heroic endurance. He had a body and temperament which exposed him to suffering. The childlike simplicity, which magnified the originality of his vision and character, made the sight of evil, physical and spiritual, shocking to him. But he never broke faith with his ideal ; he never turned in on himself and made a cult of his emotions ; he never left the ranks to whine in the ditch. In that poem " in honour of St. Alphonsus Rodriguez " he used once again the image of the soldier and announced that no trumpet was to salute his part in the battlefield. But the last lines of the poem were, though he knew it not, prophetic. " God (that hews mountain and continent, earth, all, out ; who, with trickling increment, veins violet and tall trees makes more and more) could crown career with conquest . . ." Hopkins' career was crowned with conquest, and that crowning seems to me more like the making more and more of tall trees than the veining of the violet.

DOM BEDE CAMM, O.S.B., M.A.

DOM HILDEBRAND DE HEMPTINNE

First Abbot Primate, O.S.B.

A.D. 1849–1913

THE FIRST TIME I saw Abbot de Hemptinne was at the crisis of my life, my conversion to the Catholic Faith in July, 1890. It was at Maredsous Abbey, near Dinant in Belgium. I had been received into the Church by the then Abbot, Dom Placid Wolter, on June 18th of that year. Shortly after, Dom Maurus his elder brother, who was Arch-abbot of Beuron in Germany, died, and Dom Placid was elected to succeed him.

There was never any doubt at Maredsous as to who would be the next Abbot there. It was a Belgian monk, who was acting as secretary to the late Abbot Wolter. In fact, he was elected unanimously, and greeted with joy and jubilation by the whole Community. The Abbey owed its existence mainly to him. His history was a striking one. As a boy of sixteen, Felix de Hemptinne, as he was then called, had enlisted as a zouave in the Papal army, in defence of the patrimony of Peter.

Among his fellow-soldiers in Pius IX's little army, were two great friends of his, Victor Mousty and Jules Desclée. The latter was wounded in a skirmish outside Subiaco, the monastic home of St. Benedict, and was nursed back to health by the monks. He resolved that if God gave him the opportunity, he would, in gratitude to St. Benedict, found a monastery of the Order in his native land.

Meanwhile, Felix, in his camp on the Roman Campagna, had had a mysterious call to become a Benedictine. He knew nothing of the Order, had never seen any monks, yet as he knelt in prayer, he heard most distinctly an interior voice that told him he was to be a Benedictine. He often told me the story himself. His father, who was a most pious and devout Catholic, did all he could to help him. He went round Europe visiting the various Benedictine Abbeys, and at last he found at Beuron, on the Danube, the monastery which appealed to him as the most faithful to the observance of the Holy Rule. This was but recently founded. He advised his son to enter there, which he did, and he duly became Dom Hildebrand. His heart, however,

368

did not cease to yearn after his native land, and he prayed and laboured for the foundation of a Benedictine house in Belgium.

Meanwhile Rome had fallen, and the Papal army been disbanded. Mousty and Desclée returned home, and, to please his son, old Mr. Desclée appointed Mousty to be the steward or agent of his property at Maredsous. There was, however, no chapel or church where the Desclées could assist at daily Mass. " We need an Abbé to say Mass for us." " To have an *Abbé* you must have an *Abbeye*," said Mousty. The half-jesting words bore fruit, and the result was the splendid Abbey of Maredsous.

Its first Abbot was Dom Placid Wolter, one of the founders of the Congregation at Beuron. His brother, Dom Maurus, Arch-abbot of Beuron, died in July, 1890, and Dom Placid was elected to succeed him. This left Maredsous vacant, and the abbatial throne was filled by Dom Hildebrand, whose wonderful vocation had been the cause of its very existence.

This was how I first came to know this great man. I had been received into the Church by Dom Placid, and I was still there when the change came. I shall never forget my first meeting with Dom Hildebrand. I was longing to become a monk, and Dom Placid had been more than kind about it. He gave me over to Dom Hildebrand, and in August of that year I was received into the novice-ship.

Dom Hildebrand had a great future before him. He was destined to become the first Abbot Primate, or Superior General of the whole Order of St. Benedict ; a new dignity devised by Pope Leo XIII. And not only was he Abbot Primate but Abbot of the international College of Benedictine monks, that of St. Anselmo on the Aventine at Rome. He made the plans for this great building, for he was a born architect, as he also made those for the Abbey of St. Scholastica, near Maredsous, for Benedictine nuns, and the School of Arts and Crafts at Maredsous, which was dedicated to St. Joseph. They were both beautiful buildings and marvellously well adapted to the ends for which they were designed.

St. Joseph's School, close to the Abbey, had an interesting origin. When Abbot Hildebrand was elected, he found the novitiate almost empty. He therefore made a solemn vow to St. Joseph, in which he promised that, if novices came in sufficient numbers, he would make this foundation in honour of the Artizan of Nazareth for the benefit of orphans and poor boys. From that day, novices began to flow in in large numbers, so that before long the Abbot was able to accomplish his vow, St. Joseph's School became a wonderful success. The Abbot designed for it a beautiful group of buildings, with its own chapel, refectory and dormitories, grouped round a central glass-roofed hall, containing large, airy workshops, in which the boys, taught by monks of artistic ability, exercise their crafts with really remarkable success. They have earned medals in international exhibitions and their work is acknowledged by all who examine it to be extraordinary good.

At Tyburn Convent in London, an altar carved in oak by these boys, contains six beautiful oak statuettes of English martyrs. The embroidered curtain behind the altar, and the jewelled lamps which hang around it, are also the work of these young craftsmen of Maredsous.

All this was the work of Dom Hildebrand, a born artist. He also built the Abbey of Maredret for Benedictine nuns. It is more ornate, and to my mind much more beautiful than the neighbouring Abbey of Maredsous. His own sister became the first Abbess of this lovely Abbey, so that brother and sister ruled over the adjacent monasteries, recalling the days of St. Benedict and his sister St. Scholastica.

But a greater work was before him, in the planning of the great Abbey of Sant' Anselmo at Rome. I well remember seeing him working at this in his cell at Maredsous. It was to be, as it now is, a central house of studies for young Benedictines of all nations, and it was also to be the home of him who was to be elected Abbot Primate of the Order. It was only fitting that this new office, planned by Leo XIII, should be destined for him who had laid the foundations of his home.

Abbot Hildebrand became the first Abbot Primate. At first he retained his old and much-beloved home at Maredsous, and used to pass between it and the new College at Rome, spending as much time as he could spare at Maredsous. But after a time this became impossible, and he had to resign the charge of Maredsous, though it was a real grief to him. I had the honour and the happiness of being with him, both at Maredsous and at Rome. The magnificent building he had designed for Sant' Anselmo was not completed till after my ordination to the priesthood (in March, 1895) so that I lived only in the temporary college which preceded it. Still I saw it rising on the Aventine Hill, and marvelled at its beauty.

The college was then in the Via Bocca di Leone, just off the well-known Piazza d'Espagna. We had a very happy time there. The Rector was a well-known monk of Maredsous, Dom Laurent Janssens, who afterwards was promoted to the Episcopate. But Dom Hildebrand was not only the Superior, but also the life and soul of the place. The sad days of the Petrine imprisonment kept the Pope immured in the Vatican, but we were admitted sometimes to an audience.

Dom Hildebrand, meantime, was engaged in the plans for the new and permanent Sant' Anselmo, which gave great satisfaction to Pope Leo XIII. I received from him the Minor Orders, and later on became a priest at Rome, being ordained by H. E. Cardinal Parocchi. I had made my Solemn Vows of Religion also at Rome, in the hands of my beloved Father-in-Christ, Dom Hildebrand. We all expected and hoped that he would have been created a Cardinal, but it was not to be. I suppose he would have had to leave his work at St. Anselmo, if this had happened, so it was no doubt for the best as it was.

We were a band of monks of many countries and Congregations, English, Belgian, Austrian, French and American, and Dom Hildebrand seemed perfectly at home with us all. It was the English he specially loved, as it seemed to us. He had spent some years as the Superior of a small Community of Beuron Benedictines at Erdington, near Birmingham. He had learnt to speak English perfectly, and he told me that it had been a special joy to him that the first postulant to whom he gave the habit, when created Abbot of Maredsous, should have been an Englishman and a convert, myself.

So, although I had joined a foreign Community, I was completely happy and at home under his fatherly and enlightened rule. I was destined to be sent to Erdington as soon as I was ordained priest.

The ex-papal zouave was perfectly at home in Rome, and was always *persona grata* to the reigning Pontiff, the great Pope Leo XIII.

Pope Leo had a special affection for the Order of St. Benedict. His intention and desire was that this great Order should flourish once again in all its primitive splendour. He meant the College of St. Anselm to be a link between the various Congregations of the Order and a powerful support for the whole Order. And it was this intention which led him to create what was then a complete novelty, the office of an Abbot Primate, which should unite them under one head. He realized that he had found in Dom Hildebrand that wideness of spirit and depth of charity which were required for an Office which was at once a novelty and a link of union.

The Primate was not to be a General of an Order, he was to be a leader suited to the peculiar circumstances, who was to guide his brethren in religion to the unity which was so necessary in those troubled times, and serve as a central power in the Eternal City, to whom all could have recourse in the difficulties that might disturb their peace. As Abbot Butler has said, Abbot Hildebrand was far from content with the labours which the rule of his own Abbey, and the presidency over the whole Order assigned to him.

The great Catholic University of Louvain gave him the opportunity of new labours and new foundations. The Prior of Maredsous, Dom Robert de Kerchove, was sent to Louvain, to take charge of the young monks who made these their theological studies. Dom Columba Marmion, an Irish priest, who had joined the novitiate at Maredsous, went later to assist him in the work. Dom Columba was a man of extraordinary piety, and deep learning. He had been one of the foremost students at the College of the Propagation of the Faith at Rome. His entering the novitiate at Maredsous was, it seemed, a special grace of God's Providence, and it was soon evident that he was destined to become famous in the land of his adoption. He was a thorough Irishman, witty, bright and charming, and at the same time a man of prayer, a marvellous preacher, and a most learned theologian. His vocation to the monastic life at Maredsous seemed quite extraordinary. He was a complete stranger, knowing no one in the Community. He returned from Rome as a young priest, went back to Ireland for a time, and then left everything to become a monk in this Belgian Abbey. (He had visited it with a fellow-student on his way back from Rome.) He had a peculiarly difficult novitiate in this foreign land, but he knew that God called him there, and he never wavered in his obedience. He was my guide and my friend, when I came to Maredsous as a young parson, and but for him I might never have responded to God's call.

Louvain, to which he was sent, as Prior of the new monastery there, became for some years his home, till God called him back to Maredsous to take the throne left vacant by Dom Hildebrand's death.

It was in 1896 that Abbot Hildebrand founded the great monastery of Mont Cæsar at Louvain. It was on a hill overlooking the University town, and here the Abbot erected in a few years, from his own designs, a truly magnificent Abbey. Dom Robert in due time became its first Abbot. Happily he still survives, though at a great age. I am told that though he is over 90, he still rises every morning to Matins, at 5 a.m.

The Abbey of Mont César was one of the greatest works of Abbot Hildebrand, worthy to rank with St. Anselmo itself. But it was built by stages. It was in 1899, that Dom Robert de Kerchove took possession of the Monastery, which Abbot Hildebrand had named *Regina Cæli*, for the Queen of Heaven was to be the patroness of this new house of God. A few months later Dom Robert was created Abbot. He was blessed at Maredsous on September 8th, 1899—the feast of the Birthday of the Queen.

Another great work for the Benedictine Order was accomplished by Dom Gerard van Calœn, a monk of Maredsous. In the spring of 1893, he received a missive from Rome, signed by Dom Hildebrand, enjoining him to set out for Brazil, there to work for the restoration of the Benedictine Order.

Dom Gerard was a really great man. Born of a noble Flemish

family, he had been one of the very first monks to join Dom Hildebrand at Maredsous. He had been founder and first Rector of the Abbey School at Maredsous, Prior of the Abbey, and later on Prefect of the young monks who made their studies at St. Anselmo. He was chosen by Leo XIII to undertake this very difficult work of reformation in Brazil. Curiously enough I was his companion at a Papal audience in the spring of 1893, when he first was told of his future work by Leo XIII himself. It was the Feast of Candlemas, when it is customary for the various Colleges and Religious Orders to present a taper to the Holy Father.

The Pope received most graciously the splendid wax candle we presented to him, and told Dom Gerard that he was sending him to Brazil. It was an extraordinarily difficult mission which was entrusted to him, but he fulfilled it magnificently, and is now considered in Brazil with reverence and affection as the Second Founder of the Order in that country. He was eventually created a Bishop, with jurisdiction over Rio Branco. But he had already been Abbot of Rio de Janeiro, and he had transformed a land of desolation into a flourishing centre of monastic life. He was consecrated at Maredsous, under the title of Bishop of Phocæa, April 18th, 1906.

Dom Hildebrand was accustomed to leave Rome and return to Maredsous about mid-Lent. He thus spent Holy Week and Easter in his Monastery, presiding at all the functions, and then returned to Rome, until the end of June, when he came back to his dear monastic home for the summer months. It was a busy time, for the novitiate was then crowded with new postulants, and there were many young monks preparing for the priesthood. Thus on August 30th, 1903, nine deacons, all monks of Maredsous, received the priesthood from the Bishop of Namur. And there were then more than 50 priest-monks to lay their hands on the young Levites.

Many of the monks of Maredsous were employed at Rome. The Rector of St. Anselmo, Dom Laurent Janssens, later Secretary of the Biblical Commission, Dom Pierre Bastien, Professor of Canon Law, Dom Ursmer Berlière, Director of the Belgian Historical Institution at Rome, were notable names among them.

Dom Hildebrand passed the months of August and September in England in order to get to know more intimately the ancient and venerable Anglo-Benedictine Congregation. He came, as he said, " not as a visitor, whose chief duty is to look, but as a father whose great duty is to love." His visit was a great success. On both sides there was an equal desire, an equal zeal to arrive at definite constitutions. Three years after his visit appeared the famous bull *Diu quidem*, which can be considered as the charter of the English Benedictines.

In the year 1895, he visited Cluny and the other foundations due to

Dom Mayeul Lamey.   There was a very happy outcome of his visit
to the English monasteries: our Priories became Abbeys, and a decree
of the Sacred Congregation of Rites raised to the honours of Beatification those of our English Martyrs who were represented in the famous
painting in the English College at Rome.   Not only that, but St. Bede
the Venerable, " the torch of the Church lighted by the Holy Ghost
among the Anglo-Saxons," was made a Doctor of the Church, and
his Office extended to the Universal Church.   Thus English Catholics,
and English Benedictines in particular, have much to be grateful for
to the labours of the Primate.

Dom Hildebrand also had great sympathy for the Oriental Churches,
and did all he could to help on their reunion to the Catholic and
Roman Church.   The principal result of these endeavours was the
foundation of the Monastery of the *Dormitio* at Jerusalem, the spot
which marks the place of the falling asleep of the Mother of God.

On the feast of St. Martin of Tours, November 11th, 1900, there was
celebrated with truly Roman magnificence, the Consecration of the
Church of St. Anselmo on the Aventine Hill.   The Prelates and
Abbots of the Order were invited to this ceremony.   Cardinal
Rampolla del Tindaro, as Legate *a latere*, presided, and there assisted
twelve archbishops and bishops, seventy prelates, nearly all of them
abbots, while in the Tribune, twelve cardinals, and the diplomats
of foreign countries accredited to the Holy See, found their place.
The Abbot-Primate offered the Holy Sacrifice in the crypt.   On
November 13th, Feast of All Saints of the Benedictine Order, he sung
Pontifical High Mass in the new Basilica, which had been designed
by his own hands.   On the octave day, Leo XIII gave a private
audience to Dom Hildebrand and to the Benedictines who had taken
part in the consecration ceremonies.   The aged Pontiff received them
with the greatest possible kindness, and in his speech begged them to
do all they could to help the College of St. Anselmo.

Meanwhile a new persecution was raging in France.   In the summer
of 1901, Dom Hildebrand received some of the victims at Maredsous:
the Abbots of Ligugé, St. Wandrilla and Glanfeuil.   He helped them
with funds as far as he was able, and offered them the new building
of St. Joseph.   But as their time of exile promised to be a long one,
they preferred to seek more permanent places of refuge.   Solesmes
was already settled at Quarr in the Isle of Wight, and those of Marseilles
in Italy.   The other communities established themselves in Belgium.

In 1903, the great Pope Leo XIII died.   Six days before his end,
his trembling hand had written a Latin poem in honour of St. Anselm,
which he sent as a last pledge of his paternal affection to Dom
Hildebrand.   He had intended to make him a Cardinal before he died,
but he yielded to the opposition of certain important persons.

He was succeeded by Pius X, who made a point of receiving Dom Hildebrand in special audience before the year was out. The Abbot addressed the Holy Father in moving terms. He thanked the new Pope for having, like his predecessor, taken over the protectorate of the Order. He offered him the filial devotion of all the sons of St. Benedict. " If we must fight, suffer, die perhaps to uphold the truth and defend the Pope from his enemies, we are ready, as we always have been ready."

Great feasts had already been prepared for to celebrate the thirteenth centenary of St. Gregory the Great. Pius X was determined to use this occasion to restore to the Church the ancient and venerable Gregorian Chant, which was one of the special legacies of the great Apostle of the English. The flood of modern music used in the Roman Churches, and indeed throughout Europe, had all but extinguished the work of St. Gregory. But Pius X was to restore it to its ancient glory. The Benedictines, especially in France, had been working on it for years. And it was an immense joy to them, and to the whole Order, when the new Pope took the chant under his special protection, and did all he could to make it known and used throughout the Catholic Church.

Dom Hildebrand was naturally anxious to do all he could for the furtherance of the Holy Father's wishes with regard to the ancient chant. The thirteenth centenary of St. Gregory the Great culminated in a magnificent Gregorian festival, a Papal Mass sung in St. Peter's, on April 11th. There were no less than 1,250 in the choir, which was formed by seminarists and religious from all parts of Rome, led by a choir of 150 cantors (the *Schola Cantorum*) from the Benedictines of St. Anselmo and St. Paul's outside the Walls. The Pope assisted in person at the ceremony, and after all was over he received in private audience the famous Dom Pothier, to whom the resurrection of the ancient chant was mainly due. Dom Hildebrand presided at a similar solemnity at St. Paul's, the Primate being authorized to use the Papal altar, the high altar of the Basilica usually reserved strictly for the Pope.

Meanwhile Dom Hildebrand devoted himself to his enormous correspondence. He wrote, as he said, " from morning to evening ; " he replied to all his correspondents, however simple and unknown. It was said of him later that " he had killed himself by writing letters." He wrote in many languages, English, French, Italian, even in German, though that he always found difficult.

In 1907 he decided to convoke the Abbots-President of the various Congregations to a Synod, in which the various needs of the Order could be discussed, and a decision taken on difficult points. Among the important works undertaken at this assembly was the Commission to deal with the Vulgate. It was desired to restore it as far as possible to its original text. The work was entrusted to Dom Aidan Gasquet, afterwards Cardinal, and to Dom Laurent Janssens, who was already Secretary of the Biblical Commission. Later on, the principal figure connected with this work was Dom John Chapman, who was destined to become Abbot of Downside.

In 1909, Dom Hildebrand ceased to be Abbot of Maredsous, the Pope wishing him to be fixed at Rome. It was a great grief to the monks of Maredsous to lose their beloved Father, but it was impossible to go on combining in one person two such important charges.

Abbot Hildebrand spent the last years of his life in Rome. In 1913 he made a pilgrimage to Monte Cassino to pray our Holy Father St. Benedict that his successor as Primate might be a worthy President of the Order he loved so dearly. His prayers were heard when the choice of the electors fell on Dom Fidelis von Stotzingen, Abbot of Maria-Laach, who is still happily reigning as Primate, having been but recently re-elected to his post.

Dom Hildebrand retired to the Abbey of Beuron. He spent his time in prayer : his Mass, celebrated with heroic sacrifice, was now always the same, the Mass of Our Lady—*De Beata*. His love and devotion for the Blessed Virgin had always been the keynote of his life. It was on the Feast of the Assumption, in 1870, that he had made his monastic vows. The ring he wore, given to him by M. Desclée, had engraved inside it, *Hildebrand servus Mariæ*, but a few years before his death, he had the inscription altered to *Filius Mariæ*. He loved indeed the Mother of God with a truly filial devotion. But his health gradually declined, and it was evident that he was approaching his end. He had been hoping to return to Rome in October, but it was not to be.

From the 20th July, of this year (1913) he was worse and it was clear that the end was near. He received the Last Sacraments on August 11th, and he prepared to meet death with serenity and indeed with supernatural joy. To the infirmarian he said " It is the will of God, I must depart, I am happy." Wednesday, August 13th, was to be his last day on this earth. That evening he blessed with the Sign of the Cross those who were gathered round his bed. After kissing the crucifix, he was given the relic of his beloved Saint, St. Mary Magdalen de Pazzi, which he always wore, and he was asked if he accepted her advice, " Not to die but rather to suffer ! " " Yes," was his reply. Then, a few moments later, he whispered, " Jesus, all for love of Thee ! " They were his last words.

He was 64 years of age, in the 43rd year of his monastic profession, and in the 42nd of his priesthood. He had been Abbot-Primate of the Benedictine Order for more than 20 years.

On the Feast of the Assumption, two days later, crowds of pilgrims came to venerate his body. Among them was a Protestant who on seeing it, exclaimed, " Truly this spectacle would be sufficient to convert an unbeliever to faith in the future life."

He was buried in the Abbey Church of Beuron. The Abbot-Primate, Dom Fidelis von Stotzingen, presided at the ceremony, which was attended by bishops and abbots from all parts of Europe. He was laid to rest at the foot of the ancient altar of Our Lady of Sorrows, close to the tombs of the Beuron Arch-Abbots, Dom Maurus and Dom Placid Wolter. A beautiful monument was erected to his memory at St. Anselmo : it is surmounted with his bust, and decorated with the coats-of-arms of the 15 Benedictine Congregations. But his best memorial is the Abbey of St. Anselmo itself. There everything speaks of him, the monk, the artist, the Abbot-Primate.

Those who knew him can never forget him, and long after their departure, his name will go down to history as the great and glorious Abbot, who was so dear to God and to man. *Requiescat in pace.*

MAUD MONAHAN

MOTHER JANET STUART

A.D. 1857–1914

WHEN IN 1914 Mother Stuart died at the age of 57, her loss seemed to many an irreparable one. "I looked forward to great things which I expected her to do," wrote a priest, and another saw in her death "a public calamity . . . a disaster to the cause of religious education and the Catholic Church."

But on the evening of her death, October 21st, Fr. Roche, S.J., speaking in the Chapel of Roehampton, assured his hearers that their petition to Our Lady to prolong the life of their mother had not been made in vain. "You asked a lesser thing, Our Lady will give a greater. Mother Stuart will come back to you to be a greater power in your lives than if she had stayed with you. . . . Her biography as a world-wide power began this morning."

And when, about seven years later, her life was published, some of those who deeply grieved for her loss, not only as for a friend, but as for one who could have helped so many souls, prayed that through its pages and those of Mother Stuart's published writings, which followed her biography, she might continue the work she had begun on earth, and teach and guide and strengthen souls unceasingly.

No one could have lived with Mother Stuart and failed to realize that she was unlike the great majority. There was about her a mystery of peace ; she seemed, as Père Charles, S.J., said, when he first met her, "to have recaptured, with the help of grace, that state of blessed liberty which preceded the original fall." Had the conquest been won by pain, had the goal been attained after arduous struggle— all trace of painful effort had disappeared. Her supernatural perfection seemed natural.

Père Charles met her in the last years of her life, but 35 years earlier Father Gallwey had declared she was "the most *complete* person he had ever met." Gifted in every way, mind and heart and will, yet over all her gifts she was the master, and able to use them as she willed. A rarer gift indeed than all the rest in our unbalanced race. She exemplified in her life what she urged on others : "Take yourself as you are, whole, and do not try to live by one part alone and starve the other. *Control*, but do not kill."

Many in presence of her almost incomprehensible manifestation of leisure and repose in a life, which seemed filled to the brim with unending work—one item of which alone " the mere burden of correspondence " would, as it has been said, " have daunted any but the bravest "—have tried to explain it by saying : times were quieter, she had fewer calls upon her than we have to-day. And they have not understood that the secret of her success lay then, as it would assuredly have done to-day, in her complete self-mastery. Under her strong rule there was harmony between soul and body.

She made no noise, as it is generally understood, in the world. She neither founded a religious order, nor faced the labours of the mission fields, nor did she revolutionize our methods of educating the young. Her unbounded influence over people was established by the gentlest and most imperceptible outward action and means. And this was as it should be for a chosen instrument of God, who as Ruysbroek says dwells in a sublime stillness, and who came to His fiery prophet, not as Elias seemed to expect, " in a great and strong wind overthrowing mountains and breaking the rocks in pieces, nor in the earthquake that followed, nor even in the fire " ; these things went before the Lord, but He Himself came " in the whistling of a gentle air." " So too," wrote Mother Stuart, " after the long preparation for the Incarnation, It came in great silence and tranquillity, only a few words, and only one to hear them."

And so perhaps is it most often in His direct action upon souls. Many zealous seekers after them have found it to be true that

> . . . While the tired waves, vainly breaking
> Seem here no painful inch to gain,
> Far back through creeks and inlets making,
> Comes silent flooding in the main.

Of her thirty-three years in religious life, thirty were spent in the comparative obscurity of Roehampton, and the last three in journeys round the world. " Having made a beautiful thing," wrote Fr. Roche, " God took her as it were by the hand and led her through His world for all to see." But that which all saw, and which won their love and admiration was the outcome of her thirty years of hidden life. A life like that of many others in the religious state, filled with duties and interests common to all whose lives are consecrated to God. It was in these years and by these means that she had become " joined unto Our Lord in everlasting love."

She had entered the Society of the Sacred Heart with the fixed determination to lead a perfect life, and that determination never faltered. But unlike so many seekers after sanctity, she realized, as she wrote, that " surrender in daily life is the solution of the great problem : how is my soul to get to God." She never waited for the great occasion, for the magic word, the magic hour or thought which would change all things and land her in the embrace of God ! " We are so earthly minded," she wrote, " that we are a long time before we stop looking for something great ; yet see God's choice of means to His great ends— the matter of the Sacraments ; the trivial apparent chances of word or act that make a hinge, and turn the direction of whole lives."

She gave all, as she said to another setting out on the same path, " and went in for death or life or whatever God might choose." And this, wrote Abbot Marmion, is the whole of sanctity.

God's choice of the path by which each soul shall reach Him is His own secret. As in the Easter Apparitions, He comes in a different guise to every one. " We know so little of what each one's secret is," wrote Mother Stuart, " ours to ourselves is everything . . . Every friendship with God and every love between Him and a soul is the only one of its kind . . . A unique relationship—love, friendship, prayer, union, whatever you choose to call it, and in this unique relationship *quis nos separabit.*"

But though no one can fathom another's secret, and write the history of their spiritual life, we can see how three great virtues were conspicuous in that of Mother Stuart : Faith, Hope and Charity, and these as the Catechism tells us are those which unite us most completely to God. " Those elemental forces of our souls," wrote Mother Suart, " by which we hold on to God are according to the teaching of the Catechism Faith, Hope and Charity. Beyond all controversy, beyond all human understanding, all human will-power (without the help of grace) these fundamental acts of the soul attach us to God, and this attachment to Him is the one thing necessary . . . Faith is the light of our life. That which gives it what we all long for above everything—certainty . . . Not a certainty that is exempt from difficulties, but one that glories in them. The act of Faith is the daring, willing venture of the soul out of sight of land ; an act of the will supreme over the restive mind."

Boundless is the horizon of the soul that lives by faith. " It makes us treat with realities, when we only see the symbols." And describing the fruits of a strong Faith, she drew her own portrait. " . . . As faith strengthens and matures," she said, " the mind becomes singularly hopeful, tender, patient about human things. It finds no stumbling blocks in the frailties of fellow Christians, no astonishment in failure or scandals, but persists in seeing the good, the hopeful, the victorious, the eternal . . . and in finding Our Lord through every disguise."

Hope she called the victory of our life. It must be she said not only firm, but large and glorious and full of expectations of the knowledge and life we shall have when we see God face to face. When as she wrote to another " all crooked things will go right, and the word will come into the riddle and the key into the puzzle, and we shall be so delighted to think that it was right all along and that we trusted Him when things were darkest and most incomprehensible."

Ten years after her death a very beautiful appreciation of Mother Stuart appeared in the *Messenger of The Sacred Heart*, in a series of papers by Fr. Mangin, S.J., entitled Studies in Saintship. The following passages which speak of her Hope and Charity have been taken from it.

" Mother Stuart was a woman born to rule . . . Yet her danger was self-distrust. Fostered, this weakness might have wrecked all ; combated, it gave to her soul an unusual degree of confidence in God, and to her intercourse with others a simplicity and sympathy which won all hearts. ' Human ' said someone, ' was the word that best described her.' This note of humanity, a singular appreciation and love of every human creature, is the dominant note of her character. She was a great administrator, a great educator, with a mind at once daring, original and disciplined ; a tireless worker also ; but the manifestation of God through her, remains the manifestation of His Infinite Goodness.

"The spirit of her letters too breathes every hope and courage and cheerful confidence in God. . . . ' There must be pain and doubt and insoluble difficulties,' she wrote, ' but as the screws said to the rivets, when the ship was straining in a gale : In case of doubt, hold on ! Wait for God to explain Himself in Eternity. It would be childish to think that we could understand in time. But never let go of the belief that He is the All-Good.' Her hope and patience were indefatigable. . . . But the greater the love, the more protracted and trustful the patience, so much deeper was the pain of disappointment at failure and ingratitude. . . .

" Here it is, in the deepest difficulty of her practice of charity, that we strike the source from which it sprang. ' The Charity of Christ presseth us.' He had given Himself so entirely to them, she wrote of Our Lord and His Disciples, ' that their failure did not disturb His affection for them. He looked beyond it.'

"And in a letter written some years earlier, her method of working is plainly shown : ' As to loving many people, I think the point of the problem comes in the question : From loving many people shall I not rise to loving God ? And I think the answer is, no ; very few people can manage it that way . . . But from loving God alone I can get intuitions of Him in everyone and then love them, and have them in

my heart and not only in my eclectic head, with a very high priced
ticket of admission ' . . . One facet only of her many-sided character,
one virtue only of her strong and gifted soul has been presented here.
But since God is love, and His new Commandment is that we should
love one another as He has loved us, it is the most Christ-like, and
therefore the most attractive of her virtues.   And she bears for us this
further comfort, that assuredly God cannot have abandoned the
country from which even in our own time He has raised so faithful
a servant and so rare an image of His all-embracing Goodness."

When Mother Stuart died she had indeed a vast concourse of friends,
the members of her own Society and many more with whom, from her
position and her world-wide travels, she had come in contact.   But
since that time she has made her way to countless others who had never
heard of her in life.   Some of their testimonies to her influence are
gathered here.

Priests, religious of many Orders, men and women in different
paths in life, and in places far apart, have united in declaring that
she has been to them a channel of God's Grace.

" As one reads her wise and witty sayings," wrote Canon Burton,
" how the memory of St. Thomas More arises in the mind.   Surely
she was spiritually akin to him, as he is summed up by the Church in
the collect for his festival : *hilari fortique animo crucem tuam amplecti
tribuisti*.   Gaiety, strength and always the Cross."

A well-known Benedictine having been brought by a friend, a priest
likewise, to visit Roehampton, wrote to him : " It was very good of
you to spend time in showing me the home of Mother Digby and
Mother Stuart.   I have had a great reverence for both of them ever
since I read their lives and especially for the latter.   Of Mother
Stuart, what you said, is, I am sure true, that she was one of the
very greatest women of her time, even judged by a merely human
standard."

" The world might go a thousand years and not produce the equal
to Mother Stuart, a wonderful personality and a singularly lovable
woman," wrote a Jesuit, and another added : " Her life not only
gives a perfect exposition of religious life, but is the most complete
exposition of Catholic spirituality in England since the reformation."
These words were re-echoed from America where more than one priest
recommended her spirituality as being, said one, " the best to be found
in the Church in the present day."

" Mother Stuart helped me more that I can say in my retreat,"
wrote a priest in London, and his words were echoed from many other
places.   From India a missioner wrote asking for a copy of her life :
" I shall soon be making my retreat.   Last time I had the help of
Mother Stuart, but in this poor mission we have got no such book."

" *Non est similis illi*," wrote a Franciscan Father. " I won't make any other comment, but simply say with St. Francis of Sales : ' I will do something.' "

As might have been expected many of these new friends of Mother Stuart have been found among those whose lives, like her own were consecrated to God.

" I have had a great treat during my illness : the *Life of Mother Stuart !* " wrote the Abbess of a contemplative Order. " What can I say to give you to understand how I love her. No wonder that Our Lord ' longed for her.' She was surely the most beautiful and perfect soul of her generation. While she lived I was never privileged to have a word from her. *Now* I do, and I think she knows how I love her . . . I have never felt so at home, and so one with anyone for ages."

From a number of letters from Poor Clare Convents in many parts of the world, the following may be quoted : " I cannot tell you the benefit I have derived personally from the perusal of your late Mother General's biography, nor how it is urging me to live my own life as a Poor Clare Colettine with increased fervour and inwardness."

From a lonely missioner in Calabar, who had asked that the writings of Mother Stuart might be sent to help her, as she was so far away, the following word of appreciation came : " I want to tell you all the consolation and profit that I got from *Mother Stuart's Life and Letters.* I have read it again and again and always with new joy. How good God was to give her to you and *to us all.*"

" When I was a young Mistress at X," wrote a member of an Order devoted to teaching, " a priest made me a present of *Mother Stuart's Education of Catholic girls.* The book made a great impression on me and I often wished I could have met its author, but this happiness never fell to my lot. I feel I have met her now, and the meeting, which has been an unmixed spiritual joy came to me in the reading of her life . . . When I read and re-read it I feel I shall not need another spiritual-reading book for years ! The spirituality is so strong and so true, so far reaching and so practical . . . When you are kneeling by dear Mother Stuart's grave . . . pray sometimes for one who will always love and revere her as a great religious and a friend of Heaven's choosing and giving."

But it is not only, nor even chiefly among priests and religious that Mother Stuart has found new friends. Going through the highways and the byways of the world she has gathered many round her. Some say, they owe to her the grace of conversion to Catholicism, and many have found in her words, help and comfort to bear the daily wear and tear of life.

A nurse, a convert to Catholicism writes : " For several years I was stationed at the West London Hospital, and I have spent hours on the flat roof of the nurses' home that overlooks the Convent grounds. I used to watch the nuns, and in my ignorance, I pitied them for their enclosed life . . . The first Catholic book I ever read was the *Life of Mother Stuart.* I was thrilled by it. I read about her death over and over again, and I had a longing to go and pray at her tomb in Roehampton. I thought the nuns would not admit a Protestant, and anyhow I was down here at B., so I used to say every day : Mother Stuart pray for me. I had no knowledge of the Catholic dogma of prayer, either to or for the dead, and I was not used to saying prayers at all worth the name, so I didn't know why I did it or what I wanted. But within 18 months I was under instruction."

In an office in a factory in a foreign land another friend appeared. A convert to the Church, she wrote : " During the days of my conversion I had no troubles of any kind, they all came afterwards . . . One day when it was very dark all round me—inside me just as well, I bought a book which does wonderful things for me, and always does, the more I read it . . . It is the German translation of the book of your beloved Mother Janet Stuart . . . I can never say what happiness it has brought me . . . If I am unhappy, grumbling about my destiny, furious with the whole world ! I have just to read a few lines and I get another view. She must have been the most wonderful person, and I think we never can learn enough from her . . . I would recommend the book to every person who has any religious troubles . . . If you could perhaps give me the titles of the books she has written personally . . . I would be so thankful to you . . . I know there are other good books, but I like, before all, her style." Then having spoken of some special anxieties of the moment, she added, " I need therefore distractions, and where could I get better ones than in the books of dear Mother Stuart . . . If you have a photo of her would you send one to me please. She would always remind me that with good will . . . we can get holy."

From the United States one among numbers of testimonies may be given, that of a person who described herself as " one of those tired mothers, who have no leisure, excepting at the end of a long day . . . Mother Stuart came into my life just when I needed her most . . . About four years ago I had the joy of reading her life . . . daily she is in my mind and in my heart always . . . Have you for distribution a picture or leaflet, a prayer perhaps of hers that I may have . . . Spiritually I am very needy and perhaps your reply will be the closest I can ever be to your beloved Janet Stuart . . . At present we, like thousands of others are going through a terrible ordeal, trying to live, trying to be hopeful in a very hopeless world . . . You can understand why *Mother Stuart's Life* appealed so strongly to me and helped me. She taught me to have a mighty faith. And in face of the most discouraging circumstances, I wanted to be brave to the end. I wanted to think of Our Lord as the tender Shepherd as she did . . . A few days ago I received, from Roehampton, a package of the loveliest books by Mother Stuart. It was a joy I never dreamed of, it has been a breath of heaven to me . . . I can't help feeling that from her heavenly home Mother Stuart understands and is trying to help me . . . I never needed strength and guidance in all these past hard years as I did the day the books arrived . . . It was like a message from Mother Stuart herself."

From the other side of the world, the Editor of a paper in Manchuria wrote : " I was profoundly impressed by the greatness of Mother Stuart . . . It has given me much satisfaction to impress on friends and acquaintances the ' inspiration of the life,' in places as far apart as Denmark, Manchuria and India . . . In my own case the book is a constant companion, very much worn, having accompanied me round the world. I am sure that Mother Stuart herself would enjoy knowing that not only is my faith renewed and strengthened under her guidance, but I get an enormous amount of downright fun out of her enjoyment of life, which she found so constantly refreshing . . ." And when business brought this friend to England for a short time, he came to Roehampton to visit " the Chapel so intimately connected with Mother Stuart.

The next witness is called from, as she said : " out back in the Australian bush, far from church and spiritual counsel . . . By a great chance I was enabled to get the loan, from a friend, of *Mother Stuart's Life.* Before I returned it I read it three times . . . Will you pray for me and mine and ask her to take us under her special protection once for all." Then referring to some passages in Mother Stuart's letters she added : " if unfortunately I have not the pleasure to be a friend of either yours or hers, I would like to be. If you can spare me any of her booklets I would deem it a very great favour, for I am sure my spiritual life would gain by it . . . please ask her to guide my mind so as to enable me to make the best of her advice."

And yet another traveller on the upward path wrote to a friend, " What a beautiful soul was hers. Such intellectual gifts coupled with the most fragrant humility. It left me breathless with admiration and quite fired with a desire to start afresh by being good in little things, obedience, selflessness, charity."

" One feels assured," wrote a Jesuit, " that there is not an unbeliever however bigoted who, if he made acquaintance with these letters of Mother Stuart, permeated with religion though they are, would not pay tribute to the spell they exercise." And it is a fact that Mother Stuart has won countless friends outside the Church.

" Dear friend of many years ago," writes one of these, " I feel I

must write to you because I seem to have been so near to Roehampton
for the last two weeks. You will wonder why, until I say that I have
been reading the *Life of Mother Stuart*, and cannot remember any other
book, except the Bible, which has given me such joy and inspiration
and a wonderful vision of holy things. Will you forgive a ' heretic '
for saying this ? As 'I read and re-read the book, I never felt an out-
sider—the Mother's great, loving heart seemed big enough to take
in all the world, to overstep barriers and separation in the glorious
sweep of her love for Christ."

Another Anglo-Catholic writing to ask permission to visit Mother
Stuart's grave added : " I am, like many others, one who has found
enormous and continual help from her writings and her life, and
feel that I should like so much to make a little pilgrimage to her old
home and resting place. I am afraid you think me a heretic, but I
assure you I am not a heretic about that great lady."

And another sending a thanks offering for Mother Stuart's teaching
said : " She has shown me how my life (not the one I would have
chosen) can be lived to the glory of God."

I lent the life to X, an Anglican, wrote one who had known Mother
Stuart, and she wrote as follows to thank me : " My gratitude to you
for lending me Mother Stuart's life is very real. I soaked myself
in the book all through the last days of Holy Week and Easter, and
I really think that was largely why it was the happiest Easter inside,
that I can remember. . . . Though, of course, one is used to looking
up to see the top of the ladder, from very low down on it, to see the
Saints, she made me feel that, with all my straining, I was only
looking up from the very bottom rung, and that the top was hidden
in luminous clouds. Mother Stuart is so delightful too—intellect,
humour, and that wonderful freedom to be individual, that comes
with perfect surrender and correspondence with grace. A tide of
wonder and abasing admiration swept through and over me." And
when this reader passed the book on to another member of her Church
it was with the words : " I am afraid it will make you feel that those
Romans have got something we have not."

Another member of the Church of England, far away in Africa
wrote : " having read the *Life of Janet Stuart*, I am most anxious to get
her various published works." And when obliged to return to England
for some weeks she wrote again : " I am not a Catholic, but I have
found Mother Stuart's writings so very helpful in the spiritual life,
that I would appreciate greatly this opportunity to pay a visit to
Roehampton." And having returned to Africa, when Mother
Stuart's anniversary came round in 1937, flowers came from London
by order from South Africa : " In memory of and in gratitude for
Mother Stuart."

As in her earthly life, so also in her heavenly life, her interests have been universal. These are but a few of the many testimonies received. They unite in declaring that she has been, as Cardinal Bourne foretold she would ever be to those who knew her " a strong and holy influence in their lives."

JOHN GIBBONS

THE VERY NOBLE THE VISCOUNT
CHARLES DE FOUCAULD

A.D. 1858–1916

THERE ARE WHOLE books upon this thing in different languages, big books, scholars' books. It is not a light task, then, for a man with my sins of carelessness and flippancy to try to compress within a few thousand words a Life which may possibly one day come in calendars as that of a Saint of the Catholic Church. If in a volume full of the names of famous writers I dare attempt this story at all, then it is because of a particular reason. For once I got a commission for a book on the French Foreign Legion, and I went to North Africa and even got ever such a little way into the desert itself. And there on four separate occasions amongst the legionaries, not usually accounted as men of any very startling piety, I heard the name of Père de Foucauld and always with the greatest possible honour and almost reverence. I even got as far as Taghit, one of the little desert forts that was particularly famous in his story.

It is one of the most marvellous stories in the world, and now I know a little about it. And let us begin with 15 September, 1858, and the birth of Charles Eugène de Foucauld. That was at Strasbourg, but the family really came from the south. Genealogists have worked the pedigree out back to the time of the Crusades. It was a noble family with generation after generation of fighting men, and his father was the Vicomte which young Charles became at the age of six. Actually the Republic, of course, grants no titles ; but it does recognize the patents of the old nobility as being part of their surnames, and it is still something to be a Vicomte of France. Charles was a wealthy one at that, and, of course, he had to follow the family tradition and go into the army. He was a young officer of hussars, and a very dashing young officer. St.-Cyr military college means nothing particular to me, because I have never been there ; but I was interested when I read that he had passed through Saumur, where I have been. It is the cavalry riding-school of the French army, and one has to be rather a picked man to be sent there ; it's the place that turns out the sort of teams which we see at international horse-shows, those men who apparently ride up the side of a house.   When one has been at Saumur, in fact, one does not hold on by one's horse's ears !

Then Lieutenant Charles was not a very virtuous young officer, and perhaps he had come into too much money too young.   Would he in the '70s be an " exquisite " or a " dandy " ?   He had to have his own brand of cigars especially imported for him, and it was the same with everything else.   There was too much card-playing, too many (shall we say ?) lady-friends.   Even in the hussars one can be over-dashing, and his military superiors were not pleased with him ; in fact the famous Père de Foucauld of the future was quite often under officers' arrest, and the champagne parties had to be held in his own quarters.   There was worse, with a serious scandal when the young hussar was openly flaunting one special lady much too publicly for even the not particularly squeamish etiquette of the army ;   and would he kindly get rid of the lady, or would he in short be " broke " ?   And the grave seniors of his family with centuries of soldiers' honours behind them shook their heads ;   wild oats should have a limit, and the wise and prudent French Law was appealed to for the appointment of a guardian.   " It is true that you have so many thousands a year," they said, " but it had better pass through the account of the family solicitor ;   he will know how to check these bills for diamond bracelets and the like."   And so life became a little more serious.

Next there was Africa, and the young gentleman's particular hussars had now somehow turned into the famous Chasseurs d'Afrique, those people with the wonderful horses and with the *musique* with the pride and glory of the kettle-drums.   But now there was no more extravagance and folly ;   this was soldiering, and soon there was the desert.   This North Africa must have been to the France of the earliest 1880's something like the Cecil Rhodes Africa to our England of the '90's, and here was a whole new world of Empire to be reached out for by the strong of heart.   And now the ex-dandy of the scandals of the garrison-towns is leading real men in an expedition down in the then uncharted *Sud.*   This was what an army was for, and here were the burning sands of the wilderness and nights of a gigantic silence that terrified and appealed at the same time.   This Africa which he was seeing now, with its solitudes and its unbelievable hardships, was something which was to colour the whole future life of the young officer.   It is queer, but in one of his letters he refers to the men whom he was leading, rough troopers who would go anywhere and put up with anything ;   and they might, he says, in their discipline and self-sacrifice have been monks.

Very soon, however, he was an ex-officer.   The expedition was successfully over, and it was inconceivable to think of a return to garrison life. What about going through Morocco, the unknown parts where nobody had ever been before, and making a survey of it? What about, say, a year's officers' leave, and he would pay his own expenses? But France said " No "; and probably his early record wasn't much recommendation. In that case if there was no more fighting for the moment, he would throw in his commission and be a civilian and still serve France. And Charles de Foucauld started off on one of the very great journeys of modern exploration-history.

What he actually did and exactly where he went comes in all the learned books on North Africa, and this and that Geographical Society voted their highest honours and their gold medals for the business. Take it here that he went through the unexplored part of Morocco when it was still the Forbidden Empire of the 1880's and when a European Christian if caught would have been tortured to death. In his planning of the journey he was helped by an extraordinary old Irishman called Oscar MacCarthy whom he found in Algiers. MacCarthy had spent nearly all his life in North Africa, he knew more than any other white man about the Moors, he had himself been to extraordinary places, and this particular journey through still more extraordinary places had been a dream of his for years. But he had never done it; he had not had the money or the strength. Now here was a young man with both; let him share the old man's knowledge. The two settled down together to plot out the details of that incredible journey. In the end, De Foucauld went through as a Jew. He had to have his skin dyed and to be instructed in all sorts of customs of eating and drinking and everything else; he had to be dressed in filthy rags of the proper colour prescribed for a Jew to wear, he had to take his shoes off to walk through a Moslem village, he had to be prepared to be spat on by any Moor who met him and he had to learn to cringe convincingly. Perhaps worst of all, he had to live with his Jews. Now I have had Jewish friends, of course, just as probably many of my Catholic readers have also had Jewish friends; but they have not been Moroccan Jews! Those people are something like human rats. And then with it all, De Foucauld did exactly as he planned and went precisely where he had intended to go. Eleven months and three days that journey took, with one man's courage and endurance and resource matched against a barbarous and bitterly hostile nation; and for every single minute of all that time he was in danger of mutilation and death. He did it rather on the lines of the man in our Kipling's *Kim*, making his secret survey-notes at night for the better guidance and glory of his France, and his *Reconnaissance au Maroc* stands out as one of the geographical land-marks of his age. Even the Moors, the very people whose country he had penetrated, had their word about him

as at least a man in a million for bravery.   Years later and when
the explorer had changed into something like the Saint, there came a
Moor's letter to the Algiers garrison with an address mis-spelt to
" *L'Officier Foukou.*"   There were those, it seemed, who had not
forgotten that trip.

But is not this volume titled *Great Catholics*, and when is
there any Catholic part ?   So far there had not been much !   That
boy had been brought up by a good Catholic mother, and in fact in
earliest childhood had shown signs of a more than usual piety.   But
the signs had vanished, and with youth and young manhood there
had succeeded a blank nothingness.   It was not that he just neglected
ever to go to church ;   it was that he believed in nothing.   There was
Glory, perhaps, and of course France ;   but for the rest De Foucauld
was a professed infidel.   And then something happened.   Perhaps
it was due to that mother's prayers ;   perhaps the seeds of Catholic
childhood were not quite withered after all.   Or was it an effect
of that awful trip through Morocco, and De Foucauld mentions
it himself.   He had been so " alone," he puts it.   The Mohammedans
had their religion, and the humble Hebrews were spat at for having
theirs and then still kept it ;   and he who was liable to torture and
death as a Christian had nothing at all.   In this sort of short summary
it is probably impossible to go too deeply into spiritual motives.
Better put it, perhaps, that Something Happened.   Put it that Charles
de Foucauld returned to the Practice of the Faith which he had so
long and so grievously neglected.   Say simply, if you like, that he
" Got Religion."

He got it very thoroughly !   Here is an old French priest, and
here is a man in his confessional but not kneeling down ;   he has
not come to confess, he says, but to be told how To Believe.   " Kneel
Down," the priest says, and the man protests ;   that is not what he
had come for, and can he not be first instructed ?   " Kneel," says
the priest ;   and he wins.   Then we find a Jesuit Father as Director,
and at another period there is Solesmes Abbey and a effort to test a
Benedictine Vocation.   He tried three great Orders, and it is significant that the silence of the Trappists came nearest to his soul's ideal.
Hard to please, wasn't he, the gay young man turned suddenly pious
and wanting to pick and chose his own way of salvation !   But it
wasn't really so at all.   His great biographer gives up scores of pages
and many chapters to reports and letters written about him by this
great Abbot or that famous Superior, and they all say much about
the same thing.   Here is a man of exceptional grace and of positively
heroic humility and obedience.   He himself is only too painfully
anxious to be told what to do, and it is his Superiors who are in doubt.
This man is plainly marked out by God Almighty for some great duty,

he is clearly set apart for some special path. Only what path ? And could it be the Holy Land? De Foucauld had visited it between his explorations of Morocco and of Religion, and had found a consolation in it ; for it had the solitudes and silences of his beloved Africa, and it was, besides, a land which was Holy. And now as Brother Marie-Albéric of the Trappist Obedience, monk but not priest, professed but not yet under permanent vows, he is begging for permission to be sent out there again. There is a Trappist House in Syria, and can he be transferred ? He is transferred.

Now he is leaving the Trappists altogether, and how do I get it on paper without giving all the wrong impression ? This is not the discontented would-be Religious, trying Rule after Rule and satisfied by none. This is a rare soul, almost a soul apart, and recognized as such by Trappists, Jesuits, Franciscans, and everybody else he comes in contact with. Everyone is anxious to help. Here is a wonderful instrument for God in the forging. If only his humility can be overcome. They are discussing him in Rome itself, and there is a report of a Trappist Superior. Fifty years professed, he has never yet " met with a soul so entirely given to God." Now before the irrevocable life-vows are taken, the man leaves the Trappists and he is back in Palestine again as a layman. There is a silence and a sanctity in the Holy Land ; this man wants to be quiet and to think. He wants to be alone, but he is never going to be lonely as he once had been ; for he wants to be alone with God and learn His Will. He has ideas of his own ; can he use his private fortune, untouched for so long, to purchase from the Turkish Government the Mount of Beatitudes and erect an oratory on it ? It would be a kind of lighthouse of salvation ; perhaps he himself might be a hermit-priest to serve the altar. Always the idea of the Hermit ! Always the Solitude and the Hidden Life ! But, of course, his ideas must be guided by God ; that plan was impossible, and so God had meant " No." Now he is living as servant to the Poor Clares at Nazareth, an odd-job man mending walls, feeding chickens, running errands. There is an old shed for him at the bottom of the field, and M. le Vicomte is beginning to be happy ; Nazareth is a very holy place, and he has the freedom of the nuns' chapel and time to think.

Now the great decision is made. He is a priest at last, and has permission, extra-special exceptional permission from Rome, to be a very extra-special sort of priest, a Solitary in the Sahara. Here is an extract from one of the many high-ecclesiastical letters about him, and in a way it sums up the old life and points to the glories of the new.—" Monsieur le Vicomte Charles de Foucauld, long a lieutenant in the African Army, then an intrepid and skilful traveller in Morocco, then a novice with the Trappist Fathers in Syria, afterwards devoted

to the service of the Poor Clares of Nazareth, lastly received Holy
Orders and the priesthood.   You will find in him heroic self-sacrifice,
unlimited self-endurance, a vocation to influence the Mussulman world.
—Never have I seen such prodigies of penance, humility, poverty,
and of the Love of God."

Now he is back in his Africa at last.   I have used half my space,
and the story is just going to begin.

May we for a moment consider the Grand Sahara, three thousand
miles from east to west and, say, a thousand miles from north to
south.   There are oases, of course, where the roots of almost shadeless
palm-trees can tap the moisture of some underground stream ; but
for the most part it is desert, an infinity of either sand or of sand with
patches of black rock.   It is an uncannily queer country, with sand-
dunes that are often hundreds of feet high standing up against the
intolerable blue of the African sky ; and with the wind those miniature
mountains can move.   The moistureless and over-heated air gives
a clarity of view in which it is possible to see for many miles, though
with odd distortions ; but for many miles there is nothing to see,
neither road nor tree nor anything at all to break that terrifying mono-
tone of sheer space.   Somewhere in the furthest distance of that arid
awfulness might seem to be some stream or pond ; but really it is
only the sun reflecting unevenly from burnished and almost red-hot
rock.   There is no water.   The traveller caught unprepared would
just die.   The sun would be dangerous to a European by perhaps
ten o'clock in the morning, and by high noon it would mean death ;
to get anywhere at all he must start his journey by possibly five in
the morning.   There are, however, no European travellers in the
ordinary way ; one cannot enter the Sahara except by permission
of the French military authorities, and permission will not be readily
given.   It is too expensive ; the traveller will probably break down,
and aeroplanes or cavalry will have to be sent to his rescue.   Let the
traveller deposit so many thousands of francs in advance to make
an insurance that will help pay for the rescue party.   He may quite
likely need a military escort, too, and the garrison headquarters will
radio so many scores of native irregular horsemen to stand ready to
protect his route.   Against whom ? Against Arabs.   One is never
sure with that desert ; it looks so empty, but there may be fifty men
hidden behind those rocks.   Every Arab will have a rifle.   The
soldiers may not be able to find the rifles ; they may perhaps be
buried in the dry sand.   But they are there somewhere, and the
Arabs will know where to find them.

But, of course, I have only seen the fringe of the circumference of the desert, and perhaps it was only a hundred kilometres or say sixty miles that I was taken by very special permission and under very careful escort.   The Père de Foucauld country was five hundred miles deeper into the Sahara ! And he had no escort.   Indeed there was no communication at all when he first went there, though France later on set up a monthly courier ; the ultimate boast was that official telegrams could be delivered within twenty-two days.   Tamanrasset is where Fr. Charles went, and it is fairly remote ! It is in the Tuareg country.   The Tuaregs are the " Veiled Men " of the romances, and there are all kinds of legends about them.   Probably, however, nobody really quite knows who they are.   They are not Arabs or Moors ; they are possibly the descendants of the pre-Arab aboriginals of North Africa driven down here to their last strong-point.   They are nominal Mohammedans, but with their distinctive customs.   They are a slave-owning people, of course, but with their own system of slave-tribes ; which means anybody whom they are able to conquer. Their slavery is probably the most horrible in the world, and even amongst the Arabs, themselves not a particularly humanitarian people, the Tuaregs are known as " The Merciless," and their treatment of the boys and young women of the conquered tribes cannot possibly be set down in English print.   There are comparatively few travel-books with any genuine account of a race so remote and so dangerous, but Mr. W. B. Seabrook, the American travel-author, says that the most dreadful and unspeakable thing in the whole modern world is the slave trade which works some salt mines somewhere down in the Sahara.   Those are, of course, Tuareg slaves.   In a short summary it seems impossible and unnecessary to say more about them, except perhaps that another native name for them is the " Abandoned of God."   And except that these were the people amongst whom Père de Foucauld chose to make his home.

Now this part of the story is hardest to write, and probably nobody but a religious could properly explain it at all.   Père de Foucauld had no idea of being a missionary in the ordinary way ; there were the Pères Blancs for that, the White Fathers of Africa doing their own wonderful work.   Father Charles was different ; he was not to teach or preach in the ordinary sense of those words.   He was less to do some-thing than to be something, a Solitary leading a certain life which would open the door to an Inner Life with God ; and God would do the rest.   His " parish," he said, had 100,000 souls ; and actually with the oases there are far more people in the Sahara than the old maps showed.   Prayer was something that literally worked, every Mass was a spiritual dynamo.   Come, let us light up the dark places ! Who served the Mass, then ? Inconceivable as it sounds, there nearly always was somebody.   He was learning the Tuareg language, and was beginning to make converts without asking for them. There were soldiers, odd men in odd outposts. That is not the Foreign Legion of the films, and really there are plenty of decent men in it. There are practising Catholics even in the Legion, and there are more men who are nominal Catholics. Could not one try to remember the Responses to Mass which one learned as a boy and before life went wrong? This ex-officer, ex-nobleman, living on starvation diet and putting up with worse than any legionary for the sake of his God, mightn't one make an effort to oblige him and serve his Mass? It was a miracle, but almost always even in the desert there was somebody.

If ever there was proof of the force of example, Père de Foucauld lived that proof. Seven francs a month he allowed himself to live on ; at pre-war rate, say five-and-threepence. What need of more than bread and water and a few dates? His Lord of the Blessed Sacrament of the Altar (for which he had special authority for Reservation), had He lived sumptuously? And when the Legion officers so to speak sent the hat round that an ex-comrade might at least have enough to eat, he smilingly acknowledged the money and would be grateful for more. It came in beautifully for buying slaves from the Tuaregs ; perhaps they turned into catechumens, or at worst the poor creatures were a little happier. Wasn't life wonderful? His personal fortune, however, he wouldn't touch, and really he disposed of most of it to relations. Our Lady of Nazareth, had she any private income to draw on? Only once in all those years did Father Charles touch his own money. That was years later when he visited France and took with him the son of a Tuareg chief. Then the man who had lived on fifteen pence a week must travel first-class and with all that money could buy ; it must be *de luxe*, and he must stop at the château of this and that old friend. For here is a soul which will be able to influence other souls ; this African must be impressed by the glories of the country of the Christians.

Meantime here was Père de Foucauld in his desert, gorgeously happy at last. He was living a kind of strict monastic Rule, only all by himself, sleeping on the earth and starting his prayers in the middle of the night. And it was working! The Tuaregs were coming in ! Yes, one knows the usual scoff ; that the slightly insane, the " Afflicted of God," are treated with respect. But it wasn't so. They were calling him the Christian Marabout, the " Good Man " ; they came to his tiny home-made church to see what kind of a God could fashion a man like that. By and by that church even boasts a real bell. Back on Oran quay over a thousand miles away is a huge barrel consigned to Père de Foucauld down in the desert, and of course it must be altar-wine. What a pity ! With the heat of the interminable journey it will all go sour. And from rail-head for hundreds of desert miles the Legion outposts, the Devil-May-Cares of Hollywood Heroics, are sparing a little of their precious water to damp that cask and keep it cool. Then it isn't wine, but a bell sent by some admirer in France. Father Charles is getting famous.

Even in Tuareg social circles he was becoming a notable! He knew more than any other white man of the language and customs. He was translating the Holy Scriptures ; for light recreation he was compiling a Tuareg dictionary. Those people had their princes of a sort, and he knew them and himself ranked as a kind of chief and adviser. He even found and translated such Tuareg poetry as there was ; but it must never be published in Paris under his name. Had Our Lord written books for publicity ? Very well, then ! And when the troops advanced so many more leagues and built a new *poste* and meant to call it " Fort de Foucauld," Father Charles with his terrible and uncompromising Latin logic forbade that too.

France recognised him, of course, and the great people were his friends. There was Marshal Lyautey as his staunch admirer ; he could have a cavalry escort any time from this place to that. But no ! That one needs no escort ; he can walk alone where a regiment could never go. There was Colonel Laperrine, one of the tremendous figures of the *Sud*, and as a cadet he had been at the Academy with Father Charles ; he never followed him into religion, but he was his life-long friend. That was the man who tried the first aeroplane flight across the desert ; the thing crashed and drove his ribs through his pulped body. They were trying to bring him back, carrying him by day and camping every night. The army of Africa has a discipline, and each night the colonel punctiliously drew his ration of water ; but when it was dark he put it back into the common supply, for he knew himself a dying man. That was the man who was the great friend of Father Charles. There was a camel he once sent him, and the priest was most grateful ; it was the very thing wanted to carry some altar furniture to a new oratory in the still remoter desert. What a fine chance, too, for a little joyous penance for sins of a life-time back. Some of those camels can go quite fast, and of course a man can always run behind the beast.

Did Père de Foucauld ever stop belonging to the African army in his spirit ? And one suspects that at the back of the human part of his mind he always remained a soldier. Here in his " parish " were those hundred-thousand souls to be recruited for the standard of Christ the Captain ; the Sahara was Satan's citadel, something to be stormed with many Masses, besieged with infinite prayer. Certainly he was a soldiers' priest, almost a soldiers' idol. There was his famous ride to Taghit, and down in Africa the story has passed almost into legend. That place is a *poste*, the first fort in the real desert. Over the gateway is a stone, and it says that—Here the Undermentioned, so many men of such-and-such a company under Captain So-and-So, such-and-such another company and so forth, they held out for four days against six thousand armed Moors. There were four hundred and seventy of that garrison. At the start. Then when the news reached Beni-Abbes, nothing would serve Père de Foucauld but that he must borrow a horse and go to Taghit at once. It is seventy-five miles; but desert miles. And he was off on the instant without an escort. It took twenty-three hours, and he was in time to find forty-nine wounded still alive. He remained twenty-five days in that fort and was given an officer's room and never once slept in it. The place of the chaplain of the Sahara was with his wounded.

That, by the way, was in 1903; and in 1935 I was visited in London by an old man carrying a brown-paper parcel. As a young man he had served in the Legion, he said, and he had tried to write out some of his memories; could I look at the manuscript and advise him how to get it printed? He had seen things. Yes, he had even seen Père de Foucauld. He had been one of the wounded in Taghit Fort when that one came riding in from his twenty-three hours' ride. That was at nine o'clock in the morning, and he did not take one single minute for rest or food or even drink. It was straight off his horse and in with the wounded. The old man was proud he had seen Père de Foucauld; it was something to remember. Certainly Father Charles was a soldiers' priest!

Certainly, too, he never stopped being a Frenchman. Indeed we are not sure that he did not die for being a Frenchman, for when his earthly story came to an end in 1916 he was murdered by unknown natives at his chapel in the Sahara. Now why? He had next to nothing to steal; he had no local enemies. But it was war-time; this man had more influence over the tribes than any other white man, and his influence was French. And one suggestion is that he was assassinated by hired agents of an enemy power. We do not know. An odd thing, however, is that while his two native catechumens were found later as skeletons, the body of Father Charles was said to be mummified. (*In Quest of Lost Worlds*, Count de Prorok.) "Incorrupt" is a word which we must not at present use of that body, but other people are wondering the same thing! The Saint of the Sahara, and will he one day be canonized?

There is one thing more to say. All those years in the desert, he had prayed for helpers; can we possibly say that he wanted a " Community " of Solitaries, men vowed to God? He had his Rule drawn up and approved, but there was nobody to share it. One man came out as a sort of disciple, an ex-zouave of the African army; zouaves are strong men, but that one failed to stand the severity of the life and had to go back and find another vocation. Father Charles was still alone. He had even prayed for Sisters, and outlined the marvellous work they might do under God. But of course it was impossible. No woman could go out there. It was all a glorious dream, and had Père de Foucauld failed ? He had done his life-work, and a marvellous work it had been. Was it now to die with him ?

And years later those prayers are answered. The miracle has come. There is an Order of " Brothers of the Solitude " and they are in the desert and living the Rule. There are even the Sisters, too, of the many prayers, not at present in the desert but praying and planning for the desert from a " Solitude " in France. Père de Foucauld's work is not dead but alive ; the Legion of the Lord is arming for the conquest of the Sahara.

Mine is the merest summary of the story, and is mostly taken from René Bazin's monumental biography. My information on the " Brothers of the Solitude " came first from an article by Miss Constance Davidson in the *Catholic Fireside*. Miracles still happen. I saw that article by accident, and when I wrote to the lady I found perhaps the only woman in Great Britain in touch with the French headquarters of those who are following up Père de Foucauld's work.

There are those who will read my story who will know far more about it than I do myself ; of them I would ask pardon for my omissions, and perhaps too for inconsequences and flamboyances which may have grieved them. But other readers will know as little of Père de Foucauld as I once did, and of them I would beg that they would go and find out more. Mine is only the outline. Go now, please, and read the real books.

If I apologize for even my outline, it is not in the least to make any " literary " finish, but because I know how sadly imperfect is my very summary of the story. It glosses over the important part, the spiritual part ; there is one place where into a paragraph or so I have condensed eight or nine years of life and a whole æon of spiritual voyage. To tell the truth, I am half sorry now that I ever undertook this story at all. The writing of it has frightened me. Really I am not sure that it may not be a kind of blasphemy for any common sinner to undertake the life of Père Charles de Foucauld, the Marabout of Christ.

FRANCIS THOMPSON

A.D. 1859–1907

A S WE LOOK back at the works of the great figures of the past it will sometimes give us a strange, and most painful shock if we realize how very few of them can be still said to live. A variety of interests may lead us to inquire into the circumstances relating to the person whose doings we wish to understand. But it is not often that this enquiry is facilitated by an equal amount of biographical incidents, or rewarded by a number of suggestive details.

Difficult as it is to appreciate at its true value contemporary endeavour—distance alone enables one to view things in the right perspective—very few of those for whom Francis Thompson possesses an appeal, will deny to him the title of genius or the adjective " great." The phrase " those for whom the poet possesses an appeal " is used advisedly, for there is no middle course with Thompson as there is none with Meredith. One must either possess the talisman that admits to his magnificence or stay outside. For many his magnificence is overpowering, his artistry, his involution, his inversion, his conceits, all act rather as irritants than attractions. But those who can follow him up to the heights, he rewards with wonderful gifts of sheer beauty and grandeur.

When Francis Thompson was living and writing, an understanding few valued and treasured the pure gems of poetry with which he was so lavish, but of the fact that a great force was working quietly in their midst the general reading public was unaware. Then came the merciful death, the finale of a life crowned rather with the thorn than with the laurel, and lo ! came the discovery that a poet in the direct line of English poetry had passed away. The sudden vogue of Francis Thompson is one of the curiosities of literature. Singing for some ten years to an audience few and fit, he then fell almost silent, and for another ten years produced nothing but occasional criticism, not always of much value. He wound up with his *Life of St. Ignatius Loyola*, a characteristic work of Pegasus in harness. Then the inexplicable thing happened. The English people discovered that there had been a prophet among them, a Popish prophet and therefore suspect, but a prophet, who had written—there was no telling when—one of the imperishable masterpieces of prophetic song. All the world was clamouring for a copy of the " Hound of Heaven," and no self-respecting preacher could go for a month without quoting from it.

G. K. Chesterton in his brilliant study of Victorian literature said that the spirit of it might well be described by saying that Francis Thompson stood outside it. Knowledge and appreciation of Thompson have widened during the last few years, but the present age is still unspiritual and antagonistic to the supernatural. Thompson's genius shed a new glory on Catholicism, and it should therefore be a duty as well as a delight for Catholics in particular to try to increase the fame and influence of the poet who sang :

> " the songs of Sion
> By the streams of Babylon."

There is no middle way of love with him, even as there is no middle way of love with Blake—whose *Songs of Innocence* were found in his pocket, together with Æschylus, when a timely hand was stretched to him adrift in the whirlpools of a cruel great city. And, indeed, the heart of the difference is deeper still.

One can imagine what would have been Francis Thompson's scornful amusement of sudden popularity had this happened before his death. Now—well, perhaps he is not too wise for scorn. While still capable of it, this avowed disciple of De Quincey—not in one thing only—was entirely without De Quincey's itch for notoriety. The little Opium-Eater was also scornful, but he demanded the very attention that he scorned. What Francis Thompson cared for was the attention of his friends. That he had ; and when they lost his presence, they suddenly found themselves called upon to share the memory of him with an army of discoverers. And one has not read Thompson rightly unless the memory of what he wrote comes with a strong and tender impulse to fill the whole of life, its thoughts, its efforts, and its desires, with the lilies of whiteness and of wisdom.

The setting of the sun, which moved him more deeply than any other sight of nature, is the true symbol of Thompson's life and poetry. The solemnity of evening invests all his utterance, but it is the solemnity of the sunset sky. His art in words is to be matched with Turner's. The poet, too, is a painter of skies, a sublime colourist. And as the sunset gathers up in a final pageant the day's light and glory, so Thompson reveals in his verse the infinite beauties of poetic utterance in the past. His sensitive ear has caught the floating harmonies of every age of song. He is most often compared with Crashaw, Herbert and others of their group. But if he is of the old school of Donne he is also of the school of Shakespeare, he is the disciple of Milton, the familiar of Pope and Dryden, in sympathy with the Lake poets, and a companion spirit with Shelley and Keats. The poet nearest to his own time with whom he has affinity is Coventry Patmore, and the direct inspiration which, we are told, he owed to the verse of Mrs. Meynell, is clearly discernible. Nor are his derivatives all of one civilization for Greek and Latin poets live in his diction. Withal, Thompson has the original authentic note of the great singer. In their poignancy his poems are the expression of his own life. Phœnix-like, they sprang from the ashes of his youth. To him more than to most poets the too-familiar lines may be applied :

" Most wretched men
Are cradled into poetry by wrong.
They learn in suffering what they teach in song."

It is easy to liken Francis Thompson's poetry to a cathedral. His frequent employment of dogmatical and liturgical figures makes such a reference unavoidable. Yet at the heart of it there is a similarity that is not quite so obvious, that has part of the same paradox even. For the zeal which built the cathedral at Milan was yet the same zeal as drove St. Francis to the ways of discipline. The two not only co-existed, they were part and lot of the same inspiration. So it was with Thompson. If he was content, nay, glad, that pain should prune his spirit, it did not follow that the towering wildness of his verse should be pruned in the same process. If he could bring the light of earth to a narrow focus in his own disciplined soul, it could then widen as broadly as it would on the further side in the spiritual realm.

Some are so dazzled and deafened and thrilled by the thronging pictures, the organ-blasts, the flute-notes, that they do not perceive the sadness and terror and glory of what is sung. Perhaps if our hearing and seeing were sharpened to notice one or two particulars of lesser importance, we might be less likely to content ourselves with a vague and profitless wonder at the magnificence of his imagination and language ; the wonder has its place, and will be increased when we perceive how that magnificence enhances or conflicts with a tremendous or austere burden. All through his few volumes appears the poet's own perception that his days are consumed and gone up in the smoke of sacrifice. But by some alchemy of the spirit his loss and misery were converted into the ethereal substance of art, and out of his poverty he enriched humanity. It is a fact of life and poetry that may give Eugenists pause.

For the many, for that large audience which has neither the scholarship nor the taste to hear the music of " a poet's poet,"

Thompson will live chiefly as a voice religious. He has, indeed, wrapped most of his utterance in diction which sets it apart from the narrower range of appreciation. The language of Milton is not further removed than Thompson's from the common speech of this day. In all but a few ballads and lyrics of almost Wordsworthian simplicity, Thompson adheres to his chosen vocabulary, the vocabulary of a man whose muse was nursed by a bygone literature. He uses words archaic, words obsolete, words coined from classical mints, and phrase-words of a rich invention—a vocabulary of which poets have the heritage and privilege, but such as passes slowly into the wider currency. And yet, in his highest expression of emotion, in the perfection of his form, this wealth of borrowed ornament is no veil between his thought and common understanding. His jewelled verse is like some old poem in stone, a Gothic temple, the secret of whose material loveliness is lost, but whose enshrined appeal to the springs of human feelings is instant and unchanging.

To use a metaphor, Francis Thompson's life resembles a telescope ; his life interest was focussed to a very small compass, but his vision was prolonged to an almost incredible extent. It is written : " Blessed is the people that knows its prophets before they die," yet *mutatis mutandis* the poet had a deep gratitude for the past, a love for the present, and faith in the future. Thompson was not left without the praise of those from whom it was worth having. On his coffin lay roses from Meredith's garden, with the testimony of the aged Titan, " A true poet, one of the small band." Previously Coventry Patmore heaped praise upon his work in the *Fortnightly*, H. D. Traill in the *Nineteenth Century ;* while Arthur Symons followed suit in the *Saturday Review* with the much quoted critique : " Other poets have deeper things to say, and a more flawless beauty ; others have put more heart into their song ; but no one has been a torch waved with so fitful a splendour over the gulfs of our darkness." A torch ! But let it be remembered that if a man has written one fine poem it is best to forget that he has written five hundred failures. There is a sense in which complete editions are the unkindest service that can be rendered to poets.

In the less eclectic space of a collected edition it is now possible to see the truth of this more clearly in Thompson's own work. If in the " Ode to the Setting Sun " his diction is somewhat feverish, as though the writer were not sure of expressing adequately the thing that he saw, or sought rather than affirmed it, the poem is yet saturated with his vision, and so, however one ranks it, it is stamped with his idiom ; whereas in " Of Nature : Laud and Plaint " the vision is gone ; the poet feels his way through the poem along the lines of cogitation and loses his title to poet thereby. That the cogitation itself should be none too satisfactory is only a small part of the trouble. The cogitation would have come right or would not have mattered if, as was his wont, the poet had been content to see steadily. His simplicity allied to exquisite art finds hardly more delicately beautiful expression than in the poem " To a Snowflake," which poem is, however, run very closely by the beautiful " Field Flower."

The Catholic has already been presented with one of the keys of his work, for his was essentially Catholic vision, and much of the high mystical beauty of his work is due to the Catholic basis on which it rests and to the analogies within it, drawn from Catholic faith and ceremonial. Others—many others—outside the faith have happily been enabled to climb with him, and have testified to the greatness of the man who was their guide.

In the highest sense all poets are religious in the precise degree of their poetry ; and in that affirmation Francis Thompson enrolled himself of their number. The fact that he sang his songs from the cave that so generously and nobly found him shelter when he was like to be destroyed in the storms without has not altogether served him well. Some have disparaged him as the poet of a circle ; others have thought of him as a " religious poet," meaning something between a poet proper and a hymn-writer. Whereas he was altogether of the wider company, having his place in the highway of the poets, with a fame that will increase when many more notable names have diminished in glory.

So, from those who share in this belief, a knowledge of Thompson comes weighted with moral and spiritual obligation beyond the duty which gratitude should hasten to fulfil of heightening his fame and of doing everything possible to ensure for posterity the mighty heritage of his work. Catholic lovers of Thompson should show the sincerity of their appreciation by reflecting in their lives the starry splendour of his message. In the " Motto and Invocation " to the prose volume, after a request for saints' assistance, comes this perfect little prayer :

> " Last and first, O Queen Mary,
> Of thy white Immaculacy,
> If my work may profit aught
> Fill with lilies every thought !
> I surmise
> What is white will then be wise ! "

And what can be said of the " Hound of Heaven " that could add anything to the tributes that acclaimed it upon its first publication ? Critics and poets—Coventry Patmore one of the latter—artists, Burne-Jones among others—hailed it with surprising unanimity, as the greatest religious poem in the language.

The main region of Thompson's poetry is the inexhaustible mine of Catholic philosophy, and never was a more splendid tribute paid to the theologians than is furnished by this shrinking, modest, diffident, and most eloquent disciple of the Muses. No one who has read, however cursorily, the "Hound of Heaven" has ever had a moment's doubt that the author is veritably a poet as well as a philosopher and a religious thinker. That he is also a mystic and a symbolist does not alter the estimate. Nor yet does his exhaustless vocabulary of abstract terms destroy his pretensions to be a thinker. In the one case, as in the other, the elemental bigness of the man overpowers all minor considerations or differences. We yield ourselves captive to his charm, and, as in the "Hound of Heaven," recognize with a certain awe that we are in the presence of a genius. The theme of the "Hound of Heaven" is the Divine pursuit of the sinner, the long struggle before the resisting soul acknowledges its final defeat. The everlasting arms are round the fugitive from the start to the finish ; but the human instinct to resist and preserve an obstinate independence has kept the sinner in his attitude of reluctance and refusal of God's mercies. The Hound who pursues is the abounding love which at the last overcomes all obstacles and welcomes the hunted soul to eternal peace.

Agonies of mortification are endured and even sought out by the spiritual athlete, not for their own sake, but because pain is known to be a condition of sanctity, as of all supreme attainment. To this *via dolorosa* succeeds the state of illumination, when mysterious gates are opened and a world of hidden things is made visible to a soul over which appearances have lost their power, thanks to the cleansing discipline that has prepared it for this revelation of the ultimate Reality. The true artist's resignation of prosperity and of happiness as common minds understand happiness is, like that of the saint, complete and irrevocable.

For mysticism usually appeals only to the very simple or to the very learned. You may become a mystic by communion with nature, and by cultivating a certain childishness of character. Thompson himself said "Look for me in the nurseries of Heaven." But it is also natural for the mystic to be extremely learned, and, indeed, to those who are not mystics the studies of the mystic seem to be the most recondite possible. To have read the Early Fathers is fantastic erudition. And learning has been lately the mystic's chief approach to the truths which he is bent on discovering, as the example of Yeats will show or of Lionel Johnson. Moreover, the proper understanding of a mystical poet is often an end to be reached in much the same way as the mystic reaches his truths, by elaborate historical researches which enable the student of a mystical poet to get within the minds of many past mystics and to put himself in their age, in an age when mysticism, so it would seem, was a natural and easy thing.   If we wish to understand a satirical poet it is not necessary to read Juvenal in order to appreciate the strange mind of a satirist, any more than it is necessary to read Darwin in order to understand the kind of mind which can believe in evolution.

The magnificence of the " Hound of Heaven " diction, the daring of its conception, its almost bewildering intricacy of ornament—sometimes, it must be confessed, perilously near to pulling down the structure— must place it on a plane by itself.   In its poetic value the " Hound of Heaven " must be ranked as one of the treasures of English literature, and its human value seems greater now the full story of Thompson's life is known.   The " Hound of Heaven " and " New Year's Chimes " are as sure of their life as anything that has been written since Shelley sang—are not only great things in themselves, but are full of that incommensurable quality that marks the highest.

Thompson also wrote a *Life of St. Ignatius,* and a series of essays of which the greatest is on Shelley.   In its exquisite imagery it comes as near to poetry as ever prose can.   *Health and Holiness* is an article not solely of spiritual intention but of practical good sense.   The sensitiveness of Thompson's literary ear is curiously illustrated in *A Renegade Poet on a Poet.*   To read a few lines is to be instantly reminded of Robert Louis Stevenson, and presently it is discovered that the essay was prompted by one of Stevenson's.   Indeed, says Thompson of that haunting stylist, " I cannot get him out of my head."   Thompson's essays are precious as criticisms of life and literature, and they must be read with the poems for a full interpretation of the author.   They exhibit the sanity of his genius, his equability, and own, though rarely, as might be expected, traces of the Stevensonian humour.

Few of his writings were written so much *con amore* as the essay on Shelley ; it is an *Apologie for Poesie,* an apology for Shelley, an *apologia pro vita sua.*   Shelley's sins, which were many, are to be extenuated because he was always a child.   Something of romance clings about this essay.   Written in the first days of Thompson's rescue from the " nightmare time," it was sent to the *Dublin Review,* to be declined as scarcely suited to so definitely ecclesiastical a magazine ; found among his papers after the writer's death years later, it was submitted again to the same *Dublin Review,* and, being printed, it sent that staid quarterly for the first time to a second edition.   The late George Wyndham hailed the essay as " the most important contribution to pure Letters written in English during the last twenty years."

Little need now be said about this essay, with its powerful plea for poetry in general and its tender justification of Shelley in particular as " a straying spirit of light."   It revealed to Christian readers a non-Christian poet in a new and more gracious setting ; no less did it reveal Thompson's own close poetic kinship with the author of *The Cloud*.

" Remember me, poor Thief of Song ! " So Francis Thompson prayed to his beloved Queen of Heaven, and the echoes of that heart-cry, so poignant in its dear simplicity, should fall as a personal message on the ears of all who call themselves Catholics and children of their Mother-Queen. " Remember me ! " The remembrance which should spring in response to that plea should mean more than prayer or more than mere joy in the magnificence of the song which the poet stole from the Muses to offer unto God. Thompson essayed to bring the modern unbelieving world back to Faith and spirituality ; he made all things of earthly knowledge and sight flash back even to blinded eyes a revelation of Divine governance and Divine love.

An artist more than any man needs faith ; and his faith has been given him ; the faith that his urge for self-expression is worth transmuting into writing, painting, or sculpture. The world does not find that necessary. The artist proceeds from the beginning against— not exactly hostility—but utter apathy on the part of the world. The world will eventually acclaim·him and crown him if he pursues his undeviating way and so enhances his original gift as finally to produce work of indubitable power and scope. But he may expect no real assistance from it in the meanwhile. The rigour of this condition kills off the small artists, drives them into megalomanias and persecution manias, fills them with phobias, introduces into their lives elements that sap and undermine their original gift, but the major talents proceed and attain. It has always been so and it will always be so. It may be a cruel rule of creation, but it is a salutary one.

A quality peculiar to Dr. Johnson's criticism is that it seldom fits very exactly the writer of whom he is speaking, but it often fits a writer of whom he never spoke or who came after his time. Thus he said that Dryden " delighted to tread upon the brink of meaning " and again, when speaking of the poetic diction before Dryden's time, he says that " words to which we are nearly strangers, whenever they occur draw that attention on themselves which they should transmit to things." These criticisms would be exact and just if they were made about Francis Thompson or about his diction.

A century is an inadequate test of the eternities of literary fame, and it is still too early to be certain that his poetry is really destined " to un-edge the scythe of time, and last with stateliest rhyme." But the striking change which has taken place in literary fashions since the close of the Victorian era makes it at least worth while inquiring whether he has succeeded in crossing that first barrier of oblivion which bounds the memory of many poets whose feet to their contemporaries seemed set securely upon the road to fame. For of all the changes in æsthetic valuations which are constantly occurring few have been more violent than those which have taken place since the beginning of the present century. How many of the favourite poets of the 'eighties and the 'nineties are still read to-day by any but the dwindling remnant of their contemporaries? Robert Bridges, whose greatest masterpiece, " The Testament of Beauty," was only published after the War, bestrides the two centuries like a Colossus ; but besides him who except Francis Thompson has retained his hold upon the imagination of the younger generation? *Pauci quos aequus amavit Jupiter.* This fact is the more remarkable because in many respects his poetic ideals are the very antithesis of modern fashion. His defects—and they are palpable enough—are precisely those which might be expected to jar most painfully upon the susceptibilities of an age intolerant of any mannerisms but its own. The wealth of classical allusion, the exotic neologisms, the deliberate richness of poetic diction—do not these " date " painfully for a generation which has taken " The Waste Land " as a model?

Prophecy, said George Eliot, is the most gratuitous form of human error. And the first praisers of Francis Thompson, when they went on from their own high appreciations to prophesy that he never could or would be read by the many, were, it would now seem, astray in their then plausible. divinings.

As a Christian and religious poet Thompson has few rivals, while as an artist he stands high on the rôle of fame. Dimly though we realize what manner of man this was, we gather enough to become aware that there was a tragedy in his career which left its mark on all he wrote and all he thought. Opium in a mild form shortened his days and left him a wreck, just as it exercised a baneful power over kindred sufferers—de Quincey and Coleridge. Perhaps the fact that all three were subject to the same tyranny brought them into some sort of sympathy with one another. At all events, we know that de Quincey was a prime favourite with Thompson and the *Confessions of an Opium Eater* never very far from his pocket. The laudanum habit began from a serious illness in 1879. He recovered to some extent and then relapsed, recovered and relapsed ; and thus with intervals alternated elation with despair.

Beyond question many of his earlier poems suffer from fantastic and meretricious ornamentation. A coldly critical judgment, ignorant of the setting in which these poems took shape, would justly condemn this ornamentation. Yet who can censure it if he remembers the circumstances of the writer ! It would be a harsh judgment which censured a dweller in a dismal slum because he tried to brighten his tenement with tinsel and tawdry pictures ; yet the kind of solace they would bring was the kind that overwrought and glittering phrases brought to this outcast of the streets.   Dazed with words and bemused with opium, he reverenced God and reeled in the gutter.

Thompson had to draw attention to single words in order that the attention might be transmitted from the single word to many things, or to one very great thing.   He had a great deal to say, and, being a poet, he had to say it as succinctly as possible.   The object of his best metaphors was to express a large idea, if possible, in one word enfolding his meaning ;   and his metaphors are successful only when this is his aim and when he succeeds in it.   When he tried, like Sir Thomas Browne, to embellish a simple statement with many metaphors and images, which are intended to open innumerable paths down which the reader's mind may wander, then he rarely achieved anything but a vague poetic enthusiasm.   The paths down which such words as " argent " and " beamy-textured " lead us are usually blind alleys.

A great deal is packed into Thompson's best poetry.   Since the poet spent so much time in packing it, the critic's task of unpacking it may seem ungrateful and unnecessary.   But our appreciation of the poetry very much depends upon observing the dexterity with which the packing is done.   God was even in the opium dreams of a divine drunkard.   Francis Thompson was not only drunk with opium, but drunk with God.   One was the servant of the Other.   He led a more or less outcast life after leaving his northern home as a medical student—even after he had been rescued and housed and warmed and praised and loved, breaking away from all these and escaping to the outcast life till he was again saved ;   but never, never did he feed on the husks of swine.   The poor poet was singularly innocent.   He was quite fit for the company of children, of whom and for whom he wrote.   He died with the child in him.   One cannot associate him with any kind of grossness.

His verse cannot always be spoken aloud with pleasure ;   it pays that single toll to the age wherein it saw the light, an age in which poetry has become a pen-craft, appealing to the eye from printed pages rather than to the ear with faintly-murmured accompaniment of lute and harp.   So it comes to pass that, although he utters many a line of perfect music, such as :

> Caved magically under magic seas ;
> And in her veins is quick thy milky fire :
> Dusk . . . like a windy arras waved with dreams ;
> All its birds in middle air hung a-dream, their music thralled—

he also violates the harmony with inadmissible discords like " cluck'dst "

" cast'st," " foist'st," " siev'dst," and with an immediate juxtaposition of words that cannot with loss of euphony support so close a contact, as in " verge shrivelled," " vaporpous shroudage," " lineage strange." A lesser poet might have escaped these pitfalls, but would certainly have missed " the exultation, the all-compensating wonder " of realities that lurk inviolably secure in those rough lairs.

Certain truths about Thompson's poetry must be taken into account whenever an estimate is framed, and they are not less worth setting down because nowadays they seem obvious. One is that, though the whole body of the poetical works is small, the gulf separating the best from the worst is in itself quite immense. Another is that the verbal tricks, the hideous neologisms, which his idolaters applauded, must be set among the faults and not the merits of the work. Our greatest poets have not needed to disfigure the English tongue in order to express their thought. Indeed, Thompson's simplest lyrics are also his best. " To a Snowflake " is vastly superior to some of the laboured and turgid Odes. It is a common experience that, especially with prentice hands, the endeavour to weave prose patterns of gleaming colour and exotic splendour tends to produce rhetoric and false rhythms. The keenest absorption in past mannerisms and repro- ductions of old diction are not in themselves sufficient to prevent a sentence ringing false.

Youth exults in displaying this cleverness. But the more mature writer of poetry grows to appreciate simplification. Of course, there are all manner of things that can be done with words and rhythms, and are still to be done. " If I cannot carry mountains on my back neither can you crack a nut." Yet the great accent, the truly great accent, seems strangely to inhere in the simpler forms. Diverse experimentation in form is an excellent thing. Sometimes it leads to fresh achievement. Oftener it is merely a practising of scales. What matters in poetry is the transference of a definite temperament, in all its many colours and eventually in its complete human values, to the printed page. When a poet writes a poem—if he is not merely practising—he is not counting syllables on his fingers or thinking in terms of cæsuras. He is saying something that is in his heart and on his mind, and suddenly finding that it takes unto itself a certain rhythm of utterance. If he achieves an onomatopoetic effect in its proper place or a triumph of deft alliteration, he is not thinking, " Come, now for an onomatopoetic effect—now for alliteration, now for synecdochy." Such pedantry and poetic creation are at opposite poles. The writer is simply seized of a vision and haunted by rhythms that express it. Afterward, the dissection of what he has done, the separating out of his effects, may prove a fascinating study ; but the taking of too much thought for technique at the inception of his poems would have ruined the poem ; it would have reduced it to a clever exercise.

Verdicts that have so slight a pretension to authority can arouse no indignation when it is remembered that a great poet belonging to the little band of " unacknowledged legislators " will ever be, in Shelley's words, " a nightingale who sits in darkness and sings to cheer its own solitude with sweet sounds," and that upon this unseen musician no power can sit in final judgment save the jury that must be " empanelled by time from the selectest of the wise of many generations."

Without rebellion, and with scarcely a lament, Thompson suffered his outward life to become the merest shuttlecock of destiny. It was as if the ordinary power of conscious choice had been denied him, so that while other men could walk deliberately, treading each the path of his own wisdom or folly, he must remain selfless and passive as blown thistledown. In this dependence upon some outward force more mighty than his own will lay the secret of his entire mysterious existence, and, perceiving it, he spoke always as if poetry were no abstraction, but a merciless queen exacting from even the greatest of her vassals a tribute of lifelong service. Under that most imperious of sovereigns he drifted upon every breath of circumstance, helpless to the last and, perhaps, more than any other master-singer, defenceless against his own power of song.

Trained as a young man for the priesthood, and, when that height seemed inaccessible, for medicine, he was not upheld, so far as can be discovered, by any sure knowledge of his real vocation. No one, himself least of all, had skill to unfold that riddle. So, in the battle with sickness and poverty he tried many a painful walk of life, descending always lower in the worldly scale until for the unprofitable outcast, bereft of resource and given over, in despair at so much waywardness, by even the kindest friends, nothing remained but days and nights of hunger and dereliction in the streets of London.

But for all the difficulty of comprehending the mystic's attitude to life, it is not Francis Thompson's mysticism which is most likely to displease but rather his diction. We usually accept without fully understanding a poetry like this :

> But (when so sad thou canst not sadder)
>   Cry : and upon thy so sore loss
> Shall shine the traffic of Jacob's ladder
>   Pitched between heaven and Charing Cross.

We know that the mystic can feel heaven near to Charing Cross ; we may not understand why or how, but the imaginative idea is magnificent and we are content to leave it at that. But we cannot so readily accept such a phrase as *coerule empery*. It is not possible to defend it by saying that only by such strange words could Thompson have expressed a strange and far-reaching idea, since all synonym for the phrase is easy to find. The sole purpose of such diction is to put the reader in a poetic frame of mind. If such strange words did, in fact, after putting the reader in a poetic frame of mind, lead his imagination down strange paths, in the same way as Browne takes the reader's mind to the Antipodes merely by saying in a particular way that it is time to cease writing and go to bed, they would, of course, be justifiable. But the word *coerule* seems as if it would lead the reader a long way, and yet when he is prepared for this journey, he can go no further in fact than to where the word " blue " would lead him. Thompson, we are told, when at the age of seven he read poetry, used to take his Shakespeare or his Coleridge and sit on the stairs " away from the constraint of tables and chairs and the unemotional flatness of the floor." No doubt *coerule empery* comes from the dislike of unemotional flatness which was characteristic of Thompson throughout his life. But it is never safe to condemn carelessly any strange word of Thompson's, and the practise of his worst faults often led to great beauties which could not have come perhaps any other way.

> Across the margent of the world I fled
> And troubled the gold gateways of the stars,
> Smiting for shelter on their clanged bars.

Here, by the one coined word " clanged " he has expressed in the noise of their meeting that the gates were shut to him, and also the vehemence of that inhospitality.

He has a vast capacity for this emotion, feeling it for those who suffer and for those by whom their suffering is caused, for the stupid whom the world hurts and who cannot appreciate the cause of their hurt, and for the clever, constrained by that composite stupidity to the limitation of the energy within them. His pity is sometimes misplaced, but that is because of his view of the world, which is essentially anarchical, rebellious and sentimental.

His prose verges from leanness and rigid explicitness to an abundance of sensuous images. His essays seem at times like a procession of metaphysical paintings.

When his death was announced it seemed natural to say that the flame had died out because all the fuel was consumed in that intense burning of the senses and the mind ; but it is clear from these lively and firmly written essays—at least the longer, more careful ones— that the extinction of the flame was sudden. There is no evidence of flicker and wane.

It has been affirmed that Francis Thompson was a great literary artist rather than a really great poet. The really great poet has noble things to say and trains himself to express them nobly. The literary artist may have few things of his own to say, but he loves the music of words, the cadence of sentences, the exquisite charm of a thing said perfectly. He steeps himself in the work of the great writers whose work most appeals to him, and when he practises the art of expression for himself—an art the practice of which gives him intense joy—the influence of those predecessors is almost always visible. All this is true of Francis Thompson. And with what great poets taught him he blended his own individual genius. Divest his longer poems of their sonority and imagery, and you may find very little in what Thompson has to say. Yet this does not diminish the frequent splendour of the way in which he says it. A poet, though decidedly not of the first order, but a superb craftsman, a lover of languages, a really great literary artist—that, or something like it, we venture to predict, will be the final verdict on the poetry of Francis Thompson.

We never think of Thompson in relation to human passion—he was more concerned with spiritual love—but his biographer tells us that he fell in love at least three times. A beautiful and distinguished woman-poet, a sparkling and deep-natured young lady whose eventual marriage was a keen disappointment to Thompson, and a young village girl—all three were objects of the poet's affection, though we can hardly believe that they left deep traces in his memory. But he never forgot an earlier episode in the London streets, and to the last cherished a hope that he might meet again a girl who had been kind to him when he was destitute and penniless. She had saved him from starvation and made him share her poor resources of food and shelter. When she learnt that friends were busying themselves about his welfare she disappeared, feeling that her work was done.

Nearly one-half of his poems are the songs of gratitude which were all that Thompson could bring to repay his friends. Noble and beautiful many of them are judged by any standard. Yet who, remembering the service of love which inspired them, can read them with a coldly critical detachment !

Such then, are the memories which may lead us to rate Thompson's poetry above its intrinsic worth. Yet there are other memories also, memories that incline the modern reader to unfair depreciation. The human service wrought for Thompson by his friends was splendid indeed. But the literary support they added was not always wise. Thanks to their efforts, he was " taken up " to quote the impartial record of the *Cambridge History of Literature*, " by a powerful coterie." Instead of helping him to purge his work of its faults, of forced and violent effects, of verbal tricks and grotesque diction, these people acclaimed his faults as his most sovereign virtues, and deliberately encouraged him to accentuate them. They shouted extravagant praises not merely of his best work, but of everything he wrote.

The tragic tone which pervades much of the world's greatest poetry is deepened by the " hierarchical vision " which, if it nerves the seer to his daily battle, exposes him also to the invasion of an unreckonable discontent. Woods and ponds and starlight can give less than customary joy to eyes that have caught even a fleeting glimpse of woods that never lose their green and waters that reflect in their untroubled mirror the image of eternally unfading stars. This is the lot of an inspired singer, who views from afar the towers of a more splendid city. Having drawn breath in remotest ether, he can find little savour in common life, and being haunted by secret memories keeps evermore a lonely habitation.

The poet knows, however, that the rhythms that often fill his head are just as clearly music to him as if the words he is fitting to them were sung by the most beautiful voice in the world. The wordless rhythms moving his mind, in fact, will often entrance him as actual music does the auditor. And when he reads other poetry on the printed page, the basic rhythms of any poem set up vibrations that cause him literally to *hear* the poem singing itself at the same time that he sees it lettered out before him. Indeed, we have sometimes thought, though we have known poets who were both poets and musicians, that a large proportion of writers of poetry were but musicians *manqués*. Denied the fullest expression of actual song, where sound alone creates forms and dissolving and merging pictorial effects, and rouses all the various emotions they turn to the medium that most nearly resembles actual song.

Of course to-day this musical aspect of poetry is regarded in another way by the more modern. They attempt to give that intricacy to their rhythms which will more nearly parallel the intricacy of musical improvisations and compositions. Curiously enough, the more they do this, the less actual music passes into the mind from a perusal of the poem, the more it becomes an intellectual exercise, a mathematical diagram. At least, so it appears to us. We may admire the agility of the presentation of images, the emotion inherent, the subtlety of statement—and then, for something to sing in our brain, we turn back to the Elizabethans. We are not saying, of course, that the musical element in poetry is the most important element. We are simply saying that we regard it as one necessary element, together with others.

Francis Thompson, like Wordsworth, wrote much about poetry as well as in poetry—and much worth remembering. One of his great sentences was " that with many the religion of beauty must always be a passion and a power, that it is only evil when divorced from the primal beauty." In Catholic poetry it can never be so divorced. It is welded as in the liturgy of the Church or in the souls of the saints.

The great mystic poets have one intensity in common, their ability to feel and convey a sense of unity. But they differ in the ways in which they arrive at this sense of unity, and, in the image or symbol or idea which they name unity. The Catholic mystics find their conception of the ultimate in the Catholic idea of God. Many of them reach the moment of utter conviction through the logic of the church. This was not true, or certainly not entirely true, of Francis Thompson.

He swept, sometimes in the one poem, through each of his masters, giving us, after all, the effect of a man who ransacks the treasuries of the world to pour their contents into the laps of those whom he loved on earth or before the altar. It is pillage, and the result is gleaming confusion ; but at any rate, these are treasures and the motive is not ostentation.

Francis Thompson was actually a great romantic poet. Although his faith demanded that he forsake the physical world and search for spiritual values, his strongest emotions sprang from the very flesh which he must renounce. He was sensuous, passionately emotional, acutely sensitive to every sound, taste and colour in the world about him. His imagery is as rich as Keats's, though sometimes lacking in the restraint which Keats finally learned, and his sense of light, of the disembodiment of all natural objects is not unlike Shelley's. He even tried the rhythms of Swinburne. He was not a thinker, but a man of such keen sensibilities, such vehement feelings, that he must arrive at any ultimate rather through his reactions to the physical world than through any intellectual conviction. This was the struggle that went on within him ; he was a devout Catholic, and he was a romantic poet. His mysticism springs from the resultant struggle.

Francis Thompson has little or nothing of the " terrifying simplicity " of Blake. He has nothing of the austere directness typical of the poetry of Mrs. Meynell herself. In order to see God he must see every light and shade of the physical universe and must penetrate through these to the security of deity. The famous " Hound of Heaven " is a record of just how, step by step, this penetration takes place. " The Dread of the Height," perhaps his most characteristic poem, is the acknowledgement of Thompson's awareness that once the height, or unity, was touched, the poet must fall to the depth of despondency in the immediate loss of that height. God, for this poet, could be known only in the highest, the most intense moments. For the rest there was the abundant beauty of nature, the exquisiteness of childhood, the desire for human love. None of these were satisfying and yet they caught his heart.

The struggle between the poet's romantic temperament and his

Catholic faith is everywhere apparent in his poetry. Searching always to see more than the outer garment of life, Thompson was profoundly aware of the beauties of the outer garment. His poems are a curious mingling of the sensuous and the spiritual. The greatest of his poems, however, attain a certain simplicity, a classical form which almost frees them from the emotionalism and elaboration more characteristic of the romantic poems. In those of Thompson's poems which express the highest, most perfect vision of God and of God's work the language is simpler, the lines more balanced, the imagery clearer.

Here all is resolved, and the poet is speaking from the heart of his most intense conviction. Intensity at its best tends always to order, is against over-elaboration. The mystical experience, being one of greatest intensity, has, therefore, the power of order. In the complete collection of Francis Thompson's poems the reader will note how certain poems, always the mystical, mount into complete clarity, how certain others, the romantic, give vent to the poet's love of delirious colour and natural beauty ; how many poems are a confusion of these two tendencies, the romantic and the Catholic mystic.

The most magical that Thompson ever wrote, " The Mistress of Vision," is interpreted according to Catholic doctrine, which is most certainly the only doctrine that could illuminate its mystery. This doctrine is an immediate key to the cipher, even in the matter of Cathay and the unenlightened Buddhists—unenlightened in the view of the Catholic Church. There is no doubt that Thompson's mind was so deeply impregnated with Catholic doctrine that this is the true interpretation of his " Mistress of Vision," although his development of the symbolism has a magical quality in this poem which actually, and marvellously, bears comparison with the magic of Coleridge's " Kubla Khan." To many it is the only poem in the English language that can bear such a comparison, save possibly Keats's " La Belle Dame Sans Merci."

Naturally the exigencies of rhyme, for he wrote always in rhyme, frequently caused him to resort to poetic license in syntax. " Trope that itself not scans," when what is meant is " Trope that cannot, itself, scan," is certainly not grammatical. Yet so swift is Thompson's attack that even his occasional crudities of this kind can be forgiven. Doctrinaire in religion he was yet one of the most daring wielders of words in imagery that English poetry has ever seen. And his imagery was never vague or indefinite. It summed up vividly a particular picture. He could even borrow Kipling's " the dawn comes up like thunder " from " Mandalay," probably unconsciously, and transmute it into line of organ-music, " the great earth-quaking sunrise rolling up beyond Cathay."

Despite the great debt Thompson owes to the many beauties and splendours found in the elucidation of the Catholic point of view through its masters of phrase, the fact remains that he is a great poet because he draws not only on these sources but on the great poetic writing of all time.

His debt to Crashaw, to Patmore and even to lesser poets, is clearly distinguishable. His attitude toward human love is by no means satisfactory, absorbed as he was in the idea of the soul's utter abandonment to God. For Thompson, as is the case with all true genius, had in himself the seeds, if not at times, the fine flower, of absolute fanaticism. One of the most interesting things he ever wrote, though it has been often passed over in the face of his more splendid lyrical achievements, is the sequence called " A Narrow Vessel," which he speaks of in his sub-title as being upon " the aspect of primitive girl-nature towards a love beyond its capacities."

Thompson was fortunate in utterly believing in all the ramifications of Christian doctrine as expounded by the most astute and subtle Catholic minds, and that in the ritual of the Catholic Church with its tremendous accretions of symbolism, he found infinite riches of imagery. His definite faith supplied his poetry always with a strong underlying framework and the oscillating needle of his sensitive reasoning always returned to what for him was true North. Added to this was his mystical recognition of the validity of the poetic imagination which did not disdain the imaginatively scientific.

Somehow Francis Thompson has managed to survive, while most of his contemporaries, dead or alive, are almost forgotten, because his work embodies the essential qualities which everywhere and in all ages are known as the mark of true poetry. He was indeed " one smitten from his birth, with curse of destinate verse," and though his appeal is not so wide as that of the greatest names in English poetry, chiefly because he was pre-occupied so intensely with the more Roman aspects of the Catholic religion, he will continue to be read even by those who have little sympathy with his particular creed. For richness of imagination, for metrical skill and sublimity of thought, he is surpassed only by the great master poets of our language, and even where his greatest fault—the exaggerated luxuriance of his diction—is most apparent, his " cloth of gold," as he himself has said of Shelley, " bursts at the flexures and shows the naked poetry." Few poets in any language have known as he did " to teach how the Crucifix may be, carven from the laurel tree." He is the victim of no optimistic delusions. He has studied Nature and human life too closely not to admit their " mean ugly brutish obscene clumsy irrelevances " ; but man, the highest product of Nature, is endowed with consciousness and judgment, and of what good is judgment if it does not choose the best ?

There were, besides, little personal episodes that perhaps even more instantly affixed the laurels. Barbellion, in a passage held over from the *Diary of a Disappointed Man*, and appropriately included in *Enjoying life*, said that, despite all his sufferings, he was glad to have lived to see men fly through the air like birds and to have read the poems of Francis Thompson. And Burne-Jones, saying that no words since Gabriel's " Blessed Damozel " had so moved him as this newcomer's " Hound of Heaven," went on to confess that he undressed, and dressed and undressed again, not knowing what he did in those minutes of verbal intoxication.

Thompson was a true Catholic who lived in the shadow of the Cross, and so much of the haunting poetry of the book of Job lingers in his lines that one may divine him to have been a regular reader of the Office for the Dead. Fr. McNabb was present in the Hospital of Ss. John and Elizabeth in St. John's Wood when Francis Thompson died, and he passionately pleads from first-hand evidence that it is a travesty to portray the poet as a helpless drug addict. For Fr. Vincent was present when two surgeons discussed the dead poet and one of them stressed to the other that the amount of drugs Thompson ever took or could have taken was indeed very small.

Thompson's poetry sprang from his love and contemplation of the Cross and Passion, from the Blessed Sacrament, from the Bride of Christ (and Christ was for him the True Orient), from the Lady Poverty of St. Francis (he espoused her in London streets), and not the Coleridge inspirations of intoxicants or drugs.

Fantastically absurd was the claim once made by some Theosophist writers—twisting mystic passages to fit the Reincarnation invention—that Thompson was a perfect Theosophist poet. And an article in the *London Mercury* contained much nonsense about the religious side of the poet's work. It was suggested that he belonged to no church, to any church. Now all this is to " miss the many splendoured thing " of Thompson's burning Catholicism.

We find some Catholic critics who have objected to Thompson because they think his work savours of the pagan spirit ! Even though from the outset the poet pleaded ; " I began my career with an elaborate indictment of the ruin which the re-introduction of the pagan spirit must bring upon poetry." Or " I would far prefer to be the poet of the return to God than of the return to Nature." For Thompson denounced paganism old and new ; the old paganism which he saw concerned with the expected Christ, the new paganism which he saw brooding over the rejected Christ. He demanded that St. Thomas and Dante should walk hand in hand as defenders of the Church's Sacred Literature. " I find I cannot do without Eternal Poetry," he wrote. Then there are his lovely lines of prayer " To Chastity."

> But thou, sweet Lady Chastity,
> Thou, and thy brother Love, with thee——
> Out of the terror of the tomb,
> And unclean shapes that haunt sleep's gloom
> Yet, yet I call on thee,
> " Abandon thou not me."

As a poet, he went in robes all his life. In that he was not alone in his generation, for Lionel Johnson did the same. But Johnson, with far less imagination and ardour, and far severer scholarship, got his poetry out of the robes. It was truly necessary for him to appear in the garb of the scholar or the vestments of the priest : we cannot conceive of him as a poet, though we know he had other and lamentable aspects as a man, in any but ceremonial and learnedly correct dress. His ceremony was his way of inducing order into the disorder of his life, of achieving decorum , and—though the remark may sound absurd—for readers with imagination there is pathos in the unusual, scholarly punctuation of that poem, " The Dark Angel," into which he put the tragedy of his always losing, never quite lost, battle with drink.

Thompson's quick-change splendour of costumes, for all that he was so much the more considerable poet, has nothing like as much justification. He has got at the wardrobe ; and, without a scholar's purist concern about anachronisms and incongruities, though he has his own sort of scholarship, he can resist nothing that is brilliant. Only one thing saves him. There is no cold posing. He really is enraptured and he really conveys that to us. But what incompatibilities !

Thompson has taken hold upon the imagination of the younger generation. And this although some of the distinctive features of his verse—his wealth of classical allusion, his exotic neologisms, the deliberate richness of his diction—might be expected to jar painfully upon the susceptibilities of an age intolerant of any mannerisms but its own. He has managed to survive because his work embodies the essential qualities which everywhere and in all ages are known as the mark of true poetry. For richness of imagination, for metrical skill and for sublimity of thought he is surpassed only by the great master poets of our language.

Rev. J. KEATING, S.J.

CHARLES DOMINIC PLATER, S.J.

A.D. 1875–1921

IN LONDON THERE is a " Plater Dining Club," which meets periodically to discuss the questions of social betterment to which Fr. Plater devoted nearly the whole of his Jesuit life. In Oxford there is a Catholic Labour College, established as a permanent memorial of that wonderfully beneficent career. All over Great Britain, the continued and growing activities of what was largely his creation, the Catholic Social Guild, testify to the spiritual vitality of the ideas with which he inspired it from the first. These phenomena are indications of an exceptionally vigorous personality which made a definite and lasting impression on its age, and entitles its owner to rank permanently amongst Catholic leaders. Even now a " Catholic social sense "—a realization that modern industrial conditions are in many ways at variance with the principles and ideals of our Faith—is by no means general amongst us, but we can truly say that, only for Fr. Plater and the band of fellow-workers who drew their inspiration from his wisdom and zeal, that sense of what our Catholic profession demands of us would be even less keen and less wide-spread. Accordingly, it is well to keep alive amongst us the memory of what he accomplished and of what he projected, since the need for the extension of his work is ever growing more pressing.

It is interesting to note that Fr. Plater's remote paternal ancestors came to England from the Catholic country of Poland, although somehow they had managed to lose their Catholic heritage by the change. Thus his great-grandfather and grandfather were beneficed Anglican clergymen, as was one of his uncles. His father was converted in 1851 at the age of 17, and married in 1865 a Miss Margaret Harting, a member of an old Catholic family, eminent in the practice of the law. Charles Plater was born of this union on September 2nd, 1875, the youngest of a family of four, three sons and one daughter. Apparently from his earliest years he was of a delicate constitution, and so was educated at home under the care of his talented and deeply cherished mother until he was twelve years old. Even then, although he was entered at the famous College of Stonyhurst in the Ribble

Valley, he spent his first year at the Preparatory School, Hodder, on the banks of the picturesque river of that name. In 1888 he joined the College proper where he at once became distinguished both for intellectual ability and a capacity for leadership.

Association with a school like Stonyhurst, steeped in ancient Catholic tradition, a school founded abroad during the Elizabethan persecution and driven from one Continental refuge after another—St. Omer, Bruges, Liège—during the French Revolution, until, " exiled from exile " it settled in 1794 in the old Lancashire mansion of the Shireburns, must have been an education in itself to a highly-gifted and impressionable boy like Charles Plater. Its history, illustrating the fortunes both of Church and State in England during several centuries, its many relics of the past preserved in its very structure, and in museums and libraries, the old traditional customs concerning both work and play, the constant process of its material growth, the remarkable men numbered amongst its pupils and its staff, the allusions to it embodied in English literature—all this creates an atmosphere productive of love and pride and loyalty even in the average schoolboy, and is well-calculated to fire the imagination and broaden the intelligence of the more receptive. Charles Plater, so to speak, absorbed " Stonyhurst " with every pore, and became a complete embodiment of its spirit and outlook, so much so that his portrait might fitly be added to those of the worthies which adorn the great banqueting-hall, a roll of men who have deserved eminently well of their *Alma Mater*. At the same time, it may reasonably be urged by the athletic that the name of the boy Plater never figures in the College teams of football or cricket, nor shines forth in sports records. That is true but, after all, it only goes to show—and to that extent he falls short of schoolboy perfection—that he had not that combination of inclination and capacity which makes for full physical development. He did not shirk games, and probably played as much as was good for him.

He was fortunate in that his six years at the College fell within the headmastership of Fr. John Gerard, a brilliant scholar of many-sided interests, who had the gift of exciting enthusiasm in the most diverse subjects in all who came within reach of his influences. He it was who founded the present Debating Society and the College periodical, called *The Stonyhurst Magazine*, thus providing ambitious boys with the means of acquiring fluency of speech and writing. His strongest bent was for natural science, but he was as well a competent classical scholar and a student of history. His influence on boys like Plater, thus brought into contact with so capacious and energetic a mind, was very marked. Charles laid the foundation of genuine classical culture, became a ready debater and developed a faculty for excellent prose-writing, which secured him the chief Essay Prize for five years running and, in the last two years of his school-life, the post of sub-editor of the *Magazine*. In 1894, when the Centenary of the College on English soil was celebrated, it was Plater who was selected to deliver the school address at the commemorative banquet.

It is certain too, that the desire for the priesthood which, in common with many boys in pious homes, Charles Plater evinced at a very early age, easily blossomed into a vocation, both because of the Catholic traditions of the College and neighbourhood, and from his admiration of Fr. Gerard and others of his religious masters. They were conspicuous illustrations of the truth that devotion to God's service may make a man more, rather than less, capable of helping and serving his fellows. Anyhow, two years before the end of his school course, he applied for admission into the Society, and duly entered the noviceship at Roehampton in September, 1894, in his nineteenth year. He might be described at this stage as a youth of remarkable promise whose solid and sensible piety had prevented his popularity with his companions and academic successes from spoiling his essentially simple and loveable character, but who had not yet guessed in what particular direction his life-work would lie. Nevertheless, even in his school-days, he showed, in the ready way in which he forgathered with the rustic worthies whom he met, when in search of copy for his periodical, evidence of what was a salient feature of his later life.

The traditional training of the young Jesuit follows the well-tested lines laid down in the Institute of the Society, and at first it is almost entirely spiritual. During the two years of his novitiate, the aspirant makes three retreats, one of which lasts for thirty days, wherein he studies and puts into practice that matchless method of properly orienting human life, the " Exercises " of St. Ignatius. Of these, what is called the " First Principle " sets forth the foundation of all human perfection and ultimate salvation—the praise, reverence and service of God. This is followed by the famous meditations—the " Kingdom of Christ," the " Two Standards," " Three Classes," etc.—all designed to put before the postulant the very highest ideals and to provide means and motives for their accomplishment. These are further elaborated by a detailed study of our Lord's life and a sustained endeavour to emulate that Divine Model—" to put on Christ," as St. Paul advises. On this basis, the Jesuit's spiritual edifice is erected : on these themes he continually ponders, not only on the formal occasions of his annual retreat, but practically every day of his life. No clearer indication need be given of the spiritual background of Charles Plater's future career. A mind so keen must have readily grasped and held the all-importance of the life to come, in spite of the inevitable lag between ideal and practice : a will so strong and unselfish must have kept steadily to that course in spite of recurrent human weaknesses. It is practically impossible for teaching so clear and so constantly repeated to be forgotten or in practice ignored. At the end of the two years' novitiate are taken the three vows of poverty, chastity, and obedience, which constitute the religious state, and then, normally, two years more are spent in the novitiate, engaged in the study of science, of the humanities, or of whatever branch of learning that the subject may need the most. After this, the Jesuit scholastic is sent to the seminary to apply himself to a three years' course of philosophy. Accordingly, in 1898, Charles Plater found himself back at Stonyhurst, not now at the College but at the neighbouring philosophate, St. Mary's Hall. He was not, however, destined to complete his course there, for in September, 1900, he was sent with others to fill the vacancies in the Jesuit Hall at Oxford, lately bereft of its first master by the death of Fr. Richard Clarke, and then restarting under Fr. J. O'Fallon Pope.

As is well known, it took a long time before, in the mind of Catholic authorities, the intellectual advantages of study at the famous University were held to outweigh the moral dangers of contact with a culture which had for generations ceased to be distinctively Christian. It was not until 1870, that the abolition of the Test Act made it possible for Catholics to attend Oxford, and not until 1895 that the Holy See allowed them to take advantage of that possibility. The next year the Jesuits established a private Hall there for their own scholastics, now known as Campion Hall and available for others besides members of the Society.

The four years which Charles Plater spent at Oxford could not but have been, for a mind so receptive and a zeal so all-embracing, a period of immense development, not merely or even mainly, in the academic sense. He had, of course, the great advantage, denied to all but the inheritors of the Catholic tradition, of a fixed yet rational standard of belief and a clear-cut consistent philosophy, whereby to assay all new forms of learning. His knowledge of the classics widened and deepened through contact with the experts who tutored him, and he even acquired a passion for Mycenæan archæology, but he never took a specialist's interest in languages or aspired to scholarship as such. For that reason and because already the needs of the day were competing for his attention with the records of the past, he did not, to the great disappointment of his friends, secure more than a Second in the Honours Lists of classical " Mods " and " Greats." Moreover, he was handicapped always by precarious health and a tendency to overwork. But it was during the vacations, which University customs so lavishly provide, that Plater's zeal got that definite orientation towards social work which it thenceforward never lost. He spent the

Easter vacation of 1903 at the French Jesuit House of Studies at Canterbury, where he came into contact with a number of Fathers conversant with every aspect of Catholic activity in France, and felt stirred to emulation. The "long" of the same year he spent in Holland studying German, and also the highly organized Catholic life of that country, and in Belgium where he met for the first time what seemed to him *the* remedy for manifold social evils—the provision of Retreats for workers. His immediate reaction finds expression in the following lines addressed to a friend in England—"I am quite mad on the subject of the Belgian retreats for working-men. It is really unspeakable—the cure for all our troubles, I'm sure : results really miraculous."[1] In the summer of 1904, when he finally went down, he had a similar experience in France where he visited the House of Retreats at Epinay and studied methods of organization. From this time may be dated what may be called his Apostolate of the Pen, whereby in articles or letters to the Press, he did all that he could to rouse Catholic public opinions to the need and the methods of social reform. He was a born organizer. When advocating a cause, he was careful first to learn all about its history, and particularly how far it had been projected or attempted by others. He neglected no source of enlightenment, experimental or theoretical and he excelled eliciting the co-operation of all who could help. Later, as we shall notice, he employed the platform as well as the Press. Without being an orator or a stylist, he made very effective use of both voice and pen— a pleasing clear articulation, a vivid phraseology, spiced with anecdote and humour helped to convey his message easily to all varieties of hearers or readers. What is remarkable is that he began his fruitful apostolate whilst he was yet himself in training, as if he foresaw that his years of work would be few. A greater measure of repose, a fuller cultivation of leisure, might have won him a longer span of life, but the projects before him would not brook delay. Although he never neglected his relative duties, the charity of Christ urged him to *make* time and opportunity so as to set on foot matters of greater moment. *His* "man of Macedonia," saying—"Come over and help us" was the long-neglected working-class, robbed not only of their natural rights but also of that compensatory Christian faith which makes earth's trials endurable or even turns them to gain.

He was only 29 when he left Oxford and still only an "approved scholastic." Normally, he would now have been sent to teach boys in some college for several years, to serve in this highly practical fashion,

---

[1] He set forth his impressions more at length in an article in *The Month* for November of that year (1903) the first of a long series on that and kindred subjects ; one of which, now thirty years old (Feb. 1908), bears the significant title—"A Plea for Catholic Social Action."

the Society which had educated him. As a matter of fact this experience, for which he was so well equipped, was denied him, for he had still to complete his course of philosophy at Stonyhurst, as well to embark on the formidable four years of theology, preparatory to ordination and to what may be called his professional career.

To St. Mary's Hall, accordingly, he returned in 1904 to study ethics and to revise his previous philosophical course : to this was added the task of " coaching " in Classics the scholastics who were destined for an Oxford career. Thus he was not wholly a student or altogether a professor : however, his ambiguous status helped rather than hindered his exercising his qualities of leadership. His own class were taught, but hardly in the spirit of Mr. Squeers, not only to study primitive archæology but also to excavate the Roman remains in the neighbouring hamlet of Ribchester—a work the results of which attracted the attention of the *Athenæum*. And he encouraged others of his charges and fellow-students to exercise the apostolate of the pen ; and in this way historical accounts of various Catholic societies and enterprises were put before the public,[1] always with an eye to the future and greater development which he contemplated. At the Catholic Truth Conference at Brighton in September, 1906, a paper of his on " Retreats for Working-Men " was read, which may be regarded as the formal opening shot in a campaign which has resulted, so far, in the establishment both in Scotland and England of various Houses for that specific purpose, and the prospect of still more. This cultivation of the press had gratifying, if sporadic, results ; the Catholic conscience began to be less drowsy ; little social enterprises sprang up here and there, which had their centre in him, but now the time had come for the temporary retirement of their zealous inspirer. He started his theological course at St. Beuno's College, North Wales, in September, 1907.

Some may wonder why this zealous young man, bent on doing everything possible to remedy the ravages of industrialism amongst the British working-classes, should have hit upon and stressed the specifically Catholic practice of " going into retreat." It seems rather a remote and indirect means of attacking economic injustice and the distressing phenomena of destitution. But, in essence, it is a sound means and indeed the only sound means : the means taught by Infallible Truth when he said—" Seek ye *first* the Kingdom of God and His justness, and all these things shall be added to you." Catholics know that the existing chaos of human affairs, national and inter-national, results from men and nations ignoring the Kingdom of God altogether, and that the only remedy is to restore to human relations the observance of Christian principles. . Now, in a retreat a man faces

[1] Notably a series called " Our Social Forces " which appeared in *The Universe*.

the realities of time and eternity, God's purpose in creating, the creature's responsibilities, the comparative unimportance of this world except as a training-ground for the next. It is only in the light of eternity that the things of time can be seen in their proper perspective and proportion. And man is further taught that God is best served by his own service of his fellow-man for God's sake. A retreat puts charity, the love of God and man, in its proper place in life. And it is love, not mere justice, that will save the world. Moreover, let us remember that, although Charles Plater laboured to bring the means of making retreats within the reach of those who are normally too busy or too poor to secure the privilege, he would have all classes, employers and employed, women as well as men, rich and poor, employ from time to time this hallowed way to set their lives in order, to realize both their duties and their privileges and to combine for effective action. In a retreat, the great basic doctrines of God's fatherhood and the brotherhood of men are especially emphasized, and the way paved for that Christian unity in good works which is meant to enlighten and preserve the world.[1]

During his theologate, although his intercourse with the outer world was necessarily much restricted, Plater's superiors wisely allowed him to relieve the strain of study by writing and correspondence on his various social interests and even by occasional excursions in pursuance of them. News came to him in 1908 that the first Retreat House had been opened—Compstall Hall near Romily—and he was, to his great delight, allowed to visit it. In the course of the next year came the first idea of a " Catholic Sociological Society," for which the ground had been prepared by discussion and correspondence with various friends. The Silver Jubilee Conference of the Catholic Truth Society in September, 1909, at Manchester brought together a number of these, at a luncheon presided over by Mgr. Parkinson, of Oscott. The new organization was discussed and approved, to be formerly constituted under the title of " The Catholic Social Guild," about a month later at Oscott. The name of Charles Plater whilst he was at St. Beuno's and for several years afterwards does not appear amongst the officers or even on the committee of the Guild, although every one felt that he was its principal originator and the mainspring of its early activities. At the first (Leeds) Catholic Congress of 1910, the Catholic Social Guild took a prominent place amongst Catholic societies, and was welcomed generally by the hierarchy and thenceforward, up to a point, grew rapidly in numbers and influence. In that year was published by the Catholic Truth Society the first *Catholic Social Year Book* compiled at St. Beuno's by the busy theologian largely

[1] All that can be said in commendation of this means of personal and social regeneration may be found in Fr. Plater's own *Retreats for the People*, published in 1911.

out of previous writings, and containing an account of another recently founded Catholic society, the Catholic Women's League, which also owed much to his counsel and inspiration.[1]   He continued to edit, and to contribute copiously to successive *Year Books*, which served admirably both to chronicle and to direct Catholic social effort, till a twelve-month before his death.   We may mention especially that issued in 1918 towards the close of the Great War, called " A Christian Social Crusade," which was later issued as a separate publication and ran into a third edition.   It was based upon a " statement of principles and proposals " put forward in 1917 by the Inter-denominational Conference of Social Service Unions, a body on which the Catholic Social Guild was represented almost from its foundation in 1911.

In the September of the previous year, 1910, the culminating event of his career, his ordination to the priesthood, took place at Roehampton.   Thenceforward as a member of the *Ecclesia Docens* his status as a leader was to be more assured, but he was not yet freed from the long training of the Society.   Another year of theological study, diversified by a certain amount of pastoral work, preceded his final successful examinations and then, he departed for St. Stanislaus College, Tullamore, Ireland, for his " Third Year of Probation," a sort of second noviceship which every Jesuit has to undergo before admission to his last permanent vows.   He returned in time for the Third Catholic Congress, in August, 1912, which marked some further progress of the Catholic Social Guild and then put in some strenuous parish work in the slums of Glasgow, an experience calculated to fire still further his already fervent zeal for the victims of modern industrialism.   His appointment as Professor of Psychology at St. Mary's Hall, Stonyhurst, in September, 1912, was explicitly provisional: he had not been professedly trained for the part, yet it enabled him as usual, to inoculate his charges with enthusiasm for social work, whilst it gave him many opportunities of evangelising the industrial North and spreading the work of the Catholic Social Guild by lectures, retreats and the founding of study-clubs.   He was relieved of his Psychological Professorship after July, 1914, and spent the vacation giving retreats in the Midlands, until the outbreak of War occurred to change the lives and destinies of millions.   In the first year of the War, Charles Plater was still employed at Stonyhurst, teaching philosophy and classics and beginning to add to his social apostolate that care for refugees and wounded soldiers that grew daily more clamant and absorbing.   Then the scene of his work was changed, but not its volume, by his appointment in September, 1915, to teach

---

[1] As showing the extent of his activities he had also a large share in the foundation of the Catholic Medical Guild which came into being in July 1910, and has since proved of immense service to Catholic doctors all over the country.

a class at Wimbledon College. This post brought him within reach of the large camps around the metropolis and he entered with zest upon that purely spiritual crusade for souls, which found in the realities of war unparalleled opportunities of preaching the truths and administering the consolations of religion.

Fr. Plater as we have implied had always been a " good mixer " ; now in the widely-varied composition of the huge civilian armies he could indulge his capacity to the full, and his geniality and manifest affection brought hundreds back to the practice of religion. And, of course, he speedily instituted retreats for soldiers.

Then quite unexpectedly in January, 1916, he was appointed to a rectorship, which involved his becoming Master of the Jesuit Hall at Oxford.

One feels that, in normal circumstances, this position at one of the main centres of the intellectual life of the country would have given Fr. Plater the very widest scope for the exercise of his exceptional powers of leadership and inspiration. But though the upheaval caused by the War did prepare the public mind for radical changes in industrial and social life—as witness the extensive movements for " national reconstruction " set on foot by every Christian organization, by various political parties and even by associations of business men— yet the immediate necessity continued to be the welfare of the actual victims of the War, who, in growing numbers began to fill the hospitals of England. Those in Oxford and the neighbourhood soon became familiar to the Master of Campion Hall and to others of its staff, notably Fr. C. C. Martindale, and when once week-end retreats were started the Catholic public contributed generously to the support of this novel but very real form of charity.[1] Innumerable were the friendships formed in those few crowded years, when the University, depleted of its usual inhabitants, was filled by an even more transient *clientèle*—cadets in training for the great adventure overseas and those who returned from it, alive yet broken in body and often in mind. Many were Colonials, and in time large encampments of German prisoners gave further scope for the devotion of Fr. Plater and his colleagues, during what Fr. Martindale calls " those tragic, laughable, bewildering, exhausting, exhilarating, but always happy and always holy years." (*Charles Dominic Plater*, p. 228.) Direct literary fruits of this time were *A Primer of Peace and War*, a compilation in which others took a share, and of value as giving the Church's teaching on the many moral problems connected with the practice of warfare ; *How to Help Catholic Soldiers*, *Letters to Catholic Soldiers*, four

[1] Fr. Plater never lost the chance of embodying his experiences or his projects in permanent form, and his *Retreats for Catholic Soldiers* gives an inspiring account of this enterprise.

in number which met the needs of the moment and, towards the end of the War, another compilation, *Catholic Soldiers, by Sixty Chaplains and Many Others*—an attempt, necessarily incomplete, to show how the profession of Catholicity served the fighting forces who possessed the faith.

But work for soldiers, hale or wounded, was not allowed wholly to interrupt his strenuous advocacy of the ideals of the Catholic Social Guild. Every University vacation was for him a time for a vigorous crusade through the great industrial districts of the North, carrying the social message of the Gospel, in spite of his frail and uncertain health, to the multitudinous manual workers, that class so oppressed by iniquitous social conditions and so exposed to perversion by the false principles of Communism. His "Tyneside tours" became traditional and his enthusiasm was such that everywhere he became a *colporteur* of the Guild's increasing literature.[1] His audiences were often socialistic yet, once it was explained to them, very appreciative of Catholic economic teaching. He continued these exhausting but most useful expeditions up to a year before his death, made innumerable friends among the clergy and established a solid tradition of social study amongst Catholic industrial workers.

It was not often that he had the opportunity of addressing that other factor in industry, whose need of evangelization is certainly not less than that of labour—the capitalist employers. But as late as December, 1919, before the brief glimpse of better things revealed by the explosion of the War had become clouded again by the mists of human selfishness, he was called upon, as representing Cardinal Bourne, to address a Mansion House meeting of the controllers of industry on the resolution —"that whole-hearted co-operation among all classes to secure prosperity in industry and satisfactory conditions of life for workers is essential in the national interest." It is perhaps characteristic of the business world, then and now, that the workers' welfare is put in this resolution second to industrial success ; anyhow, there was nothing in the proposal to suggest that radical reform in the ideals of industry which the crisis called for. Fr. Plater spoke plainly and bluntly, like another St. John Baptist, on the need to Christianise industrial relations. " Christianity," he said, " is something very revolutionary and something very strong. I venture to say that if you were to introduce a little real Christianity into directors' meetings or on to the Stock Exchange or into a Trade Union Congress, or into the House of Commons, you might get some surprising results." The

---

[1] Amongst the most successful pamphlets issued about this time by the Catholic Social Guild was Cardinal Bourne's famous Lenten Pastoral of 1918 *The Nation's Crisis,* regarding the form and contents of which it is generally believed that His Eminence consulted Fr. Plater. It states in clear and convincing language the only sound lines on which national reconstruction can proceed.

audience cheered, but he immediately asked them if they really meant it ; were they ready to pay for the introduction of charity and justice into business by sacrifice, " by carrying a cross." " There is no power that can lift up this conflict between employers and employed above the level of mere brute force except Christianity."

Fr. Plater's eloquence and sincerity in which was practically his last public speech in England, might win applause but more was needed to uproot the evil traditions of centuries. The only official organization of employers since the War is the Federation of British Industries and this has formally declared, regarding the Living Wage, " that the real ultimate test (of its justice) must always be what industry will bear." Instead, therefore, of the " Two Nations " managing to combine in their common interests, the lists are now being set for their final conflict which only the principles so assiduously preached by Fr. Plater and his Guild can avert.

I have said above that the Catholic Social Guild rapidly made its way to a point where it stuck. Had Fr. Plater lived, it might at last have won support from the Catholic business world, whereas that world on the whole has from the first boycotted it. In spite of all the Popes have written—and since Fr. Plater's death *Quadragesimo Anno* (1931) has come to endorse and extend the teaching of *Rerum Novarum*—in spite of all the efforts of the English hierarchy down to the latest pastoral of the Cardinal Archbishop, " Brotherhood in Christ," there is little sign yet of that combination of Catholic employers and professional men with Catholic workers, through which alone the social message of Christianity can be made articulate and effective. In his Mansion House speech Fr. Plater laid his finger on the reason. The workers on their side gladly embrace Catholic teaching because it upholds their rights, proclaims their dignity and saves them from servitude, whereas for the employers the Christianising of industry would involve, to start with, a certain amount of sacrifice. And, as the Pope Pius freely admits in *Divini Redemptoris* (the great Encyclical against Communism) the employers are saddled with " the heavy heritage of an unjust economic regime whose ruinous influence has been felt through many generations." Accordingly, there is need of association between themselves and dissociation from those whose principles are unchristian ; a process likely to be troublesome ; a process calling for the help of grace as well as of reason and therefore linked, as all Fr. Plater's apostolate was, with the practice of " seeking God " in retreats. Apart from this failure to enlist the support of the Catholic employing class as a whole—many individuals were more enlightened and generous in help—in the Christian Social Crusade, one must, for completeness, note that, especially at the beginning, the Catholic Social Guild roused opposition even amongst good and zealous people. It was the same hostility, born of righteous but mistaken zeal, that Cardinal Manning encountered in his time : the word " social " frightened all that were afraid of Socialism. Opposition grew so strong that it was thought opportune that Mgr. Parkinson, the President of the Guild, should, at the Cardiff National Congress of 1914, fully declare its attitude towards all social theories and programmes which were not specifically Catholic. This vindication effectively cleared the air and henceforward, no educated Catholic has doubted that the Guild is fully trusted both in England and at Rome, although from time to time both " Right " and " Left " have found fault with its central position.

In *The Nation's Crisis* Cardinal Bourne used these significant words : " We should co-operate cordially with the efforts which are being made by various religious bodies to remedy our unchristian social conditions. Without any sacrifice of religious principles we may welcome the support of all men of good will in this great and patriotic task." From the first Fr. Plater put this counsel into practice and he became one of the best known and most helpful members of the Annual Summer School at Swanwick, held since 1912 by the Interdenominational Conference of Social Service Unions. Fr. Martindale records that, in the opinion of some non-Catholic members, although Catholics stood uncompromisingly aloof in worship, they and especially Fr. Plater diffused a *really unifying spirit*. (*Charles Dominic Plater*, p. 203).

The last nine months of this devoted life were spent in what some one called " strenuous rest-cures." He had long known that both heart and arteries were out of gear, and he extracted from his doctors the admission that a rest, even two years, would give him no guarantee of future fitness, so he quite evidently determined to wear out rather than rust out. But obedience and indeed prudence obliged him to slacken off to some extent,· and he was sent in March, 1920, to recuperate for a month in the West of Ireland. He resumed his life at Oxford for a while and gave all his time to the first Catholic Social Guild Summer School in June of that year : whereat the idea of a Catholic Workers' College began to take shape. The Summer School has survived even the blow of his death and has been held without a break ever since. He was well enough to attend the resumed National Congress in Liverpool at the end of July, 1920, but grew steadily worse during the autumn. At last, it was suggested that, as his doctor as well as himself needed a rest, they should go together to Malta. He was there about a month, lecturing, preaching and helping in the formation of a Maltese Social Guild, before the end came, as he would have wished : a sudden cerebral hæmorrhage following on a charitable visit to the sick. In that brief period of apostolic work, he had so endeared himself to that Catholic people, high and low, had so impressed them by his whole-hearted devotion to their interests, that both Archbishop and Governor were only answering a popular demand by giving him a splendid public funeral.

The final words of this brief sketch of a great Catholic social pioneer are actually being penned on the seventeenth anniversary of his holy death. So comparatively short was the span of life in which he " fulfilled many days," that many of his colleagues and intimates are still alive, not to mourn him but rather to try to carry on his work. What, indeed, would we not give to have amidst us still that lovable personality, that fountain of contagious energy, that mind of clear vision and that God-inspired will, now that all the problems we faced under his leadership are growing more instant and more complex before our eyes. But his inspiration is with us yet to give us courage and hope and perchance he can now help us even more effectively than when alive, to fulfil his splendid ideals.

ISABEL C. CLARKE

AUBREY BEARDSLEY

1872–1898

A CONSIDERABLE AMOUNT OF attention has of late been bestowed, and not unworthily, upon the little group of men and women who won fame in the last decade of the nineteenth century. It was a time of passionate literary and artistic revival, being indeed one of those periods of collective genius which occur from time to time to startle and even dismay a world unprepared for and even suspicious of novelty. It owed its inception to the ambition, initiative and rebellion of a handful of young people, inspired by an energetic impulse that could not be disregarded. And to us it must now seem that the Victorian age, so prolific in literature, was to go down in a blaze of glory, ephemeral, fugitive, yet nevertheless imbued with the germ of immortality. That narrowly defined epoch was destined, despite its errors and exaggerations, to influence succeeding generations. It constituted a break with tradition of a very definite character. While *fin-de-siècle* was the adjective frequently and contemptuously applied to that group by those reared in an earlier and more robust tradition, its votaries did undoubtedly possess those flaming attributes of brilliancy and genius which, however wayward, must leave an indelible mark upon their period. The Wilde scandal and the South African War combined to end it, while the death of the aged Queen, the inauguration of a new epoch, produced an entirely different type of poet and writer actuated by widely divergent ideals—men who were preparing, albeit unconsciously, for that grim ordeal which was destined to earn for them the name of the sacrificed generation. Many of the survivors of the 'nineties were absorbed into that newer tradition, and in many cases lived to obtain recognition in a very different field.

The interest evoked by those artists and writers is in no way based upon any necessity to rescue their names from oblivion. For despite their youth, and in many cases their premature and tragic deaths, the work they accomplished was such that no student of Victorian art and literature can afford to ignore. And among those who perished early, three names stand out with a certain hectic and feverish brilliancy—those of Aubrey Beardsley, Ernest Dowson, and Lionel Johnson. The Church claims them all as her children. And in his book *The Beardsley Period* the late Mr. Osbert Burdett affirmed unhesitatingly that if one of the men who formed that group was lacking and " whose art the decade would feel its greatest loss, that personality is undoubtedly Aubrey Beardsley."

When in 1894 John Lane planned the publication of the *Yellow Book* he could not possibly have foreseen the immediate fame, even the immense notoriety it was destined to achieve. It was primarily instituted for the encouragement of those young writers and artists whose work he had already in many cases begun to publish. Looking back upon the list of contributors we can discern little that was in the slightest degree abnormal in the majority of those whom he thus assembled to assist him in his new venture. Such names as Edmund Gosse, Henry James, William Watson, Kenneth Grahame, Arnold Bennett, Maurice Baring and Henry Harland suggest nothing to us now of those peculiar qualities with which the periodical was then considered to be imbued. Many of them were indeed destined to survive honourably in English literature long after that ephemeral quarterly had perished. Lord Leighton and Walter Sickert were among the illustrators, but the post of art-editor was given to a young man of twenty-two, Aubrey Beardsley.

Since the appearance of the *Germ* in the early fifties nothing in the least resembling it had been seen. The *Germ* perished even more rapidly than did the *Yellow Book*, yet it gave two deathless lyrics to the world—Christina Rossetti's *When I am dead my Dearest* and Dante Gabriel Rossetti's *Blessed Damosel*. Nothing in the letterpress of the *Yellow Book* achieved a like fame, although the names of many of its contributors can never be forgotten, but the drawings of Aubrey Beardsley, disquietingly original, are of perdurable value in the history of British Art.

It is still almost universally believed that he owed his fame to that brief and abruptly ended connection with the *Yellow Book*. But his genius had already been recognized and encouraged. At the age of twenty-one he had been commissioned by Dent to illustrate the *Morte d'Arthur* for an important edition de luxe which was intended to rival the productions of the Kelmscott Press. Beardsley made over five hundred drawings for this book alone. Decorative, delicate and beautiful they were stylized to a degree that revealed the young artist's preoccupation with the Primitives. The exquisitely wrought designs for the headings and tail-pieces are full of a certain medieval charm. But he was then as always the despair of his publishers. " The most sacred engagements, the loudest imprecations," wrote one of his biographers, " failed to move him if they conflicted with his humour of the moment."

Even earlier his drawings published in the *Pall Mall Magazine* and the *Pall Mall Budget* had attracted the attention of connoisseurs by their singular force and originality. To such an one the association with the *Yellow Book* could bring only notoriety rather than fame.

Born at Brighton in 1872 Aubrey Beardsley died at Mentone in March, 1898 in his twenty-sixth year. He was educated at Brighton College where, however, he seems to have left but little mark, since the public school system, so admirable in many ways, has almost invariably failed to discover, recognize or foster genius. Nor can it be said that his ill-written and ill-spelt letters were a credit to his instructors. From childhood he was very delicate, with the Damocles sword of inherited disease hanging perpetually and menacingly above his head. His mother, left a widow with two young children, Aubrey and Mabel, could not afford to keep him at school after he was sixteen, at which age he found employment for a time in an architect's office, an experience that was not without its formative influence upon his future work. But his health broke down, and his next effort to earn his bread was as a clerk in the Guardian Assurance Company. While his days were spent at a desk in the City his evenings were devoted to attending the art-classes held by Professor Brown for students at Westminster. The long hours must considerably have taxed his fragile physique, and in his twentieth year he abandoned office life for ever and embarked upon the hazardous career of an artist. Nor was his chance long in coming, since as we have seen he was but twenty-one when Dent gave him his first remunerative commission.

During those last five years of his life Beardsley produced with ferocious energy and industry an incredible amount of work which was perfectly mature, definitely original, and certainly during its early and final phases of rare and unique beauty. Had he lived he would undoubtedly have gained many of those qualities which men and women of artistic impulse must acquire with fresh experience of life and by contact with those shaping influences which inevitably enlarge the mind and expand the soul. Indeed that the process of an immense change was at work within him during that last year of his life is amply evidenced by one of his latest and most perfect drawings, Mademoiselle de Maupin, which in delicacy of pattern and execution surpassed all his former work, as well as in one his final letters to Smithers in which he wrote : " I have definitely left behind me all my former methods." The Beardsley who had boasted that he was " nothing if he was not grotesque " was gone. The spiritual change that came to him during the last eighteen months of his life had already begun to affect his art, transmuting it to nobler purposes. But it would be idle to speculate upon the particular form which that progress and development would have taken. As well ask what Keats, Shelley, Emily Brontë, and that genius of our own day, Katherine Mansfield would have achieved had they survived to middle age. The man or woman who dies young has often completed his task, and offered his little gesture. . . .

In appearance Aubrey Beardsley was at any rate towards the end of his life extraordinarily pallid and emaciated. Someone wittily described him as a " silver hatchet with green hair." The large nose was strongly formed ; the great haggard sunken eyes were shadowed by the heavy lids so frequently to be observed in the victims of phthisis. From a narrow forehead the rather long hair was parted and brushed back from the brows. But it is always a boy's face that looks out from his photographs—an eager wistful face as of one aware of his approaching, untimely end.

The few survivors of the Pre-Raphaelite period encouraged the young man whose passage to fame was of such dramatic swiftness. Burne-Jones was perhaps less enthusiastic than the others, but Lord Leighton was warm in his praises, despite an amusing reservation with which few people could now be found to agree. On examining his drawings he exclaimed : " What wonderful line ! What a great artist ! *If he could only draw* ! " But draw he could with an unsurpassed accuracy and precision, although it was not in the manner of Leighton, educated in an earlier and very different tradition. Of younger men Mr. Pennell was one of the first to recognize Beardsley's talent and contributed an article about him to the *Studio* which was then making its first appearance.

As art editor of the *Yellow Book* Beardsley was associated with Henry Harland, the literary editor, whose stories at that time had considerable vogue. To the first few numbers of that famous periodical, Beardsley contributed much of that work which amused, dismayed and even repelled the public of his day. But he bore criticism well, even the rather deplorable " Daubray Wierdsley " of *Punch*, and only twice replied to it through the medium of the press rather after the witty and satirical manner of Whistler. And it must be said he had a good deal to bear. " To that other thing," wrote one of his critics, " to which the name of Mrs. Patrick Campbell has somehow become attached, we do not know that anything would meet the case except a short Act of Parliament to make this kind of thing illegal ! " But the " thing " in question afterwards obtained a position of honour in the Berlin National Gallery.

In a moment of panic during the following year—1895—John Lane, aware that the odium incurred by the *Yellow Book* was practically concentrated upon Beardsley, dismissed him, an action which left the young artist with impaired reputation and in a condition that save for the generosity of a few friends would have spelt destitution. It is only fair to say that no evidence has been adduced which could justify his being thrown to the wolves in such summary fashion.

At this juncture there appeared upon the scene the man who more than any other must be regarded as the evil genius of Aubrey Beardsley. Leonard Smithers was a Yorkshireman, some ten years his senior, who had abandoned the law to become a publisher and bookseller. A drug addict, he was also a surreptitious dealer in books of doubtful quality, and owing to the risks of this unpleasant trade he was able to command large sums for his wares.

He resolved to start a rival to the *Yellow Book* to be entitled the *Savoy*, and invited Beardsley's help in this new venture, offering him the munificent sum of £25 weekly for all rights in his future drawings of which he was also to retain the originals.

To the *Savoy*, which did not prove a success and was even more short-lived than its rival, Beardsley contributed at least one memorable drawing *The Rape of the Lock*, which, executed at the instigation of Edmund Gosse, evinced his preoccupation with the elaborate artificiality of the eighteenth century. He also published the fragment of a novel in its pages, and several poems of which his translation of the *Ave Atque Vale* of Catullus is worth quoting as an example of his facile mastery of verse.

> By ways remote and distant waters sped,
> Brother, to thy sad graveside am I come,
> That I may give the last gifts to the dead
> And vainly parley with thine ashes dumb ;
> Since she who now bestows and now denies
> Hath ta'en thee, hapless brother, from mine eyes.
>
> But lo ! these gifts, the heirlooms of past years,
> Are made sad things to grace thy coffin-shell,
> Take them, all drenchèd with a brother's tears,
> And, brother, for all time, Hail and Farewell !

Almost penniless Beardsley was dependent upon the bounty of Smithers, and it was for him he executed the illustrations for the English translation of Wilde's *Salome*. Those nightmare negroid faces with their hideous suggestion of evil magic were among the most repulsive he ever drew. The theme seemed to evoke all that was morbid and sinister in his imaginative processes. One turns with relief from them to the drawings of his first and last periods. Of the early ones the *Procession of Jeanne d'Arc*, done when he was only twenty and which was always a favourite of his, is one of the most beautiful. It owed something of its decorative quality to the influence of Burne-Jones, although revealing that sensitiveness of vision, that appealing rhythm of line and superb balance so characteristic of his own art. Another of his early masterpieces, *Les Revenants de Musique*, is also conceived in this happier vein ; the man's wistful, dreaming face turned towards those indeterminate phantom forms evoked by the music is full of a delicate and imaginative charm. To the later period, the work of his last year, belong the exquisite *Mademoiselle de Maupin* and *Chopin Ballade*, both "aquatintesques," executed in line and faint wash and reproduced by the auto-chromatic process then recently invented. These were among his few adventures into colour and for that reason are profoundly significant of the change he contemplated in his methods. But by that time the influence of Smithers was on the wane, and another and more spiritual one was usurping its place. Smithers was further proving a broken reed in the matter of payments, and indeed a few months before his death when hard-pressed for money, Beardsley confessed to his sister that he never knew when he sat down to a drawing whether it would ever be paid for, or if published, whether it would be adequately produced, an even worse fate from the artist's point of view.

Fortunately for him he had another benefactor in the late Mr. André Raffalovich whose influence over him was of a very different character. A writer of some repute he was a devout Catholic, and it was undoubtedly largely due to him that Beardsley was received into the Catholic Church the year prior to his death. It was to this friend the Last Letters[1] were addressed, although for a long time it was believed they were actually written to Fr. John Gray who edited them. The priest had at one time formed part of that little group of writers and artists, and was the author of two books of verse, *Silverpoints* and *Spiritual Poems*, the latter being among Beardsley's most cherished possessions since he clung to it when compelled to sell his other books. Fr. Gray renounced the career of an author and became a priest, working in Edinburgh for many years where he was well known and greatly beloved. Both he and his friend Raffalovich died in 1934 within a few months of each other.

And as his malady increased Beardsley turned more and more towards those things which Fr. Gray and Raffalovich represented. Indeed in the *Last Letters* he made generous acknowledgment of the debt that he owed to the solicitude and prayers of the latter.

[1] *Last Letters of Aubrey Beardsley* with an introductory note by the Rev. John Gray (Longmans, Green & Co. 1904).

Beardsley was influenced by many things in the world of art, assimilating and bending them to his own genius. The Greek vases from which he learned so much (one wonders that he never illustrated Keats's famous Ode), the prints of old Japan, the Italian Primitives whom he admired so whole-heartedly, all produced their effect upon his art. Absorbed in the alembic of his fertile and energetic imagination and stimulating its processes, they contributed to his intellectual equipment without touching his essential originality. His idiom remained his own. The forcefulness of those clean firm lines, the boldness of the blotted masses of shadow, the large pure white spaces which were so intensely significant, the economy and rhythm of his composition—which in the artist would seem to be the result of a special process of subjective visualization—combined to imbue his work with a quality that has never been successfully imitated. But that he had a profound influence upon subsequent decorative art cannot be denied. Indeed it has been suggested that the Bakst *décor* for the Russian Ballet could hardly have come into existence without the strange yet beautiful work of Aubrey Beardsley.

Few people ever saw him at work. If interrupted he would thrust the paper out of sight. Yet a story exists of his being one day surprised by a friend when he was in the act of drawing an overturned chair. Sheet after sheet was cast aside and destroyed, he drew it no less than fifty times before he could satisfy his own exacting ideal. He left nothing to chance ; all his work was supremely careful. " I may claim," he once wrote, " to have some command of line. I try to get as much as possible out of a single curve or straight line."

During the day it was his habit to darken the room and draw by artificial light in order to produce the desired effects, but for the most part his work was actually accomplished at night. His industry was prodigious, giving one the impression that he was—as the French say —*un averti*, aware that the time allotted to him must prove of brief duration.

> He had, wrote Mr. Arthur Symons, the fatal speed of those who are to die young, that disquieting completeness and knowledge, that absorption of a lifetime in an hour, which we find in those who hasten to have their work done before noon, knowing that they will not see the evening.[1]

Where the flame of genius burns very fiercely it is apt to consume its frail human habitation. And in Aubrey Beardsley the flame of creative energy resembled a destroying force, a fiery impulse urging him ever to more and more work until at last his enfeebled hands could

[1] *Aubrey Beardsley* by Arthur Symons. 1905.

no longer hold the implements of his craft. " I am always burning," he told a friend who remonstrated with him outside Covent Garden Opera House one bitter winter's night because he was wearing no overcoat.

It seems to have been in June, 1896, that he first became definitely alarmed about his health though it had already aroused considerable anxiety among his friends. In a letter to Raffalovich he wrote :

> I know you will be sorry to hear that Dr. Symes Thompson has pronounced very unfavourably on my condition to-day. He enjoins absolute quiet and if possible immediate change. I am beginning to be really depressed and frightened about myself.

And a little later from Epsom to the same friend :

> My only trouble now is my entire inability to walk or exert myself in the least. The attacks of hæmorrhage have been a dreadful nuisance. Last week I had a severe one and I have been an invalid ever since.

In July he went to Bournemouth, his mother accompanying him, and this journey was to have a profound effect upon his life. For it was there that he fell almost immediately under the spell of the Catholic Church.

> There is down here a beautiful little church served by the Fathers of the Society of Jesus. I hope, when I am able to go out, to assist at their services.

And a few days later :

> I should indeed be grateful for an introduction to any of the Jesuit fathers here.

But his health grew worse and a few days later he was again seriously ill.

> I can't tell you how ill I am to-day. I am quite paralysed with fear. I have told no one. It's dreadful to be so weak as I am becoming . . . work is out of the question.

Presently he was able to enjoy Fanny Burney's novels *Evelina* and *Cecilia*. They inspired several drawings, although he said in one of his letters that no book was ever well illustrated when it had become a classic. " Contemporary illustrations are the only ones of any value or interest."

In December he had a terrible attack of hæmorrhage when ascending the Chine, and believed that he was going tó die, out there and alone. Somehow or other he managed to struggle home, but his fears were now definitely aroused and the plans he made for future work were more formidable than ever.   He wrote thus to his friend :

> My agony of mind is great at even the slightest appearance of blood, for one never knows if the first few streaks are going to lead to something serious or not.   It is nearly six weeks now since I have left my room.   I am very busy with drawing, and should like to be writing, but cannot manage both in my weak state.

He was engaged then on the illustrations for what he called Dowson's "foolish playlet," *The Pierrot of the Minute*.   Very charming in all these delicate, fanciful drawings are the garden backgrounds with their heavy foliage, sharply pointed cypresses, the stylized lilies and roses.   There is something surely fatidical in the hour-glass that appears in two of them, but all are invested with an unbearable pathos when one remembers beneath what stress of mortal weakness they were accomplished.   The subject, however, pleased Beardsley.   In his boyish moods he had always been fond of drawing Pierrots, and it is interesting in this regard to learn that the witnessing of a performance of *L'Enfant Prodigue* in the early 'nineties had made a profound impression upon him.   And " like Pierrot," as Mr. Marillier observed in his sympathetic account of him, " he wore a brave mask, and faced his tragedy with a show of laughter."

During the autumn of 1896 one of the Jesuit fathers—probably at the instigation of Fr. Gray—paid him a visit and proved " most charming and sympathetic."   He lent him books from the library and gave him a *Manual of Catholic Belief*.   " I feel much drawn towards him," Beardsley wrote to Raffalovich, " and I believe he will be a good friend to me."

And indeed the priest proved to be that good friend.   He saw that he had to deal with a dying man who was looking pitifully to him for spiritual help.   He was present on one occasion when Beardsley had an exceptionally severe attack, and " was all kindness and sympathy."

The intimacy which thus deepened was viewed with considerable alarm not only by Smithers but by a certain section of Aubrey's friends. He received long communications from " certain pillars of the Anglican faith," remonstrating with him on account of his increasing friendship with the Jesuit fathers.   " I hope you are not haunted too cruelly with visions of designing Jesuits," he wrote to Smithers shortly before he was received into the Church.

His letters to Raffalovich show that he was preoccupied with those spiritual things that must necessarily absorb the thoughts of a man who knows that any day may prove to be his last. The prayers of his friend were about to be answered in full measure.

On the 16th of February, 1897, Fr. John Gray paid him a visit at Bournemouth, and the meeting between the two men could not have been otherwise than profoundly significant. A few days later he was followed by Raffalovich. Probably both believed that Aubrey was then dying. . . .

His letters to Smithers at that time were laconic. Although regretting the latter's inability to visit him he acknowledged that he should have found anything in the way of talk too tiring. He also telegraphed to Mr. John Pollitt to put off a proposed visit. Mr. Pollitt possessed the originals of the eight drawings for *Lysistrata* concerning the destruction of which Beardsley wrote to Smithers " in his death agony." It is easy to read between the lines and see that his thoughts were now definitely turned away from his former associates and patrons, and were concentrated upon the spiritual change so surely approaching.

During the early months of 1897 Beardsley read the lives of St. Aloysius and St. John Berchmans with profound interest. Until the end of March he was comparatively well, and had even visited the Jesuit fathers at the Church of the Sacred Heart. But another and more severe attack followed upon this temporary improvement, and on March 31, Fr. B. (as he is called throughout the letters) received him into the Church. *Je suis catholique*, was his laconic announcement in a letter to Smithers, but he wrote as follows to Raffalovich to whose prayers he owed so much :

> This morning I was received by dear Fr. B. into the Church, making my first confession with which he helped me so kindly. My First Communion will be made on Friday. I was not well enough to go up to the Church, and on Friday the Blessed Sacrament will be brought to me here. This is a very dry account of what has been the most important step in my life, but you will understand fully what these simple statements mean. With the deepest gratitude for all your prayers. . . .

And on the following day :

> Fr. B. came to see me this afternoon, and brought me such a dear little rosary that had been blessed by the Holy Father. He explained to me the use of it. I feel now like someone who has been standing waiting on the doorstep of a house upon a cold day and who cannot make up his mind to knock for a long while. At last the door is thrown open, and all the warmth of kind hospitality makes glad the frozen traveller . . . It is such a rest to be folded after all my wandering. . . .

The frozen traveller. The warmth of kind hospitality. The rest after wandering. . . . In those poignant words Beardsley epitomized the progress of the convert who has waited long between the first decisive call and the ultimate submission, and who has been amazed at the sense of warmth and welcome after long hesitation upon a chilly doorstep. Heart and soul he was fully prepared. His next letter reveals a note of even deeper and more rapturous faith :

> The Blessed Sacrament was brought to me here this morning. It was a moment of profound joy, of gratitude and emotion. I gave myself up entirely to feelings of happiness, and even the knowledge of my own unworthiness only seemed to add fuel to the flame that warmed and illuminated my heart. Oh, how earnestly I have prayed that that flame may never die out ! . . .

His First Communion was made on the first Friday of April, 1897, when he had rather less than a year to live. But from that time it is clear that all fear of death had left him. His letters were no longer " a study in fear," as Mr. Arthur Symons has described them. He was fortified, and the flame, by God's mercy, never died out.

> I understand now so much that you have written to me that seemed difficult before. Through all eternity I shall be unspeakably grateful for your brotherly concern for my spiritual advancement. This afternoon I have felt a little sad at the thought of my compulsory exile from Church just now, and that the divine privilege of praying before the Blessed Sacrament is not permitted me. You can guess how I long to assist at Mass, and you will pray, I know, that I may soon be strong enough to do so. . . .

No one can read the series of letters addressed to his two principal correspondents without being struck by the extraordinary diversity they display in the thoughts of the young dying man. Those to Smithers are full of his work, of schemes for future work, with references to money and to the various persons with whom the publisher was associated. But those to André Raffalovich are written with the eager simplicity of a child, and indeed form a kind of spiritual diary of the last months of his life. They are entirely without pose or self-pity, even when he refers to the progress of his malady. He did not, like Keats, bewail his " posthumous life," and yet in this pathetic record of a young life, ebbing inexorably to its premature close, we have a human document for which we must look for a parallel to the last letters of that poet.

> Here, wrote Mr. Arthur Symons, Beardsley is as he is in his drawings, close, absorbed, limited, unflinching. . . .

In his appreciative introduction to the *Last Letters* which Fr. Gray published some six years after Beardsley's death he writes :

Aubrey Beardsley, had he lived, might have risen, whether through his art or otherwise, spiritually to a height from which he could command the horizon he was created to scan. As it was the long anguish, the increasing bodily helplessness, the extreme necessity in which someone else raises one's hand, turns one's head, showed the slowly-dying man things he had not seen before. He came face to face with the old riddle of life and death ; the accustomed supports and resources of his being were removed ; his soul, thus denuded, discovered needs that unstable desires had hitherto obscured ; he submitted, like Watteau, his master, to the Catholic Church.

For a time his health improved wonderfully, and in May, 1897, he was able to go to Paris where S. Sulpice was his favourite church.

I was at S. Sulpice on Sunday. The church was crowded. Cardinal Vaughan was the celebrant. He looked magnificent, and was admired greatly by everybody.

The doctor whom he consulted in Paris gave him hope of at least a partial recovery although not attempting to conceal the gravity of his malady. He remained in Paris until July when he went to Dieppe, a place already well known to him. But he was recommended to winter in the South and plans were made for this, his last, journey. He left Paris at the end of November and went to Mentone. He was greatly worried at the time about money, for it was then that his first suspicions of the inability of Smithers to pay were disclosed to his sister, Mabel, Mrs. Bealby Wright. Before leaving Paris he finished what was perhaps his most exquisite drawing, *Mademoiselle de Maupin*, which was intended as one of a series of twelve that he hoped to complete. The drawing is very slightly tinted, the face is tender and wistful ; the lace of the garments is most delicately indicated, and the shadowed, wooded, Corot-like background is full of a haunting mystery. It is said that this print is very rare and is only to be found in complete collections of Beardsley's work. It certainly surpassed all that he had hitherto accomplished, and held abundant promise for the future which was, alas, never to be fulfilled.

His last published letter to Raffalovich was written towards the close of February, 1898, from the Hotel Cosmopolitain, Mentone, when the end of the journey was in sight.

I am in better spirits and indeed very happy at times I have been reading a good deal of *St. Alphonsus Liguori*, no one dispels depression more effectually than he. Reading his loving exclamations so lovingly reiterated it is impossible to remain dull and sullen, I believe it is often mere physical exhaustion more than hardness of heart that leaves me so apathetic and uninterested.

Symons affirmed that only once did Beardsley say anything to him which could help him to reconcile the young artist with the devout Catholic and author of that handful of letters. He told him that as a child he had had a " singular dream or vision." He awoke one night in the moonlight and saw a great Crucifix with a bleeding Christ falling off the wall where no Crucifix had ever been. But when asked if he was in the habit of seeing visions he answered evasively : " I do not allow myself to see them except on paper."

Until almost the end of February he was at work on the initials of Ben Jonson's *Volpone* which he proposed to illustrate. But during the first week in March a definite change for the worse set in, and on the 7th of the month he wrote the well known, tragic letter to Smithers.

Jesus is our Lord and Judge.

Dear Friend,
    I implore you to destroy all copies of Lysistrata and bad drawings. Show this to Pollitt and conjure him to do the same. By all that is holy *all* obscene drawings.
                                                        Aubrey Beardsley.
In my death agony.

But that poignant death-bed appeal fell upon deafened ears. Aware of their monetary value Smithers did not destroy the drawings. It is therefore scarcely surprising to learn that after the death of her son Mrs. Beardsley wrote refusing to see him although demanding the return of Aubrey's manuscripts.

Beardsley died on the 16th of March, having received the Last Sacraments two days previously. He was lovingly tended in those final weeks by his devoted mother and sister. His end was saint-like, in its complete resignation to the Will of God. It might be said of him in the words of his gifted contemporary and fellow-convert, Ernest Dowson who, stricken by the same malady was so soon to follow him, that he had :

. . . serene insight
Of the illuminating dawn to be . . .

To that frail erring life the Church had held out strong, sustaining arms, bestowing upon him her unimaginable gifts of grace, absolution and consolation, enfolding that soul securely after its brief, tortuous and tragic wandering.

Mass was sung for him in the Cathedral Church of St. Michel at Mentone, and his sister wrote thus of the ceremony to André Raffalovich.

I want you to know how beautiful everything was ; the dear heart himself would have loved it. The road from the Cathedral to the cemetery was so wonderfully beautiful, winding up a hill ; it seemed like the way of the Cross. It was long and steep and we walked . . .[1]

There upon that sunny slope, set with the black flames of innumerable cypresses and within view of the wide blue expanse of the Mediterranean upon which his dying eyes had so often gazed, Aubrey Beardsley was laid to rest in a grave hewn out of the rocky hillside, a rosary clasped in his wasted hands. . . .

---

[1] *Letters from Aubrey Beardsley to Leonard Smithers.* Edited by R. A. Walker. First Edition Club, 1937.

THE RIGHT REV. MGR. FULTON J. SHEEN

CARDINAL HAYES

A.D. 1867–1938

CARDINAL HAYES WAS born on September 4, 1938. In that one word "born" is wrapped the greatest tribute which can be paid to any man. The world celebrates a birthday on which a man is born to physical life; for example, Lincoln's birthday is February 12th. But the Church celebrates a birthday on which a man dies to the physical life and is born to eternal life; that day the liturgy calls *natalitia* or birthday. If Cardinal Hayes were a worldly man we would have said he was born on November 20, 1867, but being preëminently spiritual and living only for eternal union with Divine Life, we set down the date on which he went to meet his God.

On the earthly plane his close identification with New York City and his mission in it was forshadowed even in infancy. Nothing could be more metropolitan than City Hall Place where he first saw the light of day; nothing could be more Irish than his baptismal name Patrick which his father gave him in protest to some anti-Irish sentiment prevalent at the time; nothing could be more prophetic than the joyful outburst of his mother at his birth that he would one day be a bishop.

His education was exclusively religious, which fact has more to do with making character than is generally believed. The basic difference between religious and non-religious education is that under the former knowledge grows by penetration, whereas under the latter it grows by substitution. Religion gives one supreme purpose to which all other purposes, social, political, and economic, are subordinated. Secular education gives not supreme purpose but multiple purposes. From the day Patrick Hayes entered the parochial school of the Transfiguration parish until he completed his university work there was never once an abandonment of a material philosophy for an idealistic one, nor the substitution of a Gestalt psychology for a Behavioristic one; there was only a deepening and unfolding of eternal Truth as an acorn develops into the oak. This spiritual background of his education echoed in all his public utterances within that field. "The tendency of modern education," he once told the graduates of the College of Mt. St. Vincent, "is to take the soul out of learning and to develop only the outward

448

form. Catholic education aims too, to give a thorough knowledge of all the facts, but it goes further and claims the need of a knowledge of God, the source of all things. . . . We follow all requirements of the Board of Regents, but the heart of all our schools is the heart of Christ ; and whenever this is true we may well understand the source of their power." On another occasion he said : "It is only right that the State should spend millions, as it does, on the educational system. But it is not right for the State to halt at the most important point of its work and to neglect the spiritual education of the child."

It was this consecration to the supreme end of life which made him such a patriot, for as St. Thomas Aquinas long ago pointed out, Piety is the root and basis of patriotism. As early as 1887 when he was only twenty-one years of age he seemed to foresee the present danger to our American liberty. In a senior essay for Manhattan College he wrote : "Our constitution tolerates as much liberty as is conducive to the prosperity of any people ; therefore all factions which wish to promote either anarchy, socialism or communism, deserve the brand of censure from the ruling power." For him patriotism and religion were inseparable as love of fellow man and love of God. For that reason he praised the Catholic Teacher's Association for "placing beside the flag the Cross of Christ. The flag is only human and may of itself, God forbid, go the way of all things human. It needs the Cross of Christ beside it. The Cross will be its teacher, protector and defense, particularly in times of crisis."

His love of America was one of the great passions of his life. The Catholic Church already had a distinguished line of patriotic prelates, such as Carroll, Ryan, Kenrick, Spalding and Gibbons. To that list must be added him who, during the World War was the spiritual lord of all Catholic chaplains. After receiving the Red Hat he pleaded : "Let no one fear that the making of the Archbishop of New York has made him less an American. Democracy is not a leveler. Democracy as we understand it here in America is something that lifts men up and, in the process of lifting up, some are bound to go higher than others. As long as America pays tribute to every citizen according to merit in right and justice, America will endure, will fructify, and will receive more and more blessings from Almighty God. Then we need never fear the future. An American spirit will be created in this country and it will be of such kind that whenever anything that is vile, anything that is un-American shows its head, it will wither away in the presence of that spirit."

Men are like sponges. A sponge can hold just so much water and a man can hold so much honor. There is always a point of saturation. Some reach it much more quickly than others. Those who take little honor too seriously prove they never should have had that honor.

Instead of their wearing a decoration, the decoration wears them. Cardinal Hayes never reached the point of saturation. He was one man who never changed either his voice or his love of the poor when he was honored. This was due to two things : his humility and his gradual ascent to eminence. Honors came slowly and rhythmically ; he hardly ever took two steps at a time on the stairs that led to Princedom. From curate at St. Gabriel's Church he became the secretary of Cardinal Farley ; the next step was to that of Chancellor and President of Cathedral College in 1903 ; from that to Domestic Prelate in 1907, and from that after seven sacramental years to the honor of Auxiliary Bishop of New York. Then in 1917 he became Bishop Ordinary of the Armed Forces of the United States and two years later Archbishop of New York, and finally, in 1924 Cardinal. Such gradual ascendency stamped him with the mark of maturity. He was always ripe for each new duty. Never being thrown into office impetuously he never exercised it impulsively. It takes radicals who suddenly bombed into proletarian thrones a long time to cool off and therefore become fit for the administration of justice. Like a piece of steel tempered by being dipped into the waters of each new office, Cardinal Hayes was always prepared for governing. A fellow chaplain during the World War told me that on many occasions Bishop Hayes refused to take a Pullman sleeper, kindly offered him by a soldier or an officer or chaplain, on the grounds that they needed it more than he. The same humility manifested itself when he refused a high military rank from the United States Government, feeling that the spiritual nature of his work would be more effective among chaplains and soldiers if he worked only as a prelate.

At the close of the World War, when he had under his direction nine hundred chaplains, his foresight, along with that of three other Bishops in the United States, was instrumental in founding the present National Catholic Welfare Conference which was then called the National Catholic Welfare Council. " In view of the results obtained through the merging of our activities for the time and purpose of war, we determined to maintain, for the ends of peace, the spirit of unity and the coördination of our forces."

Catholic Charities was organized by Archbishop Hayes in 1920 to coördinate, supervise, develop and help more than 200 existing Catholic charitable agencies in the Archdiocese. Although incorporated in 1920, Catholic Charities really had its beginning in plans formulated by the Archbishop in 1917, when he was rector of St. Stephen's Church. At the annual diocesan retreat in June, 1919, three months after his installation, Archbishop Hayes stated that he did not know fully the field of charity in New York, did not completely understand its problems, its limits, its unoccupied areas ; but felt that it was his duty to know the immense field which God had committed to his care, and to know it thoroughly before attempting to organize it. On the following September 1st, he ordered that a diocesan study be made under the direction of his Secretary for Charities, the present Executive Director of Catholic Charities of the Archdiocese of New York, the Right Reverend Monsignor Robert F. Keegan. So that there might be no mistake as to the motives and methods to be pursued, as soon as the plans had been formulated the Archbishop called a meeting of some 400 persons in charge of Catholic works. He outlined the purpose, the scope and the spirit of the study and emphasized the fact that it was to be undertaken for constructive purposes rather than for criticism.

The survey and study brought to light the vast number and great variety of Catholic charitable activities in the Archdiocese, but also revealed that despite the excellent work being done, there were three principal weaknesses — lack of unification, lack of sufficient funds to improve existing agencies, and need for the extension of Catholic charitable work in many sections of the Archdiocese.

Archbishop Hayes lost no time in setting up machinery to follow out the recommendations developed by the study. He called to his aid a dependable body of some 25,000 lay people in the 300 parishes to be known as the Archbishop's Committee of the Laity. To overcome the lack of coöperation among Catholic agencies it was recommended that there be set up immediately a central organization with the Archbishop as its president, his Secretary for Charities as its secretary and, working under the latter, six divisions — Children, Families, Health, Protective Care, Social Action and Finance — each with a full-time director and assistants.

The Archbishop also planned at once for an intensive campaign, the principal aim of which was to build up the Archbishop's Committee of the Laity of 25,000 members. It was the duty of the Committee, during the week of April 18 to 25, 1920, to accomplish the secondary object of the campaign, namely, to secure from at least 100,000 Catholics, pledges to contribute a total of $500,000 annually for the next three years. No attempt was made to obtain pledges from other than Catholics. The campaign was a remarkable success. Instead of $500,000, approximately $1,000,000 annually was pledged for the following three years. Pledges were made by a total of 223,000 individuals. The enrollment campaign ended on April 25th, and on May 1, 1920, the new central organization, known as " The Catholic Charities of the Archdiocese of New York " took up offices and began to function. The success that has attended its work since then is known throughout the country.

In the light of the facts of his life, could Cardinal Hayes be called a really great man ? Naturally, that depends entirely on what is understood by greatness. Our modern world has peculiar ideas about greatness. It generally evaluates the characters which walk across its stage either by the abundance they possess or by the power they wield. By the first standard millionaires are successes ; by the second, dictators, party and organization leaders, are great.

It need hardly be emphasized that neither of these constitutes greatness, for by such standards man would be great, not because of what he *is*, but because of what he *has* ; character would then not be something inside a man, but outside of him, like money or an army. Our Blessed Lord has warned against measuring men by such superficial standards. To those who judge worth by bank accounts He warned : " A man's life doth not consist in the abundance of things which he possesseth."[1] And to those who judged worth by power over others, He said : " You know that the princes of the Gentiles lord it over them : and they that are the greater, exercise power upon them. It shall not be so among you, but whosoever will be the greater among you, let him be your minister : And he that will be first among you, shall be your servant. Even as the Son of man is not come to be ministered unto, but to minister, and to give his life a redemption for many."[2] The conclusion is obvious : Wealth without charity is snobbery ; authority without humility is tyranny. No man is great by wealth until he has learned to be detached like the Lord of the Universe in the rôle of a village carpenter, and no man is great by power until he has learned to be obedient, as the Power of Heaven and earth was subject to parents at Nazareth.

Greatness is something in the soul of man and the extent and depth of his love for the profoundest of all realities : God and neighbor. " *Thou shalt love the Lord thy God with thy whole heart, and with thy whole soul, and with thy whole mind . . . and thou shalt love thy neighbor as thyself.*"[3]

Judged by *these* standards Cardinal Hayes was truly one of the great men of the present generation. Newspapers said he was the head of the richest diocese in America, but nothing so much missed the mark — for he considered himself as the head of the poorest diocese in America. His friends lauded him for his service as Head Chaplain of the Army and Navy during the World War, as the builder of schools, hospitals, convents, and charity organizations. But whence came this profound love of the poor and the children and country ? It came from only one source, and until we find a man who loved that one source more than Cardinal Hayes, we shall never see again such patriotism and such generosity. And that one fountain whence poured all other loves as streams was his deep and profound love of God.

We would have wounded Cardinal Hayes deeply if we spoke of this during his life, but now that we need an inspiration and encourage-

[1] Luke 12 : 15.   [2] Matt. 20 : 25-28.   [3] Matt. 22 : 37, 39.

ment for these troubled days, we would leave our wounds unhealed did we not speak of his inner and unknown life. Thousands saw him during life clothed in the richest red which the Church could bestow, sometimes seated on a throne in a great Cathedral, or at other times administering agencies involving millions of souls. But how many know how little he gloried in that red or that throne or that power? What was he like without these accidents of color or pomp?

Look at this picture of the man : Early each morning of his life you would have overheard him amidst the trickling waters of a shower saying aloud the beautiful prayer of St. Augustine : " Noverim te, noverim me " — "Lord, that I may know Thee, that I may know myself." Then as he shaved there followed the morning prayers he learned as a child, and prayers in preparation for Mass beginning with the words : " O Lord, remember not my faults " which he followed by the psalm : " How lovely are thy tabernacles, O Lord of hosts ! my soul longeth and fainteth for the courts of the Lord." This mingling of action and prayer which began his waking life was followed by prayer without action. The next two and one half hours were given over purely to meditation and prayer and, until a few years ago when physicians ordered otherwise, it was all done on a hard floor without the benefit of a prie-dieu. It was no wonder that the Holy Sacrifice of the Mass which followed was always offered with such unction and devotion. So reluctant was he to leave Calvary, which the Mass renews, that he would linger in its shadows in thanksgiving for never less than half an hour.

Nor let it be thought that it was *his* Mass which mattered, it was the *Mass*. For that reason he would serve another Mass which was read in his house, and when confined to his bed during serious illness would answer the responses to be more intimately a part of that which was the center of his priestly life.

When a priest, fortified by over three hours of spiritual and sacramental communion with God, sits down before his desk, you could walk before it and feel you were in the presence of Christ. No wonder he was never known to have lost his temper, nor to have been angry, nor to have hated anyone, nor to have rebuked with bitterness ! No wonder, when hearing of any scandal among those committed to his care, that he would weep for the wounded Christ ! No wonder that, when extremely delicate matters of administration needed a decision, he would retire to the chapel and in the presence of Our Lord in the Blessed Sacrament, pray for light and guidance !

When the day was over — and what a busy day it must have been ministering to a diocese with 456 churches, 1,650 priests, 182,298 children under Catholic care, and one million faithful — he would retire to his study and very often raise his arms as if to push someone out, saying : " Trouble and worry . . . keep out ! " He would then deliberately lock the door in the face of both and go again to the feet of His Master in the tabernacle to spend another hour in prayer. There is absolutely no doubt that Cardinal Hayes spent more time in utter and abject prostration before his Lord than he permitted himself to be enthroned among men. To the eyes of his flock he was on a throne, but he was more often before one : the throne of his Eucharistic Saviour.

Next to his love of the Eucharist and the Mass was his love of the Blessed Mother of Our Divine Lord. One particularly touching custom he had betrays the utter simplicity of his heart ; it was to take from the table after each meal a flower, carry it upstairs, and with his own hands place it at the feet of the statue of Our Lady. He lost his own earthly mother at five, but Cardinal Hayes was never an orphan. His Mother who is the Mother of us all, survives him still. The greatest events of his life took place on her feasts. He was baptized on the feast of Our Lady's Presentation ; he was ordained on the feast of her Nativity ; he was named a Cardinal on the feast of her Annunciation ; his titular Church in Rome was Santa Maria in Via ; and he was buried within a day of the same feast on which he was ordained — the feast of the Nativity of Our Lady. This is more than a coincidence. One cannot help but feel that he who carried flowers to her daily must himself have been carried by the angels, as a glorious unfading flower of the Catholic priesthood, to that Heavenly Mother, as the last and most precious of gifts.

One other special devotion of the Cardinal was to St. Raphael the Archangel, whose story, as revealed in the book of Tobias, he knew so well, and on which he often preached as a young priest. Later on in life a painting of St. Raphael which hung in his bedroom kept alive that devotion until the Master called, and, we may guess, until Raphael guided him as another Tobias to the banks of the eternal Tigris. Shortly before his death His Eminence confided to his secretary and to his chancellor, Monsignor Casey and Monsignor McIntyre, that, his memory having failed him in a few of his childhood prayers, he begged his guardian angel to recall them to his mind ; and his prayer was answered.

All the doctors of the Church, whose names he knew by heart, he loved and studied. Probably no one, not even students of the subject, loved more to read their writings than he. To Saint Chrysostom he prayed often that he might, as he put it, " preach the truths of Christ and His Church in the language of the people." But among the doctors of the Church St. Augustine was his favorite. It is indeed remarkable that as a priest he once paid a visit to the tomb of that learned saint and there prayed that he might receive something of his priestly spirit. A very short time after that visit he was named auxiliary bishop of New York, and the See to which he was appointed was that which St. Augustine himself once ruled. Until his end he daily read the soliloquies and prayers of St. Augustine, and editions of these works in Latin, French, and Italian which he used, were on his desk when he died. Those who know the style of St. Augustine will recall how often the Cardinal was like him in his preaching. The frequent use of the ejaculation " O " when speaking of the love of God, was typically Augustinian, or should we not rather say it was typical of those who love God so deeply that human words are inadequate ?

The initial address over the Catholic Hour, which he inaugurated eight and one half years ago, was typical of his views concerning the purpose of preaching. " May it serve," he said, " to make better understood the [Catholic] faith as it really is — a light revealing the pathway to Heaven . . . pardoning our sins, elevating, consecrating our common every-day duties and joys, bringing not only justice but gladness and peace to our searching and questioning hearts."

Such a truly spiritual life manifested itself in his surroundings. The furniture of his house is the same that was in it during the days of his predecessor, Cardinal Farley, who died twenty years ago. The same simple desk with cloth covering that served his predecessors served him. His bedroom was only fourteen by sixteen without an attached bath, and with only an old bed and two old chairs other than the statues of Our Lady beside his bed, the crucifix over it, and a few pictures on the wall. His personal needs were reduced to an absolute minimum. He protested that he did not have money enough to have a new bath attached to his room, and the housekeeper from time to time would put a note in his old shoes saying : " Isn't it about time to buy another pair ? " He never in his life rang a bell for a servant and was never known to have asked for anything for himself. Severe and ascetic with himself, he was most generous to others. As " Cardinal of Charities " he is well known, but the many poor whom he personally supported and who are still living are too numerous to mention. This incident is rather typical of them all. A poor old woman on Third Avenue wrote a letter to the Cardinal telling him of her poverty. The Cardinal and his Auxiliary, Bishop Donahue, both paid a personal visit to the old hovel. It was winter, the room where she lived was cold, and only a dim gas light illumined her poverty. The Cardinal had her taken immediately to St. Vincent's hospital where he cared for her until she died.

Each action of his day was mingled with prayer, but when the day was over prayer again drew the curtain on a busy life. His night prayers took an hour, and during them he would go through his entire diocese, and mention by name each institution, each work and particular problem that needed God's spiritual help. True shepherd of his flock, he lived only for his sheep. If he told anyone he would pray for them, he did so by name. I shall never forget my own joy at hearing His Eminence say he read his Resurrection Mass for my intention that souls might come to God through preaching.

In the last few years of his life his physicians would not permit him to say his night prayers on his knees. Accordingly, he said them in bed with his head propped by three pillows, one of which he would remove on retiring. Alongside his bed was a glass of water and a pill which he would take immediately after his night prayers just before falling to sleep. He turned out all the lights in his room as he prayed at night, but kept his hands folded across his breast holding a crucifix. As he lifted his soul to God, he would run his fingers over the cross and the image of the crucified Saviour — one needed no light to know that Love was there.

That was the way he went back to God — saying his night prayers. The water had not been touched, nor the pill, nor the third pillow. Without any convulsions whatever he died as he prayed, and the next morning they found him as if asleep, with his hands folded across his breast and his eyes looking down upon his Crucified Saviour. Thus died America's greatest citizen and the Church's greatest priest.

Into so many hands at death a crucifix is placed by friends to bear a tardy witness to their fellowship with the Cross. Not so with the Cardinal. He placed the Crucifix in his own hands for his own death. He whose fingers daily loved to touch the Crucified Lord at the consecration of the Mass, now dies with fingers entwined about His Cross. It was the most beautiful way a priest could die ! And that is what Cardinal Hayes was, above all things else — a priest — a member of all families yet belonging to none ; living in the world and yet not of it ; serving the poor not as one giving but as one receiving ; lifting man to God in the Consecration and bringing God to man in Communion ; going to work from prayer and to prayer from work ; being hard on oneself and easy on others ; hating sin but loving the sinner ; being intolerant about truth, but tolerant to persons ; being a priest to others and a victim to Christ. What a vocation ! That is the priesthood ! That is Cardinal Hayes !